INSIDERS' GUIDE® SERIES

# INSIDERS' GUIDE® TO
# CHARLESTON
## INCLUDING MT. PLEASANT, SUMMERVILLE, KIAWAH, AND OTHER ISLANDS

TENTH EDITION

J. MICHAEL McLAUGHLIN AND LEE DAVIS TODMAN

INSIDERS' GUIDE®

GUILFORD, CONNECTICUT
AN IMPRINT OF THE GLOBE PEQUOT PRESS

The prices and rates in this guidebook were confirmed at press time. We recommend, however, that you call establishments before traveling to obtain current information.

**INSIDERS' GUIDE**®

Text design by LeAnna Weller Smith
Maps by XNR Productions, Inc © Morris Book Publishing, LLC.

ISSN 1546-329X
ISBN 0-7627-3882-0

Manufactured in the United States of America
Tenth Edition/First Printing

*Folly Beach Pier.* CHARLESTON AREA CONVENTION & VISITORS BUREAU

*Charleston Harbor.* CHARLESTON AREA CONVENTION & VISITORS BUREAU
*Charles Street.* CHARLESTON AREA CONVENTION & VISITORS BUREAU

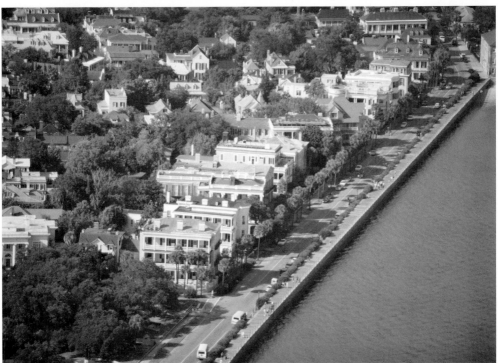

*Shops and museums line Meeting Street.* CHARLESTON AREA CONVENTION & VISITORS BUREAU
*Mansions along the Battery.* CHARLESTON AREA CONVENTION & VISITORS BUREAU

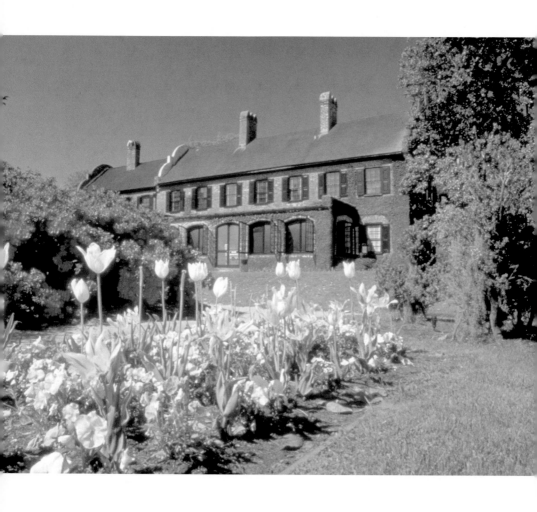

*Middleton Place plantation.* CHARLESTON AREA CONVENTION & VISITORS BUREAU

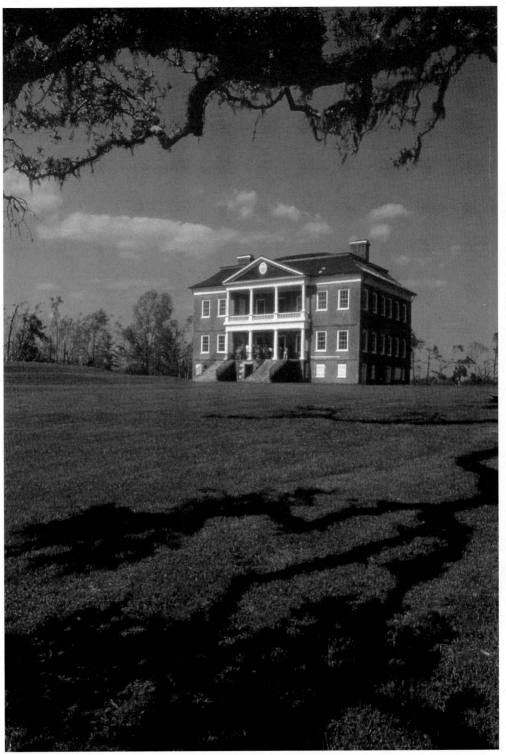

*Drayton Hall.* CHARLESTON AREA CONVENTION & VISITORS BUREAU

*Shopping at City Market.* CHARLESTON AREA CONVENTION & VISITORS BUREAU

*The Lowcountry is home to world-ranked golf courses.* CHARLESTON AREA CONVENTION & VISITORS BUREAU

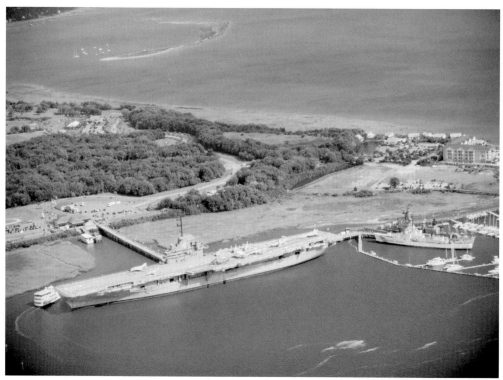

USS *Yorktown.*
*Patriots Point Naval and Maritime Museum.*

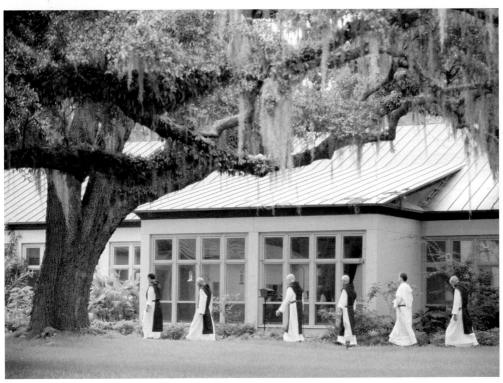

*Boone Hall Plantation's famous avenue of oaks.* CHARLESTON AREA CONVENTION & VISITORS BUREAU

*Mepkin Abbey.* CHARLESTON AREA CONVENTION & VISITORS BUREAU

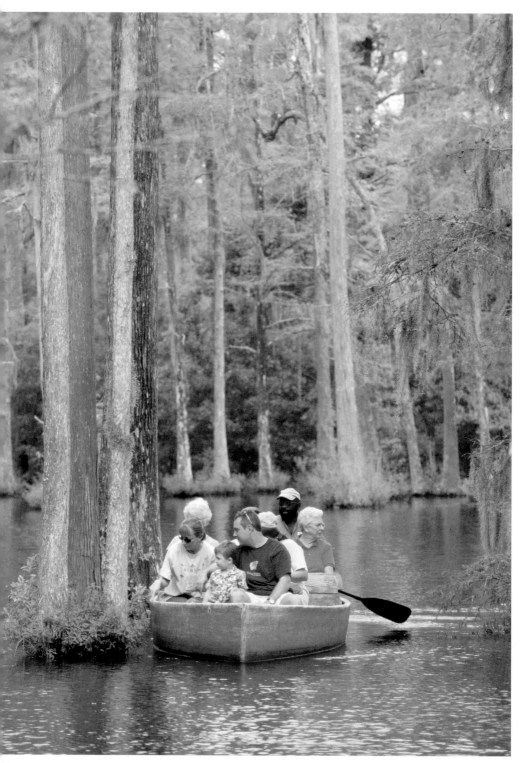

*Cypress Gardens.* CHARLESTON AREA CONVENTION & VISITORS BUREAU

*Shrimping fleet at Shem Creek.* CHARLESTON AREA CONVENTION & VISITORS BUREAU

*Dining alfresco.* CHARLESTON AREA CONVENTION & VISITORS BUREAU

*Carriage in front of Dock Street Theatre Historic District.* CHARLESTON AREA CONVENTION & VISITORS BUREAU

*Sailing in Charleston Harbor.* CHARLESTON AREA CONVENTION & VISITORS BUREAU

# CONTENTS

# CONTENTS

## Directory of Maps

Overview

**Greater Charleston**

**Charleston**
and surrounding areas

**Downtown Charleston**

N

0    0.25    0.5 km

0         0.25         0.5 mi.

# Charleston County Parks

**N**

| 0 | 5 | 10 mi. |

| 0 | 5 | 10 km |

*ATLANTIC OCEAN*

To Georgetown and Myrtle Beach

**East Cooper Airport**

Devees Island

Wild Dunes

Palm Blvd.

**Mt. Pleasant Palmetto Islands County Park**

Isle of Palms Connector

Isle of Palms County Park

Jasper Blvd.

Sullivan's Island

**Mt. Pleasant**

Long Point Rd.

Coleman Blvd.

Patriot's Point

Charleston Harbor

**Charleston International Airport and Air Force Base**

Daniel Island

**Cooper River Marina**

Cosgrove Ave.

**Charleston**

**West Ashley**

Dorchester Rd.

Ashley Phosphate Rd.

Bees Ferry Rd.

Savannah Hwy.

**Caw Caw Interpretive Center**

To Savannah and Beaufort

Main Rd.

Bears Bluff Rd.

Wadmalaw Island

Maybank Hwy.

**James Island County Park**

James Island

Folly Rd.

Ft. Johnson Rd.

Riverland Dr.

**Charleston Executive Airport**

Johns Island

Bohicket Rd.

**Mullet Hall Equestrian Center**

Kiawah Island

Seabrook Island

**Beachwalker County Park**

**Folly Beach Edwin S. Taylor Fishing Pier**

**Folly Beach**

**Folly Beach County Park**

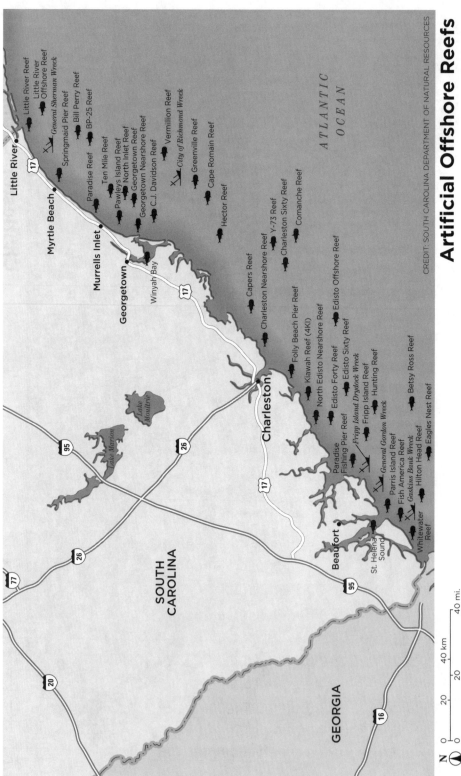

# Artificial Offshore Reefs

# PREFACE

Welcome to Greater Charleston, where three South Carolina counties (Charleston, Berkeley, and Dorchester) blend together and create the scenic backdrop for a unique and wonderful lifestyle.

This is a land of history, the home of Revolutionary statesmen. This is a city of gallantry, glory, folly, and pain—where democracy was nurtured and secession proclaimed. This is where, very early on, beauty was deemed as important as survival, whatever the cost. Pride was encouraged. Families were sacrosanct, and God was dutifully acknowledged in mind and matter.

The sociopolitical passions and turbulent economies that made Charleston such a fascinating place 200 years ago are still very much with us today. Only now the canvas is larger, the paintbrush wider, and Charleston's colorful story just gets bolder as the years go by.

One of the reasons Charleston seems so timeless has to do with geography. The historic Peninsula (the heart of Charleston's identity) is bound by two rivers, the Ashley and the Cooper. Despite whatever else those rivers have meant to Charleston and its people over time, the waters effectively impounded the 18th-century city. This watery restraint forced all real growth and change northward—pushing it upward, spilling it over onto neighboring lands. Even today, neighborhoods that were built "east Cooper" or "west Ashley" always carry the unspoken phrase "of the Peninsula" and bear indirect witness to the old city's powerful presence.

The natural containment of the Ashley and Cooper Rivers (effectively protecting the Peninsula from change) had an accomplice in the Lowcountry itself. The southeastern third of South Carolina is physically low, close to sea level, prone to swampland, marsh, and innumerable shallow creeks and streams. The land was hostile toward early settlers and planters, and it was costly to railroad builders and almost every other developer. It didn't welcome growth, and it resists change to this day.

So in many ways Charleston was isolated and remained something of a cultural island while America pushed westward into its destiny. Charleston and its captive Peninsula effectively stayed behind, surrounded by its many coastal distractions.

As it has for eons, the endless marsh still seems to change color every day. And unspoiled beaches can still be caught playing tag with a restless (occasionally punishing) sea. Charlestonians still know that not far away they can find dark and mysterious swamps that, in certain moonlight, whisper primordial secrets in the native tongue of an ancient higher power.

If this is isolation, then it's splendid isolation. This is the Lowcountry: a place, a people, a unique perspective on the world.

Is it any wonder we love living here?

# ACKNOWLEDGMENTS

For their input, expertise, and assistance in many forms, we thank all who helped with the production of this book. These include the research departments at the Charleston Area Convention and Visitors Bureau, the Avery Research Center for African American History and Culture, the Charleston County Public Library, Historic Charleston Foundation, and the Public Affairs office of the 437th Airlift Wing at Charleston Air Force Base.

So much of living here is a visual delight. We'd like to thank David Berry, Tommy Ford, John Meffert, Bill Struhs, and Larry Workman for their photography and energetic view of our city's many charms. Gracious thanks go, as well, to the various Lowcountry attractions whose staffs helped provide us with images and information enhancing our descriptions for this book. Lee and Mike would like to thank Dale Poulnot and Timm Gipe for their professional insight.

Mike would like to thank Rick Burton and the Greater Charleston Concierge Association for their support, enthusiasm, and groundwork in gaining access to so many great dining establishments and Lowcountry attractions. He would also like to express his deep appreciation to David Ratts, whose "chronological" introduction to Charleston back in 1979 was the genesis for the approach recommended in this book. His enthusiasm for the Holy City made learning about its history a delightful and life-enriching experience. Lee would like to thank her mother, Rachel Davis, for her diligent archival research. She would also like to thank Rhett Perry for his encouragement and support for the duration of the extended process.

Our thanks go to Elizabeth M. Taylor and Staci White for editing this book and for working with us on a schedule that was amazingly career-friendly for all concerned. Thanks go to The Globe Pequot Press for recognizing the value of the Insiders' Guide series and for opting to bring it to the people in markets all over the country where the information can be used and appreciated.

# HOW TO USE THIS BOOK

This guide is made up of data-packed chapters that provide the kind of practical information you need to enjoy the Greater Charleston area. The early chapters of this book are generally focused on tourism, history, and attractions. This information is useful to visitors (and residents alike) who want to know more about the city and its surrounds. Starting with Relocation, the latter chapters are especially helpful to newcomers who have decided to make the Lowcountry their permanent home.

If you are planning a visit or move to Charleston, surf the chapters to make contacts ahead of time. If you are already here, or on your way to the city, flip to the Getting Here, Getting Around chapter to determine the best route to your desired destinations, or flip to one of our accommodations chapters for information on lodging (Hotels and Motels, Bed-and-Breakfasts and Atmospheric Inns, or Vacation and Beach Rentals). And if you have arrived and are carrying the book around as a reference tool, just zip to a particular chapter to find the best or closest restaurants, entertainment, recreation, lodging, kidstuff, and attractions. There's even an index at the back of the book so you can pinpoint a specific subject or place quickly and easily.

We have worked to create chapters that stand alone but are cross-referenced so that you can easily set your own pace and schedule for getting to know Charleston. You decide when to immerse yourself in the history and culture of the community and when to make more immediate decisions about where to eat, where to sleep, what to do at night, and where to shop. Our job is to coordinate the information and organize it clearly so that you can make every minute here count.

With this tenth edition of the *Insiders' Guide to Charleston,* we hope to provide a multidimensional view of this area through description, our personal impressions, and some of our preferences. We include addresses and general directions as well as phone numbers and Web sites so you can make specific plans.

Up front, we've provided area maps to help you get your bearings here in the Lowcountry. We give you brief vital statistics, Insiders' tips (indicated by **i**) for quick insights, and more lengthy Close-ups with information that is particularly interesting, unusual, and distinctly Charlestonian.

In many of our chapters we've included quick reference information such as potentially confusing highway designations, emergency and health care phone numbers, essential contacts for newcomers, and convenient parking garages. Of course, you'll want to use our price codes in the restaurants and accommodations chapters. These are designated at the beginning of the chapter.

Our Lowcountry Day Trips chapter is designed to help you branch out from our immediate area, and a chapter called Kidstuff is offered as a collection of some of our favorite ways to show your children a healthy good time. The former is heavily peppered with historical references (because so much of the Lowcountry is all the more interesting when understood in the context of its past). The latter is a subjective overview of venues and activities that have afforded us hours of fun with children we know.

You will notice that throughout the guide we refer to four main general areas—downtown Charleston, east of the Cooper (River), and west of the Ashley (River). Downtown includes the Peninsula and the area slightly north; east of the Cooper includes Mt. Pleasant, Sullivan's Island, and Isle of Palms; west of the Ashley refers to the area just across the Ashley River bridges. We've separated the western islands, James, Johns, Folly, Kiawah, and Seabrook Islands, as a fourth area.

Within chapters such as Restaurants, Nightlife, Hotels and Motels, Parks and Recreation, Health Care, and Neighborhoods, expect to find geographical subcategories for your convenience. Further, Shopping is organized to benefit two broad categories of readers. We start with a rundown for tourists and visitors who want to explore the major shopping venues downtown. We organize the shopping opportunities by merchandise categories. Then we direct newcomers and residents who seek the convenience of shopping in the outlying areas, again, according to merchandise categories. Whether you're a visitor to Charleston or you've chosen to live here, we hope this guide proves helpful in many ways.

# AREA OVERVIEW

ere's an overview of Charleston and its surrounding areas. This chapter is arranged in the geographical order you will see again and again, and offers some information that will help provide a peek at what's here now to see and enjoy.

## CHARLESTON

Exactly 768 miles from New York City, 590 miles from Miami, and almost 2,500 miles from Los Angeles, Charleston remains an undeniably livable city for those fortunate enough to call it home. It's a city of unhurried grace and distinct Southern charm, blessed with an uncanny number of historic structures, many of which have been transformed into handsome offices, restaurants, stores, and homes.

Charleston is the second-largest city in South Carolina (Greenville takes first place). The city's 2000 Census Bureau count was 96,650. In 2003, that estimate had jumped to 101,024. The city's Standard Metropolitan Statistical Area encompasses three counties: Charleston, Berkeley, and Dorchester. This is sometimes called the "Tri-County Area" or the "Trident Area," and in 2000, the population of this area totaled 549,033. By 2003, the estimated total was 571,631. Population growth for the Charleston metro area is projected to be 625,080 people by the year 2015.

Charleston has a warm climate. In January, the average temperature is 55 degrees; in July, it's 82 on the average. But it's prudent to note that summertime temperatures can peak above the 100-degree mark, and the humidity, which is considerable in the Lowcountry during any season, makes the hot seem hotter and the cold colder. Spring in Charleston, however, more than compensates for any discomfort during the other seasons. Many consider it the best time of year in the area; days are warm, nights barely chilled, and the whole world appears to be dripping in wisteria vines and azalea blossoms.

Despite the national economic downturn after September 11, 2001, the Charleston economy continues to be sound and growing. The economic activity is most evident in the vast, newly connected lands of Daniel Island and Cainhoy. Just to the east and north of peninsular Charleston, these areas were annexed in 1991 into the city of Charleston. Daniel Island, which is 4,500 acres, is now being developed as a planned, environmentally sensitive community. (See the Neighborhoods chapter.)

Charleston also offers a wealth of job opportunities. In the banner year of 1997, the Charleston Regional Development Alliance was responsible for securing more than 4,585 new jobs throughout the area, including those at the Nucor steel plant and Mikasa, a manufacturer of tabletop products. Since then, new employment opportunities continue to accrue at a moderate rate.

In 2004 the South Carolina State Ports Authority (SPA) handled more than $39 billion in cargo through their Charleston customs facility. As the largest cargo port on the Southeast Atlantic and Gulf coasts (and still the fourth-largest container port nationwide), the port directly and indirectly provides 281,600 jobs paying $9.4 billion in wages to South Carolinians.

Throughout its history, Charleston has stood as the cultural capital of the South. The performing arts are well represented here with a symphony orchestra, community theater groups, and several ballet companies. The Gibbes Museum of Art and a growing number of independent art galleries display the city's impressive appreciation for the visual arts. The abundant examples of architectural preservation, showing the city's long-standing heritage of building excellence and craftsmanship, also bear witness to this esthetic awareness. (See the chapters called The Arts and Architectural and Historic Preservation.)

Year after year, Charleston has been recognized in popular tourist magazines as one of the top-10 domestic travel destinations. It's even been proclaimed by etiquette guru Marjabelle Young Stewart as the "most mannerly" city in America. We hope that will turn out to be your experience as well.

## MT. PLEASANT

Anyone who crosses the Cooper River via the new Ravenel Bridge into Mt. Pleasant will never forget the journey. (See the Close-up "View to Thrill over the Cooper River," in the Getting Here, Getting Around chapter.) Directly across the Cooper River from Charleston, Mt. Pleasant dates its founding to 1680. The original heart of Mt. Pleasant is the area known as the Old Village. It is designated a National Register Historic District with gracious homes from both the colonial and antebellum periods. Today, the city carefully preserves its rich heritage and small-town appeal. The 2000 Census count for Mt. Pleasant was 47,609 (a 58.1 percent jump from the 1990 Census figures). Estimates for 2003 were 54,788.

The population numbers for this thriving community certainly qualify it as a "city." But, as the name implies, the "town" of Mt. Pleasant is an apt description for the state of mind and the attitude of the businesses you'll find there. Although it serves as a major bedroom community to the Charleston Peninsula, it's still a viable community unto itself.

The days when Mt. Pleasant residents were dependent on the Peninsula for primary shopping, dining, and entertainment venues are gone. Mt. Pleasant's $40-million Towne Centre is clear proof of that with its

15 separate buildings housing about 65 tenants within 425,000 square feet of upscale shopping space.

Patriots Point, the world's largest naval and maritime museum complex, is Mt. Pleasant's biggest attraction. It is dominated by the aircraft carrier *Yorktown*, World War II's famous "Fighting Lady." You can also board tour boats at Patriots Point to visit Fort Sumter National Monument, where the Civil War began. (See the Attractions and Tours chapters.)

Adjacent to Patriots Point is Patriots Point Links, one of the area's most popular public golf courses. The 18-hole, par 72 layout provides spectacular views of Charleston Harbor and the Peninsula's skyline. (See the Golf chapter.) The Mt. Pleasant/Isle of Palms Visitor Center on the U.S. Highway 17 Bypass near McGrath Darby Boulevard is a good place to start when exploring Mt. Pleasant.

## SULLIVAN'S ISLAND

South of Mt. Pleasant and across the Intracoastal Waterway, Sullivan's Island is one of Mt. Pleasant's three true barrier islands (Isle of Palms and the private island of Dewees are the other two). Access to the island is via the Ben Sawyer Causeway (Highway 703) from Mt. Pleasant or via the Isle of Palms Connector (Highway 517) through the Isle of Palms.

Largely a quiet, residential island of old and new beach houses, the island's estimated population in 2003 was 1,854. There is also a smattering of charming 19th-century "summer homes" that have somehow managed to survive the hurricanes and changing fashions of vacation architecture. The few restaurants and pubs on the island are crowded along Middle Street and create something of a strip for strollers who might want to "pub hop" during the evening hours.

Sullivan's Island is the site of old Fort Moultrie and its accompanying interpretation center, which is operated by the

National Park Service. There you can trace the fort's 171-year history from the American Revolution through World War II. (See Forts in the Attractions chapter.)

Another interesting by-product of Sullivan's Island's military days is the fine old row of "quarters" (not far from the lighthouse) that date back to World War I. Still standing at attention along a quiet side street is a handsome line of large frame houses that once served as "officers' row" for the garrison at Fort Moultrie. Now private homes, these former examples of elite military housing speak eloquently of another time from the island's (and our country's) past.

## ISLE OF PALMS

Over the years, the Isle of Palms has grown increasingly popular as a resort and residential island. In 2003, the estimated population was 4,496. But when you add the seasonal renters and the day visitors, the island can host thousands of additional people on any given summer day. Its proximity to Charleston is one of the reasons; its 6 miles of wide, sparkling beach is another attraction.

Those who are here for the short term can enjoy a wide range of accommodations from one end of the island to the other. The island also has a full complement of shops, restaurants, goods, and services to make life very comfortable.

World-famous Wild Dunes Resort, at the northeast end of the island, offers fine restaurants, conference facilities, a fitness center, multiple tennis courts, and two championship Tom Fazio-designed golf courses. Wild Dunes is a busy destination all year long. (See the Neighborhoods and Vacation and Beach Rentals chapters.) The Wild Dunes Yacht Harbor is one of the finest marinas on the Eastern Seaboard. Maybe best of all, Wild Dunes is still only 15 miles from downtown Charleston, offering visitors the chance to enjoy the best of both worlds.

## NORTH CHARLESTON

North Charleston, incorporated only in 1972, is geographically the third-largest city in South Carolina, with an estimated population of 81,577. Its reputation as the hub of the Lowcountry is justified; it's clearly the business and transportation center for the lower half of the state. The international airport and the Amtrak station are here. Also, Interstate 26 and the Mark Clark Expressway (Interstate 526) make getting anywhere in the Lowcountry a snap. (See the Getting Here, Getting Around chapter.)

Once known as the location of Charleston's huge naval facility, North Charleston has outgrown that economic dependency. One of the city's main attractions is the Charleston Area Convention Center Complex, which includes the 14,000-seat Coliseum and the 2,250-seat Performing Arts Center. These state-of-the-art venues draw crowds from all over the area and host a wide variety of events ranging from Broadway shows to major rock concerts and ice shows. The Coliseum is also the home of the South Carolina Stingrays, our local ice hockey team. (See the Spectator Sports chapter.)

Not only does the area have more than 5,400 hotel rooms, but the rates are also generally lower than those found elsewhere in the Lowcountry (especially downtown Charleston). This makes North Charleston a favorite haunt for business types and convention travelers. If you're arriving via I-26, you may want to stop at the North Charleston Visitor Center just across from the Coliseum. You'll find plenty of area information there.

## BERKELEY COUNTY

In the 1980s, Berkeley County, just north of Charleston County, was the fastest-growing county in all of South Carolina. The boom came when major new industrial concerns invested more than $1.7 billion in the county economy.

The greatest concentration of population and residential and commercial development has been in the southern portion of the county near Moncks Corner. Berkeley's central town, however, remains Goose Creek. Other county towns include Hanahan and St. Stephen. Total population of these towns is more than 50,000, according to recent estimates.

Currently, industrial development is concentrated along U.S. Highway 52 north of Goose Creek and on the island formed by the Cooper River and the Black River and its tributary branches. The major Berkeley County employers are Santee Cooper (electric utility), Bayer Corp. (manufacturing), and Nucor Steel.

Much of the northern portion of Berkeley County is still productive, cultivated farmland. Most of the eastern portion of the county and large areas of the west remain as beautiful pine forests—one of the county's most distinctive features.

## DORCHESTER COUNTY

Dorchester's $127 million in economic development during 1997 largely came from the expansion of existing industries. The major employers in Dorchester County include the Robert Bosch Corp. (anti-lock braking systems), Industrial Products, Inc. (industrial textiles), Lieber Correctional Institute, and Dorchester County School District II.

Although St. George, with its estimated 2003 population of 2,097, is the county seat, the part of Dorchester County currently seeing the greatest amount of economic growth is Summerville. With a 2003 estimated population of 37,734, the town's healthy mix of retail, commercial, and tourist-related businesses along with light manufacturing concerns seems to be attracting both newcomers and business investors.

(For a historical perspective on Summerville and a brief driving tour of the town's historic homes, see the Lowcountry Day Trips chapter.)

## WEST ASHLEY

The City of Charleston annexed its first West Ashley tract in 1960, and the area has been growing ever since. The population figure for this area is 61,197 according to the 2000 Census.

West Ashley is a patchwork of old and new neighborhoods and businesses that line the major traffic arteries (U.S. Highway 17 S. and Highway 61). Many of the older neighborhoods have graceful old live oaks and spacious, well-tended lawns. In fact, there's a new movement afoot to do some strategic planning aimed at preserving this "village" atmosphere—especially in the area surrounding the foot of the Ashley River Bridge. And please note, the local residents don't live in West Ashley or at West Ashley, they simply "live West Ashley."

West Ashley is home to Charles Towne Landing State Historic Site, a nature/historic theme park on the site of the original English settlement. It also claims the beautiful Ashley River Road, which leads to Drayton Hall, Magnolia Gardens, and Middleton Place (see Historic Plantations in the Attractions chapter). You'll find Charleston's largest shopping center—Citadel Mall, with well over 100 tenants—in West Ashley. The area also has the "Automile," a strip of new and used car dealerships along Savannah Highway (US 17 S.) and one of the major engines of the local economy.

By far, the largest employer West Ashley (you'll get used to saying it that way) is Bon Secours–St. Francis Hospital, which relocated to a new facility in December 1996. (See the Health Care chapter.) This huge, 32-acre medical complex added 875 new jobs to the area economy, and many other spin-off businesses have followed suit.

## JAMES ISLAND AND JOHNS ISLAND

Geographically, James Island, which lies due west of the Charleston Peninsula, is less rural than Johns Island. It is essentially a bedroom community for Charleston with many shopping strips scattered along the main roads of Maybank Highway and Folly Road.

What remains of James Island's rural character may be threatened by the easy access now made possible by the James Island Expressway (Highway 30). This increasingly busy roadway connecting the island to the Peninsula is fueling rapid development—especially along Folly Road toward Folly Beach. The remaining tracts of farmland are likely victims of rising land values and are prime targets for real estate developers.

While Johns Island may be still agricultural in appearance, change is in the air. A 1997 study showed that Johns Island was home to more than half of the nearly 2,000 people employed on the resort islands of Kiawah and Seabrook (plus most of the 400 more who work there during the busy season). After the opening of The Sanctuary, Kiawah's new 255-room hotel and spa, the number of James and Johns Island employees jumped considerably. Many Hispanics joining the Lowcountry workforce have made these islands their home.

## FOLLY BEACH

This eccentric and diverse beach town likes to call itself "the edge of America." Only 10 minutes from historic Charleston, this is a tourist's world—one where there's plenty to see and do.

First of all, there's the beach—Folly's claim to fame. It runs almost 6 miles along the Atlantic side of the island. Folly has had serious erosion problems in the past. Periodically the beach is "renourished" by mechanically pumping millions of cubic yards of sand back onto the shore. But there's always plenty of sand, sun, fun, and (yes) folly to go around.

The island has a year-round estimated population of 2,197. But the population swells enormously on any summer day, when the hoards of beach lovers, young and old, come out to play. Employment opportunities are almost exclusively limited to the tourist trade.

Crabbing, sunning, surfing, swimming, surf fishing, biking, waterskiing, and sailing are going on. You name it, Folly Beach has it. Folly touts its 1,000-foot fishing pier, complete with snack bar, tackle shop, and full-service seafood restaurant. The pier is reminiscent of the old days when beach pavilions were all the rage for dance bands and swing music. (For more on area piers, see the Hunting and Fishing chapter.)

Although there are walk-throughs along the beach that lead from Arctic and Ashley Avenues to the surf for day visitors, it's best to go to the west end of the island and visit Folly Beach County Park. Admission is $5.00 a vehicle, but once you're inside you've got restrooms, showers, drinking water, limited parking, and probably the best open vistas on the island. (See the Parks and Recreation chapter.)

You'll find many reasonable short-term accommodations at Folly Beach. (See the Hotels and Motels chapter.) There are also seasonal rentals and a lot of interesting full-time residents on the island. It is Charleston's truly original beach playground. (See the Vacation and Beach Rentals chapter.)

## KIAWAH ISLAND

Only 21 miles from Charleston is Kiawah Island, renowned for its natural beauty and environmentally responsible development. The endless acres of marsh, the 10 miles of pristine Atlantic beach, the thick forests, and abundant wildlife are only the beginning. Among all this are championship golf, first-rate tennis, exclusive shopping, and fine dining. Like the beach itself, the opportunities for enjoyment here go on and on.

Golfers have a selection of courses to play. They can choose from Turtle Point by Jack Nicklaus, Cougar Point by Gary Player, Tom Fazio's Osprey Point, and the famed Ocean Course by Pete Dye (site of

# Charleston Vital Statistics

Most of these facts and figures pertaining to Charleston and South Carolina are covered in much greater detail in the following pages of this *Insiders' Guide to Charleston.* However, here's an at-a-glance overview of the area for first-timers and international visitors—plus a quick reference for those in a big hurry.

**Charleston mayor:** Joseph P. Riley Jr. (D)

**South Carolina governor:** Mark Sanford (R)

**Population:**
City of Charleston: 101,024 in 2003
Metro Area: 571,631 in 2003
South Carolina: 4,107,183 in 2003

**Area (square miles):**
City of Charleston: 88.14 square miles
Business district: 7.6 square miles
South Carolina: 31,113 square miles

**Nickname/Motto:** "The Holy City"

Translation of Latin motto from the city's official seal: Aedes Mora Juraque Curat, "She guards her buildings, her customs, and her laws."

**Average temperatures:**
January: 55° F
July: 82° F

**Average rainfall:** 52 inches per year

**City/State founded:**
First English colony of Carolina founded: 1670
Officially separated as Royal Colony of South Carolina: 1729
Incorporated as City of Charleston: 1783

**South Carolina's major cities:** Columbia (state capital), Charleston, Florence, Georgetown, Greenville, Hilton Head, Mt. Pleasant, Myrtle Beach, North Charleston, Spartanburg, Sumter

**Major colleges/universities:** Charleston Southern University, College of Charleston/University of Charleston, The Citadel, Trident Technical College, Medical University of South Carolina

**Important dates in history:**

**1670** Founding of Charles Towne colony
**1680** Colony moved to safer location on peninsula
**1719** Revolt leading to establishment of South Carolina as province of British Crown
**1783** Newly liberated city changes name to "Charleston"
**1822** Denmark Vesey slave uprising
**1861** Outbreak of War between the States
**1904** Construction of U.S. Navy Yard
**1977** Debut of Spoleto Festival USA
**1989** Devastation by Hurricane Hugo

**Major area employers:** Medical University of South Carolina, Charleston Air Force Base, U.S. Navy, Charleston County School District, Roper St. Francis Healthcare, Westvaco Corporation, Santee Cooper, Robert Bosch Corporation, Piggly Wiggly Carolina Company, Inc.

**Famous sons and daughters:** Charles C. Pinckney—youngest signer of the U.S. Constitution; John Rutledge—another signer of the U.S. Constitution; John C. Calhoun—statesman, U.S. vice president; Edward Rutledge and Arthur Middleton—signers of the Declaration of Independence; Francis Marion, "The Swamp Fox"—Revolutionary War hero; Eliza Lucas Pinckney—entrepreneur of rice and indigo culture; Dubose Heyward—author of Porgy; Philip Simmons—world-class wrought iron artisan; Septima Clark—educator and civil rights activist

**Major airports/interstates:** Charleston International Airport; I-26; I-526.

**Public transportation:** CARTA (bus system); DASH (downtown area shuttle)

**Military bases:** Charleston Air Force Base (437th Airlift Wing) and 315th Airlift Wing (Reserves); United States Coast Guard Group Charleston Station; Charleston's SPAWAR (Space and Naval Warfare Systems Center); and NOAA (National Oceanic and Atmospheric Administration) Coastal Services Center

**Driving laws:** Right turn on red permitted; seatbelts must be worn at all times in moving vehicle; headlights must be on when wipers are used; speed limit on State highways is 55 mph; speed limit on Interstates is 70 mph in designated limited access areas.

**Alcohol laws:** Legal drinking age is 21 years; blood-alcohol content of .08% or higher is DUI in South Carolina, but .06% to .09% can also be designated DUI at arresting officer's discretion.

**Daily newspaper:** *The Post and Courier;* daily circulation, 95,588; Sunday, 106,061.

**Sales tax:** 6% City/State sales tax. (1% sales tax discount for citizens age 85 and over) 12% City/State accommodations tax

the memorable 1991 Ryder Cup). (See the Golf chapter for more details.) In November 1997, the Ocean Course hosted the 43rd World Cup of Golf with teams from 32 nations competing. Televised in more than 80 countries, this was the world's most-watched golf tournament to date. In fall 2003, the World Cup returned with 24 nations participating in this much-heralded international golf championship. On Kiawah, tennis buffs have two complete tennis centers with fully staffed pro shops, and extensive instructional facilities.

The island's accommodations are all outstanding. Some guests prefer being pampered at The Sanctuary, the island's new $126-million hotel and convention facility with luxury spa, which opened in 2004. Others prefer the privacy of furnished villas or cottages conveniently scattered around the island. Bear in mind that Kiawah Island is a private community with access limited to property owners, guests of the resort, or designated rental agencies. Full-time residents number 1,110 according to a recent estimate. But seasonal visitors swell this number to more than 7,000. Public access to the beach is available at Beachwalker County Park at the west end of the island. (See the Neighborhoods, Vacation and Beach Rentals, and Parks and Recreation chapters.)

*Here is a statistic that says a great deal about the development "styles" of the resort barrier islands of Kiawah and Seabrook: Over the past decade, Kiawah's population growth has been well over 40 percent, while Seabrook's population has grown by only 11 percent. Some people are attracted to a "resort destination" image while others prefer the "quiet residential" atmosphere. Both have great appeal.*

## SEABROOK ISLAND

Seabrook Island is on the Atlantic shore just 22 miles south of Charleston. It is unique in that it is totally private and completely owned by its residents. Entry to the island is controlled by a security gate for the privacy of residents and guests. The beauty of the island is striking. Visitors can enjoy 3.5 miles of unspoiled beach along the Atlantic and the banks of the Edisto River, which flows into the ocean at Seabrook.

The Club at Seabrook offers championship golf courses: Crooked Oaks, designed by Robert Trent Jones Sr., and Ocean Winds, designed by Willard Byrd. A beach club, a tennis center, and a beautiful Island House Club with restaurants, bar lounges, and a golf pro shop are here. Also unique to Seabrook is its equestrian center.

The island has more than 450 villas available for rent as well as more than 1,194 permanent residents, whose homes are situated along the beach, marshes, lakes, and golf courses.

Bohicket Marina, just outside the Seabrook Island gate, is a superb marina with dockominiums plus an attractive shopping area. About 60 rental slips are available for all sizes of motor cruisers and sailboats. Boat rentals and charters for deep-sea fishing, crabbing, shrimping, or exploring the miles of ocean creeks are also available. (See the Boating and Watersports chapter.)

# GETTING HERE, GETTING AROUND

Visitors to the Trident area who arrive via different modes of transportation are faced with challenges unique to each form. For instance, if you drive, fly, ride the bus, or take the train, how are you going to negotiate the trip into town or—worse yet—out to the fringes? Say you come in on a yacht, or you are a passenger on a cruise ship. What next?

We've answered these questions individually, and the headings identify each transportation mode. It may seem a little lengthy, but we've tried to take you by the hand to lead you each step of the way in the Lowcountry.

## GETTING HERE BY AUTO

We have tried to give very specific directions and many options for travel into and around Charleston. Our reasoning is both practical and designed for those interested in getting more out of their drive than simply moving from point A to point B. With heavy seasonal traffic (in spring, as many as half a million visitors come to Charleston by car), seemingly constant road and bridge work, and a peculiar system of one-way city streets, getting around Charleston is not always simple on first try.

Also, parking on the Peninsula is always a problem. The city has made strides toward managing the situation to the benefit of both residents and tourists, with restricted parking hours in residential neighborhoods and parking garages for public use. Metered parking spaces are limited but convenient when you find them. To avoid costly tickets, a parking garage is your safest bet.

While there are ways to maximize speed in travel around the Lowcountry,

there are other ways to chart your journey to take advantage of the beautiful setting. Here are our suggestions for both, tailored to arrival from the main highways.

## Charleston via U.S. Highway 17 N. (Savannah Highway)

### TO JOHNS ISLAND, KIAWAH, AND SEABROOK

If you are driving north on Savannah Highway (U.S. Highway 17) and your destination is Kiawah, Seabrook, or Johns Island, the fastest route is to take a right on Main Road. Look for a major intersection with a green sign indicating Kiawah and Seabrook. When you cross the Limehouse Bridge, you are on Johns Island. To go to Kiawah or Seabrook, continue to the end of Main Road, which turns into Bohicket Road, and follow the signs. Kiawah will be on your left, and Seabrook will be at the end of the road.

### TO JAMES ISLAND AND FOLLY BEACH

If you want to go to James Island or Folly Beach from US 17, take a right before you reach the Ashley River Bridge at the intersection of Wesley Drive and US 17. Stay on Wesley until it merges with Folly Road. Cross the Wappoo Bridge and stay on Folly Road to James Island and Folly Beach.

### TO DOWNTOWN CHARLESTON

If your destination is the city, you can take either a panoramic approach or the shortest connection.

The Scenic Route: Should you have the extra minutes and the inclination, turn right at Wesley Drive as if heading to James Island or Folly Beach. Stay on Wesley until it merges with Folly Road, cross the Wappoo Bridge and stay on Folly Road until you see, on your left, the exit for the Robert B. Scarborough Bridge (also called the James Island Expressway or Highway 30).

In terms of time from Savannah Highway, this will take about 10 minutes longer than the quickest route to Calhoun Street, a main street traversing the Peninsula from east to west. However, the splendid views can make it a nice option when traffic snarls on the Ashley River Bridge. (See the Close-up "View to Thrill over the Cooper River" in this chapter.)

The Speedy Route: If you prefer the most direct route downtown, cross the Ashley River Bridge on US 17 and veer right onto Lockwood Drive. You make your next decision at the first stoplight: If you are interested in visiting the medical complexes or the College of Charleston, shops on King Street, or the Charleston Visitor Reception and Transportation Center, go left, and the road will actually curve into and become Calhoun Street. King Street intersects Calhoun, and you can turn right or left to park and shop. To find the visitor center, follow the green and white signs that will direct you to upper Meeting Street, an intersecting street that is just one block past King, off Calhoun, on the left.

But if you need to reach the southern portion of the Peninsula, follow the straight arrow at that first stoplight. This will be a continuation of Lockwood Drive. You'll drive past the City Marina and Rice Mill Building, round the corner by the Coast Guard Station, and turn onto Broad Street. Broad eventually dead-ends at East Bay Street. Take a right on any intersecting street to find addresses referred to as "below Broad."

## TO THE NORTHERN PENINSULA

To use US 17 N. to reach the northern Peninsula, cross the Ashley River Bridge in

the second from the right lane of the bridge that reads "Lockwood Drive N." Continue straight off the bridge to the traffic light, and turn left onto Lockwood Drive North. A Charleston RiverDogs sign pointing left is at this intersection. Continue up Lockwood through the next traffic light, where RiverDogs and Citadel signs direct you around onto Fishburne Street to Riley Park, sports fields, and on over to Hagood Avenue. Turn left onto Hagood Avenue at the stop sign, and the Citadel Bulldog's Johnson Hagood stadium is on the right. To reach the Citadel campus, follow Hagood Avenue until it dead-ends into one of the Citadel entrance gates.

## TO NORTH CHARLESTON

There are two ways to get to North Charleston. First, you can take a left onto Highway 7 (Sam Rittenberg Boulevard), follow it until it merges with Highway 171, then cross the Memorial Bridge (which locals call the North Bridge) into North Charleston. Another option is to take a left from US 17 onto the Mark Clark Expressway (Interstate 526), which will take you by the Charleston Area Convention Center Complex and the airport or to Interstate 26 and the commercial districts of North Charleston.

## TO MT. PLEASANT, SULLIVAN'S ISLAND, ISLE OF PALMS

To reach Mt. Pleasant and other East Cooper areas from US 17 N., take a left onto the Mark Clark Expressway (I-526), and stay on it until it intersects (again) and dead-ends at US 17 N. in Mt. Pleasant. To go to the Isle of Palms, take a left on U.S. 17 N., and after about 5 miles, look for the Isle of Palms Connector (Highway 517) exit on the right.

If your destination is Sullivan's Island, take a right on Georgetown Highway (US 17), and follow it until it intersects with Coleman Boulevard. Take a left at the light, and follow Coleman (also called Ben Sawyer Boulevard at this point) as it crosses the Ben Sawyer Bridge to Sulli-van's Island.

Another way to reach Mt. Pleasant and other East Cooper areas from US 17 is to cross the Ashley River Bridge and the overpass to the Crosstown. You'll see signs for I–26 to the left, but you'll want to stay in the right lane under the signs to Mt. Pleasant. Once on the new Arthur Ravenel Jr. Bridge over the Cooper River, negotiate into the right lane. Across the bridge, take the lane marked S.C. 703. You will see the Mt. Pleasant welcome sign on the left as you drive down Coleman Boulevard (Highway 703). Eventually, this road crosses Shem Creek near the historic Old Village residential area. It later becomes Ben Sawyer Boulevard (still Highway 703) before it crosses the Ben Sawyer Bridge to Sullivan's Island.

To reach the Isle of Palms, take a left on Jasper Boulevard (also Highway 703) and drive across Sullivan's Island to Breach Inlet. Cross the bridge over the inlet, and you are on the Isle of Palms. To find Wild Dunes, the largest resort development on the island, follow Palm Boulevard (Highway 703) and the signs to the Wild Dunes Reception Center.

If you intend to head north on US 17 to reach Mt. Pleasant destinations such as Hobcaw, Towne Centre, Snee Farm, Boone Hall or, eventually, McClellanville and Georgetown, stay left on the Arthur Ravenel Jr. Bridge over the Cooper River and cross the US 17 N. overpass.

# Charleston via U.S. Highway 17 S. (from Georgetown, Myrtle Beach)

## TO ISLE OF PALMS, SULLIVAN'S ISLAND, MT. PLEASANT

If you are headed south on US 17 and want to go to the Isle of Palms or Sulli-van's Island, take a left onto the Isle of

Palms Connector (Highway 517), which goes to the Isle of Palms. At the end of the connector, take a right to go to Sulli-van's Island and Mt. Pleasant or a left to go to Wild Dunes Resort.

## TO NORTH CHARLESTON

If you want to go to North Charleston, take a right onto the Mark Clark Express-way (I–526) off US 17 S. The airport, the Charleston Area Convention Center Com-plex, and other destinations are clearly marked along the way.

*If you just need to scoot from point A to point B downtown and you're tired of hoofing it, you can summon one of the handy rickshaws that orbit the Market area in the evenings. Eleven of the three-wheeled (bicycle-like) wonders pedal about the streets after 5:00 P.M. every weeknight, running until midnight. On weekends, they're around til 2:00 or 3:00 A.M. All are "driven" by strong-winded college kids who know the city and the bicycle rules of safety. You can just hail one anywhere you see it, or you can call the dispatch number at (843) 723–5685, and one will pedal to your location (approximate response time: five minutes). Rates are $7.00 one way (for about a 10-minute ride). Daylight hours are limited to special events or prearranged engagements.*

## TO DOWNTOWN CHARLESTON

If you want to drive into the city, follow US 17 S. to approach the Ravenel Bridge. If you want to go to the southern parts of the Peninsula, we recommend two options after crossing the bridge. For King Street (its shopping district and the nearby visitor center), stay in the left lane and take the Interstate 26 E. exit heading downtown. Follow I–26 E. and bear to the right on US 17 S. (the Crosstown). Stay right and take

# Take a Number

Bombarded by highway designations that seem to be blurring into one another? Confused by well-meaning Lowcountry direction-givers who throw out numbers faster than a lottery-ball machine? Take heart! Below is a brief listing of highways and connectors that are often referred to by locals without the state or U.S. pre-fixes.

For cross-referencing ease and your information, please note these numbers, with a few of their local incarnations:

US 17 N. (the Crosstown, the Bypass, Johnnie Dodds Boulevard, Georgetown Highway)
US 17 S. (Savannah Highway)
US 52 (Rivers Avenue)

US 78 (Summerville Highway)
Highway 7 (Sam Rittenberg Boulevard, Cosgrove Avenue)
Highway 30 (James Island Expressway)
Highway 517 (Isle of Palms Connector)
Highway 700 (Maybank Highway)
Highway 703 (Coleman, Ben Sawyer, Jasper, and Palm Boulevards)
Highway 61 (St. Andrews Boulevard, Ashley River Road)
Highway 171 (Folly Road)
I–526 (Mark Clark Expressway)

Remember, don't be afraid to ask for specifics. When true Insiders are pressed for directions, they can almost always find a way to shepherd you from point A to point B.

the first exit to King Street. Turn right at the stop sign onto King. Another option is to stay in the right lane of US 17 S. and take the Rutledge Avenue exit; then stay on Rutledge Avenue until it intersects with Calhoun Street. Take a left for destinations off the Calhoun route (such as the College of Charleston campus and King Street shopping) or a right to reach the medical complex. You can also stay on King Street or Rutledge Avenue until it dead-ends at Murray Boulevard (the Battery), getting a glimpse of some of the city's more desirable real estate along the way.

If you are looking for The Citadel or points around the school (such as Joseph P. Riley Jr. Park, Hampton Park, and sports fields), stay on the Crosstown until you come to Hagood Avenue, and take a right. You will pass sports fields and can drive straight to the back gate of The Citadel. Hampton Park is just outside the front gates of the school.

## TO WEST ASHLEY

If you're going to West Ashley on US 17 S., there are two options. First, you can take a right on the Mark Clark Expressway (I–526) and stay on it until it intersects with Sam Rittenberg Boulevard (near Citadel Mall) and eventually dead-ends at an intersection with US 17. The second option is to stay on US 17 S. until you cross the Ravenel Bridge, the Peninsula via the Crosstown, and eventually the Ashley River Bridge.

## TO OTHER POINTS WEST

For James and Johns Islands, Kiawah, Seabrook, and Folly Beach, stay on the Crosstown (US 17 S.), cross the Ashley River Bridge, then take a left at the first stoplight at the intersection of US 17 and Wesley Drive. Stay on Wesley one block until it merges with Folly Road (Highway 171). To reach destinations on James

Fall
2004

# MEMBER BENEFITS GUIDE

# AARP

>> **Write your membership number in the box below.
It opens the door to every benefit.**

AARP MEMBERSHIP CARD #

## Accessing exclusive AARP savings and services is easy!

Just look inside for details on exactly how to take advantage of these offers
and enjoy your AARP benefits to the fullest.

# Hot New Offers!

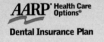

### AARP Dental Insurance Plan administered by Delta Dental Insurance Company

The new AARP Dental Insurance Plan provides coverage tailored to the dental
needs of AARP members, including the freedom to choose their own dentist.
Enrollees pay lower out-of-pocket expenses when visiting a Delta Dental dentist.
Two different plan options offer immediate coverage for the most common
services, with expanded coverage for major services after a 12-month waiting
period. Individual and family coverage options are available and premiums are
guaranteed for two years.

The AARP Dental Insurance Plan is insured by Delta Dental Insurance or
Dentegra Insurance Company and administered by Delta Dental Insurance
Company. Call 866-583-2087 or visit us online at **www.deltadentalins.com/aarp**
for more information about the AARP Dental Insurance Plan.

### Medicare-Approved AARP Prescription Discount Card

AARP Pharmacy Services has many options for prescription discounts for our
members, including the new Medicare-approved AARP Prescription Discount
Card. Save on every FDA-approved drug available at participating network
pharmacies or through the convenient mail order service. Please contact us
at **1-800-592-3069** (ask for department# JAMBG4) or visit us at
**www.aarppharmacy.com** to learn more.

**More member benefits inside >**
And visit offers.aarp.org/benefits17 **for our most up-to-date list!**

**MEMBERSHIP BENEFITS**

## Auto Club

| AARP Motoring Plan from GE Motor Club[1] | Low cost emergency road service plans | 800-555-1121 www.aarpmotoring.com |
|---|---|---|

[1] Available in California as The Amoco Motor Club for AARP Members.

## Financial Services

| AARP Automobile Insurance from The Hartford | Low rates, many discounts, great benefits | 800-932-9922 aarp.thehartford.com/ds |
|---|---|---|
| > AARP Credit Card Services from Bank One | Full 1% cash back, low interest rate, no annual fee, no telemarketing | 888-595-0542 www.aarp.org/creditcard |
| AARP Home Business Plan from The Hartford | Important protection at very low rates | 888-466-9675 aarp.thehartford.com/hb |
| AARP Homeowners Insurance from The Hartford | Lifetime renewability, many discounts | 800-423-4114 aarp.thehartford.com/hm |
| • Flood Coverage | Flood protection backed by the U.S. Government | 800-296-7542 |
| AARP Investment Program from Scudder Investments | A spectrum of 38 mutual funds, no commissions, low management fees | 800-322-2282 aarp.scudder.com |
| AARP Life Insurance from New York Life | Affordable coverage options for term & permanent life insurance | 800-449-1548 x100 www.nylaarp.com |
| AARP Mobile Home Insurance from Foremost | Superior coverage, lifetime renewal | 800-752-2461 www.aarpforemost.com |
| • Flood Coverage | Flood protection backed by the U.S. Government | 866-865-2965 |
| AARP Property & Casualty Insurance from Real Legacy Assurance Company | Personal Package Plus, Homeowners and separate Automobile Policy | P.R.:800-981-7855 U.S.V.I.:800-433-0881 |

## Health & Wellness

AARP Health Care Options is a collection of health care products and services you can trust, because they've been endorsed by AARP. Discover everything from discounts on prescriptions and eye glasses to supplemental health, dental and long-term care insurance. Call 800-874-0626 today to learn more about all the products and services you can choose from — and to experience our award-winning customer service.

For pricing and discount specifics, visit our Web site at **www.aarphealthcare.com** or contact:

| Eyewear and Eye Care Savings from *Cole Vision Corporation* | 888-352-3924 |
|---|---|
| Long-term Care Insurance underwritten by *Metropolitan Life Insurance Company* | 800-452-1393 |
| Prescription Drug Discounts, Mail Order Pharmacy, Health Essentials Catalog, and Medical Supply Services from *United HealthCare Insurance Company* | 800-456-2277 www.aarppharmacy.com |
| Supplemental Health Insurance underwritten by *United HealthCare Insurance Company* | 800-523-5800 ext. 532 |
| > AARP Dental Insurance Plan administered by *Delta Dental Insurance Company* | 866-583-2087 www.deltadentalins.com/aarp |

# Travel Products

## Hotels, Motels & Resorts

www.aarp.org/hotels

### Midprice (Continued)

| | | |
|---|---|---|
| Comfort Suites (ID#00333300) | 15% | 800-424-6423 |
| Four Points by Sheraton | 15 – 50% | 877-778-2277 |
| Hampton Inn & Suites | 10% | 800-426-7866 |
| Holiday Inn Hotels & Resorts | 10% | 800-465-4329 |
| Holiday Inn Express | 10% | 800-465-4329 |
| Howard Johnson (ID#61552) | 20% | 800-769-0939 |
| La Quinta Inns | 10 – 30% | 866-573-6722 |
| MainStay Suites (ID#00333300) | 15% | 800-424-6423 |
| > Park Plaza Hotels & Resorts | 10 – 25% | 800-814-7000 |
| Quality (ID#00333300) | 15% | 800-424-6423 |
| Ramada (ID#61552) | 20% | 800-462-8035 |
| Sleep Inn (ID#00333300) | 15% | 800-424-6423 |
| Wellesley Inn & Suites | 15% | 800-444-8888 |
| Wingate Inn (ID#61552) | 15% | 877-202-8814 |

### Luxury/Upscale

| | | |
|---|---|---|
| AmeriSuites | 15% | 800-833-1516 |
| Crowne Plaza Hotels & Resorts | 10% | 800-227-6963 |
| Fairmont Hotels & Resorts | 10 – 25% | 800-441-1414 |
| Luxury Collection | 15 – 50% | 877-778-2277 |
| > Radisson Hotels & Resorts | 10 – 25% | 800-333-3333 |
| Sheraton | 15 – 50% | 877-778-2277 |
| St. Regis | 15 – 50% | 877-778-2277 |
| W Hotels | 15 – 50% | 877-778-2277 |
| Westin | 15 – 50% | 877-778-2277 |
| > Wyndham Hotels & Resorts | 35 – 40% | 800-996-3426 |

## Independent and Escorted Travel

| | | |
|---|---|---|
| ARAMARK Parks & Resorts (lodging, houseboats, retail) | 10 – 25% | 888-272-5131 www.aarp.org/parkadventures |
| > SeaWorld/Busch Gardens (savings on adult admission) | Save $5 everyday; $8 on Tuesdays | www.aarp.org/themeparks |
| Collette Vacations | $25 – $100 | 888-332-1904 www.aarp.org/collette |
| Cosmos | $50 | 866-285-9186 www.aarp.org/cosmos |
| Globus | $50 | 866-285-9186 www.aarp.org/globus |
| National Parks Pass (savings on admission) | 10% | 888-467-2757 www.aarp.org/parkspass |

## Travel Funds

| | | |
|---|---|---|
| > American Express TravelFunds Card, Travelers Cheques and foreign currency | Special offer for AARP members | 800-721-9754 www.aarp.org/amex |

## Airlines

www.aarp.org/airlines

| | | |
|---|---|---|
| **US Airways** | Ask for "AARP Savers" | 866-886-2277 www.aarp.org/usairways |
| > **Virgin Atlantic Airways** | 11 – 17% | 800-862-8621 www.aarp.org/virginatlantic |

## Auto Rentals

www.aarp.org/autorentals

| | | |
|---|---|---|
| **Avis** (ID#A359800)[3] | 5 – 25% | 800-331-1800 |
| **Hertz** (ID#50075)[3] | 5 – 25% | 800-654-2200 |
| **National** (ID#6100120)[3] | 5 – 30% | 866-609-7973 |

## Cruises

www.aarp.org/cruises

| | | |
|---|---|---|
| > **Avalon Waterways** | $50 | 877-797-8788 |
| **Carnival Cruise Lines** | $50 – $100 | 800-227-6482 |
| **Cruise West** | $25 – $200 on-board credit | 888-396-0237 |
| **Holland America Line** | $50 – $200 | 877-724-5425 |
| **MSC Cruises** | $100 – $200 | 800-666-9333 |
| **Norwegian Coastal Voyage** | $50 – $150 | 800-323-7436 |

## Hotels, Motels & Resorts

www.aarp.org/hotels

### Economy

| | | |
|---|---|---|
| **Days Inn** (ID#61552) | 15% | 800-268-2195 |
| **Econo Lodge** (ID#00333300) | 15% | 800-424-6423 |
| **Knights Inn** (ID#61552) | 15% | 800-682-1071 |
| **Motel 6** | 10% | 877-467-7305 |
| > **Park Inn** | 10 – 25% | 800-670-7275 |
| **Red Roof Inns** | 10% | 877-467-7303 |
| **Rodeway Inn** (ID#00333300) | 15% | 800-424-6423 |
| **Super 8 Motel** (ID#61552) | 10% | 800-889-9706 |
| **Travelodge** (ID#61552) | 15% | 800-545-5545 |
| **Villager** (ID#61552) | 15% | 888-821-5779 |

### Midprice

| | | |
|---|---|---|
| **AmeriHost** (ID#61552) | 15% | 800-996-2087 |
| **Best Western** | 10% | 800-603-2277 |
| > **Country Inns & Suites By Carlson** | 10% | 800-456-4000 |
| **Clarion** (ID#00333300) | 15% | 800-424-6423 |
| **Comfort Inn** (ID#00333300) | 15% | 800-424-6423 |

**Note:** Arranged discounts do not imply endorsement of firms by AARP and are subject to change.

[3] In addition to discounts, members using the applicable car rental ID # receive special insurance-related benefits at participating U.S. locations: (1) enhanced primary liability insurance coverage of $100,000/$300,000/$25,000 from Avis, and $25,000/$50,000/$10,000 from Hertz and National; and (2) maximum personal responsibility for damages to the rental car capped at $5,000 if you decline to purchase the collision/loss/damage waiver.

> **New Offer!**

## Legal Services

| | | |
|---|---|---|
| **AARP Legal Services Network (LSN)** | Free consultation and reduced fees on additional service | 888-OUR-AARP<br>www.aarp.org/lsn |

## Technology and Entertainment

AARP Privileges

### Computers and Technology

| | | |
|---|---|---|
| **America Online**<br>AOL® Keyword: AARP | 10% savings on standard monthly rates | New: 877-523-4493<br>Existing: 888-466-2255<br>www.aarp.org/aol |
| > **EarthLink**<br>**Dialup Service** | 50% savings for the first 6 months- savings of over $77-plus an ongoing $2 monthly discount | 888-829-8413<br>Mention Code: 1018928<br>www.aarp.org/earthlink |
| **EarthLink High-Speed Internet Service** | Special offers on DSL and Cable EarthLink Internet Access! Get a free $25 Visa Gift Card. | 888-829-8413<br>Mention Code: 1020889 for DSL and 1017735 for Cable<br>www.aarp.org/earthlink |
| > **Gateway Computers** | 7% savings on consumer desktop and notebook computers | 800-270-5736<br>www.aarp.org/gateway |
| > **Gateway Accessories & Peripherals** | 7% savings on all software, peripherals and electronic accessories | 800-270-5736<br>www.aarp.org/gatewayextras |
| > **Gateway Electronics** | 5% savings on plasma & LCD televisions except for new 42" | 800-270-5736<br>www.aarp.org/gatewayextras |
| > **Gateway Training Products** | 25% savings on training offerings including in-classroom, CD-ROM & online based | 800-588-3893<br>www.aarp.org/gatewaytraining |

### Gifts, Shopping and Entertainment

| | | |
|---|---|---|
| **AARP Gift Membership Packages** | Packages that include an AARP membership | www.aarp.org/giftmemberships |
| **AARP Store** | Merchandise with the the AARP logo | www.aarpstore.org |
| > **Gold Violin**<br>Gadgets for Independent Living | Free catalog and 5% savings on every purchase | 866-206-3448<br>www.aarp.org/goldviolin |
| > **Reebok & Rockport Factory Outlet Stores** | Save 20% off your entire purchase with AARP card at checkout | 800-441-2220<br>www.aarp.org/reebok |
| **ThirdAge Gifts from GiftCorp** | 5% savings on unique, special occasion gift packages | www.aarp.org/thirdagegifts |

### Home

| | | |
|---|---|---|
| **ADT Security Services[2]**<br>(Code: AA103) | 10% savings on installation costs +$1 monthly savings on monitoring fee (new customers only) | 888-553-2430<br>www.aarp.org/adt |
| **Alternative Health and Wellness Services provided by _American WholeHealth_** | | 888-893-4639<br>www.aarp.org/althealth |

[2] For a complete list of restrictions, conditions and license numbers, please visit www.aarp.org/adt. Offer applies to new accounts only.

## Keep this guide handy and use it to take

**advantage** of the many benefits of your AARP membership. We are adding new offers frequently so check the AARP Web site, **www.aarp.org** for the most updated AARP information and news.

## Get AARP Member Benefits Updates Instantly.

The AARP Member Benefit Guide is updated quarterly. To receive an updated email version, please visit offers.aarp.org/benefitsguide

**Keep up-to-date** on all new offers by signing up for our e-mail newsletters at offers.aarp.org/emailnews4

**Note:** Some of the offers listed in this guide may have limited availability or restrictions, so please contact any of the listed providers directly to get more details on limitations. Guide sponsored by AARP Services, Inc. Discounts must be requested at time of purchase.

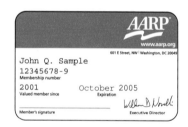

AARP
www.aarp.org
601 E Street, NW | Washington, DC 20049
John Q. Sample
12345678-9
Membership number
2001          October 2005
Valued member since     Expiration

Member's signature     Executive Director

**Write your membership** >> **number here. It opens the door to every benefit.**

AARP MEMBERSHIP CARD #

01495347¢5

**Watch for our ads** in AARP's member publications.

 **AARP** The Magazine   **AARP Bulletin**   **LIVE&LEARN**

 **SegundaJuventud**   La Publicación de Mayor Relevancia para las Personas Mayores de 50

# AARP®

*The power to make it better.*™

0904/D17166

Island, Johns Island, Kiawah, or Seabrook, cross the Wappoo Bridge, and take the first right onto Maybank Highway (Highway 700). For other destinations on James Island and for Folly Beach, stay on Folly Road (Highway 171).

For another route to James, Johns, or the resort islands, while still on the Crosstown take a left at the last light (Lockwood Drive) before crossing the Ashley River Bridge and look for the Folly Beach exit onto the Scarborough Expressway (Highway 30). This route will take you on a panoramic ride and deposit you on Folly Road on James Island. Take a left to go to Folly Beach or a right to go back toward West Ashley. If you are headed to Johns Island, Kiawah, or Seabrook, take a left on Maybank Highway (Highway 700) at the last stoplight before the Wappoo Bridge. If you are going to West Ashley or downtown, cross the Wappoo Bridge, and go straight. Then, you may either bear right to access the Ashley River Bridge into town or bear left on Wesley Drive to intersect with US 17.

## Charleston via I-26

### TO NORTH CHARLESTON

For travelers coming in on I-26 from the west, there are several options depending on your desired destination. You will pass through North Charleston on I-26, so check exits for specific locations. To go to the airport or Charleston Area Convention Center Complex, take a right on I-526 (Mark Clark Expressway) and look for signs.

### TO WEST ASHLEY, JAMES ISLAND, FOLLY BEACH

If you want to go to West Ashley, exit right at Cosgrove Avenue, which becomes Sam Rittenberg Boulevard (Highway 7). Sam Rittenberg forks at the Ashley Landing Shopping Center, and you can either bear to the left on Highway 171 toward the

Ashley River Bridge, or stay to the right on Sam Rittenberg Boulevard. The boulevard is intersected first by Highway 61, then by US 17. Take a right onto Highway 61 to go to the many historic gardens and plantations or a left to go to the Charleston Peninsula.

Another option for reaching West Ashley is to stay on the interstate as it winds around to become US 17 S. (the Crosstown), then cross the Ashley River Bridge.

To access James Island and Folly Beach, take the Cosgrove Avenue exit and cross the North Bridge, where Cosgrove becomes Sam Rittenberg Boulevard. Stay left on Sam Rittenberg (Highway 7) to Highway 171, which leads to Highway 61. Follow Highway 61 to Wesley Drive (at the In & Out Car Wash), and turn right. Cross US 17 on Wesley until it merges with Folly Road (Highway 171). To reach destinations on James Island, cross the Wappoo Bridge, and take the first right onto Maybank Highway (Highway 700). For other destinations on James Island and for Folly Beach, stay on Folly Road (Highway 171).

*Beware! Many Charleston streets and alleys are one way. With so many interesting distractions vying for your attention, it's easy to miss the signs. So keep a lookout and be careful.*

### TO JOHNS ISLAND, KIAWAH, AND SEABROOK

To go to these destinations, take a right on I-526 (Mark Clark Expressway), which will eventually merge with US 17 S. Continue on US 17 south of town, and turn left onto Main Road at the major intersection with the green sign to Kiawah and Seabrook. Cross the Limehouse Bridge to access Johns Island. To go to Kiawah or Seabrook, continue on Main Road until it becomes Bohicket Road at Maybank Highway (Highway 700), and follow the

**CLOSE-UP**

## View to Thrill over the Cooper River

The opening of the Arthur Ravenel Jr. Bridge over the Cooper River in the summer of 2005 was a major event for Charleston and the entire Lowcountry. Indeed, at a cost of $632 million, it was a major economic event as a construction project—10 years in the planning—affording employment opportunities to thousands. When finished, it provided our growing port with easier transportation to multiple markets throughout the southeastern United States. As an accomplished feat of state-of-the-art engineering, it became the longest cable-stayed span in all of North America.

Great as the opening celebration was, a certain lump remained in the throats of older locals who will always recall the two former spans, the (1929) Grace Memorial Bridge and the (1966) Silas Pearman Bridge. Each in its own time was considered a miracle of engineering. Each brought a vast improvement to the Lowcountry lifestyle.

Grace Memorial, the oldest of the former bridges, replaced a ferry system that (in one form or another) ran back and forth between the Peninsula and Mt. Pleasant since Civil War days and even earlier. The old Grace was alarmingly narrow by today's standards and crossing it was a white-knuckle experience for drivers and passengers alike. In 1946, a ship blown by gale-force winds collided with one of its pillars, causing a 240-foot section to fall into the deadly waters below, taking a car and its passengers down with it.

When the wider Pearman came along with its three lanes to help ease traffic, it was considered state-of-the-art. It offered a reversible lane that changed directions during rush hour. But the explosive growth in Mt. Pleasant soon made even this modern bridge obsolete.

Ground was broken for the new Arthur Ravenel Jr. Bridge in July 2001. Construction went well, and the span with its 8 lanes and 15 ramps was finished

---

signs. Kiawah will be on your left, and Seabrook will be at the end of the road.

### TO THE NORTHERN PENINSULA

If you want to go to the Peninsula, here are a couple of options. Take the Meeting Street exit off I-26, turn right on Meeting, and follow the signs to the Charleston Visitor Reception and Transportation Center. Another route is to follow the interstate until it ends at the Crosstown (US 17 S.), then take the Rutledge Avenue exit off the

Crosstown. Both streets run south and culminate at the Battery. If you are looking for The Citadel or points around the school, stay on I-26 until it ends at the Crosstown. Look for Hagood Avenue (just before McDonald's), take a right, and drive straight to the back gate of the school.

### TO MT. PLEASANT, SULLIVAN'S ISLAND, ISLE OF PALMS

If you are heading to East Cooper from the interstate, there are two options. For

*The dramatic profile of the Arthur Ravenel Jr. Bridge is Charleston's newest landmark.*

well ahead of initial estimates for completion. It runs 3.5 miles from Charleston's Crosstown Connector to Johnnie Dodds Boulevard in Mt. Pleasant. Its main cable span is 1,546 feet long with a 12-foot-wide bicycle and pedestrian lane along the ocean side. The two diamond-shaped tower piers include viewing platforms stretching 12 feet out over the water at a breathtaking height of 198 feet in the air. All this is suspended by 128 individual cables—each one capable of carrying over a million pounds, or 500 tons.

During most of the year, tourists marvel at how beautifully lit the Ravenel Bridge is at night. But those lights are considerably dimmed during nesting season of the Lowcountry's endangered loggerhead sea turtles. The fragile young hatchlings are guided by moonlight in their life-or-death scramble from beachside nests to the relative safety of the sea. Wildlife experts fear the massive bridge lights may confuse them.

the first, take I-526 (Mark Clark Expressway) or US 17 N. If you choose to take I-526 to Mt. Pleasant, you'll be treated to beautiful scenery, but watch your speedometer. Radar-equipped patrol cars are common. From I-526, you can go to Sullivan's Island by taking Chuck Dawley Boulevard until it intersects with Coleman Boulevard (Highway 703) at the light. Turn left on Coleman (which becomes Ben Sawyer Boulevard), and cross the Ben Sawyer Bridge onto Sullivan's Island.

If you want to go to the Isle of Palms, there are again two possibilities. First, you can take a left onto Jasper Boulevard after crossing the Ben Sawyer Bridge. This will lead to a bridge across Breach Inlet and onto the Isle of Palms. For the other route, take a left onto US 17 N. after exiting from I-526 and then a right after Sweetgrass Shopping Center onto the Isle of Palms Connector (Highway 517). This route offers direct service and allows you to bypass Sullivan's Island traffic and the inevitable openings of the Ben Sawyer swing bridge. The connector also offers a stupendous view of the island and the sparkling Atlantic Ocean spread before it.

The second East Cooper option from I-26 is to take the Mt. Pleasant exit onto the Arthur Ravenel Jr. Bridge (US 17 N.), which takes you to Mt. Pleasant and the islands. Exit the bridge following the signs to Coleman Boulevard (Highway 703). Eventually, this road crosses Shem Creek at the edge of the historic Old Village residential area. It later becomes Ben Sawyer Boulevard before crossing the Ben Sawyer Bridge to Sullivan's Island. To reach the Isle of Palms, take a left on Jasper Boulevard, and drive across Sullivan's Island to Breach Inlet. Cross the bridge over the inlet, and you are on the Isle of Palms. To find Wild Dunes Resort, follow Palm Boulevard (Highway 703) and the signs to the Wild Dunes Reception Center.

However, if you intend to head north on US 17 to reach Mt. Pleasant destinations such as Hobcaw, Towne Centre, Snee Farm, Boone Hall, or eventually McClellanville and Georgetown, stay left on the Arthur Ravenel Jr. Bridge and cross the US 17 N. overpass.

## Charleston via Interstate 95

If you are heading north on I-95 (from Savannah), the shortest route to Charleston is via exit 33. The signs will direct you to Charleston and Beaufort. See "Charleston via U.S. Highway 17 N. (Savannah Highway)," above, for further directions into the city. If you are heading south on I-95 (from Fayetteville, North Carolina), the best idea is to take I-26 just past Santee, South Carolina (exit 86). Travel about 50 miles along I-26 to access all Charleston area destinations. (See "Charleston via I-26" above.)

## GETTING HERE BY AIR

Charleston is more accessible than ever by air. The Trident area boasts a full-service international airport with major carriers taking off and touching down throughout the day. Major national rental-car agencies service the airport, limousine and shuttle services are available, and the terminal has a new, 1,200-space covered parking garage opening in 2005 plus additional surface parking on-site.

There are also four Lowcountry locations serving the needs of private pilots; one location is an auxiliary service of the Charleston International Airport. All are reasonably convenient to the downtown area, and specific amenities are noted below.

## Major Airport Service

### Charleston International Airport
### 5500 International Boulevard,
### North Charleston
### (843) 767-1100; (843) 767-7009

When newcomers need to deal with air travel in the Greater Charleston area, it's good to know a few basic facts: What major airlines serve Charleston International Airport? Who do you call to see if a flight is going to be on time or not? What are some of the route and time factors involved in getting to the airport? And what about ground transportation and parking? Answers to all those questions follow, but first, let's take a look at the historical time line of the area's major airport.

### HISTORY

In 1928, the City of Charleston leased 782 acres northwest of the city for construction of a municipal airport. A year later, the new airfield was officially opened for business. This facility served Greater Charleston until 1942, when it was turned over to the Federal government for military use during World War II (see the Military chapter).

After the war, the city resumed control of operations at the airfield, and in 1949, the first civilian airport terminal was completed. In 1952, the government got involved again, leasing the airfield to begin operations at the new Charleston Air Force Base.

In 1970, the Charleston County Aviation Authority was created, and by 1979, this entity had taken over ownership of the airport. On March 30, 1985, the greatly expanded and modernized present terminal was dedicated as Charleston International Airport.

Today's 280,000-square-foot facility has 10 gates, all served by covered loading bridges. The walking distance from the terminal entrance to the most remote aircraft gate is only about 800 feet. The international area and customs service inspection area have 25,000 square feet of space and process international passengers quickly. If you're interested in business opportunities at Charleston International Airport, contact the Aviation Authority Development Office at (843) 767-7000.

## FLIGHT INFORMATION

Major airlines serving the Trident's international flight facility include: Continental, (800) 525-0280 (reservations), (800) 335-2247 (baggage); Delta, (800) 221-1212 (reservations), (800) 325-8224 (baggage); Independence Air, (800) 359-3594; Northwest, (800) 225-2525; and USAirways, (800) 428-4322 (reservations), (800) 371-4771 (baggage).

Commuter airlines serving the Charleston International Airport are COMAIR, (800) 354-9822; and United Express, (800) 241-6522.

The number to call if you want to check an arrival time for an incoming flight is (843) 767-7009. Checking before leaving for the airport can save time and frustration. The airport's information desk always has the most updated flight schedule data available.

## RENTAL CARS/PARKING

Chances are, your preferred rental car service has an airport outlet in Charleston. The five national companies that serve the airport are Alamo, (800) 327-9633 or (843) 767-4417; Avis Rent-A-Car, (800) 331-1212 or (843) 767-7030; Budget, (800) 527-0700 or (843) 767-7051; Hertz Rent-A-Car, (800) 654-3131 or (843) 767-4552; and National Car Rental, (800) 227-7368 or (843) 767-3078.

A new terminal parking facility set to open in late fall 2005 will offer 1,200 covered spaces. A surface lot slightly farther away from the terminal offers additional parking at $8.00 per day.

## GETTING TO THE AIRPORT

As a simple rule of thumb, plan on allowing at least a half hour to get to the airport if you're driving from downtown Charleston. Allow even more time during rush hours or on busy holiday travel dates. You may want to call ahead and get time allowances for security procedures.

Take I-26 west (toward Columbia). Exit off I-26 at exit 212-B marked "Airport and I-526 Savannah." Continue approximately a mile on I-526 (toward Savannah), and exit at the Montague Avenue exit. A sign will also read, "Trident Research Authority, Coliseum, and Airport." Turn right at the light

*One way to avoid the somewhat pricey long-term parking fees at Charleston International Airport is to use one of the off-site parking facilities nearby that can deliver you to the front door of the airport in time for your flight and safely store your car while you're gone. Upon return, just call their shuttle for a quick ride to the lot where your car will be ready and waiting for you. One of the best options is Park & Go, located at 3621 West Montague Avenue. Call (843) 302-2288 for rates and information.*

*Start early on your trip to the airport. International Boulevard has gained a reputation as a notorious speed trap, so be sure to keep an eye on your speedometer. Many travelers have missed flights thanks to a heavy foot and the ever-vigilant officers.*

(at the exit to International Boulevard), and continue approximately a mile and a half to the terminal.

If you are driving south toward the city on I-26, take the Mark Clark Expressway (I-526) exit. The airport exit off this highway is clearly marked, and you'll again head into the terminal area via International Boulevard.

For local residents and those who need ground transportation to the airport from downtown or other locations, there's a central phone number through the Charleston Aviation Authority that will redirect your call to the next available option. Call (800) 750-1311 for this airport limousine pick-up information.

### TAXI, LIMO, AND SHUTTLE SERVICE FROM THE AIRPORT

Several Charleston area hotels, motels, and bed-and-breakfast inns offer shuttle service to and from the airport. Check with your reservation agent, your inn's concierge, or your hotel for specific details. Near the baggage carousel, you'll find a lighted courtesy board showing several of the area's better hotels, motels, and bed-and-breakfast inns. The attached phone offers speed-dial service to those places offering airport pickup service.

If you're left to your own resources for transportation into the city, you have a couple of options. Outside the baggage claim area, across the pick-up zone, is a small booth offering taxi and limo (van) rides to Lowcountry destinations. Various cab companies, as a service of the Aviation Airport Authority, take turns picking

up fares from this booth. Here's the gist: If you are in a great hurry, a taxi will take you immediately at a metered rate of $1.65 a mile for the first two passengers. Additional passengers will pay $10 each. The average ride from the airport to a downtown hotel will be around $19 to $23. If you're willing to wait about 15 minutes, you can catch a shuttle (really a van) with several other passengers at a much-discounted rate of $10 per person.

Passengers heading to the nearby Charleston Air Force Base can catch an immediate taxi for a flat rate of $7.00. A trip for one to Kiawah or Seabrook by taxi is about $50 for the 30-mile journey. Those heading for Wild Dunes can expect to pay about $39 for that 23-mile ride.

If you want private limousine service and make reservations in advance, you can choose from a number of limousine companies available in the Lowcountry. (See the "Limousines" listing later in this chapter.)

## Private Plane Service

Greater Charleston offers four options for private pilots, all convenient and uncongested.

### Mercury Air Center
### 6060 South Aviation Avenue, North Charleston
### (843) 746-7600

Just across the runway from the Charleston Air Force Base, off Aviation Avenue at Charleston International Airport, Mercury Air Center's terminal and service facility offers two runways (7,000 feet and 9,001 feet), nine instrument approaches, and 24-hour all-weather service. This is your best choice if you want to land a private plane in close proximity to downtown. Both jet fuel and AV gas are available. Customers not buying fuel are charged the following nightly tie-down fees: $10 for single engine, $20 for twin piston, $30 for turboprop, $40 for small jet, and $50 for mid-size jets. Larger aircraft should call for rates and facilities.

Mercury Air also offers a wide range of services—from rental cars to limousines to dinner reservations and catering arrangements.

**East Cooper Aviation**
**700 Airport Road, Mt. Pleasant**
**(843) 884-8837**
Private pilots have access to the East Cooper area (including Wild Dunes) via the East Cooper Airport in Mt. Pleasant. This facility offers a 3,700-foot runway, tie-downs, jet fuel, and AV gas service. Rental cars are available on the premises through Enterprise. The office and terminal are open from 7:00 A.M. to 7:00 P.M. in the winter, with hours extended to 8:00 P.M. after April 1. Helicopters are accommodated on site.

**Mercury Air J.Z.I.**
**2700 Fort Trenholm Road, Johns Island**
**(843) 559-2401**
**www.mercuryaircenters.com**
Private pilots wanting access closest to Kiawah and Seabrook will most likely want to choose Mercury Air's J.Z.I. airport on Johns Island, 12 miles south of the city. Charleston County and the Federal Aviation Administration spent $2.3 million on this facility in 2005, upgrading its landing strips, enlarging its jet park area, and planning for future expansion. It presently offers two runways, 5,000-by-150-feet and 4,311-by-150-feet long. The facility offers jet fuel and 100 LL gas. For customers not buying gas, a handling fee of $10 is charged for a single-engine aircraft, $20 for piston twin-engine, and $40 and up for turboprop aircraft. Rental cars are available on the premises, and limited limousine service to Kiawah and Seabrook is offered. Travelers heading for The Sanctuary on Kiawah may call the hotel for transportation to the island. Operating hours are 6:00 A.M. to 10:00 P.M.

**Pelican Aviation**
**890 Greyback Road, Summerville**
**(843) 851-0970**
This facility for private pilots flying into the Summerville area and Berkeley County has a 3,700-foot runway. It offers airplane detailing, general maintenance, and flight training, plus jet fuel and AV gas. Tie-downs are $5.00 per night (with first night waived with purchase of fuel). There's a courtesy car on site for daytime transportation to area resorts and restaurants. The office and terminal are open from 8:00 A.M. to 6:00 P.M. through the winter and 8:00 A.M. to 7:00 P.M. after April 1.

## GETTING HERE BY OTHER METHODS

# By Bus or Train

If you are arriving or departing by bus, the Greyhound Terminal, 3610 Dorchester Road, (843) 747-5341, is in North Charleston and is a routine stop for cabs. Call (800) 231-2222 or (843) 744-4247 for rates and schedules.

The Amtrak Train Station, 4565 Gaynor Avenue, (843) 744-8263 or (800) 872-7245, or visit www.amtrak.com. This is also in the north area. Amtrak runs on the CSX Railroad lines, and there are two northbound and two southbound stops each day. Call for ticket prices and train schedules.

# By Boat

There is a growing leisure craft and passenger ship industry in Charleston.

Cruise ships dock at the passenger terminal off Concord Street in the historic district. In the daytime, walking there is fine, if you have the time and the stamina, but we endorse travel by cabs or limousines at night for safety and convenience. (See the listings for taxis and limousines following.)

**CLOSE-UP**

# City and County Parking Facilities

Charleston's municipal and county off-street parking system is one of the best solutions to the city's ever-present shortage of parking spaces. In a city planned and built (and rebuilt several times) before automobile congestion was ever an issue, these lots and parking garages are a welcome oasis. In some cases, the city planners have even done a fairly good job of making the garages blend into the historic cityscape. If you're not looking carefully, you might mistake a parking garage for an old warehouse or an office building.

Some facilities near hotels offer special overnight rates for guests with proof of hotel registration. Usually, a hotel key will be convincing enough. Others offer only hourly rates. Here's the general rule for most city-owned and county-owned parking facilities: It's 75 cents for the first half-hour, 75 cents for the second half-hour, then $1.00 per hour. The all-day rate is $6.00 in county garages, $8.00 in city garages. The overnight rate (where offered) is $10 with a hotel registration, and the monthly rate (where available) is $90. City garages located near hotel facilities may be slightly higher.

In any case, unless your accommodation provides off-street parking or you want to feed a hungry meter, these parking options may turn out to be your only choices:

Aquarium Garage
24 Calhoun Street, (843) 579-7679, 1,093 spaces

Camden Exchange Garage
34 John, between John and Hutson Streets off Meeting Street, (843) 720-3866, 308 spaces

Charleston County
Health Complex Garage
21 Courtenay Drive, (843) 720-7050, 1,640 spaces

Charleston Place Garage
off Hasell Street, between Meeting and King Streets, (843) 724-7419, 404 spaces

Private yachts moor (pending availability) at any of several marinas in the Trident area. (See the Boating and Watersports chapter for more information.) Cabs or rental cars are the best solution for ground transportation unless you are docked at the City Marina, which is centrally located on the Peninsula near popular destinations and on the DASH route. (See more on the DASH system under "Public Transportation," following.) The nearby Ashley Marina has easy access via walkway to the City Marina and connecting DASH routes.

Concord-Cumberland Garage
corner of Concord and Cumberland
Streets, (843) 724-7387, 624 spaces

Cumberland-Meeting Garage
82 Cumberland Street, (843) 720-7145,
1,036 spaces

East Bay–Prioleau Garage
between Mid-Atlantic and South
Atlantic Streets, (843) 724-7403, 330
spaces

Gaillard Municipal Auditorium Garage
off Calhoun Street and Alexander,
(843) 973-7207, 596 spaces

George-Society Lot
off King Street, between George and
Society Streets, (843) 724-7384, 146
spaces

King-Queen Garage
off Queen Street, corner of King and
Queen Streets, (843) 724-6777, 454
spaces

Liberty–St. Philip Garage
corner of Liberty and St. Philip Streets,
(843) 724-7382, 540 spaces

Majestic Square Garage,
Market and Archdale Streets, behind
Saks Fifth Avenue,
(843) 853-1682, 471 spaces

Marion Square Garage
401-C King Street,
just north of the Francis Marion Hotel,
(843) 965-4104, 308 spaces

Market and Horlbeck Lot
in the block between Market and
Horlbeck Streets, (843) 724-7385,
118 spaces

Visitor Center Garage
63 Mary Street, (843) 973-7290,
723 spaces

Visitor Center Lot
375 Meeting Street, adjacent to the
Charleston Visitor Reception and
Transportation Center, (843) 720-3964,
60 spaces

Wentworth-St. Philip Garage
81 Wentworth Street, (843) 724-7383,
518 spaces

## GETTING AROUND THE LOWCOUNTRY

# Taxis, Limos, and Rental Cars

Taxis can be scarce here in the Lowcoun-

try, especially at odd hours. Because of
that, savvy travelers needing cabs should
keep a list of taxi phone numbers in their
purse or wallet. The more popular solution
is to rent a car from one of the nationally
recognized car rental companies, all of
which are represented in the area.

Limousines, it seems, are more loosely defined. A limousine can be anything from a stretch Caddy to an airport van. What follows is a list of taxi, limousine services, and rental car options.

## TAXIS

Express Cab
(843) 577-8816

Metro Cab
(843) 572-5083
North Area Taxi
(843) 554-7575

Yellow Cab
(843) 577-6565

## LIMOUSINES

Above and Beyond Limousine Service
(843) 402-0600, (800) 755-8667

Affordable Limo Service
(843) 406-1515, (800) 694-3295

Carey Chauffeur Services
(800) 336-4646

Jennings Limousine
(843) 852-0336

## RENTAL CARS

Avis Rent-A-Car
(843) 767-7030, (800) 831-2847

Budget
(843) 760-9025, (800) 527-0700

Enterprise Rent-A-Car
(843) 723-6215, (800) 736-8222

Hertz Rent-A-Car
(843) 767-4552, (800) 654-3131

National Car Rental
(843) 767-3078, (888) 868-6206

Thrifty Car Rental
(843) 552-7531, (800) 847-4389

# Public Transportation

Public bus transportation in the area is a great way to circumvent the city's automobile congestion and parking woes altogether. This service is provided in the Lowcountry by the Charleston Area Rural Transportation Authority (CARTA). Under CARTA's auspices is the Downtown Area Shuttle (DASH), a separate system generally dedicated to the transportation needs of tourists in the downtown area and historic district. Together, CARTA and DASH operate 17 routes linking downtown, West Ashley, and North Charleston.

While the green DASH trolleys are not considered tour vehicles per se, their turn-of-the-20th-century "antique" trolley look is clearly an eye catcher—and it's one way to quickly identify a DASH vehicle from the more modern-looking (yellow and green) CARTA buses that operate in the metro area. DASH trolleys and metro CARTA buses stop at designated shelters, benches, and trolley stop signs located throughout the city. For safety reasons, drivers are not allowed to pick up passengers at locations other than the designated color-coded stops.

One-way and all-day CARTA and DASH passes are available on board the vehicles. You are expected to have exact change. One-way fare is $1.25, although those with a senior-citizen or Medicare card can ride for 60 cents each way seven days a week from 9:00 A.M. to 3:30 P.M. or after 6:00 P.M. Disabled riders pay 30 cents. An all-day pass is $4.00. Transfers are 25 cents. Inside the Visitor Reception and Transportation Center and at area Piggly Wiggly (grocery) stores, you can buy a 10-ride pass for $10 or 40 rides for $35. A 31-day pass is sold for $31.25.

Police, guide, signal, and service dogs are the only pets allowed on board.

To encourage visitors to leave their cars at the visitor center garage facilities and parking lots and choose public transportation, a free hour of parking is granted in exchange for a used one-day DASH pass at the checkout booth. Call (843) 747-0922 or visit ridecarta.com for more information.

# Bicycling

If you plan on spending time on the Peninsula or out on the beaches, why not park the car and consider renting a bicycle by the hour or day? Now you can even put your bike on a CARTA bus (with their new front-loading bike racks) and enjoy the convenience of public transportation. For in-town and Mt. Pleasant service, we recommend The Bicycle Shoppe, which

offers three locations: 280 Meeting Street, (843) 722-8168, 1539 Johnnie Dodds Boulevard, Mt. Pleasant, (843) 884-7433, and the Strawmarket at Kiawah Island, (843) 768-9122. These folks rent single-speed adult cruisers and hybrids. Also serving Kiawah and Seabrook Islands is Island Bike and Surf Shop, 3665 Bohicket Road, Kiawah Island, (843) 768-1158. Another option is Mike's Bikes and Back-woods, 709 Coleman Boulevard, Mt. Pleas-ant, (843) 884-5884, or on James Island at 808 Folly Road, (843) 795-3322. For delivery and three-day or weekly rental to many of the islands, try Sea Island Cycle, North Charleston, (843) 747-BIKE.

# HISTORY 🏛

With cultural roots as deep and colorful as her surrounding blue-green waters, Charleston is a rich mixture of early English, Scots, Irish, French, Spanish, German, Swiss, Santo Domingan, African, Native American, and Caribbean influences.

While each of these cultures left its mark on the city in a unique way, no influence was stronger than that of the British. Archaeologists tell us countless generations of Native Americans lived on and around the land now called Charleston before the first permanent English settlers arrived, but little remains of their occupation outside of the archaeological record in the ground itself. The first English settlers, arriving in the spring of 1670, were adventurers coming to lands granted by King Charles II to eight Lords Proprietors, who claimed ownership of the "Carolinas"—presumably extending from the Atlantic to the shores of the Pacific.

As the settlers navigated into what is now Charleston Harbor, they passed enormous mounds of bleached, white oyster shells at the tip of a peninsula where two rivers met and named the area Oyster Point. Seeking higher ground, the colonists sailed farther up one river to a high bank they called Albemarle Point and established the first crude encampment there. They dutifully named the new settlement Charles Towne for King Charles II. The two rivers, called the Kiawah and Etiwan by local tribes, were renamed the Ashley and Cooper, respectively, in honor of one of the Lords Proprietors, Anthony Ashley Cooper, Lord Shaftesbury. The original settlement area is now a South Carolina state park called Charles Towne Landing State Historic Site. (See the Attractions chapter.) A decade later, because of their need for protection, the Charles Towne colonists were drawn back to the Oyster Point peninsula between the two rivers—clearly a more defensible location. Here, the foundations of what is now Charleston were first laid.

By 1719, the colonists were tired of being exploited by the proprietary government, and friction ensued. This resulted in the colonists coming under even more discipline from the English crown, which meant forced allegiance to a series of appointed royal governors. This troublesome governmental entity stayed in place for the colonists until the American Revolution.

In 1725 the British sent over a plan for the new settlement called the "Grand Modell," intending to guide the development of 600 prime acres on the peninsula into a proper town. Amazingly, traces of that early English plan are still evident in the plat of today's Charleston Peninsula.

Owing to the great success of this busy English port and its merchant-planter aristocracy, the town soon became a small city. To many, the 18th century will always be Charleston's Golden Age. Early travelers to this thriving colonial port took back to Europe impressive stories about Charles Towne's elegant architecture, wealthy citizenry, and sophisticated lifestyle. Indeed, during these heady, pre-Revolutionary years, rice and indigo from the plantations were sent out to eager markets all over the world. In exchange, hundreds of boatloads of enslaved Africans were brought to Charleston to ensure a cheap labor force to work the land. In stark contrast to this grim exchange, the arts flourished, and

**i** *Insiders tend to find an even kinder welcome if they show an interest in Lowcountry history. Feel free to ask questions and learn more. Most Lowcountry residents are historians at heart—they grew up with it!*

Charles Towne was considered the brightest jewel in England's colonial crown.

Many of the seeds of the American Revolution found fertile ground here in the Carolina Lowcountry. Political passions ran high, and once war broke out there were many high-profile Charlestonians deeply involved on both sides of the issue. Actually, the first decisive American victory during the Revolution occurred at the Battle of Fort Sullivan just outside the city. However, at first the war didn't go well. For a while, Charleston fell to the British, and during this time, the city suffered the first of its two unseemly "enemy occupations."

Newly liberated after the war, the city became incorporated in 1783 and adopted a new, shortened name: Charleston. As the 19th century dawned, the young city of Charleston experienced an incredible building boom. Today you can still see an extraordinary number of Adam-style buildings from this remarkable period. Among them are the Joseph Manigault House at 350 Meeting Street, built in 1803, and the Nathaniel Russell House at 51 Meeting Street, built in 1808. (See the House Museums section of the Attractions chapter.)

As cotton and tobacco were added to the plantation products earning handsome profits in the international marketplace, and even more money flowed into its thriving port, Charleston continued to grow. By the early 19th century, Charleston's flourishing middle class of merchant-tradesmen offered services and locally manufactured goods from small, street-front shops. Many of these shops were clustered along what is now King Street.

Some traders sold simple things such as household necessities and fresh produce brought in on wagons from outlying gardens. Others were true artisans in their own right and produced work such as early Charleston-made silver pieces and locally crafted furniture that are highly prized on the antiques market today. This flourishing "wagon trade" on upper King Street preceded the retail stores that make up the present shopping district.

# THE CIVIL WAR AND SUBSEQUENT STRUGGLES

Disputes over economics and slavery left unresolved by the young country's founding fathers had festered into a battle between the federal government and individual states by the mid-19th century. In April 1861, Confederate soldiers fired on Fort Sumter in Charleston Harbor, thus signaling the start of the devastating War between the States. After the city's second "enemy occupation," this time by Federal troops, Charleston was at its lowest ebb. Years of relentless bombardment, sweeping fires, and economic starvation had taken a terrible toll on the once grand city.

Because Charleston was widely known as the "seat of secession," it is probably true that Charlestonians received especially severe punishment during the Reconstruction years. Recovery was slow to come and sometimes halfhearted. Some say Charleston never did recuperate from the Civil War until the arrival of the Navy Yard in 1904 and the subsequent economic booms of the two world wars.

Fires, earthquakes, hurricanes, yellow fever epidemics, and even the boll weevil threatened Charlestonians' health and wealth during the late 19th and early 20th centuries.

After the turn of the century and the arrival of the Navy Yard, things started looking better. Phosphate, an organic fertilizer, was mined along the Ashley River and processed in several local factories. This proved to be a significant new source of income for many old plantation families who still owned phosphate-rich lands. Other landowners converted to timber farming as the South slowly rebuilt a working economy.

It has been observed that in the most difficult of times Charleston citizens were "too poor to paint," but they were also "too proud to whitewash." This inability to modernize maintained an almost timeless feeling throughout the city and actually worked to preserve Charleston's

# Hey, George Washington Really DID Sleep here!

Yup, it all happened in May of 1791. America's Founding Father, George Washington, first president of the United States, had just been inaugurated. Almost immediately, he expressed his intent to make a tour of the new country. A team of advisors was summoned to plan his visit to all 13 states. At first, in 1789, he traveled through the New England area, and the enthusiasm he received proved to be very impressive. It wasn't until the spring of 1791, however, that he found time to head south. He hoped the southern tour would shore up support for the newly formed (and centralized) Federal government, and he intended to seek out a few outstanding leaders who might be enticed to return with him and lend their talents to the new country. That may have been politically astute and a brilliantly modern "spin" on how to establish a successful first administration, but the tour turned out to be more of a giant public relations gesture. If nothing else, it enshrined Washington as a legend in the minds and hearts of Americans forever. The social aspects of the visit were never more evident than when he spent a gala week in Charleston, South Carolina.

Washington's entry into Charleston was aboard a beautifully decorated 12-oared barge manned by 13 sea captains in full dress uniforms. A flotilla of more than 40 rowboats and other vessels escorted the barge into Charleston Harbor (including two with musicians playing madly as the oarsmen pulled away at their oars in perfect unison). A 15-gun salute fired into the air as the bells of St. Michael's Church pealed. The city rented (for 60 pounds) the exquisitely furnished townhome of Judge Thomas Heyward at 87 Church Street to be a temporary "home" for the president. Arriving there, he encountered (as he wrote in his diary), a house "ornamented in front by lamps, and over the portal a triumphant arch, decorated with laurel, flowers, etc."

Charleston's display of respect for the "Supreme Magistrate of the United States" was nothing if not effusive. There were elegant breakfasts, special dinners, late-night suppers, parades, concerts, and balls scheduled all week long. Women adorned themselves with sashes, bandeaux, and medallions bearing miniature portraits of their hero. "So much beauty and elegance," reported a Charleston newspaper at the time, "were never before displayed in this country."

Washington was flattered by all this attention, but he made a strong point to avoid taking on the airs of a monarch in any way. In fact, he even refused the elaborate chairs (festooned like thrones) wherever he appeared and offered those seats to the ladies in attendance instead.

Yes, George Washington *did* sleep here. But during his waking hours, anyway, he set in place a revolutionary standard of modesty and humility that would become the American presidency to this day.

now-legendary cache of historic homes and public buildings.

## CULTURAL RENAISSANCE AND AN ECONOMIC BOOM

In the 1920s, a kind of artistic renaissance occurred in Charleston. The city's now-quaint architectural backdrop inspired a new generation of artists, writers, poets, and musicians who captured regional and national acclaim. (See the Arts chapter for more about this fascinating period in Charleston's history.)

At the same time, the aesthetic and economic value of Charleston's architectural legacy started to be realized. This was when the city's early preservation ethic was first formulated, and it was kept alive through the especially difficult Depression years of the 1930s. (See the chapter on Architectural and Historic Preservation for more information.)

World War II brought another boom to Charleston, with the Navy Yard expanding to produce war materials and more job opportunities than Charleston had seen in decades. After the war ended, many workers drawn here by the Navy decided to stay on and settle down. The sea, the mild weather, and a growing business climate kept pulling newcomers to the Lowcountry through the 1950s and 1960s.

In the 1970s, Charleston's chamber of commerce launched a national advertising campaign based on the simple phrase, "Charleston: America's Best Kept Secret." This, of course, was intended to let this cat out of the bag, and it worked splendidly. With high-profile events such as Spoleto Festival USA and the (almost always sold-out) public house tours every spring and fall (see the Annual Events chapter), the message was getting out—Charleston was a beautiful, historic, and highly desirable place to visit. Many visitors decided to move here and make the Charlestonian lifestyle their own.

## CHARLESTON IN THE NEW MILLENNIUM

Today Charleston's collection of historically significant architecture attracts visitors from around the world, and the city's remarkable preservation ethic is now a model for historic cities all over the industrialized world.

In 1996, an estimated three million tourists visited Charleston, each spending about $124 per day here. By 2003, that figure had grown to 4.6 million visitors, each infusing Charleston County with about $225 per day.

That should get you up to speed on the history of the Lowcountry's centerpiece, the historic Peninsula. Now, let's take a quick look at the historical backgrounds of the other regions making up the Greater Charleston area.

# East (of the) Cooper

Across the Cooper River east of the Peninsula is the land mass often referred to by locals as East Cooper. Actually, this is a grouping of several separate localities, all of which have proper names that further identify them to locals and visitors alike.

## MT. PLEASANT

People have been drawn to Mt. Pleasant since the late 17th century, when the lands east of the Cooper River were still wild and uninhabited. The land's proximity to the Peninsula was obvious, and local island planters built summer houses near the water (used during warmer months when plantation living was deemed "unhealthy"). One area came to be called the Old Village, and it's still a very desirable Mt. Pleasant address today.

Almost 7 miles down what is now U.S. Highway 17 N., Snee Farm was the rural home of Revolutionary patriot Col. Charles Pinckney. Pinckney helped frame the Constitution, and George Washington visited

*Charleston has been the scene of numerous historical firsts. The first regularly scheduled passenger train service in America was established here in 1830.*

his home in 1791. Today, Snee Farm is officially designated as a historic site (managed by the National Park Service) where visitors get a unique view of how the lives of slaves in the area helped mold and build a society. (See the Attractions chapter.)

Mt. Pleasant was incorporated as a town in 1837 after apparently drawing its acreage from two villages as well as former plantations on Haddrell's Point. Part of this land was once the property of Andrew Hibben, in whose honor a village street is named.

Shortly before the Civil War, Mt. Pleasant residents met at Renken's Long Room, near the old ferry wharf, and decided to follow Charleston's lead in advocating secession from the Union. Later, during the hard times of Reconstruction, Renken's Long Room housed industrious members of this community in night school and a debating society.

The local economy was based on farming for about a century, and Mt. Pleasant's vegetables were reputed to be among the best in the area. The Old Village was an important link to the mainland and the islands. When mail was transported from the north down the former King's Highway, it was brought to Haddrell's Point, then carried over to Charleston by ferry. Eventually, trolley tracks ran from the south end of Pitt Street to Sullivan's Island, transporting people and goods across what is now the Intracoastal Waterway.

When a bridge spanning the Cooper River opened in 1929, it changed the profile of Mt. Pleasant forever. Shrimping became an important industry in the 1940s, and the picturesque setting of Shem Creek, with its commercial shrimp fleet bobbing at the docks, became a major attraction.

Although some travelers then and now just pass through Mt. Pleasant on their way to the resort islands or heading north to Myrtle Beach, a percentage make the town itself their vacation destination. By the 1970s, Mt. Pleasant was booming as a bedroom community for the whole Charleston area, and real estate development here still blossoms. (See the Relocation and Neighborhoods chapters.)

## SULLIVAN'S ISLAND

The captain of the *Carolina,* one of the ships that brought the first English settlers to this area, was Florentia O'Sullivan, and it is for him Sullivan's Island is named. He was a member of the provincial parliament and held the deed to much land east of the Cooper River.

In the early days, Sullivan's Island was covered with pine trees and was used as a strategic point of defense for Lowcountry settlers. This sandy barrier island is only 3 miles long and no more than a quarter mile wide. Still, it was more than adequate to serve as a defensive buffer for attacks off the Atlantic. In 1706, the Spanish–French fleet lost footing here after a battle at the west end of the island. Here also, the British naval and land forces of Sir Peter Parker were set back in one of the most decisive battles of the American Revolution.

A lesser known fact about Sullivan's Island is its sad history as a point of debarkation for untold thousands of enslaved Africans before the American Revolution. In the years between 1700 and 1775, the number of slaves off-loaded and "processed" for sale at a now-vanished facility on the island was staggering. Today, a lone marker commemorates this site—only recently acknowledging this uncomfortable fact.

At the northwestern end of Sullivan's Island, you'll find Fort Moultrie, which is a name connected in many ways with Lowcountry history. Sergeant Jasper, whose statue graces the Battery at the tip of Charleston's Peninsula today, rescued the patriots' battle flag here during the Revolution. And 100 years later, Federal commander Maj. Robert Anderson moved his forces from Fort Moultrie to Fort Sumter and into the pages of Civil War history. Osceola, the famous Seminole Indian chief who was held prisoner at Fort Moultrie until his death, is buried outside the fort. As a young soldier, Edgar Allan Poe was stationed at Fort Moultrie and later wrote an island-inspired story, "The Gold Bug."

Charlestonians began building summer residences on Sullivan's in the 19th century to escape the heat of the city. As recently as the early part of this century, "moving to the island" meant packing up all the household essentials and making the break for several months. By the end of World War II, a school and a few shops made year-round living possible.

Today most islanders choose to live there full time, and Sullivan's is a favored residential area. Much of the island has been rebuilt since the devastation of Hurricane Hugo, but development has been closely monitored so that there is still precious little commercial activity and a relatively subdued lifestyle.

## ISLE OF PALMS

Just across the eastern tip of Sullivan's Island and over the bridge across Breach Inlet is the Isle of Palms. Although slightly larger than Sullivan's, the Isle of Palms is another classic example of a coastal barrier island. This sandy strip of land is nearly 5 miles long and a half mile wide at its midpoint.

Even in the early years, Sullivan's Islanders ventured over to this next island for boat picnics or to fish and shrimp the teeming waters. By the late 19th century, some visitors came regularly by water or the newly built railroad bridge. Records from 1941 indicate that Sullivan's Island had only 25 year-round residents at the time.

After World War II, local businessman J. C. Long, who owned the entire Isle of Palms (and plenty more elsewhere), started selling small vacation homes on

the island. During the next three decades, growth was steady. As the Isle of Palms pavilion became, like the Folly Beach pavilion, an entertainment center, the island's reputation for fun and games also grew. Surfers discovered the waves in the 1960s, and the young flocked to the oceanside strip of eateries and shops to strut their tanned bodies by day and dance from club to club by night.

By the end of the 1970s, the undeveloped northernmost point of the Isle of Palms became Wild Dunes, a self-contained, upscale, planned resort community. Today many Isle of Palms residents are full-timers who call Wild Dunes Resort their permanent home. But there's also a steady stream of short-term visitors who come out to enjoy vacation rentals or just a day's or evening's entertainment.

## NORTH CHARLESTON

According to the Smithsonian, a giant, prehistoric condor once flew over land being used for the U.S. Air Force Base in today's North Charleston. Its fossilized remains were found there not far from a much later stone hatchet, a few arrowheads, and human bones that tell us Stone Age humans lived in the area thousands of years ago.

Shortly after the first English colonists put ashore and established Charles Towne in 1670, lands in the north area were granted, sold, and resold. Early on, deer skins, pitch, tar, and turpentine from the north area's abundant pine trees became an important part of the Lowcountry economy.

By the time of the American Revolution, there were probably 60 plantations in the north area successfully raising rice and indigo. Later, regular ferry service was available on the Ashley and Cooper Rivers, making the distance to Charleston easily conquerable. Largely because the plow didn't come into general use here before 1810, and early planters neither used fertilizer nor rotated their crops, the soil in the north area was quickly played out. In fact, it was of little use for agriculture after the American Revolution.

Things took an upward turn north of the city in 1830 with the coming of the railroad. In fact, it was the destruction of these tracks and trains that had the most harmful impact on Charleston during the Civil War.

# The Important Role of Phosphate

Phosphates used in making fertilizer were discovered and mined along the Ashley River after the Civil War, employing thousands of freedmen during Reconstruction. These freedmen became landowners and formed churches and burial societies that are still in evidence today. Phosphate mining soon encouraged the building of booming fertilizer plants in the north area. These, along with successful lumber companies, provided employment, company housing, and (at last) the basis for a diversified economy not exclusively tied to peninsular Charleston.

What is now North Charleston was also the epicenter of the great earthquake of 1886. Although no Richter-scale standard for measuring earthquakes existed at the time, the tremor that shook the area that hot August night was devastating in many ways. Not only did it take 60 lives and leave thousands homeless, but it also did an estimated $6 million in damage, dealing a major blow to Charleston's priceless architectural treasures. The quake's epicenter was measured near what is now Interstate 26 and Deer Park.

But the greatest catalyst for change in the north area was not of a natural kind. Instead, it was the arrival of the U.S. Navy Yard in 1904. Suddenly land values soared, drainage plans were drawn up, and roads were built. North Charleston was slowly gaining an identity of its own.

The words "North" and "Charleston" were first put together in 1912, according to Ruth W. Cupp, a *News and Courier* writer who compiled a warm, memory-filled history of the area in 1988. The words provided the name for a vast land development plan that included 3,000 residential lots for housing "the labor force of the future." Although this would-be North Charleston real estate development went into foreclosure during the Great Depression, the momentum for a separate municipality continued to build. Workers from the Navy Yard started a savings and loan association—one of the first in the country. Then, West Virginia Pulp and Paper Co. broke ground for a new plant in the area. Things started looking up.

With the coming of World War II, thousands of newcomers settled in the north area as the Navy Yard needed employees to man three shifts working day and night. After the war, private industry and residential communities multiplied quickly. Aviation traffic increased, and an interstate highway was built. Soon the growing pains of a burgeoning city began to call for more political autonomy. The various factions and communities grafted themselves together and formed the city of North Charleston on July 12, 1972.

Residents take pride in the fact that the population center for Greater Charleston, as in the entire Trident area, is in North Charleston. Smart businesses and industries looking for a place to grow are noticing that fact in greater numbers every year.

## WEST (OF THE) ASHLEY

Here's another area that pays a kind of allegiance to Charleston's Peninsula through its very name. The neighborhood called West Ashley is, literally, west of peninsular Charleston and across the Ashley River. This was Charleston's primary artery of economic growth following World War II, and like many other similar older growth areas, West Ashley contains its share of urban sprawl. The corridor of U.S. Highway 17 S. (heading toward

# Meet You at "The Four Corners of Law"

The intersection of Meeting and Broad Streets is affectionately known in Charleston as "The Four Corners of Law." The old line (mostly used these days by carriage drivers and guides for walking tours) is meant to imply that you can do literally everything legally required in life right here at this one important Charleston intersection.

On the first corner you can get your mail (at the oldest operating post office building in South Carolina). On the second corner you can get married (at St. Michael's Episcopal Church, built in 1761 and the place where the visiting George Washington once worshiped). On the third corner you can pay your taxes (at the Charleston County Courthouse). And on the fourth corner—if necessary—you can get divorced (at Charleston's City Hall, built in 1801 and now undergoing a $9.1-million renovation).

This attitude thinly disguises the notorious Charlestonian attitude that, indeed, this intersection is (to locals) the center of the universe. The tongue-in-cheek attitude ranks right up there next to the other one-liner that graciously allows, "The Ashley and Cooper Rivers come together at Charleston to form the Atlantic Ocean."

*The Four Corners of Law at the intersection of Meeting and Broad Streets is the very heart of the Holy City.* CHARLESTON AREA CONVENTION AND VISITORS BUREAU/DAVID C. BERRY

Savannah) saw Charleston's first planned shopping center (St. Andrews) and the city's first postwar subdivision (Byrnes Downs). Its relative convenience and proximity to peninsular Charleston, along with the new connector highways, make West Ashley neighborhoods a desirable address today.

# James Island

The Cusabo Indians, whose name has been translated as "Coosawhatchie River People," lived on James Island four centuries ago and left their archaeological mark ahead of white settlers. It was probably the Kiawah tribe that first blazed a trail from the Stono River to the beach, where its leaders met to make treaties and smoke peace pipes. This path became King's Highway, an important road for European settlers, and what is today's US 17 S.

On the map, the land mass of James Island can be located southwest of the Peninsula. It is bordered by the Stono River, the Intracoastal Waterway, Charleston Harbor, and the Atlantic. Its protective barrier island is Folly Beach. James Island was called Boone's Island in early records, named for the colony's agent, Joseph Boone. Around 1671, James Towne, the second settlement in South Carolina, was officially established on one of this island's creek banks.

In the 19th century, plantations were built along with the village of Secessionville—a summer retreat for plantation owners. It is believed that the first shots of the Civil War were fired from the island's Fort Johnson onto Fort Sumter in 1861. (See the Forts section of the Attractions chapter.)

By 1866, all but a handful of dwellings—from stately plantations to gin mills—had been destroyed by the war. The island then became a farming community, where first cotton and then vegetables were the major cash crops. Today there are many businesses and residential areas covering this once sparsely populated land. James Island residents are enthusiastic about the convenient highway connector, Highway 30, which opened in 1993. It channels traffic directly to and from the Peninsula and has initiated the next chapter of James Island's history.

# Johns Island

Larger, more agricultural Johns Island is due west of the Peninsula—past the West Ashley suburban sprawl and James Island. It's technically an island because it is surrounded by the Intracoastal Waterway, the Stono River, the Kiawah River, and Bohicket Creek. Cusabo Indians also inhabited Johns Island before the British arrived. By 1695, there were perhaps 14 white families farming the land, which was also home to wild animals such as buffalo, wolves, and cougars. With the plantation system came the development of Legareville, a summer village of homes built by plantation owners.

Johns Island has developed as a patchwork of natural waterways separated by farmland, residential property, and commercial development. The island has always been something of a breadbasket for the Greater Charleston area.

After the Civil War, when many black families were disenfranchised, Johns Island became a refuge for them. On and around what had once been plantations, little hamlets and church parishes (called "Praise Houses") formed. Small farms and garden operations were soon flourishing—many of which are still in operation today. Tomatoes, strawberries, sweet corn, zucchini, pumpkins, blueberries, and melons are only some of the produce that grows beautifully in the rich Johns Island soil.

# Folly Beach

Fun-loving Folly Beach is the geographical barrier island due south of James Island.

This 6-mile-long, half-mile-wide sandy stretch of land makes up for its diminutive size with a rich and colorful history embracing both good times and bad.

It is believed that the Bohicket tribe of Cusabo Indians summered on Folly as late as the 17th century. During the Civil War, there were Union batteries at both ends of the island with thousands of men. For many years after the conflict, war-ravaged Folly Beach was described as a "tent city" because of the many temporary dwellings still used for shelter there. More permanent beach houses were built by the turn of the century, and George Gershwin stayed in one during the 1920s while he was writing his famous folk opera, *Porgy and Bess.*

It was the giant pier and pavilion that put Folly on the map. Famous names such as Tommy Dorsey, Artie Shaw, Guy Lombardo, Vaughn Monroe, and the Ink Spots played at Folly's Atlantic Boardwalk in the 1930s. The unique venue and nationally known entertainers drew crowds from the Charleston area and far beyond.

Around 1936, a township form of government was established. Fire destroyed the boardwalk in 1957, but it was reopened in 1960 as the Ocean Plaza. During the next decade, Folly became a mecca for surfers. Drawn to the sizable waves, they congregated around the pier—a popular surfing spot. Again, in 1977, fire destroyed this landmark, and eight years later, a high-rise hotel (now a Holiday Inn) went up in its place.

Hurricane Hugo scrambled homes and businesses on this island as well, but Folly is once again a popular destination, and condos are the newest trend in housing. A handsome new fishing pier lures anglers and sunbathers alike to this quaint and colorful beach community.

## Kiawah Island

Kiawah Island is 21 miles from the Peninsula—due west of James Island and Folly Beach—but it has a history and a natural ambience all its own.

It was home to the Kiawah Indians as early as the 16th century. Europeans arrived in 1688, when the island was granted to Capt. George Rayner by the Lords Proprietors of the Carolina Colony. By 1739, ownership had passed to John Stanyarne, who cleared much of it for growing indigo. In 1807, the title passed to Stanyarne's son-in-law, Arnoldus Vanderhorst.

Vanderhorst was an influential public servant and helped to establish the College of Charleston, among other accomplishments. He introduced the planting of cotton on Kiawah and eventually passed the island on to his son. All in all, various members of the Vanderhorst family owned Kiawah Island for the next 180 years.

During the Revolutionary War, British troops occupied the island, and Union forces raised their flag on Kiawah for two years during the Civil War. When the war was over, the Vanderhorsts resumed farming on the island, but ultimately lost the battle with the boll weevil in 1914.

The 10,000-acre island was unoccupied and used as a private hunting reserve between 1952 and 1974 under the ownership of Mr. C. C. Royal of Aiken, South Carolina. Old-timers still talk about the profit turned in 1974 when Royal sold the island—which he had purchased for $50,000—to the Kiawah Island Co., a subsidiary of the Kuwait Investment Co., for $17.4 million.

Under Kuwaiti ownership, the island became a world-class luxury golf and tennis resort and residential community. In 1988, when Kiawah once again changed hands, the selling price had jumped to $105 million.

## Seabrook Island

Just off the eastern tip of Kiawah—due west of Johns Island—is Seabrook. This barrier island is roughly 2,200 acres in size and located about 22 miles from downtown Charleston.

# HISTORY

Like Kiawah, Seabrook has a known archaeological history dating back to approximately 200 B.C. Nomadic bands of Native Americans roamed these lands for thousands of years, leaving shell ring deposits that are still evident today. These piles of shells from edible marine animals were once huge mounds, perhaps 25 to 70 feet in diameter.

In 1666, British subject Lt. Col. Robert Sanford arrived on Seabrook as an explorer in royal service to King Charles II. He described these shell rings as being "discernable a good way out to sea." By 1684, the local Stono Indians were persuaded to cede their lands (for mere beads, cloth, and trinkets) to the proprietary government, which, in turn, sold the property to English settlers.

The island was used as a staging area for Hessian and British troops during the American Revolutionary years of 1779 and 1780. In 1816, the island was sold to William Seabrook of nearby Edisto Island, hence the present name. Under Seabrook's ownership, the island was used for growing cotton.

At the height of the Civil War, Seabrook sold his island to William Gregg, who tried to reestablish the cotton plantation after the war. He failed and rented the land to Charles Andell of New York City, who, with a group of missionaries, tried to establish schools on the island for newly freed blacks. After Andell's death in 1876, his brother William continued the cotton-growing operation, introducing a new, finer grade of cotton with longer, silkier fibers that became world-famous as "sea island cotton."

After the turn of the century, natural and artificial disasters (such as hurricanes and fires) along with the boll weevil brought an end to Seabrook's highly profitable cotton-growing years. Hardship caused Gregg's widow to sell off Seabrook's oceanfront land to sportsmen for hunting, fishing, and recreation.

In 1939, the Episcopal Diocese of South Carolina rented land on Seabrook to establish a summer camp for underprivileged children. In 1951, about 1,408 acres of land were given to the church, some of which is known today as Camp St. Christopher.

In 1970, the diocese sold about 1,100 acres to private developers who planned the private, residential community that Seabrook Island is today. Eighteen years later, the town of Seabrook was incorporated, and it celebrated a decade of private ownership and self-government in 1997.

# RESTAURANTS

Believe it or not, you won't have to go very far to find a Charlestonian who will tell you that as recently as 20 years ago there were only a few white tablecloth restaurants in the entire city. That seems incredible today, when there are easily two dozen truly fine dining options to choose from on any given evening out on the town.

Charleston's dining traditions go way back—to England, in fact, where high tea was served in the late afternoon. In colonial Charles Towne, that habit evolved through the influences of time and climate into a late lunch, usually served at 2:00 P.M. or so. This meal was the heaviest of the day.

Before the era of air-conditioning and the advent of a more homogenized American lifestyle, Charlestonians held on to this Anglican dining custom for many generations. It moved the effort of meal preparation away from the hottest time of the day and left the shank of the daylight hours essentially uninterrupted for commerce and industry. Until the 1960s (and even later in some cases), schools dismissed their children promptly at 1:50 P.M. for "2 o'clock dinner" and resumed the business of formal education at 8:00 or so the next morning. Most downtown businesses closed at 1:00 P.M. for an hour or so—as did the banks and law offices—so the business owners could saunter home, enjoy 2 o'clock dinner, and return by mid–afternoon.

It goes without saying that fine dining was still not neglected in the evening hours, especially where entertaining was concerned. The elegant formal dining rooms of Charleston's famous houses attest to that.

The concept of going out to a restaurant for dinner is a Johnny-come-lately idea to die-hard Charlestonians. That's why there were so few fine restaurants here before the late 1970s.

With the revitalization of our downtown area and the draw of people to all places South, there has been an accompanying influx of outstanding new culinary talent and the interest to match. In fact, Charleston has been home to some of the country's most respected culinary institutions. This deepens the talent pool for dining establishments all over the Lowcountry. Now establishments and styles fit almost every whim while making a true effort to share and preserve the traditional cuisine of the Lowcountry. We have included information, typical fare, and opinions in this chapter that may help you with your selections. Menu items are frequently seasonal and subject to change.

The list here is not exhaustive but gives, we feel, a fair representation of what is available on the downtown Peninsula, in Mt. Pleasant, on the islands east of the Cooper, and in the areas and islands west of the Ashley River. Not included in our descriptions are the familiar national restaurant chains. Eateries are categorized geographically, not by type of food offered. So pin down the location where you want to dine, then dive into the listings to see what is available. Bear in mind that many of the downtown restaurants are housed in old and historic buildings that may not be wheelchair accessible. If that's an issue for you or your party, it's always good to call ahead.

Whatever your budget, we feel confident you'll find in the following listings the perfect setting for enjoying Lowcountry meals that will augment your stay in the Trident area.

## PRICE CODE

The reference guide should be used to translate the average price ranges of dinner for two persons, minus cocktails, wine, or gratuity. We caution that prices, hours, menus, and means of payment are frequently subject to change, so if you have any doubts about an important issue, call ahead. Since most restaurants will accept cash, traveler's checks, and all major credit cards (but almost never personal checks), we inform you only of those establishments that do not take plastic.

Here are our breakdowns for average entree prices for two and the correlating symbols.

| | |
|---|---|
| $ | Less than $20 |
| $$ | $20–35 |
| $$$ | $36–60 |
| $$$$ | More than $61 |

# CHARLESTON

## Anson                                    $$$
### 12 Anson Street
### (843) 577-0551
### www.ansonrestaurant.com

This elegant restaurant on Anson Street is between the Market and the trendy Ansonborough neighborhood. Anson is as well appointed as it is deserving of its reputation for fine food and good service. The nouvelle American menu includes a decadent whole crispy flounder with apricot shallot sauce that should not be missed. If you're among those who enjoy steak tartare, Anson's consistently gets rave reviews. Other temptations include outstanding first-course fried scallops and oysters in spicy tomato relish and cucumber crème. When it's time for dessert, look for their dense, moist house-made chocolate cake. Dinner is served seven nights a week; reservations are recommended.

## A. W. Shuck's Seafood & Oyster Bar   $$
### 70 State Street
### (843) 723-1151
### www.a-w-shucks.com

More than a decade has passed since Shuck's first opened its doors, and a lot has changed in the Market area since then—at Shuck's in particular. What was originally a cozy, popular bar packed with locals has become a bigger, fancier eating establishment where the bar is no longer the major draw. Shuck's features both indoor and outdoor dining. Oyster connoisseurs will be interested to know the mollusks are sold raw or steamed at market price. Beef, fowl, shrimp, grouper, scallops, snapper, and children's plates are all on the menu. A. W. Shuck's is open daily for lunch and dinner. Locals and visitors alike enjoy the abundance of early artwork by local painter John Doyle throughout the restaurant.

## Baker's Café of Charleston        $–$$
### 214 King Street
### (843) 577-2694
### www.bakerscafe.com

Baker's Café is a romantic little gem tucked away in the block below Charleston Place. Much more than a bakery (although what's baked is delicious), it is a sophisticated but comfortable restaurant that's open daily for breakfast and lunch. Sunday brunch at Baker's, lasting until 2:30 P.M., is particularly delightful, with unusual dishes such as Eggs Charleston (with a bed of snow crab substituted for the Canadian bacon), mimosas made with freshly squeezed orange juice, and a basket of hot-from-the-oven baked goods. Wine and other spirits are also available. Dress is nicely casual.

## Blossom Café                   $$–$$$
### 171 East Bay Street
### (843) 722-9200
### www.magnolias-blossom-cypress.com

Blossom Café is another see-and-be-seen place downtown but offers the bonus of being as affordable or extravagant as your budget allows. The cafe, open every day, has indoor and outdoor dining, an in-house bakery, a cappuccino bar, and an extensive New American menu with Italian and Mediterranean influences. The menu is the same for lunch, dinner, and late-night dining, featuring pastas, seafood entrees, and gourmet pizzas from the oak-burning oven. An added bonus is free parking just next door.

## Bocci's          $$-$$$
158 Church Street
(843) 720-2121
www.boccis.com

This cozy Northern Italian family restaurant near the Market keeps them coming back for more calzones, salads, seafood, and pasta topped with a choice of four fabulous sauces. Mozzarella lovers go for the hand-pulled cheese. Another favorite is scallops wrapped in prosciutto. Try the veal saltimbocca, too. There is a front-room view looking onto historic Church Street. Bocci's is open every day for dinner.

## The Bookstore Café          $-$$
412 King Street
(843) 720-8843

Near Marion Square and upper King Street, the Bookstore Café serves breakfast and lunch and sells freshly baked goods. Far enough from the madding crowd, this cafe offers some serenity along with its daily specials. Menu items include its signature potato casseroles. Specials might be quesadillas, a focaccia sandwich, roast pork, and fried green tomatoes. Take home some rhubarb-raspberry jam and beer bread. The cafe opens at 9:00 A.M. Monday through Friday; Saturday and Sunday hours begin at 8:00 A.M. Closing time is 2:00 P.M.

## Carolina's          $$$
10 Exchange Street
(843) 724-3800
www.carolinasrestaurant.com

Carolina's is on the site of old Perdita's, a much-respected restaurant of days gone by. There is little in the decor reminiscent of the establishment's roots, as Carolina's is designed for today. There are three main areas: the noisy, see-and-be-seen front dining section, with its showy wine collection (said to be one of the largest in the Southeast); a central bar with tables on two sides; and a more secluded, traditional dining room to the right of the entrance. The menu is expansive, and the style nouvelle American with seafood, veal, and lamb—grilled in many instances.

One favorite is the sweet potato–crusted grouper. Their pecan brittle basket with vanilla bean ice cream and fresh fruit berries is ample for two and a perfect ending. Carolina's is open every day for dinner only, and the dress, while generally casual, edges toward the snazzy side. Reservations are suggested. (See the Nightlife chapter.)

## Charleston Chops          $$$-$$$$
188 East Bay Street
(843) 937-9300

Don't let the name mislead you—this is not your mother's Sunday pork chops. This is an elegant dining experience with possibly the largest list of gourmet specialties in town, including a wine list with over 180 choices. Still, it's the place (on East Bay Street, anyway) to go for good prime rib, a thick veal chop, or ginger and lemongrass seared tuna. Charleston Chops is an excellent source for roasted rack of lamb and succulent seafood, too. If you need to go exotic, try the appetizer list, where you'll find ostrich brochettes, beef tartare, and much more. As for steaks, the beef is 21-day-aged Certified Black Angus—consistently tender and served as ordered. Their non-beef specialties include garlic-and-herb-crusted salmon, pan-seared duck, and a mixed grill of wild game. Classical and contemporary tunes from the piano bar will entertain you throughout the evening. Charleston Chops serves dinner Monday through Sunday beginning at 5:30 P.M., with the bar opening at 5:00 P.M. Reservations are recommended.

## Charleston Grill          $$$-$$$$
224 King Street (in Charleston Place)
(843) 577-4522
www.charlestongrill.com

This is the grande dame restaurant in Orient Express' Charleston Place. In this richly wooded and traditionally decorated eatery, quality is the byword. Service is exuberant, for those who demand close attention, and the wine list can compete with any in the South. It isn't exactly stuffy, but the atmosphere is definitely upscale. The food is simply superb. Its nightly specials are always as billed, but the regular menu is abundant in attractive choices. Try the young zucchini blossoms stuffed with Maine lobster with fried oysters for starters. And the local Burlill duck with Vidalia hash pie makes for an exotic entree. Desserts are announced nightly for those with a taste for excess. Live jazz begins at 7:00 P.M. and adds a cool balm to the well-orchestrated scene. Dinner is served nightly, and the bar opens at 4:00 P.M. Reservations are welcomed.

---

**i** *A sweating glass of sparkling iced tea is a Southern tradition, and most restaurants will gladly refill your glass gratis. Be sure to let them know, however, if you are specifically looking for our good old-fashioned sweetened tea.*

---

### Circa 1886     $$$-$$$$
**149 Wentworth Street**
**(843) 853-7828**
**www.circa1886.com**

When the giant landmark Victorian townhouse on Wentworth Street opened as a high-end B&B, the whole concept for the genre in Charleston expanded upwardly—in more ways than one. Not only would the envelope for luxury accommodations be expanded, an on-site restaurant of similar caliber would be opened for the convenience of the mansion's guests and other discerning diners. Thus, Circa 1886 was born (about a year later), and it seems well worth the wait. Named for the date of the Wentworth Mansion's construction, this small and intimate dining venue in what was once the carriage house offers seasonal cuisine that conceivably might have been served to the home's owner at that time. Executive Chef Marc Collins rotates the menu seasonally—presenting his unique and modern take on old Charleston recipes. Look for the sautéed grouper over mushroom and goat cheese potatoes. Another find is their

cornmeal-fried, locally raised soft-shell crab with chive potatoes and creamed succotash.

Desserts sure to please include pan-fried angel food cake with fresh berries and peach ice cream or chocolate soufflé.

An intimate bar and attentive but unobtrusive service add to the ambience here—and Circa 1886 provides a quiet evening of fine dining clearly intended to be a cut above the rest of the downtown restaurant crowd. An impressive wine list with more than 280 labels is available. Dinner is served Monday through Sunday from 5:30 to 9:30 P.M. Reservations are required.

### Coast     $$-$$$
**39-D John Street**
**(843) 722-8838**
**www.coastbarandgrill.com**

Tucked away on Hutson Alley behind Rue de Jean (on John Street) is this seafood restaurant now making big waves with locals as well as out-of-towners. When the question arises, "Where will you find good seafood?" this is always a great answer. The menu lists dozens of options—all prepared in different as well as traditional ways. Their coastal dishes from around the world can take the adventuresome diner on an exciting journey to Thailand, Peru, Chile, Baja, and the rocky coast of Maine in addition to our own Lowcountry waters. Some dinners come in small or large sizes so every appetite can be well accommodated. A full raw bar is part of the scene, but you can order your seafood wood-grilled, steamed, smoked, or fried. Open daily for dinner starting at 5:30 P.M.

### Cru Café     $$
**18 Pinckney Street**
**(843) 534-2434**

There's nothing quite like Cru Café in Charleston. Sure, we have other restaurants in single houses (see the Close-up on single houses in the Architectural and Historic Preservation chapter), and you can dine on the porch at those as well. But Cru

Café is unique. The menu features "upscale comfort food" that's nourishing and desirable to the palate and the eye—but not so exotic as to be intimidating. For instance, there's their lobster bisque, salmon and lemon risotto, four-cheese ravioli primavera, and herb cornmeal grouper. Lunch is Tuesday through Sunday; dinner is served Tuesday through Saturday. Seating is limited, so we recommend that you avoid the peak hours of noon to 1:00 P.M. Reservations are suggested.

**Cypress Lowcountry Grille**         **$$$$**
**167 East Bay Street**
**(843) 727-0111**
**www.magnolias-blossom-cypress.com**
Many Charleston visitors have tried Magnolia's on East Bay Street and raved about it. Here's another restaurant from the same owners and chefs with a slightly different twist. Cypress is contemporary American cuisine with Asian overtones, and the result is delightful. Wine lovers will appreciate the 21-foot-tall "wine wall" with choices for the most discriminating palate. The 4,500 bottles kept on hand make a stunning background for a memorable evening. The 1834 building that houses Cypress retains a Charleston feel while the decor is smart and trendy by any standard. The menu is large; for instance, you choose from 13 different appetizers. The cold-shrimp-and-beef spring rolls are one popular option. Among the dozen or so main dishes, smoked salmon with Wellington butter with sautéed spinach, horseradish-whipped potatoes, and lemon butter is divine. The desserts are equally attractive. Try the coconut tapioca brûlée served with blackberries, mango compote, and passion fruit sorbet. The chocolate banana torte is memorable, as well. Cypress is open for dinner daily starting at 5:30 P.M. Reservations are preferred.

**Diana's Restaurant**         **$$–$$$**
**155 Meeting Street**
**(843) 534-0043**

Diana's has accomplished an alchemy that few Charleston restaurants have been able to achieve. Here's a simple, convenient, friendly place to get an amazingly hearty breakfast, lunch, or dinner that's unpretentious and yet creatively prepared and, best of all, affordable. Located in what was formerly the coffee shop of the Days Inn on Meeting Street, Diana's is that rare "find" that's become almost extinct in downtown Charleston. The chalkboard outside the door lists an array of daily specials that are American and Lowcountry favorites. There's even a happy hour. Don't forget to save room for Diana's old-fashioned homemade pastry when the question of dessert is posed. Come hungry; portions are generous. She's open daily starting at 6:30 A.M. for those who want to get an early jump on the day.

**Doe's Pita Plus**         **$**
**334 East Bay Street**
**(843) 577-3179**

**5134 North Rhett Avenue,**
**North Charleston**
**(843) 745-0026**
Doe's offers healthy fast food that's a hit with the lunch crowd. The fresh-baked pita bread for pocket sandwiches and salads is prepared to order (right there in plain view) while you wait. Although there are several tables and chairs in the front and back, most people think takeout when they think of Doe's. The Tasty Chicken Pocket is very popular—bursting at the pita seams with plums, celery, chicken, green onions, lettuce, tomatoes, and alfalfa sprouts. For variety on the side, sample Doe's ethnic fare such as baba ghanouj, tabouleh, or Lebanese potato salad. Children love the banana-and-peanut-butter pocket and do well in the high-chair stationed in the rear dining area. Nonalcoholic beverages are sold. Doe's is open daily from 8:00 A.M. to 8:00 P.M. Monday through Friday and until 5:00 P.M. on Saturday and Sunday. American Express, cash, and checks are accepted.

**East Bay Deli**                                    $
**334 East Bay Street**
**(843) 723-3354**

**159 Market Street**
**(843) 723-4443**

Sometimes, what's called for is a quick bite grabbed en route to somewhere else—when the art of fine dining and fancy dress must wait in the wings for another time. Still, you want that bite to be tasty and prepared with care. You want it served with cleanliness and pride, too, and available from a location easy to find. That's exactly what East Bay Deli has to offer, and it's become a hit with downtown shoppers and business types on the go, as well as students and hungry visitors entering the city via the busy East Bay corridor. Here you'll find traditional deli sandwiches, wraps, salads, giant spuds, chicken wings, hot dogs, plus prepared fin and fowl—good to enjoy on-site or take with. They open at 8:00 A.M. and stay around until 9:00 P.M. or so Monday through Saturday.

**82 Queen**                                    $$$
**82 Queen Street**
**(843) 723-7591**
**www.82queen.com**

This multi-award-winning restaurant has several personalities—one of which is sure to please. Exploring the 11 dining rooms at 82 Queen is an adventure in itself. The grounds include three 18th-century town houses, two inside bars (one full-service and one just for shots), an outside raw bar that is a very popular hangout for the after-work crowd, a partly glassed-in romantic gazebo, and outdoor tables for dining. Lowcountry seafood, beef, lamb, and fowl are specialties of their updated traditional Southern cuisine. Farm-fresh herbs and vegetables are locally grown for their kitchen. The wine list includes more than 140 selections. Lunch and dinner are served daily. Reservations are encouraged. (See the Nightlife chapter.)

**FIG**                                    $$-$$$
**232 Meeting Street**
**(843) 805-5900**
**www.eatatfig.com**

Locals fondly remember an affordable Italian restaurant at the corner of Meeting and Hasell Streets that is no more. But in its place came FIG, a new and delightful offering spearheaded by Michael Lata, formerly of Anson. He brings an equally pleasing menu to FIG, inspired by his frequent travels in France where fine dining is a way of life. Local farmers supply the freshest ingredients at peak flavor and the results are reflected in every meal served. Vegetarians love the fresh plate of today's best produce specially prepared by the chef for maximum enjoyment. The ever-changing menu frequently includes a tomato and onion tart with creamy goat cheese or their shrimp radicchio and pancetta salad as starters. Look for their braised lamb with fresh mint pesto or—if you like—have your shrimp served in a tasty stew with chorizo in a light tomato and tarragon-infused broth. Seasonal desserts like blueberry cobbler make a rewarding finale. Wines—domestic and imported—are plentiful and served by the glass. They're open Monday through Saturday for dinner only starting at 6:00 P.M.

**Fish**                                    $$-$$$
**442 King Street**
**(843) 722-3474**
**www.fishrestaurant.net**

As the name implies, this is a small restaurant on upper King Street that's mostly about (but not exclusively dedicated to) seafood. You can count on the fact that none of the seafood brought to table will be more than 36 hours from its native waters. The fun decor is part of the charm. You enter through a courtyard past a fountain and discover an environment that's creative and unusual without being too cute. Don't overlook the risotto-encrusted calamari tossed with cabbage and peppers or the tempura asparagus drizzled with hollandaise. If you're game for it, one of their specialties is the mako shark. Another favorite is sweet Thai barbecue grouper. You might like to try the Captain's Seafood Pot, a traditional steam pot in saffron broth, suitable for two seafood-lovers. The dessert they're all talking about is the mudslide cake. Fish is open for lunch Monday through Friday. Dinner is served Monday through Saturday, 5:30 to 10:00 P.M.

## Fulton Five                        $$$
5 Fulton Street
(843) 853-5555

Fulton Five is an authentic taste of old Italy tucked away on Fulton Street, just off King Street in the heart of the antiques district. The building looks Old World enough to be European, and the al fresco dining experience is definitely continental in feel. An upstairs dining area adds another perspective on the charms of quaint and narrow Fulton Street. The menu is constantly changing with new and more exciting entrees, but if the following dishes are available, we heartily recommend them. Start with antipasto Spoleto (grilled fresh mozzarella and prosciutto rolled into a romaine leaf with tomato vinaigrette). Next, move to the pumpkin ravioli with a sage-and-brown-butter sauce. Then enjoy the caper-crusted tuna loin with lemon-and-fennel butter. For a light, sweet touch, order a grapefruit, orange, or tangerine ice made in-house or tiramisu—the perfect finale. A fine selection of Italian and other wines is always on hand. Fulton Five is open only for dinner Monday through Saturday starting at 5:30 P.M. Reservations are suggested.

## Garibaldi's                        $$$
49 South Market Street
(843) 723-7153

Garibaldi's is a charming Southern Italian restaurant that has survived, apparently without flinching, the continuous ebb and flow of popularity on Market Street. There is service downstairs, with a small bar and a few romantic outside tables, and there's also a formal dining room upstairs. Try the outstanding, crispy scored flounder, and enjoy any of the five pastas. Another favorite is the American red snapper au poivre. Garibaldi's Italian take on our Lowcountry seafood is worth the trouble of finding parking in the congested Market area. Dinner is served each evening. Reservations are required.

## Gaulart & Maliclet
## (Fast and French)                  $-$$
98 Broad Street
(843) 577-9797

Tucked neatly into what was once a long, narrow doctor's office, with lovely old molding, G&M (called Fast and French by locals) is a tiny Parisian-style cafe serving delicious, contemporary French fare. The counter-style service offers cheese plates, salads, and house specials. The owners (French, of course) know what they are doing and are pleasant while doing it. Some favorites are the curried sesame chicken and the Swiss fondue with French bread. They serve breakfast, lunch, and dinner almost every day except Sunday. No dinner is served on Monday.

## Grill 225                   $$$-$$$$
225 East Bay Street
(843) 266-4222
www.grill225.com

When the Market Pavilion Hotel opened near the Market on East Bay Street, they promised a restaurant of distinction, and clearly, it was a promise they kept. Fashioned in the style of the great steak houses of yore, Grill 225 prides itself on garnering the freshest and highest-quality beef, veal, lamb, and seafood available. The fare is deliberately simple in its creation, proportion, flavor, and presentation—so the exceptional quality of each ingredient can (and does) carry the day. For starters, try their tuna tower, and then tackle their generous cut of prime beef or double-cut lamb chops. From the sea come their jumbo lump crab cakes and, of course, lobster of almost any size you specify. If you're willing, the dessert menu tempts with banana bread pudding or flaming baked Carolina. Reservations are recommended, and they can even be made online. Lunch is from 11:30 A.M. to 3:00 P.M. Monday through Saturday. Sunday brunch is from 11:00 A.M. to 2:00 P.M.

---

*Check the menu or specials board at Lowcountry eateries for Beaufort Stew (sometimes called Frogmore Stew), a hearty one-dish supper that's a staple meal on the islands. It's smoked sausage, fresh ears of corn, and shrimp all boiled together with special spices. This fare is often served at Lowcountry oyster roasts as an alternative menu item.*

---

**Hank's Seafood Restaurant**          **$$$**
**10 Hayne Street**
**(843) 723-3474**
**www.hanksseafood.com**
Old-time Charleston Insiders remember a place called Henry's which was part and parcel of this city's colorful "renaissance era" in the 1920s and '30s. It was a seafood joint down in the Market (which was a whole lot rougher in those days), and among other distinctions, old Henry's served liquor throughout Prohibition with (apparently) no interference from the city fathers. Hearty "receipts" for seafood soups and dishes laden with cream and flavor were always offered at Henry's, and generations of Charlestonians were raised on it. Hank's is today's reincarnation of that tradition, with a lot of sophistication added to the mix. An old warehouse has been carefully outfitted with a quasi-period-looking fish-house decor without being too cute about it. And several of the old Henry's dishes have been reproduced or improved upon for patrons with modern palates who now flock there from all over the world. This is where she-crab soup is done right (lovingly flavored with crab roe and sherry), and oysters are still served on the half-shell atop beds of crushed ice. Look for some of the old

Henry's casseroles, if you like, or try the specialties (like sea scallops or seared tuna). There are several fried seafood platters that feature a variety of old Lowcountry receipts, as well. Spirits are still high and served at Hank's willingly. Reservations are taken from 5:00 until 10:30 P.M. Sunday through Thursday and until 11:30 P.M. on Friday and Saturday.

**High Cotton**          **$$$$**
**199 East Bay Street**
**(843) 724-3815**
**www.high-cotton.net**
A relatively recent addition to Charleston's array of fine eateries along the East Bay corridor just north of the Exchange Building is High Cotton. This is another one of the Maverick Southern Kitchens' restaurants (which also brings us Slightly North of Broad across the street and Old Village Post House over in Mt. Pleasant). They call this one "an unabashedly masculine and American saloon," but don't look for anything Wild West about it. Instead, there's dark mahogany woodwork, exposed brick walls, lots of alligator skin upholstery, and a hearty menu of meats, game, lobster, and fresh fish. Local dishes include South Carolina squab, rabbit loin, venison, and spit-roasted quail. Fresh seafood is also available—for which out-of-town visitors from inland locations all seem to call. The spirits served and the service rendered are up to Maverick group's high standards. Dinner hours are 5:30 to 10:00 P.M. Sunday through Thursday and 5:30 to 11:00 P.M. Friday and Saturday. Their weekend brunch is popular, too. Call for reservations.

**Hominy Grill**          **$$**
**207 Rutledge Avenue**
**(843) 937-0930**
**www.hominygrill.com**
On Rutledge Avenue, within a stroll from the huge MUSC hospital and medical office complex, there's a small but worthwhile cafe that's anything but institutional. This is a favorite with the medfolk, as you would imagine, so the best time to find a

table is off the peak meal rush hours—
although breakfast, lunch, and dinner are
all offered. The cuisine is contemporary
Southern, with several attractively served
specials listed daily on their chalkboard
menu. Look for some Lowcountry
favorites like McClellanville crab cakes
with Hoppin' John and pickled cucumber
salad. Or, there's a sesame-crusted catfish
with sautéed okra, baked cheese grits,
and Geechee peanut sauce. Desserts are
terrific, and their bread-pudding with
raisins and caramel sauce is a special
treat. Hominy Grill opens for breakfast at
7:30 A.M., Monday through Friday. Sunday
brunch starts at 9:00. Dinner is served
from 5:30 to 9:30 P.M. on weekdays and
until 10:00 on Saturday and Sunday night.

## Hyman's Seafood Company $$
### 215 Meeting Street
### (843) 723-6000
### www.hymanseafood.com

A casual, always-crowded seafood dining
experience for lunch or dinner, Hyman's
offers a large selection of fresh-caught
fish and a wide variety of shellfish. A raw
bar and lounge are upstairs. Hyman's regularly fries in vegetable oil for those who
want traditionally fried seafood. But you
can order your fish broiled or blackened.
Try the okra soup, even if you have always
shied away from the vegetable. The she-
crab soup is award-winning. Open every
day, the restaurant serves meals all day
long. We suggest parking in the
Charleston Place garage.

## Jack's Café $
### 41 George Street
### (843) 723-5237

The turnaround at Jack's is fast, and the
food is as typically American as the no-
frills apple or peach cobbler. College of
Charleston students, professors, and
alumni as well as King Street merchants
frequent Jack's for old-fashioned burgers
(served in plastic baskets) and milk
shakes. The value is definitely part of the
draw, but so is the vegetable soup (and, in
fact, all of the food). People eat at booths,

the counter, or around a few tables. It's all
very low-key and functional. Take-out
service is available. Jack's is open weekdays only for breakfast and lunch. No
credit cards.

## Kaminsky's Most Excellent Café $
### 78 North Market Street
### (843) 853-8270

### 1028 Johnnie Dodds Boulevard,
### Mt. Pleasant
### (843) 971-7437
### www.tbonz.com

Kaminsky's downtown location is an A-
plus addition to the list of indulge-thyself
Peninsula eateries. The surprise is its just
wonderful desserts and the right coffees
and spirits to accompany them here. The
handsome brick walls of the Market Street
location make a backdrop for a nice
showcase of art, and the cafe's intimate
size contributes to its appeal. Try an
exotic coffee or nonalcoholic drink with a
delicious dessert. The milk shakes, for
instance, are legendary. Be prepared to
face a dilemma: There are 150 other
choices. Relax with a beer or glass of
wine; both lists are international and
impressive. Kaminsky's is open every day
from noon to 2:00 A.M. (For more about
the Mt. Pleasant location, see the East
Cooper section of the Nightlife chapter.)

## Magnolias Uptown/Down South $$$
### 185 East Bay Street
### (843) 577-7771
### www.magnolias-blossom-cypress.com

Magnolias tops the list of hot restaurants
on the Peninsula. In fact, *Travel & Leisure*
called it "the place in downtown
Charleston." This is new American-
Lowcountry cuisine, and the chef's specialties include spicy shrimp and sausage with
tasso gravy over creamy white grits, and
tomato bisque dotted with generous
lumps of fresh crabmeat. The expansive
menu will remind you of the restaurant's
California, Tex-Mex, and Cajun inspirations,
but the atmosphere is strictly refined New
South. Enjoy eating in the beautiful dining

rooms at Magnolias, but also try your hand with Magnolias' recipes at home: Former executive chef Donald Barickman's Magnolias Southern Cuisine is a hot seller cookbook. Lunch and dinner are served daily. Reservations are definitely encouraged.

### Marina Variety Store & Restaurant    $$
### City Marina, 17 Lockwood Drive
### (843) 723-6325

Enjoy good food as well as a magnificent view of the Ashley River at what regulars call the Variety Store. Offering breakfast, lunch, and dinner in a very casual setting, the restaurant serves basic, good food. For instance, you can order eggs, bacon, and toast for breakfast after church and come back for a tuna salad sandwich and cup of vegetable soup after the noon regatta. If you want to return that night, a dinner of fresh fish with red rice and a salad is a distinct possibility. Spirits are available, and children are welcome. Open daily, except no dinner service on Sunday.

### McCrady's    $$$-$$$$
### 2 Unity Alley
### (843) 577-0025
### www.mccradysrestaurant.com

McCrady's experienced a new incarnation several years ago that retains much of the old tavern's charm but adds new space and sophistication. The dark wood and exposed brick interiors hark back to the days when George Washington supposedly supped here, and the huge fireplaces add their own charm. But the service and—most of all—the cuisine are the reasons to go there. Here, fine dining is a major event. McCrady's serves appetizers like house-cured salmon "pastrami" served with toast points and a zesty mustard sauce. There's a lobster and new potato salad, too. For entrees, try the rack of lamb marinated in herbs with thyme-whipped potatoes. But delicious variations of duck, chicken, beef, pork, and fish are always on the menu. If you're still able, try a dessert like the pear and almond tart or the molten chocolate cake with caramel ice cream. The sommelier's wine list is extensive and impressive. It's open daily for dinner. (See the Nightlife chapter.)

### Mellow Mushroom    $-$$
### 309 King Street
### (843) 723-7374
### www.mellowmushroom.com

Some visitors to Charleston may be familiar with the earlier version of this specialty pizza den that was a big draw in Atlanta when it first opened in the 1970s. Our version is new to the King Street crowd and the College of Charleston kids who weren't around for the "groovy" version in Hot 'lanta. In addition to the specialty pizzas, like their Mega-Veggie with a garden's worth of fresh non-meat ingredients, their dough is made with spring water. Calzones, hoagies, and salads are on the bill as well. The location is ideal for students, but MM attracts out-of-towners, too. It's especially popular with late-nighters and lunchtimers from King Street's business district. They're open daily for lunch and dinner, and the bar stays open until 11:00 P.M.

### Mistral    $$-$$$
### 99 South Market Street
### (843) 722-5708

Mistral is a very cozy, small, and intimate bistro. Lunch and dinner are served in a French country atmosphere with an emphasis on seafood and sauces. Their house pâté is a favorite with locals. This is understated elegance—a place where you can go light or heavy, from salads to seafood. Don't miss the homemade bread! Many locals enjoy their live music every evening starting at 9:00 P.M. Lunch service begins at 11:00 A.M.

### Oak Steakhouse    $$$-$$$$
### 17 Broad Street
### (843) 722-4220
### www.oaksteakhouserestaurant.com

What locals remember as the little luncheon eatery called BJ's took on a whole new identity when restaurant entrepreneur Brett McKee (formerly of Brett's, Union Hall, and Brett's at the Wickliffe

# The Taste of Charleston: Buy the Book

One of the best ways to a city's (dare we say?) stomach . . . is through the dog-eared pages of its local Junior League cookbook. But perhaps the granddaddy of all tomes dealing with a city's bounty for the table is Charleston's 30-times reprinted, $1-million fund-raising, five-decades-old, classic-of-all-classics Junior League cookbooks. Its official name is *Charleston Receipts* (in the South, recipes are traditionally referred to as "receipts"), and this venerable publication of The Junior League of Charleston, Inc., is clearly a legend in its own time.

As the oldest Junior League cookbook still in print, the publication remains essentially unchanged since its first printing back in 1950—which says a great deal about its popularity and success throughout the years. This classic compilation of Southern gentility and gastronomical goodness was gleaned from cherished old family recipes collected by 21 Sustaining Members seeking to raise funds for a community speech-and-hearing center—the first of its kind in the state. Many of the recipes were family secrets passed down by word of mouth from generation to generation and never before seen in print.

Originally, the cookbook retailed for $2.50 and featured 350 pages with 750 recipes plus quaint sketches of the city by local artists. Interspersed among the recipes were colorful Gullah verses harking back to the days when African-American servants did most of the cooking in proper Charleston households. These days, if you order one by mail, it'll cost you $19.95 plus $3.00 shipping and handling. But it's still a bargain at twice the price. Visit www.jlcharleston.org or write The Junior League of Charleston, Inc., 51 Folly Road, Charleston 29407.

House) decided to create for Broad Street a New York–style steakhouse par excellence. He started by taking the 1840s-era building (originally a bank) through a $3-million renovation and expansion, which took seven months to complete. When done, the stage was set for high drama, and Brett stepped up to the plate with his usual panache. This is an upscale source for steaks, chops, Italian specialties, veal, and seafood—all served with Brett's usual flair. They use only prime Angus beef, and you may order from a number of specially prepared sauces to complement your selection. Among the favorite starters is the tuna tartare, a sashimi-grade yellowfin tuna in spicy ginger soy sauce with chopped scallions, shaved cucumbers, and a fried wonton. A popular steak for the hearty (read: enormous) appetite is the marinated 36-ounce bone-in rib eye. For those not in a beef state of mind, there's whole Maine lobster, Italian pastas, and fresh local seafood. You might want to go for the pan-seared blackened grouper with melted leeks, shiitake mushrooms, and shellfish consommé. The wine selection is served up from a vault that in an earlier life held Confederate bonds (before the "Recent Unpleasantness"). There's even live music in the air as a gentle sere-nade for diners. Valet parking is offered along busy Broad Street, which is a wel-come gesture of true hospitality. Reserva-tions are definitely called for, as space is limited. They're open Monday through Saturday from 5:00 to 11:00 P.M.

### Olde Towne Restaurant          $$
### 229 King Street
### (across from Charleston Place)
### (843) 723-8170

Owners Spiros Fokas and Steve Ferderigos have been serving authentic Greek lunches and dinners here daily for more than 20 years. The menu includes seafood, salads, Greek chicken, and the ever-popular Steve's Special—a sampler, good for the whole gang. Pictures of classical Greece line the walls, and a grill in the front win-dow offers a tempting display of chicken being roasted on a turning spit.

### O'Reilly's Irish Pub
### & Seafood Tavern              $
### 288 King Street
### (843) 577-0406
### www.charlestoncrabhouse.com

Formerly Mike Calder's, O'Reilly's is a sports-friendly pub that pleases its clien-tele with deli-style food and a colorful atmosphere. Such favorites as chef salads, soups, and club sandwiches are always available. Try the Reuben or the toasted tuna sandwich. O'Reilly's has five imports on draft and is popular with the College of Charleston crowd that seems ever-present on King Street at night. O'Reilly's is open daily. (See the Nightlife chapter.)

### The Palmetto Café            $$$
### 130 Market Street, Charleston Place
### (843) 722-4900
### www.charlestonplace.com

This restaurant is inside the large Charleston Place complex and serves breakfast and lunch in a relaxed but upscale cafe atmosphere. The breakfast buffet on Sunday is a very elaborate event with several choices of entree and salad, fresh vegetables and fruits, plus desserts.

The garden atmosphere is particularly attractive and convenient to those staying in the hotel or shopping downtown. It falls in the pricier category, but everything is beautifully presented and it is well worth the price on a special occasion (like your first visit to Charleston). For lunch, there's nothing like their chilled red and yellow Johns Island heirloom gazpacho. Follow that with crab cakes served with black-berry, rhubarb, and roasted tomato sauces. This stylish restaurant features optional courtyard dining and is open daily.

### Peninsula Grill          $$$-$$$$
### Planters Inn, 112 North Market Street
### (843) 723-0700
### www.peninsulagrill.com

The restaurant in the Planters Inn is the Peninsula Grill, an elegantly simple and altogether comfortable dining experience that has "extraordinary" written all over it. For instance, half the menu is devoted to the Champagne Bar, which offers an Old World selection of champagnes by the glass and a list of mixed cocktails that reads like a page from Noel Coward's *Private Lives*. The Champagne Bar menu includes a full selection of oysters, lobster (fresh from Maine), and other seafood specialties. Try the sautéed jumbo shrimp scampi with lima bean, corn, okra, and tomato gumbo. The steaks, chops, and accompanying side dishes are equally fine, and you're tended to by a courteous and capable staff. As for wine, there's an extensive list—mostly from France and California. Several labels are available by the glass. Peninsula Grill is open Monday through Sunday for dinner only starting at 5:30 P.M. Reservations are suggested. (See the Nightlife chapter.)

### Poogan's Porch          $$-$$$
### 72 Queen Street
### (843) 577-2337
### www.poogansporch.com

Poogan's Porch is in a charming old Charleston house where lunch and dinner can be enjoyed fireside or outside beneath the stars on the porch or patio.

Expect casual family dining (including a children's menu) with such Lowcountry favorites as Albertha's she-crab soup, shrimp creole, okra gumbo, seafood specials, and even—on the wilder side—an occasional alligator dish. Lunch and dinner are served seven days a week; reservations are recommended for dinner. Sunday brunch is from 10:30 A.M. to 2:30 P.M.

### Robert's of Charleston $$$$
182 East Bay Street
(843) 577-7565,
(800) 977-7565 (outside S.C.)
www.robertsofcharleston.com

Starting in 1976, one of the most popular restaurant experiences in Charleston was Robert Dickson's one-man show that married music and fine dining for a delightful evening on the town. He closed in 1994 to lead small tours to Italy and do private catering, but the call of the crowd brought him back in 1998. Reservations are required well in advance for his five-course, *prix fixe* meal ($75) and a menu that changes seasonally. You might start with baked scallop mousse in creamed lobster sauce followed by breast of duckling in a cabbage and curry sauce. Then for your main course, he'll serve beef tenderloin with béarnaise sauce accompanied by fresh vegetables in interesting combinations. Desserts are very special with chocolate pâté plus tropical fruit in mango and wildberry sauce being just one example. But get this: Your chef is also your entertainment! Robert is an accomplished baritone with a vast repertoire of popular Broadway musicals to his credit. He sings while his guests dine, and his pianist fills in as he slips away to the kitchen between songs and prepares your next course. Your wine is pre-selected from a list of the chef's international favorites. The fare for the entire evening seems pricey, but it's always an unforgettable night. Many patrons are celebrating special occasions, which adds to the electricity of the event. This is a performance that takes place every Thursday through Saturday with a 7:30 P.M. seating. Don't dare be late.

### Saffron $-$$
333 East Bay Street
(843) 722-5588

This is a light and airy restaurant, contemporary in design and good for solo ventures or joining friends. This pitched-roof, modern building is divided into a gourmet product section with imported pastas and olive oils; a full bakery (you'll be seduced by the scent and leave with a loaf of bread); and a dining room with booths and tables scattered about. Popular menu items include the seafood and spinach salads, pasta dishes, and the classic carrot cake. It's open for breakfast, lunch, and dinner seven days a week. Saffron does a Sunday brunch from 9:30 A.M. to 2:30 P.M.

### Sermet's Corner $$
276 King Street
(843) 853-7775

After the success of his first eatery west of the Ashley, Sermet's creative artist and chef opened a new location on King Street several years ago to rave reviews and standing-room-only crowds. The cuisine is Mediterranean-influenced, with spicy pastas and fresh green salads, and it's a refreshing option on the King Street luncheon and dinner scene. Look for their lavender-honey-and black-pepper marinated pork tenderloin with creamy ricotta polenta. The desserts are straight from heaven. In season, there's a rhubarb and raspberry pie that is definitely to die for. Sermet's is open daily from 11:00 A.M. to 3:00 P.M. for lunch; and they reopen for dinner starting at 5:00 P.M.

### Slightly North of Broad $$-$$$
192 East Bay Street
(843) 723-3424
www.slightlynorthofbroad.net

In one of the many 19th-century cotton warehouses that line East Bay Street, there's this trendy option for S.N.O.B. types. Cute name notwithstanding, the folks here are very serious about good food. It's what they call a "maverick Southern kitchen" with multicultural overtones. The sautéed shiitake mushrooms

*The footsore traveler who's already enjoyed a full dose of Charleston's charm may be in the mood for a brief respite for some tea and sympathy. The Charleston Tea Company, at 24-B Ann Street, across from the visitor center, has just the right medicine—a glass of refreshing mint tea (locally grown right here on Wadmalaw Island) or a cup of coffee and soups or sandwiches or other light fare. There's also cold beer and wine if the mood strikes. In any case, you'll be sustained for further adventures in the Holy City.*

is all about French food served in the best tradition of the genre. Located across John Street from the visitor center, this is a great place to begin a dining tour of Charleston. They're known for their braised short ribs with espanole sauce and their steamed mussels available in six different presentations. If you want, a large assortment of French wines is available, but domestic labels are offered too. The full-service bar is a popular stop for locals as well as first-time visitors to our city. A favorite dessert is their crème brûlée. Rue de Jean is open for lunch or dinner every day from 11:30 A.M. until late night.

with foie gras mousse filling on a bed of fresh sautéed spinach with a port wine sauce are divine. This restaurant is a favorite of those who want to lunch with friends (Monday through Friday) or have a special evening on the town (any day of the week). Reservations are encouraged.

### Sushi Hiro                    $-$$
### 298 King Street
### (843) 723-3628

Sushi Hiro is a small sushi bar nestled between M. Dumas and Sharky's Pizza on King Street. In addition to à la carte sushi, there is a varied appetizer menu including tofu salad, shrimp tempura, and even soft-shell crab. Complete dinners range from chicken or beef teriyaki to a combination sushi plate. If you like your seafood unscathed by the flame, this is the downtown place for Japanese delicacies. In addition to stools around the prep station, there are several freestanding tables for those seeking more privacy. Management does not welcome tank-top-clad patrons. Sushi Hiro is open only during dinner hours, Monday through Saturday.

### 39 Rue de Jean             $$-$$$
### 39 John Street
### (843) 722-8881

Here's a little bit of Paris right here on South Carolina soil. That is, this restaurant

### Tommy Condon's Irish Pub
### and Seafood Restaurant        $-$$
### 160 Church Street
### (843) 577-3818
### www.tommycondons.com

The most authentic Irish pub in Charleston, Tommy Condon's has live Irish music Wednesday through Sunday and serves a wide variety of imported beers and ales such as Bass and Newcastle Brown. The menu is a mixture of Irish and Lowcountry items including shrimp and grits, seafood jambalaya, and fresh fish of the day. There is a covered deck for outside dining, and patrons are welcome for lunch or dinner any day of the week. The kitchen closes at 10:00 P.M., but the bar stays open until 2:00 A.M. (See the Nightlife chapter.)

### Vickery's Bar & Grill          $$
### 15 Beaufain Street
### (843) 577-5300

### 1313 Shrimp Boat Lane (Shem Creek),
### Mt. Pleasant
### (843) 884-4440
### www.vickerysbarandgrill.com

Vickery's Bar & Grill is in the Market Corner, a strip of shops just north of Saks Fifth Avenue and Majestic Square at the downtown end of Beaufain Street, and is as talked about for its unusual bar as for its good food. There's always an eclectic bunch of interesting folks to meet—young professionals and rebels with a cause. The fare here is vaguely Cuban, with a Southern twist. The original Vickery's is in Atlanta and has always earned good reviews there. Grab a booth or a table, inside or out, and order a burger (with piping hot, hand-cut fries) or a delicious seafood entree. Vickery's is open for lunch and dinner seven days a week. Sunday brunch is from 11:00 A.M. to 3:00 P.M. Their Mt. Pleasant location is currently attracting the East Cooper after-work crowd. (See the Nightlife chapter.)

**Wild Wing Café**     **$**
**36 North Market Street**
**(843) 722-9464**

**644 Coleman Boulevard, Mt. Pleasant**
**(843) 971-9464**
**www.wildwingcafe.com**
Wild Wing Café is popular with the younger-than-30 bar crowd, but also has appeal to those of us who have topped out the age group but not our attraction to a good time. Wild Wing serves a wonderful platter of chicken wings (of course), dressed in all kinds of herbs and spices—from the Ginger Wing to the Flying Fajita. There are great dips, sandwiches, and salads as well as buckets of beer for a table packed with thirsty friends. The bar serves a variety of bottled beer and spirits as well as nonalcoholic beverages. Wild Wing is open for lunch and dinner every day. The companion restaurant in Mt. Pleasant has more of the same for the East Cooper crowd.

## EAST COOPER

From all-American to Italian, health food to junk food, there are dozens of restaurants in the East Cooper areas of Mt. Pleasant, Sullivan's Island, and Isle of Palms—enough to suit anyone. Here we highlight some of the local favorites, whether they fall into that category for the food, atmosphere, staff, or all those combined. Remember, this list is not exhaustive. These areas are growing so fast, there are new options opening almost every week. The point is, don't feel you've got to go downtown for a good dining experience. East Cooper can compete with downtown's offerings any day.

# Daniel Island

**Queen Anne's Revenge**    **$$-$$$**
**160-B Fairchild Street**
**(843) 216-6868**
**www.qarevenge.com**
Beside the Hampton Inn on Daniel Island is this unique steak and seafood restaurant that's a cross between a pirate museum and an upscale eatery. Don't mistake this for a theme restaurant; this is all about fine food. But the setting just happens to be the home of a rare and fascinating collection of art and artifacts reflecting the golden age of piracy—once very much a part of the Charleston scene. Among the armor, rapiers, and blunderbusses handsomely displayed, the food is served fresh with flair and style. The pan-roasted mussels in garlic white wine sauce are as good as any from Chesapeake Bay. The barbecue ribs fall off the bone, and the steaks are equally well-prepared. Of course, a full array of fresh seafood entrees is offered nightly. Because the atmosphere is so interesting, this is a good choice for family dining, and a children's menu is available. They're open for lunch and dinner seven days a week. Grown-ups will enjoy the roomy bar where life-size pirates Stede Bonnet and Blackbeard sit and plot their next raid on hapless Charlestonians.

**Sienna**    **$$$-$$$$**
**901 Island Park Drive**
**(843) 881-8820**
**www.siennadining.com**
Time was, the dining choices on Daniel Island were somewhat limited. That's why Sienna is a welcome addition to the small group of eateries convenient to residents

of this fairly new addition to the City of Charleston. (See the Neighborhoods chapter.) Sienna is the dominant color in the handsome earth-toned interior—thus, its name. But the fare, which changes daily, is decidedly Italian as interpreted by Chef Ken Vedrinski, formerly of the Woodlands Resort & Inn in Summerville. He brings to the table treasured recipes from his own family's archives including Grandma Volpe's Italian Wedding Soup—all prepared with the freshest ingredients available. Braised veal is another family favorite along with scaloppini of Sonoma duck in Chianti saba jus. There's a full array of pasta including bucatinni carbonara and mostachioli with broccoli sauce—available in half or full portions. For those with a hearty appetite, there's the Sienna Ultimate Tasting menu, which is a seven-course indulgence in the best of Chef Vedrinski's specialties. They're open seven days a week for dinner. The bar opens at 5:00 P.M.

## Mt. Pleasant

For the most part, Mt. Pleasant's restaurant fare is family-oriented. There are exceptions, of course, for fine dining and special occasions. Here are some of the local favorites in Mt. Pleasant.

### Alex's Restaurant $
### 302 Coleman Boulevard
### (843) 881-7714

Open 24 hours a day, this Alex's is a popular spot for breakfast on the way to the beach or a late-night meal on the way home. Recently, the Sunday lunch crowd has been thick too. The restaurant is large and attractive, and draws locals as well as visitors to the area. You can't beat its standard bacon, eggs, and biscuits with plenty of hot joe. Other Alex's Restaurants are scattered throughout Greater Charleston, especially in the north area.

### Andolini's Pizza $-$$
### 414 West Coleman Boulevard
### (843) 849-7437

### 82 Wentworth Street, Charleston
### (843) 722-7437

### 1117 Savannah Highway
### (843) 225-5200
### www.andolinis.com

Fine dining is one thing, but sometimes nothing beats a good pizza. Especially when the kids are involved or when appetites of the young-at-heart come to the fore—a good pizza is a joy forever. Here in Mt. Pleasant is one of the best pizza parlors around. Andolini's Pizza uses marinated hand-tossed dough, homemade sauces, and the best cheeses in their array of pizzas, calzones, and salads. They're open for lunch and dinner Monday through Sunday.

### Capriccio Ristorante $
### 1034 Chuck Dawley Boulevard
### (843) 881-5550

This affordable and friendly Italian restaurant is actually owned by a Frenchman. That's the beauty of the place—it's for those who love to go out several times a month and customers who love to dine well. All the entrees are around $10, and yet the menu reads like an Italian cornucopia. There's a special every day, such as vitello (veal) parmigiana topped with mozzarella pomodoro sauce or rigatoni contadina. Try one of the numerous linguini with Capriccio's special gift for sauces. Mussel lovers say these are the best in town. All the dolces (desserts) are $5.50, and they change daily. There are a number of Italian coffees for after-dinner reflection. This restaurant is for serious lovers of Italian cuisine. Lunch is served Monday through Friday. Dinner is served Monday through Saturday. Reservations are preferred.

### Carpentier's Deli Wine and Cheese $
### 976 Houston Northcutt Boulevard
### (843) 884-9386

Insiders know the deli at Carpentier's is a gourmet's delight. Choose from prepared meats, European breads and cheeses, homemade pâté, and daily specials. The distinctive aroma of roasted coffee and fresh-baked cookies and pastries fills the air. A selection of imported beers and fine wines is available, and there are a few small tables for dining in the store. Carpentier's is open for breakfast and lunch Monday through Saturday.

## Coco's                                   $$
### 863 Houston Northcutt Boulevard
### (843) 881-4949

Charlestonians and frequent visitors to the city's busy restaurant scene were understandably crestfallen when the French restaurant called Le Midi burned and was closed. Things looked up, however, when it was learned that chefs François Rivalain and Alain Saley (from Le Midi) had found a new home at Coco's in Mt. Pleasant. Here, the menu is a mix of French classical and provincial, the atmosphere is warm and bistro-like, and best of all, some of the favorite dishes from Le Midi are revisited here. Try Le Flounder Alain, for instance, which is pan-fried and topped with a brown butter sauce. Their roasted half duckling with cherry sauce is another big hit. The wine list includes about 30 labels, a dozen of which are available by the glass. Enjoy a leisurely paced dinner at Coco's—you won't want to hurry this good thing. When it's time for dessert, try the classic mousse au chocolat or the crème caramel. Neither will disappoint. Catch lunch weekdays starting at 11:30 A.M. Dinner is served Monday through Saturday from 5:30 to 10:00 P.M. Reservations are a very good idea.

## Fonduely Yours                          $$
### 853 Coleman Boulevard
### (843) 849-6859

It is safe to say that Fonduely Yours is a one-of-a-kind dining experience in this area. As the name suggests, this restaurant specializes in fondues. Try cheese, vegetable, seafood, teriyaki, and sirloin fondues, and don't miss the chocolate fondue for dessert. The food is tasty and the whole concept is lots of fun. With fondue, you're the chef and you do the cooking right at your table. Dinner is served each evening starting at 5:30 until 9:30 P.M. Friday and Saturday until 11:00 P.M.

## Gourmet Blend                           $
### 354 W. Coleman Boulevard
### (843) 849-8949

For a delightful treat, try Gourmet Blend's salads (sometimes shrimp), sandwiches, muffins, and the like while taking advantage of the large selection of fresh-brewed coffees and teas. One exciting plus is that Gourmet Blend has a drive-up window to make it handy for pick-up lunches or java-to-go. It's open Monday through Saturday from early morning until late afternoon.

## J. Bistro                            $$-$$$
### 819 Coleman Boulevard
### (843) 971-7778
### www.jbistro.net

This is one of Mt. Pleasant's most stylish restaurants. *Upwith,* a hip, local tabloid when J. Bistro opened in 1995, rated it the best new restaurant in town when it first hit the scene. Obviously, it's a casual bistro setting, but New American cuisine is served with real flair. There are many evening specials designed to entice—look for their pecan-crusted catfish fillets over creamy grits, topped with spicy hollandaise or the jumbo lump crab salad. J. Bistro is open for dinner Tuesday through Sunday, and there's a wonderful Sunday brunch. Reservations are not accepted. You may have to wait, but it's worth it.

## Langdon's                               $$$
### 788 Shellmore Boulevard, Suite 105
### (843) 388-9200

A popular choice with Mt. Pleasant residents is this small restaurant and wine bar in what locals call the Bi-Lo Shopping Center. The decor is upscale, or "urban chic," if you please. The crowd is young and hip, thus so is the menu. For starters, try their creamy wild mushroom soup with lump crabmeat. Or, you might ask for the arugula salad topped with goat cheese, pear slices, and bacon vinaigrette. When it comes to entrees, look for the pan-seared grouper atop brie grits served in a sauce of apple-wood-smoked bacon, chardonnay, and basil crème. Their lightly fried duck breast finished with a red curry, garlic, and ginger crème sauce served with sweet potato puree is another favorite. The dessert menu changes seasonally, but you can usually find their berry crisp with fresh blueberries and orange liqueur a la mode. The global wine list is ample with more than a hundred varieties offered. How 'bout that for a shopping center location? This surprisingly refreshing dining adventure is open Monday through Saturday for dinner. Reservations are strongly recommended—especially Wednesday through Saturday.

**Locklear's Fine Seafood** $$
**320 Coleman Boulevard**
**(843) 884-3346**

**1920 Maybank Highway, Charleston**
**(843) 762-2549**
**www.locklears.com**
Locklear's has been one of the most popular seafood restaurants in Mt. Pleasant for years. Now there's a James Island location, too. But it's known for the chicken salad plate and she-crab soup as well. It's also considered a bargain. Call ahead for take-out lunch, and remember to consider the Heart Choice health-conscious items on the menu. Locklear's is open seven days a week for lunch and dinner. The Folly Road location has a Sunday brunch starting at 10:00 A.M. Reservations are accepted.

**Max & Moritz** $$
**920 Houston Northcutt Boulevard**
**(843) 856-9511**
There was a time when Charleston had several good German restaurants, but these days the options are somewhat limited. Happily, there's this cozy neighborhood spot in Mt. Pleasant which offers a

touch of Old World, Central European cuisine. There's a wine list with reds and whites from California, Germany, and France to set the mood. Then, try one of their appetizers like the Bavarian liver sausage spread with pickles, tomato wedges, mustard, and good German bread. Next, the Wiener schnitzel served with spätzle makes a good choice. Of course, the desserts are hearty and good (if not for the waistline). Try the Black Forest delight or the *rote grutze* served with French vanilla ice cream. Dinner is served from 5:00 until 9:00 P.M. Tuesday through Thursday. They're open until 10:00 P.M. on weekend nights. Sunday brunch is offered from 11:30 A.M. to 3:00 P.M., and dinner follows from 5:00 to 9:00 P.M.

**Melvin's Southern BBQ & Ribs** $
**925 Houston Northcutt Boulevard**
**(843) 881-0549, (888) 635-8467**

**538 Folly Road, Charleston**
**(843) 762-0511**
**www.melvinsbbq.com**
The delicious barbecue, cole slaw, onion rings, hamburgers, and vegetables at Melvin's make it a good bet for a quick meal. This has been a Lowcountry outlet for barbecue for at least 50 years. The prices are quite reasonable too. Melvin's is open Monday through Saturday for lunch and dinner.

**Mustard Seed** $$
**1220 Ben Sawyer Boulevard**
**(843) 849-0050**

**1978 Maybank Highway, Charleston**
**(843) 762-0072**
This simple, yet sophisticated, eatery is a big hit with the vegetarian crowd—although the Mustard Seed offers pork and seafood, too. And clearly, not everyone who frequents "the Seed" has abandoned beef; they simply enjoy the varied and creative menu offered here. In addition to a regular menu, there's a blackboard with daily specials that shows why there's sometimes a waiting line out the door. The artichoke, spinach, and Parme-

san fritters are one example. The huge and authentic Greek salad is another. Desserts are very special, too. Their coconut cream cake and chocolate cream pie are superb. A conservative but adequate wine list keeps customers amused if, in fact, a short wait is necessary. Be patient; it's worth it, and the food is a good value, too. Lunch is Monday through Saturday 11:00 A.M. to 2:30 P.M. Dinner is served from 5:00 to 9:30 P.M. on weekdays and to 10:00 on weekends.

**Old Village Post House**  $$-$$$
**101 Pitt Street**
**(843) 388-8935, (800) 549-POST**
**www.oldvillageposthouse.com**
This is the newest of the dining options presented by Maverick Southern Kitchens, Inc. This one is combined with a six-room inn nestled in the heart of Mt. Pleasant's quaint Old Village. The beautifully restored 1888 structure now houses two dining rooms and a charming tavern available to inn guests or a la carte visitors looking for fine food at affordable prices. For starters, you can expect to find Lowcountry favorites on the menu like she-crab soup, but check out the shrimp and mussel bruschetta with artichoke hearts, tomatoes, and capers served in a spicy wine broth. The main dishes making a hit with patrons include seared scallops with leek and corn custard, asparagus, and tomato coulis. Along with the roast stuffed quail with truffle pistachio chicken mousse you can find steaks and even a burger on the creative and varied bill of fare. They're open for dinner nightly, with lunch served Monday through Saturday, and a popular brunch is on Sunday.

**R. B.'s Seafood Restaurant**
**and Raw Bar**  $$
**97 Church Street**
**(843) 881-0466**
**www.rbsseafood.com**
Another casual spot where diners get a view of Shem Creek, R. B.'s is the newly reopened seafood landmark risen from the ashes. They serve oysters, scallops,

*Try spending lunch at one of the monthly noontime Friday Feast lectures given at the Gibbes Museum of Art. Folks bring their own sandwiches (or snag one at a nearby eatery) and get an in-depth view of an exhibit or a chance to personally meet an artist.*

fish, and shrimp as well as landlubber fare such as hamburgers, steaks, and prime rib.

R. B.'s is right on the creek, where shrimp boats dock, and boaters cruise, to see and be seen. R. B.'s colorful atmosphere makes this a happenin' place for young singles, especially on weekend nights. R. B.'s is open daily from 11:30 A.M. to 10:30 P.M.

**Shem Creek Bar & Grill**  $$
**508 Mill Street**
**(843) 884-8102**
**www.bigguynet.com**
To experience dining out the way the locals enjoy it, go to Shem Creek Bar and Grill (just Shem Creek to the regulars) and you'll find yourself surrounded by loyal Lowcountry patrons. (See the Nightlife chapter under East Cooper.) The menu has something for everyone, from burgers and steaks to lobster and grilled seafood specials, and Sloppy John's Oyster Bar is always a temptation. During the warmer months, Shem Creek is the hangout for the boating set, many of whom arrive by power craft. There is casual dining inside and out, with views of the creek from most seats. John and Angie Avinger also own and operate the One-Eyed Parrot and Banana Cabana on the Isle of Palms (see subsequent listing).

**Sticky Fingers**  $-$$
**341 Johnnie Dodds Boulevard**
**(843) 856-7427**

**235 Meeting Street, Charleston**
**(843) 853-7427**
**www.stickyfingersribhouse.com**
If you're a parent, the place to go on Tuesday night is Sticky Fingers. This barbecue

restaurant has a special menu and room set up just for kids, so the parents can take advantage of the option of dining alone (or not). Any day (or night, for that matter) is great for ordering Sticky Fingers' famous ribs. They come in about every style possible: Tennessee Whiskey, Carolina Sweet, Memphis, and Texas Style, to name a few. The eatery also serves chicken, salads, and sandwiches. It offers a full bar and is open seven days a week for lunch and dinner.

**Village Chop House**  $$$-$$$$
508 Mill Street
(843) 884-8103
www.bigguynet.com
Located just next door to Shem Creek Bar & Grill, this Mt. Pleasant venue for steaks and seafood is fairly new to the Creek scene. Indeed, the creek and marsh views seem to make a difference when it comes to evoking an appetite for red meat and fresh catch from the Lowcountry's bountiful waters. To that end, there's a rooftop bar for unencumbered views and sunset cocktails. Certified Angus beef is served exclusively, and the seafood comes straight from local boats through Crosby's Seafood. Locals and visitors enjoy the high-end steaks and chops, but entrees from the sea are equally popular. Try their 12-ounce beef tenderloin if you can handle that kind of portion. You can even dress the meat with a selection of custom sauces for an additional fee. The flounder Albert is an option for those who shy away from huge cuts of red meat. Fried seafood platters, lobster, crab, and shrimp are offered, too. The usual sides are available as well—hash browns, grits, asparagus with hollandaise, twice-baked potato, and more. Some side choices come a la carte, so be sure to ask. When it comes time for dessert, it's hard to beat their pecan pie. They're open Monday through Saturday for dinner only.

**Water's Edge**  $$$
1407 Shrimp Boat Lane
(843) 884-4074
www.watersedge.com

Water's Edge is an upscale seafood and beef restaurant on Shem Creek. Specialties include local seafood, Maine lobster, and king crab. You'll also find one of the most comprehensive wine and champagne lists in Mt. Pleasant. Patrons park themselves, if possible, at a table next to the window for a view of the shrimp boats. Water's Edge is open for lunch and dinner every day and serves a nice Sunday brunch as well.

**The Wreck of Richard and Charlene**  $$
106 Haddrell Street
(843) 884-0052
Tucked between Magwood and Wando seafood companies in the Old Village of Mt. Pleasant, two flags (there's no official sign or designation) will help find the Wreck. The restaurant is very unpretentious, and you can arrive by your own boat if you don't mind crawling around on the docks to disembark. You may dine on the deck or screened-in porch, if you like an outdoor feeling. Try the shrimp and grits or the lightly fried scallops. Portions come in either Richard's size (large) or Charlene's size (not as large, but plenty), so order according to your appetite. Beer and wine are available except on Sunday. The Wreck is open for dinner seven days a week. No credit cards.

# Sullivan's Island, Isle of Palms

Patrons often expect tropical, ocean fare when dining on the islands. These restaurants offer that with a twist of old Charleston thrown in as well.

**Atlanticville Restaurant & Café**  $$
2063 Middle Street, Sullivan's Island
(843) 883-9452
www.atlanticville.net
Not far from the cluster of businesses, restaurants, and bars across from the island's playground-like park is this small and casual option for New American cuisine. Locals and tourists alike go for the

grilled chicken satay with Thai peanut dipping sauce or the calamari appetizer in Asian spices. Along with the seafood, Atlanticville offers a full array of steaks, pork loins, and pastas. On Tuesdays, the menu is delightfully and authentically Thai, already a local legend. There's a covered deck for outdoor dining and an extensive wine and beer list. It's open Tuesday through Sunday for dinner only starting at 5:30 P.M.

## The Boathouse at Breach Inlet    $$-$$$
101 Palm Boulevard, Isle of Palms
(843) 886-8000

## The Boathouse on East Bay
549 East Bay Street, Charleston
(843) 577-7171
www.boathouserestaurants.com

Right on the infamous stretch of water known as Breach Inlet, with spectacular sunset views, is this unique restaurant. The decor is nautical but nice, and the menu includes pastas, grilled fresh fish, and house specialties such as coastal crab cakes with green Tabasco sauce and fried red onions, and the fresh catch of the day. The sides are as interesting as the entrees. Look for stone-ground grits, bleu cheese coleslaw, and collard greens. Landlubbers on the Peninsula have their own Boathouse on East Bay Street with free parking serving the same fare. Dinner is served seven days a week. Their Sunday brunch is from 11:00 A.M. until 2:00 P.M.

## Long Island Café                    $$
1515 Palm Boulevard, Isle of Palms
(843) 886-8809

Long Island Café became a local favorite soon after its doors opened, and it still has a loyal following. The changing menu is always interesting. Their herb-grilled sea scallops, the sesame-crusted salmon, and the pork loin with ginger-garlic sauce are all popular with patrons. A nice selection of soups, salads, and sandwiches is also available. The management is terrific with children and sometimes displays kiddie artwork on a wall. Long Island is open every day for lunch and dinner. Its Sunday brunch, where the cheddar-ham-and-apple omelet is a favorite, is from 11:00 A.M. to 2:00 P.M.

## One-Eyed Parrot and Banana Cabana $$
1130 Ocean Boulevard, Isle of Palms
(843) 886-4360, (843) 886-4361
www.bigguynet.com

The One-Eyed Parrot and the downstairs Banana Cabana are fun restaurants with good food, served ocean-side. John and Angie Avinger have stamped their winning sense of style on this eatery. The menus include various versions of shrimp, scallops, oysters, dolphin, tuna, a Bimini stew (a tomato-based seafood and sausage dish), and steamed oysters in season. One favorite is the crab cake, as a sandwich or alone. Seafood aside, Caribbean chicken (baked or fried), steak, salads, and pasta specials are also on the menu. Children love an early supper outside on the deck at the Cabana. They play with other children and occasionally get the mojo and start dancing right in front of the evening's featured musician. Both restaurants are open daily, but the Banana Cabana serves lunch and dinner. The One-Eyed Parrot is open for dinner only. (See the Sullivan's Island and Isle of Palms section of the Nightlife chapter.)

## Sea Biscuit Café                      $
21 J. C. Long Boulevard, Isle of Palms
(843) 886-4079

This is one petite charmer—complete with a tiny front porch, substantial side porch (for dining), and fabulous island fare. The Sea Biscuit, tucked away on one of Isle of Palms' less chaotic streets, serves breakfast or brunch with the house specialty: fabulous biscuits. Try shrimp and gravy with grits and eggs, seafood omelets, quiche, and even eggs Benedict. The cafe serves a delicious house tea, and children can order a pancake that's a Mickey Mouse look-alike. Get there early, or expect a wait. Lunch is served after breakfast Tuesday through Friday; breakfast only is served Saturday and Sunday. No credit cards.

**Sea Island Grill**                    $$–$$$
**The Boardwalk Inn, Wild Dunes Resort,**
**5757 Palm Boulevard, Isle of Palms**
**(843) 886-2200**
**www.wilddunes.com**

The premier restaurant at the upscale Wild Dunes Resort is called the Sea Island Grill, formerly the Grill. As the name implies, the cuisine has changed to feature the freshest Lowcountry seafood creatively served up by Chef Enzo Steffenelli, who has served up his magic at some of the best seafood restaurants in downtown Charleston during his impressive career. In addition to the wide selection of seafood dishes, entrees include creative presentations of steaks, chops, and poultry. Try the Flounder Boardwalk, crabmeat-stuffed flounder filet served on a bed of shrimp and corn succotash and drizzled with herb butter sauce. If you are up to it, finish off with the Ultimate Chocolate Cake for two, a thick slice of a rich, multilayered chocolate cake made with bittersweet chocolate mousse and raspberry marmalade. The Sea Island Grill is open for breakfast, lunch, and dinner seven days a week. Call ahead for reservations and the required gate pass for entrance into Wild Dunes.

**Station 22**                    $$–$$$
**2205 Middle Street, Sullivan's Island**
**(843) 883-3355**

Casual, but not quite flip-flops and a T-shirt, Station 22 offers variety on its menu and island history on its walls, which showcase dozens of photographs of turn-of-the-century Sullivan's Island. Find appetizers like their "world famous" Poblano Chile Pepper, roasted and stuffed with feta, parmesan, and mozzarella cheese. For an entree, try the Portuguese-style mussels with shrimp and sausage on linguini or the almond-coated salmon filet over a warm spinach salad. Save room for Uncle William's Brownie Fudge Pie. Open every day for dinner.

**Sullivan's On the Island    $$**
**2019 Middle Street, Sullivan's Island**
**(843) 883-3222**
**www.sullivansrestaurant.com**

A favorite with the islanders and others in the know, Sullivan's is a family restaurant with affordable, good food. Not fancy, Sullivan's is just what the regulars want—a place to order delicious, traditional specials that include steaks, burgers, shrimp and grits, or oysters and scallops with a veggie and dessert for less than $12. Dinner is served Monday through Saturday. There is a children's menu, and Sunday brunch is served from 11:00 A.M. to 2:00 P.M.

# WEST ASHLEY

Because the West Ashley area is so widespread and residential in nature, the restaurants tend to be located along the main traffic corridors. Both family restaurants and ethnic favorites are represented here.

**Avondale Station**                    $$$
**828 Savannah Highway**
**(843) 377-1300**
**www.avondalestation.com**

This popular spot for the West Ashley crowd is in a rehabbed service station where the transformation is surprisingly effective and creatively done. Diners occupy the Highway 17 side of the building with indoor and outdoor seating available. The fare is decidedly this side of Havana, and the South Beach overtones are quite evident in the tropical decor. For starters, try the papaya-glazed sea scallops or the sugarcane-skewered guava shrimp. Entrees getting lots of attention include the braised pork shank simmered in *sofrito* and a red wine sauce. The plantain-encrusted red snapper served in a mango coulis atop Spanish rice is another favorite. Dessert time means Cuban mocha torte or orange mango chiffon pie. Of course, you'll want a café Cubano to end the evening in the right spirit. They're open daily for dinner until late night with a Sunday brunch from 11:00 A.M. to 3:00 P.M.

## Bessenger's Barbecue                $
### 1602 Savannah Highway
### (843) 556-1354

Bessenger's serves tasty Southern meals featuring ribs, chicken, fried catfish, country-style steak (that means pounded, floured, and fried), barbecue with various sauces, and, of course, spirits. Their "buffeteria" is always a daily favorite—as is their next-door sandwich shop. It's open Monday through Sunday, late morning to late evening. The catering operation is open seven days a week.

## The Bluerose Café            $$-$$$
### 652 St. Andrews Boulevard
### (843) 225-2583

This little bit of Ireland may seem out of context located as it is just across the Ashley from downtown Charleston. But the Bluerose Café is a welcome find for all who seek it out.  Chef and owner Denis O'Doherty has all the blarney you'd expect of a true son of the Emerald Isle, but he makes true believers of a growing list of happy locals who know his skills in the kitchen are the real thing. The key word here is value. Luncheon specials are always well under $10 and range from Irish curry chicken salad with golden raisins to piled-high roast beef sandwiches. Dinner entrees include a shepherd's pie that's hearty and nourishing as is the seafood chowder with scallops, shrimp, and salmon. There's also a choice of chops or chicken in a number of presentations, and there's always plenty of soda bread, scones, and authentic Irish jams to satisfy the palate. A choice of imported wines and beer is offered if you like. They're open for breakfast and lunch Monday through Saturday.  Dinner is served on Thursday, Friday, and Saturday from 5:00 to 9:00 P.M. Sunday brunch is from 9:00 A.M. to 2:00 P.M.

## Bull & Finch Restaurant & Pub      $-$$
### 2070 Sam Rittenberg Boulevard,
### Citadel Mall, Charleston
### (843) 766-7429

This is a mall eatery; but in this case that's not the kiss of death. In fact, this one is quite charming and modeled after the *Cheers* pub of TV fame in Boston. There's a band or singer on hand every night, which is a big plus for the up-front bar. There are 14 English and Irish draft ales and stouts to choose from, plus 16 others (mainly American) in the bottle. Wine and port are available by the glass or the bottle, with an international selection. You'll find a very good dinner in the quieter back room. Beef Wellington topped with portobello mushroom duxelles inside puff pastry is one of the favorites. Another standout is their New Zealand lamb loin chops marinated and drizzled with fresh mint oil. The Duke's Shepherd Pie is for die-hard Anglophiles. The pub is open daily for lunch and dinner. (See the Nightlife chapter.)

## California Dreaming Restaurant
## and Bar                        $-$$
### 1 Ashley Pointe Drive
### (843) 766-1644
### www.centraarchy.com

You can go to California Dreaming by car or by boat (yes, you can tie up at a dock), and it's always an adventure. The kids pretend it's an old fort (although it isn't), and the views of the Ashley River are mesmerizing. The restaurant and the bar do an incredible, nonstop business year round. The interior is colorfully decorated with flags and divided into two dining levels with seating for 260 (and the place is often full). The little ones are welcome and can order nonalcoholic drinks (such as a blue concoction called a Smurf) and food from a special menu. Patrons really go crazy for the soft, buttery croissants and the house salad (topped with eggs, almonds, ham, and bacon—almost a meal in itself). The twice-baked potato is another big hit. All fish is fresh and local, and the burgers, ribs, and Mexican dishes are popular. A decadent dessert list includes the fabulous house special— apple-walnut cinnamon pie. Lunch and dinner are served every day, and hours are extended on weekend nights. Reservations are suggested. (See the West Ashley section of the Nightlife chapter.)

### Easterby's Family Grille $$
### 2388 Ashley River Road
### (843) 556-5707

Easterby's on Ashley River Road (Highway 61) is a comfortable, affordable place for casual dining and local seafood. It's a popular lunch stop for tourists heading out to the plantations along the highway (see our Attractions chapter). Dinner patrons enjoy the same seafood (fried or not), steaks, and pastas, she-crab soup, catfish stew, shrimp creole, and soft-shell crabs. Spirits are available, and reservations are not necessary unless you're in a large group. Lunch and dinner are served Monday through Saturday until 10:00 P.M.

### Emperor's Garden $-$$
### 874 Orleans Road
### (843) 556-7212

West Ashley gained a popular eatery with the opening of Emperor's Garden. This Chinese restaurant across from Citadel Mall prepares crispy Peking duck (a participatory dish put together, like crepes, at the table) to perfection, and it stuffs its egg rolls with substantial portions of real ingredients—no mystery meat or imitation soybean product here. Their pot stickers are the real thing, too. Customers come from all over, and children are welcome. Lunch and dinner are served seven days a week.

### Kim's Korean and Japanese Steak and Seafood House $$
### North Bridge Shopping Center
### 1716 Highway 171
### (843) 571-5100

Kim's Korean and Japanese Steak and Seafood House offers authentic "table show cooking" for dinner seven days a week. Not only is this a fun experience, but

the food is also well prepared and a delight for the palate. Choose either the beef or pork *bulgoki* with the spicy Korean sauce, a house favorite. Takeout is available, and reservations are not required.

### Mediterranean Delicatessen & Café $-$$
### 90 Folly Road
### (843) 766-0323

Talk about your neighborhood magnets. The Med Deli, as locals call it, is a real draw for West Ashley and downtown diners. It has a high-tech look with lots of chrome and glass, and desserts are now the specialty. Not only is the food good and predictable (the menu doesn't change, and favorite specials are repeated), but it's also just five minutes from the city, and parking is no trouble. Connoisseurs of spirits will enjoy the great selections of wine and imported beers here. Regulars are partial to the pita pocket sandwich with gazpacho or black bean soup at lunch. For dinner, try their pasta specials; they have plenty of variations on the theme. There is live jazz on Wednesday and Friday evenings. The Med Deli is open from late morning to late night every day but Sunday.

### Miyabi Japanese Steak House $$
### 688 Citadel Haven Drive
### (843) 571-6025

This Japanese steak and seafood restaurant rates high on the family entertainment scale because of the hibachi style of tableside preparation and the knife-juggling Japanese chefs. Meals include a light soup, salad, and entree, and the food is consistently good. If you have never experienced this form of dining, be advised you may be sharing grill and dining space with strangers. Try the steak and shrimp for a sample of what the hibachi does for surf and turf. Try the sushi bar if you like yours untouched by the flame. Dinner and drinks are served seven nights a week, and early-bird specials are common. Call for reservations.

**Outback Steakhouse** $$
1890 Sam Rittenberg Boulevard
(843) 763-8999

715 Johnnie Dodds Boulevard,
Mt. Pleasant
(843) 849-9456
www.outback.com

This steakhouse so dominates the mini-mall it occupies that the mall itself has taken on the Outback name with locals. And for good reason: This Aussie-style beef and barbecue restaurant and bar is a standing-room-only watering hole for young up-and-comers. The huge bloomin' onion is the signature side dish, and it comes with a secret sauce that kicks like a kangaroo. Kids are welcome, and dinner is served seven days a week. There's another location in Mt. Pleasant, so East Cooper types can dine "down under" and never cross a bridge.

**Sunfire Grill and Bistro** $$-$$$
1090 Sam Rittenberg Boulevard
(843) 766-0223
www.sunfiregrill.com

The white tablecloth dining options in West Ashley are somewhat limited. That's why it's good to know there's Sunfire Grill and Bistro on Sam Rittenberg Boulevard across from the Park Center office complex. This trendy restaurant and pub is popular with business folk at lunch and locals after work and when the dinner hour comes. The salad bar is plentiful and fresh. But more ambitious appetites are well-served by entrees like their bacon-wrapped colossal shrimp with asparagus and lemon-herbed orzo. Friday nights are for lobster lovers. Steaks and daily specials round out the menu offered Monday through Sunday. The after-church crowd enjoys their Sunday brunch.

**T-Bonz Gill & Grill** $-$$
1668 Old Towne Road
(843) 556-2478

80 North Market Street
(843) 577-2511

1028 Johnnie Dodds Boulevard,
Mt. Pleasant
(843) 971-7777
www.tbonz.com

Another vibrant, happening spot with several locations throughout the city, T-Bonz serves a wonderful filet mignon (when you say rare, they take you at your word) as well as fresh gourmet burgers and even seafood. There's plenty of beer on tap, including T-Bonz' own custom-brewed ales. The Mt. Pleasant location has its own brewpub. Photographs of regular customers and Western paraphernalia adorn the walls, and you can't miss the enormous painting of the renegade cowboys on horseback. Regular customers order side veggies (sautéed and delicious) and feel comfortable having the kids along. Takeout is another option. They're ropin' 'em in for lunch and dinner seven days a week.

---

*Health food shoppers have found a proverbial mecca in Earth Fare over in the South Windermere Shopping Center. Their other location in Mt. Pleasant's Towne Centre attracts the East Cooper crowd. This large, well-stocked supermarket specializing in natural and organically grown foods also has a handy corner cafe equipped with simple tables and booths. You select your meal from a cafeteria-style line or deli and seat yourself. Bringing home the bacon was never so inviting. You don't even have to be a health nut to dine there.*

---

**Trotters Restaurant** $$
2008 Savannah Highway
(843) 571-1000
www.thetownandcountryinn.com

Trotters Restaurant, in the Town & Country Inn, is a good find for an all-out buffet—breakfast and lunch as well as weekend seafood spreads. Sunday brunch is popular with the after-church crowd. The buffet table always groans with a wide selection of meats, seafood, vegetables, and desserts. There's no Saturday lunch or Sunday dinner, but Trotters is open for all other meals every day. (See the West Ashley section of the Hotels and Motels chapter.)

### Ye Ole Fashioned Ice Cream and Sandwich Café $
**474 Savannah Highway**
**(843) 766-4854**

**1502 U.S. Highway 17 N., Mt. Pleasant**
**(843) 849-3698**

This is a quick stop but a change from the usual fast food. There are several locations within our coverage area and a few more beyond. This cafe serves sandwiches, soups, and, of course, lots of ice cream. There are scores of flavors. If you use the drive-through window, you may want to call ahead for soup and sandwich take-out orders. All the food is delicious, and local kids love this place. Hours are midmorning through late night daily.

## JAMES, JOHNS, AND FOLLY ISLANDS, KIAWAH, AND SEABROOK

People come from all over the Greater Charleston area to dine at some of the establishments on these islands. Whether you're looking for a quick deli sandwich or an elegant evening experience, you'll find it here.

### Alano's Pizza $
**The Shops at Bohicket, Seabrook Island**
**1880 Andell Bluff Boulevard**
**(843) 768-2424**

If you are looking for pizza and want free delivery to the resorts, try this eatery between the entrances to Kiawah and Seabrook Islands in the Bohicket Marina Village. Alano's has good pizzas made fresh daily in three sizes, with a choice of 15 fresh toppings. It also has lasagna, wings, hoagies, and salads. Lunch hours are 11:00 A.M. to 2:00 P.M. with dinner served from 5:00 to 8:00 P.M.

### Athens Greek Restaurant $$
**1939 Maybank Highway, James Island**
**(843) 795-0957**
**www.athensofcharleston.com**

The line moves quickly at Athens, in the Cross Creek Shopping Center, where there is usually a crowd eager to dine. Specialties at this popular Greek place include Greek chicken, spanakopita, lemon chicken soup, Greek salad with feta cheese, and baklava. A full range of spirits is available. Athens is open every day from lunch until late night.

### Bear-E-Patch Café $-$$
**1980-A Ashley River Road, Charleston**
**(843) 766-6490**

Every once in a while a simple, affordable, neighborhood restaurant strikes gold with the right combination of good food, generous portions, nice atmosphere, and friendly service. And that's what the Bear-E-Patch has going for it. This relatively small and unpretentious eatery is popular with locals.

The breakfast menu is so hearty and creative with several specials offered daily that it's available until 3:00 P.M. and makes a dandy lunch. A deli-like lunch menu is offered also, along with grilled burgers and such. But at least one down-home special is right out of Grandma's Lowcountry cookbook. An on-site bakery turns out fresh bread (sourdough is a specialty) and pies, which adds to the allure. And now, dinner is served Monday through Friday until 9:00 P.M. Saturday hours end at 8:00 P.M.

### Bohicket Creek Grill $$-$$$
**1880 Andell Bluff Boulevard**
**(843) 768-1500**

Those on the resort islands of Kiawah and Seabrook may remember a spot called Café St. Tropez in Bohicket Creek Marina. Now this handy and scenic location boasts Bohicket Creek Grill with a different menu and management but an equally loyal following of locals and even patrons who feel it's worth the drive from town.

The fare is sophisticated and contemporary with an emphasis on fresh ingredients and a nod toward the Mediterranean tradition. For starters, look for their carpaccio—a dry, aged tenderloin with aged cheddar, Dijon, arugula, and olive oil served with baked crostini. Their lobster mop comes in a rich brandy cream broth with lots of claw meat and rustic bread served on the side. Popular entrees include a veal chop stuffed with roasted tomatoes, fava bean and sweet corn succotash, and braised cippolini onions. Or you may go for their grilled Carolina wreckfish with caramel glaze, coconut rice, and tomato-cucumber slaw. A selection of sides is offered a la carte. The dessert choices change daily and woe be to those who forget to save room for a tasty finale. They're open daily for dinner starting at 6:00 P.M. Reservations are encouraged.

### Café Suzanne $$
### 4 Center Street, Folly Beach
### (843) 588-2101
Here's an unexpected oasis of genuinely good food and wine in a funky little building on the main drag at Folly Beach. The menu changes daily, but a number of tempting offerings are always ready to challenge the beachcombing gourmand in all of us. The secret to Café Suzanne's success is the tremendously talented staff, who never seem to run out of new and delicious ideas. You'll like the pan-seared, crab-encrusted salmon with shrimp basmati rice or the grilled tenderloin of beef with rosemary cabernet sauce. Officially, the fare is New American. Unofficially, it's just plain good eatin'. They even put a gourmet spin on the classic burger. Café Suzanne has seasonal hours, but they're usually open only for dinner Tuesday through Saturday, and there is a Sunday brunch that's very popular.

### Charleston Crab House $$
### 145 Wappoo Creek Drive, James Island
### (843) 795-1963

### 41 South Market Street, Charleston
### (843) 853-2900
### www.charlestoncrabhouse.com
On the Intracoastal Waterway, the Charleston Crab House is open for lunch and dinner every day. The restaurant specializes in steamed garlic crabs (cooked until they are red, then placed before you for what locals call a "crab crack"). There is a raw bar, and outside tables for dining are close to the water. You can arrive by boat and moor at the restaurant dock. No reservations are necessary. They're open daily for lunch and dinner. There's a kid's menu, and Mom and Dad may enjoy frozen tropical drinks. (See listing in the James and Johns Islands section of the Nightlife chapter.)

### Cynthia's Restaurant $$-$$$
### 1956 Maybank Highway
### (843) 406-4989
In the far corner of the shopping center where the Terrace movie theatre draws crowds to James Island (see the Nightlife chapter), there's a bit of the Pacific Rim. To the uninitiated, that's a mix of Asian cuisine infused with Hawaiian and California influences. This is a fortunate marriage of cooking techniques and Lowcountry seafood. One example is their spicy teriyaki chicken wings countered with crunchy cabbage slaw and mango chutney. Popular entrees include a number of beef specialties (the filet mignon is excellent), especially when they are served with herbed butter. There are interesting vegetables served as they come into season, fresh and flavorful. The dessert menu is a garden of delights with crème brûlée and coconut crème pie among the favorites. They're open for lunch weekdays from 11:00 A.M. to 2:30 P.M., except Tuesday. And dinner is from 5:00 to 9:30 P.M. nightly.

### Dragon Gate Chinese Restaurant $
### 1739 Maybank Highway, James Island
### (843) 795-3398
Dragon Gate, in the James Island Shopping Center, serves authentic Chinese

food. It has a full bar and a lunch buffet with all your favorite Chinese dishes such as sweet-and-sour pork, Szechwan beef and egg drop soup. The restaurant is open Monday through Sunday from lunch through late night.

### General Store Deli                    $
### 1 Beachwalker Drive, Kiawah Island
### (843) 768-9541

For a quick take-out breakfast or lunch, try this deli. The bakery items are fresh, but what kids like best are the fried chicken and enormous french fries. This is Kiawah's version of a convenience store (read, "upscale"), and sometimes that's just what's called for. Handy, quick, and close to everything on the resort island, the General Store is open daily from dawn to late night.

### Gilligan's Steamer and Raw Bar    $$
### 160 Main Road, Johns Island
### (843) 766-2244

### 1475 Long Grove Drive (Seaside Farms),
### Mt. Pleasant
### (843) 849-2244
### www.gilligans.net

Gilligan's Steamer and Raw Bar has a great family atmosphere and delicious fresh steamed seafood. There are steaks and chicken as well, and the cooks will fry the seafood if you like. This is a place where you can order oysters by the bucket in season. Two veggies, a choice of salad or slaw, and hush puppies round out each meal. Crayons are available so the kids can draw while they wait. Gilligan's is open for lunch and dinner every day.

### The Hickory Hawg                        $
### 2817 Maybank Highway, John Island
### (843) 577-1121

Bring up the subject of whose Southern barbecue is best and you can always count on an argument. In fact, we don't even agree on how to spell the subject—but we sure like to eat it. One place on Johns Island getting a lot of business from barbecue lovers is this little gem tucked away

next to Kerr Drugs where River Road crosses Maybank Highway. The Hickory Hawg, as the name suggests, is nothing fancy; just a storefront location with all wood-cooked, Lexington, North Carolina–style barbecue and all the fixin's that go with it. We're talking homemade hash, baby-back ribs (you can order by the slab), barbecued chicken, green beans with bacon, coleslaw, and fries. Banana pudding is always available for dessert, and there are a number of tasty combo plates available where you get a little of all your favorites. Hickory Hawg is also a caterer, so many folks choose them for parties and family get-togethers where barbecue is a staple. They're open for lunch and dinner Monday through Saturday.

### Jasmine Porch                   $$$-$$$$
### 1 Sanctuary Beach Drive, Kiawah Island
### (843) 768-6253, (877) 683-1234
### www.thesanctuary.com

The Sanctuary at Kiawah has one dining option that revisits a much-loved tradition for those who know Kiawah from years ago. That's a dining room known as Jasmine Porch—a reincarnation of the first dining room from Kiawah's former Inn. Here the cuisine is Lowcountry fare— kicked up a notch or two. The emphasis here is on the purest and finest ingredients, so when you order shrimp and grits, the shrimp is the freshest caught available and the grits are stone-ground and cooked to perfection. Same is true for the she-crab soup and the oysters on the halfshell. Same goes for the Huguenot torte and the pecan pie. Breakfast, lunch, and dinner are served daily and spirits are on call. It doesn't hurt that Jasmine Porch with its outdoor terrace overlooks The Sanctuary's spectacular pool area and the Atlantic Ocean. Nearby is the Loggerhead Grille offering additional outdoor dining when the weather permits.

### Live Oak Café and Coffee            $
### 2867 Maybank Highway, Johns Island
### (843) 557-1795
### www.liveoakcafe.net

Not every little roadside oasis on Johns Island is noteworthy as a quick place to grab a breakfast sandwich and coffee or a quick lunch en route to the resorts of Kiawah or Seabrook. But then, not every little roadside oasis has a full-time Johnson & Wales–trained chef manning the kitchen. This one does, and area locals know it. Live Oak Café is tucked away under the trees along Maybank Highway past River Road (across from the Johns Island Post Office) with plenty of parking out back. Inside this smartly refurbished bungalow, they serve custom-roasted coffees and espresso bar drinks, chilled Nantucket juices, and sodas along with a delicious menu of breakfast and luncheon items that change daily. The pastries are prepared on-site and the biscuits, grits, and sausage gravy are clearly "down home." For lunch they have a number of very creative signature sandwiches, wraps, entree salads, and sides that are gourmet-tasting but very casually served across a counter. There's even a children's menu for youngsters. They're open Tuesday through Saturday, 7:00 A.M. to 2:00 P.M.

## Noisy Oyster                              $$
**2408 Maybank Highway, Johns Island**
**(843) 559-3552**

**24 North Market Street, Charleston**
**(843) 723-0044**

**7571 Rivers Avenue, North Charleston**
**(843) 824-1000**
**www.noisyoysterseafood.com**
What old-timers knew as Cappy's Restaurant is now called Noisy Oyster, located near the new Stono River Bridge. It's fun to go by boat and tie up at the Buzzard's Roost Marina. The fresh seafood and view of the Stono River are splendid. Noisy Oyster always has a number of daily specials with fresh shrimp, scallops, and fish. Look for their oysters Rockefeller or their blue crab fingers. Dining is possible inside and out, and spirits are available. Lunch and dinner are served daily. (See the James and Johns Islands section of the Nightlife chapter.)

## The Ocean Room                          $$$$$
**1 Sanctuary Beach Drive**
**Kiawah Island**
**(843) 768-6253, (877) 683-1234**
**www.thesanctuary.com**
The signature dining venue at Kiawah's new 255-room hotel and spa called The Sanctuary is the Ocean Room. Up a dramatic staircase from the lobby is a handsome bar that introduces the Ocean Room's dining adventure, where expansive views overlooking the Atlantic give the place its name. Elegant decor and excellent service are expected here—the cuisine is New American and presentation is one of the points of focus. Chef de cuisine Chris Brandt brings his special touch to the ever-changing menu, which includes some favorites like the baby beet and goat cheese salad tossed in truffle oil and lemon. Or the crab gratin topped with a crust of broiled Asiago cheese. Favorite entrees include the roasted rack of lamb and the Colby beef steak. Of course, the sommelier directs guests through an extensive wine list to recommend the perfect accompanying vintage. Pastry chef Claire Chapman, formerly of the Woodlands, presents a tantalizing array of fantastic desserts for the Ocean Room's finale. (For more on the Woodlands, see the Bed-and-Breakfasts and Atmospheric Inns chapter.) Reservations are definitely recommended. (For more on The Sanctuary, see the Hotels and Motels chapter.)

## The Privateer Restaurant              $$-$$$
**1882 Andell Bluff Boulevard,**
**Seabrook Island**
**(843) 768-1290**
**www.privateerrestaurant.com**
With its "sophisticated casual" atmosphere, the Privateer serves delicious gourmet seafood and other entrees that appeal to landlubbers. Outstanding shrimp and scallop dishes, seafood pastas, broiled pink snapper, tempting veal, and steaks are all part of the menu. The views at the Bohicket Marina Village location are lovely. Try to arrive in time to watch the sunset. The Sunset Lounge opens at 4:30

P.M. and dinner is served from 5:00 to 10:00 P.M.

**Rosebank Farms Café** $$
**1886 Andell Bluff Boulevard, Seabrook Island**
**(843) 768-1807**

Here's a delightful place to get typical Lowcountry cuisine (in other words, "Suh-thun cookin'") done with a modern twist. Rosebank Farms Café is in the marina atmosphere of Bohicket Creek. This spot is especially popular during fishing tournaments at Seabrook. Along with choice steaks and fresh vegetables, try the honey and buttermilk fried chicken. Rosebank is open for lunch daily and reopens for dinner every night.

**Starfish Grille** $$
**101 East Arctic Avenue, Folly Beach**
**(843) 588-2518**
**www.starfishgrille.com**

Here is the answer when the question is, "Where can we eat and look out over the ocean?" This attractive little bistro is perched right at the base of the 1,045-foot-long Folly Pier. (See the Fishing Piers and Bridges section of the Hunting and Fishing chapter.) Waves break under the dining room, and seagulls ply the air around you. Atmosphere is the draw here, and the feeling inside is strictly casual. The Grille offers a full gamut of sandwiches, salads, and pasta dishes. Appetizers include coconut shrimp and spinach-and-fried-oyster salad. Entrees range from Carolina crab cakes to fresh yellowfin tuna in a spiced red sauce. Of course, there's always a fresh catch of the day. The place is open for lunch and dinner every day of the week. It's a pleasant option for Sunday brunch, too. No reservations are required, but call ahead for parties of six or more. There's a full bar with 16 varieties of beer and a limited wine list by the glass. Don't forget their appealing array of frozen and dessert drinks. Note that the $5.00 parking fee at the pier is deducted from your bill if you show your receipt.

**St. John's Island Café**
**& David's Bakery** $-$$
**3410 Maybank Highway, Johns Island**
**(843) 559-9090**

It's hard to know what to praise first at St. John's Island Café. The menu is typically American, with a definite Southern flair. The chalkboard lists the daily specials, which read a little bit like the dinners at Grandma's house when we were kids. Look for lasagna, pork chops, and meat loaf to die for. The added pleasure of fresh-baked breads, pies, and other desserts also draws a steady crowd of regulars from the offices in downtown Charleston and the resort islands of Kiawah and Seabrook. A new and casual bar adds a friendly neighborhood feel to the place. It's possible to order home-cooked food for takeout; the cafe even offers catering services these days. They're open for breakfast, lunch, and dinner Monday through Saturday. On Sunday, St. John's closes at 2:00 P.M. following brunch.

# NIGHTLIFE ⓨ

When the sun goes down, not all the people in Greater Charleston pack it in. In fact, locals and visitors who seek nighttime entertainment are met with an abundance of choices.

If you are interested in listening to live contemporary music, dancing, or just hitting the bar scene, start with the spots we've described below—you won't be bored. If you like beer and want to sample it straight from the folks who create it, try one of the brewpubs. Since many nightspots are actually lounges at restaurants where dining is the primary focus, we have added an indicator at the end of each club listing—ⓓ—for those places that are described in greater detail in the Restaurants chapter. We also have a category called Dinner Cruises for those who want to spend an evening on the waters of Charleston Harbor cruising and dining with live music and dancing as after-dinner options.

While Charleston is affectionately called the Holy City in reference to its many lovely churches, it also has a reputation for entertaining where socializing has a long and rich tradition. If you plan on enjoying a few beers or cocktails as part of the fun, be aware of the legal restrictions in the Charleston area, and know that area police departments actively enforce these laws. The minimum drinking age is 21 in South Carolina, and open containers are not allowed in moving vehicles. A charge of driving under the influence may be levied against anyone whose blood-alcohol content is measured at .08 or higher. In the city of Charleston, last call for liquor is usually 1:30 A.M., and closing is mandatory at 2:00 A.M.

The coffeehouse phenomenon has taken a firm hold in this area. We have several Starbucks these days, and there are at least a half-dozen non-chain houses to explore around the Peninsula. There are a number of conventional movie theaters showing first-run films here in the Lowcountry. There's even a movie house on James Island, Terrace Theatre, which shows first-run films in a setting where you can enjoy light fare, wine, and beer while you watch the flick. We've listed theater names and phone numbers and suggest you call for titles after checking the local paper's movie listings.

For information about other entertainment options and cultural happenings, we suggest consulting the Arts and Annual Events chapters.

## BARS AND NIGHTCLUBS
# Downtown Charleston

**Bar 145**
**145 Calhoun Street**
**(843) 937-0314**
Here's a spot with just about everything to offer: dancing, a great martini bar, cabaret shows on occasion, dinner theatre performances, live music ranging from jazz to Top-40 bands, snazzy DJs, and even a fashion show now and then. Located on the second floor below the Terrace on Marion Square (see subsequent listing), this is a sophisticated venue while offering spontaneity and action at the same time. You'll see patrons dressed to the nines as well as some more casually attired. A full menu of creative drinks keeps the crowd well satisfied with the ever-popular metropolitan, the lemon-drop, and even an espresso martini for java lovers. Everyone is encouraged to dance to the groove du jour. The doors open at 6:00 P.M. and when a show is on the bill, it usually begins at 8:00 P.M. Admission prices vary according to the entertainment on tap.

## Blind Tiger Pub
### 36 and 38 Broad Street
### (843) 577-0088

If you are looking for British pub atmosphere, escape into this friendly environment with its dark English mahogany walls and cast-iron stools. Order Bass Ale or Guinness Stout, or try a Black and Tan (Bass on bottom, Guinness on top). Fear not: The beer is chilled appropriately for Charleston, not served lukewarm as in England. A nice selection of appetizers is available until 10:00 P.M. There is live music some nights and a crowd that just keeps coming back. The back courtyard is a nice option when weather permits.

## Carolina's
### 10 Exchange Street
### (843) 724-3800
### www.carolinasrestaurant.com

The bar at Carolina's restaurant is an upscale alternative and a very popular meeting spot for professionals. Seating is available at the bar proper and in the surrounding areas. Bar customers often feel comfortable staying on for dinner. Carolina's has an additional private dining room. Both areas are nice places to meet after work or after other events for a nightcap. ⓓ

*Late-night revelers who need a rule of thumb to remember Charleston's bar-closing hours, try this: All bars in the Market area close at 2:00 A.M. If you're getting a (very) late start or you feel the need to party even later than that, you'll have to go elsewhere.*

## Charlie's Little Bar
### 141 East Bay Street
### (843) 723-6242

In Saracen Restaurant, you'll find this cozy bar upstairs overlooking the dining room below. It also has a thriving following of neighborhood patrons and after-work professionals who enjoy the atmosphere and premium spirits, cocktails, and hors d'oeuvres. Patrons who only want what the bar has to offer can enter through a small gate and rear back door off the bank's parking lot to the side. The service is friendly and the ambience is a little like the speakeasy days of the 1920s. Open nightly after 8:00 P.M. Great fun.

## Club Habana
### 177 Meeting Street
### (843) 853-5900

Located in the swanky, upscale space directly above the Tinder Box (where all manner of tobacco products are sold), this is a late-night destination for a cigar and an after-dinner drink. The cozy spot has both male and female aficionados, so the company is always varied and interesting. Their plush couches and tasteful decor encourage patrons to puff away and sip a fine brandy in perfect comfort. Through a brilliant feat of air-conditioning engineering, the atmosphere is actually breathable. They open daily for happy hour at 4:30 P.M. On Sundays, they open at 8:00 P.M.

## Cumberland's
### 301 King Street
### (843) 577-9469
### www.cumberlands.net

Happy hour here is a crowd-pleaser, particularly with the college crowd and 20-somethings who rally to the cause most nights except Sunday. There is a full-service bar, and live music is a main drawing card—Cumberland's features all kinds. Cumberland's even has its own ticket information line, so you can see who's on the docket for the night: Call the number above to see who's on the bill.

## 82 Queen
### 82 Queen Street
### (843) 723-7591
### www.82queen.com

A long-standing, favorite hangout for the local Broad Street business set and others, the bar at 82 Queen is narrow (but comfortable enough) and a good place to see friends. You'll find a fine mix of people there knowing and not knowing each other's names. Patrons especially like the back bar if the weather is nice. They enjoy hanging out in the courtyard while waiters zip by with tempting appetizers, and outdoor diners enjoy their fare beneath the stars. **ⓓ**

## The Griffin
### 18 Vendue Range
### (843) 723-1700

A popular hangout for young professionals is the Griffin, a cozy English pub with an easy, friendly atmosphere. Especially busy at lunchtime, workers from the financial and legal offices on East Bay and Broad streets stop here for simple, but hearty, sandwiches and maybe a cool brew. Others check in for happy hour and some stay for dinner. They're open each evening (except Sunday) and attract a nice mix of locals and tourists out and about on East Bay.

## Henry's
### 54 North Market Street
### (843) 723-4363

### 816 Johnnie Dodds Boulevard
### (843) 971-1777

Henry's used to be known for its Old Charleston meals and clubby side bar. Today, under different ownership, it has updated trappings and a new reputation for light food and live acoustic music. The ambience is contemporary New Orleans, and the second-floor lounge is open Friday and Saturday nights. There is a happy hour from 4:00 to 7:00 P.M. on Monday through Thursday.

## McCrady's
### 2 Unity Alley
### (843) 577-0025
### www.mccradysrestaurant.com

Neatly tucked down Unity Alley, off the hustle and bustle of East Bay Street, is this small but attractive haven for a quiet drink. It lays claim to the fact that George Washington tipped a few here back in

1793. Today, this beautifully turned-out restaurant has an adjoining upscale wine bar that is a favorite with downtown business types and professionals because of its cozy atmosphere. Its nice wine list and premium bar serve happy-hour specials to please the after-work crowd. And its popular dining room close by makes a natural progression from an after-work respite to an evening on the town. **ⓓ**

## Mills House Hotel
### 115 Meeting Street
### (843) 577-2400
### www.millshouse.com

Easily the best location in Charleston if you're looking to be at the center of things, the Mills House Hotel is home to two nightspots that deserve your consideration. The handsome bar just off the Barbados Room Restaurant is a classic Southern setting that oozes charm. There's a grand piano, and often someone is on hand to play your favorite Gershwin tune. The Best Friend Lounge is a separate, more intimate bar with quiet entertainment Tuesday through Saturday.

## Music Farm
### 32 Ann Street
### (843) 722-8904
### www.musicfarm.com

Now in its second decade on the Peninsula, one of the most popular nightspots for contemporary music enthusiasts is the Music Farm—affectionately referred to by regulars as the Farm. The beat goes on at weekly gigs when live bands—yes, favorite city sons Hootie and the Blowfish were once among them—perform here. The Farm's concert line, (843) 853-3276, has recorded information about upcoming entertainment. Sometimes there's a cover charge. The college crowd is thick, but also expect to see 30-somethings, 40-somethings, and older-somethings elbowing their way toward the bar. The Farm is across the street from the visitor center, and parking is available on the street as well as in the nearby garage.

## O'Reilly's Irish Pub & Seafood Tavern
**288 King Street**
**(843) 577-0406**
www.charlestoncrabhouse.com

There is live entertainment Tuesday through Saturday at this pub, which has recently added a full complement of seafood entrees and salads. The College of Charleston students love the fact that it is close to campus and tend to hang out here during Happy Hour from 4:00 to 7:00 P.M. Monday through Friday. The atmosphere is decidedly Irish, though, with plenty of tables and booths for gathering with friends. After happy hour, O'Reilly's appeals to past-college-days crowds or just anyone who appreciates a clean, not-too-well-lighted place that offers a wide assortment of draft and bottled beers and other bar beverages. ❶

## Peninsula Grill
**112 North Market Street**
**(843) 723-0700**
www.peninsulagrill.com

The Peninsula Grill at the Planters Inn offers a very beautiful, romantic, upscale bar tucked inside the restaurant. In warm weather, we recommend a drink here before and after dining outdoors in the gas-lit courtyard. This bar always attracts a well-dressed, attractive crowd and is a classy oasis amidst the carnival atmosphere of the Market at night. Their delightful Champagne Bar carries 40 labels, and six are sold by the glass. ❶

## Roof Top Restaurant & Bar
**23 Vendue Range**
**(843) 414-2341**
www.vendueinn.com

On the roof of the Vendue Inn in downtown Charleston is this rare find on the Peninsula—a place (for cocktails) with a rooftop view and refreshing sea breezes. (See the Vendue Inn in the Bed-and-Breakfasts and Atmospheric Inns chapter.) With two separate levels, the Roof Top Bar was much anticipated by locals. This place is a lovely location for starting a summer evening in Charleston catching the sunset

over the rooftops of Charleston. The service is friendly, and you can enjoy live entertainment most nights.

## South End Brewery and Smokehouse
**161 East Bay Street**
**(843) 853-4677**
www.southendbrewery.com

Here's a restaurant with its own microbrewery. Ice-cold hand-crafted brews, made on the premises, are served with baby-back ribs, oven-baked pizzas, and specials off the wood-burning grill. The glass elevator takes you up to a third-floor cigar lounge and billiard and game room with spectacular views over the city. South End has live entertainment on weekends and serves both lunch and dinner seven days a week.

## The Terrace at Marion Square
**145 Calhoun Street Upstairs,**
**Corner of King and Calhoun**
**(843) 937-0314**
www.terracerestaurant.com

Locals call this the Terrace, and it's a trendy late-night hot spot for meeting and greeting friends who are dining or partying downtown. Built on top of the Millennium Music store, with views overlooking the recently refurbished Marion Square, this place has the charm of a roof garden in a decidedly urban setting. The dramatic, high-pitched roof offers some protection from the weather, but the feeling is clearly open air. The crowd is young and enthusiastic (partly because the College of Charleston is only blocks away), and you can dine or imbibe or choose a munchie that's somewhere in between.

## Tommy Condon's Irish Pub and Seafood Restaurant
**160 Church Street**
**(843) 577-3818**
www.tommycondons.com

Every day is St. Patty's Day at Charleston's only authentic Irish pub owned by an Irish family. In fact, families are indeed welcome here. Tommy Condon's has traditional Irish sing-alongs Wednesdays through Sundays and serves Irish spirits as well. The layout of the facility, with its big horseshoe bar, makes for a good party flow, and people mix and mingle all around. **Ⓓ**

### Toucan Reef
### 360 Concord Street, Suite 111,
### Fountain Walk
### (843) 853-5752

There's a great option right on the waterfront near the South Carolina Aquarium, IMAX Theater, and Ft. Sumter Interpretive Center (an area also known as Fountain Walk). Toucan Reef offers "deep drinks, fearless fare, and an awesome view" of the harbor. They bill themselves as purveyors of "international comfort food." Their Happy Hour is popular with visitors to the area attractions and with downtown office workers at the end of a busy day. Dancing into the night is a major draw here. Validated parking is available from the city garage nearby.

### Vickery's Bar & Grill
### 15 Beaufain Street
### (843) 577-5300

### 1313 Shrimp Boat Lane, Mt. Pleasant
### (843) 884-4440
### www.vickerysbarandgrill.com

Vickery's is a popular spot for a drink with friends. The restaurant does a booming daytime business with its Cuban-American cuisine, and there's a festive Latin flavor in the bar at night. There's a large outdoor seating area for imbibing or dining. Vickery's is just off King Street and offers limited (but possible) parking in the Market Corner Shopping Center's own lot. **Ⓓ**

### Wet Willie's
### 209 East Bay Street
### (843) 853-5650
### www.wetwillies.com

Across the street from the Custom House is this watering hole that's popular with the young professionals working up and down East Bay Street. Tourists are lured in as well because it's right on the street and very inviting by day or night with its big,

wide open doors. On Sunday and Wednesday, there's karaoke; Friday and Saturday offer dancing with a DJ on site. You'll also find pool, pinball, and Foosball. Wet Willie's will ask you to support global cooling by drinking a famous frozen daiquiri.

# East Cooper

## MT. PLEASANT

Although Mt. Pleasant is still a family-oriented community, there are plenty of exciting destinations for grownups when the sun goes down. The tremendous growth of the Mt. Pleasant area and the subsequent boom in population has created a whole new market for after-hours entertainment. That's especially true now that all bars on Peninsular Charleston are mandated to close at 2:00 A.M. The days when this quiet East Cooper neighborhood was strictly a bedroom community for downtown Charleston are over. Some of Mt. Pleasant's night spots howl until 4:00 A.M.! Mind you, this is no passport to drive irresponsibly or misbehave, and the Mt. Pleasant fuzz are out and about at all hours to prove it.

### Charleston Harbor Resort & Marina
### 20 Patriots Point Road
### (843) 856-0028, (888) 856-0028
### www.charlestonharborresort.com

At the Hilton Hotel in Mt. Pleasant on the Point, which extends into Charleston Harbor, is a delightful venue for sunset watching and a taste of coastal nightlife. (See the Hotels and Motels chapter.) Every other week, hotel employees construct added outdoor bars and light bonfires in the sand for the hundreds of people who come to enjoy the music, spirits, and invigorating night air. Charleston Harbor

*The minimum drinking age is 21 in South Carolina, and open containers are not allowed in moving vehicles.*

Resort and Marina is the sponsor bringing in entertainment from near and far. Jazz, rock, beach music—it's all here at one time or another. They start pouring signature drinks at 6:00 P.M. and continue until long after sunset. Light dining options may include beachside barbecue and a seasonal seafood raw bar. Located just over the Cooper River Bridge, this is a popular destination for Peninsula folk and East Cooper residents alike.

### Kaminsky's Most Excellent Café
**1028 Johnnie Dodds Boulevard**
**(843) 971-7437**

**78 North Market Street, Charleston**
**(843) 853-8270**
**www.tbonz.com**
Kaminsky's Mt. Pleasant location (there's a sibling establishment downtown in the Market area) is a wonderful cafe that has broken new ground since the management designated Tuesday nights for live music. This has brought out an interesting crowd of music-loving revelers. The action starts at happy hour after work. For more about Kaminsky's, see the Charleston section of the Restaurants chapter. **D**

### Shem Creek Bar & Grill
**508 Mill Street**
**(843) 884-8102**
**www.bigguynet.com**
High on the list of casual nighttime destinations, Shem Creek is one of the most popular watering holes in the area. It certainly has some great things going for it—namely, the dockside bar overlooking the marsh, the raw bar inside, and the salty characters who make it their home away from home. The mood is usually upbeat, and the munchies are delicious. **D**

## SULLIVAN'S ISLAND AND ISLE OF PALMS

Although the islands east of the Cooper River are considered family beaches, there are several notable watering holes nestled behind the dunes. A word of warning: Don't let the casual setting lull you into ignoring the open container laws. In other words, don't stroll outside with an unsealed alcoholic beverage. Police officers take it seriously.

### Banana Cabana
**1130 Ocean Boulevard, Isle of Palms**
**(843) 886-4361**
**www.bigguynet.com**
The Banana Cabana is open seven nights a week and offers a volleyball net and putting green as well as lots of cool, refreshing libations and munchies. Locals and visitors seem to delight in visiting this place after a day at the beach. Sometimes the volleyball court is where you'll find macho men and their female challengers fresh from the beach boasting their sports prowess and their perfect tans. **D**

### Bert's Bar
**2209 Middle Street, Sullivan's Island**
**(843) 883-3924**
Many years ago, Bert's was Sullivan's Island's pharmacy and soda fountain. Gone are the ammonia Cokes and grilled-cheese sandwiches. Blues and rock 'n' roll are what Bert's whips up these days. The kitchen serves burgers, soups, and salads. And Bert's even has an occasional Friday fish fry that draws a steady group of island characters. There is sometimes a cover charge for the live entertainment; it is generally a noisy, boisterous good time.

### Dunleavy's
**2213-A Middle Street, Sullivan's Island**
**(843) 883-9646**
A welcome watering hole for the island, Dunleavy's is an Irish pub with indoor and outdoor dining. The outdoor picnic tables are replete with dog bowls for patrons on a leash. The bar regularly attracts the beach crowd, and it's very family-oriented at the dinner hour. On weekends they feature live music. Bill Dunleavy is usually on hand and makes one and all feel welcome.

# All that Jazz...

If anything about the City of Charleston is known and recognized the world over, it has to be the 1920s dance craze that swept the country and set the tone for America in the Jazz Age. Relatively few people, on the other hand, know the origins of the dance or the story of how it captured the imagination of an American generation bursting with pent-up energy after the so-called war to end all wars.

The popular dance known as the Charleston is said to have begun on the street beside Charleston's Fort Sumter Hotel (near the Battery) with the energetic dance steps of the Jenkins Orphanage Band. In 1892, the Rev. Daniel Jenkins founded an orphanage in the city for homeless black children. To fund his charity, he organized the kids into a band that played on street corners for pennies donated from passersby. These young musicians were a delight to locals and visiting tourists alike. Eventually several bands and choirs evolved that were invited to perform in Florida, the northern states, and eventually Canada and Europe.

The Jenkins Orphanage Band and its jaunty jazz tune called the Charleston spawned the careers of several great jazz musicians who eventually played in the world-class orchestras of jazz greats like Count Basie, Louis Armstrong, and Duke Ellington.

**Station 22**
**2205 Middle Street, Sullivan's Island**
**(843) 883-3355**
A handsome, comfortable bar, with walls adorned with wonderful old pictures from the early days on the island, Station 22 has been a local favorite since it opened some years back. You can experience a quiet evening here as well as those occasional nights when the jukebox (said to be one of the best in town) is cranked loud. Revelers have been known to even cut a rug here. A charming train encircles the bar proper, and bartenders blow the whistle when the time is right. **①**

# West Ashley

Nighttime activity west of the Ashley River is often on or near the water, in settings that are attractive but casual. Most nightspots are part of restaurants, and some with docks cater to the boating crowd.

**Bull & Finch Restaurant & Pub**
**2070 Sam Rittenberg Boulevard,**
**Citadel Mall, Charleston**
**(843) 766-7429**
For those living in or visiting West Ashley, the convenience of Citadel Mall is a pull with all its shopping opportunities. But when the shopping is done, and it's time to kick back for a brew or a refreshing libation after a movie, there's this neat English pub to nicely fill the bill. They have a full menu of pub fare that runs the gamut from Lowcountry crab cakes to beef Wellington, but the billiards, sports TVs, wide selection of domestic and imported brews, and friendly service are big draws as well. They open for business daily at 11:30 A.M. **①**

## California Dreaming Restaurant and Bar
**1 Ashley Pointe Drive**
**(843) 766-1644**
**www.centraarchy.com**
This is the fort-like restaurant whose lights beckon from across the Ashley at night. After sundown, the scene is busy, lively, and fun. The bar is a great place to have a drink with a friend or a group of friends. You can see the lights of the Ashley and City Marinas, and it's adjacent to Ripley Light Marina, so the view is breathtaking. Because diners come here by droves, the bar is also a natural place to wait for a table. There's even a small floating dock for boat tie-ups. **D**

## Gene's Haufbrau
**817 Savannah Highway**
**(843) 225-4363**
Recently remodeled, this West Ashley spot claims to be Charleston's oldest bar. Nothing luxurious, the new place is a comfortable neighborhood bar, friendly and spacious, with pool, shuffleboard, darts, good pub food, and more than 120 beers and 12 draft labels from which to choose. This bar is popular with the after-work crowd who toil across the Ashley River bridge. And it's still close enough to The Citadel to draw the thirsty (and legal) cadets who can smell a beer at 40 paces.

# James and Johns Islands

## Charleston Crab House
**145 Wappoo Creek Drive, James Island**
**(843) 795-1963**

**41 South Market Street, Charleston**
**(843) 853-2900**
**www.charlestoncrabhouse.com**
This popular spot on the Intracoastal Waterway near the Wappoo Cut Bridge has dockside tables and space for mooring boats. There is live entertainment on weekends after Memorial Day, and it always seems to be packed during the summer months. The deck is a lot of fun

for drinks, appetizers, and watching those giant yachts go by. **D**

## Noisy Oyster
**2408 Maybank Highway, Johns Island**
**(843) 559-3552**

**24 North Market Street, Charleston**
**(843) 723-0044**

**7571 Rivers Avenue, North Charleston**
**(843) 824-1000**
**www.noisyoysterseafood.com**
Just across the new Stono River Bridge at Buzzard's Roost Marina is this recently renovated seafood restaurant right on the water. The friendly little bar offers service inside and out with libations that seem to taste better in the salty sea air. The lights on the boats moored at the nearby marinas add to the ambience, and the restaurant always has a number of seafood specials sure to please. Lunch and dinner are served daily. **D**

# COFFEEHOUSES

## Gourmet Blend
**354 Coleman Boulevard, Mt. Pleasant**
**(843) 849-8949**
Here's a trendy coffeehouse that's actually a cross between a place to grab some tasty hot java and a drive-thru dry-cleaner. Instead of freshly laundered shirts, they dispense coffee, gourmet sandwiches, and salads—to go. It's a favorite with morning commuters, who can buy a newspaper while waiting in line for their coffee and/or lunch. It's open until 9:00 P.M. on weekends, so it's a good stop before an early movie, and it makes a fun but inexpensive date. The fare here is far more creative than fast food and almost as convenient. **D**

## Port City Java
**387 King Street, Charleston**
**(843) 853-5282**

**261 Calhoun Street, Cannon Park Place, Charleston**
**(843) 937-9352**
**www.portcityjava.com**

This trendy, chic coffee bar has two locations. The one at the corner of King and Calhoun Streets in the Francis Marion Hotel caters mostly to tourists and students. The draw there is all kinds of exotic coffees and some pretty fancy desserts. The Port City on Calhoun Street offers a menu of small plates, salads, soups, and savories in addition to its selection of coffees and coolers. It is supported by the MUSC crowd and does a sizable lunch business. Both Port City Javas have hours that vary according to location.

## COMEDY CLUBS

### The American Theater
### 446 King Street
### (843) 853-6687

This is the home of a very popular improv comedy troupe known as the Have Nots! This three-member troupe has built a strong following in Charleston by finding the funny bone of local audiences and those out-of-towners who came for Piccolo Spoleto, alike. Somehow, they always manage to take the ordinary and turn it into the absurd from point-blank audience suggestions. Having their own space gives them an option of using creative lighting as a prop, which seems to be a trick all their own. Audiences range from teens to tourists of the senior persuasion. Everybody seems to have a great time. They sometimes tour, so call ahead to be sure they're playing at their American Theater venue. Admission is $10.

### The Comedy Zone
### 6610 Rivers Avenue, North Charleston
### (843) 853-8669

Inside T. J. & Tommy's Guitar Bar & Grill is a late-night destination for laughter. They normally mount two shows a night on weekends—at 8:00 and 10:00 P.M. Friday and Saturday. And the best part is—the first show is "smoke-free," and you'll be exposed to the comedy of nationally recognized talent. This is a hit with locals and tourists alike who enjoy a bit of clean, non-offensive mirth after a busy day. The dinner show package is $19.95, and the show is only $12.50 per person.

## DINNER CRUISES

### SpiritLine Dinner Cruise
### 40 Patriots Point Road, Mt. Pleasant
### (843) 722-2628
### www.spiritlinecruises.com

Dining and dancing aboard this 96-foot luxury tour boat while cruising historic Charleston Harbor make for one of those quintessential Charleston experiences. The *Spirit of Carolina* serves a three-course meal of she-crab soup, house salad, and a choice of five entrees such as prime rib, chicken, or seafood per prior request. All menu items are served with a nod toward the Lowcountry tradition of cooking. The boat makes its rounds up and down the waterways at sundown and is always a lot of fun. Live music and dancing are part of the weekday bill of fare. Entertainment is provided by a live band who can perform jazz, blues, shag, and country music as per your request. *Spirit of Carolina* is part of the Fort Sumter Tours group and conveniently departs from the docks at Patriots Point Naval and Maritime Museum, where there's free parking at the clearly marked boarding dock. The boarding begins at 6:30 P.M., and the cruise departs at 7:00 P.M. and returns at 10:00 P.M. Rates and schedules change seasonally, but tickets are in the $41 range for adults (Sunday through Thursday) and $45 range on Friday and Saturday. (See the Cruise and Boat Tours section of the Tours chapter.)

## MOVIE THEATERS

# Downtown Charleston

### IMAX Theatre Charleston
### 360 Concord Street
### (843) 725-4629
### www.charlestonimax.com

The IMAX movie format is technically a

whole new world for those who've never experienced it. In a nutshell, the screen is five stories tall, and the sound comes through the screen in quadraphonic fidelity at the audience, who sit in Italian leather seats that feel like those in sports cars. The subject matter of the films is different, too. Every movie is shot exclusively for IMAX theatres throughout the world, and the level of creativity is nothing short of mind-bending. There's an IMAX film (usually about 40 minutes in length) for everyone in the family, and several titles are shown daily at various times throughout the day. Call ahead for what's playing.

# James Island

**Terrace Theatre**
**1956 Maybank Highway**
**(843) 762-9494**
**www.terracetheatre.com**
In the Terrace Oaks shopping center, this first-run, wide-screen movie house features current hits and classic films in an upscale and comfortable atmosphere. Its cafe and lounge features gourmet snacks, coffee, and microbrews on tap. Desserts, wine, and champagne are also available to accommodate every taste. Call their information line (listed above) to hear what's on the current bill and to get matinee and nightly showtimes.

## CONCERT INFORMATION AND VENUES

Greater Charleston's appetite for entertainment and artistic diversions is satisfied by a wide range of performance venues today. From the rafter-filling rock concerts attracting thousands to the most intimate recitals at the College of Charleston, we have a concert hall or a major facility that can handle the crowd.

Ticketmaster is the high-tech way to get tickets to almost any concert or special event in the Lowcountry. This company, with nationwide ticket distribution,

adds a surcharge for the convenience of buying tickets through them. You can get tickets by phone or at local kiosks in venues such as Publix and Piggly Wiggly grocery stores which work like bank machines (handling charge cards). But the added cost is worth it for some. Others prefer to shop for their tickets to Spoleto and other hot concerts the old-fashioned way, by standing in line at the Gaillard Auditorium ticket window. You can access Ticketmaster by calling (843) 554-6060, or go to www.ticketmaster.com. The Gaillard's box office is generally open from 10:00 A.M. to 6:00 P.M. year-round. Before and during Spoleto, the hours are extended. (For more on Spoleto Festival USA and other performing arts events, see the chapters on the Arts and Annual Events.)

**Gaillard Municipal Auditorium**
**77 Calhoun Street, Charleston**
**(843) 577-7400**
Built in 1968, Charleston's 2,734-seat Gaillard Auditorium is the premier venue in the city for major arts events. It was named in honor of longtime Charleston Mayor J. Palmer Gaillard Jr., and it always houses the major opera productions of Spoleto Festival USA (see the chapters on Annual Events and The Arts). The Charleston Symphony Orchestra performs here, and Gaillard hosts productions of the Charleston Concert Association and touring off-Broadway shows. At Christmastime, Charleston's children are awed by the Charleston Ballet Theatre's glittering presentation of *The Nutcracker.* The auditorium is easy to find: It occupies the half-block bounded by Anson, George, Alexander, and Calhoun Streets. A city parking garage is next door. The Gaillard's box office hours are 10:00 A.M. to 6:00 P.M. Monday through Saturday.

**North Charleston Coliseum**
**5001 Coliseum Drive, North Charleston**
**(843) 529-5000**
Opened in 1993, the North Charleston Coliseum is the largest and most diverse indoor entertainment facility in South Car-

olina. Various seating configurations are possible, but generally speaking, the coliseum's capacity is 14,000 seats. Because of this, Greater Charleston is now a viable audience for some of the biggest traveling shows and sports attractions in America. The coliseum has attracted the likes of Rod Stewart, James Taylor, the Ringling Brothers and Barnum and Bailey Circus, Reba McEntire, the Eagles, World Cup figure skating, NHL hockey, and NCAA basketball, to name just a few. The coliseum is also the permanent home of the South Carolina Stingrays minor league hockey club, members of the East Coast Hockey League. (See the Spectator Sports chapter.) To get to the Coliseum, take the Montague Avenue exit off Interstate 26 and follow the signs, or take the Montague Avenue exit off Interstate 526 (Mark Clark Expressway). Ample parking is on-site, but be prepared to pay the price. Tickets for all Coliseum events may be purchased at their box office from 10:00 A.M. to 5:00 P.M. Monday through Saturday.

## North Charleston Performing Arts Center
## 5001 Coliseum Drive, North Charleston
## (843) 202-2787

With the advent of the 2,300-seat Performing Arts Center at the Charleston Area Convention Center complex, the Lowcountry won a place on the "road" itinerary for almost everyone who's anyone (or who's going to be) in the music industry. Finally, greater Charleston qualified as a viable destination for major shows and for artists who only want to visit venues that seat audiences of 2,000

or so. When it opened in August of 1999 with Harry Connick Jr. and his "Big Band" of 16 hot New Orleans musicians, the $18-million facility was off to a roaring start. Since then, touring road companies of major Broadway shows, big name artists like George Winston and Melissa Manchester, and events that were inappropriate for the 14,000-seat North Charleston Coliseum have found a home. Their on-site ticket office is open from 10:00 A.M. to 5:00 P.M. Monday through Saturday.

## The Sottile Theatre
## 44 George Street, Charleston
## (843) 953-5623
## www.cofc.edu/sottile/

The Sottile Theatre began life back in the 1920s as a venue for live vaudeville acts and the latest movies from Hollywood. Back then, Charleston had a number of downtown movie houses and this was among the most elaborate. Old-timers who remember it from its movie house days were gratified to see the ceiling restored to its former dazzle—as "pretend" stars twinkle in the darkness as the houselights go down. It fell on hard times and was vacant for many years until, in 1976, the College of Charleston bought the building for college and community use. A decade later, renovations began and continued for a full year. Today, the beautifully restored and technically updated Sottile seats 785 patrons and hosts a wide variety of performing arts. It is a venue for Spoleto Festival USA, Charleston Ballet Theatre, Charleston Symphony, Charleston Men's Chorus, and many other arts organizations.

# HOTELS AND MOTELS

If the Lowcountry knows a thing or two about putting up guests, it's because 4.6 million of them visited the Trident in 2004, and no one sees an end to this upward trend in sight. To accommodate these visitors, developers are poised to build new and better tourist accommodations both downtown and in the burgeoning North Charleston and Mt. Pleasant areas to reap the benefits of this incoming tide of dollars. Through the years, Southerners have established a reputation for hospitality, and they often compete to maintain the highest standards. Research and experience tell us that Charleston area visitors arrive with varying expectations, and a diverse accommodations industry has evolved to meet those needs.

We have included in this chapter and the one that follows what we consider to be good choices for people who may be looking for vastly different accommodations. We start with Trident area hotels and motels—some for the bargain-minded, some that are large and grand—then discuss the more intimate bed-and-breakfasts and atmospheric inns and vacation and beach rentals in the next chapters. Like friends in an eclectic gathering, each accommodations category has something different to offer. Prices vary greatly as well.

Downtown Charleston has the greatest number and the widest variety. We start our listings with downtown properties, then extend our coverage using the geographical order detailed in the How to Use This Book chapter. We end with information specifically helpful to the Lowcountry visitors who arrive by air and those among them seeking accommodations convenient to the airport. Unless we tell you otherwise, expect that these lodgings offer smoking and nonsmoking rooms and access for wheelchairs and that they do not allow pets.

There are several viable lodging options in the East Cooper and West Ashley areas. The resort islands of Kiawah and Seabrook feature a vast array of cottages, villas, condominiums, and private homes. For the most part, rental companies for the resorts and other traditional vacation spots (Isle of Palms, Sullivan's Island, and Folly Beach) prefer to deal with stays of one week or longer. See our Vacation and Beach Rentals chapter for a list of companies that handle resort and vacation properties.

A friendly word of advice: Charleston attracts droves of visitors year-round (there are major events scheduled nearly every month; see the Annual Events chapter), and we strongly recommend that you make reservations well in advance. For major events like Spoleto Festival USA and holiday weekends, it's advisable to plan up to six months in advance.

## PRICE CODE

Although rates are subject to change, we use the following pricing code to indicate the average rate for a one-night stay, in season, for two adults. Note that these rates do not include taxes (12 percent accommodations tax), gratuities, or add-on services such as room service or premium TV channels. Off-season rates are, of course, lower. March through July and October through December are usually considered peak seasons.

| | |
|---|---|
| $ | Less than $65 |
| $$ | $65–95 |
| $$$ | $96–150 |
| $$$$ | $151–200 |
| $$$$$ | More than $201 |

# DOWNTOWN CHARLESTON

## Best Western King Charles Inn   $$$-$$$$
237 Meeting Street
(843) 723-7451, (800) 528-1234
www.kingcharlesinn.com

The King Charles Inn, another in the Best Western chain, completed a major renovation of its facade and common areas a few years back. The location is ideal for those wanting to explore King Street shopping and the Market area on foot. (See the Shopping chapter.) Those of us who drive past on sweltering Charleston afternoons envy the guests we see frolicking in the second-level outdoor swimming pool. The nearby fountain makes a sparkling show for guests in the dining room. The decor is "traditional Charleston," with mahogany reproductions and Lowcountry art. Rooms feature 19th-century-style furniture, and some have adjoining guest rooms or balconies. The parking garage is underground and free for guests. The north area location is referred to as the Charleston International Best Western and is an atrium-styled hotel with many of these same amenities. (See the subsequent listings for other area Best Western locations.)

## Charleston Place   $$$$$
205 Meeting Street
(843) 722-4900, (800) 611-5545
www.charlestonplacehotel.com

In terms of size, the former Omni is the granddaddy of Charleston hotels with 490 luxury suites and superbly appointed rooms in the massive complex in the city's downtown shopping district. The hotel, with its impressive lobby and reception area, opens into the walkway of a minimall that includes such famous stores as Gucci, Talbots, and Godiva. (See the Shopping chapter.)

The full-service European spa with its on-staff masseur and masseuse has an indoor-outdoor swimming pool among the luxury amenities. Under the auspices of Orient Express, the rooms at Charleston Place have taken on the aura of Europe in the 1930s. Expect to find marble bathtubs and gold fixtures in the roomy baths, and notice the little touches in the rooms, such as art deco lighting and the subdued use of color. They add just that much more romance to your lodging experience. Several superb dining options are available right under the Charleston Place roof. Foremost among them is the Charleston Grill on the main floor tucked away among the shops and boutiques. (See the Restaurants chapter for more on the Charleston Grill.)

## Charleston Riverview Hotel   $$$
170 Lockwood Drive
(843) 723-3000, (800) 968-3569
www.charlestonriverviewhotel.com

If you are crossing the Ashley River Bridge into Charleston, look to your left to see the towering Charleston Riverview Hotel behind riverside Brittlebank Park. There are 333 rooms and suites in this option, many with views of the river, and this venue is a popular one for conventions and meetings. A swimming pool is part of the facility, and the rooms have premium channels and movie rentals. Abundant parking is available at no charge.

## Comfort Inn Riverview   $$-$$$
144 Bee Street
(843) 577-2224, (800) 228-5150
www.choicehotels.com

As part of the Comfort Inn chain, the Riverview's 129-room version offers a string of discounts and other standard features plus its most desirable asset, views of the Ashley River. It is just outside the historic district (but still on the Peninsula), and tours are available from the hotel. A fitness room appeals to many travelers, and the outdoor pool with its river view is a big hit with all ages. Continental breakfast is included in the price of the room, and there is no charge for parking. This location makes it a popular option for visitors to The Citadel, area hospitals, and the College of Charleston.

**Courtyard by Marriott/Riverview**
**35 Lockwood Drive** **$$$$**
**(843) 722-7229, (800) 321-2211**

**2415 Mall Drive, North Charleston** **$$$**
**(843) 747-9122, (800) 321-2211**
**www.marriott.com/chscy**
Overlooking the Ashley River at the base
of the Peninsula is Charleston's newest
hotel offering from Marriott. It opened in
the fall of 1997. The 179 spacious guest
rooms all have two analog dataport
phones, voice mail messaging, and a work
desk. In-room coffeemakers and movies
on demand via cable are some of the
other amenities. A waterfront swimming
pool, an indoor whirlpool spa, and a fit-
ness center are available, as well as a daily
breakfast buffet in the Courtyard Café.
Golf packages are available for 19 Low-
country courses. And there's ample on-
site parking. This Courtyard by Marriott,
which is near the Calhoun Street medical
complex, cuts a high profile for those
entering Charleston via Highway 61, U.S.
Highway 17, and Highway 30. A similar
version is located along the Interstate 26
corridor and convenient to the airport.

---

*The average daily rate for a room in
Charleston peaks in April. In 2004 that
average was $112.67 per night (accord-
ing to the city's Convention and Visitor's
Bureau). The occupancy rate for the
city's hotel and motel accommodations
is a healthy 65.2 percent.*

---

**Days Inn Historic District** **$$$$**
**155 Meeting Street**
**(843) 722-8411, (866) 683-8411**
**www.daysinn.com**
The 124 units of this Days Inn are air-
conditioned and fairly typical of the rooms
in this chain—clean and comfortable, with
few frills. Enjoy a swimming pool and
being only one block away from the Mar-
ket, fine restaurants, plus shops and gal-
leries. Limited free parking on-site is

available. You can't beat this option for its
ideal location and standard reliability. (See
the East Cooper and I-26 Corridor sec-
tions below for other Days Inn locations.)

**Doubletree Guest Suites/**
**Historic Charleston** **$$$-$$$$**
**181 Church Street**
**(843) 577-2644, (877) 408-8733**
**www.doubletree.com**
A relative newcomer to the Market area,
and formerly known as the Hawthorn
Suites, this comfortable courtyard hotel
consists of oversized suites. Units have
"the Charleston look" and include com-
plete kitchens, separate bedrooms, and
living rooms. Life is made easy with a
complimentary breakfast buffet, and you
can unwind with on-the-house refresh-
ments at the afternoon reception. For
those who enjoy burning the calories they
consume, there's a fitness center and a
heated whirlpool spa in the courtyard that
seats at least 12 comfortably (great for
relaxing while gazing at the stars). When
energy levels diminish, the hotel's VCR
tape library is available to complement
your cable television service. Five suites
are completely wheelchair accessible. The
hotel provides valet covered parking.

**Embassy Suites Historic**
**Charleston** **$$$$-$$$$$**
**337 Meeting Street**
**(843) 723-6900, (800) 362-2779**
**www.charleston-hotels.net**
This is one of Charleston's newest, all-suite
luxury hotels. It's in the historic district in
what was originally The Citadel's first
home (ca. 1820). Unmistakably a military
building, the echoes of young cadets
marching off to the Civil War still seem to
bounce off these old walls. Enjoy 153
handsomely furnished two-room suites
with private bedrooms and living rooms.
The decor recalls the grandeur of the
colonial West Indies. All guest suites open
onto a stone-floored atrium with giant
palms and a three-tiered fountain. Ameni-
ties include in-room wet bars, telephones
with voice mail and dataports, free,

cooked-to-order breakfast, and complimentary beverages each evening. This is
an ideal location, a stroll from the visitor
center, the Charleston Museum, and special events in Marion Square. (See the I-26
Corridor section, which follows for the
north area location.)

### Francis Marion Hotel $$$$$
387 King Street
(843) 722-0600, (877) 756-2121
www.francismarioncharleston.com
Built in 1924 and beautifully renovated, the
Francis Marion is now one of the city's
most popular hotels. In all, there are 226
guest accommodations ranging from
rooms with two double beds to two-room
king suites. All have been handsomely re-
appointed with custom detailing. Twelve
stories tall, the hotel affords visitors a
bird's-eye view. It's near upper King
Street's fast-developing shopping district,
the Charleston Museum, the College of
Charleston, and the visitor center. The
hotel's signature restaurant, the Swamp
Fox Room, offers a very pleasant atmosphere on the first-floor King Street side.
Ample parking is just next door in a city-
owned garage.

### Hampton Inn Historic District
345 Meeting Street $$$-$$$$
(843) 723-4000, (800) 426-7866

4701 Saul White Boulevard $$-$$$
(843) 554-7154, (800) 426-7866

1990 Daniel Island Drive $$-$$$
(843) 216-6555, (800) 426-7866

7424 Northside Drive,
North Charleston $$$-$$$$
(843) 820-2030, (800) 426-7866
www.hamptoninn.com
There are 171 rooms in the downtown
Hampton Inn Historic District, conveniently
located across from the visitor center, trol-
ley transportation, and the Charleston
Museum. One of downtown Charleston's
newer inns, the Hampton offers the attrac-
tive features of an older, restored building
mellowed with time but beautifully decked
out in crisp, new furnishings. The courtyard

is probably the largest on the Peninsula,
and the large pool is a welcome oasis for
travelers. Double rooms have two queen
beds, and an impressive continental break-
fast is part of the deal—muffins, bagels,
other breads, cereal, and coffee cake. Their
Hampton Inn Airport/Coliseum location—
just off Ashley Phosphate on Northside
Drive—is handy for airport travelers and
convention visitors. This latest addition to
the North Charleston convention complex
serves the north area's sprawling industrial
development.

---

*Low-cost accommodations on
Charleston's historic Peninsula are few
and far between. A couple of hostel-
style inns have opened recently that
offer a no-frills, economy-minded alter-
native. Visit www.notsohostel.com and
www.charlestonhostel.com to explore
your options.*

---

### Holiday Inn Historic District $$$$
125 Calhoun Street
(843) 805-7900, (877) 805-7900
www.charlestonhotel.com
For almost 40 years, the corner of Cal-
houn and Meeting was known by frequent
Charleston visitors as the location of a
convenient and affordable 1960s-style
high-rise motel. It went by a number of
names over the years and is now open as
a Holiday Inn with a recent $6-million
facelift. Now there are 126 guest rooms
and suites, a full-service restaurant and
lounge, a fitness center, valet laundry, an
outdoor heated pool, and courtyard. Best
of all, it's still just steps away from King
Street shopping, Marion Square, the visitor
center, and Gailliard Auditorium. Business
travelers have three phones with two lines,
voice mail, and dataports in-room.

### Market Pavilion Hotel $$$$-$$$$$
225 East Bay Street
(843) 723-0500, (877) 440-2250
www.marketpavilion.com

A recent addition to the landscape on peninsular Charleston and to the heart of the Market area, you'll find this hotel at the corner of South Market and East Bay Streets. Called a "boutique" hotel with an emphasis on service and design, this option features guest rooms and suites for tourists and business travelers. For the latter, there are meeting rooms and banquet facilities, and an executive boardroom on tap. Guests have access to a rooftop pavilion with a pool and an open-air bar providing spectacular views from this popular reception area. An upscale restaurant, Grill 225, completes the picture for this newcomer to the local hospitality industry. (See the Restaurants chapter.) Valet parking is available, and the location couldn't be more convenient to the Market's shopping adventures and its after-hours nightlife.

### Mills House Hotel        $$$$-$$$$$
**115 Meeting Street**
**(843) 577-2400, (800) 874-9600**
**www.millshouse.com**
Of the city's grand hotels in the historic district, the Mills probably enjoys the oldest, grandest reputation. Now managed by Six Continents, it is on the corner of Meeting and Queen Streets, next door to the imposing white-columned Hibernian Hall (site of many a debutante ball and home of the Hibernian Society). Modern in its comforts and antebellum in its decor, the Mills House has always been a favorite with affluent travelers. The original (1853) Mills Hotel standing on that site was deemed unworthy of restoration in the early 1960s, so it was razed and replaced with a new, fire-safe structure taller by a couple of floors but with lobby areas and public rooms copied from the original hotel. So exacting are the reproduced details and antebellum appointments that frequently the Mills is used as a backdrop for movies and TV shows needing a "period" hotel setting. The beautiful courtyard, outdoor pool, and deck add a casual side to the Mills experience. The in-house restaurant and bar, called the Barbados Room, draws local patrons as well as the international set. You'll find live entertainment somewhere on the premises each night, and turndown service is part of the pampering. It's hard to beat the Mills for location, as it is only a stone's throw from the Four Corners of Law, the King Street antiques district, several museums and galleries, plus the bustling Market area.

### Renaissance Charleston Hotel        $$$$-$$$$$
**68 Wentworth Street**
**(843) 534-0300, (800) 468-3571**
**www.renaissancehotels.com**
Opened in early 2001 in the heart of the city's downtown business district, this is one of Charleston's newest major hotels from Marriott. It is steps away from King Street shopping and area restaurants, and the location is ideal for visitors to the College of Charleston campus just a short stroll away. Their 166 elegantly appointed rooms are decorated in a Charleston decor with bonnet beds and other charming details. Some rooms open onto the pool deck; others (32 of them, in fact) have balconies with city views. The on-site restaurant, Brasserie des Amis, serves a Southern-French-Mediterranean cuisine with a Charleston flair. There's a fitness center, a heated outdoor pool, and ample meeting space for business travelers and conventioneers. Hotel valet and self-parking is just across Wentworth Street.

# EAST COOPER

### Comfort Inn        $$-$$$
**310 U.S. Highway 17 Bypass**
**(843) 884-5853, (800) 228-5150**

### 5055 North Arco Lane,        $$
### North Charleston
**(843) 554-6485, (800) 228-5150**
**www.choicehotels.com**
This East Cooper motel has more extras than you might imagine and is a good value. Complimentary continental breakfast and a daily paper start the day off right. There is free cable TV with premium channels as well as laundry facilities for

taking care of the beach sand in your shorts. Business guests will find phones with voice mail and dataports. You'll also find one of the two heated swimming pools available to tourists in Mt. Pleasant. The Comfort Inn Coliseum, where pets are welcome, is just a mile from Charleston International Airport and the North Charleston Coliseum.

**Days Inn Patriots Point**          $$–$$$
**261 Johnnie Dodds Boulevard
(US 17 Bypass)
(843) 881-1800, (800) 329-7466
www.daysinn.com**
One of the most popular amenities at this Days Inn is the pool area—sheltered for privacy by mature shrubbery. All rooms are air-conditioned, and the 24-hour on-site restaurant is a plus in our book for early risers who like to be close to that first cup of coffee. The rooms are in the standard Days Inn tradition. They're clean, comfortable, economical, and kid friendly.

**Hampton Inn at Patriots Point**     $$$
**255 Johnnie Dodds Boulevard
(843) 881-3300, (800) 426-7866**

**1104 Isle of Palms Connector
(843) 856-3900, (800) 426-7866
www.charleston-hotels.net**
This is a 121-room Mt. Pleasant hotel with inside hallways rather than the outside breezeways that characterize many motels. There is no charge for local calls (often important to business travelers), and children younger than 18 stay free. The rooms here are a little grander than in most off-highway accommodations. The service says hotel, but the price says motel. A deluxe continental breakfast is on the house. Hampton Inn has added a new location on the Isle of Palms connector with deluxe suites, which are popular with traveling families.

**Hilton Charleston
Harbor Resort**          $$$–$$$$
**20 Patriots Point Road
(843) 856-0028, (888) 856-0028
www.charlestonharborresort.com**

The 131-room Hilton Charleston Harbor Resort was a long time coming to this breathtaking waterfront spot at the very tip of Mt. Pleasant overlooking the Holy City. After 13 years, two different developers, and a major hurricane, this prime real estate resisted successful completion of a planned resort until Hilton arrived to save the day. Now the hotel and marina complex is one of Charleston's newest destinations for fun, sun, sea, and golf. The Hilton's decor is maritime—teak-trimmed and nautical. The state-record blue marlin catch is triumphantly displayed in the main foyer.

Indoor facilities include meeting rooms, the Rockfish Grille restaurant, a cocktail lounge called the Reel Bar, and a ballroom. Suites and rooms are available with king-size beds or two double beds. Room phones have voice mail. Outdoors there's a swimming pool as well as a man-made, private sandy beach. The USS *Yorktown* and Patriots Point Maritime Museum are just next door. Golfers have discounted greens fees at the Patriots Point course just outside the gate (see the Golf chapter), and the 459-slip marina opened in the summer of 1998. (See the Boating and Watersports chapter.)

**Holiday Inn/Mt. Pleasant**       $$$
**250 Johnnie Dodds Boulevard
(U.S. Highway 17 Bypass)
(843) 884-6000, (800) 290-4004
www.himtpleasant.com**
This elegant, full-service hotel has views of Charleston Harbor and the Cooper River and is only minutes away from the city as well as Patriots Point. Rooms are furnished with period reproductions, and a concierge level provides additional service and convenience. Visitors can enjoy a fitness center with a sauna, an outdoor pool, on-site restaurant, and bar.

**MainStay Suites**             $$$
**400 McGrath Darby Boulevard
(843) 881-1722, (800) 432-6423
www.choicehotels.com**
This 71-unit, three-floor, all-suite hotel

opened in Mt. Pleasant in February 1999 and offers unique accommodations to business travelers and vacationers who enjoy traveling as families. Half of the units at MainStay have two bedrooms and two baths with doors that separate the kitchen, living area, and bathrooms from the sleeping rooms. The other half are roomy efficiencies with full kitchens equipped with all the necessities for preparing meals. All units have 25-inch TVs and VCRs. You'll also find a heated pool, an exercise room, and guest laundry services. There's even a barbecue area for outdoor cooking. The check-in desk is manned only from 6:00 A.M. to 9:00 P.M. Monday through Friday. On weekends, it's open until 6:00 P.M. If you arrive outside of that envelope, follow the check-in instructions in the lobby.

**Masters Inn** $$
**300 Wingo Way**
**(843) 884-2814, (800) 633-3434**

**6100 Rivers Avenue, North Charleston**
**(843) 744-3530, (800) 633-3434**
**www.mastersinn.com**
This 120-room option is a bargain and offers great proximity to the city (3 miles) and the Isle of Palms (7 miles). There are some extras as well, such as a pool, cable television, and free local phone calls. A lounge and restaurant are on-site, and free continental breakfast is served each morning. Efficiencies with kitchenettes are also available. Children younger than 18 stay free with parents. The North Charleston location is convenient to the airport and the Air Force Base.

**Shem Creek Inn** $$$-$$$$
**1401 Shrimp Boat Lane**
**(843) 881-1000, (800) 523-4951**
**www.shemcreekinn.com**
With views of the shrimp boats moving in and out of their docks and the sun sparkling off miles of marsh, Shem Creek Inn is fun for both children and adults. Each of the 50 rooms has a private bal-

cony, and king-size rooms have garden tubs. There is convenient parking under the building, and continental breakfast is served each morning. All the Shem Creek nightlife goes on close to the inn, and boat dockage is available.

## SULLIVAN'S ISLAND, ISLE OF PALMS

These two islands are popular vacation destinations and abound with rental property. With no hotel, motel, condominium, or resort development, Sullivan's Island has less to offer in terms of overnight rental but has an assortment of old and new island homes for rent in weekly or monthly increments. See our Vacation and Beach Rentals chapter for a list of companies that handle rentals on the islands.

On the Isle of Palms, in addition to weekly house rentals, Wild Dunes, a major resort, offers flexibility in length of stay (see subsequent listing). Please note: Summer reservations on both islands are often booked by late winter, so start making plans with a rental agency or other entity at least six months ahead. Most do not allow pets, but it is always worth asking.

**The Boardwalk Inn**
**at Wild Dunes** $$$$-$$$$$
**5757 Palm Boulevard, Isle of Palms**
**(843) 886-6000, (800) 845-8880**
**www.wilddunes.com**
Opened early in 1998, the Boardwalk Inn at Wild Dunes is a $12-million luxury hotel with 92 rooms or suites near Wild Dunes' two famous golf courses and 20-court tennis center. All this is situated along 2.5 miles of unspoiled white sand beach. The Boardwalk Inn has an on-site gourmet Lowcountry-style seafood restaurant and lounge plus a tropical pool complex. Even locals enjoy their attractive bed-and-breakfast packages for special occasions. Those start at about $198 per couple/per night in the summer months (high season).

**Holiday Inn**
**Express & Suites**      **$$$-$$$$**
**1126 Ocean Boulevard,**
**Isle of Palms**
**(843) 886-3003, (800) 465-4329**

**1943 Savannah Highway,**      **$$$**
**Charleston**
**(843) 402-8300, (800) 465-4329**

**7670 Northwoods Boulevard,**
**North Charleston**      **$$$**
**(843) 553-1600, (800) 465-4329**
**www.hiexpress.com**
New to the Isle of Palms, this beachfront hotel is a moderately priced option for traveling families. These rooms and suites are comfortable without the extras. There's still little more to be desired with a pool, laundry facilities, sundeck, computer access ports, and free off-site parking. You're located near many of the island's most popular restaurants, too. The "Express" concept for this familiar chain seems to be growing, with locations in West Ashley and North Charleston.

**Wild Dunes Resort**      **$$$$-$$$$$**
**5757 Palm Boulevard, Isle of Palms**
**(843) 886-6000, (800) 845-8880**
**www.wilddunes.com**
Rental possibilities at Wild Dunes are widely varied. This 1,600-acre oceanfront golf resort is 20 minutes north of Charleston. Accommodations include one- to four-bedroom villas next to the ocean, golf courses, tennis courts, or lagoon. You can rent three- to six-bedroom homes with ocean, fairway, and Intracoastal Waterway views. Guests choose their location based on proximity to the beach, pool, tennis courts, marina, or fairways and, of course, on price. The accommodations provide linens, dinnerware, televisions, and washers and dryers, plus a cleaning staff takes care of the messy parts of vacationing. You just focus on the fun. Golf is a big attraction, with two excellent courses: the Links, designed by Tom Fazio and ranked as a top course by Golf Magazine, and the Harbor Course, with holes along the Intracoastal Waterway. (See the Golf chapter.)

There are Har-Tru tennis courts for day and night play, and tennis clinics and lessons are available. Of course, the sandy beach is beautiful, and there are many activities for families. Wild Dunes does not allow pets but will recommend local kennels.

## WEST ASHLEY

The following West Ashley options provide good value with proximity to the Peninsula. At most, you'll be about 20 minutes from the hustle and bustle of the historic district. Note that most properties are on or near US 17, which is called Savannah Highway throughout this area.

**Best Western Sweetgrass Inn**      **$$-$$$**
**1540 Savannah Highway**
**(843) 571-6100, (800) 528-1234**
**www.lodgingcharleston.com**
This Best Western is only 3 miles from the Peninsula and is a very tasteful, affordable option. Continental breakfast is complimentary, and everyone loves the large outdoor pool. We think this is one of the area's real values, particularly since the spacious rooms have been recently refurbished. This motel is convenient to the gardens and historic plantations along Highway 61.

**Hampton Inn Riverview Hotel**
**11 Ashley Pointe Drive**      **$$$**
**(843) 556-5200, (800) 426-7866**

**678 Citadel Haven Drive**      **$$-$$$**
**(843) 573-1200, (800) 426-7866**
**www.hamptoninn.com**
Out of the mainstream, this Hampton Inn is on a road called Ashley Pointe Drive, off Albemarle Road west of the Ashley. Other nearby landmarks are Ripley Light Marina and California Dreaming restaurant at the end of the street (see the Restaurants chapter). Ideal for visitors to the Lowcountry arriving by boat, this motel is a modern, multistory facility with great views of the Ashley River and the adjoining marina. There are 175 rooms in all. Some have one double bed, others have

two doubles, and there are VIP rooms with king beds and whirlpool baths. Continental breakfast is complimentary.

### Holiday Inn Riverview                 $$$
**301 Savannah Highway
(843) 556-7100, (800) 766-4451
www.holiday-inn.com**
For obvious reasons, locals refer to this circular hotel just across the Ashley River Bridge as the Round Holiday Inn. Many of the 181 units and four suites have spectacular water views unmatched by any other accommodation in the city. Up top, a restaurant and bar offer panoramic vistas of peninsular Charleston and the meandering Ashley River. The pool area is an outside appendage to the hotel, unusual because of its elevated height and the view it provides. Guests enjoy the complimentary shuttle downtown and free on-site parking.

### Lands Inn                 $$
**2545 Savannah Highway
(843) 763-8885, (800) 432-6423**
This Lands Inn is about 6 miles from the city, which makes it more private and relaxing, not to mention more affordable. Guests can choose rooms with a king-size bed or with two doubles. It's basic lodging, a little farther from the maddening crowd. A pool and private fishing dock for guests, cable TV, and a continental breakfast in the morning are available. Dogs (only) are welcome too (with a $10 fee), and Citadel Mall is minutes away.

### SpringHill Suites                 $$-$$$
**98 Ripley Point Drive
(843) 571-1711, (888) 287-9400
www.springhillsuites.com**
Across the Ashley just past the round Holiday Inn you'll find this all-suite Marriott hotel, which is popular with boaters tying up at Ripley Light Marina. Proximate to downtown and Highway 61 (out to the plantations), this hotel also offers many luxury amenities. Each suite has a mini-kitchen, a sitting area, cable TV, two-line telephones with dataports, voice mail

messaging, and a spacious work area. Guests also enjoy a free continental breakfast, outdoor pool and whirlpool spa, fitness center, and same-day valet service. Next door is the slightly more upscale Marriott Residence Inn offering one or two bedrooms, fully equipped kitchens, some suites with fireplaces, and other luxuries. Call (843) 571-7979 or (800) 331-3131 for reservations or more information.

### Town & Country Inn &
### Conference Center                 $$$
**2008 Savannah Highway
(843) 571-1000, (800) 334-6660
www.thetownandcountryinn.com**
What will strike you first about this West Ashley establishment is the electronic billboard out front that gives a running message about the services within. Next, you are likely to be amazed by the fact that this is as much a fitness center as it is a motel. Guests have access to facilities, and locals can buy memberships. With an indoor pool, racquetball courts, exercise equipment, sauna, and more, a stay here can qualify as a fitness vacation.

The regular rooms feature two queen beds or one king-size bed, and the bathrooms have marble tubs and built-in hair dryers. The phones offer voice mail service, and the TVs all have 56 cable channels including HBO. Laundry service is an option and, if you are traveling light, efficiencies are available. The restaurant, Trotters, is popular as well (especially with the after-church crowd on Sundays) and runs unusual specials—just check the sign! (See the Restaurants chapter.)

## FOLLY BEACH

Visitors interested in staying on Folly Beach will find a range of accommodations, including an oceanfront high-rise hotel (see listing) and old-style beach houses available for rent. Again, to rent a beach home, see the list of agents in the Vacation and Beach Rentals chapter.

**Charleston on the Beach**     **$$$$**
**1 Center Street**
**(843) 588-6464, (800) 465-4329**
**www.charlestononthebeach.com**
A Holiday Inn property, this is the only oceanfront hotel, restaurant, and bar in this part of the Lowcountry. Half the hotel's 132 rooms overlook the ocean at Folly Beach, and private balconies make wave-watching all the nicer. Standard rooms have either one king-size or two double beds. There is an oceanfront pool for those who do not dip in the salt water, and Chancy's on the Beach has terrific food and flowing spirits at its bar.

# KIAWAH AND SEABROOK

These world-class resort destinations offer some extraordinary rental options that might be just what you are looking for: everything from a private villa to luxury homes to an upscale hotel. Look for descriptions of Kiawah and Seabrook in the Neighborhoods, History, Area Overview, and Parks and Recreation chapters.

**Kiawah Island Resort**     **$$$$-$$$$$**
**12 Kiawah Beach Drive, Kiawah Island**
**(843) 768-2121, (800) 654-2924**
**www.kiawahresort.com**
Called "South Carolina's joy of a resort isle" by *Vogue* magazine, Kiawah Island is a 10,000-acre, semitropical island with rental options galore. Choose from villas, cottages, and private homes. Kiawah's newest addition to their medley of luxury accommodations is The Sanctuary, a $126-million hotel, spa, and convention complex with 255 rooms. (See following listing.)

There are actually three resort areas, or villages, within walking or biking distance of island shopping and dining. Villas and cottages are fully equipped and have as many as four bedrooms, while luxury homes for rent in adjacent residential areas have as many as seven bedrooms and elaborate extras.

Other accommodations are basically clustered in the West Beach Village, the East Beach Village, and the Vanderhorst Plantation. In the West Beach Village, villas have views of the forest, ocean, lagoon, tennis courts, or golf courses. East Beach villas are parkside, linkside, courtside, or oceanside and offer some very appealing options. There are two pools for guest usage, one of which is an Olympic-size option in the 21-acre Night Heron Park, where guests will also find a covered pavilion, arcade, soccer field, and lake for fishing. The Vanderhorst Plantation is an exclusive gated community with very large homes and ample privacy.

Plan to swim, bike, shell hunt, boat, and fish, and explore the many nature trails that encircle the island. Oh, and expect to break out the clubs too. According to *Golf Magazine,* Kiawah is one of the best golf resorts in America (see the Golf chapter). It was home of the 1991 Ryder Cup Matches, the 1997 World Cup of Golf, and the 2003 WGC World Cup. Kiawah's tennis program, with state-of-the art facilities at two centers, also ranks high nationally. Kiawah's kids' programs are a hit with young families.

**The Sanctuary**
**at Kiawah Island**     **$$$$$**
**1 Sanctuary Beach Drive, Kiawah Island**
**(843) 768-6000, (877) 683-1234**
**www.thesanctuary.com**
The Sanctuary at Kiawah Island opened in 2004 with much hoopla and anticipation among locals and regular visitors to the Lowcountry. The opening of this 255-room hotel and spa built right on Kiawah's legendary 10-mile, pristine beach came after a decade of planning and construction— marking a new era in luxury accommodations for coastal South Carolina.

Guests of The Sanctuary may think of it as a destination unto itself, although the island's world-class golf and tennis programs are major draws. Nearly all the unusually large rooms and suites offer sweeping ocean views, and the hotel's decor harks back to the gilded age of beachfront mansions built by America's 19th-century aristocracy.

Two dining rooms vie for hungry guests' attention; the Jasmine Porch (with its Lowcountry cuisine) and the Ocean Room (a fine-dining option serving dinner only with a New American menu—see the Restaurants chapter). An on-site full-service spa tempts guests with an ample selection of relaxing and healthful pamperings available to both men and women. Along with every imaginable beach amenity (including indoor and outdoor pools plus an outdoor bar and grill), The Sanctuary offers guests an arcade of smart shopping boutiques, and an on-site staff of wildlife experts is available to lead guests on a variety of nature adventures—all Kiawah style.

**Seabrook Resort                 $$$$-$$$$$**
**1002 Landfall Way, Seabrook Island**
**(843) 768-1000, (800) 845-2475**
**www.discoverseabrook.com**
This resort offers family vacations in a residential, island setting. Here you'll find one, two, and three-bedroom villas—some in the maritime forest, others overlooking the sea. There is no inn on Seabrook; the resort offers one-, two-, and three-bedroom privately owned villas for rent. These properties come equipped with spacious kitchens, sundecks or screened porches, cable hookups, and everything from linens to dinnerware. Some have maritime forest views, and others overlook the marsh or ocean. All are in proximity to one of Seabrook's two golf courses, Ocean Winds and Crooked Oaks.

Along with these championship courses (see the Golf chapter), Seabrook has a tennis complex and the area's only resort equestrian center. Swimmers choose between glistening pools and a beautiful stretch of beach along the Atlantic Ocean. Children can enjoy supervised, old-fashioned fun such as puppet shows, finger painting, and ice-cream making while their parents relish precious private time.

# I-26 CORRIDOR (CHARLESTON INTERNATIONAL AIRPORT)

For business travelers, commuters to Charleston Area Convention Center meetings (in North Charleston), and vacationers who need accommodations convenient to the airport, a number of options await them along the I-26 corridor and the Interstate 526 loop around the heart of the Lowcountry.

We've listed many of these options in the listings of well-known chain hotels and motels above. Here are a few more choices offering a variety of amenities and prices.

**Clarion Hotel**
**Charleston Airport                 $$-$$$**
**7401 Northwoods Boulevard,**
**North Charleston**
**(843) 572-2200, (800) 252-7466**
**www.clarioncharleston.com**
Conveniently located just off I-26 at Ashley Phosphate Road, this 197-room tropical atrium hotel has an indoor/outdoor swimming pool with separate whirlpool and sauna. There's a volleyball court as well as a game room for youngsters. A full buffet breakfast comes with the room, and there's free shuttle service to and from the airport. Rooms have premium channel cable TV, and guest laundry service is available.

**Days Inn Airport/Coliseum                 $$**
**2998 West Montague Avenue,**
**North Charleston**
**(843) 747-4101, (800) 329-7466**
**www.daysinn.com**
The familiar name in affordable comfort has 149 rooms with cable TV, pay-for-view movies, and refrigerators (on request). Like most others in the chain, this has an on-site family restaurant, an outdoor pool, and playground. This location is ideal for sports fans attending events at the Coliseum, only three blocks away. There's also free airport transportation for guests.

**Embassy Suites Hotel
Airport–Convention Center   $$$-$$$$
5055 International Boulevard,
North Charleston
(843) 747-1882, (800) 362-2779
www.embassysuitescharleston.com**
One of the first full-service hotels built to serve (and literally connected to via a climate-controlled skyway) the north area's convention center complex, this 256-suite high-rise hotel is very impressive. Facilities include ample meeting space, a pool, and a state-of-the-art business center for conventioneers. Services at the Embassy Suites include a complimentary breakfast as well as an evening reception and a free airport shuttle to make doing business here as pleasant and convenient as possible.

**Hilton Garden Inn
Charleston Airport      $$-$$$
5265 International Boulevard,
North Charleston
(843) 308-9330, (800) 445-8667
www.charlestonairport.gardeninn.com**
Hilton's bid for the business travelers' attention is minutes from Charleston International Airport. Their Garden Inn boasts a full array of amenities to please visitors to the area in search of business or pleasure. A complimentary airport shuttle is another plus. The 128 rooms feature refrigerators, microwaves, and coffeemakers plus work desks, adjustable lighting, and ergonomic chairs for comfort and on-task productivity. When work is done, the Great American Grill offers cocktails and dinner service, and a hearty breakfast too. The indoor pool and fitness center add another option for relaxation. There's

evening room service for those who wish to stay in. All this convenience is two blocks from the North Charleston Convention Center and Coliseum, yet downtown Charleston's many attractions are only a short drive away.

**Ramada Inn Coliseum/
Convention Center            $$
2934 West Montague, North Charleston
(843) 744-8281, (800) 272-6232
www.lodgingcharleston.com**
A slightly more affordable alternative to the Convention Center hotel choices is this familiar name-brand hotel just off I-26. The 154-room facility has an outdoor courtyard pool, room service, in-room voice mail, and video entertainment, plus some rooms have limited kitchen facilities and laundry service for long-term stays. The on-site restaurant is called the Porter House Grill, and a sports bar always has a game on the big screen TV. The Ramada offers complimentary airport transportation.

**Sheraton North Charleston     $$-$$$
4770 Goer Drive, North Charleston
(843) 747-1900, (888) 747-1900
www.sheraton.com**
This recently renovated, 296-room hotel is right off I-26 at Montague Avenue, five minutes from Charleston International Airport. Its refreshing indoor–outdoor pool and fitness center are a boon to the busy convention business. The Café is its on-site restaurant, and the nearby lounge is a favorite with guests and locals alike. Parking is free, and so is the hotel's shuttle to downtown destinations as well as to the airport.

# BED-AND-BREAKFASTS AND ATMOSPHERIC INNS

For many visitors, the quintessential Charleston experience is staying in one of the city's many fine bed-and-breakfast inns. Indeed, some would say Charleston has raised bed-and-breakfast hospitality to an art form.

The real draw of our bed-and-breakfast inns is that they allow you to temporarily assume native status with a prime Charleston address. For a fixed price, you enjoy elegant lodging, breakfast, and a string of extras ranging from cocktails to turndown service, which usually means that your host folds back your bed linens and leaves delicious chocolates and a nightcap at your bedside.

There is some confusion over what constitutes a bed-and-breakfast in the strictest sense, and much of the discussion centers on the size of the operation and the amount of contact with the host family. It's even possible to find a small bed-and-breakfast establishment where personal contact with the owner never happens at all. Some operate as entities in houses that are not private homes, and some are rental arrangements in the primary residences of homeowners. The former operate as freestanding business establishments, while the latter are businesses operating in the midst of family routine. Each type appeals to certain travelers and not to others. We offer separate listings in this chapter for the larger properties that offer similar amenities (following the bed-and-breakfast inns listings). We call them atmospheric inns.

Both small bed-and-breakfast establishments and larger atmospheric inns are becoming more popular with business travelers. The requirements for doing business on the road are relatively simple: fax access, a private phone line and e-mail, a little desk space, plus some peace and quiet usually fill the bill. If business entertaining is involved, you may want to clear that with your host to avoid any embarrassment.

Decide which type of accommodations you prefer, and call ahead for detailed information. While you have a contact person on the phone, ask a few questions to narrow your search. Make certain you understand what the host or hostess is offering. Ask if the guest quarters are in the owners' home, and if there will be interaction with the family. Ask if the accommodation has a private entrance. Does it have kitchen facilities? What about a private telephone line, local calls, and long distance charges? What about parking; is it on-site and convenient or offered at a discount from a nearby garage? Is security for valuables provided? Ask what constitutes breakfast, and clear any special dietary needs. Find out about the inn's proximity to sightseeing and public transportation. Is concierge service part of the package? Be sure to ask if there are any curfews and if guests are issued keys.

If handling luggage is an issue, mention it to your potential host. Most bed-and-breakfast inns don't have staff available for handling your baggage unless special arrangements are made. Discuss whether children or pets are welcome, and find out what time you check in and check out. These details may seem picky, but they can color the experience and make a real difference to your stay. It's always best to know these things ahead of time to avoid unpleasant surprises.

Because bed-and-breakfasts and atmospheric inns are frequently in historic homes with architectural barriers, wheelchair accessibility is rare. If that's a matter of concern, ask in advance. As for smoking, most of these properties are thumbs down, but there's usually a veranda, piazza, or nearby courtyard where you can light up.

When contacting these establishments, be sure to ask which forms of payment are accepted. Credit card policies vary, and some inns will take personal checks. We note in our listings those accommodations that do not accept credit cards, but if you want to rest more easily, it's worth a call to the property. When traveling with children, be sure to ask about roll-away beds and children's rates. Also, if there's a pet in your party, you will want to ask the inn personnel if pets are allowed.

If you would rather have someone else screen the possibilities, consider calling Historic Charleston Bed & Breakfast, (843) 722-6606 or (800) 743-3583 (www .historiccharlestonbedandbreakfast.com), a local business that has been matching guests with in-home accommodations since 1981. The reservation service books more than 50 different private homes and carriage houses within the historic district. With very few exceptions, these accommodations date from 1860 or earlier. Agents for Historic Charleston Bed & Breakfast know each property intimately. They know which ones are appropriate for children, and which are not; they know which ones are accessible to persons with disabilities and the elderly and which are not; and they can arrange for late arrivals and special transportation. Historic Charleston Bed & Breakfast also sends out excellent pre-arrival materials, including maps and shopping and dining recommendations.

Accommodations booked through Historic Charleston Bed & Breakfast can range from $95 to $295 for two adults in a one-bedroom setting; an average of $275 for a two-bedroom accommodation; and as high as $500 to $600 for luxury three-bedroom offerings during high season. Rates can be slightly higher for special events and peak weekends like Cooper River Bridge Run, Spoleto Festival USA, and New Year's. Off-season rates are, of course, lower. March

through July and October through December are usually considered peak season. Note that our pricing code does not reflect taxes, gratuities, and add-on services such as room service.

Sometimes finding the right guest house or bed-and-breakfast inn to suit your needs and desires can be the start of a long-term relationship. Many proprietors and hosts entertain the same guests year after year, and properties are sometimes booked months in advance.

When choosing a bed-and-breakfast or an atmospheric inn, realize prices vary based on season, location, amenities, and various other factors. Properties in the historic district obviously are the pricey option, but the payoff may be greater than you think. Being able to walk to major sites, stroll along the Battery, and sleep in an antique canopy bed make for a wonderfully traditional Charlestonian experience. It may warrant the price tag for many visitors.

Also note that an additional 4 percent accommodations tax is added to your bill for lodgings in smaller accommodations. At larger bed-and-breakfasts and guest houses (with six rooms or more), your total tax (including state sales tax) will be 12 percent.

## PRICE CODE

Although rates are subject to change, we use the following price code to indicate our listed properties' average rate per night, in season, for two adults.

| | |
|---|---|
| $ | **Less than $65** |
| $$ | **$65-95** |
| $$$ | **$96-150** |
| $$$$ | **$151-200** |
| $$$$$ | **More than $200** |

## BED-AND-BREAKFAST INNS

All properties listed, except for one Summerville and two Mt. Pleasant options, have Charleston addresses. They are arranged alphabetically.

**Ann Harper's Bed & Breakfast**    $$$
**56 Smith Street**
**(843) 723-3947**
Ann Harper's charming suite is in an 1870 Charleston single house that is near King Street shopping, the College of Charleston, and the Medical University of South Carolina. This air-conditioned, two-bedroom suite is furnished with antiques, wicker, reproductions, and cherished family heirlooms. Couples may rent the guest suite with a double bed, a separate sitting area with television, and a private bath with one of the deepest tubs you've ever seen. A party of three persons might find this same suite to be just what they need, with its additional bedroom with a single. Full breakfast is served. The menu varies, but often you'll find Ann's famous shrimp and grits. Off-street parking is provided. No credit cards.

**Ashley Inn Bed-&-Breakfast**    $$$$
**201 Ashley Avenue**
**(843) 723-1848, (800) 581-6658**
**www.charleston-sc-inns.com**
A real taste of Charleston, this home was built around 1832 and is a mansion even by today's standards—six bedrooms and a suite, with fireplaces throughout the house and a lovely garden. All rooms have private baths and are tastefully furnished with antique, four-poster pencil-post, or canopy rice beds. Breakfast is served on the piazza and features such gourmet delights as savory sausage soufflé or French toast with hazelnut-peach syrup. Afternoon tea and evening sherry are part of the hospitality. The inn has bicycles for guests to use and provides off-street parking. This may be the best option for guests wishing access to MUSC facilities. They are literally across the street.

**Barksdale House Inn**    $$-$$$
**27 George Street**
**(843) 577-4800, (888) 577-4980**
**www.barksdalehouse.com**
This bed-and-breakfast inn is in proximity to King Street shopping and the College of Charleston. In fact, the facility was once a fraternity house. No one would guess that fact today, as the Barksdale House Inn includes 14 beautifully appointed rooms, each one different from the others. All have cable TV and private telephones. Five rooms are equipped with fireplaces and whirlpool baths (oh, what the frat brothers would have given . . . ). Continental breakfast is served in your room or in the rear garden, and a nightly turndown service and sherry are included. Free parking is available.

**Battery Carriage**
**House Inn**    $$$$-$$$$$
**20 South Battery**
**(843) 727-3100, (800) 775-5575**
**www.batterycarriagehouse.com**
The Battery Carriage House (ca. 1843) is located right on the Battery, Charleston's very best address for a couple of hundred years. You couldn't be closer to the picturesque, historic park and beautiful views of Charleston Harbor. The 11 guest rooms to the rear and under the piazza are small, but completely charming—most with queen-size canopy beds and interesting furnishings. Three rooms are available with king-size beds. All rooms have cable TV with HBO, and you'll find individual controls for heating and air-conditioning. Some rooms have large steam showers; others have whirlpool tubs. Fluffy terry cloth robes and down pillows add to the pampering. Silver-service continental breakfast is served in the room or in the garden under the loggia, your choice. Happy hour wine is served in the lobby. The service here is very cordial, the ambience very European—a bit like an Italian pension. And there's usually plenty of parking just across the street.

**Bed, No Breakfast**    $$
**16 Halsey Street**
**(843) 723-4450**
Although this listing doesn't fit the bed-and-breakfast category in the strictest sense, it's a close relation. In fact, this is what the *New York Times* called "the no-frills option" in Charleston. You'll find two

large, light-filled, air-conditioned rooms with a private entrance but, sorry, no eggs and grits. Actually, coffee, tea, and a refrigerator are available in each room, which means you can easily prepare your own continental breakfast. Both rooms are nonsmoking, and there's a shared bath. Guests have their own TV and an in-room extension of the family phone line. There's a delightful courtyard, too, with a hammock that's ideal for an afternoon siesta. Guests appreciate the off-street parking and the fact that the College of Charleston and MUSC and the hospitals are within easy walking distance. No credit cards.

**Belvedere Bed & Breakfast**   **$$$-$$$$**
**40 Rutledge Avenue**
**(843) 722-0973, (800) 816-1664**
**www.belvedereinn.com**
The Belvedere gets its name from the handsome, Adam-style interior woodwork that was rescued from the 1785 Belvedere Plantation (torn down in the 1920s). Three rooms are offered in this handsome old mansion that faces Charleston's ornamental basin called Colonial Lake. Eclectically furnished with Oriental rugs, family heirlooms, and Charleston reproductions, you'll find a nice collection of antique Canton china along with several wonderful silver pieces throughout the public rooms. Guests all have keys to the front door and private keys to their rooms. Smoking is permitted on the balconies and porches. Local TV is available in each guest room, and a downstairs TV room offers premium cable channels and a VCR. Daily continental breakfast is provided, along with afternoon sherry and smashing views of the sunset over the lake. No credit cards.

**Bennett-Hayne House**   **$$$**
**113 Ashley Avenue**
**(843) 577-6056**
The Wades have worked wonders in restoring their beautiful historic home (built in 1799) one block south of Calhoun Street on the Peninsula. From the spectacular Adam woodwork throughout the house (in particular on the second floor)

to a lovely winding staircase, it's a tribute to 18th-century craftsmanship and 20th-century preservation efforts. One former drawing room is now used as a guest bedroom, and there are two more rooms on the third floor that offer interesting views of the city skyline and the Cooper and Ashley Rivers. Guest rooms are smoke-free, but smoking is allowed on the wide porch overlooking the garden, where guests enjoy an old-fashioned swing and tranquil surroundings. Breakfast at the Bennett-Hayne House is a major production, served in the formal dining room with all stops pulled out. Mrs. Wade does the cooking, and Mr. Wade serves as waiter and raconteur. Menus vary according to season and whim, but expect to find items like Belgian waffles with fresh strawberries or local creek shrimp with sausage and grits. Judging from guest evaluation cards, the Wades are serving up Charleston hospitality in tall order. No credit cards.

**Cannonboro Inn Bed & Breakfast**   **$$$$**
**184 Ashley Avenue**
**(843) 723-8572, (800) 235-8039**
**www.charleston-sc-inns.com**
This historic 1853 home has eight beautifully decorated rooms for guests—all of which offer antique four-poster or canopy beds. The all no-smoking rooms are done in a handsome palette of mauves and pinks that complement the original hardwood floors. The house is furnished with an assortment of period antiques, and all rooms have air conditioning and private baths. Guests have TV and private telephones too. Complimentary tea and sherry are served each afternoon along with an assortment of home-baked goods. Awake to the aroma of sizzling sausage and freshly baked biscuits. A full gourmet breakfast is served each morning on the columned piazza overlooking a Lowcountry garden and fountain. Off-street parking is provided, and complimentary touring bicycles—an especially nice option in this part of town—are available for guests.

### 1837 Bed & Breakfast and Tea Room $$$-$$$$
126 Wentworth Street
(843) 723-7166, (877) 723-1837
www.1837bb.com

Two artists have restored this historic (ca. 1837) house near the College of Charleston and King Street shopping. All nine rooms and the brick carriage house have air-conditioning and are beautifully decorated. Guests are treated to a sumptuous gourmet breakfast and have access to off-street parking. Afternoon tea for registered guests is complimentary. Rooms have private entrances and baths, refrigerators, and televisions. To quote the *New York Times,* it is "a perfect place to unwind."

### Fantasia Bed & Breakfast $$$-$$$$
11 George Street
(843) 853-0201, (800) 852-4466
www.fantasiabb.com

Here in this 1813 classic Charleston Single House (see the chapter on Architectural and Historic Preservation), you'll find a charming bed-and-breakfast in Charleston's tradition of hospitality. The main house's two bedroom suites are upstairs over a pair of first floor drawing rooms that give visitors the feel and flavor of Charleston life before the Civil War. The piazza with its lazy hammock overlooks a handsomely landscaped garden accented with fountains and a cobblestone drive. A carriage and kitchen house with another bedroom actually sleeps four with a pull-out couch. A full breakfast is served in the main house, and a continental breakfast is available for kitchen house guests. Wine and soft drinks await visitors after a busy day of shopping and touring the city's sites. Off-street parking is available, and short-term lease agreements are offered for the carriage and kitchen house facilities.

### Gateway House Inn $$$-$$$$
20 and 22 Burns Lane
(843) 722-3969, (800) 706-1802
www.gatewayhouseinn.com

Tucked away in the center of downtown Charleston on a tiny lane between King and Meeting Streets, this recently renovated bed-and-breakfast is convenient to several popular destinations. Shopping, restaurants, nightlife venues, and the College of Charleston are only steps away. Queen or twin beds are offered along with an expanded continental breakfast served in the dining room or courtyard, or delivered bedside.

### The Hayne House $$$$-$$$$$
30 King Street
(843) 577-2633
www.haynehouse.com

Situated just one block off the Battery, the Hayne House was built in 1755 by Gen. Arthur Hayne, a hero of the Revolutionary War. Innkeepers Brian and Jane McGreevy offer a total of six rooms and suites, each one with its own bath and interior theme. Furnished with heirloom antiques and artwork, the ambience of family and tradition is all-prevailing at Hayne House. Guests enjoy the family's private garden and piazza and spending time in the drawing room and library. Expect to find plenty of good books and music, but no TV. A huge Southern breakfast is served in the formal dining room every morning at the family table. Well-behaved children of all ages are welcome.

### King George IV Inn $$$-$$$$
32 George Street
(843) 723-9339, (888) 723-1667
www.kinggeorgeiv.com

At this four-story, Federal-style house with decorative fireplaces, wide-planked hardwood floors, and three porches, you're just off King Street with its many antiques shops and fashion boutiques. And Charleston's colorful City Market is only a five-minute walk away. This was originally the 1790s home of Charleston writer and early newspaper publisher Peter Freneau. Freneau was of Huguenot descent, and his brother Philip was called the "poet of the Revolution." All 10 rooms are furnished with antiques, TVs, and telephones, and have air-conditioning. Eight of the rooms have private baths. Each morning, a continental breakfast is served with pastries, cereals, coffee, and juices. There is off-street parking for guests.

## The Kitchen House $$$$$
### 126 Tradd Street
### (843) 577-6362
### www.cityofcharleston.com/kitchen.htm

This block of Tradd Street, with its 18th-century homes and gardens, is in the historic district. The Kitchen House (ca. 1732), which was the former home of the surgeon general of the Continental Army, offers guests complimentary full breakfast, sherry, and wine. Guests can use the private patio to enjoy an herb garden and fish pond. There are two charmingly restored rooms in the original kitchen house and both have cable TV and air conditioning. *Colonial Homes* and the *New York Times* raved about this one. Ask about the honeymoon packages if you're in that market.

## The Long Point Inn
## Bed and Breakfast $$$–$$$$
### 1199 Long Point Road, Mt. Pleasant
### (843) 849-1884
### www.charleston-longptinn.com

On an oak-draped, marshfront property next to historic Boone Hall Plantation in Mt. Pleasant, a large, rustic-looking log cabin has been lovingly renovated for Lowcountry visitors looking for a unique bed-and-breakfast experience. Each of the five guest bedrooms is individually decorated with an elegance that belies the informal exterior of the building. Inside, the rooms are furnished with a wide assortment of antiques and family heirlooms. Most guest rooms feature queen-size beds along with private baths. All rooms have cable TV and VCRs. A cozy fireplace dominates the common great-room, and a charming glassed-in porch is the setting for a full breakfast each morning. Vistas of the marsh can be enjoyed from the upstairs open-air porch, and the view from the shrimping dock is a special joy at sunset. Nestled among 300-year-old live oaks, the Long Point Inn offers an unforgettable stay.

*A memorable and unusual accommodation for your Charleston visit would be to book a stateroom on a yacht moored in Charleston Harbor. Spend your night "on the waters" off Mt. Pleasant near the Yorktown aboard Voyager at "C" Dock, Charleston Harbor Marina at Patriots Point. Contact the yacht at (803) 240-0997 for rates, availability, and reservations, or visit www.mv voyagerbb.com.*

## Lowndes Grove Plantation
## Bed-and-Breakfast $$$
### 266 Margaret Street
### (843) 723-8438
### www.lowndesgrove.com

Now listed on the National Register of Historic Places, Lowndes Grove (ca. 1786) is the only plantation on the Ashley River actually within today's city limits. The house and grounds, with spectacular views of the water, make a lush setting for wedding receptions and other festivities. There are six air-conditioned guest rooms with private baths and an air-conditioned guest cottage for families (babysitting is available). As elegant as the house is, the spacious grounds, pool, Jacuzzi, and river dock also make it a comfortable, almost rural setting. Continental-plus breakfast is served daily and includes at least one hot item—usually a Lowcountry favorite such as shrimp and grits. The house is especially convenient to The Citadel and Hampton Park, once the site of the 1901 West Indies Exhibition, a world's fair–like extravaganza that attracted dignitaries from all over the world. At the time, Lowndes Grove hosted former President Theodore Roosevelt.

## Old Village Post House $$$–$$$$
### 101 Pitt Street, Mt. Pleasant
### (843) 388-8935, (800) 549-7678
### www.oldvillageposthouse.com

There are six bedrooms in the newly renovated Post House, formerly the Guilds Inn (ca. 1888), each beautiful and typically

"Old Village." Every room has a private bath, and the on-site restaurant offers three gourmet meals a day. There's even a full-service pub, too. Rooms vary in size; there's an executive suite, and honeymooners can request the special bridal suite with Jacuzzi. Guests enjoy the charm of this quaint neighborhood, where evening walks are a popular pastime. (For more on the Old Village Post House restaurant, see the Restaurants chapter.)

### The Palmer Home
### Bed & Breakfast          $$$ and $$$$$
### 5 East Battery
### (843) 853-1574, (888) 723-1574
### www.palmerhomebb.com

This bed-and-breakfast is in one of the most high-profile mansions on the Battery. This huge pink Italianate single house (sometimes called the Pink Palace) offers spectacular views. From the piazza, guests can see across all of Charleston Harbor with Fort Sumter silhouetted on the horizon. There are four guest rooms on the third floor (there is an elevator) and a swimming pool in the garden for cool refreshment. There's also a more expensive carriage house (recently featured on a Travel Channel TV special) with two bedrooms that can accommodate up to eight adults. Continental breakfast is served in the rooms or on the piazza at your choosing. There's plenty of off-street parking, too.

### Phoebe Pember House       $$$-$$$$
### 26 Society Street
### (843) 722-4186
### www.phoebepemberhouse.com

This elegant, 200-year-old Federal-style home in Ansonborough was the birthplace of Civil War heroine Phoebe Pember. She was the wealthy daughter of a 19th-century Charleston businessman. As a nurse, she traveled to Confederate hospitals during the war and wrote about her experience in her memoirs, *A True Southern Lady's Story.* The interiors here are remarkably authentic yet very comfortable. The four guest rooms have fireplaces

and canopy beds. Business travelers like the fact that rooms have desks, telephones, and fax machines. There's cable TV to enjoy once the work is done, and a popular day spa is just around the corner. The carriage house, with its gardens, is available for business meetings as well as short-term or long-term rental. You're only blocks from the City Market (see the Shopping chapter) and all the nightlife offered there. Special events at Gaillard Auditorium are virtually across the street. The College of Charleston is close by as well. There is off-street parking, and a silver tray continental-plus breakfast (this usually entails fruit, a selection of breads, and coffee, tea, or juice), plus evening wine and cheese is included.

### Rutledge Victorian Guest House    $$$$
### 114 Rutledge Avenue
### (843) 722-7551, (888) 722-7553
### www.charlestonvictorian.com

This is the kind of guest house we can remember from the old days in Key West. The atmosphere is relaxed, the surroundings colorful and Bohemian. Take the exterior, for example: bright, painted Victorian, showcasing a large front porch filled with rocking chairs. Inside there are 11 rooms in all, some with hardwood floors, 12-foot ceilings, and fireplaces. Guests on business appreciate the private telephones and fax machine. There's afternoon sherry for guests as well as nightly turndown service with chocolates and brandy. A continental-plus breakfast is served daily, and the dining room always features some kind of fresh-baked pastries, cookies, and teas available anytime. This guest house is not recommended for children under age 12.

### Thirty-Six Meeting Street
### Bed & Breakfast             $$$-$$$$
### 36 Meeting Street
### (843) 722-1034
### www.36meetingstreet.com

This handsome (ca. 1740) home is only a little more than a block off the Battery and offers three guest rooms. Two are on the second floor and have queen beds and private baths. From there a spiral staircase leads to a third bedroom and bath. All rooms have queen-size beds and kitchenettes, and there's an inviting walled-in garden with tables and chairs for relaxing after a busy day. A continental breakfast is provided in the kitchenette—ready whenever guests rise and wish to partake. Off-street parking is available.

## The Thomas Lamboll House    $$$$
**19 King Street**
**(843) 723-3212, (888) 874-0793**
**www.lambollhouse.com**
Named in honor of colonial-era Judge Thomas Lamboll, this Charleston single house (ca. 1739) is now a private home with two lovely third-floor guest rooms offered to bed-and-breakfast guests. Each is elegantly furnished with reproduction and antique furniture, has central air-conditioning, a fireplace, cable TV, and a telephone. French doors lead onto the third-floor piazza with distant views of Charleston Harbor over the peninsula's treetops. Continental breakfast is offered in the formal dining room every morning. Children are welcome, and off-street parking is available.

## 21 East Battery
## Bed & Breakfast    $$$$$
**21 East Battery**
**(843) 577-8289**
**www.21eastbattery.com**
Within the urban compound of Charleston's historic 1825 Edmundston-Alston House (see House Museums in the Attractions chapter), is this charming bed-and-breakfast created in the property's former stables, carriage house, and slave quarters. The old hayloft is now the master bedroom overlooking a lovely garden. And where carriages were once stored are now a spacious living room and a dining room with hidden kitchen facilities—stocked for a gourmet breakfast. Additional rooms in the museum house's rear dependency can accommodate up to a total of 10 people. This high-end option located right on Charleston's famous High Battery is ideal for multiple couples celebrating a special event or traveling families.

## Two Meeting Street Inn    $$$$-$$$$$
**2 Meeting Street**
**(843) 723-7322**
**www.twomeetingstreet.com**
This elegant 1890 Victorian mansion is at the intersection of Meeting Street and South Battery facing White Point Gardens. Guests stay in one of nine air-conditioned rooms, each of which has a private bath. The rooms are all different, but each carries out the Victorian theme in every detail. Continental breakfast is served in the garden or the formal dining room depending on the weather. The fare ranges from bakery-fresh lemon-blueberry muffins to fresh local strawberries to whatever is in season served with yogurt sauce. Afternoon tea is included in the rate. Much of Two Meeting Street's charm comes from the lacy Queen Anne–style veranda stretching across the front of the inn. Its lazy ceiling fans and rocking chairs make the scene an inviting option for afternoon tea. No credit cards.

## Villa De La Fontaine
## Bed-and-Breakfast    $$$-$$$$
**138 Wentworth Street**
**(843) 577-7709**
The owners of this columned mansion (ca. 1838), with its spacious formal gardens, terrace, and fountain, offer four centrally air-conditioned rooms with canopy beds. Full breakfast served in the solarium is a special treat with homemade breads, jellies, and (depending on the day) Spanish omelets, eggs Benedict, and fresh waffles among the menu items. Two of Villa De La Fontaine's rooms have separate entrances. All rooms are furnished with exquisite museum-quality pieces, making the Villa quite a showplace. On-site parking is available. No credit cards.

## Zero Water Street    $$$-$$$$$
**31 East Battery**
**(843) 723-2841**
**www.zerowaterstreet.com**

Zero Water Street is actually a quiet, private entrance to 31 East Battery, one of Charleston's classic mansion houses built on the Battery in 1836. Water Street is in the very heart of the old city's historic district, and 31 East Battery directly overlooks Charleston Harbor and Fort Sumter. Your room (with its private bath) and the adjoining piazza will offer spectacular views. Two guest suites with 12-foot ceilings are available plus an additional guest room. All rooms have air-conditioning, private telephone, TV, and off-street parking. A continental breakfast is provided either in your room or in the lovely Victorian garden with its antique play house. Children over age 12 are welcome. A two-night minimum is required. No credit cards.

---

*When negotiating your way through Charleston streets, you may encounter several street names that Charlestonians choose to pronounce in their own inimitable fashion. Here's a quick translation: If somebody mentions "Le-GREE" Street, it's Legare Street. And when directed to Hasell Street, note it is called "Hazel."*

---

## ATMOSPHERIC INNS

Many inns in Charleston offer some of the same personalized touches that make the bed-and-breakfasts special, but on a larger scale. Most, but not all, operate in modernized facilities either renovated or built specifically for lodging. You can usually expect a great deal of charm along with complimentary continental breakfast, afternoon wine or sherry, and evening turndown service. What distinguishes one from another is location, authenticity of decor, trendy amenities, and management style. Prices per night vary with the seasons, and our price guides reflect the

same coding ranges and caveats used for the bed-and-breakfasts. Unless otherwise indicated, all addresses are in Charleston.

**Anchorage Inn**                    $$$-$$$$
**26 Vendue Range**
**(843) 723-8300, (800) 421-2952**
**www.anchoragencharleston.com**
Close to the Waterfront Park and some of Charleston's best restaurants, this fascinating luxury inn is one of the city's premier accommodations. While so much of Charleston revisits the 18th century, this inn replicates the ambience of a 17th-century English coachman inn. Every detail is delightfully conceived—period antiques and one-of-a-kind handcrafted reproductions, made specifically for the inn. Continental breakfast is served in the dining room. Afternoon wine and cheese is offered, and guests enjoy turndown service at night. There are two suites included in the inn's 19 rooms, and four rooms have Jacuzzi tubs. Ample parking is available in the city garage (at a rate of $10 for 24 hours) just to the rear of the inn.

**Andrew Pinckney Inn**              $$$-$$$$
**40 Pinckney Street**
**(843) 937-8800, (800) 505-8983**
**www.andrewpinckneyinn.com**
The Andrew Pinckney Inn is at the corner of Church and Pinckney Streets on the very edge of Charleston's historic Market. All of the Market's famous diversions— quaint shops, craft stalls, nightclubs, and fine restaurants—are nearby. Even the horse-drawn carriage tours are just a few steps away. The recently remodeled and expanded inn features a rooftop garden terrace for catching Lowcountry sunsets, and the attentive concierge service can arrange special golf and fitness packages on request. A continental breakfast is part of the package, and all rooms feature handsome antique-style furnishings. There's even a fully equipped conference room available for business or group travelers.

### Ansonborough Inn          $$$-$$$$
**21 Hasell Street**
**(843) 723-1655, (800) 522-2073**
**www.ansonboroughinn.com**

The award-winning Ansonborough Inn is at the end of Hasell Street off East Bay. Thirty-seven suites have been cleverly fashioned out of a turn-of-the-century warehouse. Heart-of-pine exposed beams (measuring 12 inches by 12 feet) and locally made red brick have been incorporated into the decor to give the inn a remarkably warm feeling, even with its magnificent 16- and 18-foot ceilings. The facility's three floors are wheelchair-accessible and laid out around an open central atrium. The suites are equipped with full kitchens, and some have lofts. There's an on-site English-style pub and rooftop bar. Guests receive complimentary afternoon wine and a 24-hour monitored parking lot is available. One favorite amenity is the continental breakfast with fresh-baked breads. Choose from banana, apple-raisin, and blueberry muffins delivered each morning from Saffron's, a popular bakery just down the street. The business traveler is treated to multiple dataports and on-site conference facilities.

### Elliott House Inn          $$$$
**78 Queen Street**
**(843) 723-1855, (800) 729-1855**
**www.elliotthouseinn.com**

Elliott House is next to the popular 82 Queen restaurant (see the Restaurants chapter) and across the street from the Mills House Hotel. This is life as it should be in the refined fast lane—breakfast served on silver service, afternoon champagne in the courtyard, and a heated Jacuzzi at night. Guests stay in one of 24 air-conditioned rooms, complete with Oriental rugs and period furniture. Since 82 Queen draws a big (but respectable) crowd to its bar, the action is just a few strides away for Elliott House guests. Complimentary bicycles are available for exploring the neighborhood, and parking is across the street in a city garage.

### 4 Unity Alley          $$$$
**4 Unity Alley**
**(843) 577-6660**
**www.unitybb.com**

Unity Alley is steeped in history; according to legend, George Washington quartered his horse here on his visit to Charleston back in 1791. Today, this quiet alley in the bustling French Quarter boasts a renovated warehouse beautifully transformed into a grand home with charming guest accommodations.

Furnished with antique and reproduction furniture, the building surrounds a restful atrium garden perfect for entertaining and dining. Opened in 1998, 4 Unity Alley offers three suites, each with a private bath. A full breakfast is served each morning, and rarest of all, there's indoor parking available for guests.

### French Quarter Inn          $$$$
**166 Church Street**
**(843) 722-1900, (866) 812-1900**
**www.fqicharleston.com**

Located in Charleston's original French Quarter district in the historic Market and Church Streets area, this independent offering opened in January 2002.

There are 50 rooms and suites elegantly appointed with an eclectic array of French pieces, Provençal beds, European-style bed dressings, and imported down comforters. Some of the rooms feature working fireplaces, whirlpool tubs, and balconies overlooking the festive Market area. Amenities include silver service breakfast in the room, afternoon wine and cheese, turndown service, and complimentary 24-hour coffee, tea, and snacks. Valet parking is part of the upscale service.

### Fulton Lane Inn          $$$$$
**202 King Street**
**(843) 720-2600, (800) 720-2688**
**www.charminginns.com**

This cozy inn is a nonsmoking facility nestled just off King Street in the heart of Charleston's fascinating antiques district. Built post–Civil War by Confederate blockade runner John Rugheimer, the inn is a fascinating taste of a time gone by. The 27 rooms are decorated in Southern plantation style, and some feature fireplaces, king-size canopy beds, luxury baths, and whirlpool tubs. Nightly turndown service and a continental breakfast delivered on silver service are part of the hospitality here. Public parking is available just outside the door. This inn is part of the Charming Inns of Charleston group.

*If you arrive in Charleston without reservations, help is available at the Charleston Visitor Reception and Transportation Center at 375 Meeting Street. Open daily from 8:30 A.M. to 5:30 P.M., the visitor center offers help finding rooms at inns, hotels, and motels in the Greater Charleston area. This is, in effect, a clearinghouse of last-minute accommodations and a real life-saver for those impromptu visitors to the city. Later in the business day, these rooms are often offered at discounted rates. The desk personnel cannot secure reservations for you via phone; you must be there in person. They can, however, make a room reservation using your credit card once you're there.*

**The Governor's House Inn   $$$$-$$$$$**
**117 Broad Street**
**(843) 720-2070, (800) 720-9812**
**www.governorshouse.com**
Built in 1760 by John Laurens, this is the oldest house in Charleston currently being used as a bed-and-breakfast. Edward Rutledge, the youngest signer of the Declaration of Independence and once governor of South Carolina (1798–1800), lived here. Today, the house boasts 12 elegantly appointed guest rooms. The Grand rooms feature 12-foot ceilings with fireplaces and private verandas. The Roofscape room provides lovely views over the area's historic architecture. The Kitchen House suite

has a separate living room, private porch, wet bar, and an original 1760 fireplace. A Southern continental breakfast is served, as are afternoon tea and evening sherry. The location is ideal from several standpoints. You're at the edge of the original Grand Modell city and today's prestigious Below Broad residential area, and you're within easy walking distance of King Street's shopping and antiques district. No credit cards.

**HarbourView Inn   $$$$**
**2 Vendue Range**
**(843) 853-8439, (888) 853-8439**
**www.harbourviewcharleston.com**
This is one of Charleston's newest luxury inns right in the heart of the downtown historic district. Its location, directly across from Waterfront Park, is one attraction. The 52 high-end, luxury rooms and suites close to the area's many fine restaurants, shops, galleries, and nightclubs are another. Opened in May of 1998, the inn, with its handsome nautical appointments throughout, offers nightly turndown service, elegant in-room continental breakfast, and afternoon refreshments in the atrium. Top-floor rooms have spectacular views over Charleston Harbor—hard to find on the Peninsula. Ask about their special rate packages for honeymooners.

**Indigo Inn   $$$$**
**1 Maiden Lane**
**(843) 577-5900, (800) 845-7639**
**www.indigoinn.com**
The Indigo Inn fronts on Meeting Street and is across from a bustling shopping and restaurant district not far from Charleston Place. The three-story inn has 40 rooms around a private courtyard and fountain, and it prides itself on impeccable service. The traditionally decorated rooms feature massive four-poster beds and evoke a plantation atmosphere. A hunt (continental-plus) breakfast and the morning paper are complimentary, as is the on-site parking, a blessing in the heart of the city. Well-behaved pets are welcomed at an additional charge.

## The Jasmine House     $$$$$
**64 Hasell Street**
**(843) 577-5900, (800) 845-7639**
**www.jasminehouseinn.com**

This classic Greek Revival (1843) mansion sits in the historic Ansonborough neighborhood, between the Market and Gaillard Auditorium. Six guest rooms are in the main house and feature 14-foot ceilings, Italian marble baths, and original architectural details. Four others in the carriage house open onto the private courtyard and Jacuzzi area and have charming brick floors and second-level piazzas. Guests enjoy a hot continental-plus breakfast and complimentary parking. Rooms in the main house are handsomely decorated in themes appropriate to the period of the house and Charleston's pre–Civil War heyday. Check-in is handled at the sister property, Indigo Inn, at the corner of Maiden Lane and Meeting Street.

## John Rutledge House Inn     $$$$$
**116 Broad Street**
**(843) 723-7999, (800) 476-9741**
**www.charminginns.com**

Built in 1763 by John Rutledge, a signer of the U.S. Constitution, the house at 116 Broad Street has been completely renovated and transformed (as part of a three-building complex) into a swank inn with 19 rooms in all. The house is a designated National Historic Landmark, and the National Trust for Historic Preservation named it among the top 32 Historic Hotels of America for good reason. George Washington himself had breakfast here and was one of many patriots, statesmen, and presidents who came to call on Mr. Rutledge. The main residence contains elaborate parquet floors, Italian marble mantels, and molded plaster ceilings. Rooms have been modernized to include private baths, refrigerators, televisions, and individual climate controls. Afternoon tea is served in the ballroom, and evening turndown service includes chocolates at bedside. Continental breakfast and a newspaper are delivered to guests each morning. A full breakfast is available for a small additional charge. This inn is part of the Charming Inns of Charleston group.

## Kings Courtyard Inn     $$$$-$$$$$
**198 King Street**
**(843) 723-7000, (800) 845-6119**
**www.charminginns.com**

The Kings Courtyard Inn has an interesting history in that the building has come full circle in its lifetime of nearly a century and a half. It began as an inn catering to 19th-century plantation owners and businessmen; then it was a private residence; after that, the downstairs housed some of Charleston's most fashionable shops; and now it once again serves guests with luxury accommodations. The Greek Revival–style inn is nestled among many fine antiques shops on King Street.

Rooms and suites are modernized with air-conditioning and private baths, and no two are exactly alike. Some offer canopy beds; others feature fireplaces, and many offer views of a lovely courtyard below. Wine or sherry is provided upon arrival. You may expect a continental breakfast and a newspaper delivered to you each morning, or you can have breakfast in the courtyards or the breakfast room. Guests may order from a menu if they like. One of our favorite details at the Kings Courtyard is the garden spa, used by guests year-round. Cocktails are available in the courtyard bar, and brandy is provided each evening on the first floor. This inn is part of the Charming Inns of Charleston group.

## Maison Du Pré     $$$$-$$$$$
**317 East Bay Street**
**(843) 723-8691, (800) 844-INNS**
**www.maisondupre.com**

There are 12 elegant, air-conditioned guest rooms plus three suites at Maison Du Pré (ca. 1804). Each has a private bath and is beautifully furnished with Oriental rugs and antiques appropriate for this charming compound of single houses in Charleston's fashionable Ansonborough section. In the spring and other temperate seasons, the garden patio—alive with flowers and the therapeutic splash of fountains—is a big draw.

In typical Charleston fashion, the piazza is a focal point for socializing with other guests and enjoying the garden views. The continental breakfast is complimentary as is the afternoon Lowcountry tea. Sometimes it's wine, cheese, fruits, and hors d'oeuvres with little tea in sight. Parking is $8.00 per day in a lot just across the street from the compound. This location is ideal for those attending Spoleto events at Gaillard Auditorium. Maison Du Pré has been featured in *Country Inns, Bed and Breakfast* magazine, and on cable TV's Travel Channel.

### Meeting Street Inn          $$$$-$$$$$
### 173 Meeting Street
### (843) 723-1882, (800) 842-8022
### www.meetingstreetinn.com

In the heart of the city on bustling Meeting Street, this is a convenient option for a Charleston inn experience. The front portion of the inn is 140 years old, while the back section is a recent addition. Four-poster rice beds in every room add to the 19th-century ambience of this elegant accommodation, convenient to many fine restaurants, antiques shops, and the colorful City Market area. Continental breakfast may be taken in your room or out in the courtyard. The courtyard's heated Jacuzzi is popular with guests any time of the day. Afternoons at the Meeting Street Inn include complimentary seasonal refreshments and bar service in the lobby. Evening turndown service means a freshened-up room and bath plus a delicious chocolate on your bedtime pillow.

### Middleton Inn          $$$$
### 4290 Ashley River Road
### (843) 556-0500, (800) 543-4774
### www.middletonplace.org/inn

In our estimation, Middleton Inn is the kind of place you really want to write home about. Situated on the grounds of one of the most beautiful and historic plantations in the South, Middleton Inn overlooks the Ashley River and the nation's oldest landscaped gardens and is just 14 miles from downtown Charleston. Guests have access to the nature trails, gardens, a swimming pool, and tennis courts. You'll also find croquet, canoeing, and an on-site cafe for continental breakfast. Middleton Place's famous restaurant is just a stroll away through the woods. The facility itself is of national award-winning design, contemporary and starkly modern in its simplicity. It has 55 rooms with charming fireplaces and European baths. (See the Attractions chapter for more about Middleton Place.)

### Planters Inn          $$$$-$$$$$
### 112 North Market Street
### (843) 722-2345, (800) 845-7082
### www.plantersinn.com

As charming and roomy as an antebellum Charleston home, this inn has a European flavor and an understated elegance that radiates quality. It came as no surprise to us some years back when Planters Inn captured *Lodging Hospitality* magazine's first-place award in the guest room category. From four-poster beds to mahogany armoires, authentic Charleston reproductions are showcased in spacious rooms with traditional high ceilings. The inn is in the colorful City Market area and is home to the popular Peninsula Grill (see the Restaurants chapter). Silver-service breakfast is delivered to your room, and an evening wine and hors d'oeuvres reception is a great way to meet other guests of the inn. Parking is available—a rarity for this busy location.

### Vendue Inn          $$$$-$$$$$
### 19 Vendue Range
### (843) 577-7970, (800) 845-7900
### www.vendueinn.com

Situated between East Bay Street and the famous "walk through" fountain of Waterfront Park is this upscale European-style inn with one of the best reputations going for fine service and attention to detail. There are 65 rooms and suites in all—each one carefully furnished with authentic antiques and 18th-century reproductions.

Junior and deluxe suites offer gas fire-places, marble baths, separate showers, and whirlpool tubs. Deluxe suites even go so far as to include separate living rooms, stocked wet bars, and fresh fruit baskets. A rooftop terrace and bar offer one of the best views in the city, and the Vendue's on-site restaurant, the Library, is one of Charleston's great dining adventures. (See the Restaurants chapter.) Guests start the day with a complimentary Southern breakfast buffet or enjoy a continental breakfast in their room. Business travelers will find two-line phones in every room, making computer hook-ups easy. Wine and cheese in the Garden Room is available every afternoon.

**Victoria House Inn**               **$$$$–$$$$$**
**208 King Street**
**(843) 720-2944, (800) 933-5464**
**www.charminginns.com**
The Victoria House Inn is a 16-room luxury inn created within an 1889 Victorian build-ing on King Street. Following the tradi-tional inn format of serving light spirits in the lobby, providing evening turndown, and offering continental breakfast, the Victoria is another addition to the corpo-rate family that includes Kings Courtyard Inn, Fulton Lane Inn, and the John Rut-ledge House Inn. Some rooms offer cozy gas fireplaces and relaxing whirlpool baths. Expect impeccable service and tasteful Victorian-style decor, but best of all is your handy access to the downtown antiques shops, restaurants, and watering holes.

**Wentworth Mansion**               **$$$$$**
**149 Wentworth Street**
**(843) 853-1886, (888) INN-1886**
**www.wentworthmansion.com**
This elegantly refurbished inn was built from 1885 to 1887 as one of Charleston's few great Victorian townhomes. Articu-lated in what is called the Second Empire style of architecture (after a French fash-ion popularized during the reign of Napoleon), it was originally the private estate of Francis Silas Rodgers. Rodgers

was a Charleston cotton merchant who made a fortune in phosphate after the Civil War. His mansion survives today as the city's most opulent ode to the long-lost Gilded Age of Innocence. Remarkably unchanged over the last century, the property has recently been converted into an inn of uncompromising luxury. It fea-tures 21 rooms and suites individually dec-orated and furnished with 19th-century antiques. All rooms have king-size beds and baths with oversize whirlpool tubs. Most have working gas fireplaces.

Guests enjoy the mansion's common rooms such as the Rodgers Library, the Harleston Lounge, and the atrium-like Sun Porch—where guests savor leisurely ele-gant breakfasts, afternoon teas, and evening wine and hors d'oeuvres. Local guides lead guests on tours of the city, and an on-site fine dining restaurant, Circa 1886, opened in the fall of 1999. (See the Restaurants chapter.) With its private spa making its debut in the fall of 2004, Went-worth Mansion brought a whole new level of service to Charleston's already renowned tradition of unparalleled hospi-tality.

**Woodlands Resort & Inn**               **$$$$$**
**125 Parsons Road, Summerville**
**(843) 875-2600, (800) 774-9999**
**www.woodlandsinn.com**
Although this upscale option is beyond the geographic boundaries of this listing, it is so extraordinary that it should not be overlooked. Woodlands Resort & Inn is a unique venue in the best tradition of the "English country house hotel." Only this one has a decidedly Southern flair. The 42-acre estate now called Woodlands was once the winter retreat (ca. 1906) of a wealthy Northern industrialist. But today it is a 19-room luxury inn and conference center with tennis facilities, a croquet lawn, heated pool, and upscale spa facility. Each room is handsomely appointed and stocked with thoughtful personal ameni-ties ranging from monogrammed robes of thick terry cloth to fresh-cut flowers and soothing glycerine soaps. The inn's on-site

spa offers special pamperings such as fibrotherapy massage, herbal wraps, and body masques.

Perhaps best of all is the Woodlands dining experience. Their chef has consistently earned rave reviews from local and international food critics alike. He calls his cuisine "contemporary regional American," but we call it unforgettable.

Summerville is 30 minutes from downtown Charleston via Interstate 26 (see the Day Trips chapter), and many Charlestonians plan mini-vacations to Woodlands just as their ancestors did a century ago when Summerville offered a pine-cooled retreat from Charleston's muggy humidity.

# VACATION AND BEACH RENTALS

Beach rentals, especially those on the barrier islands of Kiawah, Seabrook, Sullivan's Island, Isle of Palms (home of Wild Dunes Resort), and Folly Beach, are considered a real estate specialty here in the Lowcountry. Several companies deal exclusively in resort properties, while others target the less organized, more laid-back beach life on Sullivan's Island and Folly Beach.

Many of these beachfront accommodations are the second homes or would-be retirement homes for out-of-town owners. And it's fairly common to find the same real estate company that sold the property representing the owners in short-term lease arrangements to carefully screened area visitors.

Other companies, which deal in rental properties alone, offer vacation packages that make renting a beach house or ocean-side condo a one-stop, one-call proposition.

Every company will have its own rules for renters, but keep these tips in mind when you're planning (and packing for) a Lowcountry beach rental. You can generally count on the rental company (or owner) to provide sheets, towels, blankets, pillows, paper products, kitchen cleaners (including dishwasher detergent), laundry products, bath soaps, and all your basic housewares.

You, on the other hand, will need to bring your own beach chairs and recreational equipment. You buy your own groceries—including staples like salt, pepper, and other spices plus condiments like ketchup and mayonnaise. You may want to throw in some plastic wrap or foil for leftovers. Also, ask ahead about bike or Moped, crib, and high chair rentals, when appropriate. Don't forget your camera and plenty of film.

Many families make long-standing reservations with the same company and make return visits for several years. They soon establish trusting relationships with agents and property owners that work to everyone's advantage. Here are some of the best options for beach rentals here in the Lowcountry.

## Beachwalker Rentals
**The Island Center, 3690 Bohicket Road, Suite 4-D, Johns Island**
**(843) 768-1777, (800) 334-6308**
**www.beachwalker.com**
This independent resort-rental company specializes in Kiawah and Seabrook Island vacations. With more than two decades of experience, the company has built a solid reputation for value and friendly service. Many loyal families return to Beachwalker year after year, with these folks handling all the arrangements from bike rentals to golf. Call for the annual catalog of beachfront and nearby properties, and ask about the off-season discounts.

## Carroll Realty
**103 Palm Boulevard, Isle of Palms**
**(843) 886-9600, (800) 845-7718**
**www.carrollrealtyinc.com**
This firm, which started in 1981, specializes in the sale and rental of resort homes on Isle of Palms and Sullivan's Island. Its offices are between the islands on Palm Boulevard.

## Dunes Properties of Charleston
**1400 Palm Boulevard, Isle of Palms**
**(843) 886-5600**
**www.dunesproperties.com**
Specializing in coastal real estate and vacation rentals, Dunes Properties of Charleston has been doing business in the Lowcountry since 1989. Its staff of 17

agents handles rentals on Kiawah, Isle of Palms, Wild Dunes, Sullivan's Island, Dewees Island, Seabrook Island, and Folly Beach. About half this company's business comes from repeat customers who use its services year after year. Vacation planners can request Dunes Properties' annual catalog describing rental listings on the East Islands, West Islands, and Folly Beach. To ask about rental properties on Wild Dunes, call (888) 843-2322. For information about rental properties on Kiawah, call (800) 476-8444.

*Vacationers to Kiawah and Seabrook islands can take advantage of the seasonal fresh fruits and vegetables grown on Johns Island and sold by vendors in roadside stands along Bohicket Road. Rosebank Farms is the largest of these, and Newton Farms supermarket (at the southern end of Betsy Kerrison Parkway) offers the gourmet version.*

### Fred Holland Realty
**50 Center Street, Folly Beach**
**(843) 588-2325**
**www.fredhollandrealty.com**
Experience is the key word for Fred Holland Realty when it comes to Folly Beach real estate and rentals. He's been finding vacation homes for Folly visitors for more than 25 years. The company handles about 150 beach rentals every year ranging from two- and three-bedroom condos to oceanside beach houses and even small apartments. The agents also arrange about 100 long-term (yearly) leases annually. About 65 percent of their business is repeat customers coming back for more. Their spring brochure features the year's offerings for summer rentals. Call for more information.

### Great Beach Vacations
**1517 Palm Boulevard, Suite C,**
**Isle of Palms**
**(843) 886-9704, (800) 248-1125**

### Two Great Beach Center, Kiawah Island
**(843) 768-2300, (800) 246-4815**
**www.greatbeach.com**
This company offers rental homes, cottages, and villas on Wild Dunes, Isle of Palms, Sullivan's Island, Kiawah Island, and Seabrook Island. Accommodations range from one to nine bedrooms (depending on the island). Golf packages and kids' programs are available. They have a yearly catalogue of rental listings that's free upon request.

### Island Realty
**1304 Palm Boulevard, Isle of Palms**
**(843) 886-8144, (800) 905-6290**
**www.islandrealty.com**
Since 1977, this firm has been a major player in property sales and resort rentals on Isle of Palms (at Wild Dunes) and Sullivan's Island. Island Realty has 12 sales agents and 20 full-time employees in its resort-rental division. It also has a beachfront meeting and convention center with resort amenities available and golf packages at Wild Dunes.

### Islands West
**83 Center Street, Folly Beach**
**(843) 588-6699, (800) 951-2470**
**www.islandwestrealestate.com**
This company handles real estate in the West Ashley area and exclusively handles Folly Beach rentals. Its office is in the first two-story building you'll see on Center Street as you come off the bridge to the island. It offers a variety of accommodations ranging from the most rustic of basics to oceanfront luxury condominiums. The 10-year-old company is "big enough to serve you and small enough to know you." Write or call for its yearly brochure of Folly Beach properties.

**Pam Harrington Exclusives**
**The Island Center, 3690 Bohicket Road,**
**Suite 2-C, Johns Island**
**(843) 768-0273, (800) 845-6966**
**www.kiawahexclusives.com**
This company, with headquarters near Kiawah in the Island Center, has a lion's share of business on Kiawah Island. It's been helping visitors secure luxury accommodations and premium real estate on Kiawah, Seabrook, and Johns Island since 1978. For sales information, call (843) 768-3635.

# SHOPPING

For a city that's famous for all that's old and historic, Charleston offers shoppers today easier-than-ever access to all things that are new and exciting. From fashions to home furnishings, from bestsellers to sporting goods, the Lowcountry has it all. The older shopping haunts have been updated and expanded, plus whole new shopping destinations have sprung up in high-growth areas where the expanding population has called for them.

No matter how you look at it, the shopping opportunities here in the Lowcountry are almost unlimited. Communities that were geographically isolated only a dozen years ago are now within an easy commute to a diverse and interesting commercial/shopping adventure. The future looks bright, and more shoppers are drawn to the area every day.

The variety ranges in size from specialty shop enclaves in downtown nooks and crannies to major shopping centers and the seemingly endless random strip malls. To provide a useful index for your shopping needs, we've categorized these shopping adventures by location and merchandise.

We'll start with the major shopping areas of downtown Charleston. Some of these famous old streets have been shopping meccas for two hundred years. Other streets have only recently become decidedly commercial. Much of downtown's historic district houses a mix of shops and homes and every other aspect of daily life—with a certain deference made to keeping the historic fabric of the city intact.

Next, we'll survey the brightest and best shopping opportunities in the surrounding areas, as we've done with our chapters on accommodations, restaurants, nightlife, and neighborhoods. Within each geographic designation, however, we've categorized stores by the type of merchandise that's dominant there. Included are the most exclusive boutiques and the just-as-welcome discount stores catering to the dollar-conscious consumer. In each case, we've tried to identify businesses with items of particular interest for our visitors and those frequented by a local clientele. In general, we've omitted descriptions of the major chain retailers with which you are already familiar. Some of the best of these are the high-end shops featured in The Shops at Charleston Place.

Finally, we'll offer newcomers a brief rundown of the major shopping malls here in the Lowcountry. We hope our guide is a tempting sample of the variety and quality of shopping options in this area. We do encourage you, however, to venture off the beaten track from time to time—new and hidden surprises are everywhere!

## DOWNTOWN CHARLESTON

## King Street

Let's start with King Street, the mother of all Charleston shopping districts. This is the essence of downtown shopping, and it has been for a couple hundred years. While the street actually begins high on the Peninsula and ends as a narrow throughway past an extraordinary collection of pre-Revolutionary private homes, the real business and shopping district begins at about Mary Street and continues with greater intensity until it crosses Broad Street.

King Street is a busy two-way street until you reach Calhoun Street, where it becomes narrower and one-way heading south toward the Battery. Time was that King Street, like many of the other shopping thoroughfares in America's downtowns, was said to be dying. But the building of Charleston Place, a huge hotel and shopping complex, turned the tide. (Charleston Place was first an Omni hotel and later an Orient Express property; see the Hotels and Motels chapter.) It didn't hurt at all that Charleston Place contained a ground-floor shopping arcade featuring world-famous labels and merchandise. Today, all of King Street is alive and well and enjoying a latter-day renaissance (particularly above Calhoun Street) that's amazing to watch. Old storefronts and facades are being restored, and new construction seems always under way, from Calhoun to Mary Street and above. Apparently, there's no stopping in sight.

The area from Queen to Beaufain Streets is generally considered King Street's Antiques District (extensively covered in the Antiques chapter). Most other shopping adventures on King Street are found in the blocks between Beaufain and Calhoun. With the refurbishing of the Francis Marion Hotel at Calhoun and King, plus the complete renovation of Marion Square (park), the shopping options don't necessarily cease at Calhoun anymore.

You'll find several major chain stores along King Street. For fashions you can check out Abercrombie & Fitch, 260 King Street, (843) 853-5888; Ann Taylor, 267 King Street, (843) 722-8231; Banana Republic Men, 249 King Street, (843) 722-6681; Banana Republic Women, 245 King Street, (843) 958-8050; Gap, 269 King Street, (843) 577-2498; Express, 230 King Street, The Shops at Charleston Place, (843) 577-0379; Saks Fifth Avenue, 211 King Street, Majestic Square, (843) 853-9888; Talbots, 238 King Street, (843) 723-4802. You're also sure to recognize Victoria's Secret, 254 King Street, (843) 723-0332; The Body Shop, 216 King Street, (843) 723-3300; and Williams-Sonoma, 281 King Street, (843) 723-5373.

Listed below, by category of merchandise, are some of the more unique shops you'll find on or near King Street.

## BOOKSTORES

### Books, Herbs and Spices
### 63 Spring Street
### (843) 722-4747
This is primarily a health-food store, but for those willing to venture a bit further, there's a large section of books about foods, herbal remedies, and other health-oriented matters. While you're shopping, treat yourself to something tasty from the kitchen or the blender. There's also a refrigerator case that's always filled with fresh vegetarian sandwiches and exotic juices promising health benefits. Look for them near the corner of Spring and Coming Streets.

### Boomer's Books & Collectibles
### 420 King Street
### (843) 722-2666
This upper King Street bookshop buys, sells, and trades books. While popular reading material is the main thrust of the store, rare books, collectibles, Lowcountry memorabilia, and souvenirs are also for sale. Mind you, this store is a fooler. Its tiny storefront belies the seemingly endless series of rooms housing a vast selection of reading matter for every taste.

### College of Charleston Bookstore
### 160 Calhoun Street
### (843) 953-5518
### www.cofc.bkstr.com
The College of Charleston's bookstore, actually on Calhoun Street just off King, is typical of university bookstores. But it also carries a nice section representing local authors and local interest books as well as faculty publications. It's also fun to poke around in the college textbook sections just to see what's happening these days. Time flies.

### The Preservation Society of Charleston Bookstore
### 147 King Street
### (843) 723-4381
### www.preservationsociety.org
The Preservation Society of Charleston

Bookstore has what may be the most comprehensive area collection of books about Charleston, the Lowcountry, and all things Southern. Many Charleston and Lowcountry authors are represented here. You also can shop for art books, academic works, entertaining literature, and even some recorded material. (See the Architectural and Historic Preservation chapter, plus the Attractions chapter, for more on The Preservation Society of Charleston.)

**University Books of Charleston
360 King Street
(843) 853-8700
www.ubc-cofc.com**
This bookstore is not officially affiliated with the College of Charleston, but is a popular source for college students and a place to browse for interesting academic titles. Along with textbooks and reference materials, University Books sells school logo items—everything from T-shirts to bumper stickers for your favorite college team.

## CANDY

**Godiva Chocolatier, Inc.
The Shops at Charleston Place
142 Market Street
(843) 722-6045
www.godiva.com**
Tucked seductively inside Charleston Place's trendy shopping arcade, this is where you'll find those famous Godiva chocolates loved the world over by serious chocoholics. Go all out, and take home a whole box, or taste just the individual confections that catch your eye. Be prepared for the not-too-subtle aromatherapy when you walk in the door. It's very beguiling.

## CHILDREN'S CLOTHING

**Sarah Anne's Ltd.
279 King Street
(843) 722-8675**
In addition to wonderful toys and gifts, Sarah Anne's sells adorable children's clothes and accessories. You'll find Viva La

Fete, Bailey Boys, Simi, and Feltman Brothers among the lines in this upscale boutique. This is the exclusive outlet in downtown Charleston for Madame Alexander dolls and Steiff. Check out the hair accessories too. (Also see the Women's Clothing listing in the King Street section of this chapter.)

**Worthwhile
268 King Street
(843) 723-4418
www.shopworthwhile.com**
This boutique sells 100 percent cotton clothing for children and adults (See the Women's Clothing section under King Street in this chapter.) Shop here for earth-friendly, contemporary clothes that feel comfortable in the Charleston heat.

## FLOWERS

**Tiger Lily Florist
131 Spring Street
(843) 723-2808
www.tigerlilyflorist.com**
Oftentimes, visitors to the Lowcountry are especially impressed with the floral displays that grace private parties, special events, and hotel lobbies throughout the city. When asked who did the arrangement, the answer is frequently, "Tiger Lily." This creative and popular florist is located at the corner of Spring Street and Ashley Avenue (a short drive from upper King Street). They're in what was once an art deco-styled auto dealership from the 1930s. The creativity they brought to rehabbing this distinctive building can be found in their floral arrangements, which range from the most elaborate affair to the single rose on the pillow of a honeymoon bed. One nice touch to Tiger Lily's marketing is their Web site, which shows shoppers an array of creative displays recently produced by their designers. Shoppers can choose or modify their orders from a visual starting point, which is very helpful. They also carry accessories and furnishings for outdoor gardens and patios where flowers and design are the main focus.

## GARDEN ACCENTS

**Charleston Gardens Catalog Outlet**
**650 King Street**
**(843) 723-0252, (800) 469-0118**
**www.charlestongardens.com**
This popular outlet offers discounted home and garden furnishings. Here, you'll find English garden furniture, statuary, fountains, hand-thrown pottery, hand-crafted ironwork, garden books and tools, topiary, paintings, and prints. Some items are slightly damaged or distressed. Charleston Gardens always has a great gift idea for that hard-to-shop-for friend with a green thumb. Open Monday through Saturday from 9:00 A.M. to 5:00 P.M.

## GIFTS

**Brittain's of Charleston**
**180 King Street**
**(843) 723-7309**
**www.brittains.com**
When it's time to shop for a wedding or anniversary gift, this should be your first stop. Brittain's deserves a gold star for its complete selection of crystal and fine china. It carries Baccarat, Orrefors, Lalique, and Tiffany as well as a wonderful collection of accent pieces and decorating accessories. This is where many Charleston brides register their china and sterling patterns.

**The Preservation Society of Charleston Bookstore**
**147 King Street**
**(843) 722-4630**
**www.preservationsociety.org**
Along with all that's printed on Charleston and the Lowcountry, this terrific store offers local crafts, art prints, even recordings of Lowcountry lore told in the local Gullah dialect. Here, too, are the architectural drawings of Jim Polzois, whose studies of the city's architectural vernacular are beautifully done. They're simply the best available. (See previous listing under Bookstores.)

## HOME ACCENTS AND DECOR

**Aubergine Home Collection**
**511 King Street**
**(843) 722-3838**
**www.auberginehome.com**
One of the most exciting aspects to the renaissance of Upper King Street is the proliferation of shops and outlets catering to the home decor enthusiast. In fact, Upper King is getting to be *the* address for the hottest decorators and suppliers of home furnishings and design services in Charleston. Adding to the growing selection of home furnishing options here is Aubergine Home Collection, a factory outlet specializing in bed linens, pillows, fabrics by the yard, and even distinctive bathroom shower curtains. The choices range from traditional to contemporary—all offered at a discount of 50 to 70 percent off retail. They carry samples, discontinued lines, and trade-show display items, all of which give shoppers a nice pricing advantage. They encourage shoppers to bring paint chips, fabric swatches, and carpet samples to mix and match colors for the best designer look.

**Fred**
**237 King Street**
**(843) 723-5699**
**www.fredstore.com**
This smart, trendy resource for kitchen basics, high-tech housewares, and contemporary nifties is so chic you'll think you stepped into the culinary fantasy of a Danish designer. The emphasis here is on line and function, and almost everything you see is stark white. What a concept! What a neat store! But who the heck is Fred?

**Le Creuset**
**241 King Street**
**(843) 723-4191**
**www.lecreuset.com**
Most folks don't know that the famous French enameled cast-iron cookware known as Le Creuset has a manufacturing plant right here in the Lowcountry. It's in

Yemassee, South Carolina, about an hour's drive from Charleston, and the good news is the factory outlet on King Street. The ordinarily pricey cookware is considerably discounted here—a boon to gourmets who happen across this downtown store. You're likely to pick up some wine and champagne accessories, too, along with some nifty cooking gadgets.

### Maine Cottage
### 525 King Street
### (843) 722-7188
### www.mainecottage.com

Maine Cottage is one of the newcomers to upper King Street, which is blossoming anew as one of Charleston's hippest shopping venues. This shop features the hot new trend for painted furniture for use as a vibrant accent for the contemporary apartment or home. Whether you're looking for a large piece or something zany and small, this is a must-see for young homemakers or the young-at-heart with a zest for color in their domestic decor.

### Raymond Clark
### 307 King Street
### (843) 723-7555
### www.raymondclarkgallery.com

Located between George and Liberty Streets on King, Raymond Clark offers affordable but original American crafts. From interesting, one-of-a-kind gifts to handmade jewelry and very arty home accessories, the look is contemporary and distinctive. Half store, half gallery, this is really fun to see.

### Yves Delorme
### The Shops at Charleston Place
### 246 King Street
### (843) 853-4331
### www.yvesdelorme.com

This is the store for fine French linens—everything for the bed, bath, and table. All the merchandise is natural fiber—either linen or Egyptian cotton. Palais Royal also carries goose-down duvets and pillows that veritably evoke pastel mornings on the Left Bank. To complete the scene, the shop carries a variety of hand-painted porcelain and other table graces. If you love Paris, there's a little bit of it here.

## JEWELRY

### Croghan's Jewel Box
### 308 King Street
### (843) 723-3594
### www.croghansjewelbox.com

This is a shop that some will remember as a tiny space unobtrusively tucked away behind a small awning on King Street but filled with quality merchandise. It's tiny no more. After more than 80 years as a Charleston shopping institution, this family-owned jewelry store finally has the space to show its worth. Now, expanded into the space next door, Croghan's carries exquisite jewelry and wonderful gifts for all the important occasions. The rings are to die for, and there seems to be no end to the trays of earrings, shelves of silver and crystal, and other delights. A Croghan's package delivered to your door or under the tree—sometimes the smaller the better—is cause for real excitement. (See the Antiques chapter.)

### Dazzles
### 202 King Street
### (843) 722-5997

### 86 Queen Street
### (843) 722-5950

### The Shops at Charleston Place
### 226 King Street
### (843) 722-5951, (800) 722-5951
### www.dazzlesjewelry.com

This family of jewelry stores is best known for its 14-karat-gold slide bracelets that have the look, style, and feel of an heirloom. Dazzles has a large selection to choose from, or you may design one of your very own. Gold slide bracelets can be set with diamonds and precious stones in various shapes and motifs. Dazzles also has a large selection of gold enhancers for Omega necklaces too.

**Joint Venture Estate Jewelers**
**185 King Street**
**(843) 722-6730**
**www.jventure.com**
Joint Venture is unusual in that it focuses on jewelry on consignment. The inventory at any time can include heirloom and contemporary jewelry as well as watches, and the staff is happy to appraise, restore, or repair your possessions. (See the Antiques chapter.)

**Norma May International**
**315 King Street**
**(843) 577-8884**
This high-end resource for truly distinctive fashion art and accessories offers an international collection of one-of-a-kind and limited edition jewelry. Also, check out their selection of beautiful silk shawls, scarves, and wraps. This is clearly one for the bold and the beautiful and those who dare to wear the different.

## MEN'S CLOTHING

**A. J. Davis & Company**
**296 King Street**
**(843) 577-3088**
**www.ajdavis.net**
This store joined the King Street cadre of men's clothiers several years ago and has been a pacesetter ever since. The accent here is on quality and service—the store even delivers to downtown hotels. Look for designer names such as Barry Bricken, Zegna, Ike Behar, Zanella, Kenneth Cole, Joseph Abboud, and Corneliani. You'll find everything from formal wear to sportswear and accessories, to boot. A recent addition, a ladies' boutique, A. J. Davis for Her, carries such designers as Bernard Zins, Margaret O'Leary, and Barry Bricken.

**Ben Silver Collection**
**149 and 154 King Street**
**(843) 577-4556, (800) 221-4671**
**www.bensilver.com**
Here is a must-see, whether you're shopping for men's or women's clothing. Ben Silver maintains shops only in Charleston and London, so here's your one chance on this side of the Atlantic. Along with ultra-fine British and American clothes and furnishings, you'll also discover exclusive blazer buttons for virtually every college or university in the United States and abroad. In fact, Ben Silver carries button sets for more than 600 fraternal organizations and military schools as well. It's a classy place for a nifty gift idea.

**Berlin's Clothiers**
**114 King Street**
**(843) 722-1665**
**www.berlinsclothing.com**
Since 1883, Berlin's has been a Charleston institution. Four generations of young Charleston gentlemen have purchased their first good suit from Berlin's. You can find all the classics here, from wing-tip shoes to navy blazers, knit shirts to madras shorts. Look for European designer names, too, among the classics, such as Brioni, Canali, Hickey-Freeman, Hart Schaffner & Marx, and more. Berlin's offers custom sizing, a complete formal-wear department, and a big-and-tall section. Patrons love the convenient parking across the street for their own shopping or shopping for something nice for the lady in their life from Berlin's for Women next door. (See listing under Women's Clothing.)

**Grady Ervin & Co.**
**313 King Street**
**(843) 722-1776**
The sign says, "Classic Clothiers to Gentlemen," and that pretty much sums it up for this shop. This smart store is among King Street's collection of fine men's shops, and it's a real contender. You'll find a complete selection of traditional blazers, yachting wear, sports clothes, and accessories. Expect quality, style, and gracious Old World service.

**M. Dumas & Sons**
**294 King Street**
**(843) 723-8603**
**www.lowcountry.com/dumas**

Charleston men and boys have been buying their outdoor sports clothes at M. Dumas since 1919. This store is all about practicality mixed with style and boasts one of the most complete inventories—hunting jackets, camouflage hats, flannel shirts, corduroy pants, shoes, and even snakeskin boots—in town. Dumas was doing the "hunting look" before doing the hunting look was cool.

### Margaritaville
**282 King Street**
**(843) 577-4145**
**www.margaritaville.com**
"Parrot Heads" will recognize the name instantly. This new store is Jimmy Buffett's own 2,000-square-foot retail outlet on Charleston's King Street, selling men's and women's super-casual clothing, Buffett's compact discs, and assorted Jimmy Buffett memorabilia. JB loves Charleston, and this is one of 10 retail stores—some of the others being in Key West, New Orleans, Orlando, and Jamaica. Here is a haven for chilled-out college kids and good fun for the laid-back crowd.

### 319 Men
**316 King Street**
**(843) 577-8807**
Part of the King Street men's clothing scene for 17 years now, this shop is a favorite among discriminating shoppers whose tastes edge toward Italian designs. The owners of 319 Men claim to carry the most recognizable designer labels in town, and they probably do. You can always count on personalized service and a pleasant shopping experience.

## NATURAL BEAUTY

### Spa Adagio
**387 King Street**
**(843) 577-2444**
**www.spaadagio.com**
This is one of those places you can go for those special pamperings that bring back harmony to your life. The Spa Adagio therapists know just the song your sore

muscles need to hear (through massage). Their soft aromas sing to your senses, and their relaxing sounds soothe your soul. You'll find Spa Adagio in the lower level of the Francis Marion Hotel.

### Stella Nova
**292 King Street**
**(843) 722-9797**

**78 Society Street**
**(843) 723-0909**

**2048 Sam Rittenberg Boulevard**
**(843) 766-6233**

**1320 Theatre Drive, Towne Centre,**
**Mt. Pleasant**
**(843) 884-3838**
**www.stella-nova.com**
Stella Nova sells Aveda pure plant products and services for the hair, skin, and body. Check out the natural solutions to stress, ranging from aromatherapy to basic, old-fashioned pampering. Ask about the Micro Nova Botanical Salon at 84 1/2 Society Street, (843) 577-2500, with Stella Nova's natural hair-color process and skin-care programs. Call (843) 723-0909 for day spa appointments.

## SHOES

### Bob Ellis
**332 King Street**
**(843) 722-2515, (843) 722-2605,**
**(843) 723-5204, (800) 253-8628**
**www.bobellisshoes.com**
Experience the shoe-store phenomenon that is Bob Ellis. People from all over the country make the pilgrimage to Charleston to do just that. Suffice it to say that the downtown tradition's three telephone lines into the women's section say something about the store's popularity. High fashion, a huge selection, and friendly, highly qualified sales folk create the magic. They carry women's sizes 3 1/2 to 12 AAAA, AAA, AA, and B. In men's, they carry sizes 6 to 16 and widths from A to EEE. If you love shoes (and fine matching bags), don't miss Bob Ellis.

## Mephisto
**324 King Street**
**(843) 722-4666**
**www.mephistousa.com**

Sometimes the challenge of walking around downtown Charleston is just too much for the feet. Footsore tourists are always happy to encounter the Mephisto logo displayed outside the shop at 324 King Street. Mephisto is famous for making the world's most comfortable walking shoe, and this store carries the Southeast's largest collection of their styles. Devoted fans call these shoes "health food for the feet." And many visitors to Charleston have decided to go on a Mephisto diet for the duration of their stay. Best of all, they're open seven days a week.

## Pete Banis Shoes
**297 King Street**
**(843) 577-0950**

This is a great shoe shop for the young and trendy at heart. It carries women's shoes by names such as Van Eli, Franco Sarto, Steve Madden, and BCBGirls. Expect to find style, selection, service, and smart shoes with a little sass.

## Rangoni of Florence Shoes
**270 King Street**
**(843) 577-9554**
**www.rangonishoes.com**

Many think the level of personal service here is simply the best in town. Rangoni's fine collection of Italian-designed shoes for men and women is superb in both quality and style. For women, the store carries (even in hard-to-find sizes) the elegant Rangoni shoes, along with the more fashion-forward Anne Klein, Claudia Ciuti, and Clark. Also, look for Donald J. Pliner, Andre Assous, and others. For just the right accessory to complement those stylish new shoes, choose from one of the largest selections of handbags in town. Men's lines of footwear include Cole-Haan, Bally, Moreschi, Donald J. Pliner, Clark, and Johnston & Murphy, among others.

## Susan Michelle Shoes and Accessories
**338 King Street**
**(843) 722-4612**

**Building 644-I Long Point Road,**
**Belle Hall Shopping Center, Mt. Pleasant**
**(843) 971-7625**
**www.susanmichelleshoes.com**

The idea of Charleston having a shoe store that attracts customers from all over America is not a new concept. Finding such a store where the prices are conquerable and the styles super trendy and chic may be the big news here. Shoppers are hotfooting it to this newcomer to King Street, where they can find Italian lines like Prevata, Gama Studio, Aquatalia, and Pazzo. Comfortable lines like Berne Mev and Uffizi join the ranks with Tsonga from South Africa. Handbags by Matt and Nat, Cynthia Rowley, and Monsac complete this stylish scene for happy shoe shoppers.

# SPORTS

## The Extra Mile
**336 King Street**
**(843) 853-9987**
**www.theextramileinc.com**

This is a service-oriented, specialty sports shop with products preferred by competitive runners and swimmers. It sells Nike, New Balance, Asics, Saucony, Zoot, Sugoi, and other name brands.

## Half Moon Outfitters
**280 King Street**
**(843) 853-0990**

**861 Coleman Boulevard, Mt. Pleasant**
**(843) 881-9472**
**www.halfmoonoutfitters.com**

When friends were gearing up to travel through South America one Christmas season, where did they head first? That's right—Half Moon. They were after brands such as Patagonia, Simple Shoe, and Birkenstock. Half Moon carries other lines in its wide assortment of supplies for outdoor sports and adventure-seeking activity.

**Sportsman Shop**
**359 King Street**
**(843) 722-0072**

**Wando Crossing Shopping Center,**
**Mt. Pleasant**
**(843) 884-6640**

Shop here for sporting equipment of all types, plus clothing and accessories. For years, the simply named Sportsman Shop has served the needs of area school teams as well as the serious and weekend athletes of Charleston.

## WOMEN'S CLOTHING

**Anne's**
**312 King Street**
**(843) 577-3262**

Anne's has developed a loyal following among petites in the community because of the wonderful selection, all the way down to size three. There are happy customers in all the other sizes as well, because Anne's carries name-brand merchandise and gives personalized service. Many a bride has dressed herself and her wedding party in beautiful gowns from Anne's. Shop here for contemporary clothing appropriate for business and casual occasions as well as evening attire.

*Along King Street at about Wentworth Street, you'll note a section of roadway paved in bricks bearing the names of individuals and businesses. In the early 1980s, the construction of Charleston Place required a complete rebuilding of the immediate area's infrastructure. City leaders initiated a fund-raising campaign to cosmetically revitalize the area, and the bricks of the street commemorate those who donated to the cause.*

**Berlin's for Women**
**114 King Street**
**(843) 723-5591**
**www.berlinsclothing.com**

At the corner of King and Broad is family-owned Berlin's, one of Charleston's oldest and nicest clothing stores. Established in 1883, Berlin's built a reputation as a fashion landmark specializing in sportswear, lifestyle, and special occasion dressing. It carries one of the largest selections of evening and special occasion dresses in the Southeast and attracts customers from all over. Some of its designer lines include Nicole Miller, Tahari, Wolford, and Zelda. A beautifully renovated store, excellent service, and free parking across the street make it a pleasure to shop here. A spin-off of this store in I'On Square called "ellen b" caters to the Mt. Pleasant crowd. (See the Neighborhoods chapter for more on I'On.)

**Bits of Lace**
**302 King Street**
**(843) 577-0999**
**www.bitsoflace.com**

For sexy, pretty lingerie, visit Bits of Lace. Please note: These are undergarments that should be treated with care. In fact, many are silk and should be washed only by hand. Most items are simple, top-of-the-line articles of clothing that definitely give the impression that someone cares.

**Christian Michi**
**220 King Street**
**(843) 723-0575**

At the corner of King and Market Streets, across from Saks Fifth Avenue, Christian Michi offers collections for women by fashion designers such as Etro, Piazza Sempione, Strennesse, and Alberta Ferretti. The shop also sells Kiehl's cosmetics and toiletries plus assorted home furnishings like imported crystal, and Diptyque candles. Check out their handmade 22-karat gold jewelry.

**Ellington**
**82 Society Street**
**(843) 722-7999**

Classic style with a new arrangement is Ellington's claim to fame. Located just off King Street, the retailers say they are to clothing and furniture what jazz is to music. Some of the chic lines of women's clothing they offer include Barry Bricken, Margaret O'Leary, and Zanella. Accents and accessories include Joan & David belts and purses. Things for the home include lamps (new and old), bedding, and some American and European antiques (from couches to accent tables). Look for names like Pacifica and (Italian) Dialogica. Ellington ships anywhere.

## The Finicky Filly
**303 King Street**
**(843) 534-0203**
**www.finickyfilly.com**
The shop of exquisite women's fashions is a delight for the discerning shopper on King Street. In addition to their private-label jackets and accessories, look here for Italian fashions and leathers, Parisian couture, hand-loomed fabrics, and cashmere items. Their hand-embellished silks are the inspiration for many a formal ensemble worn here and in other fashionable places. Some of the names you'll find here include Louis Féraud, Bernard Zins, and Rena Lange. The in-store fashion consultant is available for private appointments.

## Granny's Goodies Vintage Clothing
**301 King Street**
**(843) 577-6200**
**www.grannysgoodies.net**
This is a decidedly acquired taste, but for those who love the avant-garde, Granny's Goodies is a gold mine. Everything from old designer labels to castoffs from estate sales—the goods are there for the getting. It's not unheard of to choose an ensemble from Granny's, hit the club or the art gallery openings, and make a fashion splash. Movie makers and costumers love this place. And the prices are right.

## Luna
**334 King Street**
**(843) 853-5862**
**www.shopluna.com**
Like its sister store in Columbia, South Carolina, this King Street shop features clothing, jewelry, accessories, shoes, can-

dles, Mexican pottery, and home furnishings. Eclectic style, lots of color, and sheer exuberance are the keynotes here.

## Moo Roo
**316 King Street**
**(843) 724-1081**
**www.mooroo.com**
This is the dream of handbag designer Mary Norton that spread like wildfire from her own kitchen table manufacturing plant to the red carpets of Hollywood and the fashion runways of New York and Paris. Charleston shoppers compete with the likes of major stars like Halle Berry, Ashley Judd, and Meryl Streep for Ms. Norton's one-of-a-kind designs. They're made with simple satins and applied silk flowers and exotic beads from distant lands. These handbags are not for the faint of heart when it comes to cost. But this is another example of Charleston's emergence on the fashion fast track of the world at large.

## Nancy's
**342 King Street**
**(843) 722-1272**
Nancy's is another interesting, upscale boutique on King Street that's a must-see for ladies with a strong sense of style. Look here for such designer labels as Parameter, Sheri Bodell, Jill Stuart, View Collection, and Essendi. Of special note are the one-of-a-kind metal bracelets imported from Europe exclusively for Nancy's. Belts of leather, chain, and even rhinestones are among the accents found here. The look is chic but timeless—appropriate for the young and the merely young at heart.

## The Oops Co.
**326 King Street**
**(843) 722-7768**

**696 Coleman Boulevard, Mt. Pleasant**
**(843) 881-6935**

**975 Savannah Highway, St. Andrews Shopping Center**
**(843) 556-3222**
**www.theoopsco.com**
The shop is every catalog shopper's

dream come true. They exclusively feature the clothing overruns and irregulars from your favorite name-brand mail-order catalogs. The prices here are about half the regular fare when you order from the book, and the merchandise is plentiful for folks of all ages and sizes. They also carry a nice collection of South Carolina logo items like polos, T-shirts, caps, belts, key bobs, and pet accessories. They may be the "find" of your whole shopping day.

### Putumayo
**445 King Street**
**(843) 958-0900**
**www.putumayoclothing.com**
Formerly of New York City, this company moved lock, stock, and barrel to Charleston in 1997 and opened its retail outlet on Charleston's King Street. The shop sells fashions collected from exotic markets all over the world. Its contemporary, well-priced women's apparel consists of exclusive prints, embroideries, and tapestries that are comfortable and casual yet unusual and bold. This shop appeals to women from ages 18 to 60.

### RTW
**186 King Street**
**(843) 577-9748**
**www.rtwcharleston.com**
For interesting clothes that are always on the cutting edge of fashion, visit RTW. Look for designers such as Sylvia Heisel, Peter Cohen, and Loree Rodkin Jewelry, and others who present trunk shows here with some frequency. RTW is diagonally across King Street from George C. Birlant & Company. (See the Antiques chapter.)

### Sarah Anne's Ltd.
**279 King Street**
**(843) 722-8675**
Sarah Anne's sells novelty sweaters, tops, and jackets for women by designers such as Michael Simon, Marisa Christina, Christine Rotelli, Robert Scott, David Brooks, Susan Bristol, and Geiger of Austria. In addition to good-looking, fun clothes, Sarah Anne's offers entertainment for

impatient youngsters with toys and live animals on the prowl or in the pen, depending on the need for confinement. (See the previous listing under Children's Clothing.)

### Worthwhile
**268 King Street**
**(843) 723-4418**
**www.shopworthwhile.com**
Selling unique casual and contemporary clothing made from only natural fibers, Worthwhile is, well, a worthwhile boutique on Charleston's trendy King Street. Look for brand names such as FLAX, Kishori, and Krista Larson, and shoes by Giraudon. (See the previous Children's Clothing listing in the King Street section of this chapter.)

## Meeting Street and the City Market

The cross street that, along with Broad Street, defines the "Four Corners of Law" is Meeting Street, another wide avenue of history, prosperity, and faith. Here, after all, is the location of the original church that gave the street its name (see the Historic Churches section of the Attractions chapter). Meeting Street runs virtually the length of the Peninsula and ends at White Point Gardens.

Meeting Street boasts many of Charleston's most famous and historic homes, but above Broad Street, the scenery changes from residential to commercial. Here, again, the options run the gamut from banks to museums to office buildings, hotels, and churches. But you should get to know a gem or two along the way that offer valuable information along with quality merchandise.

Meeting Street takes you smack-dab into the historic Market, one of the most colorful and popular tourist destinations in the city. The Market's shopping area is flanked by busy, one-way streets (called North and South Market Streets) and East Bay Street.

The Market may be one of the oldest "shopping malls" in the United States. It was built on land that Charles Cotesworth Pinckney, who was a signer of the U.S. Constitution, ceded to the city in the 18th century for use as a public market. Made up of low brick buildings that have survived hurricanes, earthquakes, tornadoes, fires, and even Civil War bombardment, these sheds also were used by vendors selling fish, meat, and vegetables in bygone days.

The figurehead building that gives a dignified front to all the Market's craziness is the 1841 Market Hall, designed by Charleston's famous 19th-century architect, E. B. White.

This faithful copy of a Roman temple, sitting where Market Street intersects Meeting, is now owned by the city and has recently undergone extensive renovation. But the building is better known to locals as the Confederate Museum, run by the Daughters of the Confederacy. To visitors, it's a prelude to the cornucopia of color and noise, food, and fun the legendary Market has in store.

Originally built as a municipal shelter for merchants and farmers bringing their wares and produce into the city for sale, the spirit of the Market survives today. Everything from odd pieces of sterling silver flatware for the table to handmade children's toys and even tie-dyed clothes is offered on tables and from booths set up daily by a cadre of merchants. The traditional Charleston "basket ladies" are here in force with their signature sweetgrass baskets galore (see the Close-up on sweetgrass baskets in this chapter). Artists ply matted and framed prints of famous Charleston scenes, and you can even buy packages of mixed rice and beans—all ready to cook up as "Hoppin' John"—a traditional black-eyed pea and rice dish.

The Center Market, stretching from Meeting to Church Streets, is a string of specialty shops, boutiques, and eateries. Here, vendors of all types rent spaces and booths to hawk their wares.

Then at North Market Street, Rainbow Market is an unusual cluster of small shops. Each has a separate facade but is situated within the parameters of two 19th-century buildings. From Birkenstock shoes to needlepoint patterns, the merchandise and services in Rainbow Market appeal to a varied clientele.

Continuing along the open air section, between Church and East Bay Streets, local artisans and international importers sell their wares. Here you can watch the basket ladies actually weaving their regional treasures—sweetgrass baskets of all sizes and shapes.

Sooner or later, everybody ends up at the Market, Charleston's traditional melting pot. For shoppers looking for the unusual in jewelry, art, or crafts; for tourists in search of the quintessential souvenir; for college kids on spring break too sunburned for the beach; and even for the occasional out-of-work musician who will play for loose change, all Charleston roads lead to the Market.

Galleries and restaurants flank the Market on both sides—some of which come alive at night as jazz clubs and gourmet restaurants. All the chefs have their own slant on Charleston's "she-crab soup," and the seafood is always fresh and succulent.

The Market has become something of a second stop for any and all other events going on in the city, so it's a popular nighttime destination for the young and restless.

The Market is a must-see for every Charleston visitor, and its magic seems to lie in its eternal spontaneity. It's an ever-changing kaleidoscope of things and smells and sounds and people who all seem to be in a carnival mood. It's different every day, and it's always the same. The Market is a Charleston enigma. Don't miss it.

## BOOKSTORES

**Historic Charleston Foundation Museum Shop and Bookstore**
**108 Meeting Street**
**(843) 724-8484**
**www.historiccharleston.org**

This store is in the Frances R. Edmunds Center for Historic Preservation and, as you might expect, stocks books regarding preservation and restoration. From beautiful coffee table books to fascinating reference material, choose from works about everything from gardening to selecting Victorian house colors. The store's selection of gift items also is keyed to the Charleston taste with brasses and china accents and linen tableware. (For more, see the Attractions chapter and the Gifts listings in the Meeting Street section of this chapter.)

## CANDY

**Lucas Belgian Chocolate Inc.**
**73 State Street**
**(843) 722-0461**
**www.lucasbelgianchocolate.com**
You can't miss the cheerful pink awning just a half-block south of South Market Street next to Häagen-Dazs Ice Cream Shoppe. This was one of the first truly fine chocolatiers to open in the Market area, and its longevity is fair testimony to the quality of its chocolate and presentation skills. Not only is just about every chocolate confection offered, but your purchases are also beautifully wrapped, and the service is charming.

**Market Street Sweets**
**100 North Market Street**
**(843) 722-1397**
**www.riverstreetsweets.com**
As if the distractions of the Market aren't enough, here's a candy store that hands out free samples. Woe be to the poor dieter who happens to pass by here. Market Street Sweets opened in this location in 1984 selling gourmet Southern candies. The devil has had his way with sweet-tooth sufferers here ever since. The shop is most famous for its pralines but also turns out beautiful bear claws, chocolates, and other homemade specialties. This is a first stop for many Charleston visitors who have passed this way before. Market Street Sweets ships anywhere, so no one is really immune.

## GIFTS

**Alpha Dog Omega Cat**
**40 Archdale Street**
**(843) 723-1579**
**www.alphadogomegacat.com**
In Majestic Square on the corner of Market and Archdale Streets, this shop is strictly for the dogs (and cats). Gifts range from gourmet pet biscuits, designer collars, and leashes to jewelry, toys, and clothes. We're talking indulgence here! And this shop is serious about it all. Only a pet lover would really understand.

**Cat's in the Doghouse**
**40 North Market Street,**
**Rainbow Market**
**(843) 853-1915**
As the name implies, this is a shop for pet lovers who go all out when shopping for their four-legged friends. There are gifts galore for the humans, too, who love (and spoil) their pets. Collars, toys, treats, and other goodies await, plus name-brand art objects and humorous gifts dedicated to pet lovers. Located in the Rainbow Market where so many other gift items are found, this shop is an impromptu reminder that our furry friends are worthy of our devotion, as well.

**Charleston Luggage & Leather**
**61 South Market Street**
**(843) 577-4773, (877) 881-0030**
**www.charlestonleather.com**
Down in the Market where all the action can be quite distracting, there's a very nice resource for leather goods and luggage. They carry a number of brand names like Fossil, Rolfs, Dopp, and Scully for leather items. Look for Boyt, London Fog, Vera Bradley, and Travel Club for luggage. This collection of luggage, duffles, totes, and travel gear can take you to your next destination in style.

**The Charleston Museum Gift Shop**
**360 Meeting Street**
**(843) 722-2996**
**www.charlestonmuseum.org**
Here in America's oldest municipal

museum, there's a gift area that's both comprehensive and tasteful. The emphasis is on items (such as books, jewelry, models, textiles, and educational toys) that have some connection to Charleston and the Lowcountry. It's an ideal place to pick up a souvenir from your vacation while visiting the must-see museum. (See the Other Sites and Museums section of the Attractions chapter as well as the Kidstuff chapter.)

## Gibbes Museum of Art Shop
**135 Meeting Street**
**(843) 722-2706**
**www.gibbesmuseum.org**
The shop at the Gibbes is just inside the front doors of the museum and is open to the public with no admission charge. This is one of the Lowcountry's best stops for art books, jewelry, stationery, small reproductions, and art prints of all kinds. Many locals go in early November for the best selection of fine Christmas cards in the city. (For more on the Gibbes Museum of Art, see the Attractions, The Arts, and Kidstuff chapters.)

## Historic Charleston Foundation Museum Shop and Bookstore
**108 Meeting Street**
**(843) 724-8484**
**www.historiccharleston.org**
A stop at the Frances R. Edmunds Center for Historic Preservation is usually for visitor orientation and resource offerings on preservation and restoration, but this also is easily one of the best gift boutiques in town. Miniatures, reproductions in brass and china, books, textiles, and even some crafts abound here. Quality reigns, even in gifts for the children. (See the Attractions chapter and the Bookstores listing for Meeting Street earlier in this chapter.)

## Kites Fly'n Hi
**40 North Market Street,**
**Rainbow Market**
**(843) 577-3529**
Something about flying a kite brings out the best in people. That's the philosophy

behind this colorful little shop in Rainbow Market that is all about kites—of every kind and size. Look here for diamonds, deltas, boxes, and dragons plus wind socks and flags of fantastic design. The shop even has stunt kites for advanced fliers. Put the products to use here on the Lowcountry beaches or take them home to your own sky.

## Market Leather of Charleston
**40 North Market Street, Rainbow Market**
**(843) 722-1156**
**www.marketleather.com**
Here's a shop in the Rainbow Market that's all about leather accessories for men and women. They import several lines of ladies' handbags, belts, and worktotes for the home or office. For men, they have a wide selection of billfolds, duffles, and utility kits. Look for leather backpacks, passport covers, attachés, briefcases, garment bags, wallets, computer briefs, plus handsome cases for phones and palm pilots. This is a gold mine of gift ideas when holidays and birthdays come around.

## The Mole Hole of Charleston
**94 North Market Street**
**(843) 723-0881**
Here's the Market's version of the staple shop for arty collectibles and accents for the home and garden. Folks into Bovano and Wee Forest Folk will find a nice selection here. The shop features cut glass and birdhouses, Wolfard oil lamps, and Hummel figurines—a myriad of beautiful keepsakes from which to choose.

## Noah's Nook
**City Market, Shed A**
**(843) 722-8002**
For those travelers who like to find a year-round Christmas shop and buy that special ornament for the tree that's sure to recall their Charleston vacation, here's a shop that nicely fills the bill. This shop, tucked away in the Market between Meeting and Church Streets, is a division of Light Be and features exclusive lines of

hand-painted, locally made ornaments with a Charleston theme. Their collectible lines include Byers' Choice, Annalee, Seraphim Angels, Fontanini, and many others. Even on the hottest days of summer, there's a little bit of the North Pole here.

### Toy Soldiers of Charleston
**40 North Market Street**
**(843) 722–0228**
**www.toysoldiersofcharleston.com**
Collectors look for these things wherever they go, and in Charleston this is where they are. We're talking about Toy Soldiers of Charleston. This store carries more than 1,500 of the popular military miniatures representing nearly every major conflict since the American Revolution. They even carry color guards from The Citadel, vintage 1860 as well as today. They carry 54 mm soldiers by Conte, Britains, Soldat, Mundiart, and Frontline. Find these gems inside the Rainbow Market.

## HOME ACCENTS AND DECOR

**Metropolitan Deluxe**
**164 Market Street**
**(843) 722–0436**
**www.metropolitandeluxe.com**
Ever since it opened, the Metropolitan Deluxe has been the home furnishings store that marches to a different drummer. This seductive and eclectic mix of European-style furniture, bedding, and linens is across Market Street from Majestic Square and straight out of the latest magazines. Look here for tableware that's chic beyond the pale and for special accents and accessories that delight decorators and casual browsers alike. The collection of candles and dried flowers alone is worth the trip. A corner devoted to cards and stationery is one of the major pulls, as is the bit of free parking in front of the store.

## JEWELRY

**Nice Ice Fine Jewelers**
**145 Market Street**
**(843) 577–7029**
Cross Market Street from Charleston Place to find Nice Ice. Check out the many cases of costume designs along with displays of the real stuff. Expect to be a bit surprised by the good prices. Some of the most unusual pieces seen around town have been created by Nice Ice. Look here for Stephen Dweck, Doris Panos, Hidalgo, Barry Kronen, and Judith Ripka.

## WOMEN'S CLOTHING

**Everything But Water**
**130 Market Street,**
**The Shops at Charleston Place**
**(843) 722–5884**
**www.everythingbutwater.com**
If you are looking for a bathing suit, try Everything But Water in Charleston Place. The store carries contemporary swimwear and accessories by such designers as Anne Cole, Gottex, La Blanca, Calvin Klein, and Oscar de la Renta in sizes 4 through 26.

# Church Street

This is a street with romantic charm to spare. It's the heart of Charleston's French Quarter, where the Huguenots first set up their houses and shops in the 18th century. It was once the very center of the old city, and much of its early ambience and heritage remains in evidence today.

Although Church Street runs from the Market area to White Point Gardens, past houses where presidents slept and folk operas were inspired, the shopping section is largely limited to the area between Market and Tradd Streets. Here you'll find everything from charming little fashion boutiques to bookstores and antiques shops.

## BOOKSTORES

### The Southern Literary Tradition
### 83 Cumberland Street
### (843) 722-8430

Here's a bookstore that's an adventure in architectural history and the city's rich literary tradition. It's located in the Nicholas Trott House (1709), next door to the Powder Magazine, in what is said to be Charleston's first brick residence. The store offers formal tea and a house tour as well as rare first editions and books about the South and the Lowcountry. You can see a wonderful private collection of rare books, but many volumes are for sale, as well. A $5.00 admission charge includes a house tour (given between 10:00 A.M. and 2:00 P.M.) plus tea. If you're looking for a hard-to-find book, the proprietors will search for lost titles for you and watch the marketplace for your favorite author's work.

## GIFTS

### Baby's Nook
### 168-C Church Street
### (843) 722-8404

Just off Market Street next to the French Quarter Inn is a great venue for the parents and the grandparents (and the uncles and aunts) who seek a very special gift for a much-loved child. The Charleston visitor obligated to bring home something from the Holy City will find inspiration in this unusual shop exclusively for the wee ones. They carry Christian gifts, quilts, classic children's books, dolls, teddy bears, tea sets, and tutus. Brand names like Gund, Taggies, Blankies, Demdaco and Sesame Street plus others assure the gifts are of the highest quality. This is the place to find special baby shower gifts and birthday surprises.

# East Bay Street

This was once a street of bustling cotton warehouses in the mid-19th century, where silks and satins from exotic lands were bought and sold by the rice and indigo merchants who labored here. The old warehouses that survived the rigors of war and economic stagnation were "rediscovered" in the late 1970s, when a new epoch for the street began. Although below Broad Street, East Bay can claim the famous Rainbow Row of town houses and the High Battery along Charleston Harbor. Today you'll find a concentration of galleries, nightclubs, restaurants, and bookstores along East Bay between Market and Broad Streets. Beyond this area, other clusters of shops have emerged worth noticing. Here are some of the shopping venues you won't want to miss.

## GIFTS

### Harbor Specialties
### 190 East Bay Street
### (843) 722-3722, (800) 369-2999
### www.harborspecialties.com

People who love boating and the sea are naturally drawn to Charleston. Therefore it follows that a store would specifically cater to their nautical fancy with merchandise (clothes and gifts, mostly) centered around the maritime theme. Harbor Specialties carries Sperry, Tervis Tumblers, boat models, canvas bags, and clothing for male and female seafarers. Best of all, they are set up to same-day monogram almost any item you buy, which makes this store a hit with birthday gift-givers and holiday shoppers.

### Indigo
### 4 Vendue Range
### (843) 723-2983
### www.indigohome.com

If you gravitate toward the eclectic, you'll love Indigo. The inventory ranges from antique luggage to Mexican folk art to Brazilian textiles. In this shop, you'll find village baskets nestled near Shaker boxes next to Edwardian bamboo and old Italian marble. You'll never fail to find something wonderful here.

**Luden's**
**78 Alexander Street**
**(843) 723-7829**
**www.ludensoutfitter.com**
Since 1867 Luden's has been selling Charlestonians top-quality, brand-name clothing, equipment, and gear for hunting, fishing, and boating. Anyone who goes for this outdoor gear will love Luden's for the myriad of gift items available here. Shop here for tide clocks, ship's logs, nautical cookbooks, and all kinds of rigging and boat accessories. Luden's is a block off East Bay Street, just below Charlotte Street on Alexander. There's free parking on-site. (Also see Luden's in the Hunting and Fishing chapter.)

**O'Hara & Flynn, Ltd.**
**160 East Bay Street**
**(843) 534-1916**

**1640 Palmetto Grande Drive,**
**Towne Centre, Mt. Pleasant**
**(843) 216-1916**
**www.oharaflynn.com**
Here's a direct importer of fine wines and gourmet cheeses plus fresh pâtés, smoked salmon, and *saucissons* for the discerning connoisseur. With a shop downtown near Harris Teeter and another in Mt. Pleasant's Towne Centre, they're handy for locals who know their tastes and want the best. They even have in-shop tastings every Friday evening from 5:00 to 7:00 P.M.

**The Smoking Lamp**
**189 East Bay Street**
**(843) 577-7339, (800) 745-7465**
**www.smokinglamp.com**
Forget the no smoking signs. Between Magnolias restaurant and Lodge Alley Inn, this always-fragrant tobacco shop features a complete selection of fine pipes, cigars, tobacco, cigarettes, and smoking accessories.

## HOME ACCENTS AND DECOR

**Charleston Cooks!**
**194 East Bay Street**
**(843) 722-1212**
**www.charlestoncooks.com**
For gourmet cooks and those who just love cooking, Charleston Cooks! is a little bit of heaven right there on East Bay Street. The concept is part kitchen store, part cooking school—where Lowcountry visitors can take one-time-only classes in how to prepare those Southern dishes that are so tasty. Executive Chef Frank Lee from the Maverick Southern Kitchens group heads up a program of daily classes that feature guest chefs from restaurants all over the city and beyond. The model kitchen where classes take place holds 40 "students" with a video overview allowing close-up observation of the magic at hand.

Next door is the retail side of the operation with a complete array of fine cooking utensils, cutlery, pots and pans, small appliances, and many cookbooks (some locally inspired). You'll even find some delicious prepared Southern accent foods like relishes, jams, and sauces. Shoppers don't necessarily have to be enrolled in the cooking classes to take away some culinary souvenirs. But to enroll in the classes, call the number above or visit their Web site.

## JEWELRY

**Geiss and Sons Jewelers**
**116 East Bay Street**
**(843) 577-4497**
**www.geissjewelers.com**
Geiss is on the first floor of a charming little 18th-century brick building on East Bay just south of Broad. While the shop sells custom-designed diamond and colored-stone rings, it is also known for its inventory of watches by Rolex and Tissot.

## NATURAL BEAUTY

**Earthling Day Spa**
**245 East Bay Street**
**(843) 722-4737**
**www.earthlingdayspa.com**
Located in the old Roxy Theater building,

Earthling Day Spa is a great source for skin and body products and books and tapes on health and well-being. Earthling also offers the unique Pilates method of conditioning. With Pilates, clients work out with trained professionals who guide them through a therapeutic body-conditioning regimen of stretching, strengthening, alignment, and toning exercises. There are other gifts for the mind and spirit such as aromatherapy candles, spa treatments, therapeutic massage, and a nice selection of natural cosmetics.

# Broad Street

This is the major Charleston thoroughfare that crosses King, Meeting, and Church Streets, ending at East Bay with the impressive facade of the Exchange Building (see the Attractions and Kidstuff chapters). It is the one made famous by the adage "Below Broad Street," which indicates the mother lode of pricey Charleston real estate south of this line. Historic Broad Street has always been a center of business and political activity since colonial days, but recently the street is primarily commercial between East Bay and King—home to many banks, law offices, and real estate firms. Nowadays, you'll also find a few high-end art galleries and restaurants in the mix, plus a few creative retail venues.

## CHILDREN'S CLOTHING

**82 Church Street**
**1 ½ Broad Street**
**(843) 723-7511**
**www.82church.com**
Moms have been shopping at 82 Church for generations. That's why (when the shop moved up the street) they kept the well-known name. Here you'll find conservative, traditional clothing for children and a shopping adventure that is charming in its own right. The "Charleston Bonnet" for baby girls (puffed with a front-top bow and chin tie) and hand-smocked dresses

are sold here. A full range of imported and American-made merchandise is available, and the shop's precious display windows are always an escape into fashion innocence.

## GIFTS

**The Boutique**
**47 Broad Street**
**(843) 722-1441**
Without a doubt, the Lowcountry's most gorgeous nightgowns, bathrobes, slips, and the like come from the Boutique. This store, located at the corner of Church and Broad, is where the "hat man" is painted on a wall. The shop also sells fine costume jewelry, linens, and other quality gift items, including the Lilly Pulitzer collection.

**Cabbage Row Shoppe**
**13 Broad Street**
**(843) 722-1528**
**www.cabbagerowshoppe.com**
Needle artists in the know say this is a great place to find cross stitch and needlepoint supplies. Look for antique samplers and charts, kits, and hand-painted canvases of Old Charleston and the South. Brand names include DMC, Medicis, and Paternayan—to name a few. This shop also handles custom framing and finishing of heirloom pieces. Look here for fine linen, needlework stands, and reference books.

**Clowns' Bazaar**
**56 Broad Street**
**(843) 723-9769**
This is Charleston's only tax-exempt showcase for folk art, collectibles, and gifts handmade by challenged artisans. By "challenged," the shopkeepers mean crafted by people in Third World countries and faraway lands too-seldom accessible by international traders. You'll find crafts from India, Pakistan, Kenya, Cameroon, Chile, Peru, Jerusalem, Bangladesh, and Indonesia. Along with tableware, hand-loomed cloth, ceramics, pottery, carvings, and baskets, there's even some clothing

# CLOSE-UP

## Lowcountry Tradition: Sweetgrass Baskets

The art form practiced here in the Low-country has been recognized and celebrated virtually all over the world. Examples of this rare craft are found in the art museums of New York and Rome and among the Smithsonian collections in Washington, D.C.; yet the work is evident all along the sidewalks of Charleston's Four Corners of Law at Meeting and Broad Streets. You'll easily find it downtown in the Market and in makeshift stalls along Lowcountry highways—especially U.S. Highway 17 N.

We're talking about the weaving of sweetgrass baskets, a traditional African-American art practiced here in the Lowcountry since the early 18th century.

These baskets are handmade of long bunches of sweetgrass, pine needles, and bulrush that are bound together with fiber strips from native palmetto trees. The bunches are coiled and formed to create a wide variety of baskets—all shapes and sizes, each one unique. The baskets are both functional and beautiful.

Creating these baskets requires skilled craftsmanship and long hours of hard work. A simple, average basket may require 12 hours or more to make, while larger, more complicated versions may take up to two or three months.

The craft of weaving sweetgrass baskets has been a part of the Lowcountry since the earliest days of slavery. The skills are largely passed on from generation to generation. Traditionally, the men harvest the fiber and other plant material from the local marshes and swamps; then the women weave the baskets.

While the bulrush, pine needles, and

---

from Tibet. (See the listing in the Arts chapter under Galleries.)

**The Wine Shop**
**3 Lockwood Drive**
**(843) 577-3881**
Sometimes, there's nothing like having a nice bottle of wine to enjoy in your hotel, yacht, or B&B room at night after a day of shopping or sightseeing in Charleston. This shop, next to the City Marina, is the place to find just the right vintage. They carry a wide selection of wines and champagnes for all budgets as well as cheese, glassware, and wine accessories. It's a good resource for finding a nice gift bottle for a friend or house-sitter keeping the pets back home.

### HOME ACCENTS AND DECOR

**Historic Charleston Reproductions Shop**
**105 Broad Street**
**(843) 723-8292**
**www.historiccharleston.org**
The Reproductions Shop for the Historic Charleston Foundation is at the corner of King and Broad Streets. It's the showroom for home furnishings, accessories, and gift-

palmetto strips are indigenous to and traditionally obtainable throughout the Lowcountry, coastal land development has begun to threaten the artisans' supply. Today, some weavers have to travel as far as Florida and along the Savannah River in Georgia to find natural stands of sweetgrass growing in roadside marshes. Because of this threat to one of the Lowcountry's most endearing traditions, Historic Charleston Foundation sponsored a test project on James Island to cultivate the growing of sweetgrass as a crop. It is hoped the sweetgrass basket tradition will continue to be an integral part of the Charleston experience. Each sweetgrass basket is utilitarian and beautiful, rich in the natural tones of the varied grasses and elegant in its ethnic simplicity. The baskets are true objects of art, and so they're not cheap. We feel the investment (usually $50 or $60 for a standard basket) is very worthwhile. Be sure to discover the wonderful sweetgrass baskets of the Lowcountry for yourself.

*A Lowcountry artisan works on a sweetgrass basket.* CHARLESTON AREA CONVENTION AND VISITORS BUREAU/ DAVID C. BERRY

ware authorized by the foundation. All items for sale have an accompanying product card explaining the item's historical significance to Charleston's history and the Charlestonian lifestyle. The shop features Baker Furniture's Historic Charleston collection of 18th- and 19th-century reproductions of furniture from famous Charleston homes. It also carries dinnerware patterns and brass accessories, fabrics, and wallpaper as well as rugs, books, and jewelry. Because of its non-profit status, no sales tax is charged. (For more, see the chapter on Architectural and Historic Preservation.)

## EAST COOPER

### CHILDREN'S CLOTHING

**Gwynn's of Mt. Pleasant**
**916 Houston Northcutt Boulevard,**
**Village Pointe Shopping Center,**
**Mt. Pleasant**
**(843) 884-9518**
**www.gwynns.com**
The department for children at Gwynn's is special indeed. For infants through teenagers, Gwynn's offers top-line brands, attractive accessories, and shoes. It's another of those Charleston

traditions: outfitting the little one at Gwynn's.

### Radical Rags
210 Coleman Boulevard, The Common, Mt. Pleasant
(843) 884-8763
www.theragamuffinshop.com
Radical Rags in the Common sells cute, traditional clothing for girls size 7 to 16, along with some preteen outfits. Boys' sizes range from 8 to 20. The staff is friendly and helpful, and the selection is terrific.

### Ragamuffin Shop
210 Coleman Boulevard, The Common, Mt. Pleasant
(843) 884-4814
www.theragamuffinshop.com
Also in the Common, Ragamuffin Shop shares staff and floor space with Radical Rags. Its specialty is clothing for infants up to size 6X in girls and 7 in boys.

### Southern Belles
280 West Coleman Boulevard, Mt. Pleasant
(843) 881-1741
This shop is near Wonder Works in Northcutt Plaza and carries traditional clothing for preemies through preteens. Expect lots of smocked outfits, coordinated sibling attire, and crib shoes. It also has toys, picture frames, signature gift items, and scrapbook supplies.

## GARDENING

### Abide-A-While Nursery & Garden Center
1460 U.S. Highway 17 N. Bypass, Mt. Pleasant
(843) 884-9738
Here in Charleston, where gardens are so beloved, there has to be a nursery where people go to get perennials, seeds, shrubbery, trees, and ornamentals. One of the best is Abide-A-While. Its selection is enormous, the quality is good, and you can always count on getting knowledgeable gardening advice.

### Mrs. Capper's Plants N' Things
228 Coleman Boulevard, Mt, Pleasant
(843) 884-4963

1608 Palmetto Grande Drive, Towne Centre, Mt. Pleasant
(843) 971-1002
A long-standing tradition for Charleston area gardeners is a visit to Mrs. Capper's for fine hand-crafted home and garden decor—especially when the spring blossoms arrive. Her hanging baskets of geraniums and petunias are colorful, healthy, abundant, and irresistible. She also carries a vast array of lush, green interior and tropical plants. And there's a good selection of pottery and decorative garden accents to transform a home into a virtual Eden. Treat yourself or brighten someone else's day.

## GIFTS

### Rana
280 West Coleman Boulevard, Suite A, Northcutt Plaza, Mt. Pleasant
(843) 884-1983
This exclusive gift boutique tucked away in Northcutt Plaza is a veritable cache of fine china, crystal, linens, and gifts you'd be proud to give or receive. Locals find Rana inspiring when wedding gifts are called for and Santa needs a little help for someone very special. Parking is free.

### The Scratch Pad
409 Mill Street, Mt. Pleasant
(843) 884-3433
Here is the stop every newcomer should make to buy those smart change-of-address notices to tell friends and family "back home" that you've arrived in Charleston. Located in Mt. Pleasant near Shem Creek and the Common, this store carries the area's best selection of stationery, invitations, note cards, and small gift items that make Lowcountry entertaining very special. This is the place to order wedding invitations and announcements, too. They represent brand names like Crane's and William Arthur. They carry cocktail napkins in every color scheme available to match any party's decor and

ensure your event is truly in theme. Their paper tableware for children's parties is especially fun. Birthday shoppers find a wide variety of cards as well as other fine gifts like picture frames and address books. Even visitors to Shem Creek's seafood restaurants enjoy browsing here before or after a meal.

**Wonder Works**
**624-D Long Point Road, Mt. Pleasant**
**(843) 849-6757**

**975 Savannah Highway, Charleston**
**(843) 573-9300**
**www.wonderworkscharleston.com**
This is a toy store with an educational theme for kids and adults. Departments include geography, nature, arts and crafts, and a special section with developmental toys for infants and toddlers. There are many of the most famous names in educational toys, such as Brio and Playmobil, and Wonder Works is the largest seller of telescopes in the southeastern United States.

## HOME ACCENTS AND DECOR

**The Brick House**
**1465 Stuart Engals Boulevard,**
**Mt. Pleasant**
**(843) 881-8911**
These folks have created a unique and fun marketplace for very fine gently used and new home furnishings. They say good taste doesn't have to be expensive, and this store proves the point. Designer and owner Mary Chason will also visit your home for consultation on items you wish to consign. You'll find the Brick House on the bypass frontage road near Wal-Mart and Wando Crossing Shopping Center.

**Celadon Home Furnishing & Accessories**
**621 Johnnie Dodds Boulevard,**
**Mt. Pleasant**
**(843) 884-7005**
**www.celadonathome.com**
Celadon Home Furnishing & Accessories is one of those stores where you could almost outfit a home from cellar to dome.

Its large inventory of affordable sofas, chairs, tables, and accessories is outdone only by the number of options available "by order." Choose from more than 700 fabrics, and your upholstered sofa or chair can be delivered in about two to four weeks.

**East Bay Gallery**
**121 Coleman Boulevard, Mt. Pleasant**
**(843) 216-8010**
The latest incarnation of this well-known gallery of home accents and objets d'art is located near Shem Creek. Here's a treasure chest of contemporary decorative accessories that range from hand-crafted, one-of-a-kind art pieces to the eclectic object that makes a home truly distinctive. Look for blown glass, wrought iron, jewelry, mirrors, accent chairs, clocks, wind chimes, children's toys, and interesting collectibles. More than 100 artists and craftspeople are represented here—carefully juried by the owners. (See the listing in The Arts chapter, under Galleries.)

**gdc**
**695 Coleman Boulevard, Mt. Pleasant**
**(843) 849-0711**

**975 Savannah Highway,**
**St. Andrews Shopping Center,**
**Charleston**
**(843) 571-5142**
**www.gdchome.com**
More than a yard goods outlet, here's a one-stop option for the home, carrying rugs, gifts, lamps, mirrors, furniture, framed art, accessories, and fabrics. The store offers complimentary design assistance from a well-trained staff of friendly sales folk.

**Kitchens By Design**
**234 Mathis Ferry Road, Mt. Pleasant**
**(843) 849-6890**
Since 1980, this unique shop has offered creative design services for new and renovated kitchens and baths. The showroom displays and sells fine kitchen furnishings, gourmet cookware, and tools.

## JEWELRY

**Skatell's Manufacturing Jewelers**
**1036 Johnnie Dodds Boulevard,**
**Mt. Pleasant**
**(843) 849-8488**

**1798 Ashley River Road, Charleston**
**(843) 763-8925**
www.skatells.com
The outstanding thing about Skatell's is that customers come here to have jewelry made to their own specifications. Skatell's is a direct importer of diamonds, and it tries to pass the savings on to the buyer.

## MUSIC

**Millennium Music**
**1732 Towne Centre Way, Suite L,**
**Towne Centre, Mt. Pleasant**
**(843) 971-2005**

**372 King Street, Charleston**
**(843) 763-2000**
www.milleniummusic.com
There are two locally owned Millennium Music stores (East Cooper and down-town), and we recommend both for your listening and music purchasing pleasure. The Towne Centre location is handy for Mt. Pleasant residents who love to spend time and money there. Purchasing a mem-bership gives you a break on costs for CDs and tapes (be sure to ask about the initial membership charge to determine if it's worth your while), but listening—at a long wall of sampling stations where you can pick a CD and don the headphones—is free.

Both Millennium Music stores have an area dedicated to children and their music, and behind a lovely set of doors down-town is a glassed-in classical music listen-ing room. Millennium carries all major categories of music and then some.

## NATURAL BEAUTY

**Gallery for Hair & Skin Care**
**320 West Coleman Boulevard,**
**The Shops of Mt. Pleasant, Mt. Pleasant**
**(843) 881-4546**
This full-service hair- and skin-care shop

offers massage by a certified therapist and specialists in hair color, skin care, and makeup. For women who know their skin- and hair-care products by name, this op-tion carries Paul Mitchell, American Crew, Kenra, Nioxin, Joico, Biolage, Matrix, Gold-well, Sebastian, and Tigi, among others.

**Stella Nova**
**1320 Theatre Drive, Towne Centre,**
**Mt. Pleasant**
**(843) 884-3838**

**292 King Street, Charleston**
**(843) 722-9797**

**78 Society Street, Charleston**
**(843) 723-0909**

**84½ Society Street, Charleston**
**(843) 577-2500**

**2048 Sam Rittenberg Boulevard,**
**Charleston**
**(843) 766-6233**
www.stella-nova.com
Stella Nova's location in Towne Centre makes a pleasant stop before or after a movie. They carry Ahava, Kusco-Murphy, Terax, and Le Clerc make-up, among many other lines. They have Aveda pure plant products and services for the hair, skin, and body. Services include haircuts, styling, pedicures, facials, and scalp treat-ments. Ask about their day spa programs.

## WOMEN'S CLOTHING

**Copper Penny**
**280 West Coleman Boulevard,**
**Northcutt Plaza, Mt. Pleasant**
**(843) 881-3497**

**1228 Belk Drive, Towne Centre,**
**Mt. Pleasant**
**(843) 881-9889**

**311 King Street, Charleston**
**(843) 723-2999**
www.shopcopperpenny.com
This boutique sells stylish clothes for con-temporary women. In Northcutt Plaza near Wonder Works, this shop is a good source for unique, casual yet sophisticated clothing that works from day into evening.

Gifts and distinctive accessories fill out the inventory, and its popular shoe department has spawned two new retail stores called Copper Penny Shooz.

## From Here to Maternity
**1055 Johnnie Dodds Boulevard,
Crickentree Village,
Mt. Pleasant
(843) 884-8250**

For those anticipating a visit from the stork, here's a Mt. Pleasant option that's more than a maternity store. They carry designer labels to take mothers-to-be from the beach to the most formal black-tie event. Look here for names like Japanese Weekend, Belly Basics, Olian, and Majama's. The staff is experienced at fitting patrons who may be new to the excitement of buying quality maternity wear. The shop is prepared to serve you even after the baby arrives. To outfit the nursery, look here for custom-designed iron cribs and baby bedding, unique toys, and accessories. The Baby Room specializes in newborn-size clothing to toddlers' wear. They carry designers like Zutano and Royal Child to welcome your baby to this wonderful world.

## Gwynn's of Mt. Pleasant
**916 Houston Northcutt Boulevard,
Village Pointe Shopping Center,
Mt. Pleasant
(843) 884-9518
www.gwynns.com**

Locals have shopped at Gwynn's in several locations through the years, and they have always been pleased. A nice thing about this store is the wide range of departments under one roof. Women's clothing is a specialty, and the shoe and accessory departments carry top-of-the-line merchandise. Sales consultants are most helpful and will coordinate outfits to your specifications.

# WEST ASHLEY

## BOOKSTORES

### Book Exchange
**1219 Savannah Highway
(843) 556-5051**

The Book Exchange sells new and used paperback and hardback books as well as collectible comics. Reader-friendly, this is where the serious mystery novel addicts go for a fix, and where the neighborhood kids swap comic books.

### Books-A-Million
**832 Orleans Road
(843) 556-9232**

**2150 Northwoods Boulevard,
North Charleston
(843) 764-2377
www.booksamillion.com**

Books-A-Million is one of Charleston's largest chain bookstores. With its small coffee shop section and expansive inventory, Books-A-Million has a lot to offer. For instance, it stocks nature-related gift items, calendars, and toys. The magazine section covers a big back wall, and the children's section has a video area to entertain the young ones while parents shop. Books-A-Million offers several discounts, and you can buy a one-year club membership for $5.00 to maximize your savings.

### Indigo Books
**3714 Betsy Kerrison Parkway,
Johns Island
(843) 768-2255**

A great hit with the Kiawah and Seabrook crowd, this small but well-stocked bookstore in the Island Center Plaza is the place to pick up a great summer vacation read. The shopkeepers do a great job of keeping a wide variety of books on hand, and they special order anything you cannot find post haste. Their section of Southern authors is especially interesting, and the inventory of Lowcountry titles is as good as the major chains. Even wintertime islanders find Indigo a good place to shop for holiday gifts to send grandkids up North.

## Ravenous Reader
**520 Folly Road, James Island**
**(843) 795-2700**
This is a favorite bookstore on James Island, and thanks to the James Island Connector, it's now very convenient to those coming from town as well as those traveling Folly Road. The Ravenous Reader is expanding and has great books and a friendly staff who'll answer your questions and order just about anything you want.

## GARDENING

**Cross Garden Center**
**840 St. Andrews Boulevard**
**(843) 766-1687**
**www.crossgardencenter.com**
You can always tell spring is coming to the Lowcountry when Cross Garden Center starts displaying the new early-blooming plants along the front of their West Ashley store. Charleston gardeners for generations have shopped at Cross Garden Center for gardening supplies, pet products, and all things natural for the well-dressed outdoors. Along with seeds and bulbs, here's a great source for information on when to plant and how to nurture the quintessential Charleston garden.

**Hyams Landscaping and Garden Center**
**870 Folly Road**
**(843) 795-4570**
Here's another favorite of Charleston gardeners. The selection of room-filling house plants is spectacular, but you'll also find bedding plants, seeds and bulbs, fountains, birdbaths, hanging planters, and more. And there's always someone nearby with helpful answers to your gardening questions.

## GIFTS

**Charleston Collections**
**625 Skylark Drive**
**(843) 556-8911**
This shop sells an incredible assortment of things Charlestonian. Look for Charleston wind chimes, Charleston art prints and originals, Charleston seashell lamp kits, Charleston cookbooks, Charleston note cards, and even Charleston jewelry. Get the drift? The clerks are prepared to ship goods anywhere, so this is a great stop for souvenirs to send home.

## HOME ACCENTS AND DECOR

**Charleston Lighting and Interiors**
**1640 Sam Rittenberg Boulevard**
**(843) 766-3055**

**1109 Johnnie Dodds Boulevard,**
**Mt. Pleasant**
**(843) 352-0188**
**www.charlestonlightingandinteriors.com**
Locals and newcomers looking to brighten their homes with distinctive chandeliers, lamps, ceiling fans, and interesting accents in occasional furniture are discovering this new option west of the Ashley. Their collections include both period and high-tech pieces that work well in traditional as well as contemporary settings but still have that Charleston touch of class. Look for names like Quoizel (Tiffany), Iris, Wilshire, Minka, and Tech Lighting to name a few.

**In Good Taste**
**1901 Ashley River Road**
**(843) 763-5597**
This is a store for the serious gourmet, with all kinds of kitchen items, live herbs, wines, cheeses, coffees, teas, and gift baskets. It often sponsors wine tastings and fun cooking classes that have proven very popular with a devoted clientele. Look for In Good Taste near the Charleston Crab Shack restaurant.

## JEWELRY

**Polly's**
**2048 Sam Rittenberg Boulevard**
**(843) 763-0017**

**270 King Street**
**(843) 722-9228**

**1492 U.S. Highway 17 N., Mt. Pleasant**
**(843) 884-2447**
**www.pollysjewelry.com**
Just across from Citadel Mall on Sam Rittenberg Boulevard, you will find Polly's, a large, locally owned jewelry store. Polly's specializes in diamonds, gold jewelry, and watches. There is ample free parking, and the staff is most helpful. The downtown and Mt. Pleasant stores are a similar source for diamonds, gold, and watches. Customers can have jewelry designed or repaired on the premises.

**Traditions by Garfield**
**86 Folly Road,**
**South Windermere Shopping Center**
**(843) 571-3099**
Traditions by Garfield is South Windermere Shopping Center's unique jewelry store. Traditions is not only a full-service shop with cases of pretty jewelry and nice watches, it is also a good source for estate jewelry (be sure to check out the little case of lovelies in the back) and gorgeous children's gifts. The shelves around the front part of the store are filled with handsome gifts.

## MEN'S CLOTHING

**Barton & Burwell**
**47 Windermere Boulevard,**
**South Windermere Shopping Center**
**(843) 766-3220**
**www.bartonandburwell.com**
Serious anglers know Barton & Burwell like they know the back creeks of the Lowcountry. Anything and everything associated with the sport of fishing is here to be found: clothes, shoes, boots, reels, lures, and any other kind of tackle. Any 10-year-old kid worth his or her spinning

rod would be thrilled with a gift certificate from here. (See the Hunting and Fishing chapter for information on where to put your new equipment to use.)

**Stein Mart**
**975 Savannah Highway,**
**St. Andrews Shopping Center**
**(843) 763-2444**

**600 Long Point Road, Mt. Pleasant**
**(843) 971-5466**
**www.steinmart.com**
The men's (and boys') section of this high-end discount store is quite extensive. You can find a good selection of suits and sport coats in short, regular, and long sizes. Expect to see designer labels as well as fine Italian cuts among the lot. Shirts, ties, sport clothes of all kinds, and underwear complete the selection.

## NATURAL BEAUTY

**Urban Nirvana**
**8 Windermere Boulevard**
**(843) 720-8000**
**636-D Long Point Road, Mt. Pleasant**
**(843) 881-1160**
Here's a day spa with locations convenient for downtowners and visitors to the resort islands, as well. Relax and indulge yourself with massage therapy, skin care, body wraps, hydrotherapy, Swiss and Vichy showers—the works. They have complete men's and women's locker rooms plus a relaxation lounge open daily.

## TOYS

**The Learning Center**
**67 South Windermere Center**
**(843) 556-1200**
**www.the-learning-center.com**
The Learning Center offers educational books and toys. Located behind the South Windermere Shopping Center, the shop is staffed by knowledgeable employees who are prepared to help parents, teachers, and interested friends and relatives find appropriate learning tools for kids with an appetite to learn as well as play.

## WOMEN'S CLOTHING

**The Resort Shop**
**526 Freshfields Drive, Kiawah Island**
**(834) 768-4466**
**www.theresortshop.com**
When famed Palm Beach fashion designer Lilly Pulitzer first introduced her gaily flowered prints, the casual look of beach clothes made a sea change for the better. Even though that seems like eons ago—as fashions change—the vivid Lilly Pulitzer look has never gone out of style. Every new generation seems to rediscover this distinctive, sports-minded brightness and make it their own. In the Lowcountry, one place to find Lilly these days is at the Resort Shop on Kiawah Island.

**Stein Mart**
**975 Savannah Highway,**
**St. Andrews Shopping Center**
**(843) 763-2444**

**600 Long Point Road, Mt. Pleasant**
**(843) 971-5466**
**www.steinmart.com**
It claims to be the only "upscale, off-price specialty store in America," and it may be true. Stein Mart has frontline women's fashion apparel in its Boutique section and accessories that are considerably discounted. There are hats, shoes, purses, jewelry, hair accessories, and hosiery too. The store also carries a large selection of gifts, linens, and special things for the home.

## SHOPPING CENTERS AND MALLS

**Citadel Mall**
**2070 Sam Rittenberg Boulevard**
**(U.S. Highway 17 and Highway 7**
**at Interstate 526)**
**(843) 766-8511**
**www.shopcitadel-mall.com**
When Citadel Mall opened in the early 1980s, it was the merchandising hit of the decade. Major anchors are Dillard's, Sears, Parisian, Belk, and a Target that opened in the spring of 2002. The whole mall has undergone a complete refurbishing with updated and relandscaped bench areas for footsore shoppers, a new children's play area, and a multinational food court for catching a quick bite before launching into further shopping expeditions. There are more than 100 shops to satisfy every shopper's needs. The location, at the intersection of I-526 and US 17, makes Citadel Mall convenient for almost anyone in the Lowcountry. Call the Customer Service Center for information as to business hours and special events.

**South Windermere Shopping Center**
**22 Windermere Boulevard**
**(at Folly Road)**
**(843) 766-0261**
With shops that front on Folly Road and others on a second row behind, South Windermere is a popular shopping center in the West Ashley area. There is also a shopping strip that borders the center itself, and those stores have addresses on Windermere Boulevard as well. The major anchor is Staples, but there are other worthwhile stops in the complex. There's Robinson's Bicycle Shop, founded in 1888 and still very popular with bike enthusiasts. The Open House is a gift shop with elegant paper goods ranging from Crane stationery to whimsical gift wrap. Traditions by Garfield is a jewelry store and gift shop that always has enticing window displays (see previous listing). A more recent tenant called Earth Fare is a popular outlet (set up like a chain grocery store) for all-natural, organically grown food. Shoppers at Earth Fare can also order from a counter and dine in a convenient on-site cafe. Other shopping options are Phillips Shoes and Barton & Burwell, a favorite of local anglers (see previous listing).

**St. Andrews Shopping Center**
**975 Savannah Highway**
**(843) 556-9442**
Generations of Charleston kids have identified St. Andrews Shopping Center by the Coburg Cow revolving on a sign at the

edge of its parking lot on Savannah Highway. The life-size plastic bovine lights up at night and signals to travel-weary kids that they are almost home (or at the shopping center). The major anchor here is Stein Mart, the upscale, off-price department store that features items for the home and clothes for men, women, and children (see previous listing). Other stores include an old-fashioned barber shop called Mooney's and gdc, a large fabric store that also carries lamps, rugs, furniture, and accessories (see previous listing). St. Andrews is the handy location of a Weight Watchers and Ladies Choice Fitness Center, as well.

## Towne Centre
**U.S. Highway 17 N., Mt. Pleasant**
**(843) 216-9900**
**www.mtpleasanttownecentre.com**
This is the Lowcountry's first major offering to shoppers of the newest trend in retailing—the replication of a traditional downtown shopping district in a suburban setting. The fantastic growth of Mt. Pleasant and the whole East Cooper area provoked Towne Centre, a whole "new town" that has the best of the old and all the convenience of the new. The look of Towne Centre is based on Charleston's famous King Street—with traditional-looking storefronts (more than 60 of them so far) and attractive sidewalk settings. The difference is—ample free parking with lush landscaping added to avoid the "vast sea of asphalt" look offered by the shopping malls of yore.

Towne Centre was a $40-million, 47-tenant project when it opened in the summer of 1999. Since then, new stores and entertainment options have been climbing aboard at a steady rate. Among the pioneers in this venture were the major anchors of Belk, Old Navy, Barnes & Noble, Millennium Music, plus Bed, Bath & Beyond. Soon, a 16-screen, 3,100-seat movie theater called Palmetto Grande joined the crowd. Newcomers include Banana Republic, Game Pro, Casual Corner, Chiço's, Chili's Grill & Bar, Hallmark Creations, Old Navy, Learning Express, Gap, and Pier 1. Even Victoria's Secret moved to Towne Centre to be part of the action.

Towne Centre is located on US 17 in Mt. Pleasant. The location is convenient to nearly everyone because of the nearby Isle of Palms Connector (Highway 517) and the proximity to I-526, which almost completely encircles the Lowcountry.

# ANTIQUES

For the Insider who wants to buy, sell, study, or just window shop for antiques, Charleston is a mother lode. Because it was first an English city, the Charlestonian sense of taste in antiques is decidedly British. And fittingly, Charleston's many antiques shops and galleries, many of which are clustered along King Street, tend to reflect that English bias.

The affluent, British-educated, 18th-century Charlestonians proudly decorated their homes with the latest in English good taste as an obvious symbol of their cultural status and social position. If they couldn't import their heart's desire for finery and furniture, they imported tradesmen who could re-create it for them on this side of the Atlantic. Eventually, Charleston produced a new generation of silversmiths and cabinetmakers who earned their own reputations for fine craftsmanship. Indeed, early furniture from Charleston is among the best of the pre-1830 furniture crafted in this country. But it's safe to say that long after Britain ceased being a political factor in the colonies, Americans still looked to Mother England for direction in taste. In fact, this artistic and cultural co-dependency has lingered in Charleston for more than 200 years.

During the late 18th and mid-19th centuries, drastic events greatly altered the city's economic health. There were earthquakes, wars, fires, and storms, all of which took their toll on Charleston's grandeur (including the city's remarkable resource of period antiques). The collapse of the indigo and rice trades, the hardships of Reconstruction, and the opening of America's vast Western frontier left poor Charleston with few viable resources to rebuild its economy.

Many of the elegant old homes fell into neglect as Southern families struggled to cope with all the social and economic changes swirling around them. In many cases, their only recourse was to sell some of the old family furniture, silver, crystal, and china remaining from the former days of glory. Charlestonians did what they had to do to survive.

By the early 1900s, a few savvy antiques dealers from New York had discovered Charleston's cache of fine English furnishings. They soon learned the quality of the furniture was outmatched only by the city's economic distress. By the 1920s, what amounted to an antiques industry was going strong in Charleston. Unfortunately, it was mostly out-going. Along with fine furnishings, dealers were carting off architectural details like wrought iron balconies, shutters, and even whole paneled rooms.

Today, Charleston no longer relies on furnishings from her local homes and the misfortunes of her old families to fill today's antiques shops and galleries. Local dealers and buyers attend auctions and estate sales up and down the Eastern seaboard, and some make regular buying trips to Europe. Ships carrying 40-foot containers filled with early-to mid-19th-century English antiques arrive regularly in Charleston Harbor. Much of the merchandise is sold in local shops, while some of it goes to discerning dealers all over America. Still, Charleston enjoys the lion's share of the top-quality merchandise, largely because of the demand. Many of Charleston's old homes were built to showcase such furnishings, and each new owner cherishes the opportunity to refurbish his or her home appropriately.

From St. Michael's Alley and King Street to the shops in Mt. Pleasant and along Savannah Highway, there are dozens of opportunities to shop for some of the best antiques sold in America.

One particular section along King Street, between Beaufain and Queen Streets, is sometimes referred to as the Antiques District, where you'll find a high concentration of quality shops and fascinating merchandise. But shoppers who really want to "do" the antiques market in Charleston will have to expand their search well beyond King Street these days. Quality shops are found tucked away in nearly all the commercial areas, plus small areas of West Ashley, Mt. Pleasant, and James Island. Seeing them all is getting to be something of a crusade. Lookers are almost always welcome, but if you're a serious collector or a dealer, be sure to talk to the proprietor and make your wishes known. Often, there are back rooms or upstairs galleries available only to those interested enough to ask.

At the corner of King and Queen Streets is a good place to start. Walking north from there, you'll find some of the best antiques stores the city has to offer. Most shops are open Monday through Saturday, but hours of operation can be as eclectic as the selections at many of these shops, so if in doubt, call ahead. We've alphabetized the following store and merchandise descriptions for easy reference.

## Acquisitions
### 273 East Bay Street
### (843) 577-8004, (843) 722-0238
This shop offers full interior design services and specializes in English pine originals and beautifully made reproductions of English mahogany and antique painted furniture. It is a great resource for accent pieces as well. These designers are very popular with the Kiawah and Seabrook Island crowd, and one look at their handsome displays tells you why.

## A. Fairfax Antiques
### 200 King Street
### (843) 853-2400
Even casual window shoppers can tell from first glance—this is a resource for top-quality 18th- and early 19th-century antiques. Shop owners Ann and David Silliman say their emphasis is on Southern Americana, although their collection can be varied at any given time. Each piece is handsomely documented and displayed to

its best advantage. Quality is the key word here, and it really shows.

## Alexandra
### 156 King Street
### (843) 722-4897
Walk through the King Street doorway to discover this exclusive shop of 18th- and 19th-century French furniture, decorative wares, fine linens, pillows, china, and oil paintings—all reflecting the French Provençal ambience now gaining popularity in Charleston.

## Antiques Market
### 634 Coleman Boulevard, Mt. Pleasant
### (843) 849-8850
Only 10 minutes from downtown Charleston, you'll find this mall with antiques and collectibles that are fun and decorative. This market hosts more than 100 booths under one roof, with furnishings, sterling silver, antique button jewelry, and other interesting treasures for the finding. Less serious, perhaps, than some of the King Street antiques stores, this is a great place for browsing through the keepsakes and surprises. Parking is free and convenient just off Coleman Boulevard.

## A'riga IV
### 204 King Street
### (843) 577-3075
Open since 1976, this shop carries a wide assortment of interesting early ceramics, decorative arts, and period accessories. There are no reproductions here at all. Look for an eclectic assortment of 17th- through 19th-century furniture. A'riga IV is best known, however, for its fascinating assortment of antique medical and scientific instruments. This is a special treat for the many docs and nurses who come to Charleston for medical conventions. A'riga has been the subject of a nice write-up in the *New York Times*.

## Carolina Galleries
### 188 King Street
### (843) 723-2266, (800) 328-6256

**91 Church Street**
**(843) 722-4773**
**www.carolinagalleries.com**
This shop deals in pre-1945 American art, antique prints, sporting and Southern genre art, and museum-quality framing. It has an extensive assortment of art from Charleston's "Renaissance Period" of the 1920s and 1930s, including works by Alfred Hutty, Elizabeth O'Neill Verner, and Alice Ravenel Huger Smith. Purchases can be framed and shipped anywhere.

**Carolopolis**
**814-A St. Andrews Boulevard**
**(843) 763-7080**
Away from the King Street crowd at their West Ashley location, this is a treasure hunter's delight. Carolopolis is John Brown's constantly varying selection of antique and vintage furniture, along with offbeat lighting, mirrors, paintings, architectural items, and other assorted finds. Some items are rustic, while others are finished and ready to use. All are fun to browse through on a rainy day.

**Charleston Antique Mall**
**4 Avondale Avenue (at Savannah Highway, U.S. Highway 17 S.)**
**(843) 769-6119**
**www.charlestonantiquemall.net**
Here's another option for those willing to travel away from traditional King Street in search of more affordable antiques and a wide, eclectic selection of merchandise. Look for the large blue awning, which marks the 5,500-square-foot, climate-controlled mall filled with furniture, sterling, jewelry, clocks, books, antique dolls, lighting, collectibles, china—and even a

---

*Footsore antiques shoppers find iced tea and maybe a dessert at Baker's Café. (See the Restaurants chapter.) Its location near the Antiques District makes it within walking distance so you can sit down and plan your assault on all the antiques shops yet to be seen.*

---

bridal registry service. This is also where you can find rare craftspeople doing expert caning, rush, and splint seat work. They're open Monday through Saturday.

**Chicora Antiques**
**102 Church Street**
**(843) 723-1711, (888) 343-8775**
**www.chicoraantiques.com**
This is C. Lyman McCallum Jr.'s collection of finer pre-1840 American furniture and decorative arts with an emphasis on Federal and Classical period pieces. An especially nice aspect of this shop is the detailed documentation of every piece for sale. He proudly guarantees the authenticity in writing of every item offered and maintains a client request file to notify customers when objects of special interest become available. Mr. McCallum also offers an inspection and authentication service, by commission, for any piece offered at an estate sale or auction anywhere in the country. This is a must-see for the serious connoisseur of fine American furniture.

**Church Street Galleries**
**100 Church Street**
**(843) 937-0808**
Here you'll find fine English and American furnishings from the 18th and early 19th centuries along with exceptional Oriental screens and accessories. These dealers proudly say they've been in the trade for more than 27 years and have been collecting for more than 47.

**Classics of Charleston, Ltd.**
**154 King Street**
**(843) 853-0333**
Here is a resource for extremely high-quality and well-documented English period antiques. Owner Lynn Anne Christensen also does appraisals and consultations for clients here and all over the country. The shop shows only a fraction of her entire inventory, and some out-of-town customers shop here "electronically." Accent pieces include American sterling, Staffordshire dogs, gilt mirrors, Oriental porcelains, and cranberry glass.

## Consignmart
## 440 King Street
## (843) 722-1373

This is the exception among antiques shops on King Street in that it carries only consignments. Instead of imported merchandise from "away," you'll find an ever-changing selection of beautiful things gleaned from some of Charleston's finest homes, where owners are always updating and improving their collections of furniture, estate jewelry, fine art, silver, collectibles, and lovely porcelain. The surprises found here are amazing.

## Croghan's Jewel Box
## 308 King Street
## (843) 723-3594
## www.croghansjewelbox.com

Croghan's is another Charleston institution. Many a sterling wedding gift or baby cup has come from here. Croghan's specializes in antique jewels and elegant jewelry, children's jewelry, rings, estate silver, hollowware, and unusual gifts. Here is where you can find those wonderful Charleston (or plantation) rice spoons—traditionally found on every well-set Charleston table. (See the Shopping chapter.)

## Dailey-Grommé Twentieth Century
## 208 King Street
## (843) 853-2959
## www.dailey-gromme.com

Here is a distinct and refreshing anomaly on the King Street antiques scene. This shop is all about Art Deco and 20th-century modernist furniture and design. They carry an array of sassy and chic European furniture, paintings, decorative objects, and lighting. The shop also has an extensive research library where serious shoppers can learn more about this fascinating period in decorative arts. Visitors to this trendy venue almost get the feeling Noel Coward has just stepped out for a pack of cigarettes or to jot down a smart new song.

## The Design Gallery
## 28 Hasell Street
## (843) 722-6099

What long-time Charleston antiques shoppers remember as Poppe House (on King Street) has its newest incarnation here at the corner of East Bay and Hasell Streets in trendy Ansonborough. Two different and gifted dealers/designers have joined forces in this expanded retail expression of their individual talents. Merrill Benfield Interior Design is headquartered here, and the shop houses his fine collection of 18th- and 19th-century antiques for sale. Joining him is Grace Snead and her unusual assortment of fine period paintings. And yes, the two (otherwise very friendly) West Highland terriers are still around—trained to growl at mention of the word "Yankees."

## English Patina, Inc.
## 179 King Street
## (843) 853-0380

Here is a direct importer of quality English and European 18th- and 19th-century furniture and accessories. The major specialty here is the large collection of handsome English chests, but we saw some fine Country French pieces as well. Be sure to see the large selection of antique brass spyglasses a la Captain Ahab and Moby Dick.

## George C. Birlant & Company
## 191 King Street
## (843) 722-3842
## www.birlant.com

This is one of Charleston's oldest and largest antiques stores, having been around since 1929. The owners are direct importers of 18th- and 19th-century English furniture and faithful English-made reproductions. They also specialize in antique silver, china, crystal, and brass. Birlant is the exclusive source for replicas of a Charleston Battery Bench like those found in White Point Gardens. It actually owns the original cast-iron molds.

**George C. Williams, LLC,**
**American Antiques**
**155 King Street**
**(843) 723–2362**
**www.georgecwilliams.com**
Mr. Williams carries a wide assortment of fine early American 18th- and 19th-century (pre-1830) furniture, plus Oriental rugs, prints, paintings, and other decorative accessories. The focus is on Charlestonian and Southern furniture, and the owner keeps a keen eye out for interesting local estate sales. Mr. Williams carries no reproductions. Every effort is made to authenticate (and document) every piece on display. Past customers have the right to exchange previously purchased items for current merchandise or store credit. The owners are exclusive distributors of the video series Authenticating Antique Furniture, by noted expert John Bivins, an excellent reference for beginners and professional collectors alike.

**Golden & Associate**
**206/197 King Street**
**(843) 723–8886, (843) 853–4706**
Clearly, this is one of King Street's largest displays of imported and locally acquired pieces. The vast array of merchandise includes, but is not limited to, furniture, mirrors, chandeliers, sconces, fireplace accessories, and garden items from the 18th and 19th centuries.

**Helen S. Martin Antiques**
**169 King Street**
**(843) 577–6533**
The specialties here are antique weapons with names like Remington and Williamson. There are 19th-century English, French, and even Confederate firearms to see, plus fine bronzes and rare antique books. Look for Oriental rugs, European ivory, and a large collection of sterling silver. We especially admire the shop's collection of fine European beer steins.

**Hungryneck Antique Mall**
**401 Johnnie Dodds Boulevard,**
**U.S. Highway 17 Bypass, Mt. Pleasant**
**(843) 849-1744**
Here is one of the largest antique malls in Mt. Pleasant, with more than 60 dealers sharing 15,000 square feet under one roof. They buy and sell antiques and collectibles of all kinds. Look for sterling silver, mahogany and oak furniture, Victorian pieces in wicker, and ornamental iron. We've seen wicker, dolls, architectural pieces, and even linens here. It's always a changing scene, and there's plenty of parking right out in front of the mall.

**Jack Patla Co.**
**181 King Street**
**(843) 723-2314**
Established back in 1951, this name has long been associated with fine 18th- and 19th-century antiques and English garden ornaments in the classic Charleston tradition. The ownership changed in 1997, but the tradition goes on, and the reputation for reliability still applies. Even the same management is on hand. Look for the extensive collection of antique brass fireplace fenders, English-made lead garden ornaments, and wooden boxes of all kinds. Shipping is never a problem.

**John Gibson Antiques**
**183 King Street**
**(843) 722-0909**
This firm has been dealing in antiques on King Street for about 20 years. Because genuine 18th-century pieces are getting increasingly difficult to find (not to mention more costly), this shop can make up remarkably convincing pieces by combining different old but incomplete antiques. Many handsome pieces of furniture have resulted from this practice, but be advised that their value (like the price) has been compromised. This crowded, fascinating shop features mostly 19th-century furniture along with some fine old reproductions. Estate appraisal, interior design, restoration, and gold-leafing services are offered.

**Joint Venture Estate Jewelers, Ltd.**
**185 King Street**
**(843) 722-6730**
**www.jventure.com**
This is the area's largest estate and pre-owned fine jewelry consignment shop. The inventory ranges from the most elaborate Victorian ornaments to a very modern, contemporary look. Variety is the strong suit here—with more than 1,200 consignors offering jewelry, flatware, and hollowware for every taste and pocketbook. Specialties found here are platinum, diamonds, sapphires, emeralds, rubies, pearls, and a large assortment of vintage watches. Repairs, restorations, and appraisals are done on-site.

**King Street Antique Mall**
**495 King Street**
**(843) 723-2211**
**www.kingstantiquemall.com**
Here is the only antiques mall, per se, on the Charleston Peninsula—which means you see a whole lot of merchandise under one roof. There are more than 40 dealers currently participating in this 9,000-square-foot showroom of affordable antiques, collectibles, and fine art. You'll find everything from costume and estate jewelry to furniture and rugs to garden statuary and Civil War memorabilia. The location, only a block from the visitor center, puts you near convenient parking and (DASH Trolley) transportation elsewhere downtown.

**Khoury Oriental Rugs**
**71 Wentworth Street, Suite 102**
**(843) 720-7370**
**www.khouryorientalrugs.com**
This retailer, just off King Street, handles the finest in hand-knotted Oriental rugs. Their selection is considerable, with something for every discerning shopper. They have old and antique Persian rugs, Indian tea-stained rugs, kilims, Savonneries, and Aubussons as well as needlepoints from China and assorted tapestries. Free shipping is available for out-of-town buyers.

**Livingston & Sons Antiques Inc.**
**163 King Street**
**(843) 723-9697, (843) 556-6162**
**www.livingstonantiques.com**
Livingston is a direct importer of fine English and European antiques whose displays can be seen at either its King Street shop or in its 39,000-square-foot warehouse at 2137 Savannah Highway. Look in these locations for an eclectic mix of merchandise from larger pieces such as chests and cabinets to handsome old wood boxes and clocks plus collectible majolica, Wedgwood, and Staffordshire.

**Midsummer Common Antiques**
**& Interiors**
**152 King Street**
**(843) 727-1212**
Located in the heart of the King Street antiques district (not far from Queen Street), Midsummer Common offers one-of-a-kind antique textiles imported from Europe. Look here for interesting period quilts, château toiles, and paisleys, too. Their selection of 18th- and 19th-century furniture is unique and always changing. An exclusive line of custom-upholstered furniture is yet another asset to the professional interior design services also available from this store.

**Moore House Antiques**
**150 King Street**
**(843) 722-8065**
Here is a delight for fanciers of Chinese export porcelain. There's always a fine assortment of Canton, Rose Medallion, Fitzhugh, and others from the early 19th century. Look for the shop's 18th- and 19th-century furniture, including rare Charleston-made pieces. This merchandise is beautifully documented, and safe shipping to anywhere is never a problem. Owner Bryan Riddle has been serving King Street antiques shoppers for many years.

**Page's Thieves Market**
**1460 Ben Sawyer Boulevard**
**(843) 884-9672**

Since 1959, folks heading for the beach at Sullivan's Island via the Ben Sawyer causeway have been rubber-necking as they pass Page's Thieves Market in the old red barn off to the right. This colorful and eccentric display of antiques, used furniture, knick-knacks, and collectibles is always an adventure to explore—rain or shine. You'll never know what you'll find here; this is for the free-spirited shopper with time to hunt for that illusive gem of a buy. Many a rustic beach house, starter home, or college apartment was furnished from this place. They even have new bedding.

## Period Antiques
## 194 King Street
## (843) 723–2724

Period Antiques is a small shop with an interesting, unusual, and ever-changing selection of choice 18th- and 19th-century American and European antiques including furniture, paintings, mirrors, and decorative accessories. Owner Chris Kellogg grew up in the antiques trade and really knows his stuff. Quality and value are the bywords here. Framed prints and wall hangings are a special forte.

## Queen Charlotte Antiques, Ltd.
## 61 Queen Street
## (843) 722–9121

A relative newcomer to the Queen Street antiques scene is this shop, a sister to the original store open for a number of years in Charlotte, North Carolina. Their specialty is 18th- and 19th-century English and French fine antiques and decorative accessories. They also carry garden ornaments that are either old or reproductions of old garden decorations (recreated in new, more durable materials). The philosophy here is to provide merchandise for the Charleston market that has the formal elegance of 18th-century England combined with the livability and casual charm of the French countryside. A nice collection of coffee table books illustrating that delightful mix makes this shop a pleasure to visit.

## Roumillat's Antiques
## 2241 Savannah Highway
## (843) 766–8899
## www.a-a.com

This is something of a departure from the veddy, veddy serious antiques tradition of King Street in Charleston, but it's an awful lot of fun. Roumillat's has a vast array of used furniture and antiques that can surprise you. Some people find real gems in the rough. Roumillat's says the selection includes American and English antiques, Victorian, Edwardian, and plain old-fashioned stuff. Call ahead for directions to its West Ashley warehouse and the twice-monthly auction dates, then go and enjoy.

## Shalimar Antiques
## 2418 Savannah Highway
## (843) 766–1529

Five miles south of the Ashley River Bridge on U.S. Highway 17, Shalimar has a large stock of quality antiques, clocks, and furniture. It carries the area's largest stock of American primitives, which are definitely hard to find here in the Lowcountry.

## The Silver Vault of Charleston
## 195 King Street
## (843) 722–0631, (843) 571–4342
## www.silvervaultcharleston.com

This is a hard-to-find resource for silver-plating, repairs, and full restorations of all metals, including brass and pewter. This is the companion shop of the Brass & Silver Workshop at 758 Street Andrews Boulevard. The owners, Alfred and Charlotte Crabtree, have more than 30 years' experience in silver repair and restorations.

## Southern Accent
## Designer Showcase Market
## 630 Coleman Boulevard, Mt. Pleasant
## (843) 856–9131

Over in Mt. Pleasant, you'll find the area's only high-end designer showcase market selling to consumers and professionals alike. Along with antiques selected by more than 60 vendors, you'll find a nice selection of fine art, Oriental rugs, accessories, and other decorative items galore.

Located in Moultrie Plaza, there's plenty of parking, and hours are Monday through Saturday, 10:00 A.M. to 6:00 P.M.

## Terrace Oaks Antique Mall
### 2037 Maybank Highway, James Island
### (843) 795-9689

Terrace Oaks is a fun place to browse for unexpected finds. It houses 20 antiques dealers and 11,000 square feet of American, European, and primitive furniture along with a wide variety of other related goodies, including porcelain, collectibles, estate jewelry, and sterling. Shipping is available, and there's ample free parking.

## Village Antiques
### 709 Coleman Boulevard
### (843) 881-2072

Another option for antiques lovers and one located in Moultrie Plaza where there's plenty of parking is Village Antiques. The specialty here is fine art, consignment items from an assortment of local sources, books, vintage lighting fixtures, sterling silver, crystal, and much more. Hours are Monday through Saturday 10:00 A.M. to 5:00 P.M.

## Wine & Pine
### 269 East Bay Street
### (843) 958-8466

Just north of the City Market along East Bay Street you'll find this slight anomaly that—when you stop to think of it—is actually a great idea. The shop is an offshoot of the owner's other East Bay Street store, Acquisitions, which is described earlier in this chapter. Here you'll find English and European wine cabinets and armoires (both antique pine and reproductions) as well as other interesting furniture associated with fine dining. But the surprise here is their vast collection of European and California wines plus the best accessories to go with them. The staff is well versed in domestic and imported wine as well as antique pine furniture, so stopping here is educational as well as fun. Picking up a nice bottle of wine to enjoy after a day's antiques shopping is nothing short of inspired.

## Zinn Rug Galleries
### 76 Wentworth Street
### (843) 577-0300
### www.zinnruggallery.com

Zinn is a direct importer of exquisite antique and semi-antique Oriental, Caucasian, and Turkish rugs, kilims, and kilim accessories. It features a large selection of Aubussons and needlepoint as well. Also look for suzanis and Ottoman furniture.

# ATTRACTIONS

However varied the attractions of the Lowcountry and Greater Charleston may be, this is a place where people are drawn to, captured by, and never completely released from the clutches of history. In fact, it's fair to say we focus more on history—a deeper, richer, more romantic history (and more of it)—than any other colonial city in America. At least, that's the traditional and prevailing Charlestonian attitude.

Whether you're a newcomer to the Lowcountry (and soon to be an Insider yourself) or just a visitor to this gentle land, it's easy to be overwhelmed by the amount of history offered here and the seriousness with which Charlestonians deal with it in their daily lives.

Charlestonians very much want to share their history with newcomers and guests. They'll proudly do so as long as you pay close attention, clearly make an effort to learn, and seek factual information from reliable sources. People here aren't very interested in the tired Southern clichés put out by Hollywood and the peddlers of all that moonlight and magnolia nonsense. The true story of Charleston's past is far more interesting than any of the fiction you might have read or heard. Good listeners are richly rewarded for their investment of time and attention.

For obvious economic reasons, and for other reasons equally valid in this community (such as pride and passion), the subject of tourism in historic Charleston is seriously studied. There are many points of view, of course, but tourism has for many years been a rather sensitive and often volatile topic of discussion.

A good example of this debate can be found in a Charleston Chamber of Commerce brochure published for attracting the tourist market in 1904, a time when the city's fortunes were at a rather low economic ebb. Charleston is described as a

lady—one of unquestionable breeding and dignity—who has been forced onto the wicked stage of tourism by unseemly circumstances far beyond her control:

"The conservatism which has always characterized Charleston has hitherto prevented her merits from becoming so widely known as they should be," the pamphlet reads. "But conservatism in matters connected with the welfare of the community is no longer in accord with the spirit of our times. Charleston has always been justly famed for her hospitality and still delights to honor all those who are deserving of (her) respect and admiration."

Then, with further Victorian modesty, the brochure goes on to laud the city's apparently unlimited historical attractions:

"The lover of history finds deep interest in her (Charleston's) connection with every important historical event from the planting of the early colonies down to the present day and the sentimentally inclined can discover in the city and vicinity the scenes of many a legend and story."

Obviously, tourism and Charleston have a long working (if sometimes strained) relationship. Charleston and tourist management, on the other hand, are relatively recent and wary acquaintances. In other words, the sheer volume of visitors (especially during the past decade) has begun to seriously impact the fragile charm Charlestonians have stubbornly held onto for the past 200 years.

The quaint, genteel, quiet residential flavor of the 18th-century peninsular city (even with its 19th- and 20th-century scars) is by definition threatened by the economic, cultural, and environmental consequences of 4.6 million tourists visiting annually. This collision of mores and economics has resulted in a very carefully planned and closely monitored tourism experience for today's Charleston visitor. We, as the city's guests (whether for a

week or a lifetime), are very much the fortunate winners in this tug-of-war between
then and now.

Because we truly care, and because it
helps to preserve our city's unique cultural
identity, Charleston's historic attractions
are, for the greatest part, well organized,
highly accessible, and intelligently interpreted. In short, there are delightful experiences in Charleston for visitors of all ages
and all areas of interest.

In this chapter, we will begin by steer-
ing you to visitor centers and information
outposts. Then we'll take you on a written
tour of the Lowcountry's brightest and
best attractions, beginning with the house
museums, followed by plantations and gardens, forts, historic churches, and other
museums. There is a lot to see and do
here, and we hope this guide will help you
plan well and miss nothing of interest to
you. Unless otherwise noted, all addresses
are in Charleston.

## VISITOR INFORMATION

**Charleston Visitor Reception and
Transportation Center
375 Meeting Street
(843) 853-8000, (800) 868-8118
www.charlestoncvb.com**
Because parking in the old historic district
is nearly always a problem, visitors are
encouraged to make their first destination
the Charleston Visitor Reception and
Transportation Center. Its location on
upper (meaning the northern end of)
Meeting Street offers visitors a welcome
opportunity to leave their cars behind and
see Charleston's large historic district
(mostly on the southern end of the Peninsula) by any of several alternative transportation options. This is the major, general
information resource site in Charleston
proper, and when we make a general reference to "the visitor center" in our guide,
the Visitor Reception and Transportation
Center is the place to which we refer.

The visitor center building, erected in
1856 by the South Carolina Railroad and

originally used as a freight depot, makes a
perfect place to get your bearings and
plan your adventure in historic Charleston.
Inside, you'll find a three-dimensional dio-
rama model of the peninsular city, while a
multi-screen video display introduces you
to the sights and sounds you're likely to
encounter here. You'll find a comprehensive collection of free brochures, maps,
fliers, and other publications detailing the
special tours, dining adventures, and lodging options in the city, along with information on various recreational offerings and
transportation venues. There is also a central ticket office for most of the area's
attractions, special events, and performances.

If you're arriving without reservations
for lodging, there's even a desk here that
can offer visitors a rescue for last-minute
accommodations. The Lowcountry Reservations desk, near the ticket and information counter, keeps track of the city's hotel,
bed-and-breakfast, and motel rooms that
are still available as of that day and of their
sometimes discounted prices. Bear in
mind, this is risky business during spring
and fall or on weekends when it is entirely
possible that the city's visitor accommodations are fully booked. But on the other
hand, if you're looking for a last-minute
room, this is the place to go first. And
sometimes you can get a great deal.

Once you've taken in the city's
overview of itself, it's time to go out and
see the real thing. It's always best to start
with a professional tour of some kind. If
you're new to Charleston, this will be your
only "first impression," so why not make it
an informed one with a guided tour?

Guided walking tours usually begin in
the morning and last from one to two
hours. They start from various central locations in the historic district—at most of the
large hotels and bed-and-breakfast inns.
The cost is about $15 per person. You may
also choose to ride in a comfortable, air-
conditioned minibus. These guided, motorized tours take about an hour, and prices
range from $15 to $20. Or you might want
to take one of Charleston's famous car-

riage tours and see the city at a clip-clop pace. (See the chapter on Tours for complete information on tour options and prices.)

Inexpensive and convenient motorized shuttle buses called DASH (Downtown Area Shuttle System) cost $1.25 per ride, leave the old depot behind the center at 15- or 20-minute intervals, and carry passengers to the old City Market in the heart of downtown. So, it's very possible to "do" the city and leave your car at the visitor center lot or garage.

Also at the Visitor Reception and Transportation Center, you'll find the 20-minute slide presentation called "Forever Charleston." This audiovisual introduction to the cornucopia of Charleston history and culture is a good one, well worth seeing. The work includes some remarkable photography by three of Charleston's nationally known photographers: Tom Blagden Jr., Ron Anton Rocz, and Bill Struhs. In air-conditioned comfort, you'll see breathtaking vistas over and beyond the city and check out (up close) some of the architectural detail that has been the signature of historic Charleston for at least 200 years. You'll hear tidbits from some of the city's local philosophers, and you'll get to peek behind usually closed gates into a few Charlestonian gardens and lifestyles.

"Forever Charleston" is shown every 30 minutes from 9:00 A.M. to 5:00 P.M. daily. The admission charge is $2.50 for adults and teens and $2.00 for seniors. It's $1.00 for children. The visitor center is open daily from 8:30 A.M. to 5:00 P.M.

### Frances R. Edmunds Center for Historic Preservation
### 108 Meeting Street
### (843) 724-8484
### www.historiccharleston.org

Those who find themselves downtown in the vicinity of 108 Meeting Street (across from the Mills House) have another option for starting their historic Charleston odyssey. The Frances R. Edmunds Center for Historic Preservation is its official name, but it's the Historic Charleston

Foundation's version of visitor orientation. You'll find a well-planned cultural and architectural overview and free and friendly tourist advice.

The center's museum shop carries a fine array of merchandise, including many items from the foundation's Reproduction Collections. You'll find a comprehensive selection of books and reference materials relating to preservation, restoration, and Charleston's 18th- and 19th-century cultural life. You can also buy tickets for the foundation's signature house museum, the Nathaniel Russell House, and Middleton Place Foundation's Edmondston-Alston House. (See the House Museums section of this chapter.) The Frances R. Edmunds Center is open Monday through Saturday from 10:00 A.M. to 5:00 P.M. Sunday hours are from 1:00 to 5:00 P.M. Admission is free.

### The Preservation Society of Charleston
### 147 King Street
### (843) 722-4630
### www.preservationsociety.org

Another friendly informational oasis for the sore-footed traveler (especially handy for those touring the many antiques venues scattered along King Street) is the Preservation Society of Charleston.

Its bookstore offers a fine collection of books, reference materials, and gift items pertaining to Charleston and the Lowcountry. The accommodating staff of volunteers offers free tourist information as well.

Every fall, starting in mid-September and running through October, the Preservation Society's evening candlelight tours of private homes and gardens are very popular. This is a lovely time of year to see the city. Tickets are priced at $45 a tour and often sell out early, but you might check here at the bookstore at the last minute and still be able to join one of these self-guided, neighborhood walking tours. (See the Annual Events chapter for more on the tours.)

The 147 King Street location serves as headquarters and resource center for the organization (founded in 1920) originally known as "The Society for the Preservation of Old Dwelling Houses," one of America's premiere preservation organizations. (See the Architectural and Historic Preservation chapter for more information.) The Preservation Society bookstore is open from 10:00 A.M. to 5:00 P.M. Monday through Saturday. (See the Shopping chapter.)

## HOUSE MUSEUMS

According to a recently completed study, peninsular Charleston contains more than 2,800 historic buildings rated as "architecturally significant." Overwhelming as that may seem, it's even more amazing to realize the vast majority of those buildings are private homes. And of these homes, literally hundreds could legitimately qualify as house museums—not only for their exterior architectural sophistication, but also for their sumptuous interiors. In fact, preserving these homes and their remarkable collections of art, china, fine furniture, and fabrics has become an integral part of today's Charleston lifestyle.

It's staggering to think that even after Charleston's devastating earthquakes, wars, fires, and hurricanes—not to mention the ever-changing tides of the city's economy—these houses still stand. More than a few of them contain many of their original furnishings and treasured family heirlooms, some having been in place since before the American Revolution.

While most of these historic homes remain in private hands and are rarely opened to public tours, seven Charleston house museums offer visitors unique adventures behind normally closed doors.

Most of the following house museums are open year-round and operated by various nonprofit preservation organizations in the city. (See the Architectural and Historic Preservation chapter for more information.) Others are privately owned and run as businesses. In either case, Charleston's house museums afford a fascinating glimpse into the style the city's interiors during a number of heydays in the development of American decorative arts.

From 18th-century Georgian to late-19th-century Victorian, Charleston's house museums are presented here in the chronological order of their construction dates.

As a quick reference for those who don't happen to keep the eight basic architectural styles of historic Charleston constantly top-of-mind, the following definitions (courtesy of the Historic Charleston Foundation and the National Trust for Historic Preservation) are offered:

• *Colonial* refers to the period from 1690 to 1740. Look for a very low foundation, beaded clapboard siding, a high-pitched gable roof (sometimes with flared eaves), hipped dormers, and raised panel shutters. A good Charlestonian example is the John Lining House, 106 Broad Street at King Street.

• *Georgian* refers to the architectural style popular in England during the reign of Anne and the four Georges. Here in America, the style is generally assigned to the years 1700 to 1790. Look for a hipped roof, box chimneys, triangular pediments (often with oval lights), columns, a raised basement, and a belt course between floors. An excellent Charleston example is the Miles Brewton House, 27 King Street.

• *Federal* is the American architectural style seen chiefly between the years 1790 and 1820. In England, the style is called "Adam," in reference to the English-Irish architect Robert Adam. Look for geometric rooms, ironwork balconies, a low-pitched roof, decorative bands around interior rooms, exterior trim, spiral stairs, and elliptical fan lights. The Nathaniel Russell House, 51 Meeting Street, is a fine Charleston example.

• *Classical Revival* is the architectural return to the lines and look of ancient Greece (and later, Rome). It was popular in America from about 1820 to 1875. Look for large, heavy columns and capitals, temple pediments, triglyph and guttae, and all the other details in classic Greek architectural order. In

Charleston, a great example is Beth Elohim Synagogue, 90 Hasell Street.

- *Gothic Revival* refers to the period between 1850 and 1885, when many American building designs borrowed from the upreaching lines of western European architecture between the 12th and 16th centuries. Look for pointed arches, buttresses, stone tracery, and finials. At 136 Church Street, the French Huguenot Church exemplifies this style.
- *Italianate* is shown in the popular building style seen here between 1830 and 1900. Look for paired brackets and round head arches, balustrades, a low-pitched roof, and the loggia (or veranda). A classic Charleston example is the Col. John Algernon Sydney Ashe House, 26 South Battery.
- *Victorian* refers, of course, to England's Queen Victoria, who reigned from 1836 to 1901. In American architecture, however, it was a popular style between the years 1860 and 1915. Look for a multi-gabled roof, elaborate wood bracket work (sometimes called gingerbread), turrets, and roof decorations. A rare Charleston example is the Sottile House, on the College of Charleston campus at Green Street.
- *Art Deco* is exemplified in the highly stylized look that many American buildings took during the years between the world wars, roughly 1920 to 1940. Look for decorative panels, narrow windows, flat roofs, and multicolored bands. Charleston's most outstanding example is the beautifully restored Riviera Theater, 225–227 King Street.

## Calhoun Mansion (1876)
## 16 Meeting Street
## (843) 722–8205

Recently reopened after a brief hiatus during which there was a change in ownership and the installation of a dynamic new collection of furnishings and art, this house museum is one of Charleston's few great Victorian-era palaces. Architecturally, it represents a brilliant expression of the Italianate style, which became extremely popular in America during the last half of the 19th century. This style is a rarity in Charleston's rich display of domestic architecture, possibly because when it was built, in 1876, the city's economy was still devastated by the loss of the Civil War. During the post-war period known as Reconstruction, very little mansion-building was going on in Charleston. But the builder, George Walton Williams, a wholesale grocer and banker, was financially undaunted by the war. Unlike most wealthy Southerners, he had invested heavily in England and in the North before the war. When Mr. William's huge, new Charleston home was completed, newspapers in New York, Atlanta, and Charleston immodestly described it as "the handsomest and most-complete home in the South, if not the country." Indeed, it is still the largest privately owned home in Charleston with its 25 rooms, 24,000 square feet of living space, 19 fireplaces, three-tiered piazza, Italian water gardens with fountains, and a cupola soaring 90 feet in the air overlooking Charleston Harbor. The Calhoun name comes from the fact that the builder's son-in-law, Patrick Calhoun—grandson of John C. Calhoun, "The Great Nullifier"—lived here until 1929 when he lost the house and his fortune in the stock market crash of that year. Subsequent owners failed to find a viable use for this venerable old mansion. It slowly slid into decline until it was finally condemned by the City of Charleston in the 1970s. A young local attorney bought it and spent a considerable fortune and much of the next 25 years restoring its structural and artistic integrity. Today, it houses a new owner's extensive personal collection of English and American furniture of the 18th and 19th centuries—with an emphasis on Southern decorative arts. In addition, his fine collection of impressionist art, Chinese ceramics, and other *objets d'art* look amazingly at home in this huge Victorian-era forum originally designed to create an impressive display. The Calhoun Mansion has been featured in many national magazines and used as a set for the very memorable television miniseries "North and South." Guided tours of the main two floors take place on the hour and half hour starting at 11:00 A.M., Tuesday through Friday and by appointment. Admission price is $15 per person. Children under age six are free. Toddlers must be carried by a supervising adult; no strollers allowed. In-house photography is prohibited. Group tours are handled through JMC Charleston. For more information, call (843) 577–1100.

## Thomas Elfe House (1760)
**54 Queen Street**
**(843) 722–9161**
This delightfully miniature single house is one of Charleston's wonderful little treasures that, for the past several years, has been open to the public on a limited basis. (For more information on single houses, see the Close-up on this architectural idiom in the Architectural and Historic Preservation chapter.) Built well before the American Revolution, it was a modest craftsman's home like many others throughout the city. The particular craftsman who owned this one, however, was most extraordinary.

Thomas Elfe arrived in Charleston from England in about 1747, bringing along a unique skill for woodworking. Here in Charleston, he became one of the most prolific and acclaimed cabinetmakers of the Colonial era. His work appears in many other house museums and private homes throughout the city, as well as in other fine museums all over the country.

During the period of 1768 to 1775, his own records show that Elfe created more than 1,500 pieces of cabinetwork. He worked primarily in mahogany, with distinctive fretwork, unique leg design, and inner-drawer construction being telltale signs of Elfe's craftsmanship.

Restored in 1970, the house interiors show many finishing touches that are attributed to its first, now-famous owner. All four rooms display exquisitely proportioned fireplace walls of cypress paneling. There are china cabinets and deftly scaled

closets artfully worked into each chimney alcove. The slightly lowered dados give the effect of higher ceilings and greater space.

The fact that its first owner was a major contributor to the art and lifestyle of colonial Charleston makes it interesting today. Any serious student of fine, Charleston-made, 18th-century furniture or an antiques buff with a nose for history will want to see this house. It is a showplace for 18th- and early-19th-century furnishings. The tour schedule is Monday through Friday from 10:00 A.M. until noon. Occasionally, the house is open afternoons and weekends, so call ahead to check. Admission is $7.00.

## Heyward-Washington House (1772)
**87 Church Street**
**(843) 722–2996**
**www.charlestonmuseum.org**
This handsome, early Charleston "dwelling house" is now known by two names because of two prominent Americans associated with it—one an owner, the other a distinguished guest.

It was built in 1772 by Daniel Heyward, a wealthy rice planter and the father of Thomas Heyward Jr., a South Carolina signer of the Declaration of Independence. It is documented that the younger Heyward lived in the house until 1794.

In 1791, President George Washington made a grand tour of the new nation and included Charleston on his itinerary. In anticipation of this distinguished visitor, the city rented Heyward's house for Washington's accommodations, and Heyward was thus displaced to his country house for the duration. In Washington's diary, he recorded his visit to the property, saying, "The lodgings provided for me in this place were very good, being the furnished house of a gentleman at present residing in the country; but occupied by a person placed there on purpose to accommodate me."

Today the house is furnished with a magnificent collection of period antiques, especially some fine Charleston-made furniture of the 18th century. Look for the famous Holmes bookcase that still bears the scars of an incoming British mortar from the days of the American Revolution. This is the only 18th-century house museum in the city with original outbuildings (kitchen, carriage house, and necessary) still a part of the courtyard. You'll also find a small formal garden, in keeping with the period of the house.

Heyward-Washington House was saved from destruction in the early 1920s by the Preservation Society of Charleston. It is now a National Historic Landmark owned and operated by the Charleston Museum. It's open daily, Monday through Saturday from 10:00 A.M. to 5:00 P.M. and Sunday from 1:00 to 5:00 P.M. No entry is allowed after 4:30 P.M. Admission is $8.00 for adults and teens and $4.00 for children ages 3 to 12. Note that the Charleston Museum offers discounted combination ticket prices for this house and the Joseph Manigault House—$14 for the two museum sites.

### Joseph Manigault House (1803)
### 350 Meeting Street
### (843) 723-2996
### www.charlestonmuseum.org

At the beginning of the 19th century, Charleston architecture was still very much dominated by what was fashionable in Mother England. This house, designed and built in 1803 by Charleston gentleman-architect Gabriel Manigault for his brother Joseph, was certainly no exception. Today it remains one of America's most beautiful examples of the graceful Adam style.

Both Manigault brothers were wealthy rice planters with sophisticated tastes. Gabriel had studied in Geneva and London, where the Adam influence was at its height, and he maintained an extensive architectural library of his own.

The house is distinguished by one of the most graceful staircases in the city and displays an outstanding collection of Charleston, American, English, and French furniture of the period. Don't miss the charming gate temple in the rear garden. During the 1920s, when the Manigault

House was very nearly torn down in the name of progress, Gabriel Manigault's classical gate temple was used as the restroom for an oil company's service station, then on the garden site. Later, during World War II, the house served as a USO canteen for servicemen passing through Charleston's busy Navy Yard en route to battle stations overseas.

Today it is a National Historic Landmark owned and operated by the Charleston Museum. Hours are 10:00 A.M. to 5:00 P.M. Monday through Saturday and 1:00 to 5:00 P.M. on Sunday. The last tour begins at 4:30 P.M. Admission is $8.00 for adults and teens and $4.00 for children ages 3 to 12.

### Nathaniel Russell House (1808)
### 51 Meeting Street
### (843) 724-8481
### www.historiccharleston.org

Prominent shipping merchant Nathaniel Russell decided to build his great "mansion-house" on Meeting Street, practically within sight of the busy wharves that produced his wealth. When his house was completed in 1808, Russell was 71, and he had reportedly spent $80,000 on the project—an enormous sum at that time.

Like the Manigault house, Russell's new home was inspired by the work of English architect Robert Adam, whose delicate style was influenced by the airy classical designs only recently uncovered (literally) in the Italian excavations of Pompeii and Herculaneum.

Today's visitor is immediately dazzled by the dramatic, free-flying, elliptical stairway floating up through three floors without any visible means of support. Finely proportioned, geometric rooms are furnished with another outstanding collection of Charleston, English, and French pieces, including rare china, silver, and paintings.

Unlike most other Charleston house museums, the Russell House has never been through a sad period of decline and disrepair. First as a fine town house, then as the home of a South Carolina governor, and later as a school for girls and even a convent, 51 Meeting Street has always been a respected and cared-for landmark. Today it is owned and operated by Historic Charleston Foundation, an organization that has done much to preserve and illuminate the city's architectural heritage (see the Architectural and Historic Preservation chapter).

The house is open for tours Monday through Saturday from 10:00 A.M. to 5:00 P.M. and Sunday from 2:00 to 5:00 P.M. The last tour begins at 4:30 P.M. The house is closed on Christmas Day. Admission is $8.00 per person; for children younger than 6, admission is free. A combination ticket for this and the Aiken-Rhett house at 48 Elizabeth Street is $14. Call (843) 724-8482 for tickets and group tour information.

### Edmondston-Alston House (1825–1838)
### 21 East Battery
### (843) 722-7171
### www.middletonplace.org

In 1825, Charles Edmondston, another wealthy merchant and wharf owner, built this handsome dwelling where he could enjoy an uninterrupted view over the expanse of Charleston Harbor. In 1828, the house was bought by Col. William Alston, a rice planter. His son, Charles, redecorated the house in the 1830s, favoring the fashionable Greek Revival style.

Incredibly, today's visitor can still find many family documents, portraits, silver pieces, and fine furnishings—including Charles Alston's almost-intact library—in place. Much of it dates back to the 1830s. The house is notable for its unusual Regency woodwork, as well as its uncompromising views of the harbor. The intimacy and authentic details of the house may leave guests feeling as if the Alstons only recently left the property, perhaps on a visit to the country.

The Edmondston-Alston House is owned by Middleton Place Foundation. Tours are offered from 10:00 A.M. to 4:30 P.M. Tuesday through Saturday and 1:30 to 4:30 P.M. Sunday and Monday. Admission is

$10.00 per adult, $8.00 for students, and free for children age 7 and younger.

### Aiken-Rhett House (1817, 1833, 1857)
### 48 Elizabeth Street
### (843) 723-1159
### www.charlestonmuseum.org

Unlike any other house museum in Charleston, the Aiken-Rhett house is a time capsule of Charleston's history and taste. It was the home of Gov. William Aiken from 1833 through 1887, and it owes most of its eerie charm to him.

The structure was built in 1817 by John Robinson as a typical Charleston single house, much like many others built in the city at the time. However, under the later ownership of South Carolina railroad magnate Aiken (who was governor at the time of the Civil War), the house was drastically altered and enlarged. In 1833, it was remodeled to conform to the bold Greek Revival style popular then. Again in 1857, alterations were made, this time in the heavily ornamented Rococo Revival style that was gaining popularity in antebellum Charleston. Rococo Revival, which was popular in 18th-century France, is noted for curvilinear lines, as in shells, foliage, and scrolls.

Here again, an uncanny amount of furnishings and other objects belonging to Governor and Mrs. Aiken can still be found, including portraits, statuary, library volumes, and elaborate chandeliers the couple brought back from Paris in the 1830s. The difference here is that much of the house is unrestored. It is instead preserved, largely as it was presented to the Charleston Museum in 1975 by descendants of the Aiken family.

As a result, the visitor can almost feel the presence of Jefferson Davis, president of the Confederacy, who was a guest in the house in 1863. You can easily picture Confederate General P. G. T. Beauregard using the house as his headquarters during the almost relentless Federal bombardment of Charleston in 1864. And the haunting, life-size portrait of Mrs. Aiken dressed in her finery belies the emotional and economic hardship she suffered after the war when the governor was arrested and briefly imprisoned for treason.

Another miracle of the Aiken-Rhett house is the remarkably well-preserved (but unrestored) slave quarters and out-buildings (including stables and a privy) to the rear of the house. A high masonry wall surrounding the stable yard and slave quarters somehow managed to keep out the forces of time and change. They're shown as they are, unrestored and unro-manticized, making an eloquent statement about slavery and the sociology of the 19th-century South. If woodworking detail is any measure of worth and respect, the horses at the Aiken-Rhett house were more important than the slaves who worked as house servants. The horse stalls have Gothic arches and turned pillars; no such adornment graces the utilitarian slave quarters.

The fragile textures of time and the changing fortunes of war very much show in this remarkable house museum. Surely this is its most romantic and tragic charm. The Aiken-Rhett House is a must-see. The 45-minute audio house tours are given from 10:00 A.M. to 4:30 P.M. Monday through Saturday. Last tour starts at 4:15 P.M. On Sundays, tours are from 2:00 to 5:00 P.M., with the last tour starting at 4:45 P.M. Admission is $8.00 per person; for chil-dren age 6 and younger it is free. A com-bined ticket that includes admission to the Nathaniel Russell house is $14.

## PLANTATIONS AND GARDENS

Without a doubt, no visit to Charleston is complete without a journey to the planta-tions. And nowhere is Charleston's late, great plantation culture more evident than along the old route to Summerville via the Ashley River Road (Highway 61).

This is the state's oldest highway, and it once provided secondary, back-road access to some of the most beautiful colonial plan-tations in the Lowcountry. Primary access

to the early plantations was by river—a much faster, more convenient route.

It might be helpful to remember that much of the wealth and sophistication of Charleston in the 18th and 19th centuries was derived from the plantation system. And the plantation system was, after all, an agricultural economy based on the prac-tice of slavery. As beguiling as it may appear to be, the opulence and wealth so evident in the downtown Charleston houses and outlying plantations built dur-ing these years may be viewed with a newfound perspective when remembering this grim reality.

This is where the Charleston visitor may fall prey to a trite old Southern cliché: namely, that there was a time when the bucolic romanticism of the Old South largely swirled around the moonlit, magno-lia-scented lives of Southern aristocracy. While some of that romantic imagery may be true, it by no means tells the whole story.

Today, much more than in the past, greater emphasis is being placed on show-ing visitors a realistic picture of the society as a whole. That includes the lives of slaves, trades people, merchants, women, and children. Look for that emerging slant as you go about your adventures on the old plantations.

It might also be helpful to know that America's version of the plantation system did not originate here at all. Like almost everything else in the early colonies, it was imported. It came to Charleston from Eng-land through the West Indies. In fact, many of Charleston's early planter families emi-grated from older plantations in Barbados.

While a number of influences brought its concept to America, slavery clearly flourished here in the Lowcountry. Today's visitor has a rare opportunity to see the plantation system in its various forms and eras. Indeed, today's more enlightened stance offers the chance to see where slavery took root in South Carolina—and where it ended.

Here's a suggested route you may want to take:

Starting on the Peninsula, take U.S. Highway 17 S. Once across the Ashley River bridge, you'll drive through some of Charleston's post–World War II urban sprawl. You may choose to start your plantation tour at the very beginning—at Charles Towne Landing State Historic Site, South Carolina's unique state park at the site of the colony's original settlement. There, you'll explore a reconstruction of an early settler's cabin and see the "experimental garden" where test crops of various kinds held the settler's best hope for survival in this brave new world.

Next, you may want to take the same architectural quantum leap Charlestonians did—from that early, crude settler's cabin to the classical grandeur of Drayton Hall (begun in 1738), which was built along the Ashley River's west bank only a generation later.

At Middleton Place (developed ca. 1740) and Magnolia Plantation (started in the 1680s, then expanded about 1840), you can explore the vast gardens so important to these early planter families. Magnolia's informal design (typical of 19th-century gardens) makes an interesting contrast to Middleton's strict geometric patterns (so popular in 18th-century France).

In fact, the geometrically designed formal gardens at Middleton Place show the incredible strength of Europe's artistic influence here in Charles Towne, just 40 years before the American Revolution. At Middleton Place House (1755) you can trace the story of the distinguished Middleton family, which included Arthur (1742–1787), a signer of the Declaration of Independence. At the Middleton Place stable yards, you can interact with some of the daily activities of a working plantation.

In the spring, you'll want to include Cypress Gardens, originally part of Dean Hall plantation on the Cooper River. Follow Highway 61 from Middleton Place to Highway 165, join U.S. Highway 17-A through Summerville to Moncks Corner, and follow the signs. There, in a 163-acre, black-water cypress swamp, is an incredible azalea garden started in the 1920s and now owned and operated by the City of Charleston Department of Parks. You'll find charming little bateaux (flat-bottomed boats) to use, and there are 3 miles of walking paths through the vibrant spring colors reflected in the mirrorlike waters.

Back through Charleston and 6 miles north along U.S. Highway 17 is Boone Hall, the picturesque, 738-acre plantation used extensively in the ABC TV miniseries "North and South," filmed in and around Charleston several years ago. Boone Hall's best features include the famous avenue of live oaks and the original "slave street" of nine brick slave cabins (ca. 1743).

You won't be able to visit all these plantations in a single day. If you must select only a sampling of Greater Charleston's plantation culture, the following in-depth review of these sites should help you choose.

You won't regret the investment of time and travel it takes to digest these plantations and gardens. They're so much a part of the city, so vital to its development, that to see just one side of Charleston life and not the other might seriously handicap your understanding of the area as a whole.

### Charles Towne Landing
### State Historic Site
### 1500 Old Towne Road, between
### Interstate 26 and Highway 171
### (843) 852-4200
### www.southcarolinaparks.com
Surely this is one of the most unusual state parks in South Carolina, if not America. Charles Towne Landing State Historic Site was created as part of South Carolina's 300th anniversary celebration in 1970 on the plantation belonging to Dr. and Mrs. Joseph I. Waring. Today, the property isn't presented to the public as a plantation per se. Rather, the vast acreage is devoted to re-creating and interpreting the first English settlement in the Carolinas, which existed on this plantation site back in 1670.

Once inside the gate, visitors travel down a long alley bordered by ancient live oaks and swamp. Eventually you come to a parking lot and a large complex of modern buildings that serve as a starting point for your adventure.

A giant interpretive center at the main pavilion once included an unusual underground museum that interpreted the first 100 years of the colony with artifacts, exhibits, recordings, and art. This area was torn down because of damage sustained in Hurricane Hugo. Today, Charles Towne Landing is a working archaeological site where visitors can interact with historians literally unearthing the early story of South Carolina's first English settlement and the Native American history that preceded it. Visitors can also tour the Legare-Waring plantation house and observe many fascinating artifacts found at the site.

Along the river, you may observe a full-scale replica of a typical 17th-century trading vessel called the *Adventure,* currently under restoration. Picture it as a common work vehicle of the early plantation system, plying the waters loaded with fur pelts, indigo shipments, and rice to sell on the wharves in Charleston. These boats also carried people and supplies to the widely scattered plantations upriver.

The post-Hugo redesign of the Animal Forest boasts a 20-acre natural habitat zoo with wolves, pumas, bears, bison, snakes, and alligators—all part of the Lowcountry landscape when settlers first arrived in the 1670s.

The Settlers' Life Area, with its replica colonial buildings, is a handsome example of what early colonists saw every day. You'll see candle-making, open-fire cooking, woodworking, and, depending on the season and the weather, even the colony's first printing press in action. Special exhibits and demonstrations can be found here on holidays.

Charles Towne Landing is open all year. The hours are 8:30 A.M. to 5:00 P.M. Picnic tables, a snack bar, and a gift shop are all on-site. The park is largely accessible to visitors with disabilities. Admission is $5.00 for adults and teens older than 15, $3.00 for children ages 6 to 15, and free for handicapped visitors and children younger than 6. Bicycle rentals are $3.00 per hour with a $3.00 deposit.

## Drayton Hall
**3380 Ashley River Road**
**(843) 769-2600**
**www.draytonhall.org**

Not a tour of a reconstructed working plantation or the collected decorative arts from a bygone era, Drayton Hall offers an adventure in architecture. Yes, architecture and a great deal more.

If for no other reason, Drayton Hall should be seen and experienced as the sole survivor of the ugly 1865 rampage by Union troops, who looted and burned nearly every other plantation house along the Ashley River. But there is more to Drayton Hall, as it also stands as a survivor of many other changes, influences, forces, and times.

It was built between 1738 and 1742 as the country seat (primary home) of John Drayton (1716–1779), whose family had emigrated to Charles Towne from Barbados and settled nearby at Magnolia Plantation a generation earlier. The house is considered one of the oldest and finest examples of Georgian-Palladian architecture in America. Its recessed, two-story portico may have been inspired by Italy's Villa Pisani, designed in 1552 by Andrea Palladio. The portico is one of the architectural signatures of Palladianism, and Drayton Hall's portico may be one of the earliest built in America.

The story of how this very sophisticated English Palladian villa came to be built along the west bank of the Ashley, and how it survived the ravages of time, wars, earthquakes, and hurricanes, is a fascinating saga.

Maybe the greatest curiosity of all is how the old Drayton house survived the enormous forces of changing architectural taste. Oddly, the house was never modernized for 20th-century use. Drayton Hall has never seen plumbing or central heat; it never had gas installed for lighting or heating purposes. Its only link with modern electricity is the one meager line that brings life to its sadly necessary modern security system.

Quite simply, Drayton Hall is an architectural time capsule. The structure remains almost untouched as an eloquent statement about 18th-century thinking, craftsmanship, technology, and design. It's one of the few sites left in colonial America so pure, unaltered, and uncompromising.

Visitors will find the Drayton Hall story—how it all came to pass—interpreted by a small group of professional guides. These storytellers lead you through 250 years of time, family genealogy, architectural history, and a smattering of the economic and social realities of the plantation system.

A word or two about "interpretation" might be helpful here. Because each guide at Drayton Hall develops his or her own perspective of the house, every tour will be slightly different. That is, each guide bears the responsibility of interpreting and synthesizing the tremendous amount of research data collected about the property. You hear the guide's words, not a written script. Thus, return visits will only deepen your understanding of the house, its people, and its times. The bare fact that you're touring virtually unfurnished rooms is hardly noticeable, since each room is chock-full of interesting information and rich architectural detail.

Drayton Hall comes to life because imagination is a wonderful artist. Imagination can paint in the faded colors of Drayton Hall's early days, when the settlement of Charles Towne was barely 70 years old. It can flesh out the heady, pre-Revolutionary days when the Ashley River plantation system was at its zenith. Now, through imagination, the visitor can even see Drayton Hall in the grim, dark days following the Civil War, when vagrants and vandals used it at will. Imagination can find the returning prosperity and almost hear the laughter of the Drayton parties and other family occasions held here as recently as

the 1960s. All it takes is an informed interpreter and your attentive ear.

Research is an ongoing process at Drayton Hall. The staff has recorded oral histories of the Drayton family as well as the African Americans so closely associated with the house and its survival. Preserved but unrestored, Drayton Hall and its faded hues and subtle shading, its frayed places and telling stains are all pure Charleston. The house serves to illuminate the whole Ashley River plantation system in a rare and strangely haunting light.

In the spring of 1997, Drayton Hall added another dimension to its interpretation of the site. A map is now provided to visitors for a self-guided nature walk through the Drayton property. You can walk through various natural environments including marsh, riverfront, and forest areas. Minimal signage along the trail offers interpretation of each environment. Archaeological as well as historic sites can be seen and understood as to their relevance to the 18th- and 19th-century Drayton Hall lifestyle. Major portions of the nature trails are wheelchair-accessible.

An ongoing project at Drayton Hall is an education program for students in kindergarten through grade 12. Several curriculum-coordinated programs feature student tours, plantation games, archaeology studies, and preservation workshops for both teachers and students.

This historic site is now jointly owned by the National Trust for Historic Preservation and the South Carolina Department of Parks, Recreation, and Tourism. Admission prices include a professionally guided tour of the historic house and a self-guided tour of the grounds, including the African-American cemetery and their interactive Connections program. Tours are offered on the hour from 9:30 A.M. to 3:00 P.M. November through February and 9:30 A.M. to 4:00 P.M. March through October. A written tour in English, French, or German can be purchased. Group rates, AAA and military discounts, wheelchair access, and prearranged student programs are available. Regular

---

# Ashley River Road:
# Back Road to the Plantation Life

Before Hurricane Hugo struck the Low-country in September 1989—destroying an estimated seven million board feet of prime, standing lumber—the Ashley River Road (Highway 61 from Church Creek to Bacons Bridge Road) was oak-lined, moss-laden, sun-dappled, and almost unbearably beautiful. Certainly, that's how many Lowcountry old-timers remember it.

Most of the huge oak trees were hundreds of years old and stood so close to the road they became a hazard to speeding cars. So, for several years, every serious accident (and there were many) became a new excuse to remove more trees and more of the road's ambi-ence. Then came the slow but relentless encroachment of commercial businesses and the addition of more and bigger real estate developments, each taking an even higher toll on the once scenic high-way.

In the late 1990s, however, preserva-tionists woke up to the fact that old S.C.

Highway 61 was a unique natural resource—of Lowcountry history and beauty—and it was quickly vanishing in the name of progress and development. Turning back these forces, once under way, turned out to be nearly impossible. But through years of planning and nego-tiation, a new plan has emerged which hopes to preserve as much of the old road's ambience as possible. The group seeks to qualify the road for National Scenic Byway status after winning State Scenic Byway status in 1998.

The stretch between Drayton Hall and Middleton Place still has the densest tree canopy. That is, the live oaks reach up and over the road, creating a sun-fil-tered canopy through which you'll feel you're driving into the past.

Remember, the Ashley River itself is always on your right—sometimes just through the trees. Bear in mind, too, that the old road (originally a trail for Native Americans) was only a back road to the

---

admission is $12.00 for adults, $8.00 for ages 12 to 18, $6.00 for children ages 6 through 11. A "Connoisseur Tour" is avail-able by reservation. Call extension 630 for details. Admission is always free to members of the National Trust and Friends of Drayton Hall who show their membership cards. (See the Annual Events chapter for information on the Annual Spirituals Concert at Drayton Hall.)

**Magnolia Plantation and Gardens**
**3550 Ashley River Road**
**(843) 571-1266, (800) 367-3517**
**www.magnoliaplantation.com**
This is where Thomas Drayton Jr., father of Drayton Hall's John Drayton, settled when he came to Charles Towne in 1676. Early on, the home that Drayton, a suc-cessful English planter from the island of Barbados, built for himself and his family was destroyed by fire. The house built to

Ashley's colonial plantations. It was slow, rutted, and practically impossible to navigate in wet weather. Most social and business traffic to and from the far-flung plantations went by water. Thus, the great houses were actually built facing the river, the avenue to all agricultural wealth. Still, European settlers are recorded using the back road as early as 1707.

If you look carefully, you'll notice some unexplained low ridges along the roadside. Chances are, these are old rice dikes indicating where the land was flooded and the fields cultivated for rice.

In other places through the forest (now drastically thinned by Hugo), you'll see larger, unnatural-looking mounds—especially noticeable in the wintertime. These are the outcroppings from old, abandoned phosphate mines. After the Civil War, during the late 1870s, phosphate (an early fertilizer product) was discovered in the ground along the west bank of the Ashley. For a brief but reckless period, this entire landscape was crudely strip-mined. As ecologically careless and harmful as these practices

were, the phosphate era provided desperately needed income for a few of the old planter families that had somehow managed to hold onto their properties through the war and Reconstruction.

If the phosphate mining years were not the Ashley River's finest hour, at least they helped rescue what little was left of the plantations after the cataclysmic year of 1865. In February of that year, as the war was winding down, Union troops advanced toward Charleston on the Ashley River Road, looting and burning as they came. Of all the great houses once standing along the high, west bank of the river, only Drayton Hall survived.

Once, there were scores of plantations along the Ashley. They had wonderful, lyrical names: MacBeth and Runnymede, Millbrook and Schieveling. Today, three of the old properties are open to the public. These are Drayton Hall, Magnolia, and Middleton Place. (See entries in text.) Each is unique and remarkable in a different way and each offers special insight into the Ashley River's fascinating plantation story.

replace it was subsequently burned by Union troops in 1865. The present structure is said to have been a Drayton family hunting lodge that was moved down the Ashley River in 1873 and placed atop the foundations of the old plantation house. Magnolia Plantation is the original (and continuing) home of the Drayton family, now owned and managed by a ninth-generation descendant. It is famous for its expansive, informal, English-style gardens,

which are the legacy of the Reverend John Grimke-Drayton, the plantation's owner during the Civil War, whose parish was nearby at Saint Andrews. In 1843, Grimke-Drayton imported numerous specimens of *Camellia japonica,* and in 1848, *Azalea indica.* Due to a bout with tuberculosis in the late 1840s, he left his parish for a time and devoted himself entirely to his garden.

By 1870, despite the tragedy of the war and the burning of the main house,

---

i

*Looking to add a splash of color to your spring visit to Charleston? Wade into the vast sea of fuchsia, pale pink, and white azalea blossoms during the annual spring bloom at Magnolia Plantation and Gardens. It's truly an overload for the senses.*

---

the gardens at Magnolia Plantation had grown in size and reputation. That year, the property was first opened to the public. Paddle-wheeled steamboats from Charleston made regularly scheduled excursions to Magnolia, where tourists relaxed, took picnics, and strolled along the blossom-laden paths. But for all its lacy bridges arching gracefully over mirror-like cypress ponds, one little-known, smaller area is well worth finding.

Look for the garden called Flowerdale. This is where it all began. Here is Magnolia's earliest garden area (planted in the late 1680s), and it was possibly the inspiration for Grimke-Drayton's larger, more ambitious plan a century and a half later. Surely the reverend sat here in the 1850s, pondering the moral issues facing his plantation world as the political storm clouds gathered over the South. Perhaps it was amid the beauty of Flowerdale that Grimke-Drayton first thought of expanding the garden plan to create an oasis of beauty so large and lasting it might someday sustain his family home.

Today, the gardens boast 250 varieties of azaleas and 900 varieties of camellias. These, plus many other flowers added through the years, keep Magnolia Gardens in colorful bloom all year long. Its most spectacular season, however, is spring, when the dazzling, vibrant azalea colors seem to vibrate on the landscape as far as the eye can see.

Visitors can get an overview of the property in a 12-minute video on the plantation's history shown at regular intervals in the orientation theater. Magnolia Plantation offers additional activities for nature lovers. Canoes can be rented to glide

through the eerie beauty of its 125-acre waterfowl refuge. There are walking and bicycle trails, plus a wildlife observation tower that's very popular with bird-watchers. There's an herb garden, a horticultural maze, an antebellum slave cabin, a typical Ashley River rice barge, and even a petting zoo for children (as well as adults). You'll find picnic areas, a snack shop, and a gift shop there too. (See the Kidstuff chapter.)

The property is open daily from 8:00 A.M. to 5:00 P.M. Group rates are available. Basic admission is $14.00 for adults, $8.00 for ages 6 through 12, and free for those younger than 6 (an additional $5.00 provides admission to the Audubon Swamp Garden as well). The house tour is an additional $7.00, but children under 6 cannot tour the house. However, the 30-minute Nature Train tram ride is $7.00 for adults, $5.00 for ages 6 through 12, and $3.00 for children under 6.

### Audubon Swamp Garden at Magnolia Gardens
### Highway 61
### (843) 571-1266
### www.magnoliaplantation.com

In the 1980s, Magnolia Plantation and Gardens added a new element—the Audubon Swamp Garden. This separate attraction encompasses a 60-acre, black-water cypress and tupelo swamp. The visitor has the opportunity to see an otherwise inaccessible natural area via boardwalks, dikes, and bridges that provide an intimate view of the horticultural beauty and wildlife, including a few alligators.

The swamp garden gets its name from the great 19th-century American naturalist and wildlife artist, John James Audubon, who visited Magnolia in search of water-bird specimens during his many lengthy stays in Charleston.

This attraction, a 45-minute self-guided walking tour, is operated apart from the rest of Magnolia Plantation and may be seen at half the price of Magnolia's general admission. That means $6.00 for adults, $5.00 for ages 6 through 12, and free for those younger than 6.

## Middleton Place
**4300 Ashley River Road**
**(843) 556-6020, (800) 782-3608**
**www.middletonplace.org**

Middleton is one of the Lowcountry's most famous plantations and another National Historic Landmark along the rich and fascinating Ashley River. This was the home of Henry Middleton, president of the First Continental Congress, and his son Arthur, a signer of the Declaration of Independence.

The sheer size and scope of Middleton's gardens tell a great deal about the man and his grand vision. When he began his garden plan in 1741 (the framework for it remains unchanged today), the French influence for adopting a formal, geometric design was still very much in vogue. This was the Age of Reason, during which philosophy held that the essence of true beauty lay in humankind's conquest over nature. Thus, all great gardens of the time imposed order and geometric form over the otherwise natural, unruly landscape.

Legend says it took 100 slaves almost a decade to complete the sweeping terraces, walks, and artificial lakes—vistas that are still pleasing to the eye today. But the gardens at Middleton Place are only part of the plantation story interpreted here. Unlike some of the plantations closer and more convenient to Charleston, Middleton Place was a world unto itself. The 12-acre greensward, with its grazing sheep and strutting peacocks, creates an unforgettable image for the first-time visitor. This bucolic, pastoral scene belies the frenzy of activity and the vast labor force needed to maintain this busy world.

Now open on the Middleton Place grounds is Eliza's House, an actual freedman's dwelling. It is furnished as it might have been found in the 1870s, when African Americans who stayed on the plantation after emancipation lived there. Middleton Place Foundation conducts ongoing research into the lives of the slaves, freedmen, and tradespeople who were so important to the Middleton Place scene. The lively plantation stable yards,

with active displays of day-to-day life, provide another glimpse into that busy world. Chances are you'll find a blacksmith, a potter, weavers, and carpenters all busy at work and eager to explain and demonstrate their skills.

The main house, built sometime before 1741, was—like Magnolia's—burned in 1865 by Union troops. It is said the soldiers drank wine and dined in splendor at Middleton Place house, then set fire to it as they left.

The south flanker building (added about 1755) was least damaged by the fire, and it was essentially rebuilt in the early years of the 20th century in its present form. Inside, you'll find Middleton family memorabilia displayed, along with a remarkable collection of important family portraits that include works by Benjamin West and Thomas Sully.

Not to be missed is the view of the Ashley River from the high terraces of the gardens. The green grass ripples down the hillside to the graceful butterfly lakes below. Off to one side, the old rice mill counterbalances the picture-perfect composition of the landscape.

The Restaurant at Middleton Place serves authentic Lowcountry cuisine, and a daily lunch is available to visitors from 11:00 A.M. to 3:00 P.M. At night, from 6:00 to 9:00 P.M., the restaurant serves a delightful candlelight dinner, and there's no admission charge for entry to the property after 5:30 P.M. with dinner reservations. (See the Middleton Place Web site for details on dining there.)

In addition to the sensitive and skillful interpretation of the plantation's glorious past, there's an unexpected contemporary side to its present-day life. Just past the rice mill, a path leads into the forest and up a hill to the Inn at Middleton Place, a 55-room riverside oasis for discerning overnight travelers. The Inn was designed by Charleston architect W. G. Clark, and it seems to have been born "of" the forest rather than "in" it. With vine-covered stucco and unblinking modern glass walls, each suite looks out over a green, woodland setting or the quiet waters of the Ashley River. A visit to the Inn is well worth the short stroll from yesterday into the present. (See the Bed-and-Breakfasts and Atmospheric Inns chapter for more.) The Inn has won numerous architectural awards, plus a place in *Time* magazine's "10 Best of '86" list and a spread in *Architectural Digest Travels.*

Middleton Place is open daily. Hours are 9:00 A.M. to 5:00 P.M. for the gardens and stable yards. House tours begin at 10:00 A.M., except on Mondays when they begin at 1:30 P.M. House tour admission adds $10.00 per person to Middleton Place rates: $20.00 for adults and teens and $5.00 for children ages 7 to 15. An optional carriage ride through the property adds $13.00 to the admission charge for adults and children. Group rates are available; special events with food service may be arranged on the property. (See the Annual Events chapter for special events at Middleton.)

**Cypress Gardens**
**Off Highway 52**
**8 miles south of Moncks Corner**
**(843) 553-0515**
**www.cypressgardens.org**
For those with time and the inclination to go even farther afield, there's yet another treat in store. Discover the beauty and wonder of Cypress Gardens—a true Southern cypress swamp and a 162-acre water forest of uncommon natural beauty.

This park, once part of Dean Hall Plantation, is now owned and operated by Berkeley County. You'll find meandering footpaths for hikers, but the traditional way to see Cypress Gardens is by bateau—a flat-bottomed boat poled or paddled by expert young boaters who are always on hand to do the work for a small price. You have the option of rowing yourself if you like, but the serenity of the black waters mirroring springtime azaleas, dogwoods, daffodils, and wisteria deserves your undivided attention.

In a separate building, Cypress Gardens' 24,000-gallon aquarium features fish and turtles native to the Lowcountry and has a display of venomous and non-venomous snakes.

Cypress Gardens is closed the entire month of January. Call ahead for seasonal hours and special admission prices. Hours are usually 9:00 A.M. to 5:00 P.M. No admittance is allowed after 4:00 P.M. In-season admission is $10.00 for adults and teens, $9.00 for seniors, and $5.00 for students ages 6 to 12. Admission free for children younger than 6.

## FORTS

Among the most visited attractions in the Lowcountry are the area's famous forts—standing today in mute testimony to the great strategic role Charleston Harbor played during the conflicts of the past 300 years.

Of course, the most famous of these fortresses is legendary Fort Sumter, where the Civil War began. But Greater Charleston has a number of other forts and former military fortifications that offer fascinating stories, both for the serious historian and for us regular Insiders too. There's Fort Moultrie on Sullivan's Island, Fort Johnson on James Island (now site of the South Carolina Wildlife and Marine Resources Center), and Battery Wagner on Morris Island.

We'll sketch brief histories of these sites—just enough to send you off to see the real thing with a taste of the very real drama and sacrifice associated with these places.

**Fort Sumter National Monument**
**Charleston Harbor**
**(843) 881-7337, (800) 789-3678**
**www.nps.gov/fosu**
Almost every Charlestonian knows the story by heart: The year was 1861. South Carolina had seceded from the Union. And yet, just a few miles east, there at the mouth of Charleston Harbor, Union forces were still stationed at Fort Sumter. The Confederacy officially demanded that Fort Sumter be vacated, but the North

adamantly refused. At 4:30 A.M. on the morning of April 12, a mortar shell burst over the fort, fired from nearby Fort Johnson. The Civil War had begun.

At first—largely as a matter of honor—the Union forces defended Fort Sumter. But after 34 hours, they surrendered. It was practically a bloodless battle—no one was killed, and only a few men were wounded.

Amazingly, the Confederates held the fort for the next 27 months, against what was the heaviest bombardment the world had ever seen. Over the course of almost two years, no fewer than 46,000 shells (about 3,500 tons of metal) were fired at the island fort. In the end, the Confederate troops abandoned Fort Sumter, but they never surrendered. It was February 17, 1865. By April, the war and the cause would be lost.

Today, Fort Sumter is a national monument administered by the National Park Service of the U.S. Department of the Interior. It is still accessible only by boat, and the only public tour of this tiny man-made island and world-famous fort is offered through Fort Sumter Tours, Inc.

You can board the Fort Sumter tour boat at the National Park Service's new facility at the foot of Calhoun Street on the Cooper River. The impressive $15-million interpretive center took three years to build and adds a dramatic new dimension to the Fort Sumter experience. Here, visitors are immersed in the Fort Sumter story with interactive displays and graphics, while Park Service rangers are on hand to answer questions. Among the sights found here, you'll find the actual 33-star Garrison Flag that flew over the fort that historic first night of the Civil War. The trip out to Fort Sumter takes about two hours and 15 minutes. The boat ride affords delightful views of Charleston's waterfront and includes a narrated history of Charleston Harbor given en route. The specially built sightseeing boats are clean, safe, and have on-board restrooms.

Once you're at Fort Sumter itself, you can walk freely about the ruins. There's another interpretive museum area on-site

with National Park Service rangers there to answer any questions you may have.

You'll need to check in for your tour at least 15 minutes early for ticketing and boarding. Departure times vary according to the season and the weather, so call the number listed for departure information. During the busy summer season, there are usually three tours a day. Prices are $13.00 for adults and teens and $7.00 for children younger than 12. Children younger than 6 are admitted free, but a boarding pass is required for them. Wheelchair access is available. Group rates are available, but advance reservations for groups are encouraged. (Visit www.spiritlinecruises .com or see the Kidstuff chapter for additional information.)

## Fort Moultrie
## 1214 West Middle Street, Sullivan's Island
## (843) 883-3123

From the earliest days of European settlement along the Eastern seaboard, coastal fortifications were set up to guard the newly found, potentially vulnerable harbors. In this unique restoration, operated today by the National Park Service, visitors to Fort Moultrie can see two centuries of coastal defenses as they evolved.

In its 171-year history (1776 to 1947), Fort Moultrie defended Charleston Harbor twice. The first time was during the Revolutionary War, when 30 cannons from the original fort drove off a British fleet mounting 200 guns in a ferocious, nine-hour battle. This time, Charleston was saved from British occupation, and the fort was justifiably named in honor of its commander, William Moultrie.

The second time the fort defended the city was during the Civil War. For nearly two years, the Charleston forts (and the city itself) were bombarded from both land and sea. The walls of Forts Sumter and Moultrie crumbled under the relentless shelling, but somehow the forts were able to hold back the Union attacks.

Today, the fort has been restored to portray the major periods of its history. Five different sections of the fort and two outlying areas each feature typical weapons representing a different historical period. Visitors move steadily back in time from the World War II Harbor Entrance Control Post to the original, palmetto log fort of 1776.

Fort Moultrie is open from 9:00 A.M. to 5:00 P.M. year-round. It is closed on Christmas Day. Groups should make reservations for guided tours. Pets are not allowed. Admission is free.

From Charleston, take U.S. Highway 17 N. (Business) through Mt. Pleasant to Sullivan's Island and turn right on Middle Street. The fort is about 1.5 miles from the intersection.

### Fort Johnson
### Wildlife and Marine Resources Center
### 217 Fort Johnson Road, James Island
### (843) 762-5000

Fort Johnson is another Charleston area fortress steeped in history and adaptively reused for modern needs. Since the early 1970s, the waterfront James Island site has been the home of the South Carolina Wildlife and Marine Resources Department, which researches and promotes the state's marine industries.

But savvy military buffs know Fort Johnson in another role. Like Fort Moultrie, this site has military significance that dates back several hundred years.

No trace now exists of the original Fort Johnson that was constructed on the site in about 1708. It was named for Sir Nathaniel Johnson, proprietary governor of the Carolinas at the time. A second fort was constructed in 1759, and small portions of that structure remain as tabby ruins there today. (Tabby is an early building material made from crushed lime and oyster shell.)

Records show the fort was occupied in 1775 by three companies of South Carolina militia under the leadership of Lt. Col. Motte. During the American Revolution, the fort remained in colonial hands until 1780, when the British forces advancing on Charleston reported finding it

abandoned. A third fort was built in 1793, but a hurricane destroyed it in 1800. Some work on Fort Johnson was done during the War of 1812, but the following year another storm destroyed that progress. Shortly afterward, Fort Johnson was dropped from official reports of U.S. fortifications.

During early 1861, South Carolina state troops erected mortar batteries and an earthwork of three guns on the old fortress site. Unbeknownst to most Americans, the actual signal shot that opened the bombardment of Fort Sumter and marked the beginning of the Civil War was fired from the east mortar battery of Fort Johnson on April 12, 1861. Fort Sumter was fired upon, not vice versa.

During the Civil War, building activity increased until Fort Johnson became an entrenched camp, mounting 26 guns and mortars. However, apart from routine artillery firing from the site, the only major action at the fort occurred on July 3, 1864, when its Confederate defenders repulsed two Union regiments totaling about 1,000 men. The Union forces sustained 26 casualties and lost 140 men as captives. The Confederate loss was one killed and three wounded. On the night of February 17, 1865, Fort Johnson was evacuated during the general Confederate withdrawal from Charleston Harbor.

After the Civil War, Fort Johnson became a quarantine station operated by the state and the city of Charleston. It continued to be used in that capacity until the 1950s. Today's inhabitants at the site (the Marine Resources folks) do not prohibit exploration, so you might find this history-drenched spot worth a visit.

### Battery Wagner, Morris Island

Of all the forts and battlegrounds that dot the Lowcountry landscape and pay quiet tribute to the area's military history, perhaps the most muted one is Battery Wagner on Morris Island. The story is a brief one in the long struggle of the Civil War, but it is a significant one that is especially poignant today. In 1989, the story of Battery Wagner was portrayed in the acclaimed film *Glory*, which starred Matthew Broderick, Denzel Washington, and Morgan Freeman.

Time and tides have long since removed all traces of Battery Wagner. Today, Morris Island is vacant and uninhabited. It is hoped that one day Morris Island will become a National Historic Landmark and interpreted for visitors as the battleground and graveyard it is. Although a monument at Battery Wagner is planned, the site remains remarkably overlooked by the public for now. But whatever its future may hold, the story of Morris Island will always include the story of Battery Wagner and the 54th Massachusetts Regiment.

Because Charleston was the "cradle of Secession," it was a primary target for the Union's high command. On June 16, 1862, the Union forces' first attempt to capture the city failed at the Battle of Secessionville on James Island. Union commanders decided to mount a two-pronged attack using both land and naval forces. There were two possible lines of approach to the city: through Sullivan's Island, which was heavily defended, or through Morris Island, which was more lightly guarded. On Morris Island, the main defense was Battery Wagner, a quickly built fortification with thick sand walls and more than a dozen cannons.

Choosing the Morris Island approach, Union forces landed on July 10, 1863, and opened fire the following day with little success. A week later, they tried again. Even after a 10-hour artillery bombardment, Battery Wagner stood firm.

At dusk on July 18, the Union infantry advanced up the beach toward heavily defended Battery Wagner. Spearheading the attack was the 54th Massachusetts Regiment under the leadership of Col. Robert G. Shaw, the 25-year-old son of a wealthy Boston abolitionist. The regiment under Shaw's command was made up entirely of free blacks from the North. It was one of the 167 black units that fought against the Confederacy in the Civil War.

The bloody, hand-to-hand struggle at Battery Wagner saw 272 men from the 54th (more than 40 percent of the unit) fall dead, and 1,500 Union forces were lost, including Col. Shaw. The valor and courage displayed in the battle proved once and for all to Northern and Southern leaders that black soldiers could and would fight. The story of the 54th was widely publicized at the time, and as a result, the Union Army began to enlist blacks in growing numbers. By 1865, a total of 178,895 black soldiers had enlisted, which constituted 12 percent of the North's fighting forces.

The fight for Battery Wagner continued for 10 more weeks until the Confederates finally abandoned the work on September 6. The 54th continued to serve along the southeast coast for the remainder of the war. It was mustered out of service in Mt. Pleasant on August 20, 1865.

# HISTORIC CHURCHES

In a city that was a major contributor to the American ethic of religious freedom, there's a deep reverence for church architecture. The "Holy City," as it likes to be called, has dozens of beautiful 18th- and 19th-century churches that bear witness to this history and the 21st-century pride that goes with it.

Several churches are notable because of their early dates of construction, while others impress with their architectural grandeur. Some are survivors of cataclysmic events; a few speak volumes about their ethnic and sociological origins. Here are some churches whose history enriches Charleston and her citizenry, but remember, they are only a few of many. Unless otherwise noted, all are in the downtown vicinity and are still active houses of worship. They are listed in alphabetical order.

**Cathedral of St. John the Baptist (1890–1907)**
**Broad and Legare Streets**
**www.catholic-doc.org/cathedral/index.html**

The first Cathedral of St. John the Baptist was completed in 1854. It was an outstanding example of Gothic architecture, built of Connecticut sandstone with a 200-foot spire. The building was completely lost in the great fire of 1861. By 1890, work had begun on what is almost an exact duplicate of the 1854 building. It was designed by P. C. Kelly of Brooklyn, New York, and followed closely the plans for the original structure. The exception is the square tower that, for monetary reasons, replaced the tall spire. The newer building is made of Connecticut brownstone. The nave is tiled, measures 150 by 80 feet, and seats 700 people.

### Cathedral of St. Luke and St. Paul (1815)
### 126 Coming Street

The church that is now the Cathedral Church for the Episcopal Diocese of South Carolina was originally known as St. Paul's, Radcliffeborough. It was organized as a mission in 1806.

This building, designed by the architects James and John Gordon, was completed in 1815. At the time of its building, the load of the tower proved too heavy for the supporting walls, and the tower was dismantled. A lighter, Gothic Revival–style parapet was added, which is in contrast to the Classical Revival building below. Inside, the original color schemes have been reproduced as part of the intensive

restoration of the building following severe damage in Hurricane Hugo.

### Circular Congregational Church (1891–1892)
### 150 Meeting Street
### www.circularchurch.org

This church was originally called the Independent Church of Charles Towne and was established in 1681 by some of the first settlers of Charleston. It was one of the first two congregations created in the settlement (the other being St. Philip's Church; see subsequent listing).

The first building was of white brick and was known by locals as the White Meeting House. It is from this early euphemism that Meeting Street takes its name. That building was outgrown and replaced in 1806 by the first "Circular Church," an impressive structure designed in the Pantheon style by Charleston's famous architect Robert Mills. It is said to have seated 2,000 people, both black and white. The great fire of 1861 swept across the city and took this building with it. The ruins stood mutely until the earthquake of 1886 turned them to rubble.

A third (and the present) building on this site was completed in 1892 and is circular in form but Romanesque in style. The church's graveyard is the city's oldest, with monuments dating from 1696. This is the burial ground of Nathaniel Russell. (See the Nathaniel Russell House listing under House Museums in this chapter.)

### Emanuel A.M.E. Church (1891)
### 110 Calhoun Street

The African Methodist Episcopal Church had its beginnings in 1787 in Philadelphia with the founding of the Free African Society, based on the doctrines of Methodism and the teachings of John Wesley. A similar organization was founded in Charleston in 1791 by the Rev. Morris Brown, a free black preacher affiliated with another Methodist church in the city. This show of independence from the blacks led to a secession from the Methodists and the founding of three

---

*Some downtown churches are open to visitors who respectfully wish to see these historic interiors during weekday daytime hours. The schedules may be erratic because these are active, working religious organizations with busy calendars of church events scheduled for the congregations. However, if the doors are open, the sanctuary is deserted (usually there's a sign posted for visitors), and you know you're disturbing no one, feel welcome to quietly enter and briefly look around.*

---

black churches in Charleston, known as the Bethel Circuit.

The Emanuel A.M.E. congregation is one of those churches. The original building was in the Hampstead neighborhood in the east side of the city. By 1818, it had 1,000 members. In 1822, Denmark Vesey, a carpenter who bought himself out of slavery, laid plans in the church for an insurrection. Word of the rebellion leaked out, and Vesey and some of his followers were executed. The Hampstead church was burned to the ground. By 1834, all black churches in South Carolina were closed by the state legislature.

During the years following the Denmark Vesey incident, some of the congregation returned to white churches, but others continued the traditions of their African church and met underground. The congregation resurfaced in 1865—3,000 strong. Today's building was completed in 1891. The original gas lamps that line the sanctuary have been preserved. With seating for 2,500, the church has the largest seating capacity of Charleston's African-American congregations.

## First Baptist Church (1822)
## 61 Church Street
## www.fbcharleston.org

Here is the oldest Baptist church in the South. The congregation originally emigrated from Maine to the Carolinas in 1783. The building was designed by the first American-born architect, Robert Mills, in the popular Greek Revival style. Mills didn't mince words, saying of his creation, "[it is] the best specimen of correct taste in architecture in the city. It is purely Greek in style, simply grand in its proportions, and beautiful in its detail." Wood for the solid mahogany pulpit was brought from the West Indies for the staggering sum (in 1822) of $1,000. First Baptist's fabulous organ dates from 1845 and was made by Erben.

## First (Scots) Presbyterian Church (1814)
## 53 Meeting Street
## www.first-scots.org

The Scots Kirk (or Scots Meeting House) was organized in 1731 by 12 Scottish families who believed in a strict subscription to the Westminster Standards (church laws) and the Presbyterian form of church government. Their first simple structure on this site was built in 1734. It was replaced in 1814 by the present structure, which is the fifth-oldest church building in Charleston. By unanimous vote of the congregation, the church bell was donated to the Confederacy in 1862 and has never been replaced.

Although the church was badly damaged by a fire in 1945, it was lovingly repaired. In the window over the main door appears the seal of the Church of Scotland, the burning bush, with a Latin motto that reads, *"Nec Tamen Consumbatur"* ("Nevertheless it was not consumed").

## French Huguenot Church (1845)
## 136 Church Street
## www.frenchhuguenotchurch.org

French Huguenots were followers of the 16th-century French reformer John Calvin. After Louis XIV revoked the Edict of Nantes (1685), there was an enormous flight away from France by Protestants, many of whom came to the Carolinas.

The Huguenot Church in Charleston was organized in 1681, and groups of believers arrived in this area between 1680 and 1763. In 1706, the Church Act established the Anglican Church as the official religion in South Carolina, and slowly, most Huguenot churches were absorbed into what became Episcopal congregations. The Huguenot Church in Charleston is the outstanding exception; it is the only remaining independent Huguenot congregation in America.

This church was the city's first to be built (1845) in the Gothic Revival style. It was designed by Edward Brickell White, a noted Charleston architect who is credited with popularizing the Gothic style in America. The church was damaged by shelling during the Civil War and nearly demolished by the 1886 earthquake. Each time, it was painstakingly restored. The building underwent a major refurbishing in 1997.

The church's famous Tracker organ, restored in 1967 by the Preservation Society of Charleston and the Charleston chapter of the American Organists Guild, is one of the city's true musical treasures. It is one of the last of its kind anywhere in the country.

## Grace Episcopal Church (1848)
## 98 Wentworth Street
## www.gracechurchcharleston.org

Another magnificent example of Gothic-style church architecture in Charleston is Grace Episcopal Church, designed by Edward Brickell White. This building was completed in 1848.

The memorial windows in Grace Church are teaching windows, each containing scenes from the life of Christ as well as lay persons and clergy associated with the church. The largest window, over the rear doorway, took more than a year to complete and contains more than 10,000 pieces of glass. A small window on the Epistle side of the narthex contains an angel with the face of a small girl who drowned on Sullivan's Island.

Grace Church was closed for a year in 1864 because of the terrible bombardment from Morris Island, but it reopened soon after the evacuation of Charleston, during Federal occupation.

## Kahal Kadosh Beth Elohim (1840)
## 90 Hasell Street
## www.kkbe.org

This is the oldest synagogue in continuous use in the United States. The present congregation was organized in 1749. It is also the longest surviving Reform synagogue in the world. Beth Elohim is acknowledged as the birthplace of Reform Judaism in the United States, tracing its origins back to 1844. This is a branch of Judaism that places more emphasis on traditional religious and moral values, instead of rigid ceremonial and ritualistic detail. The present 1840 Greek Revival structure was designed by Cyrus L. Warner. The graceful

but massive wrought-iron fence that faces onto Hasell Street dates back to the original 1749 synagogue.

## St. John's Lutheran Church (1817)
## 10 Archdale Street
## www.stjohns-lutheran.org

This is Charleston's mother church of Lutheranism, with a history spanning more than 250 years. The congregation was organized in 1742 and worshiped in various places until the present structure was completed in 1817. Frederick Wesner was the architect. The steeple is said to have been designed earlier by famous Charleston miniaturist Charles Fraser and was constructed in 1859. The original bell was given to the Confederate cause (bells were often melted down for use in ammo, cannons, ships, firearms, and the like) and was not replaced until 1992.

## St. Mary's Catholic Church (1837–1839)
## 89 Hasell Street
## www.catholic-doc.org/saintmarys

Called "the Mother Church of the Carolinas and Georgia," St. Mary's was the first Catholic church established in the English colony. Its first pastor came from Ireland in 1788. Originally known as "The Roman Catholic Church of Charleston," St. Mary's officially took its present name in 1837. The Greek Revival building on the site today was consecrated in 1839, replacing an earlier edifice lost in the city's great fire of 1838. Early communicants were mostly Irish immigrants and French refugees from the West Indies. In fact, church records were kept in French until 1822. Today, the crowded churchyard contains gravestones written in Latin, French, and English representing a congregation that spanned 17 nationalities, three continents, and two centuries. Inside, over the main altar, hangs a painting of the Crucifixion painted in 1814 by John S. Gogdell, a noted Charleston artist. The current organ is a Jardine (built in 1874 and restored in 1980) that is often featured in Piccolo Spoleto concerts held in May.

## St. Matthew's Lutheran Church (1872)
### 405 King Street
www.smlconline.org

The huge influx of German immigrants to Charleston during the first half of the 19th century caused the city's second-oldest congregation of Lutherans to greatly expand their house of worship. The magnificently Gothic church, with its tall, German-made stained-glass windows, was finished in 1872 with a 297-foot spire that stands taller than any other in the state. It was designed by John H. Devereaux.

In a spectacular 1965 church fire, the spire collapsed into the street below—the very point, in fact, piercing the sidewalk just to the left of the church's front door. That steeple point is still there (encased in concrete) and commemorated by a plaque honoring the congregation's courage and determination to restore the architectural treasure.

## St. Michael's Episcopal Church (1752–1761)
### 80 Meeting Street
www.stmichaelschurch.org

While St. Philip's can claim to be the oldest congregation in Charleston, St. Michael's lays claim to having the oldest church structure. There is some mystery as to whom the actual architect of St. Michael's might have been, but there's no question that this magnificent edifice is one of the great treasures of the city.

The church has remained essentially unchanged over the centuries, with the exception of a sacristy added in 1883. However, the structure has undergone major repairs several times because of natural and man-made disasters. In the earthquake of 1886, the steeple tower sank 8 inches, and the church cracked in several places. St. Michael's was damaged by a tornado in 1935 and again in 1989 by Hurricane Hugo. During both the American Revolution and the Civil War, the spire was painted black to make it less visible as a target for enemy gunners.

During his visit to Charleston in 1791, President George Washington worshiped at St. Michael's, where he sat in the Governor's Pew—so marked by a small plaque. In later years, the Marquis de Lafayette and Gen. Robert E. Lee sat in that same pew. Buried in St. Michael's churchyard are several distinguished members of the congregation, including Gen. Charles Cotesworth Pinckney, Revolutionary hero, signer of the Constitution, and Federalist presidential candidate; and John Rutledge, signer of the Constitution and member of the U.S. Supreme Court.

## St. Philip's Episcopal Church (1835–1838)
### 146 Church Street
www.stphilipschurchsc.org

St. Philip's is the mother church of the Episcopal Diocese of South Carolina, and for more than 300 years, this church has been a vital force in the life of Charleston. Today, there are more than 1,500 communicants. It is believed the name is derived from the Anglican parish in Barbados, the island from which many early Charleston planters came after emigration from England.

The first St. Philip's was built in 1680–1681 on the site of what is now St. Michael's Episcopal Church at Meeting and Broad Streets. A new edifice was authorized for what was considered to be the "new" gates of the city (the present site on Church Street) in 1710. This building was destroyed by fire in 1835. The present building was designed by Joseph Nyde, who was influenced by the neoclassical arches inside London's St. Martin's-in-the-Fields Church (1721) designed by James Gibbs.

The history of Charleston is traceable just by reading the names of the memorial plaques around the walls of the sanctuary and in the churchyard outside. Buried here are Col. William Rhett, officer of the Crown; Edward Rutledge, signer of the Declaration of Independence; Charles Pinckney, signer of the U.S. Constitution; and the Hon. John C. Calhoun, statesman and vice president of the United States. Here, too, is the grave of DuBose Heyward, author of *Porgy* and collaborator with

George Gershwin on the libretto for the folk opera *Porgy and Bess.*

### Unitarian Church in Charleston (1780, 1854)
### 8 Archdale Street
### www.charlestonuu.org

The first building on this site was under construction when the American Revolution began. During the British occupation of the city, the church was used as quarters for the British militia, and its newly installed pews were destroyed. The church, of Georgian design, was finally repaired and in use by 1787. For the next 30 years it formed one corporate body with the Meeting Street Independent Church (now Circular Church; see previous listing), but in 1839, this congregation was re-chartered as the Unitarian Church.

Charleston was experiencing a period of great prosperity in the 1850s, and the Unitarians hired the young architect (and church member) Francis D. Lee to remodel the building in the popular Gothic Revival style. He was commissioned to incorporate the old walls and tower into his new design. Lee was inspired by the Henry VII chapel at Westminster Abbey—especially the delicate and lacy fan tracery ceiling there. He duplicated that amazing ceiling in this church, and it is considered to be some of the finest Gothic Revival work extant in America.

## MUSEUMS AND OTHER SITES

### American Military Museum
### 360 Concord Street
### (843) 723-9620
### www.americanmilitarymuseum.org

Directly underneath the food court in the IMAX theatre at Fountain Walk (near the S.C. Aquarium) is the American Military Museum, which will be of interest to dedicated reenactment buffs. Here you'll find hundreds of uniforms, patches, and insignia plus legions of military miniatures and toy soldiers. The 7,000-square-foot

museum's collection includes items from Desert Storm, the Vietnam and Korean wars, World Wars I and II, the Spanish–American War, Indian wars, the Civil War, and the American Revolution. Admission is $6.00 for adults, $3.00 for children ages 6 to 12, and free to military personnel in uniform. Hours are 10:00 A.M. to 6:00 P.M., Monday through Saturday. Sunday hours are from 1:00 to 5:00 P.M.

### The Battery

One can argue that Charleston's White Point Gardens, which most people know as the Battery, shouldn't officially be called an "attraction," like a museum or a fort. On the other hand, it's a darn good bet that no first-time visitor to the city ever left here without making it a point to walk there or at least drive by.

In a city where almost every other building or street holds some historical significance, few sites have afforded a better view of Charleston's 300-year-long parade of history than the Battery.

That seaside corner of land at the end of East Bay Street, where it turns and becomes Murray Boulevard, is now a pleasant park with statues and monuments, long-silent cannons, and spreading live oak trees. There's even a Victorian bandstand that looks like it could sport a uniformed Sousa band any Sunday afternoon. But the atmosphere on the Battery hasn't always been so serene.

The Battery has been a prominent feature in Charleston since the earliest days of the English settlement. Then, it was known as Oyster Point because it was little more than a marshy beach covered in oyster shells—bleached white in the Carolina sun.

At first, it was mostly a navigational aid for the sailing vessels going into and out of the harbor. The peninsula was still unsettled, and the first colonial effort was farther upstream on the banks of the Ashley River at what is now called Charles Towne Landing. Later, when the settlement was moved to the much more defensible peninsula site, the point was a popular fishing area—too low and too easily flooded to be much of anything else. Charts used during the years 1708 to 1711 show only a "watch tower" on the site and just a few residences built nearby.

Remember, Charles Towne was still a walled city at that time, the southernmost wall being several blocks north, near what is now the Carolina Yacht Club on East Bay Street. The point was definitely a "suburban" location. The area took a decidedly higher public profile about a decade later, when the pirate Stede Bonnet (pronounced bo-NAY) and some 40 or 50 scalawags like him were hanged there from makeshift gallows. These executions were apparently quite effective in bringing an end to the pirate activity that had plagued the Carolina coast.

The first of several real forts built on the site came along as early as 1737. This and subsequent fortifications were crudely built, however, and none lasted long against the tyranny of the sea. By the time of the American Revolution, White Point was virtually at the city's door and no longer considered a strategic site for defense.

Hurricanes in 1800 and again in 1804 reduced whatever fortification remained there to rubble. Another fort, this version constructed for the War of 1812, apparently gave White Point a popular new name—the Battery. At least, the new name appears on maps beginning about 1833.

The seawall constructed along East Battery (the "high" one) was built after a storm in 1885. Storms and repairs have traded blows at the seawall for many years—in 1893, 1911, 1959, and, of course, with Hugo in 1989.

The area's use as a park dates back to 1837, when the city rearranged certain streets to establish White Point Gardens. It was from this vantage point that Charlestonians watched the battle between Confederate fortifications across the river and the small band of Union troops holed up in Fort Sumter on April 12, 1861. This, of course, was the beginning of the Civil War. Once the war had started, this peaceful little garden was torn up and convulsed into

two massive earthwork batteries—part of Charleston's inner line of defense. And while one of these battery sites housed a huge Blakely rifle (one of the two largest weapons in the Confederacy), neither battery ever fired a shot in anger. (Some incoming artillery rounds probably landed here during the extended bombardment of the city from late 1863 until Charleston fell in February 1865.)

The end of the Civil War was the end of the Battery's role in Charleston's military defense, although several subsequent wars have left poignant souvenirs behind for remembrance. Today no fewer than 26 cannons and monuments dot the Battery's landscape, each of which is described on a nearby plaque or informational marker.

Over the years, the Battery has become something of a balm for the Charlestonian soul. In 1977, Warren Ripley wrote a detailed booklet called *The Battery*, which is still available through the *Post and Courier* offices. In it, Ripley sums up the reasons the Battery is so special:

"It has watched the elaborate drill of colonial militia and the 'goose step' of Hitler's sailors on parade before WWII. It has suffered through 're-enactments' of

---

*Parking can be a hassle in Charleston. See our Getting Here, Getting Around chapter for a list of the city's parking garages. For the lucky few who happen upon a parking meter, here's the story: Most of the older meters have a two-hour maximum time limit and take nickels, dimes, and quarters. If the meter is painted red, you're limited to only fifteen minutes. Here and there, we're starting to see new digital meters that take only quarters. But here's the worst news of all: The meter maids (and misters) in Charleston tend to be quick on the draw when issuing tickets. If you want to be a good citizen, you can report a broken meter by calling (843) 724-7368.*

historic events it witnessed in the first place, seen parades, air shows, and fireworks displays without number.

"It has observed three centuries of ocean traffic, watched the evolution from sailing ship to steam and nuclear propulsion as warships and cargo slipped in and out of port.

"It has echoed Sunday afternoon band concerts and heard the weekday cries of street vendors hawking wares to the neighborhood homes. It has harked to the whispers of countless lovers and warmed to the daylight shouts of happy, playing children."

For Charlestonians, clearly the Battery is more than a pleasant little park. Far more, indeed.

## The Bells of St. Michael's
## Meeting and Broad Streets

If your timing is lucky, a visit to the very heart of Charleston and its "Four Corners of Law" at the intersection of Broad and Meeting Streets will be delightfully punctuated by the resonant chime of mighty church bells ringing overhead.

Indeed, the bells of St. Michael's Episcopal Church make more than just a pleasant sound. Their ringing is very much a part of Charleston—one of its oldest and most endearing attractions. In fact, their ringing is another of Charleston's object lessons in faithful perseverance, stubborn Southern survival, and the fleeting passage of time.

St. Michael's Episcopal Church, built in 1761, is the oldest church edifice on the Peninsula and the second-oldest congregation in the city. (See previous listing in the Historic Churches section of this chapter.) This is the church where George Washington worshiped on his famous 1791 presidential tour that included a stay in Charleston (see Heyward-Washington House listing in the House Museums section of this chapter).

The eight bronze bells hanging in St. Michael's spire were originally cast at the Whitechapel Foundry of London in 1764. Church records say the bells first sounded here in Charleston on September 21 of that same year, having safely made their first journey across the Atlantic Ocean. Amazingly, the bells have made that long journey back to England three times since.

Their first journey "home" was in 1782 during the War of Independence. The bells had rung in defiance of the Crown during Charleston's protest of the Stamp Act in 1765, and British soldiers confiscated them as a punishing prize of war. Once back on English soil, however, the bells were purchased by a private speculator and promptly returned to Charleston and again placed in St. Michael's steeple.

In 1862, during the Civil War, seven of the bells were removed from the steeple and taken to Columbia for what was hoped to be safekeeping. Charleston was such a likely target that many of the city's treasures were sent to Columbia at that time to escape the Union's wrath. Only the large tenor bell was left behind, to ring the alarm for Charlestonians still in the city. In 1865, the year Charleston fell, the bell rang dutifully until it cracked. Meanwhile, Gen. William T. Sherman's Union army selected upstate Columbia as an artillery target, and South Carolina's entire capital burned in what was one of the most dramatic episodes of the war.

In 1866, St. Michael's vestry arranged to have the seven charred bells from Columbia and the one cracked bell remaining in the church returned to England to be recast once more in their original molds at the Whitechapel Foundry. When they were returned in 1867, church records show that the melodies of "Home Again" and "Auld Lang Syne" rang from St. Michael's steeple.

The last journey of the bells back to England and the Whitechapel Foundry—still in business after all these years—was in 1993. Their recasting, once more in the original molds, was part of St. Michael's $3.8 million restoration and repair project undertaken as a result of damages suffered in Hurricane Hugo.

The bells of St. Michael's rang anew on July 4, 1993, in a special, daylong hand-ringing ceremony done in the English style.

Nostalgic Charlestonians from all denominations made special trips past St. Michael's all day to hear the bells celebrate Independence Day and to acknowledge another homecoming for the bells of St. Michael's at the Four Corners of Law.

**Children's Museum of the Lowcountry**
**25 Ann Street**
**(843) 853-8962**
**www.explorecml.org**
This long-planned museum, which opened in September 2003, was the realization of a dream stubbornly defended by its founders for several years. They envisioned a hands-on learning place for children ages three months to 12 years celebrating their unique Lowcountry surroundings and the vast creative opportunities available to them here. For example, youngsters can explore the ocean and the life of a shrimper on their very own shrimp boat, the *Ann Marie*. They can also imagine themselves as medieval royalty living in a mighty castle. They can create artistic masterpieces in an "art room" designed for spirited young minds. And throughout the year, programs, day camps, and special classes will support educational experiences in the arts, sciences, and humanities. The museum is open to Lowcountry children, visitors, and their families from 10:00 A.M. to 5:00 P.M. Tuesday through Saturday, Sunday 1:00 to 5:00 P.M. General admission is $5.00.

**The Charleston Museum**
**360 Meeting Street**
**(843) 722-2996**
**www.charlestonmuseum.org**
Directly across Meeting Street from the Visitor Reception and Transportation Center is one of Charleston's finest jewels: the Charleston Museum. Because it is the first and oldest museum in America, having been founded in 1773, the museum's collection predates all modern thinking about what should be kept or discarded in preserving the artifacts of a culture.

Instead, the Charleston Museum is heir to the collected memorabilia of real American patriots, early Charlestonian families, and early colonial thinkers, explorers, scientists, and planters. It is their opinion of what mattered then, and what they thought should matter to us today. Although the collection is housed in modern buildings and has the benefit of modern conservation methods and enlightened interpretation, the collection is uniquely eloquent. It speaks of a city that already knew it was great and sought early on to record itself for posterity. That difference alone makes the Charleston Museum a must-see.

The museum's scope is the social and natural history of Charleston and the South Carolina coastal region. Objects from natural science, cultural history, historical archaeology, ornithology, and ethnology are presented to illustrate the importance each had in the history of this area. The Charleston Silver Exhibit contains internationally recognized work by local silversmiths in a beautifully mounted display. Pieces date from colonial times through the late 19th century.

Visitors will see what the museum's many archaeological excavations have revealed about some of the city's best and worst times. Some artifacts date from the early colonial period, while others are from the Civil War years. Some exhibits focus on early Native Americans who lived in this region. Others trace changes in trade and commerce, the expansive rice and cotton plantation systems, and the important contributions made by African Americans.

Children will be intrigued by the Discover Me room with amazing things to touch, see, and do. They'll see toys from the past, games children played, the clothes they wore, furniture they used, and more. The photographs, ceramics, pewter, and tools reveal a very personal portrait of Charlestonians from the past.

Because the Charlestonian lifestyle is so much a part of the city and its history, the two house museums owned and operated by the Charleston Museum are an important part of its offering. (See previous listings for Heyward-Washington House and Joseph Manigault House in the

# The "Best Friend of Charleston" Comes Home

The very first steam locomotive to offer regular passenger and freight service in the United States chugged out of Charleston in 1830. A near-exact replica of that train, known as "The Best Friend," finally came back home in 1993 to rest and to be stored in part of Charleston's original railroad complex next to the visitor center on Ann Street.

The replica (built in 1928 and refurbished in 1969) was originally commissioned by Norfolk Southern Railroad Co. to celebrate the 100th anniversary of its parent company, the South Carolina Canal and Railroad Co.

The now-famous train (consisting of an engine, a tender, and two open passenger coaches) made its first run on Christmas Day of 1830. About 140 brave Charlestonians climbed aboard this curious-looking contraption at Line Street and chugged a dazzling 6 miles out to Dorchester Road—which was as far as

tracks had been laid to date.

Newspaper accounts at the time said, "We flew on the wings of the wind at the varied speed of 15 to 25 miles per hour." Soon, the tracks were extended 136 miles, up to Hamburg, South Carolina, creating the first viable train transportation system in the country. Eventually, those first railroad tracks would find their way over the Smoky Mountains to Knoxville, Tennessee, where they would carry the first U.S. mail over the mountains and carry the first military troops into the Civil War.

As for the original "Best Friend," it sadly came to an early demise. Just six months into the operation (in June 1831), the train was idle at one of its stops en route when the engineer became annoyed by the constant hissing of the noisy escape valve. He instructed a slave fireman to tie off the valve with his handkerchief and fix the nagging problem. In due course, the engine exploded, killing

House Museums section of this chapter.) In these appropriate settings, you'll see some of the museum's remarkable collection of antique furniture and other decorative arts.

The Charleston Museum is open Monday through Saturday from 9:00 A.M. to 5:00 P.M. and 1:00 to 5:00 P.M. on Sunday. Admission is $10.00 for adults and teens and $4.00 for children ages 3 to 12. (See the Kidstuff chapter for more on children's programs.) Combination tickets, which include admission for the two house muse-

ums, sell for $14 for two sites and $18 for all three.

**Old Exchange and Provost Dungeon**
**122 East Bay Street**
**(843) 727-2165**
**www.oldexchange.com**
A public building has stood on this site at East Bay and Broad Streets since Charles Towne was moved from its original settlement to its present location in 1680. The early settlers built their court of guard here.

*The Best Friend, America's first passenger and freight train, would have been a wondrous sight to behold as it traveled the length of its run from Charleston to Hamburg, South Carolina, in the 1830s.* CITY OF CHARLESTON

the poor fireman, scalding the engineer, and destroying the original locomotive.

Plans are now under way to eventually include the "Best Friend" replica in the newly opened Children's Museum of the Lowcountry, located at 25 Ann Street. (See the Kidstuff chapter.)

They imprisoned pirates and Native Americans in the building's lower level and held their town meetings upstairs in the hall.

The British built the present building to create an impressive presence in the bustling colonial port. With its striking Palladian architecture, the Exchange surely did just that. It was completed in 1771 and quickly became the social, political, and economic hub of the growing city.

From its steps, the independent colony of South Carolina was publicly declared in March 1776. During the Revolution, the building was converted to a British prison, where signers of the Declaration of Independence were to be held. In 1788, the convention to ratify the U.S. Constitution met in the building, and President George Washington was lavishly entertained here several times during his Southern tour. From 1818 to 1896, the building served both the Federal and Confederate governments as the Charleston post office. In 1917, Congress deeded the building to the

Daughters of the American Revolution of South Carolina.

During an excavation of the dungeon in 1965, part of the original seawall of Charles Towne was discovered. Today, the Old Exchange and Provost Dungeon is leased to the state of South Carolina and open to the public as a museum. The building has two halls that are available to rent for private events. Hours are 9:00 A.M. to 5:00 P.M. daily. Admission is $7.00 for adults and teens, $3.50 for children ages 7 to 12, and free for kids younger than 6. Senior discounts and group rates are available.

## Gibbes Museum of Art
## 135 Meeting Street
## (843) 722-2706
## www.gibbesmuseum.org

Established in 1905 by the Carolina Art Association, the Gibbes Museum of Art stands a block and a half north of the Four Corners of Law. As locations go, that's fairly close to what Charlestonians traditionally believe to be heaven. And clearly, the Gibbes represents Charleston's most uplifting experiences in art.

Museum members, residents of the city, and visitors all have access to a distinguished and growing collection along with year-round exhibitions, educational programs, and special events. The building itself stands as a memorial to James Shoolbred Gibbes, a wealthy Charlestonian who bequeathed funds to the city of Charleston and the Carolina Art Association to create a permanent home for the association's collection.

Today that rich and fascinating collection includes American paintings, prints, and drawings from the 18th century to the present. There are landscapes, genre scenes, views of Charleston, and portraits of notable South Carolinians. Faces associated with history (and architectural landmarks all over the Lowcountry) seem to come to life here. You'll find Thomas Middleton painted by Benjamin West and Charles Izard Manigault painted by Thomas Sully. There's John C. Calhoun painted by Rembrandt Peale, plus an out-

standing collection of more than 400 exquisite, hand-painted miniature portraits of 18th- and 19th-century Charlestonians.

The Elizabeth Wallace Miniature Rooms offer 10 miniature interiors representing different traditions in American and French architecture, decorative arts, and design. The Gibbes also has an outstanding collection of early Japanese woodblock prints in a special Oriental gallery.

In addition to the regular schedule of exhibitions on loan from international, national, and regional collections, the Gibbes presents major exhibitions in the visual arts during Spoleto Festival USA every May through June. Members and the public are invited to join museum tours, gallery talks, lectures, seminars, and meet-the-artist events, and to see films and videos made for schools and community groups.

One of the most popular aspects of the Gibbes is the museum shop, which offers an excellent selection of art books, posters, note cards, jewelry, and other gift items. Shop early for the best Christmas cards. Museum members receive a 10 percent discount on all purchases. Admission to the shop, which is open during regular museum hours, is free.

The Gibbes has a working studio at 76 Queen Street that provides professional instruction in everything from painting and photography to textile silk-screening and jewelry-making. Classes and workshops are designed for all ages and levels of experience. Contact the Gibbes School of Art at (843) 577-7275 for additional information.

Memberships to the Gibbes Museum of Art are renewable on an annual basis. Dues are tax-deductible. You'll find applications for membership at the information desk, or you can call the Gibbes at (843) 722-2706. Guided tours are available by appointment. Ask for the education department to make arrangements. Admission is $7.00 for adults, $6.00 for seniors, military, and college students with school IDs. For youngsters 6 to 18, admission is $4.00. Members are admitted free. Museum hours are Tuesday through Saturday from 10:00 A.M. to

5:00 P.M. and 1:00 to 5:00 P.M. Sunday. The museum is closed on Mondays. The Gibbes is fully wheelchair accessible. (For more on the Gibbes, see the chapters on Kidstuff and The Arts.)

### CSS *H.L. Hunley*
**Warren Lasch Conservation Center**
**1250 Supply Street, Bldg. 225,**
**North Charleston**
**(877) 448-6539, (843) 744-2186**
**www.hunley.org**

In 1864, the CSS *H.L. Hunley* was the first submarine in history to successfully sink an enemy war ship when it launched an attack against the Union ironclad *Housatonic* off the coast of Charleston. The *Hunley* and its eight-man crew never returned to home port, however, and its fate remained unknown until divers located the sub in 1995. It was discovered partially buried in mud not far from the scene of its 1864 triumph. In August 2000, the *Hunley* made national headlines as it was carefully raised from its watery grave and brought back to Charleston for several years of painstaking conservation and analysis. It rests, for now, at the high-tech Warren Lasch Conservation Center on the former Charleston Navy Base, where scientists are slowly unlocking the mysteries of its disappearance, including how and when the crew died. Tours are available every Saturday from 10:00 A.M. to 5:00 P.M. and Sunday from noon to 5:00 P.M. Advance reservations are required to view the sub in its tank and see the fascinating exhibits of its contents and ingenious technology. Call for available tour times, tickets, and directions. Admission is $10 plus a small service charge.

### IMAX Theatre Charleston
**360 Concord Street**
**(next to the S.C. Aquarium)**
**(843) 725-4629**

Just next door to the South Carolina Aquarium, you'll find another attraction making a hit with children and adults alike. In the summer of 2000, Charleston got its own IMAX theater, which brings the moving picture experience into a new dimension. Incredible photography notwithstanding, the screen is five stories tall, and the theater seats are ergonomic delights for the weary spine—upholstered in light blue Italian leather. The ultra-dynamic sound comes literally "through" the screen at the viewer, and many of the newer IMAX movies are now photographed in 3-D. Some of the titles that locals and tourists have recently enjoyed include *Dolphins, Everest, Titanic,* and *T-Rex.* Shows run on the hour from 10:00 A.M. to 9:00 P.M., with different titles shown throughout the day. Adults are charged $8.50, and seniors and youth pay $7.50. Call for the day's movie schedule, and catch the incredible IMAX experience, if you haven't already done so.

### Magnolia Cemetery
**70 Cunnington Street**
**(843) 722-8638**

One of the most telling places in all of Charleston has to be the remarkably distinctive 19th-century cemetery at the north end of the Peninsula, not far off East Bay Street (which becomes Morrison Drive).

Not on any contemporary beaten path, and clearly not a tourist destination, Magnolia Cemetery is the quiet, final resting place of many important Charlestonians and other players in the city's long-running and colorful drama. It is also an intriguing collection of Southern funerary art in an almost unbearably romantic setting.

The site was originally on the grounds of Magnolia Umbria Plantation, which dates back to 1790 and where rice was the principal crop in the first half of the 19th century. By 1850, however, a 181-acre section of that land on the edge of the marsh had been surveyed for a peaceful cemetery, dedicated on November 19, 1850. From that time on (even to the present), many of Charleston's most prominent families chose Magnolia as the place to bury and commemorate their loved ones.

Many of the city's leaders, politicians, judges, and other pioneers in many fields of endeavor are interred beneath the ancient, spreading live oaks of Magnolia. Among them are five Confederate brigadier generals. There is a vast Confederate section, with more than 1,700 graves of the known and unknown. Eighty-four South Carolinians who fell at the Battle of Gettysburg are included.

There are literally hundreds of ornate private family plots, many of which bear famous names. You will find the monument of Robert Barnwell Rhett, "Father of Secession," U.S. senator, attorney general of South Carolina, and author. There's also the grave of George Alfred Trenholm, a wealthy cotton broker who served as treasurer of the Confederacy and organized many a blockade run for the cause. Trenholm is thought by many to be the man on whom Margaret Mitchell's Rhett Butler was based. Among the famous artists and writers buried in Magnolia are Charleston's Alice Ravenel Huger Smith and John Bennett.

To find Magnolia, drive north on East Bay (Morrison Drive), and turn right at the traffic light onto Meeting Street (Highway 52). Turn right at the first opportunity onto Cunnington Street, and Magnolia's gates (open daily from 2:00 to 6:00 P.M.) are at the end of the street.

### Patriots Point
### Naval and Maritime Museum
**40 Patriots Point Road, Mt. Pleasant**
**(843) 884-2727**
**www.patriotspoint.org**

Patriots Point is the name given to a huge maritime museum complex that consists mainly of four *in situ* ships (permanently situated): a submarine, a destroyer, a Coast Guard cutter, and an aircraft carrier with 25 vintage aircraft. For this, one of Charleston's major attractions, you'll need comfortable shoes and plenty of time.

Considering all there is to see, Patriots Point Naval and Maritime Museum is a real bargain. Admission is $14.00 for adults and teens, $7.00 for children ages 6 to 11, and free for children younger than 6. There's a $2.00 discount for senior citi-

zens and anyone with a military ID. Plan on spending the better part of your day at Patriots Point; it's open from 9:00 A.M. to 6:30 P.M. Gift shop hours are from 9:00 A.M. to 5:30 P.M. Here's a detailed rundown of the ships on display.

### USS *Yorktown* (Aircraft Carrier)

No one comes or goes through Charleston via US 17 across the Cooper River bridges without noticing the giant aircraft carrier moored off Mt. Pleasant. It dominates—no, commands—a vast stretch of the Cooper's Mt. Pleasant shore at the very gates into Charleston Harbor.

She is none other than the USS *Yorktown* (CV-10), the famous "Fighting Lady" of World War II and the proud flagship of Patriots Point, the world's largest naval and maritime museum.

Of the four vessels permanently anchored and open to the public, the *Yorktown* is the most impressive. Commissioned April 15, 1943, in the darkest days of the war, the ship fought valiantly in some of the worst engagements ever witnessed at sea, inflicting heavy losses against the Japanese at the Truk and Mariana Islands, and supporting the American ground troops in the Philippines, at bloody Iwo Jima, and Okinawa.

Shortly after the ship was commissioned and sent into battle, 20th Century Fox put a film crew onboard to record—on then-rare Technicolor film—the continuing war story of a typical Navy carrier in action. The spectacular footage shot at unnamed, secret locations during then-unnamed battles became the Academy Award–winning documentary film feature of 1944. The film was called *The Fighting Lady,* and it is shown daily at the *Yorktown's* onboard theater at regularly scheduled intervals. Don't miss it. Nothing brings the World War II drama of the *Yorktown* to life like this amazing celluloid time capsule. The terrible explosions and blistering fires, the fierce fighting, and all the brave young faces who served on the *Yorktown* are there to be seen and appreciated by generations then unborn.

But the *Yorktown* story doesn't end there. Not at all. The ship went on to patrol the western Pacific during the Cold War and even fought in Vietnam. In fact, the *Yorktown* received the crew of *Apollo 8,* the first manned space flight around the moon, in 1968.

The flight deck, hangar deck, and many of the *Yorktown* crew's living and working quarters are open to visitors today. You'll find actual carrier aircraft and Vietnam-era anti-sub planes on display—25 aircraft in all. And there are other fascinating exhibits on everything from mines to shipbuilding.

One of the newer exhibits is the true-to-scale Vietnam Naval Support Base, showing the living conditions and work areas of a typical support base during the Vietnam War. You'll also find the Congressional Medal of Honor Museum, featuring displays representing the eight different eras of our military history in which the Medal of Honor was awarded. You'll see actual Medals of Honor and some of the artifacts related to their original recipients.

Mercifully, you'll find a snack bar onboard the *Yorktown* and another in the riverside gift shop, so excited youngsters and foot-weary veterans can stop for lunch and a rest.

### Laffey (Destroyer)

The heroic destroyer *Laffey* (DD-724) was commissioned on February 8, 1944, and participated in the giant D-Day landings of Allied troops at Normandy four months later. Transferred to the Pacific, she was struck by five Japanese kamikaze suicide planes and hit by three bombs during one hour on April 16, 1945, off Okinawa. The *Laffey*'s gallant crew not only kept the ship afloat but also managed to shoot down 11 planes during the attack. After World War II, the *Laffey* served during the Korean War and then in the Atlantic Fleet until she was decommissioned in 1975.

A tour route on the *Laffey* lets you see the bridge, battle stations, living quarters, and various displays of destroyer activities.

### Clamagore (Submarine)

The World War II submarine *Clamagore* (SS-343) was commissioned on June 28, 1945, and operated in the Atlantic and Mediterranean throughout its entire career, patrolling tense Cuban waters during 1962. Twice modified, the *Clamagore* survived as one of the U.S. Navy's last diesel-powered subs until it was decommissioned in 1975.

The *Clamagore* tour route covers the control room, berth and mess areas, engine rooms, maneuvering room, and displays of submarine warfare. Note: Spaces are very cramped onboard. Visitors with health problems or claustrophobia are strongly cautioned.

### Ingham (Coast Guard Cutter)

The *Ingham,* (WHEC-35) was the most decorated vessel in the U.S. service, with a total of 18 ribbons earned during its career of more than 50 years. Commissioned in 1936, the *Ingham* took part in 31 World War II convoys, six Pacific patrols, and three Vietnam tours. In 1942, it sank the German U-boat 626 with one depth charge, called *"Ingham's* Hole-in-One."

In recent years, the cutter tracked illegal immigrants and drug runners. The *Ingham* was decommissioned in 1988 and is now open for tours.

### South Carolina Aquarium
### 100 Aquarium Wharf,
### Calhoun at Concord Streets
### (843) 720-1990
### www.scaquarium.org

In May 2000, after years of planning, controversy, and nervous anticipation, Charleston's $69-million South Carolina Aquarium opened to rave reviews as a major new attraction in the Lowcountry. This nonprofit, self-supporting institution is dedicated to educating the public about and helping to conserve South Carolina's unique aquatic habitats. Their mission is to display and interpret the state's diverse range of habitats—from rushing mountain streams to the oceanic depths of the

Atlantic. It was the first aquarium in the country to open with a complete Education Master Plan in place. Admission is free for South Carolina school children enrolled in the aquarium's academic programs. Extensive field studies and outreach programs are also in place.

Among the 60 exhibits in the 93,000-square-foot building are more than 10,000 living organisms, representing more than 500 species. The aquarium is home to otters, birds, turtles, fish, venomous snakes, other reptiles and amphibians, aquatic invertebrates, and insects. The exhibit path leads visitors through five major regions of the Southeast Appalachian Watershed as found in South Carolina—the Blue Ridge Mountains, the Piedmont, the Coastal Plain, the Coast, and the Ocean. They use a wide variety of media to enhance the visitor experience. Some are interactive, some are for very young children, some are education "stations" for discovery labs and classrooms. Admission to the South Carolina Aquarium is $15.00 for adults age 12 through 61, $13.00 for seniors age 62 and up, and $8.00 for children ages 3 to 11. Hours vary according to time of year: From August 16 to March 31 it's open Monday through Saturday 9:00 A.M. to 5:00 P.M., Sunday noon to 5:00 P.M.; from April 1 to August 15 it's 9:00 A.M. to 6:00 P.M., Sunday noon to 6:00 P.M. The aquarium is closed on Thanksgiving and Christmas Day and closes at 1:00 P.M. on Christmas Eve. Parking is available across Concord Street from the aquarium's entrance.

### The Citadel Museum
**171 Moultrie Street**
**(843) 792-6846**
**www.citadel.edu**

This museum showcases The Citadel, the Military College of South Carolina. The museum covers the history of the school from 1842 to the present. Various displays represent the military, academic, social, and athletic aspects of cadet life.

The museum is on campus, on the third floor of the Daniel Library—the first building on the right inside The Citadel's

main gates. Hours are Sunday through Friday from 2:00 to 5:00 P.M. and Saturday from noon to 5:00 P.M. The museum is closed for college, national, and religious holidays. There is no charge for admission. (See more on The Citadel in the Education chapter.)

### Karpeles Manuscript Museum
**68 Spring Street**
**(843) 853–4651**
**www.karpeles.com**

This is one of seven museums in the United States funded by California businessman David Karpeles. They are all nonprofit endeavors to "preserve the original writings of the great authors, scientists, statesmen, sovereigns, philosophers, and leaders from all periods of world history," according to the museum's mission statement.

Scholars, educators, students, and lovers of books and manuscripts are invited to enjoy these collections free of charge. This unusual but fascinating collection is housed in the former Saint James United Methodist Church (1856), one of Charleston's best 19th-century replicas of a classical Roman temple. Special exhibits change from time to time, but the permanent collection includes some of the rare, original writings that helped build our country's unique form of government. Among the Karpeles manuscripts is one of the four original drafts of the Bill of Rights and the Emancipation Proclamation amendment to the Constitution.

The museum is open Tuesday through Saturday from 11:00 A.M. to 4:00 P.M. For more information on exhibits or special programs, contact Caroline Dame at the museum. Admission and parking are free.

### John Rivers Communications Museum
**College of Charleston, 58 George Street**
**(843) 953–5810**
**www.cofc.edu/~jrmuseum**

The College of Charleston's John Rivers Communications Museum offers a unique opportunity to explore the world of broadcasting and communications. John M. Rivers was a Charleston-born banker, businessman, and broadcasting executive who introduced television to the Low-country in 1953.

Visitors to the museum can hear early sound recordings from the Kenneth Hanson Collection, learn about the lives of famous inventors such as Marconi and Edison, and trace the advancements in science from the magic lantern to television, from the phonograph to radio.

The museum is open Monday through Friday from noon to 4:00 P.M., except during College of Charleston holidays. Summer hours may vary, and group tours are conducted by appointment only, so call the museum for scheduling. Admission is free, but donations are appreciated.

## Postal History Museum
## Meeting and Broad Streets

Unknown to most of the tourists who pass through the intersection of Meeting and Broad Streets (the Four Corners of Law), there's a fine and fascinating little gem right there, deftly tucked into one of the corners.

The Postal History Museum is a special room inside the Charleston post office showing visitors some of the interesting tidbits of postal history associated with this coastal colonial town.

For instance, Charleston's first postmaster (on the job before 1694) was actually known as the city's "powder receiver." Not only was he responsible for the mail, he also collected a percentage of gunpowder from every ship that arrived (see subsequent listing for Powder Magazine). He was required to post incoming letters in a public room in his house for 30 days and collected his commission only when the letters were picked up by the recipient. Imagine being in London in 1700, addressing a letter to "John Doe, Charles Towne, Carolina," and it actually getting here.

This little museum is a must for philatelists or anyone else who ever wondered how 18th- and 19th-century mail was handled. It is open during regular U.S. post office hours, and admission is free. It's a great excuse to see Charleston's elabo-

rately detailed 1896 post office building, the oldest continuously operating post office in the Carolinas.

## Powder Magazine
## 79 Cumberland Street
## (843) 805-6730

Only a couple of blocks from the bustling market area is, quite simply, the oldest public building in the Carolinas. And yet, as Charleston attractions go, the Powder Magazine is relatively unknown to tourists and to some locals as well.

Perhaps the site is overlooked because it's dramatically upstaged by Charleston's sumptuous house museums and romantic streetscapes. And in truth, the utilitarian Powder Magazine actually predates Charleston's legendary aesthetics. It was built for a time when the still-new English settlement was predominantly interested in self-defense and basic survival.

In the early years of the 18th century, Charles Towne was still threatened by Spanish forces, hostile Indians, rowdy packs of buccaneers, and an occasional French attack. It was still a walled city, fortified against surprise attack.

In August 1702, a survey of the armament in Charles Towne reported "2,306 lbs. of gunpowder, 496 shot of all kind, 28 great guns, 47 Grenada guns, 360 cartridges, and 500 lbs. of pewter shot." In his formal request for additional cannons, the royal governor requested "a suitable store of shot and powder . . . (to) make Carolina impregnable." And so, in 1703, the Crown approved and funded such a building, which was completed in 1713 on what is now Cumberland Street.

The Powder Magazine was the domain of the powder receiver, a newly appointed city official entitled to accept a gunpowder tax levied on all merchant ships entering Charleston Harbor during this period.

The building served its originally intended purpose for many decades, but eventually, in an early colonial version of today's base closings, it was deemed unnecessary (or too small) and sold into private hands.

This multi-gabled, tile-roofed, architectural oddity was almost forgotten by historians until the early 1900s. In 1902, it was purchased by the National Society of Colonial Dames of America in the State of South Carolina. It was maintained and operated as a small museum until 1991 when water damage, roof deterioration, and time had finally taken too high a toll. What the Powder Magazine needed to survive at all was a major stabilization and restoration—something beyond the resources of the owners.

In an agreement whereby the Historic Charleston Foundation did the needed work under a 99-year lease, the Powder Magazine has undergone a $400,000 preservation effort, its first ever. This included a temporary roof over the entire structure, allowing the massive walls to dry out before necessary repairs could even begin. Much-needed archaeological and archival research was also done on the site.

The Powder Magazine was opened to the public in the summer of 1997. Inside, a new, interactive exhibit interprets Charleston's first 50 years—a time when it was still a relatively crude colonial outpost of the British Empire. Admission is free. Hours are 10:00 A.M. to 5:00 P.M. Monday through Saturday; Sunday 2:00 to 5:00 P.M.

# ARCHITECTURAL AND HISTORIC PRESERVATION

I f anything is more remarkable than Charleston's softly pastel colors, cobblestone streets, graceful church spires, and elegant old homes with their exquisite interiors—it has to be the fact that any of it still exists at all.

No other colonial city has suffered so many calamities as often as Charleston. Time after time, fire has left vast areas of the city in ashes. The city was bombarded during war twice—once by the British during the Revolution and again by Northern cannon in the War between the States.

Mother Nature has repeatedly hurled fierce hurricanes and tornadoes at the city, and it has been cracked and shaken periodically by terrible earthquakes.

And yet, as you walk through the large and little streets south of Calhoun, you find them lined with fascinating architectural relics of the past. It's hard to imagine that much of what looks so timeless and permanent today could so easily have been swept away by any number of man-made disasters or devastating natural happenstances.

Indeed, Charleston's ethic of architectural preservation and restoration comes by no accident. It's the result of hard work and sacrifice by a few early visionaries and the regularly tested courage of today's preservation organizations.

Insiders need to know about these organizations. Being savvy of the preservation laws can actually have financial benefits here. Qualified Charleston property owners (newcomers and old Charleston families alike) can donate conservation easements to either of the city's two major preservation organizations and receive cer-

tain tax benefits in exchange. This is one of the ways our federal government rewards and encourages historic preservation in the community. An easement is "partial interest in a property, set out as protective covenants or restrictions and conveyed by recorded deed." In other words, the easement runs with the land in perpetuity and affects each succeeding owner, but the grantors and successor owners retain full use and enjoyment of the property, subject to the terms of the easement. In exchange, the Internal Revenue Service recognizes a tax deduction for the gift of a perpetual conservation restriction on the use of real property.

Charleston buildings within the registered historic district that are of some architectural integrity and more than 50 years old usually can receive this certification. Properties eligible for easement donation (mostly below Calhoun Street) include agricultural, commercial or residential structures, or historically important acreage.

This award-winning preservation and tax strategy has been growing in popularity during the last few years. The Historic Charleston Foundation, for instance, holds protective covenants on more than 320 structures and easements donated by commercial and residential owners in the Greater Charleston area. This is a viable means through which concerned property owners can actively participate in the long-term preservation of Charleston.

To stand guard properly against the pitfalls and challenges that lie ahead, it is important to recognize the dues already paid. Historic preservation in Charleston

# The Steps of Market Hall:
# Getting Them Right Took Three Tries

For some visitors, the "discipline" of Charleston's preservation ethic may seem excessive (and to some homeowners, maybe even intrusive). But the result of being universally strict and having exceedingly high standards of excellence is a city whose collective architectural charm is nothing short of a national treasure appreciated the world over. A good example of this discipline is evident to every visitor who strolls through the busy downtown Market area with its colorful souvenir stalls and sweetgrass basket weavers. Dominating the entire Market area is the 1840–41 Market Hall facing Meeting Street. The Market Hall, now open as the museum of the United Daughters of the Confederacy (see the Attractions chapter), has recently undergone a $3-million renovation.

The building was designed by Edward Brickell White, one of the city's most prolific and sophisticated 19th-century architects. White used a combination of Tuscan, Doric, and Georgian elements to simulate a Roman temple in academically correct proportions.

After a century and a half of use, the building was in need of complete restoration. If the ravages of earthquake, war, and time hadn't taken enough of a toll, 1989's Hurricane Hugo came along and all but destroyed the structure. A meticulous restoration that took nearly a decade to complete was begun by the city shortly after the storm. This work included replacing the crumbling brownstone steps leading from the street level to the massive front door.

Originally, the steps had been ordered from a quarry in Connecticut that pro-

duced a unique stone with a distinctive reddish hue. Since that quarry had long since been closed, another option was chosen, and custom-cut steps were ordered from a stone quarry in Nova Scotia to simulate the originals. However, when the steps arrived, this "new" stone contained certain imperfections that were unacceptable to local preservationists on Charleston's Board of Architectural Review. In a gesture to save time and money, another set of steps were ordered—this time precast from a high-tech, dyed concrete-like material that supposedly was longer wearing than even the original brownstone. In fact, sample steps were delivered to the site and installed pending approval from the experts. But a howl of protest arose from Charleston's purists, and this solution was summarily rejected. They made the point that if owners of private homes in the historic district must be required to use appropriate, original materials when making their repairs, so should the city. Thus, Charleston officials flew to New England to the quarry site where the Market's original steps were cut in the 1840s to see if enough stone of sufficient quality could be found to complete the project and do it right. This, they did—personally overseeing the cutting and shaping of each stone.

After another $100,000, the handsome brownstone steps to Market Hall were installed, and the job was finally completed. That's the kind of restoration ethic that wins architectural awards from international critics. That's the standard of excellence you see everywhere you look in the historic district. That's Charleston.

remains an active and vital force. The organizations responsible for keeping Charleston beautiful continue to need public support and enlightened participation.

What follows is a brief description of Charleston's principal preservation organizations along with membership and other support information.

### Charleston Library Society
### 164 King Street, Charleston
### (843) 723-9912

The Charleston Library Society is one of the little gems that academics and serious researchers say is quintessentially "Charlestonian." This private, subscription library of rare and often original resource material traces its collection back to 1748. Therefore, some of their indexing may not be state-of-the-art. However, in their King Street archives is housed a rich and diverse collection of early printed matter relating to South Carolina architecture and history. They have clipping files, newspapers, maps, photographs, and manuscripts—some of which date back to the earliest days of the colony. This is an appropriate resource for serious scholars and experienced genealogists only. But the library is open to new membership, and it is possible to pay a daily research fee to work here. Hours are Monday through Friday 9:30 A.M. to 5:30 P.M. and Saturday 9:30 A.M. to 2:00 P.M.

### Historic Charleston Foundation
### 40 East Bay Street, Charleston
### (843) 723-1623
### www.historiccharleston.org

Historic Charleston Foundation is a nonprofit, educational organization dedicated to the preservation and conservation of the nation's architectural and cultural heritage as represented in Charleston and the Lowcountry.

Organized and incorporated in 1947, the Foundation has undertaken programs that concentrate on property conservation plus neighborhood and business zone revitalization. The Foundation seeks the stabilization of Charleston's architecturally significant urban environment, which traces its origin to the 1670s.

The Foundation's primary efforts have centered in Charleston's Old and Historic District, the oldest in the United States, which encompasses more than 3,600 structures and represents approximately 25 percent of the Peninsula's buildings. Additional preservation efforts and survey work extend into the outlying tri-county area, the original settlement area of the Carolinas.

Foundation programs serve as realistic alternatives to urban decay; provide protection for vulnerable buildings, housing, and neighborhoods; and promote heritage education and citizen participation in urban planning. In fact, the Foundation's efforts in these areas serve as models for many other communities throughout the nation.

The work of the Foundation is divided into five basic areas: preservation programs, house museum and curatorial efforts, heritage tours and education, Historic Charleston Foundation reproductions, and public relations and development. Staff offices and the organization's Preservation Resource Center are at 40 East Bay Street in the historic waterfront building known as the Missroon House (1808).

The Missroon House contains the Foundation's executive offices, but it also contains four public spaces including an archive where people can research individual properties and access other restoration information.

The Foundation owns and operates three of Charleston's famous museums— the Nathaniel Russell House at 51 Meeting Street, the Aiken-Rhett House at 48 Elizabeth Street, and the Powder Magazine at 79 Cumberland Street. (See the Attractions chapter for in-depth descriptions of these museums.)

The Foundation's Frances R. Edmunds Preservation Center at 108 Meeting Street provides additional offices and serves as an orientation center with free exhibits about the city's architectural history. Here,

## CLOSE-UP

# Charleston's Architectural Idiom: The Single House

You'll see a thousand examples—from grand brick or stucco structures three or four stories tall to more modest clapboard houses with one or two floors. As different as they may seem, they all share a common denominator. They all are exponents of a unique architectural invention: the Charleston single house.

In its simplest definition, the single house is one room wide (butted against the street) and two or more rooms deep. Frequently a side porch is featured—in Charleston, it's called a "piazza"—giving welcome shade and adding extra room for outdoor living. Piazzas, in turn, may also be one or multiple stories in height. All single-house piazzas, however, will have one formal opening onto the street that serves (more or less) as the property's front door.

Experts love to debate the origins of this architectural phenomenon. There are several theories. Some say the architectural roots lie in the Bahamas; others say it evolved here in Charleston as the English custom of primogeniture (whereby the eldest son inherits an entire property) began to break down. This in turn led to inherited properties being subdivided again and again into narrow, strip-like lots—the houses built on them ultimately had to conform. Another possibility is tied to residential properties being taxed according to their frontage on the street in 18th-century Charleston.

You can choose a theory and join in the fray if you like, but genuine 18th- and 19th-century single houses are quintessentially Charlestonian. And they're a point of much-deserved pride and satis-

too, you can buy tickets to the Foundation's house museums (and the annual house and garden tours). Call (843) 724-8484. Also housed in the Edmunds Center across from the Mills House is the Foundation's museum shop, where you'll find a comprehensive selection of books, gifts, Lowcountry crafts, and heritage-related items for adults and children. (See the Attractions chapter for more on the Foundation's museum shop.)

The Historic Charleston Foundation Reproduction Shop at 105 Broad Street (at the corner of Broad and King) is a retail showroom displaying exclusive, Charleston-inspired furniture as commissioned by the Foundation for reproduc-

tion. The offerings have been assembled from the Foundation's own collections as well as from the Charleston Museum, Middleton Place Foundation, and various private collections in the city. This shop is open Monday through Saturday 10:00 A.M. to 5:30 P.M. During spring and fall "peak season," the shop is open 1:00 to 5:30 P.M. on Sunday. Call (843) 723-8292.

For more information about any Historic Charleston Foundation merchandise, see our Shopping chapter or write P.O. Box 622, Charleston 29402.

A recent restoration project of the Foundation was the Powder Magazine at 79 Cumberland Street (see the Attractions chapter). This utilitarian structure, once faction for those who own or live in them.

The other side of that coin, of course, is the maintenance factor. Charleston single houses are all very old. Some of them are turn-of-the-century Victorian versions; others are Revolutionary-era houses with rare paneling and priceless interior detailing. In any case, we're talking high maintenance here. Really big bucks.

Oh, and those charming side piazzas? Be advised that, every three years or so, they need painting. Depending on the style of balustrade (railing) and the number of levels to the piazza, the paint and labor bill can run several thousands of dollars. Don't forget to plan for that in your budget along with the cost of taxes and other routine maintenance.

Charleston single houses are obviously treasured. This distinctive architectural style, indigenous to this city, is very much a part of living here. And every

*This is a typical Charleston single house, the city's distinctive contribution to urban American architecture.* THOMAS P. FORD

beautifully maintained Charleston single house you'll see is tangible evidence that the city's architectural traditions remain sacrosanct.

used for storing gunpowder, is the only public building remaining in the Carolinas from the period of the English Lords Proprietors. Today it is restored to its mid-19th century appearance and serves as an interactive interpretive center for Charleston's first 50 years. Call (843) 805-6730 for more details.

Historic Charleston Foundation has no membership, but its work is augmented by the active support of about 600 volunteers who annually donate thousands of hours to the Foundation's programs and special events. The largest concentration of volunteer support is provided by the board of trustees, homeowners, and docents for the enormously popular Festi-

val of Houses and Gardens each spring. (See the Tours and Annual Events chapters for more information.) Volunteer opportunities include duties as house museum docents and service on standing and special interest committees.

Financial support for Foundation programs comes from a variety of sources including earned and endowment income, public and private grant money, and tax-deductible gifts of cash securities or objects. The Foundation welcomes gifts from those who wish to participate in the study, conservation, and protection of Charleston's heritage. All contributions and bequests are tax-deductible.

## The Preservation Society of Charleston
### 147 King Street, Charleston
### (843) 722-4630
### www.preservationsociety.org

In the early 1920s, Charleston was fortunate to have a remarkable group of people who sensed the value of their historic town and its wealth of architecturally significant buildings. These people jealously guarded that heritage and saved a great portion of it from its two worst enemies—the many decades of past neglect and the future's natural gravitation toward urban "renewal."

The city's first preservation organization, the Society for Preservation of Old Dwelling Houses, was founded in 1920 and incorporated in 1928. It evolved into what is now the Preservation Society of Charleston.

The organization is dedicated to preserving the heritage of the city. Its varied activities include advocacy on behalf of protective acquisition and restoration of historic properties, active participation in meetings of Charleston's Board of Architectural Review, and representation at a variety of city meetings and boards dealing with preservation issues. One of the Society's most visible programs is their Carolopolis Awards. Here individual properties are identified as outstanding examples of preservation in the community. Awardees receive a small plaque bearing Charleston's official seal indicating the Society's acknowledgment of the owners' effort to protect the city's architectural heritage.

The Society works to keep both its membership and the general public informed about current preservation philosophies, techniques, and issues. To that end, the group publishes a quarterly newsletter, *Preservation Progress,* and schedules regular meetings with informative speakers.

In 1931, the Society played an important role in promoting the first historic zoning ordinance in the United States. Other successes have included the initial saving of the Joseph Manigault House, the Heyward-Washington House (see the section on House Museums in the Attractions chapter), and the East Bay Street area now known as Rainbow Row.

In its early years, the society depended on the generosity of its founding members for financial support. Today it continues to depend in large part on its membership (about 2,000 people scattered all over the country) for monetary and moral support. To augment this base, the Society engages in limited publishing efforts and maintains the beautiful, well-stocked Preservation Society Bookstore, which carries associated gift items from the Lowcountry. (See the Shopping chapter.) The store is open daily at the Society's 147 King Street headquarters. In addition, the Society sponsors the annual Fall Candlelight Tours of Homes and Gardens (see the Annual Events chapter), which are very popular with tourists. Funds earned from these activities are used to further preservation objectives.

Dues for annual membership are as follows: student and nonprofit institutional membership, $20; individual, $30; family, $40; contributor, $100; sustaining, $250; patron, $500; and benefactor, $1,000.

The Preservation Society is a nonprofit, tax-exempt institution. Membership dues and contributions may be deducted for income and estate tax purposes. Memorial gifts are invited. Write the Preservation Society of Charleston for more information at P.O. Box 521, Charleston 29402.

## South Carolina Historical Society
### 100 Meeting Street, Charleston
### (843) 723-3225
### www.schistory.org

In 1855, as the last of America's Revolutionary generation was dying off, their recorded thoughts, accomplishments, and aspirations were dying with them. The founders of the South Carolina Historical Society recognized this fact and saw the need to preserve existing records of that era for the future of South Carolina and generations to come.

That year, they invited "contributions of every sort . . . [to] illustrate . . . social, political or ecclesiastical [life], our industry, [and] our resources . . . " This 19th-century call for the vanishing evidence of South Carolina's past became the foundation for the Society's collection.

Simply restated for today, the Society's mandate is to collect information respecting every portion of our state, to preserve it, and when deemed advisable, to publish it.

The Society's holdings now constitute South Carolina's most important private repository of history. Members and researchers find and study the papers of governors, members of Congress, generals, architects, poets, artists, soldiers, and planters, along with young girls' diaries and love letters, the records of churches, banks, grocery stores, plantations, and shipping companies. Together, they all record the rhythms of daily life in South Carolina, then and now.

In addition, the Society holds more than 40,000 photographs; 50,000 maps, architectural drawings, and manuscripts; plus 50,000 books, pamphlets, and serials that trace the lives of South Carolinians. Their Tower Collection of Civil War material is especially strong. The Society maintains an internet Web site with 65,000 records pertaining to 18,000 South Carolina surnames—a boon to genealogists checking in from all over the world.

Partly as a result of the increasing awareness of heritage and the growing popularity of genealogy during the past five years, researchers—historians, genealogists, authors, lawyers, scholars, and film makers—have flocked to the Society in record numbers for the wealth of information available.

The South Carolina Historical Society seeks membership among all who share an interest in the state's past, whether they be students, adults, natives, or newcomers. Members enjoy a rich variety of programs and benefits including the quarterly *South Carolina Historical Magazine;* a newsletter, *Caralogue;* and invitations to Society-sponsored lectures, tours, and social functions.

The Society maintains its offices and collection in the Fireproof Building, built on Charleston's Meeting Street in 1826 and designed by South Carolina's premier antebellum architect, Robert Mills.

The Society is open Monday, Wednesday, Thursday, and Friday from 9:00 A.M. to 4:00 P.M., Tuesday from 9:00 A.M. to 7:30 P.M., and Saturday from 9:00 A.M. to 2:00 P.M.

Membership dues encourage easy participation by all those interested in South Carolina history. They are as follows: undergraduate student membership, $30; regular, $55; contributor, $75; and sustainer, $100. Various levels for corporate and major donor memberships are also available.

For a membership application or more information, call the number above, or write South Carolina Historical Society, 100 Meeting Street, Charleston 29401.

# TOURS

U pon first impression, visitors to
Charleston are usually taken with
the city's architectural charm. Part
of that fascination comes from the unspoken questions that leap to mind about
Charleston's early good times. People
want to know more about how a city of
such wealth and architectural sophistication did, in fact, evolve.

The next impulse many visitors have is
to seek out some kind of tour to find
answers to some of those questions.
Understandably, people want a visual, geographic, or ethnic overview, a point of reference, some kind of perspective. But
most of all, they want to hear the stories
about Charleston when everything old was
shiny and new, political independence was
still a dream, and the name of Charles
Towne was world famous as the brightest
jewel in the British colonial crown.

That's why the telling of Charleston's
story has literally become an industry. In
fact, it's so important that to become an
officially licensed tour guide here, one
must take a city-sponsored course (and
pass very tough written and oral exams).
Charlestonians, you see, care enormously
that their story be told well. That's simply
because the real truth is interesting
enough to make mere half-truths, down-
right lies (told by unscrupulous tour
guides), and corny amateurism wholly
unnecessary. It's deceitful, unnecessary,
and not at all Charlestonian.

Tours of the city are available in several
forms. Most of the walking or riding (be
that in a carriage, car, or van) tours depart
from the Charleston Visitor Reception and
Transportation Center on Meeting Street
(simply referred to as the "visitor center"
hereafter) or from the City Market area.
You may also choose to meet a private
guide at your inn or hotel and depart from
there. Ask your hotel clerks or concierges
to book your tour reservations—they have

plenty of experience doing so.

Whichever tour mode you choose,
you'll have a wonderful adventure. There
are many tours of Charleston offered these
days—privately guided, walking, by bus or
van, by carriage, and even by boat. All
have merit. Included in this chapter are
some of the tours currently available that
we consider especially good and interesting. We've listed categories of tours alphabetically, so we'll start with a little
background information to help you
explore Charleston's rich African-American
heritage.

## CHARLESTON'S AFRICAN-AMERICAN HISTORY

As we've mentioned in several places in
this book, no visit to Charleston would be
complete without gaining a better understanding of and appreciation for the
strong African influences on this society,
past and present. The folkways, lifeways,
culture, and achievements of these people
have been infused into every fiber of the
Charleston experience since the very
beginning of the 1670 English settlement.

Among the first settlers in Charles
Towne were black and white indentured
servants and enslaved Africans. Within a
decade, the English settlers had implemented the plantation system (already
flourishing in Barbados) to sustain themselves here and create a product for economic exchange. Their labor force came
from Africa—particularly the West Coast of
Africa—from areas now known as Sierra
Leone, Ghana, and Benin.

European and American traders plied
the Atlantic waters off these areas, captur-
ing Africans and imprisoning them until
they could be boarded onto slave ships.
Typically, each African was afforded a
mere 4 square feet of living space while

chained down in the hold. Under these grim and inhumane conditions, untold numbers of Africans died en route to the New World. From coastal Africa, the ships would sail to the West Indies where some of the human "cargo" would be sold into slavery. The rest were brought to the South Carolina coast.

Awaiting the slave ships on Sullivan's Island off the coast from Charles Towne were crude structures called "pest houses." Here, the unwilling passengers would be held for a period of at least 40 days to be checked for diseases and infections, during which they would be also groomed for sale. If maladies were suspected or discovered, the captives would be quarantined onboard their ships.

In just the five years between 1803 and 1808, an estimated 40,000 Africans were imported to America. The sheer volume of incoming slaves became a cause for concern among the relatively few white slaveholders, who feared an uprising. In 1808, the importing of additional slaves was banned. However, this ban did little to stem the flow, and slave trade continued as late as 1858.

Once sold, most of the Africans would toil in the fields. Their labor made the early plantation life of coastal South Carolina not only possible but highly profitable. Africans also brought with them vital knowledge of rice and indigo production, cattle tending, boat building, and ironworking. Eventually, their foods, languages, religions, and music all mingled with the European traditions to create the Lowcountry culture called "Gullah" we celebrate today.

Not all Africans living in America were enslaved. From 1690 on, a few free people of color were living in Carolina. They were mostly multiracial and usually lived in the urban areas where they could find work in various trades. There were cobblers, carpenters, wheelwrights, brick masons, and smithies. Some became wealthy and owned slaves themselves.

With the Emancipation and Proclamation and the end of the Civil War, all

*For a more extensive look at the hidden historical treasures of the Charleston area, look into one of the day-long excursions planned annually by the South Carolina Historical Society. Every year, the membership is invited to participate in a caravan tour deep into the Lowcountry hinterlands, touring private plantations and fascinating little-known sites. For membership details, you can write the Society at 100 Meeting Street, Charleston 29401.*

African Americans were technically free. However, the opportunistic post-war Reconstruction period and the advent of Jim Crow laws led to constitutional struggles over the 13th, 14th, and 15th Amendments. The much-longed-for freedom of African Americans in Charleston was shallow, indeed.

Many people of color left their rural homes and sought a better life in urban settings (sometimes moving to large Northern cities) where opportunities for work and education were better. Those who remained behind tended to live in small, rural, self-sustaining villages that were clustered around their beloved churches—mostly free of white control. Visitors to the Lowcountry today can see evidence of this social pattern in communities such as Snowden, in Mt. Pleasant, and Maryville, west of the Ashley. During the civil rights movement of the 1960s, Charleston blacks gathered at sites like the old cigar factory at 701 East Bay Street and Moving Star Hall on Johns Island to organize and peacefully gain rights granted to all Americans by the U.S. Constitution.

Because more than one-fourth of the African slaves shipped to the 13 original American colonies before the Revolution came through Charleston, this city's role in African-American history can hardly be overstated. In the years between 1700 and 1775, an estimated 200,000 slaves were put ashore on Sullivan's Island. One expert on slave history has even dubbed Sullivan's Island the "Ellis Island of black Americans" (in the symbolic, if not the literal, sense). Clearly, the Africans brought to South Carolina as slaves did not come as free-willed immigrants (like those arriving at Ellis Island). But Charleston was their point of entry and (like Ellis Island) this location was the beginning of the American experience for countless African Americans. And yet, until very recently, this fact was little known by most contemporary Americans—even South Carolinians.

Realistically, this was not a popular subject for Charleston tour guides in the pre-civil rights era. History buffs felt awkward describing the tragedy of 18th- and 19th-century slave trade along with the city's upbeat tourist attractions. As a result, Charleston has been criticized in the national media for taking a shortsighted view of its own black history.

More and more of our nation's 34 million African Americans are discovering Charleston in their efforts to explore their cultural heritage.

Today, the annual MOJA Arts Festival in October is Charleston's official celebration of its African and Caribbean culture. (See more about MOJA in the chapters on The Arts and Annual Events.) But many of our popular tourist destinations feature special exhibits and events pertaining to Charleston's African-American history.

As Charleston proceeds deeper into the new millennium, a more enlightened approach to presenting the city's rich African-American heritage is starting to bloom. The African American National Heritage Museum is a multisite, cooperative educational effort undertaken by the Avery Research Center for African American History and Culture, the City of Charleston, Historic Charleston Foundation, and the South Carolina African American Heritage Council.

At four primary historic sites, these entities are working together to provide insight into the Greater Charleston African-American experience. At these sites, visitors can start to explore the origins of the

culture and the role African Americans played in shaping Charleston, the South Carolina Lowcountry and, in fact, the nation. Historical exhibits, living history demonstrations, site interpretation, and cultural events are offered at the following venues.

### Aiken-Rhett House
**48 Elizabeth Street**
**(843) 723-1159**
**www.historiccharleston.org**
It is rare, indeed, that a property of such prominence and historic importance as this would survive to this day in so authentic a state. But here is a house museum that affords the uncanny opportunity to view an "urban" household of great privilege as it was on the eve of the Civil War.

The central section of the Aiken-Rhett House (see House Museums in the Attractions chapter) was built in 1818 in the Federal style popular at that time. However, when William Aiken Jr. and his wife bought the property in 1831, they did an extensive remodeling of the first floor in the robust Greek Revival style, which was all the rage at that time. When Mr. Aiken was elected governor of South Carolina, wings were added with a dining room and ballroom for formal entertaining, and even an art gallery eventually came along. But in effect, the decor of the house was arrested in 1857, shortly before the Civil War began. And because of the war's drastic impact on Governor Aiken and his family, the house and the outbuildings that supported it (including the on-site slave quarters) remained remarkably unchanged from that point on. In fact, the house came into the hands of the Charleston Museum in 1975 almost as a sealed time capsule of pre–Civil War taste and technology.

Most notable are the servants' quarters to the rear of the house, which are in sharp contrast to the rest of the property—far more plain and utilitarian than the horse stables and even the privies.

A portable pre-recorded tape with appropriate sound effects is available for self-guided tours of the property, and docents are on hand to answer any questions you may have.

The museum house is open from 10:00 A.M. to 5:00 P.M. Monday through Saturday. Sunday hours are from 2:00 to 5:00 P.M. Admission is $8.00 per person; for children younger than 6, it is free.

## Avery Research Center for African American History and Culture
### 125 Bull Street, College of Charleston
### (843) 953–7609
### www.cofc.edu

In Charleston, the rich culture of South Carolina's African Americans is recognized for its unique national significance. However, the materials that document this culture have been widely scattered over time, and much has already been lost. The College of Charleston's Avery Research Center for African American History and Culture was established to document, preserve, and make public the unique historical and cultural heritage of this significant group for this and future generations.

In October 1990, the center was established at 125 Bull Street in Charleston's historic district. Here, at long last, a growing archival collection and on-site museum could share the purpose of gathering together these valuable materials and encouraging scholarship on the subject.

The research center is on the site of the former Avery Normal Institute, the local normal school (for teachers-to-be) and college preparatory school, that served Charleston's black community for nearly 100 years. Avery Normal Institute was organized in October 1865, by black minister F. L. Cardozo of the American Missionary Association for (in his words) "the education of colored children." In 1868, the school moved into the Bull Street building just five blocks west of the College of Charleston. There, for nearly a century, the school produced teachers for the community and gifted leaders for South Carolina and the nation.

Today, the center is actively soliciting manuscript collections: the personal and professional papers of individuals and organizations, oral and video histories, photographic records, and other related documents. Donors may be assured their gifts will receive the care needed to store and preserve them properly.

The archival collections are regularly used for exhibits and educational programs for the public. These activities are planned in conjunction with local and national African-American celebrations and holidays.

The Avery Research Center reading room is open to the public Monday through Saturday from noon to 5:00 P.M. Morning hours are available by appointment. Walk-in visitors can enjoy tours of the building and the museum galleries between 2:00 and 4:00 P.M. on weekdays and Saturday from noon to 5:00 P.M. Group tours are available by appointment.

For more information, call Annette Teasdell at the number listed above. Written inquiries should be addressed to Avery Research Center for African American History and Culture, 125 Bull Street, College of Charleston 29424.

## Battery Wagner, Morris Island

The first Union regiment of free black soldiers, the now-famous 54th Massachusetts Volunteer Infantry Regiment, fought on Morris Island during the Civil War. The bloody battle was an undeniable confirmation of the bravery, courage, and valor of the black soldiers and their willingness to fight for the North. Although the site is not (yet) memorialized formally, the island can be viewed briefly during Fort Sumter harbor tours, which leave from Patriots Point in Mt. Pleasant or the tour boat facility at Liberty Square near the S. C. Aquarium. What you'll see are just small hills that were originally built as artillery fortifications, a few shanties, and truck-farm areas. Call (843) 881–7337 for departure times. Ft. Sumter Tours are from 9:00 A.M. to 6:30 P.M. Monday through Friday. The fare is $12.00 for adults and teens and $6.00 for children ages 6 to 11. No tours go out to the fort on Christmas or New

**CLOSE-UP**

# Gullah: A Language, an Ethic, a Lowcountry Folklore

Part of our country's growing trend toward ethnic self-awareness has been a renewed interest in Gullah, the colorful language and accompanying lifestyle that once flourished on the South Carolina sea islands from Georgetown to Daufuskie.

Researchers reported that as late as 1979, 100,000 South Carolinians spoke Gullah. But in the census of 1990, only 180 families still listed it as the language they spoke at home. Without intervention, the Gullah language will soon live only in scholarly textbooks and on fragile academic recordings.

The origins of Gullah date back to a sad chapter in America's past. When slave traders sailed to West Africa and stuffed their ships full of men, women, and children to be sold as slaves to Southern planters, Gullah was conceived. As that black culture meshed with the white, Gullah was born. A thick, lilting mix of African and English dialects, it started as a makeshift second language used among the sea island slaves, and it slowly evolved into the unwritten native tongue of their descendants.

Oddly, slavery and the antebellum South fed energy to the language. Gullah served a very practical transitional purpose, and its use and culture actually developed during those years. After the Civil War, however, the separation between the black and white cultures became highly exaggerated for nearly a century and a half. Cut off from the cultural homogenization that occurred everywhere else in America, life along the sea islands changed very little. Sea

---

Year's Day. (See more on Battery Wagner in the Forts section of the Attractions chapter.)

**Boone Hall Plantation**
**1235 Long Point Road, Mt. Pleasant**
**(843) 884–4371**
**www.boonehallplantation.com**
Once one of the largest cotton plantations in the South, Boone Hall dates back to the 1680s. At one time Boone Hall was home to more than 1,000 slaves. Nine of the original slave houses still stand on the plantation's "Slave Street." These structures, now frequently used by film makers for their stark authenticity, are open to the public on this still-working farm. Boone Hall is open Monday through Saturday from 8:30 A.M. to 6:30 P.M. and Sunday from 1:00 to 5:00 P.M. April 1 through Labor Day. After Labor Day until April 1, hours are 9:00 A.M. to 5:00 P.M. Monday through Saturday, Sunday 9:00 A.M. to 4:00 P.M. Admission is $14.50 for adults and teens and $7.00 for children ages 6 to 12. Seniors 60 and over pay $13.00. The Plantation Kitchen Restaurant is open 9:00 A.M. to 3:00 P.M. Monday through Saturday. (See the Lowcountry Day Trips chapter for more on Boone Hall Plantation.)

islanders still fished the coastline, shrimped the marsh, hunted for game in the woods, and spoke their native tongue unashamedly.

Gullah stubbornly survived in this splendid isolation, until the outside world rediscovered the islands and invested millions of dollars to develop them as resorts. Suddenly, bridges were built that introduced paved roads, indoor plumbing, better education, and access to higher-paying mainland jobs. Gullah became thought of as "bad English." Soon it was something to be ashamed of or denied. Then television, the greatest homogenizing influence of all, came along and nearly snuffed the language out altogether.

Finding true Gullah today is like finding gold. It's rare, and it's kept hidden from "outsiders." Still, there are a few islanders determined to keep it alive. There still are those who knit their own fishing nets rather than buy the ones made in Japan. There are those who still cook the Gullah receipts (recipes) and serve their families whole

*Obo Addy performs Gullah rhythms and song at the MOJA Arts Festival, a celebration of the city's African and Caribbean heritage.* CHARLESTON AREA CONVENTION AND VISITORS BUREAU

meals fresh from the sea. Thankfully, there are still those who take what's left of the sweetgrass from the riverbanks and fashion baskets of great skill and beauty—just like their ancestors did back in Sierra Leone.

## Cabbage Row
### 89–91 Church Street

This downtown area was claimed as the inspiriational setting for DuBose Heyward's 1925 book, *Porgy,* and for George and Ira Gershwin's beloved folk opera, *Porgy and Bess,* which premiered in 1935. Cabbage Row, the scene of the story, took its name from the vegetables regularly sold from carts and windowsills by the area's black residents. Today, this section houses quaint little shops, but anyone familiar with the opera and its distinctive stage settings will readily see that this place and the alleys around and

behind it could easily have been the story's original scene.

Was the story based on truth? Was there ever a crippled vendor named Porgy who won, then lost, the love of a troubled woman named Bess? Many older Charlestonians recall a poor, crippled man who lived here in the early 1920s and used a small goat cart to get around. His name was Samuel Smalls. The other details of the story are hard to pin down, but Charleston certainly had enclaves of black families who struggled against very difficult circumstances, and their sagas of survival and social interdependence were not

*If you're going to be in Charleston during the spring or early fall, chances are you can find tickets to Charleston's two most-famous house and garden tours of private properties. In the spring, the Historic Charleston Foundation sponsors its annual Festival of Houses and Gardens from mid-March through mid-April when the city's flowers are at their peak. Late in September and well into October, the Preservation Society of Charleston sponsors its Fall Candlelight Tours after the long-anticipated cooler nights have returned to the Lowcountry.*

unlike Porgy's. Charleston obviously experiences the wrath of hurricanes, and in those days, terrible storms struck with little warning. And surely then, as now, the ugly specter of drugs and violence dramatically influenced the lives and loves of these people. We may never actually know if Heyward ever heard of Samuel Smalls, but the connections are intriguing, and the story is timeless.

More avid music lovers and *Porgy* fans may want to visit Smalls' grave, which is well-marked in the churchyard of James Island Presbyterian Church, about a 6-mile drive from the Charleston Peninsula on Folly Road. The grave was unmarked for many years, until an anonymous but concerned Charlestonian took the responsibility of funding a suitable marker for this legendary Charleston icon. To get to the church, take the James Island Connector (Highway 30) over the Ashley River, and turn left on Folly Road. The church is at 1632 Fort Johnson Road, the intersection of Folly and Fort Johnson Roads. Look for the marker to Porgy just outside the fenced churchyard.

**The Charleston Museum**
**360 Meeting Street**
**(843) 722-2996**
**www.charlestonmuseum.org**
America's first museum, founded in 1773, has exhibits and art depicting African-American life in the South Carolina Lowcountry. Additional photographs and vauled information on African-American history and culture are housed in the museum's archives. Archival research is welcome; call the museum for an appointment. The Charleston Museum is open Monday through Saturday from 9:00 A.M. to 5:00 P.M. Sunday hours are from 1:00 to 5:00 P.M. Admission is $10.00 for adults and teens and $4.00 for children ages 3 to 12. The doors are closed on Thanksgiving, Christmas, and New Year's Eve. (See the Charleston Museum entry in the Attractions chapter for more information.)

**Drayton Hall**
**3380 Ashley River Road**
**(843) 766-0188, (888) 349-0588**
**www.draytonhall.org**
This colonial-era plantation house is shown to the public today as an architectural museum. It is considered to be the finest and earliest example of Palladian architecture in America. Built between 1738 and 1742, the structure serves as a monument to 18th-century European and African-American artisans, who displayed highly sophisticated building skills at a remarkably early time.

Now a property of the National Trust for Historic Preservation, Drayton Hall's research and education departments are in the vanguard of the nation's effort to document and acknowledge the contribution of African Americans to the colonial South. Special events and educational programs at Drayton Hall offer insight into this culture and its modern legacy.

Drayton Hall is open daily, except Christmas and Thanksgiving. Admission is $12.00 for adults, $8.00 for students ages 12 to 18, and $6.00 for children ages 6 to 11. Admission to the grounds only is $5.00. Admission is free to card-holding members of the National Trust for Historic Preservation. (See the Drayton Hall entry in the Attractions chapter.)

One of our most treasured exponents of African-American heritage is the Lowcountry gospel spiritual. For a little slice of heaven, attend one of the special holiday candlelight concerts performed by local African-American choirs at Drayton Hall during the Christmas season. These concerts, originally sponsored by the Friends of Drayton Hall, are now open to the public and offer a rare opportunity to hear authentic Lowcountry spirituals (with their distinctive double hand-clapping) in an original setting. See the Annual Events chapter, or call the number listed for more information.

### Eliza's House at Middleton Place
**4300 Ashley River Road**
**(843) 556-6020, (800) 782-3608**
**www.middletonplace.org**
After the Civil War, a number of freed slaves chose to remain living and working on the huge rice plantation that was Middleton Place. They were most likely responsible for constructing in the 1870s the building that was later named "Eliza's House." It was named in memory of Eliza Leach, a South Carolina African American born in 1891 and the last person to live in the building. For 40 years or so, she worked at Middleton Place performing a variety of duties from working in the gardens to greeting visitors. She died in 1986 at age 94, and almost to the end of her life, she lived in the house in much the same way her predecessors did.

The building has been restored and is now shown along with the other former plantation outbuildings that house demonstrations of weaving, spinning, blacksmithing, candle-making, carpentry, and pottery-making—all tasks of the plantation slaves. Eliza's House was originally built to house two families: One half of the building now depicts typical living quarters; plans are in the works to set up the other half for exhibits of artifacts from Middleton Place slaves.

Eliza's House is open daily from 9:00 A.M. to 5:00 P.M. Middleton Place house tours are Tuesday through Sunday from 10:00 A.M. to 4:30 P.M. Admission is $20.00 for adults to see the plantation gardens and stable yards (including Eliza's House)

and $5.00 for youngsters ages 7 to 15. There is an additional $10 charge (for adults and children alike) for a guided tour of the plantation house. (See more about Middleton Place in the Attractions chapter.)

### McLeod Plantation
**325 Country Club Drive, James Island**
**(843) 577-5245**
**www.buildingartscollege.us**
McLeod Plantation dates back to the late 17th century when it was one of the first profitable farms to be established along the Ashley River system. Its fine collection of antebellum buildings is considered to be among the best preserved in the American South.

In addition to the main house (ca. 1854), there are barns, stables, a gin house, kitchen, and a dairy plus a street of several slave cabins. According to a census taken in 1860, there were 74 slaves living in 26 dwellings on the plantation whose work was the cultivation of sea island cotton.

McLeod was occupied by both Confederate and Union forces during the Civil War. The main house served as a field hospital, and it housed officers from the famous 54th and 55th Massachusetts Volunteers. It also became the main office for the Freedman's Bureau serving the James Island area during Reconstruction years.

In 1993 the still privately owned McLeod Plantation was acquired by Historic Charleston Foundation and held in trust while they assessed how best to use this historic site. Many suggestions were aired and analyzed during the following years, but in 2004 a working plan finally emerged. The plantation will soon become the new campus for a school whose mission is to educate and train young people in the (quickly vanishing) traditional building arts. Students of the American College of the Building Arts will work here to preserve the rich heritage and diverse cultures found in historic structures. The goal is to increase the number and quality of master craftspeople—thereby raising the quality of building standards in new construction as well as in restoration of historic structures throughout the country.

## Slave Mart Museum
## 6 Chalmers Street

The one longtime local outlet for black cultural information in Charleston was the Old Slave Mart at 6 Chalmers Street. At this site, reproduction slave-made wares and crafts were sold, and actual slave-era artifacts were displayed. Unfortunately, the museum failed as a privately owned tourist attraction, and it closed in 1987. A year later, the City of Charleston bought the building, and plans are in place to reopen it soon as a museum depicting the slave-trading that went on here between 1856 and 1863.

The building encloses part of the rear yard of a now-gone tenement building known to have been used for slave auctions. First called "Ryan's Mart" and later, the "Mart in Chalmer's Street," this was one of several sites in this neighborhood where African Americans were sold into slavery.

## Snee Farm (Charles Pinckney National Historic Site)
## 1254 Longpoint Road, Mt. Pleasant
## (843) 881-5516, (843) 883-3123
## www.nps.gov/chpi

The interpretation of African-American history at Snee Farm centers on the influence of enslaved people of West African origin on the development of Charles Pinckney's colonial farm. This offering has struck a chord with a large population of Charleston tourists, and in the peak year of 1997, more than 40,000 people (individuals, families, and school groups) visited the site. Snee Farm was established in 1988 to highlight the contributions of Pinckney, a famous statesman, politician, and signer of the U.S. Constitution. The contribution of people of African descent is shown through exhibits, park handouts, archaeology displays, and a video program. These contributions were in the form of language, food, agricultural skills, and craftsmanship.

The site has a small gift shop where various publications are sold that help illuminate the African-American story. Sometimes even a maker of sweetgrass baskets is on hand to demonstrate that distinctive local art form. Park hours are from 9:00 A.M. to 5:00 P.M. most of the year, with an extended hour offered in the summer months. There is no admission charge for this site.

# ETHNIC TOURS

## Gullah Tours Inc.
## 43 John Street
## (843) 763-7551
## www.gullahtours.com

This group offers Charleston folktales told in Gullah, the distinctive language spoken by Lowcountry blacks that's a separate and unique cross between English and various African dialects. Your guide is Alphonso Brown, licensed guide, lecturer, and author of *A Guide to Gullah Charleston*. You will tour many of the important local African-American sites, including a visit with Philip Simmons, a famous local blacksmith. All tours leave from Gallery Chuma on 43 John Street, across from the visitor center. Weekday tours are at 11:00 A.M. and 3:00 P.M. Saturday tours are at 11:00 A.M. and 1:00 and 3:00 P.M. No tours are given on Sunday. These all-adult tours are $18 per person.

## Sites and Insights Tours
## 1220 Folly Road, James Island
## (843) 762-0051
## www.sitesandinsightstours.com

Visit little-known black history sites, and gain a knowledge of Charleston's past from an African-American perspective. Hear stories of slavery, free blacks, the Denmark Vesey Slave Uprising, the Stono Rebellion, Catfish Row, and Charleston's colorful sea islands. These are one- and two-hour motor tours that depart from the visitor center. Rates are $13 for adults of any age for the one-hour tour and $10 for children. The two-hour program is $18 for adults and $13 for children. A two-hour

## CLOSE-UP

# The Pest Houses on Sullivan's Island

Today there's just a bronze plaque. And even that plaque is a very recent addition to the history being interpreted for the public at Ft. Moultrie on Sullivan's Island. But it is, at least, a beginning. The plaque commemorates a grim chapter in Charleston's history—the advent of the "pest houses" on Sullivan's Island during the city's booming slave trade in the 18th and 19th centuries.

In 1707, the local government was in fear of the diseases carried by slave ships arriving at the colony from West Africa. As a remedy for this, a law was passed requiring all slave ships to dock at Sullivan's Island and unload their human cargo for a period of quarantine—usually 10 days or so. The place for holding these unfortunate people was called a "pest house," in reference to the pestilence hopefully kept inside its primitive walls. After a period of time, during which the "cargo" was inspected for disease, the captives were moved across the harbor and sold at public auction into slavery. An estimated 40 percent of black Americans have ancestors who came through the pest houses of Sullivan's Island.

There are no surviving eyewitness accounts of what actually went on in these long-vanished structures, but in 1759 a Charleston physician, Dr. Alexander Garden (for whom the gardenia blossom was named), left this description of the slave ships:

"I have often gone to visit those Vessels on their first Arrival," he writes. "But I have never yet been on board one that did not smell most offensive and noisome, what for Filth, putrid Air, putrid Dysenteries. . . . [I]t is a wonder any (people) escape with Life."

The plaque on Sullivan's Island is a step in the right direction, but a far too small (and too late) gesture of acknowledgment for what is clearly an important chapter in American history.

island tour (of James, Johns, Angel Oak, and Civil War sites) is available upon request. Rates are $23 for adults, $18 for children. Call for schedules.

### Tourific Tours African American History (843) 853-2500

This company, owned by a native Charlestonian and civic leader, offers two privately guided tours of African-American history departing from the visitor center. Tour 1 lasts two hours and takes visitors on a stroll through the streets of Charleston to the boundaries of the original walled city. You'll see typical Charleston "single houses" and antebellum mansions, historic churches, the Dock Street Theater, cobblestone streets, and the famous Four Corners of Law. Tour 2 is by car and takes visitors through the picturesque College of Charleston campus where free people of color lived prior to the Civil War. Hear about the early contributions of African Americans to the city's history and see on-site examples of work by Charleston's famous wrought-iron worker Philip Simmons. Learn about slave uprising leader Denmark Vesey, and visit African-American churches. Reservations are required for these tours, and all require a minimum of two people to begin. The walking tour is $25 per person. The auto tour is $40 (maximum, four persons per tour).

## OTHER GUIDED TOURS
# Bus and Van Tours

Bus and van tours are very comfortable, if for no other reason than the fact that these tour vehicles are air-conditioned. In the summer months, that certainly counts for a lot. Most of these vehicles have small PA systems, so hearing the driver and tour guide is no problem. Be advised, however, that only certain streets are approved for larger tour vehicles, so you'll miss some of the tiny side streets and alleys that give Charleston so much of its charm. Here are some of the best of the motor tours offered:

**Adventure Sightseeing**
**1090 Ft. Sumter Drive**
**(843) 762-0088, (800) 722-5394**
**www.touringcharleston.com**
This company offers a variety of tours of the historic district. You may choose one of the bus or van tours with special features such as The Citadel Dress Parade (Fridays only), a tour through the Old Exchange, or one of Charleston's house museums. Adventure Sightseeing offers free pick-up service from downtown hotels, the visitor center, the City Market, and the City Marina. Reservations are accepted from 8:00 to 10:00 A.M. daily.

Fares for two-hour tours are $25 for adults and teens, $16 for children under 12. For Adventure's one-and-a-half-hour tour, adult fares are $19, and $11 for children under 12. The shorter, one-and-a-quarter-hour tour is $17 for adults and $10 for children.

All Adventure tours include a complete history of the city; two-hour tours include one house museum.

**Charleston Tours Inc.**
**545 Savannah Highway**
**(843) 571-0049**
**www.charleston-tours.com**
These guides say they're "the Southern specialists for city or plantation tours." Tour A is a 90-minute city tour that includes the French Quarter and the Slave Market plus a stop at the Battery. The fare for adults and teens is $20; children ages 3 to 12, half price. Tour B goes out to the plantations and lasts about four hours. It includes a visit to Magnolia Plantation and Gardens. Adult and teen fare is $50, and the fare for children ages 3 to 12, $25. Tour C includes the Joseph Manigault House filled with fine antiques. Adults and teens go for $28, children ages 3 to 12 go for $14. Tour E is billed as an "all-day adventure" that includes the city tour (you do lunch on your own) in the Market area, then continues on to Boone Hall Plantation. Adults and teen admissions are $55.00; children ages 3 to 12 go for $27.50. All tours depart from the visitor center with free pick-up service from most downtown locations.

**Charleston's Finest Historic Tours**
**P.O. Box 263, Ridgeville 29472**
**(843) 577-3311**
**www.historictoursofcharleston.com**
This company offers three daily scheduled tours—all in a luxury touring coach. Tour A begins at 10:30 A.M. and is a city-centered adventure including seeing and hearing about noteworthy mansions and churches, Civil War forts, the Battery, and Slave Mart (allow 110 minutes). Adult fare is $17; youths ages 6 to 12, half price. Tour B begins in the afternoon at 12:30 P.M. and lasts four and a half hours. It includes an extended visit to Magnolia Plantation. Adult rates are $45; ages 6 to 12 half price.

**"Doin' the Charleston" Tours**
**P.O. Box 31338, Charleston 29417**
**(843) 763-1233, (800) 647-4487**
**www.dointhecharlestontours.com**
Here's something of a high-tech motor

tour, a new twist on historic interpretation. You travel around Charleston in an air-conditioned minibus with large windows while historic views of many of the same places you're seeing are displayed via laser disc on a screen inside your motor coach. There's even a musical soundtrack to your guide's live narration. Allow 90 minutes for this tour, which includes a stop at the Battery. Rates for adults and teens are $18, and the price is $13 for children ages 6 to 11. Daily tours leave promptly from the visitor center at 9:30 A.M., noon, 2:30, and 4:30 P.M. (during daylight savings time only). Free pick-ups from downtown lodgings are offered. Call for reservations.

**Gray Line Bus Tours**
**P.O. Box 219, Charleston 29402**
**(843) 722–4444, (800) 423–0444**
**www.grayline.com**
Gray Line offers three tours of Charleston in various configurations—all in minivans with air-conditioning and large windows.

The Historic Charleston Tour 1 (allow 90 minutes) includes a stop at the Battery and points out dozens of historic sites. Adult rates are $19, children younger than 12, $12.

Tour 2 is called Historic Charleston and Restored Home (allow two hours). This tour includes a stop at the Battery and one of Charleston's house museums (which one will vary according to season and availability). Adults and teens are charged $25, children younger than 12, $16.

Tour 3 is a combination Bus and Boat Tour with an optional all-day shuttle pass. This is a special pricing of Tour 1 along with a boat tour of Charleston Harbor. Also included is an all-day pass on the downtown area shuttle that travels to and from the boat tour as well as the City Market, the King Street shopping district, and most downtown hotels and motels. Adult and teen rates are $27, and children younger than 12 pay $16. Tours depart the visitor center every 30 minutes (on the hour and half-hour), and the tour bus stops at 102 North Market Street 20 minutes before then.

**Talk of the Towne**
**2166 St. James Drive**
**(843) 795–8199**
**www.talkofthetowne.com**
Enjoy panoramic views of the Battery, Rainbow Row, and all the major downtown landmarks from a minibus designed especially for touring Charleston. Two-hour tours, leaving from the visitor center, include a 35-minute guided tour of the Nathaniel Russell House or Edmondston-Alston House. Pickup from all major downtown hotels is available. The rate for adults and teens is $25; for children 12 and younger, it's $16. The 75-minute version, leaving from the visitor center at 3:00 P.M., is a nonstop, 7-mile ride through Charleston that includes the Battery, Rainbow Row, and the Four Corners of Law. Adult and teen fare is $15.00; for children ages 12 and younger, it's $9.00.

---

*For the connoisseur intending to become immersed in Charleston's history and culture, there's a way to save nearly 40 percent on regular admission to six of the most popular attractions. Purchase a Heritage Passport (sold only at the visitor center at 375 Meeting Street) and see the Gibbes Museum of Art, Nathaniel Russell House, Edmondston-Alston House, Aiken-Rhett House, Drayton Hall, and Middleton Place (gardens and stable yards only) at what is a very considerable savings. Ask for details at the visitor center information desk.*

---

**Taylored Tours of Charleston**
**1300 Lenevar Drive**
**(843) 832–3321, (888) 449–8687**
**www.toursofcharleston.com**
This group offers four historic tours of Charleston. Tour 1 is a general history tour (allow 75 minutes) covering more than 90 points of interest including a stop at the Battery overlooking Fort Sumter. Adults and teen admissions are $15.00; for chil-

dren younger than 12, $8.00. Tour 2 is a 90-minute trip specializing in specific subjects: the colonial period and the Revolution, the Civil War, black history, and architectural points of interest. Reservations for these tours are required a day in advance, and the cost is $18 per person. Tour 3 offers 90 minutes of general history (same as Tour 1) followed by a guided tour of one of Charleston's house museums (the Nathaniel Russell House, Heyward-Washington House, Edmondston-Alston House or the Aiken-Rhett House). Rates for adults and children are $25; children younger than 12 are charged $13. Tour 4 is a private plantation tour lasting about three and a half hours. It includes a trip up the historic Ashley River Road and a visit to one of two historic Lowcountry plantations (your choice), either Middleton Place or Magnolia Plantation. This tour costs $30 per person. Guests pay for any additional options they choose at the site. Free pickups from downtown hotels are available. All tours depart from the visitor center. Interested parties may ask about their day-long tours of Savannah, Georgia, as well.

# Walking Tours

Walking tours are great if you're up to the exercise. The pace is slow, the interpretation is personal, and the detail you'll see and hear is incredible. These tours—by definition— have the excitement and feel of a treasure hunt, and treasure is always found. Every one of these tours bears the stamp of your particular tour guide, and this seems to make the experience more intimate and fun. On the other hand, you cover a relatively small part of the historic Peninsula and see only a microcosm of all there is to see. Here are some of our favorites:

**Anna's House & Garden Walking Tour**
**122 Queen Street**
**(843) 853-2266**
**www.ghostwalk.net**

Anna Taylor Blythe is a second-generation tour guide in Charleston and has been collecting stories for Charleston visitors for many years. Her tour includes refreshments in a private home "below Broad" and a stroll through two famous Charleston private gardens, and ends in a charming shop at 61 Queen Street. Tours begin under the green awning at 61 Queen Street at 9:45 A.M. and 2:00 P.M. Monday through Saturday, rain or shine. The rate is $30 per person; reservations are required.

Her one-and-a-half-hour Ghost Walk tour is also a visit through 18th- and 19th-century neighborhoods—this one with tales of ghosts, the plateye, voodoo, graveyards, and "Hags & Haints." These tours begin at 7:00 and 9:00 P.M. in front of 164 Church. Adult fare is $15.00, children ages 7 to 12, $7.00; reservations are required.

**Architectural Walking Tours**
**173 Meeting Street**
**(843) 893-2327, (800) 931-7761**
**www.architecturalwalkingtours**
**ofcharleston.com**
These are two-hour tours of Charleston's remarkable architectural heritage. Your guide through seven local public buildings is Fern Williams Tuten, a local art historian and licensed city guide. The tour of 18th-century buildings begins at 10:00 A.M.; the tour of 19th-century buildings is at 2:00 P.M. Both tours depart from the Meeting Street Inn, 173 Meeting Street (tours depart 10 minutes earlier from Hawthorne Suites). No tours are offered on Tuesday or Sunday. The charge is $15 a person. Special theme tours and group tours are available with advance notice. These include a house museum along with public buildings.

**Charleston Strolls**
**Walk with History**
**(843) 766-2080**
**www.charlestonstrolls.com**
This is the walking tour recommended by the *New York Times* and *Southern Living*. It operates Monday through Saturday all year long, leaving from outside the Palmetto Café in Charleston Place at 9:30 A.M., and

from the Mills House at 10:00 A.M. A personal guide brings to life Charleston's history from colonial days through the Civil War to the present. You'll stroll cobblestone streets, find hidden gardens, walk in famous footsteps, and much more. Rates are $16.50 for adults and teens, and children 12 and younger are admitted free. Reservations are accepted, but not required.

### Charleston Tea Party Walking Tour
### (843) 577–5896, (843) 722–1779

These two-hour tours end with a tea served in the private garden of your guide after a walk through the oldest section of the historic district. The tours include colonial and 18th-century architecture, Civil War history with quotations from diaries, church history, Charleston gardens and interiors, plus insight into Charleston's preservation story. Tours begin at the King's Courtyard Inn, 198 King Street, and cost $15.00 for adults and children 12 and older and $6.00 for children younger than 12. For the 9:30 A.M. tour, call 577–5896; for the 2:00 P.M. tour, call (843) 722–1779. Reservations are required.

### Charleston's Original
### Ghost Hunt Walking Tour
### (843) 813–5055
### www.charlestonghosthunt.com

Here's another offering for those interested in chasing down Charleston's famous ghost stories. These "adventures" come in a number of guises these days, and this is one of the best. The tour departs from the sidewalk area in front of the United States Custom House on the corner of South Market Street and East Bay at 7:00 and 9:00 P.M. (weather permitting). The tour is appropriate for adults only and the fare is $12. A late-night tour (at 10:45 P.M.) is offered on weekends. Reservations are required.

### Civil War Walking Tour
### 17 Archdale Street
### (843) 722–7033
### www.civilwarwalk.com

This walking tour departs from the Mills House lobby, 115 Meeting Street, at 9:00 A.M. daily. You'll hear the personal accounts and colorful anecdotes of the late Charlestonians who lived through it all. The tour includes comparisons of photos of Charleston from the 1860s with those of today. Reservations are appreciated. The adult rate is $17. Children under age 12 are free. Group rates are available, and the route is wheelchair accessible.

### Ed Grimball Walking Tours
### 306 Yates Avenue
### (843) 762–0056
### www.edgrimballtours.com

Ed Grimball's walking tour of Charleston is a keeper for your memory book. He's a born-and-raised Charlestonian whose family settled on nearby Edisto Island. He knows and loves the city as only a native son can. As a registered tour guide, his entertaining insights and stories run the gamut from architecture and colonial history to the Civil War and the great earthquake of 1886. He's familiar with the stories of the heroes and statesmen, the scoundrels and bizarre characters who've helped make Charleston history what it is—endlessly fascinating. Tours last about two hours and depart from the Pineapple Fountain in downtown's Waterfront Park starting at 9:30 A.M., most Fridays, Saturdays, and Sundays. Call for more information or special tour arrangements. The charge is $16.00 for adults and $8.00 for children 7 to 12. Reservations are required. He goes rain or shine—even in the heat of summer. Complimentary ice water is provided about an hour after the tour begins (from the middle of May through the end of August). Nice touch in our Charleston climate!

### On The Market Tours
### (853) 853–8687
### www.onthemarkettours.com

Tommy Dew is your host (and licensed guide) for this ghost tour with grisly tales of murder and death, unrequited love, tragedy, and other old Charleston lore.

# CLOSE-UP

# Gateway Walk

Looking for a way to see Charleston that's a little off the beaten path? Gateway Walk is a free walking tour many find unique, and it's right through the heart of the historic district.

In 1930 Mrs. Clelia Peronneau McGowan, president of the Garden Club of Charleston, came up with the idea for a walkway that would connect the city's churchyards, garden areas, and tucked-away courtyards. She was inspired by a trip to Paris where she embraced the idea of meandering through serene gardens in the midst of a bustling cityscape. The plan was designed by noted Charleston landscape architect Loutrel Briggs and opened on April 10, 1930, to celebrate the 250th anniversary of the founding of Charleston on its peninsula site.

The walk is designated by unobtrusive plaques and foot-stone markers that lead through historic sites but depart from the sidewalk viewpoint and beckon you into the hidden core of the city blocks between Archdale Street and Philadelphia Alley. This self-guided stroll covers four blocks where you may amble through four churchyards full of fascinating old tombstones with a variety of blooming flora. It continues through the gardens of the Charleston Library Society and Gibbes Museum of Art, with its rose garden that features the Governor Aiken gates, a fountain, and sculpture. Winding your way through several centuries of Charleston history, you'll discover how Gateway Walk was named for the beautiful wrought-iron gates along the way.

Daily tours begin at the steps of Market Hall, on Meeting Street between South Market and North Market Streets, at 6:00 and 8:00 P.M. Ghost tour adult fare is $18; children (12 and under), $10.

General history tours from Tommy Dew start from the same location and begin at 11:00 A.M. and 1:00 and 3:00 P.M. Tours last approximately 1 hour and 45 minutes. Reservations are required. Adult fare is $18; children (12 and under) pay $10.

**The Original Charleston Walks**
**58 ½ Broad Street**
**(843) 577–3800, (800) 729–3420**
**www.charlestonwalks.com**
This group specializes in educational and group tours. Choose from the following eight options: the Charleston Walk, Wicked Charleston, the Civil War Walk, Pirates Walk, Patriots Walk, Lowcountry Ghost Walk, Historic Homes Walk, and In Slavery & Freedom. One of these options is bound to please the most finicky traveler. Tours depart Washington Park at the

An inscription on one of the plaques attributed to Mrs. McGowan reads:

"Through hand wrought gates,
      alluring paths
Lead on to pleasant places,
Where ghosts of long forgotten
      things
Have left elusive traces."

The walk underwent its first restoration in 1953 with the continued support of Mr. Briggs. In 1992 the garden club initiated a three-year restoration designed by T. Hunter McEaddy Associates and spearheads its ongoing maintenance through an endowment established at the Community Foundation. The Gateway Walk is free and open 8:30 A.M. to 5:00 P.M. Monday through Friday.

KEY: ●● GATEWAY WALK ENTRY PLAQUES
● GATE MARKER PLAQUE (WITHIN WALK)

N

PHILADELPHIA ALLEY

ST. PHILIP'S
EPISCOPAL
CHURCH

CHURCH                    STREET

ST. PHILLIP'S
GRAVE YARD

CIRCULAR
CONGREGATIONAL
CHURCH

MEETING        STREET

GIBBES
MUSEUM OF ART

GOV. AIKEN
GATES

CHARLESTON
LIBRARY SOCIETY

KING           STREET

ST. JOHN'S
LUTHERAN          UNITARIAN
CHURCH            CHURCH

ARCHDALE   STREET

T. HUNTER MCEADDY ASSOCIATES, INC.

Broad Street gates at the corner of Meeting and Broad Streets. Call for times and reservations. Tours are $18 for adults and $10 for children ages 8 to 14. The Historic Homes tour is $28 for adults and $20 for children (ages 8 to 14).

### The Story of Charleston
### (843) 723-1670, (800) 854-1670
### www.tourcharleston.com

Reservations are required for this walking tour that claims to show visitors the Holy City "from a Charlestonian's point of view."

In addition to architecture and history, this intimate, 90-minute-plus tour profiles some of the city's legendary personalities and recounts the impact of wars and disasters. Tours leave from in front of the circular fountain at Waterfront Park (at the foot of Vendue Range) at 10:00 A.M. and 5:00 P.M. Rates are $15 for adults and $10 for children 12 and younger.

The same company, called Tour Charleston, offers the Ghosts of Charleston tour, which is based on the book *Charleston Ghosts and Other Macabre*

*Aberrations* by Edward Macy and James Buxton. This 70- to 90-minute adventure is a big hit with those interested in the paranormal and departs from the fountain at Waterfront Park at 5:00, 7:30, and 9:30 P.M. The same pricing applies.

The company's newest offering is the Ghosts of Charleston II, wherein you encounter specters on the edge of town. This tour begins at 6:00 and 9:00 P.M. leaving from the Calhoun Monument at Marion Square.

## Carriage Tours

Carriage tours are an enduring Charleston tradition. There's nothing like seeing an 18th- and 19th-century city at an appropriately slow, leisurely, clip-clop pace. You'll ride through neighborhoods above and below Broad Street (ones that are approved for horse-drawn vehicle traffic) while your driver tells the Charleston story. The ambience is wonderful, but again, you're restricted to certain areas of the city for traffic management purposes and you receive a somewhat limited view of

**i** *With all the horse-drawn carriage tours on city streets, you will be pleased to learn that Charleston horses wear "diapers." Should a horse's diaper need changing and the street in any way become sullied (they say it can happen to even the best of horses), there's a very civilized Charleston solution. A special truck patrols the carriage routes during tour hours carrying a huge, white tank of perfumed disinfectant. In the event of an "accident," carriage drivers are carefully instructed to throw out weighted flags to mark the spot and drive on with dignity unruffled. The truck then scurries to the scene for a welcome squirt, a quick wash, and a gracious apology. What can we say? It happens.*

the city's many charms. Here are the carriage tour options now available:

**Carolina Polo & Carriage Company**
**102 North Market Street**
**(843) 577-6767**
**www.cpcc.com**
All tour guides on these carriages are city licensed and trained by a company tour director who has been doing carriage tours since 1978. These tours depart from 16 Hayne Street, 102 North Market Street, and 181 Church Street (from the lobby of the Doubletree Hotel on the corner of North Market and Church Streets). Adult and teen rates are $18; children ages 4 to 11 pay $12. Private carriage tours are available upon request.

**Classic Carriage Tours Inc.**
**10 Guignard Street**
**(843) 853-3747**
**www.classiccarriage.com**
One of the South's best-known carriage works, Classic Carriage, specializes in the construction and restoration of 19th- and 20th-century carriages, wagons, and surreys. With Percheron draft horses and experienced, licensed tour guides as drivers, these one-hour tours are popular with visitors and those planning special events in the Charleston area. These carriages are especially popular for traditional Charleston weddings. Reservations are strongly encouraged for the daily tours, which leave from the corner of Church and Market Streets in the City Market area from 9:00 A.M. to 5:30 P.M. daily. Adult and teen rates are $20; rates for children 12 and younger are $10. If you book your tour in advance by phone, there is a $2.00 discount per person.

**Old South Carriage Co.**
**14 Anson Street**
**(843) 723-9712**
**www.oldsouthcarriage.com**
These are the carriage tours narrated by licensed guides wearing red sashes (Confederate uniforms, of sorts). The 60-minute tours depart from 14 Anson Street,

at the corner of North Market and Anson Streets, every 20 minutes beginning at 9:00 A.M. daily. Adult fares are $20, and fares for children ages 3 to 11 are $10.

### Olde Towne Carriage Co.
### 20 Anson Street
### (843) 856-1730, (888) 800-5091
### www.oldetownecarriage.com
These carriage tours by licensed guides leave the company barn at 20 Anson Street near the City Market starting at 9:00 A.M. Tours are given until dusk and run from 45 minutes to an hour. Fares for those older than 11 are $19.00, and fares for ages 4 to 11 are $9.00.

### Palmetto Carriage Tours
### 40 North Market Street
### (843) 723-8145
### www.carriagetour.com
Experienced guides narrate this one-hour carriage tour that meanders through 25 blocks (2 miles) of antebellum neighborhoods at a clip-clop pace. Tours begin and end at the red barn behind the Rainbow Market, 40 North Market Street. Hours are 9:00 A.M. to dusk daily. Adult rates are $19.00, and children ages 4 to 11 are $10.

# Cruise and Boat Tours

These tours offer the absolute joy of being on the breezy waters of Charleston Harbor and the wide Cooper River, both of which offer an entirely new perspective on Charleston. It's a perspective that was, after all, the one first seen by pirate scalawags and some of our country's founding fathers. This was the first view for those aboard heavy-laden packet boats and cotton barges as well as those on the first ironclad warships and the crowded slave vessels out of Africa and the Caribbean. Maritime history is clearly one of Charleston's long suits, but we suggest you supplement a boat tour with another type of tour so you don't miss the urban story. Here are some of our favorite water tours:

### Barrier Island EcoTours
### (843) 886-5000
### www.nature-tours.com
Here is a chance to become immersed in the ecology and natural history that make the Lowcountry a marine biologist's paradise. Young and old alike will enjoy these adventures on the barrier islands led by personable guides who skillfully teach visitors some of the most fascinating aspects about this environment. Tours depend on weather conditions and availability, but you can choose from the following adventures. Capers Island is an untouched barrier island close to Charleston with diverse wildlife to see and a breathtaking landscape to explore. The three-and-a-half-hour tour goes both mornings and afternoons in summer, mornings only in winter. Fare is $32 for adults, $25 for children under 12. The Crabbing Clinic (also three and a half hours) teaches guests how to catch, cook, clean, and consume this Lowcountry delicacy. Fare is $32 for adults, $25 for children under 12. The Sunset Cruise (two hours) is an abbreviated version of the Capers Island wildlife trip and includes a 30-minute walk on the island. Fare is $28 for adults, $22 for children under 12. Call for information on their Creek Fishing Trip for adults and the Marine Biology Day Camp for children ages 5 to 12 during summer months. Reservations are recommended. All tours depart from Isle of Palms Marina at the end of 41st Avenue, Isle of Palms.

### Charleston Harbor Tours
### 10 Wharfside Drive
### (843) 722-1112, (800) 344-4483
### www.charlestonharbortours.com
These folks say they've been giving water tours of Charleston Harbor since 1908. Their current tour boat, the *Carolina Belle,* is 85 feet long and carries 300 passengers in comfort. The Harbor of History tour includes 75 points of interest including a ride past Fort Sumter and lasts approximately 90 minutes. Tour hours are 11:30 A.M., 1:30 P.M., and 3:30 P.M. Adult fare is $14.00, and children ages 4 to 11 go for

*Believe it or not, there's even a tour of the Carolina Lowcountry's unique culinary history for those seeking insights and instruction on the secrets and traditions of Southern cooking. Carolina Food Pros offers tours, seminars, gift baskets, and walking tours with the inside scoop on many of the foods that have made South Carolina famous. You meet chefs, bakers, food growers, and special artisans as you visit restaurants, markets, kitchens, and food shops throughout the city. Their standard tour leaves the visitor center at 9:30 A.M. Saturday mornings and goes until noon. The cost is $35 per person and includes three tasting stops along the way. Reservations are required; call (843) 723-3366 or (877) 728-2783.*

$8.00. Tickets are sold at the boat, at the visitor center, or on the Web site.

### Schooner *Pride*
**(843) 559-9686, (888) 571-2486**
**www.schoonerpride.com**
Ah, here's a fantasy that is delightfully achievable. See Charleston from the water—as countless settlers and 19th-century immigrants saw it—from the decks of a tall ship, the Schooner *Pride*. She's 84 feet long and U.S. Coast Guard–certified to carry 49 day passengers or 20 overnight guests. The two-hour cruise of Charleston Harbor costs $20 for adults and children 12 and older and $15 for children ages 4 to 12.

Experienced sailors and quick learners may help with the ship, or you can simply sit back and enjoy the wind, sea, and unexpected pleasure of almost soundless propulsion. Call for afternoon or evening schedules and reservations. Schooner *Pride* is moored at the Aquarium Wharf directly behind the IMAX on Concord Street. All tours depart from there. No tours are offered after November 26 until they begin again on May 1.

### SpiritLine Cruises
**360 Concord Street, Ste. 201**
**(843) 722-2628, (800) 789-3678**
**www.spiritlinecruises.com**
This is the only boat tour from Charleston that actually stops at the Ft. Sumter National Monument where the Civil War began. Tours leave daily from two locations: Liberty Square beside the S.C. Aquarium and Patriots Point in Mt. Pleasant. Tour hours vary seasonally, so call for details. Adult rates are $13.00; rates for children under age 11, $7.00.

SpiritLine also has a nonstop Harbor Tour that departs from Liberty Square at Aquarium Wharf and from Patriots Point (only on weekends in January and February). The tour lasts approximately one and a half hours and cruises past the Battery, Patriots Point Maritime Museum, Castle Pinckney, Fort Sumter, and Fort Johnson. Adult rates are $13.00; rates for children (age 6–11), $7.00.

Their dinner cruise is aboard the *Spirit of Carolina* and departs from Patriots Point at 7:00 P.M. and returns at 10:00 P.M. (boarding begins at 6:30 P.M.). A sumptuous three-course meal is served—prepared to order—with table-side service, spirits, live entertainment, and dancing. Prepaid reservations are required. The weekday fare is $41.15 per person; the weekend rate is $45.15.

## Air Tours

### Flying High Over Charleston
**202 Commons Way, Goose Creek**
**(843) 569-6148**
If getting the "overview" is something you want—literally—there are even a couple of airplane tours available to Charleston area visitors. Jim Ellison is an FAA-licensed commercial pilot with more than 20 years of flying experience in the Charleston area. His Package A: Historic Charleston & Sea Island Tour includes historic plantations, harbor and aircraft carrier *Yorktown* views, beautiful beaches and sea islands,

The Citadel, Ft. Sumter, Morris Island light-house, and 40 miles of ocean coastline vistas in addition to Historic Charleston from the air. This is an hour-plus tour in a photo-friendly airplane. His Package B: Taste of Charleston Sightseeing Tour is about 55 minutes in length and slightly more limited in subject matter, but just as exciting. Tours are available seven days a week (weather permitting) and take off from Mercury Air Center, $\frac{3}{4}$ mile from Charleston International Airport. The rate for Tour A is $170 for two passengers; Tour B is $150. A third tour, appropriate for children, is somewhat shorter in length (about 45 minutes) and goes for $130.

# THE ARTS

Some people would tell you the verdict on Charleston and the arts is still out—that after an early, spectacular (even historic) colonial-era start, the city fell asleep artistically and has stayed that way since . . . well, the Civil War. Others would have you believe this city, today, is a virtual mecca for experimental and traditional artists of all kinds, if only during Spoleto Festival USA. The truth probably lies somewhere in between. While there have been dormant stretches, there have also been times, such as the 1920s and early '30s, when Charleston experienced artistic stirrings that resulted in truly exciting art.

In literature, there was Charleston's own DuBose Heyward (1885–1940), whose legendary 1925 novel, *Porgy,* inspired a renaissance of artistic effort in and about the city and its people. The story, for those who may not be familiar with it, is based on the life of a poor, crippled black street vendor and his tragic love for an abused, drug-addicted woman. The novelist's playwright wife, Dorothy, co-wrote the successful stage play that opened on Broadway in 1927.

In 1926, none other than George Gershwin—already famous for "Rhapsody in Blue" and bound for immortality as the composer of dozens of American musical standards—was fascinated by the story. He felt *Porgy* was just the vehicle he was looking for to create a new art form: the American folk opera.

One of the city's favorite legends is about the long, hot summer George Gershwin spent in Charleston (actually, in a house on Folly Beach) working on the opera. Yes, he did come here. And no, the house isn't still standing. It washed out to sea years ago in a storm long since forgotten, although you might hear otherwise from alleged Insiders. During that summer, with the help of the Heywards and Gershwin's lyricist brother, Ira, the project eventually made the transformation from the literary page to a legitimate, hauntingly beautiful opera.

Although it took several years to finally put it on the boards, the world-famous work known as *Porgy and Bess* was at last produced by New York's Theatre Guild in 1935. While it was never a staggering financial success (not many things were in 1935), the work was universally and artistically acclaimed. Since then, the opera has played all over the world, including in Milan's prestigious La Scala. But no audience could love it more than an audience in Charleston, where it was performed most recently in 1990 in a marvelous production at Gaillard Municipal Auditorium. In 1989, immediately following the devastation of Hurricane Hugo, a bruised and battered Charleston was given a special gift when a New York City production of *Porgy and Bess* was flown in to give an impromptu performance for the people of Charleston. Over the roar of portable generators and the sound of distant buzz saws clearing streets still filled with debris, the New York cast sang a concert version of the opera on the steps of the Customs House. As they sang the part of Gershwin's score that dramatizes a violent hurricane and the awesome stillness of its aftermath, the audience wept openly—unashamed. The cathartic effect of that emotion-filled performance is difficult to describe. Suffice to say it created an indelible memory for those Charlestonians who were there to witness it.

Neither DuBose Heyward nor George Gershwin would live to see *Porgy and Bess* reach the zenith of its fame. Gershwin died of a brain tumor in 1937, and Heyward succumbed to a heart attack in 1940. The Heywards, along with their daughter, are buried in the graveyard of St. Philip's Episcopal Church, not far from the real Catfish Row on Church Street, a couple of blocks below Broad.

Another highlight of the Charleston renaissance period would be the work of Alice Ravenel Huger Smith (1887–1958), watercolorist and "preservationist" of the Lowcountry's rice plantation landscapes. In the late 1930s, when she began to realize the old plantation lifestyle—especially the rice plantation lifestyle of the 1850s—was dying out and might soon be forgotten, she recorded it in a series of paintings that are now integral to the permanent collection of the Gibbes Museum of Art (see the section on Other Museums in the Attractions chapter).

Yet another important artist of the city's renaissance years was Elizabeth O'Neill Verner (1883–1979). Her fascination with the architecture and streetscapes of Charleston can be traced back as early as 1903. One passion was etching, and her works (including many illustrations of Charleston) are highly acclaimed. The work of Verner, from about 1923 until the late 1960s, has almost come to define Charleston's renaissance school of art.

But what about today? And what is all this Spoleto hoopla about? Following is an introduction to the big event, along with a couple of other popular festivals. After that, we offer listings and information under self-explanatory headings: Festivals, Organizations and Venues, Theater, Dance, Music, and Galleries. Unless otherwise noted, all addresses are in Charleston.

# FESTIVALS

## MOJA Arts Festival
**133 Church Street**
**(843) 724-7305**
**www.mojafestival.com**
The MOJA Arts Festival in September is the city of Charleston's celebration of the Lowcountry's rich and wonderful heritage from the African and Caribbean cultures. This 16-day performance schedule offers exciting theater, visual arts, dance, music, films, and lectures.

"MOJA" is a Swahili word meaning "one" and "unity" or "the source" and "the

beginning." Hence, the city's celebration of black arts is indeed appropriately named, as Charleston was the port of entry for thousands of slaves during the 18th and 19th centuries. Their contribution to American culture is clearly enormous. The festival is sponsored by the city's Office of Cultural Affairs and is funded in part by the South Carolina Arts Commission. (See the Annual Events chapter for more on MOJA.)

## Piccolo Spoleto
**133 Church Street**
**(843) 724-7305**
**www.piccolospoleto.com**
Piccolo Spoleto (Italian for "Little Spoleto") is the city of Charleston's way of saying, "Encore! Encore!" It is Charleston's official companion festival (a series of festivals, really) running concurrently with the internationally acclaimed Spoleto Festival USA.

Piccolo's focus, however, is on local and regional talent of every artistic discipline. There are literally hundreds of events offered every year through Piccolo, most of which are relatively low cost or free. Expect to see performances ranging from chamber music and provocative theater to experimental dance and visual arts.

The city's Office of Cultural Affairs handles the project and sees to it, through its Artreach program, that the festival's high spirits and fine performances are exported to artistically neglected sections of the community. This way, the arts can be experienced by everyone, regardless of economic status or educational background. (For more on Piccolo Spoleto, see the Annual Events chapter.)

## Spoleto Festival USA
**Various locations, P.O. Box 704,**
**Charleston 29402**
**(843) 579-3100**
**www.spoletousa.org**
Not every newcomer to the Lowcountry is familiar with the city's spectacular May showcase for the arts called Spoleto Festival USA. By the same token, no one stays

**THE ARTS**

---

> *The Spoleto finale concert at Middleton Place is a great site for an all-day picnic. Go early, and spread out a blanket to reserve your spot on the open greensward before the orchestra shell. Eat, drink, and toss the Frisbee all afternoon. Stroll the magnificent gardens. Then settle down for a great evening of festival music followed by spectacular fireworks under the stars.*

---

in Charleston very long before hearing "Spoleto this . . ." and "Spoleto that . . . "

For openers, know that Spoleto (pronounced spo-LAY-toe, like tomato) is the New World counterpart to the summertime arts extravaganza in Spoleto, Italy, called the "Festival of Two Worlds." The latter was founded back in 1958 by Pulitzer Prize–winning composer–librettist–director Gian Carlo Menotti.

Menotti saw the quaint, medieval town of Spoleto's rich architectural heritage, suitable performing facilities, and central European location (about 60 miles north of Rome) as the perfect backdrop for an interdisciplinary arts celebration. There, he created a world-famous showcase and exchange for international talent both young and old, rich and poor.

By 1977, Menotti was looking for an American home for his festival, and for many of the same reasons he chose Spoleto, Italy, he thought Charleston could neatly fill the bill here in America. With support and encouragement from Charleston Mayor Joseph P. Riley Jr., other important members of the local community, and the then-well-funded National Endowment for the Arts, Spoleto Festival USA premiered as a two-week explosion of opera, jazz, theater, visual arts, and dance, including classical ballet. It explored new ways to look at traditional works as well as the cutting-edge and the avant garde. Tickets to Spoleto events are sold in packages as well as for individual events. They aren't inexpensive, but much of Spoleto's infectious

enthusiasm is palpable on the city streets—that is, free, and available to everyone.

Almost anyone would agree that Charleston takes on a special glow during the festival. Maybe the illumination comes from the corps of international critics who review performances daily in a special section of the *Post and Courier* or from the crowded restaurants and traffic-clogged streets. Perhaps it's the joyful noises that seem to be floating on the air all over town, the street performers, the sudden profusion of sidewalk art galleries and the excitement of a population swollen with young, animated, talented people. But for whatever reasons, Spoleto is a time of great fun and good art. Don't miss it.

When the festival is over, and alas, they pack up the sets and costumes and truck them off to distant parts, take heart. The arts in Charleston—and by that we mean a number of quality offerings—don't completely cease. They just slow down a bit after those hectic weeks of intense saturation. We try to think of it this way: The spirit of Spoleto fosters the development of greater and more appreciative audiences for arts activities in and around Charleston throughout the year. (See the Annual Events chapter for more on Spoleto.)

## ORGANIZATIONS AND VENUES

**City of Charleston**
**Office of Cultural Affairs**
**133 Church Street**
**(843) 724-7305**
The city of Charleston devotes this office in the Dock Street Theatre to advocating, providing services for, and helping fund the various arts organizations that contribute to promoting the city. In the summer, for example, these folks sponsor the Storefront School for the Arts, a program for inner-city children co-administered by the Parks and Recreation Department. The Office of Cultural Affairs also maintains the revolving exhibits of the City Gallery in

the Dock Street Theatre and produces the MOJA Arts Festival each fall and Piccolo Spoleto in the spring. Call Ellen Dressler Moryl, executive director, for more details.

## North Charleston Coliseum
**5001 Coliseum Drive, North Charleston**
**(843) 529-5050**
**www.coliseumpac.com**
This beautiful venue has already helped put the Lowcountry on the map for many nationally known performing arts groups. Opened in 1993, the much-anticipated North Charleston Coliseum is the largest and most diverse indoor entertainment facility in South Carolina. Various seating configurations are possible, but, generally speaking, the coliseum's capacity is 14,000 seats. Because of this, Greater Charleston is now a viable audience for some of the biggest traveling shows and sports attractions in America. The coliseum has attracted the likes of Rod Stewart, Neil Diamond, the Ringling Brothers and Barnum and Bailey Circus, James Taylor, Metallica, World Cup figure skating, NHL hockey, and NCAA basketball, to name just a few. The coliseum is also the permanent home of the South Carolina Stingrays hockey club, which began play in the East Coast Hockey League in the fall of 1993. (See the Spectator Sports chapter.) Tickets for all coliseum events may be purchased at the Coliseum box office or by phone (888) 386–8497. To get to the coliseum, take the Montague Avenue exit off Interstate 26, and follow the signs, or take the Montague Avenue exit off Interstate 526 (Mark Clark Expressway).

## North Charleston Cultural Arts Program
**Sterett Hall**
**(former Charleston Navy Base)**
**PO Box 190016,**
**North Charleston 29419-9016**
**(843) 745-1087**
**www.northcharleston.org**
The Cultural Arts Program for North Charleston was created in 1979 to plan for and support artistic and cultural activities throughout the community. It provides programs and services intended to enhance the quality of life for citizens and assists in the cultural and economic development of the area. The Cultural Arts Program is located in Sterett Hall on the former Navy Base, and many of its performances are held in the recently renovated Park Circle Auditorium.

The program's other offerings include the North Charleston City Gallery in the Charleston Area Convention Center Complex at 5001 Coliseum Drive. Gallery hours are Monday through Saturday from 9:00 A.M. to 5:00 P.M. The Dinner Theatre series in the Embassy Ballroom at the Convention Center Complex is another popular feature. By far the largest project undertaken through the program is the annual North Charleston Arts Festival, held every spring. Most events and parking are free (some tickets cost up to $10) at this weeklong extravaganza mounted in the giant North Charleston Coliseum. The festival is a kaleidoscope of color and images with original artwork, photography, arts, and crafts plus live entertainment and food concessions. For more information, call Marty Besancon at the NCCAP office or write the group.

## THEATER

In the 18th century, when Charles Towne was the capital of the colonial province and a thriving port of entry, there were reports in England that it was "the gayest, politest, and richest place in America," so naturally it follows that Charles Towne was one of the first American towns to patronize the cultural arts—including the world of drama.

According to Eola Willis and her copious 1933 study of the city's early theatrical life, *The Charleston Stage in the XVIII Century,* drama was alive and well here as early as the 1730s. The city's first newspaper, the *Charleston Gazette,* described at some length the theatrical season of 1734. That year on January 18, the *Gazette* carried the following notice:

"On Friday the 24th instant, in the Court-Room will be attempted a Tragedy called 'The Orphan, or the Unhappy Marriage.' Tickets will be delivered out on Tuesday next at Mr. Shepheard's at 40s each."

Apparently, the season's opening performance was a hit, because on February 8, the *Gazette* published its first review, in which the prologue to *The Orphan* was reprinted in its entirety. Quickly following on February 18, *The Opera of Flora* or *Hob in the Well* opened with the dance of the two Pierrots and the pantomime of Harlequin and Scaramouch. This was another first for Charleston theater—the first time a musical play had been performed on American shores. Apparently, the theatrical life of Charleston was off and running by 1734 and shines just as brilliantly today.

## Dock Street Theatre
**135 Church Street**
**(843) 720–3968, Box Office: (843) 965–4032**
**www.charlestonstage.com**

Much ado is made about Charleston's many firsts, not the least of which is the story about the Dock Street Theatre being the first and oldest theater in America.

Let's split hairs here just for accuracy's sake. It has been academically determined that the first theater in America was erected in Williamsburg, Virginia, in the second decade of the 18th century. The second was built in New York in 1732. The third was in Charles Towne in 1736, while poor old Philadelphia didn't have a playhouse until 1749.

In the early 18th century, certain buildings were called theaters though they were no more than "long rooms"—rooms big enough to hold an audience. These places lacked a traditional stage and other theatrical facilities. The 1734 production of *The Orphan,* for instance, was actually performed in a courtroom—just such a place.

Charleston's first (technical) theater was on the site of the old Planters Hotel on Church Street, which was then the only major route running the entire length of the city. It ended at White Point, which is

now known as the Battery. (See more on the Battery in the Attractions chapter.) Thus, Church Street was the thoroughfare for all the traffic to and from the bustling and noisy docks. It made good sense to build a theater near this main traffic route, so in 1736, the first building was constructed on the south side of Queen (then called Dock) Street, just a little west of heavily traveled Church Street. Records show it was less than 100 yards from the Huguenot church and St. Philip's Episcopal Church. It was said to have had a stage, pit boxes, and a gallery. Some ill fate likely soon befell this building, because no mention of it is found after 1737.

Eventually, a second theater was constructed nearby, and an early hotel was built on the rear portion of the old theater lot. The year was 1800. It was called the Planters Hotel because it was popular lodging for Lowcountry planters and their families, who would traditionally leave their plantations at certain times of the year. It was customary to be in town for the winter social season and for Race Week, an exponent of Charleston's torrid 19th-century love affair with horse racing. In 1835, the Planters Hotel was remodeled and expanded.

The old Planters Hotel is the structure that was still standing but in ruins when, in the 1930s, the New Deal's Work Projects Administration, giving work to unemployed architects and craftsmen during the Depression, rebuilt it as the theater we know today. Technically, it is the oldest building still standing that was part of a colonial theatrical enterprise. But the charming stage proscenium and the handsome paneled boxes we encounter today in the Dock Street were not around for the prologue to *The Orphan*—not in 1734, anyway. It would be more than 200 years later, on November 26, 1937, that Charleston's own DuBose Heyward, already famous for *Porgy,* would write a special dedication to reopen a new facility. The reconstructed theater was called the Dock Street in honor of those early Charleston productions on the site.

None of the above, of course, takes anything away from Dock Street Theatre's enormous popularity and charm or the tremendously important role it plays in the theatrical life of the city today.

The reconstruction of the Dock Street auditorium recaptures the spirit of early Georgian theaters. It seats 463 people, with a pit and a parquet of 13 boxes. The walls are paneled with natural local black cypress, rubbed soft and mellow. The wood was treated with an old formula of iron filings dissolved in vinegar and then waxed to bring out the grain. The lighting fixtures carry out the feeling of candle brackets, and the cove ceiling has exceptional acoustic properties, as did many theaters of the time. Over the stage hangs a carved wood bas-relief of the Royal Arms of England (obligatory in all Georgian theaters), duplicated from an original that still hangs above the altar in Goose Creek's chapel of ease, built in 1711. (See the Close-up, "Lowcountry Chapels of Ease," in the Worship chapter.)

The Dock Street's stage has a proscenium opening of 34 feet (somewhat larger than the original would have had) and features an apron forestage with "proscenium doors" on either side. This is typical of Georgian theaters. Today's Dock Street stage floor is flat, whereas the original was most likely tilted. The rebuilt Dock Street was never intended to be a museum piece or an exact reconstruction. It is, however, a modern theater capable of handling a wide variety of productions, and an integral part of Charleston's rich cultural life.

After dutiful service for almost 70 years, the venerable Dock Street Theatre is currently due for a facelift. Plans are now under way for updating the theater's stage technology and some of the fixtures and infrastructure, which will make it more comfortable for patrons and performers alike.

# Acting Companies

Whether you're a confirmed theater patron, an experienced actor, or just a thespian wannabe, there's a Lowcountry theater company that will interest you. Some of these companies are longstanding members of the Greater Charleston arts community; others are embryonic or just getting off the ground.

The College of Charleston's multi-award-winning theater department is flourishing, with four groups currently taking bows. The work is first-rate, and these quality productions stand out as some of the best bargains in town. All college productions are mounted in various venues in the Simons Center for the Arts at 54 St. Philip Street on campus. Thumbnail sketches of some of our local theater groups follow.

### Art Forms & Theater Concepts
### P. O. Box 20130, Charleston 29413
### (843) 723-5399
### www.aftcinc.com
This exciting African-American theater group with more than a decade of successful productions behind them recently presented its high-energy musical *I Sing From My Soul.* The members are always busy preparing for their next MOJA production or Piccolo Spoleto performance. The director is actor, director, playwright Art Gilliard. Call for more details.

### Center Stage
### Simons Center for the Arts
### 54 St. Philip Street
### (843) 953-8210
### www.cofc.edu/theatre
Center Stage is the College of Charleston

*The easiest ways to get the best tickets to major arts events in Charleston are to become a patron of that arts organization, participate in their annual fundraising drive, or buy series tickets whenever possible.*

student organization that, together with the school's Theatre Department, produces a varied season from October through April in the Emmett Robinson Theater. Productions are staged and directed by faculty and guest directors. Admission is free. Separate from these productions are the experimental one-act plays (also free) staged by students in the Simons Center's flexible and highly creative "black box" Theatre 220. For more information, call the number listed above.

## Charleston Guerrilla Theatre
### 217 Lucas Street, Mt. Pleasant
### (843) 762-6685

Here's a community theater group that does everything from lively classics to innovative modern works, Shakespeare to Broadway. Its venues have found the group everywhere from Dock Street Theatre to public parks and the odd warehouse for community outreach programs. Open auditions are publicly announced before major productions. Call Bill Stewart for more information.

## Charleston Stage Company
### 135 Church Street, Suite 7
### (843) 577-5967, (800) 454-7093
### www.charlestonstage.com

This group presents a full season of family-oriented plays and children's theater from September through April in the Dock Street Theatre. It also offers various educational programs that explore stage management, scene study, projection, and creative dramatics for beginners and advanced students. Volunteers are encouraged to contact Julian Wiles at the theater to become involved. For ticket information, call (843) 577-7183.

## Flowertown Players
### 133 South Main Street, Summerville
### (843) 875-9251
### www.flowertownplayers.org

This is a community theater in Summerville whose educational and literary objectives are to stimulate interest in the arts, music, literature, and drama in people of all ages. It has a regular season of productions and its own home facility in downtown Summerville. General manager is Naomi Nimmo; volunteers are welcome. Call the theater for more information.

## The Footlight Players
### 20 Queen Street
### (843) 722-4487
### www.footlightplayers.net

This group recently celebrated its 69th season of producing quality community theater in Charleston. It enjoys strong support from Charleston's theater community for its long-standing record of exposing local audiences to interesting, instructive, and cultural plays that are in keeping with Charleston's traditional mores. Since the early 1940s, the Footlight Players have performed in their converted cotton warehouse (ca. 1840) on Queen Street, easily one of the city's most charming theatrical venues. Executive director is Richard Futch; volunteers are welcome. Call for additional information.

## Main Stage
### Simons Center for the Arts,
### 54 St. Philip Street
### (843) 953-6306
### www.cofc.edu/sota

Main Stage is a series of several plays produced each semester that are exclusively directed and designed by faculty from the college's department of theater. Productions—often of classical or traditional works such as Shakespeare's *Macbeth* and Ibsen's *Ghosts*—are at the College of Charleston's Emmett Robinson Theater. They recently staged a contemporary version of Mary Zimmerman's *Metamorphoses*. For production information, call (843) 953-6306, or the box office at (843) 943-5604.

## Premiere Theater at the
## College of Charleston
### Simons Center for the Arts,
### 54 St. Philip Street
### (843) 953-6306
### www.cofc.edu/sota

These productions are contemporary plays featuring the work of local professionals as well as faculty and graduate students from the College of Charleston theater department. Sometimes, professional directors are brought in as guests for special works. For additional information, contact Evan Parry's office at (843) 953-5439, or the box office at (843) 953-5604.

### Robert Ivey Ballet Productions
### 1910 Savannah Highway
### (843) 556-1343

Although Robert Ivey Ballet is primarily a dance company with a full-time studio, this production operation offers popular musicals on a fairly regular basis. Recently, the RIB mounted their 25th anniversary gala (contemporary ballet and jazz) at the College of Charleston as ballet company in residence. For theater productions, open auditions are held, usually in the fall. Call Robert Ivey for more information on ballet, modern, and jazz dance instruction at the Charleston Dance Studio.

### Shakespeare Project at the College of Charleston
### College of Charleston, Simons Center for the Arts, 54 St. Philip Street
### (843) 953-5604
### www.cofc.edu/sota

Now five years old and still growing is the college-sponsored Shakespeare group who recently mounted a wonderful production of *Twelfth Night*. These performances by student and community-based actors are presented in August under a wing of the theatre department and are done in the Emmett Robinson Theater. There's general seating with adult tickets costing $12.00, student seating, $8.00. For more specific information, call Todd McNerney at the number above.

## DANCE
## Dance Companies

### Anonymity Dance Company
### 26 27th Avenue, Isle of Palms
### (843) 886-6104

This professional modern dance company has been Charleston-based since 1985. It performs throughout the state with a wide repertoire of styles and works. The company is available for master classes in technique, improvisation, choreography, and classroom creativity for children. Contact Jennifer D. Strelkauskas, artistic director, at the number above for more information.

### Charleston Ballet Theatre
### 477 King Street
### (843) 723-7334
### www.charlestonballet.org

This energetic group presents professional dance concerts in Charleston and throughout the Southeast. Its wide range of performances includes such classics as *The Nutcracker, Sleeping Beauty,* and *Swan Lake* as well as contemporary works. Call Don or Patricia Cantwell, artistic directors, for more information. The group's resident facility, near the visitor center, includes a 300-seat theater space, public parking, and spacious studios. Charleston Ballet offers an annual series. For box office information, call the number above.

## Dance Schools

In a town that gave its name to a famous dance step that put flappers of the '20s on the world map, it should be no surprise that Charleston is still the scene for a variety of dancing and dance instruction. Below we have listed some good schools but we encourage new residents to also check with your local area's recreation department and/or continuing education programs.

## Ballet Academy of Charleston
**1662 Savannah Highway**
**(843) 769-6932**
Ballet Academy of Charleston is under the direction of Mara Meir, former ballerina with Ballet de Paris and prima ballerina of the Israeli Opera. This is a fee-based school offering scheduled semesters of classical ballet training for children ages four to seventeen, with separate adult classes. Trial classes for children are offered. No recital performances are held. Instead, parents view their children's progress through regularly scheduled, end-of-year open classes and periodic conferences with the director.

## Charleston Ballet Studio
**477 King Street**
**(843) 723-7334**
**www.charlestonballet.org**
This school is affiliated with the professional dance company Charleston Ballet Theatre. Classes and workshops are offered for ages three through adult, and performances—a serious goal for serious students—are held at the Gaillard Municipal Auditorium and Sottile Theater.

## Charleston Dance Studio, Robert Ivey Ballet
**1910 Savannah Highway**
**(843) 556-1343**
Robert Ivey, a professional dancer and Artist-in-Residence at the College of Charleston's School of the Arts, directs this dance company and school. His professional instructors teach classes in ballet, jazz, and dance exercise. The school has a nurturing attitude toward children, and their families and friends appreciate the seasonal performances that let the students show off their talents. His groups also perform frequently at College of Charleston events and have represented the city and the United States in international competitions.

# MUSIC

## Charleston Community Band
**14 George Street**
**(843) 763-4528**
Started in 1977, this all-volunteer concert band performs 20 free concerts a year throughout the area. The group provides a wonderful opportunity for talented local adults to continue their musical pursuits. Call current band president Jeff Hooven or Susan DuPuis at the number listed above for more information.

## Charleston Concert Association
**P.O. Box 743, Charleson 29402**
**(843) 722-7667**
**www.charlestonconcerts.com**
The Charleston Concert Association (CCA) is Charleston's oldest nonprofit presenting arts organization. Founded in 1936 as a sister organization with the Charleston Symphony Orchestra (CSO), CCA's original mission was to bring internationally acclaimed musicians to Charleston as a complement to CSO. Back in 1931, the symphony's aim was to create an avenue for local musicians to develop their skills.

Today, the CCA's mission is to provide local access to classical artists of international caliber throughout the year (whereas Spoleto Festival USA is a more concentrated exposure of only two weeks). In recent years, the CCA has expanded its vision to include all of the performing arts, including theater and film as well as dance. Among the CCA's recent presentations were the highly acclaimed Opera Verdi Europa, Orpheus Chamber Orchestra, Les Ballets de Monte-Carlo, the Dresden Philharmonic, and the Duke Ellington Orchestra. Tickets are sold by subscription to the series, and individual prices range from $15 to $35. The executive director is Jason A. Nichols. Call for subscription rates and concert season details.

## Charleston Symphony Orchestra
160 East Bay Street, 3rd Floor
(843) 723-7528
www.charlestonsymphony.com

Charleston has a long, rich, and varied musical history. Records indicate several different orchestras were organized in the city during the years from 1819 to 1919. Today's organization, known as the Charleston Symphony Orchestra, has been in existence for more than 68 years.

In December 1936, Miss Maud Winthrup Gibbon and Mrs. Martha Laurens Patterson founded what is known today as the Charleston Symphony Orchestra, and they presented a concert in Hibernian Hall on Meeting Street. The orchestra provided music for the official grand opening of the newly restored Dock Street Theatre in 1936, and the Dock Street in turn became the orchestra's official home for its first three years. Through the 1940s and 1950s, Memminger Auditorium was home for the group, as it brought in such famous artists as Robert Merrill, Jan Pierce, Blanche Theirbom, and Eleanor Steber. The orchestra played under the batons of conductors J. Albert Frecht, Tony Hadgi, Don Mills, and, from 1962 to 1982, Lucien DeGroote.

In the late 1970s, the orchestra emerged as a fully professional organization with the employment of a core of full-time, conservatory-trained, first-chair players. The orchestra achieved "metropolitan" status in the American Symphony Orchestra League and adopted Gaillard Auditorium as its official home. In 1984, David Stahl became music director and conductor. Under his leadership, the CSO has become one of the leading arts organizations in the Southeast. The orchestra's budget under Stahl increased from $250,000 in 1984 to about $2.3 million in 2003. A resident orchestra of about 45 professional, full-time musicians now perform a demanding concert schedule on stage and throughout the community, including special events and school programs throughout the state every weekend from September through May.

The orchestra has several major concert series—Masterworks, Charleston Pops, Lowcountry Concerts, Casual Classics, Stained Glass Concerts, and CSO Kids (for youngsters). In addition, the CSO performs other special concerts that cover a broad range of musical tastes.

Individual ticket sales are handled through the Gaillard Auditorium box office, at Ticketmaster, (843) 554-6060, or at any Publix supermarket. Ticket prices vary according to the series, but they range from $10 to $39 for individual concerts.

*A fresh new venue for the Charleston Symphony Orchestra is their free concert at Freshfield Village on Kiawah Island. This performance, part of the Pops series, brings together local friends, family, and island vacationers.*

## Charleston Symphony Orchestra League
160 East Bay Street, 3rd Floor
(843) 766-2161
www.charlestonsymphony.com

Although it's mostly known in the community as sponsor of the annual Symphony Gala and the Symphony Designer Showhouse, the 400-member Charleston Symphony Orchestra League serves its namesake group in many ways.

Through fund-raising events, the league provides major financial support to the orchestra. It annually awards scholarships to orchestra musicians for advanced study and to school-age musicians who are members of the Charleston County Youth Orchestra. Members volunteer many hours of service in the CSO office promoting the orchestra and aiding in the sale of season tickets, and they also serve as concert ushers. The league welcomes anyone wishing to join and support the CSO.

## CSO Chorus
160 East Bay Street, 3rd Floor
(843) 723-7528
www.cso-chorus.org

First organized in 1978 as the CSO Singers Guild, to be the choral complement of the Charleston Symphony Orchestra, this group is now called the CSO Chorus. The group performs with the CSO in major works several times a year. In addition to the large concert group of nearly 125 singers, there are two smaller perform- ance groups that appear throughout the season. The Chamber Singers, under the direction of Robert Taylor, perform 20th- century music. Participation in CSO Cho- rus groups is by regularly scheduled audition. Call Mr. Taylor at (843) 953-8231.

### East Cooper Concert Series
### P.O. Box 279, Mt. Pleasant 29464
### (843) 884-9090

This annual seven-concert series, sched- uled from September through May at Christ Episcopal Church, benefits Meals on Wheels. Admission to all concert events is a monetary donation. Performers include various ensembles from the Charleston Symphony Orchestra, visiting concert choirs, and individual artists. The church is at 2304 U.S. Highway 17 N. in Mt. Pleasant. Contact Lorna Tedesco for scheduling and more details at the number above.

### International Piano Series,
### College of Charleston
### 44 George Street (Sottile Theatre)
### (843) 953-6575
### www.cofc.edu/sota

Since 1989, the School of the Arts at the College of Charleston has had an annual spring International Piano Series that's also open to the general public. The series was designed to introduce students and the Charleston community to an array of fine, established performers from around the world. This is a major inspiration to music students on campus who have come from as far away as Spain, Korea, China, and Costa Rica to study in the col- lege's piano performance program. All concerts are at 8:00 P.M. in the Sottile The- atre on George Street just off King, and admission is $15 at the door. Call the num- ber above for a performance schedule

and a calendar of School of the Arts events.

### Monday Night Concert Series,
### College of Charleston
### Simons Center for the Arts,
### 54 St. Philip Street (Recital Hall)
### (843) 953-8228
### www.cofc.edu/sota

This is one of those little gems that few people know about, and yet it's one of the best arts events going on in the city. These regularly scheduled Monday night concerts are usually presented in the Simons Center Recital Hall and feature faculty and adjunct faculty talent from the music department. The programs vary from jazz to Renais- sance music, from organ concerts (at the Cathedral of St. Luke and St. Paul, 126 Coming Street) to choral works from the College's Gospel Choir (at the nearby Sot- tile Theater, 44 George Street). The overall quality of the concerts is always quite wonderful, and the admission price of $5.00 can't be beat. Call the School of the Arts for more information and specific concert schedules.

### Vox Aeterna
### P.O. Box 13268, Charleston 29422
### (venues vary)
### (843) 556-5826
### www.voxaeterna.homestead.com

The name means "voice eternal," but the group is only about seven years old. This is a choral group of nearly 20 singers who get together to perform serious 20th-cen- tury music in four planned concerts a year. Performances are held in various churches and concert halls throughout the city to explore the many acoustical possibilities and find the appropriate space to match the music. Many of the singers hold advanced degrees in music or related fields, and the quality of their concerts is earning praise from local critics. Call Kathy Stringer at (843) 532-2351 for audition and concert information. The group is pro- fessionally conducted by Scott Atwood, who auditions new singers by appoint- ment. Admission to the concerts is free (for now), but that may change soon. Call the number above for concert dates and audition information.

# GALLERIES

With so much history and architecture to brag about, Charleston may not be terribly famous for its art. But the fact is the city has produced a number of fine artists over the years. The charming illustrations Elizabeth O'Neill Verner created from the 1920s to 1940s were certainly not the first artistic views of the city to catch the public's eye, but they were (and still are) among the most popular. Other great talents include Charles Fraser and Samuel Morse (the inventor of the telegraph), who were portraitists working here. Some of the works of those artists are on display at the Gibbes Museum of Art. (See the Other Museums section of the Attractions chapter.)

Today, downtown Charleston hosts an amazing array of fine art galleries that expand the view and viewpoint far beyond the city Elizabeth O'Neill Verner loved to draw. Generally, when you're browsing in any of the downtown galleries, you're within easy walking distance of another . . . and another . . . and another. All are free to enter.

The serious shopper with an appetite to see more than just a few galleries may want to park the car and use Charleston's DASH shuttle system between stops. If you decide to give it a try, take the Meeting–King Street route. (For more on DASH, see the Getting Here, Getting Around chapter.)

**African American Art Gallery**
**43 John Street**
**(843) 722-7568**
**www.gallerychuma.com**
There is always a colorful and changing collection at this showcase for African and African-American art. Just across from the Charleston Visitor Reception and Transportation Center, the exhibition room features original works from local, national,

and international artists. New exhibits are mounted every two months. The gallery's prints and custom framing department has more than 1,500 limited-edition prints and posters.

The African American Gallery also offers a number of educational programs for schools, local community groups, and visitors. These include gallery tours, lectures, poetry readings, meet-the-artist events, classes, workshops, multimedia presentations, and more. African-American heritage tours to areas of historic importance in and around Charleston are offered in conjunction with licensed tour guides. (See the Tours chapter.) Hours are 10:00 A.M. to 6:00 P.M. Monday through Saturday.

Downstairs, Gallery Chuma features the large-format, stunning imagery of Jonathan Green, famous Gullah artist now of Naples, Florida.

**American Originals**
**153 East Bay Street**
**(843) 853-5034**
**www.americanoriginalsgallery.com**
This unique gallery, between Broad and Queen Streets, occupies more than 2,500 square feet in an old, historic sugar and cotton warehouse. Bright and colorful, the shop carries decorative fine crafts and wearable art. They feature original works by Rogers Oglesby, Zernie Smith, and Chaz Walter. Look for oils, watercolors, mixed media works, and contemporary handcrafts made by more than 350 local and regional artists. American Originals has silks and batik, tile art, metal sculpture, pottery, jewelry, and mobiles. Hours are 11:00 A.M. to 6:00 P.M. Monday through Thursday; 10:00 A.M. to 7:00 P.M. on Friday; 10:00 A.M. to 10:00 P.M. on Saturday; and Sunday 11:00 A.M. to 4:00 P.M.

**The Audubon Gallery**
**190 King Street**
**(843) 853-1100, (888) 853-BIRD**
**www.audubongallery.com**
This is the official gallery of the annual Southeastern Wildlife Exposition with

# Philip Simmons and the Wrought-Iron Connection

The lacy wrought-iron gates, grills, and balconies seen throughout Charleston punctuate the city's eloquent architectural statement. Many of them are original 18th-century works still *in situ*— proud survivors of a nearly lost art.

But Charleston's wrought-iron artwork, thanks to a man named Philip Simmons, is still being practiced and (perhaps more important) being taught to young artisans.

Born in the city's Mazyck-Wraggborough neighborhood (see the Neighborhoods chapter) more than 85 years ago, the young Philip Simmons learned the ironworking trade from his father . . . who learned it from his father . . . and so on, back through time.

Indeed, Philip Simmons is a living example of Charleston's rich heritage in the arts passed on through the African-American community since the days of slavery.

His works, like the gate shown, have long been recognized for their fine sense of scale, balance, and craftsmanship. Mr. Simmons is a recipient of the American Folklife Award, the highest honor bestowed on folk artists in America. He is in South Carolina's Hall of Fame, and his work has been exhibited in major museums and galleries throughout the United States.

Today, more than 300 documented works by Philip Simmons—gates, fences, railings, and window guards—are scattered throughout Charleston. They meld handsomely with the surviving antique works and add a meaningful continuum to the city's architectural and aesthetic history.

*Not all wrought iron in Charleston is old. This gate is from the talented hands of legendary Lowcountry blacksmith/artist Philip Simmons.* CHARLESTON AREA CONVENTION AND VISITORS BUREAU/DAVID C. BERRY

exhibits of SEWE artists all year long and is very popular with tourists, nature lovers, and wildlife fans. You'll find old and new limited-edition nature prints, Audubon prints, 19th-century city views, engravings, and antique plates. It carries original wildlife art and a wide assortment of merchandise related to birding, stargazing, and nature study. Hours are 10:00 A.M. to 5:00 P.M. Monday through Saturday.

**Birds I View Gallery**
**119-A Church Street**
**(803) 723-1276, (843) 766-2108**
**www.anneworshamrichardson.com**
Anne Worsham Richardson is a South
Carolina artist and naturalist recognized
across America for her wildlife paintings—
especially her birds. Richardson has
received many honors over the years, her
latest being induction into the South Carolina Hall of Fame at Myrtle Beach. Gallery
hours are Monday through Saturday from
10:00 A.M. to 5:00 P.M.

**Carolina Antique Maps and Prints, LLC**
**91 Church Street**
**(843) 722-4773**
This shop exclusively carries those handsome and fascinating antique maps,
prints, and botanicals that make such a
striking addition to an office, library, or
study. Some of these maps originate from
the 16th to the 19th century and depict
various locations, both local and international. Of added interest is the shop's
location—in Cabbage Row, which Dubose
Heyward, along with George Gershwin,
immortalized as "Catfish Row" in the folk
opera *Porgy and Bess*. Hours are Tuesday
through Saturday, 11:00 A.M. to 5:00 P.M. or
by special appointment.

**Carolina Galleries**
**188 King Street**
**(843) 723-2266**

**91 Church Street**
**(843) 722-4773**
**www.carolinagalleries.com**
This gallery specializes in pre-1945 American art (including a fine selection from
Charleston's own Renaissance Period) and
what's called sporting art. Carolina Prints
has been around for almost 30 years, putting artists and collectors together. You'll
find a wonderful selection of works by
Alfred Hutty, Alice Smith, Anna Heyward
Taylor, and Elizabeth O'Neill Verner plus
antique prints, original paintings, and
botanicals by Besler, Schwert, and others.
The gallery carries Audubon prints and

architectural drawings too. The staff is
qualified to act as framing consultants.
Hours are Monday through Friday, 9:00
A.M. to 5:00 P.M., Saturday 10:00 A.M. to
5:00 P.M., or by appointment.

**Charles II**
**2 Queen Street**
**(843) 577-7101**
**www.charles2.com**
As Charleston becomes more recognized
as an art destination of note, talents from
around the country (and indeed the
world) are becoming eager to find representation here. Charles II is a gallery
catering to collectors looking for artists
with established reputations outside the
Lowcountry—in New York, San Diego,
Santa Fe, and Miami. Their subjects range
from landscapes to abstracts, but the
quality is universally superb. The gallery is
located just off East Bay Street at 2
Queen Street, and hours are Monday
through Saturday, 10:00 A.M. to 5:30 P.M. or
by appointment.

**Charleston Clay Works Studio & Gallery**
**285 Meeting Street**
**(843) 853-3345, (843) 971-9934**
Strollers down Meeting Street near
Charleston Place with a penchant for pottery will enjoy this studio featuring potters
and artists from across the country. This a
working studio, as well, so even the uninitiated can enjoy watching the creative
process. Here you'll find a special showcase of the contemporary porcelain works
of Susan Filley. Hours are Tuesday through
Sunday 11:00 A.M. to 5:00 P.M. or by
appointment.

**Charleston Crafts Inc.**
**87 Hasell Street**
**(843) 723-2938**
**www.charlestoncrafts.org**
This gallery, just next to the Charleston
Place parking garage, showcases the works
of South Carolina's finest craft artists.
Exhibits include works in clay, fiber, wood,
jewelry, metals, glass, photography, paper,
traditional crafts, basketry, leather, toys, and

even soap-making, with exhibitors chosen by a jury of other artists and gallery owners. Charleston Crafts offers a wide variety of gifts—from traditional to contemporary, from utilitarian to decorative, from affordable to exclusive. Demonstrations and featured craft artists change every week. Hours are from Monday through Saturday from 10:00 A.M. to 5:30 P.M. Sunday hours are seasonal and posted accordingly.

### Charleston Frame Works and Gallery
### 738 St. Andrews Boulevard
### (843) 556-9373

Across the Ashley River about a mile down St. Andrews Boulevard, this gallery is making a name for itself as a source for affordable artwork. Prematted and framed prints and posters are featured here. There is a custom framing department that's well stocked and creative. Hours are Monday through Friday from 10:00 A.M. to 6:00 P.M. and Saturday from 11:00 A.M. to 3:00 P.M.

### Charleston Renaissance Gallery
### 103 Church Street
### (843) 723-0025
### www.fineartsouth.com

This charming gallery is at the intersection of St. Michael's Alley and Church Street. Recently restructured to present a mix of old and new works, it appeals to visitors from all over the world as well as local Charlestonians. It features 19th-century Southern masterworks and the art of the Charleston Renaissance period (1920s and 1930s). Also, the gallery has exclusive representation of contemporary plein air painter West Fraser. Gallery hours are Monday through Saturday 10:00 A.M. to 5:00 P.M.

### City Gallery
### 133 Church Street
### (843) 724-7305

This city-owned art gallery is actually next door to (and connected with) the city's historic Dock Street Theatre. That means there's a lot of heavy traffic, and to be shown here is a real coup for an artist.

Local talent is shown exclusively, and all exhibitions are juried. Hours are Monday through Friday 9:00 A.M. to 5:00 P.M. and during all performances at the Dock Street.

### Clowns' Bazaar
### 56 Broad Street
### (843) 723-9769

Here is Charleston's only tax-exempt folk art showcase, a gallery exclusively set up to provide employment for disadvantaged artisans. It features the work of several groups of talented artists who, for one reason or another, fall under the auspices of this special category. The showcase represents artists from SERRV (which includes many Third World countries), Ten Thousand Villages (mostly African art), and Charleston Sunday Artists (local artists who are retired from the mainstream gallery scene). Hours are 10:00 A.M. to 5:00 P.M. every day except Wednesday.

### Cobblestone Studios
### 40 North Market Street
### (843) 853-5829

Look for Cobblestone Studios in the Rainbow Market in the old City Market area. It carries fantastic watercolors and oils, flowers, and exciting Charleston reproductions, plus handmade gifts and jewelry. Hours are Monday through Saturday from 10:00 A.M. to 5:30 P.M. and Sunday from 11:00 A.M. to 4:00 P.M.

### Coleman Fine Art
### 79 Church Street
### (843) 853-7000
### www.colemanfineart.com

This is the needle in the haystack for anyone looking for an art restoration specialist. Services include cleaning and revarnishing damaged or dirty oil paintings, plus museum and custom framing for art of all kinds. It carries children's books illustrated by Mary Whyte plus other original works and some limited-edition prints as well. Commissions are accepted for portraits. Hours are Tuesday through Saturday 10:00 A.M. to 6:00 P.M. or by appointment.

## East Bay Gallery
### 280 West Coleman Boulevard, Mt. Pleasant
### (843) 216-8010

Here is a gallery of eclectic, functional art that houses the work of more than 400 American artists. You'll find art glass, jewelry, pottery, contemporary wood and metal art, textile art, and much more. Although the name implies the location is on East Bay Street in Charleston, this gallery is actually in Mt. Pleasant in the specialty shops of Northcutt Plaza where there's plenty of free parking.

## Elizabeth Lyle Gallery
### 161 King Street
### (843) 723-2600, (888) 847-0937
### www.elizabethlylegallery.com

One of the city's upscale, international galleries gaining more attention these days, the Elizabeth Lyle Gallery specializes in the works of contemporary American, European, and Peruvian artists, featuring Yvonne Mora (Peru), David Fernandez (Peru), Martin Jewell (USA), David Borenstein (USA), Han Chul Jung (Korea), and Ruis de la Casa (Spain). Gallery hours are 10:30 A.M. to 5:00 P.M. every day but Sunday.

## Ella Walton Richardson Fine Art Gallery
### 73 Broad Street
### (843) 722-3660
### www.ellarichardson.com

Located next to picturesque St. Michael's church on Broad Street, this gallery seems especially blessed in its convenient downtown location. Artistically, however, the gallery is far reaching in its wonderful representation of contemporary American and Russian fine art. Wildlife sculpture, jewelry, and photography join the selection of paintings by nearly a dozen artists with impressive regional and national credentials. Visitors to the gallery also enjoy the quaint courtyard garden.

## E. S. Lawrence Gallery
### 229 Meeting Street
### (843) 853-4280, (888) 823-0228
### www.eslawrence.com

This gallery is a branch of the upscale gallery of the same name in Aspen, Colorado, and features works by Chiu Tak Hak, Steve Hanks, Graciela Rodo Boulanger, Zvonimir Mihanovic, Pino, Leon Bronstein, and Tania Dibbs. Hours are Sunday through Thursday 10:00 A.M. to 5:00 P.M., Friday and Saturday 10:00 A.M. to 8:00 P.M.

## Eva Carter Gallery
### 132 East Bay Street
### (843) 722-0506
### www.evacartergallery.com

In what used to be called the New Gallery, next to the Old Exchange Building on East Bay, is now Eva Carter's own gallery displaying her bold abstract paintings. Her sophistication in the arrangement of line, color, space, and texture creates emotional intensity even evident to drivers passing by her windows. One of Charleston's better-known artists, Eva Carter's work is a must-see for contemporary art lovers. The gallery also features abstract works of the late William Halsey and sculptural works in steel by Gretchen Lothrop. Hours are Monday through Saturday 10:00 A.M. to 6:00 P.M., Sunday 1:00 to 5:00 P.M.

## Gayle Sanders Fisher Gallery
### 124 Church Street
### (843) 958-0010
### www.gaylesandersfisher.com

This is the showcase for Gayle Sanders Fisher's imaginative originals in oil and watercolor. The Carolina Lowcountry, its unique architecture, nature, and color have been Fisher's subjects for the past 30 years. Her work is included in many private and corporate collections throughout the country. Gallery hours are Monday through Saturday 10:00 A.M. to 5:00 P.M. and Sunday 1:00 to 5:00 P.M.

## Gordon Wheeler Gallery
### 180 East Bay Street
### (843) 722-2546
### www.gordonwheeler.net

The gallery of local artist Gordon Wheeler offers original acrylic paintings of

Charleston and other Lowcountry scenes. He's mostly known for his commission work, but the shop has limited edition prints and some very popular golf art. Gallery hours are 10:00 A.M. to 6:00 P.M. Monday through Saturday; 11:00 A.M. to 5:00 P.M. Sunday.

## Halsey Gallery at the College of Charleston
### 54 St. Philip Street
### (843) 953-5680
### www.cofc.edu/halseygallery

The Halsey Gallery in the Simons Center on St. Philip Street between Calhoun and George Streets is administered by the School of the Arts at the College of Charleston. It exists to advocate, exhibit, and interpret visual art with an emphasis on contemporary art. In addition to housing seven major exhibitions each year, the gallery serves as an extension of the undergraduate art curricula and sponsors interpretive programs such as accompanying lectures and seminars. While the primary audiences served include the college's students, faculty, and staff, the gallery is open to the public, and participation in its programs is encouraged. Gallery hours vary according to the building's use for performances and school-related functions. Call for more specific details.

## The Hamlet Gallery
### 7 Broad Street
### (843) 722-1944
### www.hamletgallery.com

Only three doors from the Old Exchange building, this is one of the galleries associated with Charleston's famous French Quarter and the many fine art dealers located there. Look here for light, bold watercolors of Charleston scenes by Alexandria H. Bennington; Audrey Dillard's oils, which have a wonderful Matisse-like quality; and Kellie Jacobs' pastel landscapes. Owner Stephanie Shuler Hamlet's mixed media abstracts are intensely colored and look at home beside the vibrant handblown glass by Andrew Merrick.

Hours are Monday through Saturday from 10:00 A.M. to 5:00 P.M.

## Hatfield 2 Fine Art
### 38 Queen Street
### (843) 577-7710
### www.hatfield2fineart.com

This is one of Charleston's premier fine art galleries, housed in a 170-year-old house in the shadow of the Dock Street Theatre. The gallery represents both established and emerging artists—which means the art is of interest to both experienced collectors and beginners. There are watercolors, etchings, oils, acrylics, and sculptures in bronze. The gallery's ongoing exhibit features original oils by Jim Crompton and his wife, Louise Pinto, both of North Carolina; the Virginia landscapes and sporting scenes of Nick Mace; pastels by New Yorker Robert Rabinowitz; and bronze sculptures by Silvia Hutchins. They also carry some limited edition watercolors by Stephen Scott Young and Ed Cooper. Hours are 10:00 A.M. to 5:00 P.M. daily (Wednesdays by chance or by appointment), 1:00 to 4:00 P.M. on Sundays.

## Horton Hayes Fine Art
### 30 State Street
### (843) 958-0014
### www.berniehortongallery.com

Here you'll find fascinating marshscapes and Lowcountry images of shrimpers, crabbers, clammers, and oyster harvesters done in oils and acrylics. The works of Mark Horton are also featured. Gallery hours are Monday through Saturday, 10:00 A.M. to 5:30 P.M. and Sunday 12:30 to 5:00 P.M.

## John Carroll Doyle Art Gallery
### 54 Broad Street
### (843) 577-7344
### www.johncdoyle.com

Visitors to the Market area who stop in at A. W. Shucks for lunch or for oysters and beer are totally surrounded by the unique work of popular Charleston artist John Doyle. His bold colors and striking figures are filled with life, drama, and his very

special treatment of light. Doyle is nationally known for his energetic paintings of
blues musicians, blue marlins, and blue
hydrangeas. His studio is right on Broad
Street, and special showings of his work
or private commissions can be arranged.
Gallery hours are Monday through Saturday, 10:00 A.M. to 5:00 P.M. Doyle's print
gallery is on-site as well, with affordable
prints of his distinctive work.

## Lese Corrigan Studio
## 62A Queen Street
## (843) 270-9700
## www.lesecorrigan.com

Many Charleston art patrons know Lese
Corrigan's work from her award-winning
outdoor exhibits during the MOJA Festival
or Piccolo Spoleto. Today, her work
appears in private collections in Japan,
France, Great Britain, and throughout the
United States. She deals in portrait, still life,
architecture, and landscape subject matter,
and her colorful oil paintings balance on
the fine line between representation and
abstraction.  She also produces black-and-
white linoleum-cut prints of local citizens
at work. Formerly an instructor at the
Gibbes Museum School of Art for 17 years
and currently their artist-in-residence (for
2005), she welcomes studio visits by
appointment. Call the number above for
more information or visit her Web site.

## Lowcountry Artists Ltd.
## 148 East Bay Street
## (843) 577-9295
## www.lowcountryartists.com

Nine local artists operate this gallery on
East Bay Street's busy gallery row. The
quaint shop has a fine selection of original
watercolors, woodcuts, pottery, oils, and
prints. The specialty here is Charleston
and Lowcountry scenes. You'll also find
collages, hand-painted tiles, colored-pencil
drawings, linocuts, monoprints, etchings,
and other graphics. Portrait, fine art, and
commercial art commissions are welcomed. Every month, one of the participating artists has a show of new works.
Hours are Monday through Saturday from

10:00 A.M. to 5:00 P.M., Sunday 1:00 P.M. to
5:00 P.M., or by appointment.

## Margaret Petterson Gallery
## 125 Church Street
## (843) 722-8094
## www.margaretpetterson.com

To see the Lowcountry through Margaret
Petterson's artistic eye is to see it in a new
light. Her work blends old and new, traditional and contemporary, and you're
invited to visit with the artist as she paints
in her Church Street studio. You'll also find
original pottery by Jo Jeffers Wingfield.
Gallery hours are Monday through Saturday from 10:00 A.M. to 5:00 P.M. and by
appointment.

## Martin Gallery
## 18 Broad Street
## (843) 723-7388
## www.martingallerycharleston.com

Here's a showcase for contemporary
works by nationally acclaimed artists
working in oils and acrylics—including
works of Italian master painter Imero
Gobbato; bronzes by wildlife sculptor
Leo Osborne, marble, bronze, terra cotta
sculpture by Claire McCardle, and photography by Michael Kahn. Hours are Monday
through Saturday 10:00 A.M. to 6:00 P.M.,
Sunday 1:00 to 5:00 P.M., and by appointment.

## McCallum-Halsey Gallery and Studios
## 20 Fulton Street
## (843) 723-5977
## www.halseyfoundation.org

Work by longtime Charleston favorite Cor-
rie McCallum and her late husband,
William Halsey, is shown at their Fulton
Street studio (second right turn off King
Street past Charleston Place). The works
are primarily in oils but often incorporate
interesting textiles (sometimes even
objects). Graphics and sculptures are
included. William Halsey, by the way, is the
artist for whom the College of Charleston
named its exhibition gallery in the Simons
Center for the Arts. Hours are by appointment only for the discerning collector.

**Nina Liu and Friends**
**24 State Street**
**(843) 722-2724**
**www.carolinaarts.com**
Nina calls this "a gallery of contemporary art objects." We call it fun. This quaint gallery is quite possibly the heartbeat of Charleston's French Quarter art scene. Her gallery makes bold and changing statements with very distinctive collections of glass, porcelain, jewelry, decorative ceramics, and fiber art. Solo shows by nationally known artists are featured periodically, and you'll find paintings, photography, and sculpture as well. Her gallery/salon, which attracts an international clientele of shoppers and art patrons, is in a 19th-century town house on State Street. Hours are Monday through Saturday from 10:00 A.M. to 5:00 P.M. or by appointment.

**Pink House Gallery**
**17 Chalmers Street**
**(843) 723-3608**
**pinkhousegallery.tripod.com**
In one of the city's most picturesque buildings (first used in 1694 as a tavern) is this quaint gallery featuring architecturals, wildlife, and florals. Look here for original works by Alice Stewart Grimsley, Bruce W. Krucke, and Alexandria H. Bennington. Ravenel Gaillard's remarkable Lowcountry scenes are featured here, as well. Works are shown on all three floors, and special exhibits are held in the courtyard just off the cobblestone street. Hours are Monday through Saturday, 10:00 A.M. to 5:00 P.M.

**Steven Jordan Gallery**
**409 West Coleman Boulevard,**
**Mt. Pleasant**
**(843) 881-1644, (800) 749-4946**
**www.stevenjordan.com**
Steven Jordan's enormously popular work has always been well worth the trip over to Mt. Pleasant. He works primarily in transparent watercolor and occasionally in acrylics and pastel. Jordan's subjects range from Lowcountry to international scenes. For 10 years, Jordan was on the faculty at the Gibbes Museum of Art, and

he is a member of the American Watercolor Society. More than 40 of his works are available in print. His gallery, located at 24 Broadway Street behind the Boulevard Diner, has an entrance at 409 West Coleman Boulevard. It includes handcrafted jewelry, pottery, and some sculpture. Hours are Monday through Saturday 10:00 A.M. to 6:00 P.M.

**Tidwell Art Gallery**
**343 King Street**
**(843) 723-3167**
**www.tidwellart.com**
This gallery features prints and oils from local, state, and nationally known artists including Martin Ahrens, Irene Charles Batt, Miles Batt, Deborah Cavanaugh, Carolyn M. Epperly, Joyce Hall, Matt Constantine, Vernon Washington, and Patsy Tidwell. Look for color graphics and original watercolors too. Hours are 8:30 A.M. to 5:30 P.M. Monday through Saturday and Sunday 1:00 to 4:00 P.M.

**Utopia**
**27 Broad Street**
**(843) 853-9510**
This small fashion boutique/art gallery on Charleston's very traditional Broad Street seems like a non sequitur, but it's a welcome and refreshing break. It also displays alternative and avant-garde fashions and art, which is attracting a dedicated following. Hours are Monday through Saturday from 11:00 A.M. to 7:00 P.M.; on Sunday, it's noon to 5:00 P.M.

**Waterfront Gallery**
**215 East Bay Street**
**(843) 722-1155**
**www.waterfrontartgallery.com**
This is Charleston's largest art gallery. A cooperative gallery, the Waterfront features 18 South Carolina artists working in oils, watercolors, pastels, monotypes, and hand-colored photography. Every participating artist has works in residences and businesses around the world. Commissions are accepted, several of the artists do portraits, and others do calligraphy

and sculpture. Gallery hours are 11:00 A.M. to 5:00 P.M. Monday through Saturday, and Sunday noon to 5:00 P.M.

## Wells Gallery
**103 Broad Street**
**(843) 853-3233**
**www.wellsgallery.com**
The Wells Gallery presents a diverse palette of original work from artists who enjoy regional, national, and international success. Works range from contemporary realism to abstract expressionism, from landscape to figure, from full color to somber neutrals. Regular gallery artists include Marty Whaley Adams, Susan Mayfield West, David Ballew, Joseph Cave, Claire Farrell, Gary Gowans, Russell Gordon, George Pate, Sue Stewart, Karen Lar-

son Turner, and David Goldhagen. Gallery hours are 10:00 A.M. to 6:00 P.M., Monday through Saturday.

## The Wolf Contemporary Art Gallery
**113 Church Street**
**(843) 577-7100**
**www.thewolfgallery.com**
This relative newcomer to Charleston is making quite a reputation for itself among the local (and regional) devotees of quality contemporary art as well as traditional works. Look here for the original paintings of Martha Sharp, Fred Jamar, Dorothy Shoemaker, and Robin Smith. They carry steel works by Bob Doster, as well. Gallery hours are Monday through Saturday, 10:00 A.M. to 5:00 P.M.

# ANNUAL EVENTS

Tradition is of utmost importance to Lowcountry residents, and successful annual events always fall into that category. Events in the Trident area run the gamut from the Lowcountry Oyster Festival—where salty oyster juice stains and face-painting masterpieces serve as souvenirs—to the sophisticated and comprehensive arts festival that is Spoleto Festival USA. Charlestonians and visitors alike turn out in big numbers for all the events listed in this chapter, so we strongly suggest you make your reservations early.

For information about any of the activities, we recommend contacting the Visitor Information Center of the Charleston Metro Chamber of Commerce (part of the area's convention and visitors bureau) at (843) 853-8000 or (800) 868-8118 or visiting their Web site at www.charleston cvb.com. The City of Charleston Office of Cultural Affairs, 133 Church Street, (843) 724-7305, and the automated ticketing service Ticketmaster, at (843) 554-6060, are other good sources for information. The following listings will serve as good starting points in your efforts to dive into the traditions of the Trident. Unless otherwise noted, all events take place in Charleston proper.

## JANUARY

### Citadel Dress Parade
**The Citadel, 171 Moultrie Street**
**(843) 953-5000**
**www.citadel.edu**
Almost every Friday during the school year, the nearly 2,000-member Corps of Cadets at The Citadel marches in retreat parade or review on Summerall Field to close out each week. In addition to the family and friends turnout, the Dress Parades are a long-standing local and visi-

tor favorite due to the impressive precision of the Corps. Spectators are welcomed (for free)—just be sure to take your seat before 3:45 P.M. when the action commences. Call for a schedule.

### Make Your Own History
**Charleston Area Convention and Visitors Bureau**
**P.O. Box 975, Charleston 29402**
**(843) 853-8000**
**www.makeyourownhistory.org**
If you are a Tri-County local and haven't quite gotten around to seeing all the wonderful attractions in your own town, this is your big chance. Purchase this pass with local I.D., and play tourist during the month of January. For $20 per person and $50 for a family, this pass entitles Charleston-area residents to free admission to more than 25 of the area's best attractions. Some of the most popular house museums such as the Aiken-Rhett House and the Edmonston-Alston House are on the list. Plantations include Boone Hall, Charles Pinckney National Historic Site, Middleton Place, and Drayton Hall. Patriots Point Maritime and Naval Museum, Charles Towne Landing State Historic Site, Fort Moultrie, several county parks, and the Gibbes Museum of Art are a few more on the diverse menu of attractions that may be just a little less crowded in January and well worth checking out. (See the Attractions chapter for more on these special sites.) Passes may be ordered on-line or picked up at the visitor center at 375 Meeting Street.

## FEBRUARY

### Lowcountry Oyster Festival
**Boone Hall Plantation,**
**1235 Long Point Road, Mt. Pleasant**
**(843) 577-4030**

The very first Lowcountry Oyster Festival gathered a small but hardy crowd back in 1982. That was then. And now? Well, now we would marvel if snow scared off the thousands who loyally appear. This festival, organized by the Greater Charleston Restaurant Association, is built around the mighty oyster but is geared to the whole family's appetite for fun. The gates of beautiful Boone Hall Plantation in Mt. Pleasant open at 11:00 A.M., and ticket holders are welcomed until the gates close at 5:00 P.M. An oyster-eating contest as well as other competitions and games are held, all in the name of fun and for the support of local children's charities. Barbecue and chili fill the void for non-oyster-eaters, and if the winter temps aren't enough, there are plenty of chilled beverages—beer being the most popular—to keep things cool. Held the Sunday prior to Super Bowl Sunday in January. Festival admission is $8.00 in advance and $10.00 at the gate. Children under 10 are free with an adult.

## The Junior League of Charleston "Whale of a Sale"
**Charleston Area Convention Center**
**5001 Coliseum Drive, North Charleston**
**(843) 763-5284**

This is the rummage sale to end all rummage sales. And if you don't believe it, ask the dozens who camp out the night before in the parking lot to be the first ones through the door. Everything from large appliances, furniture, and computers to toys, sports equipment, clothing, and "you name it" is donated by the Junior League's membership, and there is new merchandise from area merchants. Of course, it's all available at rock-bottom prices. This event is a treasure hunter's paradise, so come prepared to search for loads of bargains. The doors open at 8:00 A.M. and close at 4:00 P.M., usually on the first Saturday in February.

## Lowcountry Blues Bash
**Various locations, P.O. Box 13525,**
**Charleston 29422**
**(843) 762-9125**
**www.bluesbash.com**

In the past, as many as 35 acts have participated in the Lowcountry Blues Bash. Musicians such as Dave Peabody and Rob Mason, the Love Dogs, Big Boy Henry, Lil' Brian & the Zydeco Travelers, Carl Weathersby, and Shrimp City Slim have played to enthusiastic crowds at more than 10 venues throughout the area. The event proudly showcases some of the area's older blues musicians along with ones up-and-coming on the scene. Tickets range from free to $25 per performance. The 10-day event is held in mid-February. Festival promoter, musician, and radio personality Gary Erwin runs the show, and you can call him for more information about the Bash and other blues happenings around town at (843) 762-9125 from 10:00 A.M. to 6:00 P.M. Monday through Saturday. A Lowcountry Blues Bash brochure is available by sending a self-addressed, stamped envelope to the above address.

## Kids Fair
**Gaillard Municipal Auditorium**
**77 Calhoun Street**
**(843) 571-6565**

Since 1988, the Charleston Jewish Community Center has sponsored this indoor fair for children ages 3 to 12 at the Gaillard Auditorium. We like the safety precaution of not allowing any adult to enter if not accompanied by a child, and we appreciate the wide range of age-appropriate entertainment—from face-painting, arts and crafts, and school group performances, to health-issue booths, all free of charge. The hours are 10:00 A.M. to 5:00 P.M. on a Saturday in February. In a nice change of pace, parents are admitted free with children, whose tickets are $2.00. Parking is free, too.

## Southeastern Wildlife Exposition
**Various downtown locations**
**(843) 723-1748**
**www.sewe.com**

This exposition is said to be the largest celebration of wildlife art anywhere. Incredible displays of paintings, prints, sculpture, carvings, photography, collectibles, and crafts are all inspired by the boundless wonders of nature. More than 40,000 ticket-holding guests crisscross between the dozen or so exhibition sites on the Peninsula during the three-day event. Most are also interested in the expo's conservation motif. Hence, the booths, student contests, and the like are devoted to the green theme. Tickets for the 2005 event, held on Presidents' Day weekend, were $15 a day or $35 for a three-day pass (children 5 and under are free with a paying adult). VIP packages start at $100 and include an insiders' look at the Expo. VIPs get opportunities to preview and purchase original artwork, attend special receptions and parties, and enter exhibits through separate entrances and move to the front of lengthy lines. For more information on the next annual exposition or advance ticket purchases, write the SEWE at 211 Meeting Street, Charleston, SC 29401.

# MARCH

## Historic Charleston Foundation's Festival of Houses and Gardens
**Various downtown locations**
**(843) 723-1623,**
**(843) 722-3405 (festival info)**
**www.historiccharleston.org**

Those who want to move beyond a passive, coffee-table-book enjoyment of Charleston's private homes and gardens wait for this event each year. It's a mouthful, but what the foundation undertakes and offers is also expansive. For a month's time in March and April, more than 600 volunteers make it possible to tour more than 150 private houses and gardens.

Every day the itinerary changes, with the focus on historically and architecturally distinct dwellings and gardens. To broaden the experience further, the foundation also hosts oyster roasts at Drayton Hall Plantation, and there is a series of garden-only tours. Tickets are $45 and are available from the Frances R. Edmunds Center for Historic Preservation at 108 Meeting Street or by calling the number above. Proceeds support Historic Charleston Foundation's many preservation programs. (See the chapter on Architectural and Historic Preservation for more on Historic Charleston Foundation.)

## Charleston Symphony Orchestra League ASID Designer Showhouse
**Location varies, 14 George Street**
**(843) 723-0020**
**www.charlestonsymphony.com**

Each year, a private historic dwelling is placed in the capable hands of volunteers from the Charleston Symphony Orchestra League to be presented in all its dazzling glory to the public in a one-house tour. The annual showhouse event, which opens in mid-March and continues for a month, is sponsored by the orchestra league, and each room is decorated by an ASID designer. It provides a great opportunity to tour an attractive home, shop the in-house boutique, and have lunch at the same residence in the tea room. Sometimes the boutique might be in a garage or carriage house; the tea room might be set up in the garden. It all depends on the layout of the chosen home. Tickets are $15 in advance or $20 at the door, and proceeds benefit our outstanding orchestra. Hence, it's a win-win situation and another opportunity to experience the inside of Charleston.

## Charleston International Antiques Show
**40 East Bay Street**
**(843) 720-1181**
**www.cias2006.com**

Benefiting from the rich historical, architectural, and cultural heritage of

Charleston, the Charleston International Antiques Show has quickly established itself as a premier event for collectors and browsers alike since its inception in 2004. Benefiting the Historic Charleston Foundation, the weekend kicks off the Foundation's Annual Festival of Houses and Gardens ever-popular tours (see previous listing) with world-class exhibitors showcasing a full spectrum of period furnishings, decorative pieces, and fine art from the late 17th to the 20th century. American, Asian, and European antiques are presented by some of the most recognized names from around the country. In addition to the exhibits next to the Foundation's headquarters on East Bay Street, special events such as a patrons' champagne reception, preview party, young collectors' soiree, and guided group tours as well as luncheon lectures provide even more opportunities to learn and to enjoy the display. The show runs from Friday through Sunday in mid-March. Daily passes are $15 and a three-day pass is $35. The special events range from $45 for the luncheon lectures to $150 for the preview party. Call the number above for more details.

## The Garden Club of Charleston's Walking Tour of Private Houses and Gardens
**Various downtown locations**
**(843) 762-0091**
**www.thegardenclubofcharleston.com**
Some of Charleston's finest historic district homes and gardens are showcased on the Garden Club of Charleston's tours on two Saturday afternoons in the latter part of March. The members have organized this tour for more than 70 years and continue to delight tourists and locals alike with the selection of private homes, breathtaking gardens, and their own flower arrangements that enhance the homes' interiors. Tickets are in the $35 range and can be purchased by calling the number listed or by writing to P.O. Box 20652, Charleston 29413. They also may

be purchased the day of the tour at the visitor center or Market Hall at the corner of Market and Meeting Streets.

# APRIL

## Cooper River Bridge Run
**P.O. Box 22089, Charleston 29413**
**(843) 792-0345, (843) 937-4183**
**www.bridgerun.com**
The Bridge Run, as the natives call it, is a social event as much as it is a run. Men, women, and children begin training for the run months before the race date, and some even attend clinics scattered around the area as part of their preparation. Bumper stickers dare us with words like "Gone Runnin'," and banners fly around the city for weeks ahead of time—we can't say we just forgot. Still, a 10-kilometer (6.2-mile) run or 7-kilometer (4.5-mile) walk is a bit much for some of us, if not too great a challenge for the 30,000 or so participants who pound the pavement each year (usually in early April). The race begins in Mt. Pleasant, continues across the Cooper River on the new Arthur Ravenel Jr. Bridge, and finishes downtown. The early entry fee for the shorter walk is $15, and for the run it is $25. All entrants receive a T-shirt and other goodies. A 1-mile Kid's Race is a new feature of the event at Hampton Park (see our Parks and Recreation chapter) for an entry fee of $8.00. For more information and an application, write to the Cooper River Bridge Run, P.O. Box 22089, Charleston 29413. (For more information, see the Spectator Sports chapter.)

## Flowertown Festival
**900 Crosscreek Road, Summerville**
**(843) 871-9622**
**www.flowertownfestival.org**
Summerville, a 20-mile drive from Charleston, is the setting for this wonderful small-town festival each spring (see more on Summerville in the Lowcountry Day Trips chapter). If the winter has been

kind, the city—affectionately called Flow-ertown—will be ablaze with color on the first weekend in April, and the events are nonstop. Sponsored by the Summerville Family YMCA, the festival is a three-day affair that includes arts and crafts displays with more than 400 vendors, a youth festival, sports tournaments, the Taste of Summerville food festival, and much more. There is no admission fee, but there are charges from individual vendors for food and activities.

## Lowcountry Cajun Festival
**James Island County Park**
**871 Riverland Drive**
**(843) 762-2172**
**www.ccprc.com**
Crawfish-crazed connoisseurs, take heart. There's a chance for you to get your fill this side of New Orleans at the annual Lowcountry Cajun Festival. Set in early April, it's a stompin' good time at the James Island County Park, where more than five tons of crawfish, eating contests, crawfish races, and a genuine Louisiana Cajun band make up the mix for family fun. Sponsored by the Charleston County Park and Recreation Commission, tickets for the festival are $8.00 for adults and free for children 12 and under with a paying adult.

## Family Circle Cup
**Daniel Island Tennis Centre**
**161 Seven Farms Drive,**
**Daniel Island**
**(843) 856-7900, (800) 677-2293**
**www.familycirclecup.com**
Take in some tennis at the $9-million Daniel Island Tennis Centre, the new home of the Family Circle Cup. This tournament relocated in 2001 to Charleston after a long-time run in Hilton Head, South Carolina. The nine-day Women's Tennis Association Tier I event attracts many of the top seeds in women's tennis. Some of the past competitors were Serena Williams, Conchita Martinez, Monica Seles, Arantxa Sanchez-Vicario, Jennifer Capriati, Lindsay Davenport, and Mary Pierce. Held in mid-

April, the Family Circle Cup is another highlight in Charleston's spring events lineup. Ticket prices range from $10 for qualifying matches up to $55 for the finals. Call the number above for more information. (See the Spectator Sports chapter for more on the Family Circle Cup.)

## Folly Beach Sea & Sand Festival
**21 Center Street, Folly Beach**
**(843) 588-9713**
**www.cityoffollybeach.com**
What could be better than enjoying the beach before the crowds descend for the season? The Sea & Sand Festival at Folly Beach lets fun-loving beachgoers do just that by celebrating all things "beachy" one Saturday in mid-April. The city closes down the beachfront street for leisurely strolling and browsing during this event, so break out the shorts and flip-flops. The festival is full of vendors serving up local seafood delicacies, an arts and crafts show, a martial arts demonstration, and live music. An auction, children's games, and a hula-hoop contest add to the entertainment, and the sandcastle competition gets more creative and spectacular every year. Admission is free. Call the number above for more information.

## East Coast Canoe & Kayak Festival
**James Island County Park**
**871 Riverland Drive**
**(843) 795-4386**
**www.ccprc.com**
Since 1991, the Charleston County Park and Recreation Commission has sponsored the popular East Coast Canoe & Kayak Festival at James Island County Park. The event is a full weekend of canoeing and kayaking history, technique, and hands-on experience appropriate for the beginner as well as the experienced paddler. In addition to on-water classes and boat demonstrations, lectures, workshops, and ACA instructor courses are held. There is an interpretative canoe and kayak exhibition, along with over 40 commercial exhibits by equipment designers

and manufacturers. Try out new boats, paddles, and accessories at the festival site, or shop the used boat sale to pick up used gear at bargain prices. And for the early riser, sunrise paddling trips are led by local paddling clubs and outfitters. Family activities and a kids' camp round out the weekend of fun. Festival attendees are encouraged to stay on-site at the 640-acre park which features a 16-acre freshwater lake, tidal creek access, tent and RV camping, and miles of nature and bike trails. (See the Parks and Recreation chapter for more on this park and other Charleston County Parks.) Package fees range from $15 per day up to $100 for the full weekend of events.

### Ashley Hall Annual Tour of Homes & Gardens
### Various downtown locations
### (843) 965-8547
### www.ashleyhall.org

Organized by the Alumnae Association of Ashley Hall school, this self-paced tour runs from 2:00 to 5:00 P.M. one Saturday in late April or early May. Each year, the tour features a different downtown neighborhood of historic homes and gardens, many of which will not be found on any other tours in the city. For this reason, alums, locals, and visitors jump at the chance to see inside some of Charleston's most beautiful private homes. Tickets are $30, with advance purchase encouraged; some tickets are available the day of the tour at the visitor center. For more information, contact the Alumnae Association of Ashley Hall at 172 Rutledge Avenue.

### Charleston Farmers Market
### Marion Square (between King and Meeting at Calhoun)
### (843) 724-7305

Held every Saturday from April through December at Marion Square (King, Meeting, and Calhoun Streets), the Charleston Farmers Market gives you a chance to pick out fresh fruit and veggies from our best local growers. Other vendors offer light fare such as crepes, omelets, bakery goods, and barbecue for sustenance during a leisurely stroll. Each week brings a variety of special activities, and the food and family fun are offered from 8:00 A.M. until 1:00 P.M. (or often later during Spoleto and other special event weekends). Music, arts and crafts, and "Ask a Master Gardener" are just a few of the attractions. On the December Saturdays be sure to gather loads of fresh greenery and goodies to "deck the halls." We know lots of folks who are regulars at the Farmers Market—hooked on that fresh-harvested produce and free fun.

### Blessing of the Fleet
### Alhambra Hall, 131 Middle Street, Mt. Pleasant
### (843) 884-8517

The town of Mt. Pleasant and the shrimping industry pull out their finest when they invite the public to celebrate the Blessing of the Fleet. Along with prayers for a successful shrimping season and a parade of shrimp boats, organizers offer a wide range of entertainment and culinary delights. From shrimp-eating and shagging contests to a crafts show and face painting, the formula is for fun, and the setting—beautiful. With its gorgeous view of Charleston, Alhambra Hall can't be beat. The festival is held the last weekend in April. Drawing more than 10,000 people each year, the Blessing of the Fleet is Mt. Pleasant's largest tourism event. The festival is sponsored by the town of Mt. Pleasant and the Blessing of the Fleet Committee. Admission is free, but food from a variety of East Cooper restaurants ranges from about $2.00 to $5.00.

### Lowcountry Senior Games
### St. Andrew's Parks and Playground
### 1095 Playground Road
### (843) 763-4360, ext. 119

Attention all 50 and older athletes: These senior games feature competitions in more than 25 recreational events, so display your competitive nature. No matter what your interests, there is something for you in this five-day event in late April. The events include bowling, golf, croquet, swimming, basketball, tennis, track and field, and softball, held at various locations such as The Citadel. In addition to the competitive events, other opportunities for friendship and fun include the opening social with live Big Band music, and a Senior Expo. And who knows—qualifying here may lead to the chance to compete at the state and national senior sports classics. Registration, which includes events and the banquet, is $20, with additional fees for golf, softball, and bowling. Registration forms are available at area recreation departments or by using the address or phone number listed.

## MAY

**Dining With Friends**
**Lowcountry AIDS Services**
**3547 Meeting Street Road**
**(843) 747-2273**
**www.aids-services.com**
Hundreds of volunteers host private dinner parties for friends in their homes in a joint fund-raising effort supporting Lowcountry AIDS Services one Saturday in May. (For more information on the services provided by LAS, see the Health Care chapter.) The kinds of parties run the spectrum from barbecue to black tie. Guests make a tax-deductible donation and enjoy a pleasant evening with old and new friends topped off with a Champagne and Dessert Grand Finale at 9:00 P.M. at the Charleston Maritime Center.

**North Charleston Arts Festival**
**Performing Arts Center of the**
**Charleston Area Convention**
**Center Complex**
**5001 Coliseum Drive, North Charleston**
**(843) 745-1087**
**www.northcharleston.org**
Bring the family and spend some time at the North Charleston Arts Festival. The

indoor/outdoor entertainment at this nine-day festival encompasses everything from juried adult and youth art exhibits, a photography competition, and a local arts and crafts show and sale, to puppet and magic shows, live theater, and dance performances. Just listening to the variety of musical entertainment (including reggae, school choral groups, classical music, and contemporary gospel) is reason enough to check it out. Event hours are 10:00 A.M. to 4:00 P.M. daily. Some events are free, and others are ticketed events in the $5.00 to $10.00 range. The festival wraps up with a gala priced at around $30 to $40 per person. Ample parking is available for free.

**Spoleto Festival USA**
**Various locations**
**(843) 722-2764,**
**(843) 579-3100 (Box office)**
**www.spoletousa.org**
Since 1977, Spoleto Festival USA has continued as a bright star on Charleston's arts calendar. One resident put it well when she said that anticipating Spoleto each year is "like looking forward to another Christmas, without having to dread the discarded gift paper mess." Already accustomed to an unusually strong year-round arts agenda, the city becomes blissfully hyperactive during Spoleto with world-class theater, music, dance, opera, and visual and literary presentations. It begins on Memorial Day weekend and lasts 16 days or so.

The 2005 Spoleto was highlighted by two operas, *Ariadne auf Naxos* and *I Capuleti e i Montecchi,* the Moscow Ballet Theatre, Alvin Ailey American Dance Theater, and an ever-popular chamber music series directed by Charles Wadsworth. Tickets for individual Spoleto events range from about $15 to $75. For an up-to-date schedule, contact the event box office at P.O. Box 157, Charleston 29402, or call Ticketmaster at (843) 554-6060. (See The Arts chapter for more on Spoleto.)

**Piccolo Spoleto Festival**
**Various locations**
**(843) 724-7305,**
**(843) 554-6060 (Ticketmaster)**
**www.piccolospoleto.com**
We are particularly proud of Piccolo Spoleto, the city of Charleston's creative companion to Spoleto Festival USA. Piccolo events—including jazz cruises, a children's festival, a juried art exhibit, cabaret, and "brown bag and ballet"—are held in unusual places (anywhere from boats to parks to churches) and showcase local as well as national talent. The calendar is booked, and the ticket prices are very reasonable, ranging from free events to others that are almost always less than $25. For a more comprehensive schedule of events, write the City of Charleston Office of Cultural Affairs, 133 Church Street, Charleston 29401. (For more on Piccolo Spoleto, see The Arts chapter.)

**Grace Episcopal Church Tea Room**
**98 Wentworth Street**
**(843) 723-4576**
Another of Charleston's special spring tea rooms is the one put on by the volunteers of Grace Episcopal Church, near the College of Charleston. Lowcountry specialties are the fare here, and who can pass up an opportunity to sample a few of these: crab and okra soup, ham biscuits, and shrimp rémoulade with an assortment of freshly baked desserts. Prices run from $2.00 to $5.00 an item, and you may find yourself returning several times during the two weeks the tea room is open. The dates correspond with the Spoleto Festival, the last week of May and first week of June. Lunch is served Monday through Friday from 11:30 A.M. to 2:00 P.M., and takeout is available for your own Spoleto picnic. Proceeds benefit church outreach programs.

**Greek Festival**
**Greek Orthodox Church**
**of The Holy Trinity**
**30 Race Street**
**(843) 577-2063**
**www.greekfest.us**

Another in Charleston's delectable ethnic festivals is the Greek Fest held in late May or early June during Piccolo Spoleto at the Greek Orthodox Church. Greek food, dancing, jewelry, crafts, and cooking demonstrations are some of the highlights of the weekend-long family fun. Dine in or take out the gyros, Greek chicken dinners, spanakopita, and pastries. Check out the bazaar, and take in a tour of the beautiful church. You're bound to be speaking a little Greek by the time you leave. Hours are 11:00 A.M. to 9:00 P.M. Friday and Saturday; noon to 6:00 P.M. on Sunday. Admission is $1.00 at the gate for ages 12 and older. Free admission coupons are available on the Web site and several Greek restaurants around town.

# JUNE

**Carolina Day**
**1214 Middle Street, Sullivan's Island**
**(843) 723-3225, (843) 883-3123**
Sullivan's Island in the summer is cause for celebration in itself. Add to the natural charm of the venue an event like Carolina Day, and you're in for some serious fun. No admission is charged for this annual re-enactment program at Fort Moultrie, and it is a wonderful opportunity to learn about the history of the patriots' Revolutionary War victory over the British Navy on June 28, 1776. Other Carolina Day events include a special church service and the ringing of church bells in Charleston, Mt. Pleasant, Sullivan's Island, Isle of Palms, and North Charleston. An open house at the South Carolina Histori-

*In the Lowcountry, it doesn't get much more paparazzi-friendly than the black-tie opening night of Spoleto Festival USA's major opera presentation at Gaillard Municipal Auditorium. Don the good threads and check it out, along with the gala reception that follows, if you're lucky enough to score a ticket.*

cal Society (see the Architectural and Historic Preservation chapter for more information) and a South Carolina Art Tour at the Gibbes Museum of Art (see the section on Other Museums in the Attractions chapter) are both free of charge. A procession takes place in the afternoon. It is composed of historical and lineal groups that make up the Palmetto Society of Charleston, the group that sponsors Carolina Day. The parade moves from Washington Park downtown to White Point Gardens at the Battery, where a wreath-laying ceremony and band concert wrap up the procession. The program runs from 9:00 A.M. to 8:00 P.M. (See the Kidstuff and Attractions chapters for more information on Fort Moultrie.)

## JULY

**Patriots Point 4th of July Blast!**
**Patriots Point Naval & Maritime Museum**
**40 Patriots Point Road, Mt. Pleasant**
**(843) 884-2727**
**www.patriotspoint.org**
With one of the biggest Fourth of July fireworks displays in the Palmetto State, the festivities at Patriots Point Naval and Maritime Museum on Charleston Harbor are a blast! It all begins at 1:00 P.M. with free admission to the ships of the museum, including the aircraft carrier USS *Yorktown*. Food and arts and crafts vendors add to the fun atmosphere, and the kids will enjoy a jump castle, climbing rock wall, and more in the Kids Zone. Popular area bands perform live before and after the fireworks for dancing the night away. The fireworks light up the sky usually just after 9:00 P.M. More than 10,000 people have celebrated our nation's birthday here in earlier years, so allow time for traffic and parking. (For more on Patriots Point Naval and Maritime Museum see our Attractions chapter.)

## AUGUST

**Key West Boats Fishing for Miracles**
**King Mackerel Tournament**
**Charleston Harbor Resort & Marina**
**24 Patriots Point Road, Mt. Pleasant**
**(843) 766-0011**
**www.fishingformiracles.com**
This king mackerel fishing tournament, held the third weekend in August, is one of the largest saltwater fishing tournaments in South Carolina. Based out of Charleston Harbor Resort & Marina, the tournament awards cash prizes (and we're talking more than $115,000 in total prize money) for the biggest catch as well as other categories. The tournament proceeds benefit the Medical University of South Carolina Children's Hospital (see the Health Care chapter) and the Coastal Conservation Association of South Carolina. The entry fee is $275 before August 1 and $325 thereafter. (For more on this and other fishing tourneys in the area, see the Hunting and Fishing chapter.)

## SEPTEMBER

**Scottish Games and Highland Gathering**
**Boone Hall Plantation**
**1235 Long Point Road, Mt. Pleasant**
**(843) 529-1020, (843) 856-5361**
**www.charlestonscots.com**
The tartan-clad clans gather, and traditions abound when the Scottish Games and Highland Gathering, sponsored by the Scottish Society of Charleston, is held at Boone Hall Plantation. All ages are incorporated into the festivities, which range from highland and country dancing and bagpipe music to tossing the caber. Those interested in finding out more about their Scottish roots enjoy talking to clan members at various booths, and everyone has a chance to sample Scottish culinary delights such as meat pies, scones, and shortbread. Boone Hall Plantation is a lovely setting for all of this, and September is usually a very temperate month in the Lowcountry. Advance tickets for the 9:00

A.M. to 5:00 P.M. gathering are $13.00 for adults and teens and $5.00 for children ages 6 to 12. Gate prices will be $15.00 and $6.00, respectively. Parking is $5.00 per car, which includes a program. For more information, contact the Scottish Society at P.O. Box 31951, Charleston, 29417–1951.

## The Preservation Society of Charleston's Fall Candlelight Tours of Homes & Gardens
**Various downtown locations**
**(843) 722-4630**
**www.preservationsociety.org**

Beginning in September and running through October, the candlelight tours, sponsored by the Preservation Society of Charleston, are a splendid opportunity to experience the interiors of homes and churches in Charleston at night. Tourists and locals alike enjoy the romantic walk along several city blocks between dwellings and appreciate the commentary on the architecture, history, and folklore of each property by the volunteer guides. Tours run from 7:00 to 10:00 P.M. on Thursday, Friday, and Saturday nights. The Sunday afternoon garden tea tours are enchanting, too. Tickets are $45 per tour or $120 for the weekend package of three, which features different locations in the historic district each week. You can find out more about the tours by writing the Preservation Society at P.O. Box 521, Charleston 29402. (Please see the chapters on Architectural and Historic Preservation and Attractions for more information about the society.)

## MOJA Arts Festival
**Office of Cultural Affairs**
**133 Church Street**
**(843) 724-7305,**
**(843) 554-6060 (Ticketmaster)**
**www.mojafestival.com**

Running for 10 days in September and October, MOJA—a Swahili word for "source" or "beginning"—celebrates the long and fascinating African-American and Caribbean traditions and contributions to western cultures. Charleston

becomes a stage for lectures, theater, and dance performances, art exhibits, concerts, and general festivities. Activities for the young and old provide the opportunity for sharing good times and harmony among people. Expect broad strokes of color, graceful movement, and beauty and revelry in abundance. Check the *Post and Courier* for special features and a listing of specific events with admission prices (many events are free), or call the above numbers for more information. (See the Tours and The Arts chapters for more about MOJA and Charleston's African-American tradition.)

## Bookfest 2006
**Gaillard Municipal Auditorium**
**77 Calhoun Street**
**(843) 805-6978**
**www.ccpl.org**

Organized by the Friends of the Library's volunteers to raise money for Charleston County libraries, this used-book sale just gets bigger and better. Since 1983, the event, held at the Gaillard Exhibition Hall, has included categories such as fiction, nonfiction, history, cooking, and travel, just to name a few. The books all are donated by the public—paperbacks sell for $1.00; hardbacks are $3.00. A "better book" section has individually priced books. Children's hardcover books are $1.00 and paperbacks are 50 cents. Peruse the selection of more than 50,000 books, tapes, DVDs, and CDs during the three-day event, which has a $5.00 admission fee (on Friday only) for adults and teens. Children younger than 12 are admitted free. Event hours are Friday from noon to 8:00 P.M., Saturday from 9:00 A.M. to 4:00 P.M., and Sunday from noon to 4:00 P.M.

## Festival Hispano
**Wannamaker County Park**
**8888 University Boulevard,**
**North Charleston**
**(843) 762-2172**
**www.ccprc.com**

Celebrate the sights, sounds, and tastes of

the Latino world at Festival Hispano on a Saturday in early September. In between nachos, salsa, and chicken tamales, delight in the red-hot beat of hot Latin music. The Parade of Nations and folk dances add to the colorful display of the beautiful ethnic costumes. Over 4,000 attended the 2005 festival, making it the second-largest event sponsored by the Charleston County Park and Recreation Commission—second only to the Lowcountry Cajun Festival (see April's events). Admission is $8.00 for adults, and children 12 and under are free. Food, beverages, and merchandise are purchased with tickets in $1.00 increments.

## OCTOBER

**Charleston Garden Festival**
**4300 Ashely River Road,**
**Middleton Place**
**(843) 579-9922, (843) 556-6020**
**www.charlestongardenfestival.com**
Charleston's botanical treasures are many, and the garden festival celebrates the long history of them all. From lectures to tours to hands-on activities for children and adults, the show is a comprehensive and informative mid-October weekend for the experienced and the newly interested. Vendors are on hand at Middleton Place with plant materials and garden accouterments all ready to be incorporated into your landscape scheme. It's all for sale, and widely acclaimed landscape designers are scheduled for informative sessions with participants. General admission to just take a look at the exhibits and marketplace vendors is $10.00 in advance or $15.00 at the gate. Children ages 7 to 15 are $5.00, 6 and under are free. Tickets to special events like tea or lunch or "Groovin' in the Garden Party" are additional.

**Taste of Charleston**
**Boone Hall Plantation**
**1235 Long Point Road, Mt. Pleasant**
**(843) 577-4030**

If you have ever dreamed of sampling just a bite here and a bite there from the great restaurants all around town, this event is your dream come true. The Taste of Charleston is an all-day affair at Boone Hall Plantation, where more than 50 restaurants, all members of the Greater Charleston Restaurant Association, sell their specialties in sample proportions at bite-size prices. The fare may include shrimp and grits, beef kabobs, Greek chicken, seafood dishes, and a variety of desserts. Plan to nibble your way around the plantation grounds, then watch the Waiters Wine Race (make a bet on who'll spill) and ice-carving competition. Adults love the beer- and wine-tasting booths, and children delight in the pony rides and face painting. The event is usually scheduled for a Sunday in October, and admission is $8.00 in advance or $10.00 at the gate. Children 10 and under are admitted free with an adult.

**Komen Charleston Race for the Cure**
**P.O. Box 20637, Charleston 29413**
**(843) 723-7771**
**www.charlestonrace4cure.org**
Since starting out in 1994 with 900 participants in the Charleston area, the Race for the Cure has quickly grown in popularity among runners of all ages to become the largest 5K race in South Carolina. The event is held by the Susan G. Komen Breast Cancer Foundation, which sponsors the 5K Race for the Cure around the country. It is a breast cancer awareness race, in which participants are invited to wear the name of loved ones who have battled cancer. The race takes place at Etiwan Park on Daniel Island (see the Neighborhoods chapter for more on Daniel Island), and early registration fees (before October 7) are $22 for the 5K run/walk and the 1-mile family fun run/walk. Children under five are free but must be registered. After October 7, the cost goes to $25. Race day registration is $30. Proceeds benefit both local and national grants awarded for breast cancer prevention and research.

**Mt. Pleasant Children's Day Festival**
**Patriots Point Sports Complex,**
**Mt. Pleasant**
**(843) 849-2061**
**www.townofmountpleasant.com**
On an October Sunday afternoon, the
town of Mt. Pleasant holds the Children's
Day Festival to honor the children of the
community and provide them with live
entertainment, games, food, and fun. The
event is organized by the Mt. Pleasant
Recreation Department and East Cooper
schools, all of which set up game and
food booths at the Park West Recreational Complex. Games are free, with
prizes awarded, and food sales benefit the
school PTAs and PTSOs. Last year's entertainment lineup delighted more than
10,000 children and families. The Rhine-
stone Roper, Mandrake the Magician,
Becky Becker's Box of Puppets, the Grav-
ity Brothers Comedy Juggling Duo, the
Citadel Cheerleading Squad, and the
Wando Show Choir have all performed
here. If that's not enough to make the little ones' eyes light up, there's laser tag,
jump castles, a climbing wall, a giant slide,
and mechanical animal rides. A Halloween
costume contest also puts the children in
the spotlight. Parking and admission are
free.

# NOVEMBER

**Plantation Days at Middleton Place**
**4300 Ashley River Road**
**(843) 556-6020, (800) 782-3608**
**www.middletonplace.org**
No wonder so many brides ache to marry
close by the spectacular butterfly lakes of
Middleton Place: The grounds are the
essence of romanticism and classic beauty
(for more on Middleton Place, see our
Attractions chapter). Perhaps it's a fantasy
about living in a magnificent setting like
Middleton with the mythical prince until
death do you part. Back here in reality,
consider getting a feel for plantation life
at Middleton Place's Plantation Days. On
every Saturday in November, visitors can

observe craft workers in action as they
showcase the tasks necessary for existence on an 18th- or 19th-century plantation. It's not hard to imagine the harvest
season in full swing as you watch demonstrations of actual quilting, dyeing, candle
making, leather tanning, and cider making.
Sweetgrass baskets, like those sold downtown at the City Market (see the Close-up
in the Shopping chapter), are fashioned
before your eyes as you immerse yourself
in a different era. Regular gate admission
to see the stable yards and gardens during
Plantation Days is $20.00 for adults and
$5.00 for children ages 7 to 15. An addi-
tional $10 is charged to see the house.

**Charleston Fine Art Annual**
**Charleston Fine Art Dealers' Association,**
**P.O. Box 942, Charleston 29402**
**(843) 722-3660**
**www.cfada.com**
Immerse yourself in the visual arts when
the Charleston Fine Art Dealers' Association holds its annual event weekend in
early November. Ten of Charleston's finest
galleries sponsor receptions, painting
demonstrations, and special exhibit openings with extended hours over the three
days. The plein-air painting demonstrations by CFADA gallery artists take place
under the live oaks in Washington Park on
Saturday morning. Completed paintings
are sold by the respective galleries, with
proceeds benefiting local schools' art programs. And what better remembrance of
your experience could you take home
than an original work by one of
Charleston's leading artists?

Most events are free. The gala patrons'
reception on Saturday evening is $50 in
advance or $60 at the door per person. A
Sunday brunch at High Cotton with live
jazz and blues for $25 per person wraps
up the Fine Art Annual.

**The Battle of Secessionville**
**Boone Hall Plantation**
**1235 Long Point Road, Mt. Pleasant**
**(843) 884-4371**

Sponsored by the Confederate Heritage Trust, the Battle of Secessionville is re-enacted right before your eyes with all the splendor and tragedy of the Civil War. Some of the activities to witness on this mid-November weekend include cavalry and artillery performances, battle aftermath re-enactments, uniform demonstrations, and tours of the Boone Hall Plantation house and slave village. (For more on Boone Hall, see the Lowcountry Day Trips and Tours chapters.) Camps open at 9:00 A.M., and the battle commences at 2:00 P.M. Admission prices are $14.50 for adults and $7.00 for children ages 6 to 12. (To learn more about the Battle of Secessionville, see "Battery Wagner" in the Forts section of the Attractions chapter.)

**Holiday Festival of Lights**
**James Island County Park**
**871 Riverland Drive**
**(843) 762-2172**
**www.holidayfestivaloflights.com**
Young and old delight in the more than 125 magical lighting displays set up in the James Island County Park from mid-November through New Year's. Set your own pace as you take the 3-mile driving tour, winding through the park and enjoying the spectacle. The lights burn from 5:30 to 10:00 P.M. Sunday through Thursday and until 11:00 P.M. on Friday and Saturday. Admission is $10 a car and $25 for 16-passenger vans. A Holiday Festival of Lights Fun Run and Walk the day before opening gives participants a preview of the 2,000,000 glittering lights. The 5K Fun Run or the 2-mile walk is a $7.00 entry fee for ages 13 and up and $4.00 for ages 3 to 12. Start a new family tradition of viewing the dazzling display every year.

# DECEMBER

**Gibbes Museum of Art**
**Holiday Tour of Homes**
**Various downtown locations**
**(843) 722-2706**
**www.gibbesmuseum.org**
When it's time to get in that Christmas spirit, this is the tour to inspire you. Organized by the Women's Council of the Carolina Art Association of the Gibbes Museum, the Holiday Tour of Homes regularly sells out early. Many of Charleston's finest private homes, decorated by the homeowners and volunteers for the holidays, are on display. Held in early December from 1:00 to 4:00 P.M., the tour gives locals and tourists the opportunity to experience and enjoy the holidays Charleston-style and gather some new decorating ideas for the season. Tickets are $35 and can be reserved by calling the number above. (For more on the Gibbes Museum of Art, see the Attractions, Kidstuff, and Shopping chapters.)

**Annual Spirituals Concert**
**Drayton Hall, 3380 Ashley River Road**
**(843) 766-0188**
**www.draytonhall.org**
African-American spirituals, rooted in the work songs of West Africa and developed during the days of slavery, are incredibly moving. A cappella voices and rhythmic double-clapping are characteristic of the songs. The opportunity to hear them performed is rare. This early-December event begins with an informal candlelight house tour and refreshments each night at 6:00 P.M. followed by the hour-long concert around 7:00 P.M. A matinee performance is offered on Sunday at 3:30 P.M. To order tickets at $35 per person ($30 for Friends of Drayton Hall), write Drayton Hall at 3380 Ashley River Road, Charleston, SC 29414. Seating is limited in the Great Hall of Drayton Hall, so advance reservations are required. (For more on Drayton Hall, see the Attractions chapter.)

### Family Yuletide
**4300 Ashley River Road, Middleton Place**
**(843) 556-6020, (800) 782-3608**
**www.middletonplace.org**
There's a fire for chestnut-roasting, Jack Frost could very well be nipping at your nose, and you can bet that yuletide carols are going to be sung by a choir. It's all part of Family Yuletide at Middleton Place, which is usually held on the third Thursday in December. There will be holiday storytelling by the bonfire, and crafters will be working by torchlight in their shops to get the venerable plantation ready for Christmas. The children can make angels out of corn husks, and a live nativity scene is planned. Reservations are recommended for this family event. Admission is about $10.00 per adult and $5.00 for children ages 3 to 12.

### Kwanzaa
**Various downtown locations**
**(843) 724-7305**
Like the traditions of Mardi Gras, the Chinese New Year, and Cinco de Mayo, Kwanzaa is a celebration of culture and heritage. Based on the ancient African harvest, the focus is on the African-American family, and the holiday is meant to be observed at home, where participants reflect on principles such as unity, self-determination, purpose, and creativity. A variety of events takes place around the Lowcountry, allowing opportunities to learn more about Kwanzaa. During the last week of December through New Year's Day, singing, dancing, poetry readings, and speakers are a part of the observance. A naming ceremony is held for the giving of indigenous African names. A children's ceremony and final celebration with the lighting of candles share the holiday with the community. All events are free and open to the public.

### First Night Charleston
**Various downtown locations**
**(843) 724-7305**
**www.firstnightcharleston.com**

The inaugural First Night Charleston was held on New Year's Eve 1997 and met with great success. First Night Charleston, a local interpretation of the event started in Boston in 1976, marks the passage of one year into the next with a broad selection of arts and cultural performances in the downtown historic district. The slant is a family-oriented, affordable, nonalcoholic, entertaining way to ring in the New Year. The 30- to 45-minute offerings include ballet, theater, improvisational comedy, puppetry, and an array of music from choral, chamber, and ethnic, to folk and Big Band. Much of King Street is blocked off for pedestrian-only traffic, allowing a festive atmosphere at every turn with roving musicians and actors, jugglers, facepainters, and dancing. All the events are within walking distance, and performances take place several times over the course of the evening so that participants may

*If you're thinking of spending the holidays in history, look into the "Christmas in Charleston" festival. Plan to celebrate during November and December with a variety of special events such as Christmas carriage rides, gallery art walks, holiday shopping excursions, an outdoor ice-skating rink in Marion Square, and tree lightings complete with visits from Santa. The music of the season can be experienced through children's choir performances and plantation concerts, and the tastes can be enjoyed at Victorian teas, oyster roasts, and progressive dinners in historic Charleston. Homes, churches, storefronts, boats, and parks are all decked out for the holidays, and Christmas walking tours as well as holiday tours of homes and gardens provide an up-close view of the finery. For a complete schedule of events call the CACVB at (800) 853-8000 or visit www.christmasincharleston.com.*

attend as many shows as they like. Children's programming begins at 3:00 P.M.; the major events begin at 7:00 and last until 10:30 P.M. A $7.00 button ($10.00 after December 26), $6.00 for children ages 5 to 17, gains access to more than 60 indoor and outdoor events. Buttons are available in advance at the number listed or on-site at booths the night of the event. Free parking at City of Charleston garages comes with the presentation of a button.

# KIDSTUFF 👫

For starters, know that Greater Charleston is a fabulous vacation destination. Over three million people come to the Lowcountry every year, and a majority of those visitors arrive in the form of families.

A quick glance through the Attractions chapter might give you the impression that Charleston primarily serves up nothing but history—forts, house museums, plantations, and historic sites. While this wouldn't seem to be very kid-friendly, we've found that, almost without exception, Charleston's major annual events and attractions have been designed (at least partially) with children in mind.

And don't forget that children love to learn. Greater Charleston is a living, breathing, three-dimensional, full-color, interactive classroom for learning about America (which is really learning about ourselves). And here's the best part: It's a classroom with a beautiful ocean nearby, and that means beaches! Are we talkin' fun, or what?

So, let's take stock. What have we got here? Interesting (new and old) places to go with really neat stuff to see; places where people used to live and work (and play) hundreds of years ago; ships of all types and all sizes that you can actually climb around on; and beaches close by with plenty of sand and sunburn to go around. We've got ball parks, game parks, and parks where you can swim. There are places to camp, rivers to explore, even new foods to taste. Ever eat a crawfish? We've got farms where you can pick your own strawberries and blueberries when the season is right. We've got something for every kid out there.

So this chapter is dedicated to fun activities that children and parents can do together. Let's get started.

## OUTDOOR EXPLORATIONS

As you will note in our Parks and Recreation chapter, there are many public parks in the area. We have found that some are particularly appealing to children, and we describe those in more detail below. Whatever outdoor plans you make, be sure to bring plenty of sunscreen during the warm months and bug repellent for those pesky no-see-ums (gnats) present most of the year.

**Boone Hall Farms**
**U.S. Highway 17 N., Mt. Pleasant**
**(843) 884-4371, (843) 856-5366**
**www.boonehallplantation.com**
During the spring and summer months, area farms offer you-pick-it produce, and one of our favorite spots is Boone Hall Farms, the working farm of Boone Hall Plantation in Mt. Pleasant. Children carry buckets out into the fields and delight in gathering and eating seasonal berries right off the vine. Strawberries (as well as other seasonal produce such as tomatoes, pumpkins, and peaches) are carried home by the pound and can stimulate some creative pie and ice cream making later. This can be a pleasant morning or afternoon that teaches kids that food doesn't just come from the grocery store or drive-through. The fields are open 9:00 A.M. to 7:00 P.M. Monday through Saturday and 1:00 to 6:00 P.M. on Sunday in season; call the number listed for directions and produce selections. (See the Tours and Lowcountry Day Trips chapters for more on Boone Hall Plantation.)

**Charles Towne Landing**
**State Historic Site**
**1500 Old Towne Road, between**
**Interstate 26 and Highway 171**
**(843) 852-4200**
**www.southcarolinaparks.com**

> *Take the kids to help solve the mystery of the H.L. Hunley—the world's first submarine to sink an enemy ship in combat. After attacking and sinking the USS Housatonic 4 miles off Sullivan's Island in February 1864, the Confederate sub disappeared with her brave crew. For 136 years she remained on the ocean's floor until her raising in August 2000. Archaeology and conservation are underway at the Warren Lasch Conservation Center on Charleston's old Naval Base, but visitors are allowed every Saturday from 10:00 A.M. to 5:00 P.M. and Sunday from noon to 5:00 P.M. Advance tickets are $10 plus a service charge (a limited number are available on a walk-up basis), and proceeds support the conservation work. They may be purchased by calling (877) 448-6539 or visiting www.etix.com.*

This state park is many things to many people, and it really is a terrific introduction to a hands-on history lesson. Founded in 1970, Charles Towne Landing State Historic Site is 663 acres of walking, bicycling, and in-line skating paths; an animal forest; an area dedicated to the depiction of the lives of settlers; and more. Children can expect to see native animals such as wolves, alligators, pumas, otters, bison, and maybe even a bear or two in a natural habitat setting. Children enjoy the craft-making demonstrations and appreciate the period clothing worn by the park staff. Recent archaeological digs are centered on uncovering information about the original settlement of Charles Towne prior to its relocation on the peninsular site. These excavations are bound to stir some excitement among visitors of all ages.

We recommend strolling or biking through the park passing by the original house and down to Old Towne Creek, where a reproduction of a 17th-century trading vessel named *Adventure* is currently undergoing restoration. Bike rentals are available for a $3.00 deposit plus

$3.00 an hour. Wonderful special events throughout the year as well as summer and holiday day camps attract a steady flow of young people. The park is open daily (except Christmas Eve and Christmas) all year. Hours are 8:30 A.M. to 5:00 P.M. Adult admission is $5.00, South Carolina seniors and South Carolina people with disabilities are $3.25, and admission for children ages 6 to 15 is $3.00. Children younger than 6 get in free. (See the History, Attractions, and Parks and Recreation chapters for more information.)

**Fort Sumter National Monument**
**Charleston Harbor**
**(843) 881-7337, (800) 789-3678,**
**(843) 883-3123 (National Park Service)**
**www.fortsumtertours.com**
What could be a more awe-inspiring setting and thrilling experience for a young person than arrival by tour boat at Fort Sumter, the fort where the Civil War began? In the middle of Charleston Harbor, Fort Sumter looks much like it did a century ago and affords an incredible view of the city and surrounding islands. We recommend careful supervision of children, as the fort is surrounded by water, and there are many precarious climbs. The gift shop has an array of interesting items (a kit of historically accurate paper dolls or replica buttons, for example) and Civil War books, and it is air-conditioned—a major plus after a hot day scouring the fort. National Park Service rangers are on-site to answer questions, and there is a museum.

Admission for adults and teens to Fort Sumter is $13.00; seniors, $12.00; children ages 6 to 11, $7.00 accompanied by a ticketed adult; and those younger than 6, free. Tour boats depart from the new National Park Service dock and visitor education facility at Liberty Square next to the South Carolina Aquarium in downtown Charleston and Patriots Point in Mt. Pleasant. Call for schedules; the fort is open year-round. (For more on Fort Sumter, see the Forts section of the Attractions chapter and the Tours chapter.)

## Hampton Park
**30 Mary Murray Drive**
**(843) 724-7327**
**www.charlestoncity.info**

As children, we came to Hampton Park to play around the 60 inner-city acres, so it's a particular treat to experience the park these days with the next generation. Children delight at the same simple pleasures we remember: feeding ducks and geese in the pond, smelling the gorgeous roses, and just frolicking in the wide-open spaces. The police department's horse stables are a real draw for the little ones, who can stand outside the ring and admire the animals; and the parcourse exercise trail is a favorite of older children and adults. The Piccolo Spoleto finale, a city-sponsored Easter Egg hunt, and in-line skating night during warm weather are great reasons to plan a Hampton Park visit. The park is free, but keep in mind the midtown location and possible safety concerns if you're venturing to Hampton Park at night. (See the Parks and Recreation chapter for more information.)

## James Island County Park
**871 Riverland Drive**
**(843) 795-7275**
**www.ccprc.com**

This beautiful, 643-acre park offers biking, keowees (junior-size kayaks), skating, fishing or crabbing, a climbing wall, a super playground, and much more. Splash Zone, however, is the James Island park's great water attraction. With two 200-foot tube slides, a 500-foot lazy river is enlivened by a spray-filled, waterfall-peppered "adventure channel." There's a leisure pool perfect for kiddies and a Caribbean play structure with interactive elements. Splash Zone is simply awesome. Showers, concessions, lockers, and restrooms are available. The annual Holiday Festival of Lights will dazzle young and old alike with more than 100 lighting displays on view mid-November through New Year's. (See Annual Events for more on this festival.) Park daily hours are 8:00 A.M. to 6:00 P.M. in March and October; 8:00 A.M. to 7:00

P.M. in April and September; 8:00 A.M. to 8:00 P.M. from May through August; and 8:00 A.M. to 5:00 P.M. November through February. Gate admission is $1.00 per person (2 years and under are free), but Splash Zone will run you an additional $7.99 for Charleston County residents ($6.99 for children under 42 inches tall) and $9.99 for nonresidents. Splash Zone is open 10:00 A.M. to 6:00 P.M. on weekends in May and mid-August through Labor Day; and it's open 10:00 A.M. to 6:00 P.M. daily from Memorial Day through mid-August. The Holiday Festival of Lights admission is $10 per car. (For more, see our Parks and Recreation and Boating and Watersports chapters.)

## Magnolia Plantation and Gardens
**3550 Ashley River Road**
**(843) 571-1266, (800) 367-3517**
**www.magnoliaplantation.com**

While the horticultural maze and antebellum cabin (an original, dating back to around 1840) are first stops for the little ones, the petting zoo with African pygmy goats, deer, and other friendly animals is the real calling card for toddlers and elementary school kids visiting Magnolia. They can buy handfuls of grain to feed the gentle creatures but should expect an occasional nibble on the posterior from a pushy goat or two. The topiary gardens, trimmed to resemble animals, and Barbados Tropical Garden (with plants native to Barbados—homeland of the original settling family—and points south) are also fun to see. Older children can rent canoes or bikes (or you can bring your own), and everyone enjoys the 45-minute, 4-mile tram ride through the property. Leashed pets are welcome too.

Magnolia is open 365 days a year from 8:00 A.M. to 5:00 P.M. Admission for adults is $14.00, for seniors $13.00, and the price for children varies according to age: $8.00 for ages 6 to 12; free for under 6. For the house tour, there is an additional charge of $7.00 per person. (Children under 6 are not admitted to the house tour.) For the nature train or boat there are additional

**KIDSTUFF**

charges of $7.00 per activity for adults, $5.00 for kids ages 6 to 12, and $3.00 under 6. (See the Attractions chapter for more on Magnolia Plantation and Gardens.)

*Plan to bring swimsuits, but leave the coolers at home for your day at Splash Island or Splash Zone at Palmetto Islands or James Island County Park. Proper swimming attire is required, and no outside food or beverages are allowed.*

**Middleton Place**
**4300 Ashley River Road**
**(843) 556-6020, (800) 782-3608**
**www.middletonplace.org**
In addition to being lots of fun for the kids, the incredible beauty of the gardens and forest trails of Middleton Place tends to leave parents lingering, trying to drag out the good times a little bit longer. A shady picnic area near the greensward is a delightful place to enjoy the vistas. And here's the chance for everyone to milk a cow, card wool, or grind corn. Middleton is a working plantation. Free-range farm animals mill about, and craftspeople are hard at work so that visitors can observe or even take part in the re-enactment of history.

Plantation Days are a fun, educational series of Saturdays in November when demonstrations of plantation harvesting, candle dipping, syrup making, shepherding, and more take place (see the Annual Events chapter). Gates are open daily from 9:00 A.M. until 5:00 P.M. Middleton Place is open year-round. Garden and stable yard admission is $20.00 for adults and teens and $5.00 for children ages 7 to 15. Children younger than 7 are admitted free. An additional $10.00 fee is charged for the house tour, and a carriage tour is offered for an additional $9.00 for adults and $13.00 for children. (For more on Middleton Place, please see the Planta-

tions and Gardens section of the Attractions chapter.)

**Palmetto Islands County Park**
**444 Needlerush Parkway, Mt. Pleasant**
**(843) 884-0832**
**www.ccprc.com**
This nature-oriented park is on more than 900 acres of typical Lowcountry terrain and features a mile-long wilderness trail along a boardwalk through the marsh. Little children enjoy playing at the Big Toy, a play area with lots of wooden equipment such as towers, slides, and swings; their older siblings enjoy the tunnel, slide, and view associated with the observation tower. Pedal boats and canoes are for rent, and many visitors enjoy exploring on bicycles—rent one or bring your own.

Splash Island is the hot attraction here for warm-weather patrons. A 200-foot slide, a 16-foot otter slide (no otters, just a fun name), sprays, waterfalls, geysers, and a delightful sand play area await. In addition to the park admission of $1.00 per person, Splash Island admission is $5.99 for Charleston County residents, $6.99 for non-Charleston County residents, $4.99 for children under 42 inches tall, and free for children younger than 2. A flat $3.99 is charged after 3:00 P.M. Monday through Friday. Splash Island is open from 10:00 A.M. to 6:00 P.M. on weekends in May and late August through Labor Day, and daily from Memorial Day through mid-August. Park daily hours vary by season as follows: May through August, 9:00 A.M. to 7:00 P.M.; March, April, September, and October, 9:00 A.M. to 6:00 P.M.; and November through February, 10:00 A.M. to 5:00 P.M. (See the Parks and Recreation and Boating and Watersports chapters for more information on this park.)

**Sullivan's Island Park**
**1610 Middle Street (Station 21**
**and Middle Street), Sullivan's Island**
**(843) 883-3198**
Involved parents and other residents of Sullivan's Island have worked hard to make this park the little gem that it is.

With two sections of play equipment, lots of wooden things to crawl in and on, and sliding-friendly apparatuses, children are fairly contained and easily occupied. There is even a fence around one area for additional safety for younger children. The man-made mound, left over from World War II, was built as a mortar battery to store ammunition. It is referred to by locals as "The Hill" and is the place to go if your kids are into sliding. Wear tennis shoes and play clothes, bring a big piece of cardboard and your steady nerves, then climb to the top and slide down . . . over and over and over again. At least that's the way it works with kids. While this is the same good, clean fun we had here as children, be forewarned that there is danger in the shape of a huge pit in the mound's center that is not particularly well-marked. Keep children away from the edges, and also avoid letting the kids make solo treks into the bamboo groves or other isolated areas. Although Sullivan's is an island of good neighborhoods, there is safety in numbers where children are concerned. There is no admission charge. (See the Parks and Recreation chapter for more on Sullivan's Island Park.)

**Waterfront Park**
**Cumberland Street to North**
**Adgers Wharf**
**(843) 724-7327**
**www.charlestoncity.info**
Just off East Bay Street in downtown Charleston, the lovely Waterfront Park is another nice picnic and cool-your-heels spot. Sea breezes keep the tables under the covered pier area perfect for just these pursuits. Children have fun splashing around in the pineapple-shaped fountain or getting soaked in the circular spray fountain. We've seen pictures of half a kindergarten class in one of the large swings that line the pier, a 400-foot extension into Charleston Harbor. No admission is charged. (See the Parks and Recreation chapter.)

**White Point Gardens at the Battery**
**South tip of East Bay and King Streets**
**(843) 724-7327**
**www.charlestoncity.info**
Frisbee-throwers and cannon-climbers love White Point Gardens. Children can run free beneath the canopy of trees and pretend to lift the immensely heavy and immovable cannonballs. Lots of photo ops here! There is usually a pleasant breeze off the water (the harbor circles around the point), and this open space is a much-loved haven of respite in the city. We used to search through the oyster-shell fill along the walks to find ancient shark teeth or other treasures. Don't expect any more luck than we had decades ago, but do plan to enjoy the leisurely pace of an old-fashioned park. Of course, no admission is charged. (For more info, see the Parks and Recreation, History, and Attractions chapters.)

## KID-FRIENDLY BEACHES

Though there are many great beach destinations in a coastal area like this one, one of our favorite swimming areas for children is on Folly Beach at the Folly Beach County Park, (843) 588-2426. Unlike some other area beaches, this one has its own parking, lifeguards, and facilities. Take a right off Folly Road onto Center Street, and follow it to its end. Young surfers will want to head for the midsection of the island, where waves are best. Admission is $5.00 a car.

Kiawah, most of which is a private resort community, does offer public access at Beachwalker Park, (843) 768-2395, on the west end. Lifeguards, parking, restrooms, and equipment rentals are available from April through October. Turn just before the gates to Kiawah to find the park. The ocean frontage is somewhat off-the-beaten-path, thus allowing for 11 miles of unspoiled sand and surf. A $5.00 fee is required per car.

We can cautiously recommend the beaches on Sullivan's Island and the Isle of Palms, but urge parents to keep several general cautions in mind before you send the children skipping to the surf. Note that strong, tricky currents are prevalent at each end of Sullivan's Island as well as the south end of the Isle of Palms. Convenient parking can be tough to find on both islands, but the Isle of Palms County Park, (843) 886-3863, located mid-island, offers lots of parking and lifeguards on duty during the summer months for a $5.00-per-car entrance fee. Walk-ins and bicycles are admitted at the three beach parks at no charge. (the Parks and Recreation chapter offers more information on all of these parks.)

## CULTURAL FUN

**Charleston Ballet School**
**477 King Street**
**(843) 723-7334**
**www.charlestonballet.org**
If your youngsters fancy standing on their tippy-toes, put that talent to good use by enrolling them in the Charleston Ballet Theatre's official school. Classes in creative movement, ballet, and jazz dance for ages 3 and older are offered. While the school's graduates dance with major companies throughout the country, students without professional ambition are welcome. The school and its parent theater company are located in a King Street facility downtown just a block from the Charleston Visitor Reception and Transportation Center. Call the number above for class offerings and fees. Regular ballet performances and Piccolo Spoleto tickets are $20 for adults and $10 for children. Season tickets for five performances are $140 with discounts for children younger than 18 and seniors. The annual *Nutcracker* ballet, performed by many of the ballet school students during the Christmas season, is a long-standing favorite. (See The Arts chapter for more on the Charleston Ballet Theatre.)

**The Charleston Museum**
**360 Meeting Street**
**(843) 722-2996**
**www.charlestonmuseum.org**
In addition to being the oldest history, art, and science museum in the country (founded in 1773), the Charleston Museum is one of the best resources for children in the city. We love to try to keep pace with the kids as they scamper through the modern complex (the facility is well designed and very kid-older-than-four friendly). There are interesting programs throughout the year—with such titles as "Babies, Bunnies, and Beasties," "Treasure's Ahoy," and "Mummies, Monsters, and Make-Believe"—that usually last one afternoon session and are included in admission. We've found that starting off on a rainy day in the Discover Me room, with its "touch-me" exhibits, is the best way for little ones to unwind and connect with the museum. The museum is across the street from the visitor center. It is open 9:00 A.M. to 5:00 P.M. Monday through Saturday and 1:00 to 5:00 P.M. on Sunday. Admission is $10.00 for adults and teens and $4.00 for children ages 3 to 12. Free parking is available in a small lot behind the museum. (For more information, see the Attractions chapter.)

**Charleston Stage Company**
**Theatre School**
**Dock Street Theatre, 135 Church Street**
**(843) 577-5967**
**www.charlestonstage.com**
"All the world's a stage" . . . and maybe your youngster would like a chance to learn more about it. Charleston Stage is a prime creative outlet for that dramatist in the family. The Theatre School offers a variety of acting and theatre education opportunities for children in grades K–12. The program introduces theatrical skills in classes designed to enhance acting skills, bolster self-confidence, and encourage self-expression. Advanced students may participate in KidsRep, the performing troupe for middle school students, and TheatreWings, the apprentice program for

high school students. The Theatre School students are encouraged also to audition for roles in the Charleston Stage's Main-Stage and KidStage productions each season. Classes are offered year-round in two-week summer sessions to weekly afternoon classes throughout the school year at the Dock Street Theatre downtown and in their rehearsal studios in Mt. Pleasant.

## Children's Museum of the Lowcountry
### 25 Ann Street
### (843) 853-8962
### www.explorecml.org
The newest museum on the scene with a focus on kids is the Children's Museum of the Lowcountry. Located near the visitor center in the Camden Tower Sheds, this popular concept is to inspire a love of learning in children through interactive, interdisciplinary, hands-on environments and experiences in the arts, sciences, and humanities. The fun exhibits include climbing a tower in the Castle, sliding into the art room, painting on a mural wall, playing with water in WaterWise, racing golf balls, and shrimping from a shrimp boat. This immersion environment for children and their families leads to creative thinking, problem-solving skills, and confidence. Who knows what a visit here may spark? Admission is $5.00 for all ages. Children under age 1 are free. Hours are Tuesday through Saturday 10:00 A.M. to 5:00 P.M. and Sunday 1:00 to 5:00 P.M.

## Gibbes Museum of Art
### 135 Meeting Street
### (843) 722-2706

## Gibbes Museum School of Art
### 76 Queen Street
### (843) 577-7275
### www.gibbesmuseum.org
The Gibbes is a source of pride for many Charlestonians. Not only are the collections impressive, but the facility itself and the enthusiasm of the membership also spark creativity in the young and old alike. Studio art classes at the Gibbes are very popular with Charleston children. From drawing to working with clay to watercolor art or photography, the offerings appeal to many levels of artistic interest and skill. Classes cost between $90 and $180, and semesters run about eight weeks.

A variety of special events and activities are held for children throughout the year, so call for a calendar with all the details. And to celebrate a birthday full of creative, fun art projects, call the school to schedule. The cost is $185 for members or $195 for non-members for up to 15 children.

With exhibits ranging from the contemporary to the abstract, a simple visit to the museum any time can be a visual thrill. Hours are 10:00 A.M. to 5:00 P.M. Tuesday through Saturday and 1:00 to 5:00 P.M. on Sunday. The museum is closed on Mondays. Adult admission is $7.00 (with a $1.00 break for seniors, military personnel, and college students); for children ages 6 to 18, $4.00. Annual family memberships are $100, and they include a 10 percent discount on museum shop purchases and classes. (For more on the Gibbes, see the chapters on The Arts and Attractions.)

## Old Exchange and Provost Dungeon
### 122 East Bay Street (at Broad Street)
### (843) 727-2165, (888) 763-0448
### www.oldexchange.com
Make history really come to life for your child. The period-costumed docents at the Old Exchange and Provost Dungeon tell the stories of the extraordinary events of Old Charles Towne at this site, including the imprisonment of the notorious pirate, Stede Bonnet, seizure and storage of British tea, ratification of the U.S. Constitution, and George Washington's visit. Animatronic storytellers in the Provost Dungeon entertain all ages with wonderful tales of pirates and patriots held captive within these eerie confines. Remnants of the 1698 fortification wall surrounding Charles Towne are here too. The Old Exchange is open daily from 9:00 A.M. to 5:00 P.M. Adult admission is $7.00, and children ages 7 to 12 and students are $3.50.

Children 6 and under are admitted free. (For more about the Old Exchange and Provost Dungeon, see the Attractions chapter.)

## INDOOR FUN AND GAMES

### American Theater
### 446 King Street
### (843) 853-1810
### www.americantheater.com
Make your child a "star" for the day, and line up his or her next birthday at the American Theater "Stars" room. What birthday child wouldn't be delighted to see their name in lights on the marquee? Saturday and Sunday afternoons, the party starts 30 minutes prior to the film screening so that children can gather to sing "Happy Birthday," blow out the candles (you provide the cake and your own child-appropriate video), and open presents. During the movie, food, beverages, and cake are served. Three birthday packages are available, depending on the menu selected, and range from $8.00 to $15.00 per person with a 15-person minimum. A birthday party here makes for a fun afternoon's entertainment.

### Carolina Ice Palace
### 7665 Northwoods Boulevard, North Charleston
### (843) 572-2717
### www.carolinaicepalace.com
Charleston's coolest place for family fun is the Carolina Ice Palace with two NHL-size ice rinks for recreational skating, instruction, hockey teams and leagues, and birthday parties. Open seven days a week for you to perfect that double axle, the Ice Palace's general-public hours are 11:00 A.M. to 3:00 P.M. Monday through Friday with after-school skating from 3:00 to 5:30 P.M. Monday and Friday. The palace is also open from 7:00 to 9:00 P.M. Wednesday and Thursday, and both nights are family nights with a $30 package of skate rentals, pizza, and soda for a family of

four. Friday and Saturday hours extend to 11:30 P.M., and Sunday hours are 1:30 to 6:00 P.M. Other on-site attractions are the video arcade, virtual reality center, and giant pro shop for skate rental and sharpening. Burgers and pizza can take care of the hungries, and an alcohol-free lounge with satellite TV provides a little relaxation while watching your future Olympic star. A 17,000-square-foot outdoor skate park features ramps, rails, quarter pipes, and spires for skateboarders, in-line skaters, and bikers. Call the number listed for a seasonal schedule of times and fees. Carolina Ice Palace admission prices are $6.00 for children ages 4 to 12 and seniors, $3.00 for children 3 and younger, and $7.00 for adults, with a $3.00 charge for skate rental. After-school skating is $5.00 including skate rental. Discount coupon books offer savings for 12 admissions. Of course, birthday parties are a popular option here for ages 3 to 18. Skating and hockey classes, conducted by professional instructors, are available on a group or individual basis.

### Charleston County Library Storytimes
### 68 Calhoun Street
### (843) 805-6893
### www.ccpl.org
"Tell me a story, please." Charleston County Libraries have the answer. They offer a series of storytimes for young children ages 12 months to 5 years old. "Wee Reads" is a 20-minute weekly morning program for ages 12 to 24 months. "Time for Twos" is another weekly morning program lasting 30 minutes for ages 24 to 36 months. All toddlers must be accompanied by a parent or caregiver. There is a preschool storytime for ages 3 to 5 that includes 30 minutes of interactive storytelling, sometimes with videos and crafts. Children 6 and under may come in their pajamas for the evening "Starlight Storytime" to hear stories and sing songs. Call the number above or your branch library to register. (See the Education chapter for a list of branch libraries.)

**Frankie's Fun Park**
**5000 Ashley Phosphate Road,**
**North Charleston**
**(843) 767-1376**
**wwww.frankiesfunpark.com**
This is Charleston's answer to the kiddies' cry for an amusement park. Children can spend money on a variety of activities—from bumper boats and a batting cage to go-carts and the "trampoline thing." A rock-climbing wall offers another challenge. Two miniature golf courses and a lighted, 90-position driving range offer a slower-paced, less gravity-defying experience. There is no general admission, but park activities cost between $2.00 and $10.00 each. (A $20 fee allows two hours of unlimited fun with six activities.) A family with two kids can expect to spend $20 to $30 at Frankie's if Mom and Dad don't participate; it'll likely be $40 or more if everyone joins in. There are picnic tables, a snack bar, and clean restrooms. Hours are 10:00 A.M. to midnight Monday through Sunday during the summer. September through October, and March through May, it's 10:00 A.M. to 10:00 P.M. Monday through Thursday, 10:00 A.M. to midnight Friday and Saturday, and noon to 10:00 P.M. on Sunday. Winter hours, November through February, are 10:00 A.M. to 9:00 P.M. Monday through Thursday, 10:00 A.M. to 11:00 P.M. Friday and Saturday, and noon to 9:00 P.M. on Sunday. Frankie's is closed on Thanksgiving, Christmas Eve, Christmas, and New Year's Day.

**South Carolina Aquarium**
**100 Aquarium Wharf**
**(near Calhoun and Concord Streets)**
**(843) 720-1990**
**www.scaquarium.org**
The newest major attraction in Charleston is the South Carolina Aquarium, opened in May 2000. Located at the edge of historic Charleston harbor, two-thirds of the building projects over the water, and multiple decks complete the views of the Cooper River, both the bustling activity of the shipping industry and the serene natural landscape. The aquarium interprets South Carolina's diverse variety of habitats from mountain streams to the depths of the Atlantic Ocean. The 93,000-square-foot facility displays more than 60 exhibits representing over 500 species with 10,000 living organisms. Otters, birds, turtles, fish, reptiles, aquatic invertebrates, and insects are all a part of the habitats here. Visitors will experience five major regions of the Southeast Watershed of South Carolina: the Blue Ridge Mountains, the Piedmont, the Coastal Plain, the Coast, and the Ocean. Their education master plan, developed with local teachers, naturalists, and community leaders, encompasses interactive displays, special toddler exhibits, an education center, a discovery lab, and several education stations. August 16 through March 31, the hours are 9:00 A.M. to 5:00 P.M.; April 1 through August 15 hours are 9:00 A.M. to 6:00 P.M. Sunday hours begin at noon. Adult admission for ages 12 to 61 is $15.00, seniors 62 and up are $13.00, and children ages 3 to 11 are $8.00. The aquarium is closed Thanksgiving and Christmas Day and a half day on Christmas Eve. (See the Attractions chapter for more on the South Carolina Aquarium.)

## DAY CAMPS

Many community centers, schools, and churches operate day camps around the Trident. Extended-day programs are available for many working parents and run from the end of the school day until 6:00 or 6:30 P.M. at most schools and centers. Like camps, some offer enrichment courses such as karate, piano, foreign language study, drama, and arts and crafts.

**Charleston County After School**
**Charleston County Community Education**
**75 Calhoun Street**
**(843) 937-6421, (843) 762-2172**
**www.charlestoncoce.org**
Working parents of school-age children will be glad to take advantage of the extended-day programs available in many

of the local public elementary and middle schools. These programs provide a safe, supervised, and educational environment at your child's own school. This affordable after-school alternative offers organized activities, snacks, and time to complete homework assignments, and many have a selection of enrichment courses. The average cost is $30 a week, but it varies by school and activity. The following community school directors' offices can provide additional information: Downtown, (843) 579-4827; Mt. Pleasant, (843) 881-8273; North Charleston, (843) 529-3926 or (843) 764-2236; James Island, (843) 762-2793; Johns Island, (843) 559-6460; West Ashley, (843) 573-1212; McClellanville, (843) 887-4229; Yonges Island, (843) 889-6852.

### Davis Community Center
**4800 Park Circle, North Charleston**
**(843) 745-1028**
The recreation department offers after-school programs at all 20 community center locations throughout North Charleston. Supervisors direct help with homework, games, sports, and arts and crafts. No fee is charged. Contact the number listed for more information.

## SUMMER CAMPS

It has an all-too-familiar ring: "Mom, Dad, I'm bored."

Once school is out, you better have a plan to keep the kids occupied and happy on those never-ending, lazy summer days. Fortunately, several of the recreation departments, county parks, private schools, arts organizations, churches, and scout groups around the Trident area offer a plethora of summer day-camp adventures. Lots of fun stuff is organized to pique your child's interest in something new or improve skills in a favorite pastime. A brief sampling of some of the day camps with a mix of activities are listed below, plus a few sports- and arts-oriented camps. Prices may vary slightly.

### The Citadel Basketball Camp
**McAlister Field House,**
**The Citadel**
**(843) 953-5904, (843) 723-2005**
**www.citadelsports.com**
Citadel head basketball coach Patrick Dennis serves as camp director of this popular, 20-plus-year-old basketball program for boys and girls ages 6 to 16. The staff includes Citadel basketball coaches, area high school coaches, and collegiate players. The younger Bulldog campers (ages 6 to 8) play on scaled-down facilities, and all instruction takes place in McAlister Field House, where the big Bulldogs play their college games. The one-week sessions run from 9:00 A.M. to 4:00 P.M. on Monday through Thursday and from 9:00 A.M. to noon on Friday. Fees are $190 for the week. The Citadel also offers baseball, soccer, football, and wrestling camps. Contact the school's athletic department for more information. (For more on The Citadel's academic offerings, see the Education chapter.)

### City of Charleston
**Junior Tennis Summer Camp**
**Maybank Tennis Center,**
**1880 Houghton Drive**
**(843) 406-8814**
**www.charlestoncity.info**
The city's Junior Tennis Summer Camp has an excellent program for your budding tennis enthusiast. The camp is for beginners to advanced intermediate students ages 4 to 16. It meets from 9:00 A.M. to noon or 3:30 to 6:00 P.M. Monday through Friday. Daily instruction includes working on fundamental strokes, video analysis, and personal attention. Games and prizes add to the positive, fun environment. Fees are $75/week for either session. (See the Tennis section of the Parks and Recreation chapter for more information.)

### Co-ed Summerfest
**Ashley Hall,**
**172 Rutledge Avenue**
**(843) 965-8485, (843) 722-4088**
**www.ashleyhall.org**

Ashley Hall's campus provides a perfect in-town setting for summer programs designed to entertain, educate, and challenge your children. (See the Education chapter for more on Ashley Hall.) Day camps, athletics, enrichment adventures, academic skills, and computer workshops let you sign 'em up for a variety of sessions throughout those long summer months. The day camps keep campers on the go with tennis, swimming, gymnastics, group games, and arts and crafts. Athletic challenges sap some of that boundless energy with basketball, volleyball, dance, soccer, scuba, swimming, and tae kwon do.

The enrichment adventures allow students to explore and develop new interests in areas such as guitar and piano lessons, jewelry making, fiction writing, and French. Computer skills and study and reading skills workshops are some of the academic offerings. Contact the school for a complete brochure outlining sessions. Day-camp sessions cost $200 per one-week session with an additional $50 a week for extended days. Athletic challenges start at $45 a week and go up to $120. The enrichment adventures begin at $50 and climb to $125. The Reading Skills Workshop is $220.

## Creative Spark
**757 Long Point Road, Mt. Pleasant**
**(843) 881-3780**
**www.creativespark.org**
Let your child's creativity and imagination be sparked. Creative Spark Center for the Arts presents a wonderful variety of summer camps in the performing and visual arts to do just that. Art, an improvisational drama workshop, and musical theater camps, along with creative writing, dance, and private music instruction, are among the choices for ages four and older. Call the above number for a complete brochure with details on sessions. The art camps cost around $190 for one two-week session with a 20 percent sibling or multi-camp discount. The creative camp combines singing, playing instruments, and making artistic creations for $190 for

two weeks. Drama classes start at $70, and music classes are $100 for eight weeks. Birthday parties with an art, music, or dance theme are fun options here. A cake, favors, activities, supervision, and cleanup are provided for up to 12 for $175 on Saturdays.

## East Cooper Gymnastics
**497 La Mesa Street, Mt. Pleasant**
**(843) 849-6668**
Half-day and full-day camps are offered in June and July for $115 (ages 3 to 5) to $165 (ages 6 to 12) per week. The goal of each camp is to provide a fun and relaxed atmosphere where each child can build strength, flexibility, and coordination. Instruction covers vault, bars, beam, tumbling, and TumbleTrak. Campers also have play time in the tumble jungle—an indoor, soft playground.

*Three hundred thousand and counting . . . that's the number of kids who have enjoyed a unique overnight camping experience aboard the aircraft carrier USS Yorktown at Patriots Point in Mt. Pleasant. Campers (in groups of at least 10 plus a chaperone) sleep in the bunks once occupied by the crew, dine in the ship's galley, and hop in the cockpit of a real fighter jet. Fun-filled excursions are an option, too. Call (800) 278-3508 or visit www.patriotspoint.org for more information.*

## Stono River Stable
## Summer Riding Camp
**2962 Hut Road (at 3000 River Road), Johns Island**
**(843) 559-0773, (843) 559-2737**
**www.stonoriverstable.com**
Learn about the splendor of the horse! Stono River Stable has been offering its Summer Riding Camp since 1969. They provide professional instruction taught by adult teachers with backgrounds from the

Fulmer Riding School and Park Farm School in England. The emphasis here is on safety and fun. One-week sessions are offered throughout the summer months for ages 6 to 16. The classes last from 9:00 A.M. to 1:00 P.M. daily and cover grooming and tacking up, riding lessons, and horse care. The last hour changes each day from bareback riding to games on horseback to trail rides and more. Classes are limited to 12 students per day and the one-week fee is $265. (See the Parks and Recreation chapter for more on Stono River Stable.)

## Summer Art Camp
## Gibbes Museum School of Art
## 76 Queen Street
## (843) 577-7275
## www.gibbesmuseum.org

Hands-on art and imaginary travels await your four- to six-year-old at the Summer Art Camp at the Gibbes School of Art. Each of the four one-week sessions encourages creativity, helps develop fine motor skills, and builds confidence. Classes like "Jurassic Art" (drawing and painting Earth's prehistoric creatures) and "Magical Masks" (making tribal and masquerade masks) are sure to get those little hands busy.

The Summer Art Camp for ages 7 to 12 focuses on art-inspired adventures through different eras and cultures. Past offerings have included "Picasso's Faces,"

where students learn to draw faces by painting portraits of classmates as well as a self-portrait. "O'Keeffe's Flowers," "Calder's Mobiles," and "Van Gogh's Landscapes" carry on the famous-artist projects, stimulating your child's own artistic expression. The Summer Art Camps meet Monday through Thursday from 1:00 to 4:00 P.M. Tuition is $145 per week for Gibbes members, $160 a week for nonmembers. (See the Attractions chapter for more about the Gibbes Museum of Art and the Gibbes School of Art.)

## Summer Fun on the Island Day Camp
## James Island Recreation Complex
## 1088 Quail Drive
## (843) 720-3808

Sponsored by the City of Charleston Department of Recreation, Summer Fun on the Island is a camp for youth between the ages of 6 and 12 years old. Monday through Friday from 7:00 A.M. to 6:00 P.M., campers are engaged in arts and crafts, swimming, storytelling, movies, music, aerobics, and sports divided by age groups. Once a week, campers venture out on field trips to great spots such as James Island and Folly Beach County Parks, Middleton Place, Riverbanks Zoo, and Splash Zone. Four sessions are offered from June to July, with fees for city residents set at $125 per two-week session. Nonresidents of the city pay $150 per two-week session.

# LOWCOUNTRY DAY TRIPS

H ere are some day trip adventures into the very heart of the Low-country—great excuses to go afield in search of unusual fun and a deeper understanding of what makes this area unique.

The first is a day-long journey into a land of winding rivers offering a fascinating look at some of South Carolina's early rice plantation history. The second will allow you to spend an afternoon discovering a real Lowcountry gem, Summerville, and all the strange twists of fate that have led to its various incarnations: railroad boomtown, international health resort haven, and azalea paradise (a title the community still proudly boasts). The third is a morning walk on the Lowcountry's wild side—along Marrington Watchable Wildlife Trail near the town of Goose Creek in Berkeley County. A fourth day trip is a must for families with school-age children—Old Santee Canal State Park up in Moncks Corner. Children and parents alike enjoy the interactive adventures at the park, where the Lowcountry's days of canal-building and horse-drawn barges are revisited.

## IT WAS (ONCE) ALL ABOUT RICE . . .

In the 18th and early 19th centuries, this Lowcountry land and its waters spawned a rich, romantic, fragile culture largely based on a single cash crop—rice. Any real understanding of the Lowcountry and its ethic includes an appreciation for rice and the major role it played in the development of the area.

To that end, on our first day trip we will visit the sleepy fishing village of McClel-lanville—once a cool summer home for old rice plantation families, more recently the brave survivor of 1989's devastating Hurricane Hugo.

We'll pay a call on two important 18th-century rice plantations presented to the public in totally different, but equally valid, ways. And we'll explore old Georgetown, formerly the "Rice Capital of the Carolinas." On the way, we'll encounter charming little chapels of ease that served the faithful plantation dwellers so far flung and isolated in South Carolina's earlier days.

And finally, we'll wander the quiet paths of Brookgreen Gardens, a unique and unexpected museum of 19th- and 20th-century American sculpture, built on rice plantation lands once granted to Lowcountry colonists by King George II of England.

*Start at the foot of Charleston's new Arthur Ravenel Jr. Bridge on U.S. Highway 17 N. Watch for the signs to Georgetown and U.S. Highway 17-701. Continue along the U.S. Highway 17 Bypass for about 8 miles through commercial development. Then look to your right for a small, tin-roofed chapel with an octagonal cupola. Pull into the churchyard through the open gate.*

### Christ Episcopal Church
### 2304 US 17 N., Charleston
### (843) 884-9090

Here's your first chance to encounter one of the Lowcountry's most charming undiscovered treasures, one of the little-known but much-loved chapels of ease (See the Close-up on chapels of ease in the Worship chapter.) Millions of tourists visit the area and never even know these little testimonies to the Lowcountry's bygone plantation era still exist. Amazingly, they do exist, in various forms and in varied states of repair and use. First, however, a little background information is required.

The colony of Carolina was founded with the Anglican Church as its established religious force. Early on, Anglican congregations received financial assistance from the British government to construct houses of worship. These first Anglican churches also tended to benefit from the generosity of wealthy planters in their congregations. As a result, these churches were built with greater architectural sophistication than the early buildings of other religious organizations, and it's mostly these better-built, early Anglican structures that survive today as mute witness to the strength of religion in the early colonies and the isolation of plantation life.

Christ Church Parish was one of 10 parishes established by the Church Act of 1706. The following year, a wooden building was in place on this site, serving a slowly growing number of communicants. After fire destroyed the wooden building in 1725, a brick structure was completed in 1726.

In 1782, British soldiers burned the church to the walls during the Revolution, and it wasn't restored until about 1800. In 1865, during the Civil War, fire all but destroyed the church again, and although it was once more rebuilt, regular services were discontinued by 1874. Finally, in 1925, both the structure and the congregation were restored by caring descendants of early Christ Church Parish families. Despite its long, hard struggle for survival, Christ Church is a viable, active congregation today. Sunday services offer Holy Eucharist at 8:00, 9:00, and 11:15 A.M.

*Chances are, your initial excursions into the Lowcountry's plantation past (including many of the sites documented in the Attractions chapter) led you along the Ashley River, not the Cooper. If so, you missed the opportunity to visit some of the vast plantations that once flourished along the Cooper. First, we'll stop at Snee Farm, country home of one of America's founding fathers, Charles Pinckney*

*(1757–1824), then we'll visit one of America's most photographed plantations, Boone Hall.*

*To find Snee Farm and Boone Hall Plantation, cross the four-lane highway opposite Christ Church to Long Point Road, and look for the sign. Less than a mile up Longpoint Road on your left is the entrance to Snee Farm.*

### Snee Farm
### (Charles Pinckney National Historic Site)
### 1254 Long Point Road, Mt. Pleasant
### (843) 881-5516, (843) 883-3123
### www.nps.gov/chpi

Only 28 acres remain of what was once the expansive Snee Farm, colonial plantation home of Charles Pinckney, a major molder of the U.S. Constitution. But those relatively few acres are fast becoming a home-base for thousands of African Americans who come to the Lowcountry seeking more information about their heritage and the important role Charleston plays in that story.

Let's begin with Charles Pinckney, the man. He began his public career at age 22, when he was admitted to the South Carolina Bar and the South Carolina General Assembly. Pinckney served as one of four South Carolina delegates at the Constitutional Convention in Philadelphia. He served as governor of South Carolina, was ambassador to Spain from 1801 to 1805, and held seats in both the state and national legislature. He retired from public life in 1821 and died three years later.

Originally, Snee Farm was part of a 500-acre royal grant awarded in 1698 to Richard Butler. By 1754, the farm comprised 715 acres and was purchased that year by Pinckney's father. The property was the family's "country seat" and an integral part of Charles Pinckney's life. Like many other Charleston aristocrats, Pinckney relied on slave labor (mostly imported from West Africa) to raise the "Carolina gold" (rice) that grew on Snee Farm.

Today, the contributions of those people of African descent are being unearthed by National Park Service archaeologists.

Historians working behind the scenes are following the threads of African contributions to the Lowcountry culture in the fields of language, diet, agriculture, mechanics, and craftsmanship. And the Pinckney site is a rich resource for this information.

The present house on the site, built in the 1820s, is an excellent and charming example of the type of coastal cottage once common here in the Lowcountry. Guests will find interesting interpretive exhibits in and around the house. There's an informative 18-minute video telling of Charles Pinckney, Snee Farm, George Washington's colonial-era visit to the property and the United States as a young, emerging nation. Park hours are from 9:00 A.M. to 5:00 P.M. Admission is absolutely free, a real bargain.

*Turn left back onto Long Point Road, and less than a mile down the way is Boone Hall's entrance.*

## Boone Hall Plantation
**1235 Long Point Road, Mt. Pleasant**
**(843) 884-4371**
**www.boonehallplantation.com**
Today's Boone Hall Plantation is a 738-acre estate dating back to the 1680s, when the Lords Proprietor made this sizable land grant to an early English settler, Maj. John Boone.

During the 18th and 19th centuries, Boone Hall was a thriving cotton plantation covering more than 17,000 acres. Brick was also a plantation product and was used in the construction of the original mansion, cotton gin house, slave cabins, and circular smokehouse. Later, Boone Hall was famous for its large groves of pecan trees, many of which are still productive today.

Boone Hall is a favorite of photographers and filmmakers because of its magnificent avenue of live oaks and the nine original, unrestored slave cabins (ca. 1743) that once housed the plantation's skilled craftspeople and house servants. The original Boone Hall mansion was lost in a tragic fire. The present structure dates from the

mid-1930s. Extensive location filming was done here for the ABC-TV miniseries "North and South."

Admission is $14.50 for adults and teens and $7.00 for children ages 6 to 12. The property is open every day except Thanksgiving and Christmas. Hours are Monday through Saturday from 9:00 A.M. to 5:00 P.M. and Sunday from 1:00 to 4:00 P.M. From April 1 through Labor Day, hours extend to 8:30 A.M. to 6:30 P.M. on weekdays and 1:00 to 5:00 P.M. on Sundays. (For more on Boone Hall, see the Tours chapter.)

*Return to U.S. Highway 17, and turn left. (Note that this is a four-lane highway, and use extreme caution while crossing the two oncoming lanes before turning left.) Follow US 17 and note the signs designating the Francis Marion National Forest on both sides of the highway.*

## Francis Marion National Forest
**US 17 N.**
**(843) 336-3248, (843) 887-3257**
**www.fs.fed.us/r8/fms**
This quarter-million-acre tract includes sections of both Charleston and Berkeley Counties. Once the battleground where the legendary Gen. Francis Marion—the Swamp Fox—engaged Col. Banastre Tarleton's British troops during the American Revolution, this vast park is now a wildlife reserve and a microcosm of the Lowcountry's natural habitat.

Here, as in no other place, the power and destructive range of 1989's Hurricane Hugo is dramatically apparent. The tall, mature forest was completely devastated by the storm, yet nature's recovery process is equally fascinating. Today, what is most obvious to passing visitors is not the storm's aftermath but the lush thicket of natural regrowth that has appeared since the 1989 storm.

The Francis Marion National Forest offers a wide variety of recreational activities, including picnicking and camping sites, boat ramps, fishing ponds, rifle ranges, and hiking, horse, and motorcycle trails. For more information, contact the Witherbee District Ranger in Moncks Corner or the Wambaw District Ranger in McClellanville at the numbers listed. (For more on camping options in Francis Marion National Forest, see the Parks and Recreation chapter.)

*Continue on US 17. At about mile marker 33, look for the sign on the right marking the intersection of Highway 45. Turn right to discover McClellanville.*

# McClellanville

This sleepy old fishing village, nestled among the live oaks along Jeremy Creek, was once the summer haven for 19th-century rice planters living along the Santee River. More recently, however, McClellanville is best known as one of the small towns where residents bravely and miraculously survived Hurricane Hugo in 1989.

Eons before the town was known as McClellanville, it was one of the small villages occupied by the Sewee Indians. Archaeology shows it's one of the few sites in South Carolina that have been continuously occupied by humans for thousands of years.

The beginnings of the existing village date back to the mid-1800s, when rice-planters on the Santee River built retreats here, away from the disease-ridden backwater plantations. A devastating hurricane in 1822 had completely wiped out a village of planter homes on nearby Cedar Island, and the new site was thought to be safer from storms. After the Civil War, economics forced some of the area planters to completely abandon their large plantations and move into the little summer village on a permanent basis.

McClellanville wasn't actually "McClellan-ville" for many years, until it became necessary to christen it something for postal and other municipal purposes. Several names were discussed, including "Jeremy" or "Jerryville," after the creek of the same name. Even "Romain" was considered, after Cape Romain. But the village was finally named McClellanville for

one of its early citizens, A. J. McClellan.

In the 1920s, it became one of the first places in the state where shrimpers from the west coast of Florida would come to trawl the rich coastal waters. Eventually, the town developed into one of the major shrimp ports in the state. The old buildings in McClellanville reflect the architectural development of the town from a summer retreat for plantation families to a thriving, incorporated municipality. You'll find residential, commercial, religious, and educational properties dating from the 1860s to the 1930s.

Of the hundreds of thousands of stories spawned by the forces of Hurricane Hugo on September 21, 1989, the story of McClellanville is among the most memorable.

A small plaque has been placed on a wall near the cafeteria door in McClellanville's Lincoln High School. It's a little more than 6 feet above the floor, and it shows how high the water rose that night. But no 8-by-10-inch plaque can measure the level of fear experienced by the 400 or so people who had gathered at the school for shelter against the storm.

In the pitch-black night, as the storm center pushed violently over peninsular Charleston some 35 miles to the south, the accompanying tidal surge rushed in on McClellanville with horrendous force and speed. The school was a designated storm shelter, and what was almost the entire population of the town had just settled in for what they hoped would be only a moderately uncomfortable night. There was excitement, to be sure. And dread. And worry. But the primary concern was getting the children and older people settled in as comfortably as possible. To that end, people were scattered throughout the building in various hallways and classrooms. Suddenly, they heard a strange, rushing noise above the already fierce storm. The cold, black water of Hugo's tidal surge rushed in from everywhere, pinning the exit doors shut and turning the school into a nightmarish death trap.

Some people scrambled onto the bleachers in the gymnasium as the waters quickly climbed after them. Others crowded up onto the school's stage and literally held their children over their heads as the water surged in up to their chests. They sang and prayed, cried and comforted each other throughout the seemingly endless night. Finally, the water began to recede. What the stunned survivors found outside by dawn's earliest light was unrecognizable.

Amazingly, no one drowned in the McClellanville calamity at Lincoln High School. One life was lost, later (a heart attack victim), but it could easily have been a disaster costing hundreds of lives. Today, McClellanville is remarkably recovered. If you drive into the village via Pinckney Street, note the "new" Wappetaw Presbyterian Church (ca. 1830) on the right. Turn right on Oak Street and drive about 2 blocks to St. James Santee Episcopal Church. There, the congregation dates back to 1706. This charmingly pure, shingled Gothic structure was built in 1890. Don't leave town before you drive up to the docks for a view of the McClellanville shrimp fleet harbored along the Intracoastal Waterway.

*Return to US 17 via Pinckney Street and turn right. About 5 miles up the road, a sign marks the intersection of S. Santee Road (marked S.C. Highway 857). Turn left and follow it about 2 miles to the entrance of Hampton Plantation.*

## Hampton Plantation
**1950 Rutledge Road, McClellanville**
**(843) 546-9361**
**www.discoversouthcarolina.com/sp.asp**
The origins of Hampton Plantation (ca. 1750) can be traced back to the earliest European settlement of the Santee delta. The Horry family, who built and developed the property, were descendants of French Huguenots who had immigrated to Carolina in search of religious freedom and economic advancement.

The Horrys are thought to have acquired the land on which Hampton now stands during the period between 1700 and 1730. The actual date of construction

*Drop those windows (or the convertible top) and breathe in the Lowcountry. If you're looking for a picture-perfect afternoon drive, head out in the early evening down the twisting ribbon of Bohicket Road, and enjoy the summer sun filtering through the spreading canopy of live oaks as you approach Kiawah.*

for Hampton's main house is not known, but according to early records, Col. Daniel Horry built it around 1750.

The Horry land holdings on Wambaw Creek comprised some 5,000 acres, and they all were worked by slaves like most other Lowcountry plantations at the time. Rice was grown on the swamplands along the water, and these fields were connected by a complicated system of canals and ditches. The fields were flooded and drained as the demands of the rice-growing season required.

Indigo—used in the dyeing of wool—was another Hampton cash crop. For a time, there was a profitable demand for indigo because England used it in vast quantities for the dyeing of British naval uniforms. In fact, the Daniel Horry who supposedly built Hampton Plantation married the daughter of the famous South Carolina woman Eliza Lucas Pinckney who is credited with growing the first successful indigo crop in the Lowcountry.

During the American Revolution, while most of the prominent men were off engaging the British enemy at various locations, a colony of wives and children sought refuge at Hampton—relatively isolated from the military action. The dozen or so ladies sheltered there represented something of a Who's Who of South Carolina colonial history. Women with names such as Drayton, Middleton, Rutledge, Izard, and Huger were in attendance at various times.

Hampton's famous portico played an interesting role in the plantation's long story. It may have been built specifically to impress one of Hampton's distinguished early visitors. In 1791, President George Washington made a grand tour through the still very young United States of America. On May 5, according to Washington's own diary, he "breakfasted and dined at Mrs. Horry's about 16 miles from Georgetown." The traditional story is that as the president was brought up the steps of the glorious new portico at Hampton, Mrs. Horry and her mother, along with the youngest Horry daughter, greeted Washington wearing "sashes and bandeaux" handpainted with likenesses of the president.

Another story is that Washington was asked whether a young oak tree growing directly in front of the house should be removed to improve the view. The president is supposed to have suggested the tree be spared, and so it was. At any rate, what remains of a giant old live oak can still be seen today directly in front of the house.

Circumstances found the actual welfare of Hampton Plantation left largely up to the Horry women during the busy years between the Revolution and the beginning of the Civil War. As ownership passed down (and the married name became Rutledge), Hampton faded as a viable agricultural operation.

In 1865, when he was just 22, the young master of Hampton, Henry Middleton Rutledge, joined the 25th Regiment of North Carolina. Eventually, he was elected to lead his unit through the war. Before the war was over, his regiment had suffered 200 killed in action, 280 dead from disease, and 470 wounded, with 140 of those wounded more than once.

Of course, life at Hampton was drastically altered following the war. The family struggled to cope with the financial requirements of maintaining the house, but the altered economic climate made life very difficult. Rice was no longer profitable, and Hampton was too far from the struggling markets to try to raise cotton, corn, or tobacco in any volume. Hampton, during those years, must have presented

quite a strange juxtaposition: the proud, classical portico once surrounded by a formal lawn now planted in string beans and crowded with chickens.

By 1923, both Col. Henry Rutledge and his wife, Margaret Hamilton Seabrook, were dead. Hampton sat empty and neglected for a number of years until 1937, when the colonel's youngest son, Archibald Rutledge, retired to his family's ancestral home.

Archibald Rutledge was a man of letters; he'd published his first book of poetry in 1907. His prowess with poetry and prose always reflected his love and nostalgia for life on the Santee. By 1934, in recognition of his burgeoning literary reputation, Archibald Rutledge was named poet laureate of South Carolina. In 1941, he published his most popular work, Home by the River, in which he described his efforts to restore Hampton Plantation to its former glory. Over the course of more than 30 years, hundreds of visitors were eventually received at Hampton, drawn to the plantation and its owner by the popular works of Archibald Rutledge. By 1971, in failing health, Rutledge sold the house and 75 acres to the state of South Carolina. He died in 1973 and was buried in the family cemetery on Hampton's grounds.

When Hampton Plantation became a state park in 1971, the house had been unoccupied for several years. Initial inspections quickly indicated that an extensive renovation would be absolutely necessary. While documentary research about the house and its owners went on, another story began to unfold—the evolution of the house itself.

The exposed fabric of the house revealed that most of the interior walls had been covered with modern materials at various times over the course of the previous century. As the newer surfaces were removed, the ancient framework of Hampton became exposed. This afforded researchers an excellent opportunity to display sections of the original house as well as the different patterns of modernization and change that evolved in a Lowcountry plantation house on the Santee delta.

Like Drayton Hall on the Ashley River, Hampton Plantation offers visitors an architectural look at the sophisticated lifestyles pursued by some of the Lowcountry's earliest families.

Admission to Hampton Plantation, the state park with its picnic grounds and screened cabanas, is free, and the grounds are open daily from 9:00 A.M. to 6:00 P.M. The house is open Thursday through Monday from Memorial Day through Labor Day from 11:00 A.M. to 4:00 P.M. Admission to the house is $4.00 for adults, $3.00 for youths ages 6 to 15, and free for children younger than 6.

*As you leave Hampton and return to Highway 857, turn right and go about a half-mile. This will bring you to a sandy road leading off to the left. This remote, almost abandoned stretch of wilderness eventually brings you to another early chapel of ease—this one built for the spiritual needs of the planters along the Santee delta.*

*Bear in mind, you're well off the beaten track here. Real Insiders shouldn't be daunted by a lonely, sandy road apparently leading into the pages of history and the beguiling mists of time . . . but we'd better add that if the road is wet and muddy, proceed at your own risk. If you see recent tire tracks, you can be safely encouraged to try it. When you get there, you won't be disappointed.*

## St. James Santee Church
## Off Highway 857

Finding this incredibly sophisticated, earlyw architectural treasure sitting here alone in the apparent wilderness is your first surprise. Your second jolt may be learning it was built (in about 1768) not as the first but as the fourth church to serve St. James Santee Parish. Let this simple fact dramatically emphasize just how important religion was to these early Carolina settlers.

St. James Parish was a thriving neighborhood of planters who petitioned the

church for a "new" chapel that would be more conveniently located near Wambaw Creek. The building eventually provided for them was finished shortly after the completion of St. Michael's in Charleston at Meeting and Broad streets. In fact, the impressive design of St. Michael's may have influenced this structure in that both designs employ the use of two bold, classical porticos. Here the porticos are supported by four gently fluted brick columns complete with brick bases and brick Doric capitals.

If you're lucky, the church will be open, and you can see the high-backed, boxed pews separated by a cross axis of clay tile flooring. If the church isn't open, discreet window peeking is definitely called for.

Amazingly, these beautiful, hand-hewn box pews have never been painted, never in the church's history, although sometime in the 18th century they were rearranged so the chancel might face the east wall. What is now the rear portico has been enclosed as a vestry room, and the simple pulpit on the north wall is a modern replacement, but the general ambience of this little chapel in the wilderness is overwhelmingly authentic.

Sitting here so proudly in this quiet, woodland setting, St. James Santee Church seems to generate its own will to survive. This relic of the Lowcountry's plantation past is so powerful that, although the church's communion silver was stolen during the Civil War, it was quietly returned at a later date.

In the churchyard, barely legible tombstones (best translated by paper rubbings) relate stories of fierce Revolutionary battles and the closely held relationships between the strong early families of the Santee delta.

*Turn around, go back to US 17 and turn right, heading northeast toward Georgetown. At about mile 56, there's a sweeping curve in the road that preludes the delta of the South Santee River and its plantation system. Your vista both to the right and the left is not natural marsh but what remains of vast rice fields, once worked by*

# Angel Oak: A Lowcountry Treasure

Don't laugh, but we're about to suggest taking a drive to the countryside of Johns Island for the sole purpose of seeing . . . a tree.

That's right, a tree. It's an oak tree, but it's a very special one, a very old one, and a very famous one.

The tree is called Angel Oak, and everything about it is pure Lowcountry. No visitor has really seen the Charleston area without making the trip out to the island to be summarily awed and embraced by the Angel Oak's mighty outstretched arms.

Let's start with some background information.

Live oak trees (Quercus virginiana) are native to the Lowcountry and found throughout the area, but they are especially common on the sea islands. During the 18th and 19th centuries, lumber from the live oak forests was highly valued for shipbuilding. In fact, most of the area's

ancient live oaks were harvested during those two centuries.

This live oak, however, survived. Angel Oak has been reported to be in excess of 1,400 years old, although the exact age is difficult to calculate. Very old live oaks are prone to heart rot (they become hollow at the center), which makes core sample ring-counting unreliable. This much is documented: Angel Oak is only 65 feet tall, yet its circumference is 25 ½ feet. The area of shade under this huge canopy is an incredible 17,000 square feet, and the longest outstretched limb reaches out 89 feet and has a circumference of more than 11 feet.

Clearly, the Angel Oak is ancient. It knew the Lowcountry long before the English settlers arrived. It was already an old tree when the Kiawah tribe lived on this land and no doubt enjoyed its shade. It knows more than any of us ever will about hurricanes, wars, fires, earthquakes,

*19th-century slaves when Georgetown was the "Rice Capital of the Carolinas." Just across the high bridge over the North Santee—another branch of the Santee's widespread watershed to the Atlantic—you'll encounter the painted white gates of Hopsewee Plantation on your left.*

**Hopsewee Plantation**
**494 Hopsewee Road**
**12 miles south of Georgetown**
**(843) 546-7891**
**www.hopsewee.com**
Hopsewee Plantation was built in 1740 and

was the birthplace of Thomas Lynch Jr., a signer of the Declaration of Independence. This is the only early rice plantation in Georgetown County that is currently open to the public.

Amazingly, only five families have ever owned Hopsewee. Today, it is owned by Mr. and Mrs. Franklin D. Beattie, who graciously open their home and its grounds to the public. Theirs is a remarkably refreshing attitude toward historic preservation in that the Beattie's actually live in Hopsewee, but with a respect for its place in history.

and time. To see it is to gain worthwhile perspective on the entire Lowcountry environment.

The property where the Angel Oak stands was originally part of a land grant to Abraham Waight in 1717. Waight became a prosperous planter with several plantations in the Lowcountry including one known as the Point, where the Angel Oak stands. The property passed through generations of the Waight family, acquiring the Angel name when Martha Waight married a Justis Angel in 1810.

The Angel family plantation was sold in 1959 to the Mutual Land and Development Corp., but a small parcel of land and the old tree itself were held back and leased to the South Carolina Agricultural Society for $1.00 a year. The society cared for the tree until 1964, when it became the property of an S. E. Felkel, who eventually fenced in the tree and charged visitors a small fee to view it.

The City of Charleston acquired the Angel Oak property in 1991, and it was opened to the public with no admission fee on September 23, 1991. Generations of Charlestonians have journeyed to the property for picnics, family reunions, weddings, and private parties. Permits are required for large events and the consumption of alcoholic beverages at the site.

You won't regret making the effort to visit the old Angel Oak. It's part and parcel of the Lowcountry experience. To get there, take US 17 to Main Road, looking for the signs to Kiawah and Seabrook. After Main Road crosses Maybank Highway to become Bohicket Road, look for Angel Oak Road on your right. Signs mark your route to this magnificent tree of life. For more information, call (843) 559-3496. Admission is still free.

Although the main house at Hopsewee has been modernized for today, it is handsomely furnished with fine antiques and family-owned period furniture that make it very easy to picture life here as it was in Thomas Lynch's day. Be sure to visit the two cookhouses, as so few of them survive today. These are furnished with tools, crockery, and cooking utensils appropriate to their original purpose. It's important to realize that the work in these "dependency" structures—like the backbreaking work done in the rice fields—made the more formal life of the main house possible. Guests are invited to walk along a marked trail past quiet rice fields and the foundations of 18th-and 19th-century slave cabins—mute testimony to the countless African Americans who worked the plantation in another era.

Hopsewee is on the North Santee River overlooking the river's broad, flat delta. Imagine the beautiful views Lynch was able to see every day as he pondered the dangers and daring consequences of national independence.

Hopsewee is open "by chance or by appointment," as their literature puts it, but the Beattie's have a refreshingly generous attitude about sharing their historic property. Chances are you'll find Hopsewee open and well worth the investment of your time. Tours of the house are hourly, and there's a nice gift shop to browse through if you need to wait a few minutes until the next tour. Hopsewee is usually open 9:30 A.M. to 4:30 P.M. Admission is $10.00 for adults and $5.00 for children ages 5 to 17. For carloads entering the grounds but not touring the house, the fee is $5.00.

*Continuing north on US 17 for about 12 more miles past Hopsewee Plantation, you'll cross a high bridge over the Sampit River and pass a large industrial complex, the recently reopened Georgetown Steel Corporation, on your right. Then, once in Georgetown proper, turn right off US 17, and you'll quickly find yourself downtown.*

# Georgetown

More than any other South Carolina community of its size, age, and historical importance, Georgetown is respectful of its past. What the visitor sees here today—streets and streets lined by charming 18th- and 19th-century homes—reflects this consciousness quite beautifully.

Several preservation organizations in the community can share credit for this effort. They include the Georgetown County Historical Society, the Georgetown County Historical Commission, and the Historic Georgetown County Foundation. These groups were instrumental in collecting data pertaining to the community, marking and preserving historic homes and sites, and educating new generations about the former rice capital of the Carolinas.

Downtown Georgetown was recently revitalized and now has interesting shops and restaurants backed up against the once-bustling riverfront docks. At the intersection of Front and Scriven Streets, you'll see an interesting old brick building with a clock tower. This is Georgetown's famous Rice Museum—a great first stop in your search to understand the giant rice industry that made Georgetown the thriving agricultural focus of the Lowcountry.

## Rice Museum
**633 Front Street, Georgetown**
**(843) 546-7423**
**www.ricemuseum.com**
The real story of the rice culture of Georgetown County is one of the most exciting and colorful chapters in the history of South Carolina—maybe even in the whole history of American agriculture. It's all been captured here in the Rice Museum through fascinating maps, pictures, artifacts, exhibits, and intricate dioramas that portray a rice crop from planting through processing and eventual shipment to markets all over the world.

The Rice Museum is in the Old Market Building, which locals call "the town clock." This clock tower has become the architectural symbol of Georgetown, and this is an appropriate place to browse through booklets and tourist information pertaining to Georgetown County.

Look for the exhibit called "The Brown's Ferry Vessel." This is what remains of an early commercial river vessel that plied the waters of the Carolina coast during the first half of the 18th century. Heretofore, very little has been learned about South Carolina river vessels of this early period. This one, which was carrying a load of bricks when it sank near Brown's Ferry in about 1740, has been excavated from its longtime resting place in a riverbank and laboriously preserved for this display. The remaining sections of its hull and keel shed invaluable light on a dimly lit facet of the Lowcountry's transportation history. There you'll also find a 15-minute video presentation called "Garden of Gold," which beautifully illustrates the area's rice culture. The gallery is open from 10:00 A.M. to 4:00 P.M. Monday through Saturday.

Museum hours are 10:00 A.M. to 4:30 P.M., Monday through Saturday. Admission is $7.00 for adults, $5.00 for seniors, and

$3.00 for students 6 to 21. Admission is free for children 5 and younger. Members of the museum get in free. Admission to the next-door gallery, which features changing exhibits of paintings, crafts, and sculpture relating to Georgetown, is free.

*Eighteen miles north of Georgetown, still on US 17, is the entrance to another adventure, Brookgreen Gardens. Rest assured it's well worth the long drive.*

**Brookgreen Gardens**
**US 17, Georgetown**
**(843) 235–6000, (800) 849–1931**
**www.brookgreen.com**
Brookgreen Gardens plugs nicely into the plantation theme of this day trip in that the property encompasses four 18th- and 19th-century plantations: the Oaks, Springfield, Laurel Hill, and (old) Brookgreen. But since the late 1920s, agriculture has hardly been the primary harvest here. Instead, Brookgreen now has 350 acres of beautifully landscaped gardens specifically designed to display more than 500 pieces of outdoor sculpture, all created by leading American artists of the 19th and 20th centuries.

Brookgreen Gardens was the brainchild of noted American sculptor Anna Hyatt Huntington, who, with her late husband, philanthropist Archer M. Huntington, planned and endowed a museum back in the 1930s. Today the property is managed by a private organization, Brookgreen Gardens, a Society for the Southeastern Flora and Fauna. You may choose to get an initial orientation at the visitors pavilion for an overview of the property, or you may want to wander the seemingly endless paths and encounter the breathtaking sculpture by surprise. Brookgreen has a tour boat that takes guests four times daily on a brief trip out into the swamp waters and estuaries. There's also a nature area where wild animals native to these plantations are housed and viewable in natural settings.

Brookgreen's hours are 9:30 A.M. to 5:00 P.M. every day except Christmas. They have extended hours during the summer season. Admission is $12 for adults and teens, $10 for seniors and students ages 13 to 18, and it's free to children 12 and younger. It's also free for members of the Brookgreen Society.

*To return to Charleston, follow U.S. Highway 17 S. back to Mt. Pleasant, and cross the Cooper River bridge into the city.*

## SUMMERVILLE, FLOWERTOWN IN THE PINES

Our second day trip suggestion is perfect for either a crisp spring afternoon or one of those Lowcountry summer scorchers that's so hot you will gain a true appreciation for the natural wonder that is your destination. We're headed to Summerville, the Flowertown in the Pines.

If you're coming from Charleston along Highway 61 (the old Ashley River Road), veer to the right on Bacons Bridge Road, which is Highway 165. This will lead you into Summerville at S. Main Street (U.S. Highway 17-A). If you're arriving via Interstate 26 from Charleston, take the second Summerville exit onto US 17-A, then follow the signs.

In Summerville, you're 25 miles inland from the Atlantic Ocean on a ridge that's just 75 feet above sea level. The longleaf pine forest all around you helps keep temperatures moderate and the air freshly scented with refreshing pine vapors borne on soft sea breezes.

These are the basic elements that first attracted a few planter families to build summer camps in this pineland spot away from the mosquitoes and deadly swamp fevers that plagued the lower areas. The first few families to establish summer homes in Summerville settled between the end of the Revolutionary War and 1790. By 1828, there were 23 houses in the village. Two years later, a chapel of ease to St. Paul's Episcopal Church was built, indicating a growing desire of some families to maintain full-time residences there. The summer homes were often built high on

*Try to be especially patient in Charleston traffic during April, May, and June. That's when Charleston's spring flowers are in bloom (bringing thousands of visitors), and Spoleto Festival USA is going full tilt. Traffic can be especially heavy during these months, and the city's narrow streets are easily overwhelmed by the volume.*

pilings with large, wraparound porches to catch the breezes. Today, you still find many of them scattered in the half-mile Old Town area around St. Paul's Episcopal Church.

By 1832, the South Carolina Railroad had come to Summerville, and the new areas of growth (unlike Old Town) had the benefit of better planning. There were regularly spaced streets running parallel to and at right angles with the train tracks. A large, open space was reserved for a town square, and today's town hall overlooks that site. Victorian commercial buildings soon sprang up around the square, and many of them are still standing. With its umbilical railroad connection to Charleston at last in place, the once sleepy village started to grow rapidly, and in 1847, Summerville was incorporated.

A series of fever epidemics struck Charleston during the late 1850s, sending even more new residents to this relatively disease-free locale. As a Charleston newspaper lamented during those difficult years, "The eyes of Charleston sadly turned toward Summerville . . . " By 1860, the population had grown to 1,088 residents—548 white, 540 black.

The Civil War brought an abrupt end to Summerville's growth and prosperity. Not until the end of the century would the town see another boom. When it did come, however, it would bring the pineland village international fame.

In 1889, a world congress of specialists in respiratory diseases met in Paris and named Summerville, South Carolina, of all places, one of the two best resort areas in

the world for the cure of lung and throat disorders. This widely publicized "Tuberculosis Congress" introduced a whole new era for Summerville. Special excursion trains came in from New York and St. Louis, and numerous establishments were built to accommodate the flood of health-minded visitors. The grandest of these lodges was the Pine Forest Inn (unfortunately, no longer standing), where President Theodore Roosevelt, among other luminaries, stayed.

But alas, the fame of Summerville as a health resort waned with the coming of the Depression. However, post–World War II prosperity in the Lowcountry gave the town new reason to succeed.

Summerville has traditionally been known as a center for azalea culture. The lushly landscaped gardens and homes all seem to be extensions of the city's own Azalea Park, which is a focal point on the town's Main Street. Come spring of every year, Summerville still earns the title "Flowertown in the Pines." What follows are listings that give information on places and events you will want to see on your visit to Summerville, including an auto tour of more than a dozen architecturally significant homes.

### Greater Summerville Chamber of Commerce
**402 North Main Street**
**(843) 873–8535, (866) 875–8535**
**www.greatersummerville.org**
Day trippers to Summerville may first want to check in at the city's chamber of commerce, located right on Main Street near Town Square. This green-roofed building serves as a mini welcome center with newcomer information, maps, brochures, and friendly advice. It is open Monday through Friday from 9:00 A.M. until 5:00 P.M., Saturday from 10:00 A.M. to 3:00 P.M., and Sunday 1:00 to 4:00 P.M.

### Summerville-Dorchester Museum
**100 East Doty Avenue**
**(843) 875-9666**
The Summerville-Dorchester Museum is an

easy walk from the chamber offices, and it is another must-see on your visit to Summerville. Officially opened in 1993 for the Flowertown Festival (see the following listing), this museum gives visitors a fascinating look at the city's and the county's past. The inspiration was simple enough— it was intended to be a place where the area's children could learn about their own hometown, and visitors could see some of the area's rich and romantic past. You'll find local fossils, natural history, memorabilia from an earlier Summerville, and photographic displays tracking the city and Dorchester County from the days following the Great Earthquake of 1886 to the present. There is a special emphasis on the area's historic architecture and Summerville's many memorable characters.

The building was formerly a police station and is in the same block as the chamber of commerce, less than a block from Town Square. Admission is $2.00 for adults, and $1.00 for children. Under age 5, it's free. Museum hours are Thursday through Saturday 10:00 A.M. to 2:00 P.M. They're closed during the month of August.

### Flowertown Festival
### Various sites
### (843) 873-2931

If you're lucky enough to be stopping in town sometime around Easter, chances are you'll see vestiges of Summerville's biggest annual bash, the Flowertown Festival. The entire town participates in this gala, planned for when the town is ablaze with color, and the area's spectacular azaleas, camellias, and dogwoods are all in bloom.

The fun has been going on each spring since 1973 and includes concerts, dancing, a food fair, a health fair, kiddie rides, historic house tours, and craft exhibits of all kinds. In fact, the Flowertown Festival (originally sponsored as a fund-raiser for the Summerville Family YMCA) is highly regarded in craft circles up and down the Eastern Seaboard. The quality of crafts traditionally displayed here is exceptional.

Each year, tens of thousands of visitors celebrate spring in the Lowcountry by attending the three-day event. The atmosphere is like an old-fashioned country fair. For more details, call or write the chamber at P.O. Drawer 670, Summerville 29484. Check out the Chamber of Commerce Web site, too, at www.greatersummerville.org. (Also, see the Annual Events chapter for more on the festival.)

If, however, the calendar finds you in Summerville when the flowers are not quite so showy, don't fret. There's more to see in this special little town. The following driving tour will take you through the Old Town section of Summerville, with its winding streets, architecturally significant homes, and gleaming aura of uniqueness.

# Summerville's Old Town

The cool, shady streets of this part of Summerville recall the days when this was a hot-weather retreat for wealthy planters. The charming homes and well-kept gardens seem little changed from those days in the mid-1800s.

*For a nice driving tour, turn from US 17-A—Main Street—onto West Carolina Avenue and begin at St. Paul's Episcopal Church. The church parking lot is a good place to pause and get your bearings.*

### St. Paul's Episcopal Church
### 316 West Carolina Avenue
### (843) 873-1991
### www.stpaulssummerville.org

The history of St. Paul's Episcopal Church dates back to 1828, when the Rev. Philip Gadsden, rector of another Lowcountry chapel of ease, followed the growing number of communicants moving to the thriving village of Summerville.

Services were first held in the leaky old village hall or a parishioner's residence, but in 1829 a decision was made to build a proper house of worship. The first church building, dedicated in 1832, stood just a few feet south of the present structure, but Summerville's rapid growth soon made this simple wooden building inadequate for the growing number of believers. By 1857 a new church (the present structure) was built at a cost of $5,000.

The terrible earthquake that rocked the Lowcountry on the night of August 31, 1886, badly damaged the building, but somehow the sturdy church survived. Inside, you can still note the metal earthquake rods running through the structure for reinforcement.

There was a move in the early 20th century to replace the building with a more modern structure. Fortunately, those plans were never realized. Today St. Paul's rector, vestry, and congregation work to preserve the old church, an architectural focal point for Old Town and Summerville.

*Exit the church parking lot left onto Gadsden Street, which will take you back to West Carolina Avenue. Take a right, then an immediate left onto Sumter Avenue, where in a few short blocks you will encounter at least 13 architecturally significant homes or "cottages" dating from the mid- to late-19th century. What follows are brief descriptions of the homes, arranged in geographical order for a brief but pleasant driving tour past some of the most charming houses of Summerville's Old Town.*

### Gelzer Brothers House (ca. 1819)
### 413 Sumter Avenue

This home, like several others on this end of Sumter Avenue, was actually built facing a street that's no longer in existence. You're viewing what was originally the rear of this very early Summerville dwelling.

### Brailsford-Browning House (ca. 1830)
### 408 Sumter Avenue

Here is an example of early Summerville architecture in which the house is lifted high off the ground to catch cool breezes. The lower area was once open; the present enclosure was added after 1915. Early records show this house was occupied in

1838 by a Dr. W. M. Brailsford, when it was listed among 29 houses in the growing village of Summerville.

### Brownfield House (ca. 1875)
### 320 Sumter Avenue

This residence belonged to the Brownfield family, who built on the site of a defunct boarding school for girls known as the Brownfield Academy. In 1893, the school was advertised as "particularly desirable for Northern young ladies with impaired health who would probably be successful in following their studies in this health-giving climate."

### Buckheit House (ca. 1884)
### 317 Sumter Avenue

Existing documentation indicates that, in 1862, a baker from Charleston named Philip Buckheit bought this land. Perhaps because of the war, he didn't actually build his house until more than two decades later.

### Disher House (ca. 1862)
### 303 Sumter Avenue

Deeds for this property go back to 1862 when Robert W. Disher bought 2 acres of land from A. W. Taylor. Disher's house (and presence) on this site must have been noteworthy, as the adjoining road, now called Charleston Street, was formerly known as Disher Street.

### William Prioleau House (1896)
### 302 Sumter Avenue

Built by Charleston druggist William H. Prioleau, this is one of the many Victorian homes built during the big health resort boom around the turn of the century. The lacy architectural style is called Queen Anne.

### Kinloch House (ca. 1861)
### 233 Sumter Avenue

This house was built in 1861, shortly after the shelling of Fort Sumter in Charleston Harbor, on land formerly owned by the Rev. Philip Gadsden, first rector of St. Paul's Episcopal Church.

## Purcell House (ca. 1820)
### 224 Sumter Avenue
Records date this home to between 1811 and 1828. The architecture is typical of the very early hunting lodges or summer homes built by nearby planters.

## Preference (ca. 1885)
### 223 Sumter Avenue
Note the West Indian character of this home. The broad porches and high elevation would have offered friendly shade and cool breezes to residents and guests.

Although the exact date of construction is unknown, this handsome Victorian house is thought to have been built for one Mary Webb around 1885. As for the unusual name, it seems that after the Civil War, many summer homes took on the names of the owner's former plantations, most of which were lost or sold after the conflict.

## Charles Boyle House (ca. 1888)
### 220 Sumter Avenue
This house was built by Summerville attorney Charles Boyle around 1888 on land that at one time straddled the Colleton-Berkeley county line.

## Samuel Prioleau House (1887)
### 217 Sumter Avenue
This was the home of Dr. Samuel Prioleau, in whose honor the first Summerville infirmary was named. The land was given to the doctor's wife by her mother, Mrs. Benjamin Rhett, who lived next door.

## Rhett House (1882)
### 205 Sumter Avenue
Dr. Benjamin Rhett served as a surgeon for the Confederacy and later practiced medicine in Summerville. His Victorian house was built on land that was once owned by the South Carolina Canal and Railroad Co. during Summerville's first boom days in the 1830s.

## Samuel Lord–Elizabeth Arden House (1891)
### 208 Sumter Avenue
This handsome Victorian house was built for Samuel Lord in 1891 by the same contractor who built the town's celebrated Pine Forest Inn. With its three stories and impressive double piazzas, the ornate house was purchased in 1938 by Elizabeth Arden, the famous cosmetics magnate, who used it as her winter retreat. It remained in her possession until 1954.

*To return to Charleston, stay to the right on Sumter Avenue until it intersects with West Fifth Street at the First Baptist Church. Turn right and follow West Fifth back to Main Street, take a left and follow US 17-A through town until you see signs for Interstate 26 S. That will be your quickest route back to Charleston.*

# A WALK ON THE WILD SIDE

### Marrington Watchable Wildlife Trail
### Charleston Naval Weapons Station, Goose Creek
In a city famous for its bittersweet history and sophisticated architecture, it's easy to follow that same suit when you go afield in search of some Lowcountry day trip adventures. The previous sojourns (to the fishing village of McClellanville and the quaint metropolis of Georgetown) basically offer more of the same with a country flavor. So, for the sake of variety and an adventure into another world, here's a day trip expressly for nature lovers, serious birders, wildlife photographers, and anyone who wants an up-close and personal look at the Lowcountry's true environment—the Carolina wetlands.

Marrington Plantation is on land now owned by the Charleston Naval Weapons Station outside the town of Goose Creek. It was a typical working plantation during colonial times. In the late 1600s, when rice was introduced to this area and became a major cash crop, this was only one of hundreds of rice operations flourishing here. By the 1850s, more than 150,000 Lowcountry acres were under rice cultivation.

Rice fields were man-made. They comprised an elaborate system of dikes and canals used to control different water levels needed for planting, growing, and harvesting the rice. Today, many of those agricultural fields—long since gone feral—have become natural wetlands, teeming with wildlife.

Under the Navy's Natural Resources Program and its local initiative dubbed "Watchable Wildlife," some of Marrington Plantation's former rice fields (not used for any military purposes) were developed in 1995 as a self-guided nature trail for the public. The mile-long trail opened in 1997 and includes more than 1,200 feet of boardwalk that winds its way around several ponds.

Today, these ponds offer a natural habitat for wading birds, migratory waterfowl, alligators, eagles, hawks, wood ducks, snakes, turtles, frogs, and insects. White-tailed deer, river otters, gray squirrels, and other wildlife can sometimes be seen there too.

Even winter visitors are treated to many of the Lowcountry's natural delights. Look for egrets, herons, and ring-necked ducks. But lower temperatures usually drive the alligators and snakes out of view for the Lowcountry's short cold season. (This may or may not come as welcome news to hard-core nature lovers.)

Two observation towers offer a panoramic view of the 1,000-acre plantation, and 27 numbered stations serve as markers along the way—each with a corresponding paragraph in an accompanying brochure that explains the cultural and natural history of each feature.

To find this nifty natural diversion, take I-26 to the Goose Creek/Moncks Corner exit (at Northwoods Mall) and follow Highway 52 about 2 miles, past a number of auto dealerships and commercial buildings. Turn right on Snake Road (which crosses the Goose Creek Reservoir), and turn right, again, onto Redbank Road (County Road 29). You'll pass several signs announcing the Naval Weapons Station, and after 2 miles or so you'll see a large green sign for Marrington Plantation. Follow the dirt road to the parking lot, where you'll see the trail's starting point and some accompanying brochures for interpretation. A tip to the wise: Pack plenty of insect repellent for this outing.

## THE STORY OF SANTEE CANAL

**Old Santee Canal State Park**
**900 Stony Landing Road,**
**Moncks Corner**
**(843) 899-5200**
**www.oldsanteecanalpark.org**
Another fun day-trip adventure is to Old Santee Canal State Park, a wonderful addition to the South Carolina park system just 45 minutes from Charleston. Opened about a decade ago, Old Santee Canal State Park interprets the building and operation of America's first man-made inland waterway.

To find this colorful and kid-friendly park, take I-26 north from Charleston to exit 208 (Highway 52), then follow Highway 52 about 18 miles past Goose Creek and into Moncks Corner. Two miles down the main road of the town (Highway 52), look for an Old Santee State Park sign on the right. Plan to bring a picnic basket (rain or shine—there's a large, covered picnic area with tables) and spend your day absorbing the tranquil inland beauty.

Santee Canal was America's first summit canal, a type of canal that uses a multi-lock system to raise and lower cargo-laden barges. It was praised as a great engineering and economic development in the 1800s. The canal provided a cost-efficient, dependable way to ship crops between the uplands and the coast. While ideas for such a solution had been tossed about as early as the 1700s, the Revolutionary War intervened, and it was not until 1793 that construction actually began. Seven years and $650,000 later, with the labor of 700 men who worked with shovels and picks, a canal 22 miles long, 30 feet wide, and 5 feet deep was a reality.

At first, mules and horses walked alongside the canal and pulled the heavy barges or boats with their cargo. Later, crewmen with poles replaced the beasts. In all, there were 16 years of profitable operation before severe droughts in 1817 and 1819 dried up the canal and ended operations for the time being. The rains returned, and 1830 was the canal's busiest year, with 700 cotton-heavy barges passing through the waterway.

Progress in transportation technology within the state spelled disaster for the canal, however, when a railway between Columbia and Charleston was completed in 1840 and took a substantial portion of the canal's business. The final blow came in 1846, when the railroad tracks were laid to Camden. In 1850, the shareholders threw in the towel.

Today, most of the canal is covered by the waters of Lake Moultrie. But where the still waters of Biggin Creek and the nearby swamps intersect with the southernmost section of the canal, the South Carolina Department of Parks, Recreation, and Tourism has created the Old Santee Canal State Park. Included in the park is the plan-tation house at Stony Landing bluff, built after 1840 by John Dawson. The house—restored and open to the public free of charge—faces Tail Race Canal (flowing from the Santee Cooper lakes, created during the 1940s). Throughout the 19th century, cement and building blocks were made here, and during the Civil War, gun-powder was manufactured.

After a house tour, a good place to get oriented is the park's interpretive center. There are nifty exhibits showing the canal in different phases, a 30-foot simulated oak tree with man-made wildlife inhabi-tants (we bet you can't tell the difference!), and a cave. Short films about canals and the environment are also up-to-date and well-done. If it's a pretty day, we suggest a hike on a nature trail—either the swamp walk, the creek walk, or the canal walk—or renting a canoe.

The park is open from 9:00 A.M. to 5:00 P.M. For more information, call or write Old Santee Canal State Park, 900 Stony Landing Road, Moncks Corner 29461. Admission is $3.00 for adults; sen-iors age 65 plus pay $2.00; children age 6 and younger get in free.

# PARKS AND RECREATION

The warm climate and natural resources of the Lowcountry make recreation and physical fitness top priorities with locals. This chapter deals specifically with some of the things we do for fitness and fun and offers a sampling of the public places designated for them. Spectator sports, boating and watersports, fishing, hunting, and golf are detailed in separate chapters due to the immense popularity and numerous outlets for these recreational activities.

As you will see reflected in many of the listings in this chapter, the Charleston County Park and Recreation Commission and Charleston County Community Education Program provide wonderful opportunities for recreation. The school programs are set up at public schools after regular hours to serve adults and sometimes children who are interested in non-credit self-enhancement courses. For detailed information, write to Adult and Community Education Programs, Charleston County School District, 75 Calhoun Street, Charleston 29403 (the phone is 843-937-6421, or call Charleston County Park and Recreation Commission at (843) 762-2172. Free brochures on recreational opportunities are often available at one of the public libraries.

The following is an overview of specific places, organizations, and businesses that keep the fun flowing through the Lowcountry. The listings will let you know how to go about participating in some of the Trident's most popular recreational activities. We start off with descriptions (arranged geographically) of the public parks and recreation centers where you and your family can fashion your own fun. Then we get more specific, breaking down

information on individual recreational pursuits by type of activity (arranged alphabetically).

## PARKS AND RECREATION CENTERS

The parks we like best are sizable tracts of land that give young and old alike a chance to enjoy the great outdoors. We make a distinction here between "park" and "playground" because, although the former may include the latter, "park" implies more space and characteristics that appeal to both children and adults. We list several playgrounds under a separate heading later in the chapter. For more information on the public parks, call the City of Charleston Department of Parks and Recreation, (843) 724-7327. Call the same number if you would like to schedule a special event at one of the parks.

Also included here are several community center complexes scattered throughout the Lowcountry. These offer various indoor activities, usually at a bargain price. All listings are arranged geographically, starting with parks and centers in Charleston and East Cooper (including Mt. Pleasant, Sullivan's Island, and Isle of Palms). Then we go to West Ashley and James, Folly, and Kiawah Islands. Welcome to a few of our favorite places.

## Downtown Charleston

Officially this subject comes under the auspices of the City of Charleston Department of Parks and Recreation. It offers an extensive program of activities, sports, special events, and multigenerational recreation for residents and visitors. Here are the best-known spots.

**Hampton Park**
**30 Mary Murray Drive**
**(843) 724-7327**
**www.charlestoncity.info**
Near the Citadel, Hampton Park is a 60-acre downtown park with a lake (complete with lots of resident ducks for feeding), one of the largest rose gardens in the state, grassy areas, a trail for workouts, a bandstand (the site of many an afternoon concert), and even the police department's horse stables (sorry, no touching). A giant Easter egg hunt and the Piccolo Spoleto finale are held here. Sometimes the park is closed off (usually Tuesday and Thursday evenings from April to September and Saturday mornings year-round) for walkers, runners, joggers, skaters, and bikers—a great traffic-free treat for city kids and their parents. (For more, see the Kidstuff chapter.)

**Waterfront Park**
**Cumberland Street to**
**North Adgers Wharf**
**(843) 724-7327**
**www.charlestoncity.info**
Just off East Bay Street, from Cumberland Street to North Adgers Wharf, this is one of the city's most popular and most delightful parks. On site are a 400-foot pier for viewing harbor activity and two inviting fountains in which the young and young-at-heart are allowed to play. You'll also enjoy grassy areas and swings. (See the Kidstuff chapter.)

**White Point Gardens**
**South tip of East Bay and King Streets**
**(843) 724-7327**
**www.charlestoncity.info**
At the tip of the Peninsula, boxed in by East Bay Street, Murray Boulevard, King Street, and South Battery, White Point Gardens has a beautiful view of the harbor and some of the homes of the Battery. Children love to climb on the old

cannons (and stacked cannonballs) or picnic in the grassy areas. You may even catch a glimpse of a bride and groom exchanging vows here in the old bandstand. It is often crowded on Sunday when the weather is nice, but is less so during the week. (For more on the history of White Point Gardens, see the History chapter; see Kidstuff for more on fun activities.)

# Mt. Pleasant

**Alhambra Park**
**131 Middle Street, Mt. Pleasant**
**(843) 884-2528**
**www.townofmountpleasant.com**
This simple, lovely park across from Alhambra Hall is wide open with free public admission from sunup to sundown. It offers a nice lawn and scenic view of Charleston Harbor. The selection of playground equipment (swings, slides, climbing toys, and a merry-go-round) keeps the children busy. For picnics, there are several tables under the shade of big oaks.

**Mt. Pleasant Recreation Department**
**at Park West**
**1251 Park West Boulevard, Mt. Pleasant**
**(843) 856-2196**
**www.mtpleasantrec.com**
Located just off U.S. Highway 17 in the Park West development is this new 59-acre sports and recreational complex built to serve the new communities in the upper part of Mt. Pleasant. The Park West facility has a 6,000-square-foot program building with lots of parking, lighting, and fields for baseball, softball, soccer, football, and other activities sponsored by the Mt. Pleasant Recreation Department. (See the following listing on the Richard L. Jones Recreation Complex for more on the programs.) With Mt. Pleasant's rapid population growth along U.S. 17 and Highway 41, this complex is expected to serve about 30,000 people in the area. The fourth and final phase of construction, scheduled for completion in spring 2004,

## CLOSE-UP

# A rose . . . is a rose . . . is a rose . . .

Anyone who spends any time at all in Charleston's Hampton Park will be dazzled by the ancient trees, the handsome bandstand, lovely duck pond, and refreshing fountain arranged on the pastoral grounds. In fact, the park was originally landscaped by the firm of Frederick Law Olmsted, the brilliant designer of New York's Central Park. It was all part of Charleston's 1902 "would-be" Worlds Fair, the once-glittering South Carolina Interstate and West Indian Exposition—an ill-fated enterprise that drew little attention to the city at the time. Even less of Olmsted's original plan survives today, but Hampton Park remains a pleasant oasis of beauty on the city's east side.

Ringing the park is an exercise path, part of which passes one of the city's most impressive rose gardens, and among the colorful hybrids and showy cabbage roses is a shy, pink beauty that is Charleston's very own.

In 1802, a wealthy Charleston plantation owner and plant enthusiast named

John Champneys crossed two roses to produce what he called "Champneys' Pink Cluster." One of the roses he used for his experiment was called "Old Blush," a rose given to him by French-born horticulturalist Philippe Noissette. When the seeds of "Pink Cluster" found their way to Paris and were raised by Noissette's brother, the name evolved into "Blush Noisette"—a whole new class of roses that soon became extremely popular throughout the continent. Today, Noisette roses are grown all over the world.

Of the 80 different Noisettes marketed worldwide, Hampton Park is currently growing nearly 50 as part of a special scientific study. A conference of rose experts recently gathered in Charleston and attracted visitors from as far away as South Africa, Australia, Germany, Bermuda, and France—all here to see Hampton Park's famous Noisette roses. True beauty is timeless, it seems, and apparently knows no bounds.

will include two tennis courts, an asphalt walking trail, a six-lane, 25-meter pool, another baseball field, playground equipment, and an additional 1,400-square-foot program building. This is Mt. Pleasant's largest and finest recreational offering.

**Palmetto Islands County Park**
**444 Needlerush Parkway**
**(843) 884-0832**
**www.ccprc.com**
This family-oriented, 943-acre nature facil-

ity is in a heavily wooded area, with a 2-acre pond and 1-mile canoe trail. You'll enjoy a well-designed playground, picnic sites, and boat docks. It is a perfect place to jog, walk, or rent a pedal boat or a bike. Rates are $4.00 per half-hour for boats (plus a $2.00 deposit) and $4.00 an hour or $10.00 for a full day on a bike (again, add in a $2.00 deposit). Splash Island, with its 200-foot water slide, is quite popular in the warm months. Park admission is $1.00 per person (no charge for children younger than 3) with an annual individual pass available for $15.00 for Charleston County residents, $25.00 for nonresidents. Additional fees ($5.99 for Charleston County residents and $4.99 for children under 42 inches tall; $6.99 for nonresidents) are charged for entry to Splash Island. Annual family and senior passes are available also. (For more on this park, see the Kidstuff and Boating and Watersports chapters.)

### Richard L. Jones Recreation Complex
**391 Egypt Road, Mt. Pleasant**
**(843) 884-2528,**
**(843) 884-2278, ext. 6773**
**www.mtpleasantrec.com**
Opened in March 1991, this large, modern building provides a facility for scheduled recreation programs, a gymnasium, a six-lane pool, and an activity room. There is a one-year membership fee of $2.00 each for everyone 5 and older. The pool usage fee is $2.00 a day, but it's free for children younger than 5. Non–Mt. Pleasant residents pay $100 for an annual family membership. There are separate fees for T-ball, softball, basketball, baseball, track, soccer, and a supervised skate park. Crafts, painting, dance and theater classes, swimming lessons, and gymnastics camps (half-day and full-day) are some of the activities offered. The buddy softball, basketball, and soccer leagues provide the opportunity for children with disabilities to play with children their own age. The hotline number, the second one listed previously, gives more information on programs, athletics, and current events.

## Sullivan's Island, Isle of Palms

### Isle of Palms County Park
**1-14th Avenue, Isle of Palms**
**(843) 886-3863**
**www.ccprc.com**
Everyone can hit the beach straight off

*After finishing lunch at one of the fine restaurants scattered along East Bay Street, take a stroll through Charleston's Waterfront Park. It's safe, nearby, and perfect for "taking the air," as the old-timers in this area might put it.*

the Isle of Palms Connector at one of the newer county parks. Enjoy one of the area's nicest beaches, open daily year-round, with the convenience of paved parking, outdoor showers, restrooms, a sand volleyball court, and children's play area. Just in case you forget your beach gear, you'll find chairs, umbrellas, bicycles, and boogie boards available for rent. The summer season hours are 9:00 A.M. to 7:00 P.M. with lifeguards on duty. The park is open daily from 10:00 A.M. to 6:00 P.M. in April, September, and October; and the November through March hours are 10:00 A.M. to 5:00 P.M. Admission is $5.00 per car, $10.00 per camper, and $20.00 per bus. (See the Kid-Friendly Beaches section of the Kidstuff chapter for more information.)

### Isle of Palms Recreation Department
**24-28th Avenue, Isle of Palms**
**(843) 886-8294**
**www.iop.net**
This comprehensive facility includes a big playground (complete with separate equipment and areas for different ages), a volleyball court, athletic fields (for soccer, football, and kickball), baseball fields, tennis courts, and basketball courts. An indoor center houses night basketball courts, tumbling equipment, Ping-Pong tables, and more. There are also sheltered tables and grills for picnics.

The department sponsors special programs, such as a summer day camp, youth dances, and a senior citizens group, and organizes events such as kite-flying and sand-sculpting contests. And bring your favorite canine friend to the Bark Park on 29th Avenue behind the recreation center.

*It's a Charleston tradition to enjoy an oyster roast at sunset along some Lowcountry creek when there's a nip in the air. Locals like their oysters with crackers and cocktail sauce with a pinch of horseradish.*

The park is open from sunup to sundown; the recreation building is open from 9:00 A.M. to 5:00 P.M. (with the kids' programs in the morning) Monday through Friday and from 1:00 until 5:00 P.M. on Saturday and Sunday.

### Sullivan's Island Park
**1610 Middle Street, Sullivan's Island**
**(843) 883-3198**

Sullivan's Island has a nice park at the Mound (constructed by the military during World War II) on Middle Street between stations 20 ½ and 22 (street names on Sullivan's are based on the old streetcar station stops). There is a bandstand, plus basketball courts, two tennis courts, and children's wooden play equipment in a fenced-in tot lot (see the Kidstuff chapter). Although there is no official recreation department on Sullivan's Island, one member of the town council serves as head of recreation.

# West Ashley

### Caw Caw Interpretive Center
**5200 Savannah Highway, Ravenel**
**(843) 889-8898**
**www.ccprc.com**

A bit further out, but worth the trip (about 15 miles south of Charleston on U.S. Highway 17 S.), is the Caw Caw Interpretive Center in Ravenel, South Carolina. Part of the Charleston County Park system, this 654-acre park is managed specifically for birds and wildlife. There are 7 miles of interpretive trails, a 1,200-foot swamp boardwalk, and a bird and butterfly garden. Loads of educational programs, daily walks, workshops, and demonstrations complete the natural, cultural, and historical experience. Admission is $1.00 and free for children 2 and under. Pets and bicycles are not permitted. Hours are 9:00 A.M. to 5:00 P.M. Saturday and Sunday and 9:00 A.M. to 3:00 P.M. Wednesday through Friday. The park is closed on Monday and Tuesday.

### Charles Towne Landing State Historic Site
**U.S. Highway 171, Charleston**
**(843) 852-4200**
**www.southcarolinaparks.com**

In West Ashley, this is a wonderful, low-key park for all ages on the site of the original settlement called Charles Towne. There is an animal forest, playground, replica of the ship *Adventure,* early settlement village, gift shop, restaurant, and even a movie, *Carolina,* about the history of the Lowcountry. It shows every half-hour. You can rent bikes for a $3.00 deposit plus $3.00 per hour. Ask about the annual bike passes for $10 and vehicle passes for $50 (good at any state park). They are good deals if you are going to be spending lots of time here. (For more on Charles Towne Landing, see the Attractions, History, and Kidstuff chapters.)

### West Ashley Park
**3600 Mary Ader Avenue, Charleston**
**(843) 724-7327**
**www.charlestoncity.info**

The new, 270-acre West Ashley Park includes four baseball and soccer fields, bicycle and pedestrian trails, picnic areas, a playground, and restrooms. The $4-million facility is, in fact, the largest of all the City of Charleston's parks. The unusual concept of this park is that it will remain largely undeveloped, allowing residents "to get away from the city without leaving the city." The pedestrian trails wind through the woods and along Church Creek, giving visitors a change of pace (and vista) from nearby suburbia. Fishing is a pleasant pastime in the park's large lake surrounding a 10-acre island accessible by footbridge. The playground has a tot lot with a giant slide popular with the little ones. Ask about special recreation programs offered on a seasonal basis, such as canoeing, by calling the number above. The park is open 8:00 A.M. until dusk.

# James Island

**James Island County Park**
**871 Riverland Drive, Charleston**
**(843) 795-7275**
**www.ccprc.com**
This incredible, 643-acre park offers biking, nature trails, a climbing wall, an elaborate playground, pedal boats, kayaks, Hydrobikes, 16 acres of lagoons, a Spray-Play fountain area, a fishing and crabbing dock, and picnic areas. There are 10 vacation cottages, camping sites (see "Camping" later in this chapter), and three picnic shelters that can accommodate 200 or more people each. Admission is $1.00 per person (no charge for children younger than 3). Individual passes are $15 for Charleston County residents; $25 for nonresidents. The ever-popular Splash Zone costs an additional $7.99 (residents) and $6.99 for children under 42 inches tall or $9.99 (nonresidents), but most agree it is well worth the price to escape to the land of the tropics via slides, waterfalls, and spray effects (see our Kidstuff chapter). Annual family and senior passes are also available.

# Folly Beach

**Folly Beach County Park**
**1100 West Ashley Avenue**
**(843) 588-2426**
**www.ccprc.com**
At the tip of Folly Beach, this county park is an easy-to-reach, family-oriented beach destination. Enjoy the sand and waves, or bring along binoculars for viewing feathered friends in the marsh or nearby Bird

Key. In addition to seasonal beach chair, boogie board, and umbrella rentals, you'll find a snack bar and gift shop. The Pelican Watch Shelter provides natural gas, an oyster-roasting pit, barbecue cookers, and volleyball and horseshoe equipment.

Owing to recurring winter high tides, erosion is a problem at this beach park. Each year a renourishment program replenishes the sand, but the parking has been cut to 150 spaces. This may make parking here more difficult in the summer months, so it's best to get there early in the day. Admission is $5.00 per car, $10.00 per camper, or $20.00 per bus. Walk-ins and bicycles are free. Hours are 9:00 A.M. to 7:00 P.M. from May through August, 10:00 A.M. to 6:00 P.M. in April, September, and October, and 10:00 A.M. to 5:00 P.M. November through March. (See the Kid-Friendly Beaches section of the Kidstuff chapter for more details.)

# Kiawah Island

**Beachwalker Park**
**1 Beachwalker Drive**
**(843) 768-2395**
**www.ccprc.com**
This county park, just outside the gates into Kiawah (take a right on Beachwalker Drive), is open April through October. Summer hours, May through August, are 9:00 A.M. to 7:00 P.M.; in September, October, and April the hours are 10:00 A.M. to 6:00 P.M. (weekends only in October and April); and in March the hours are 10:00 A.M. to 5:00 P.M. weekends only. November through February the park is closed. This is 10 miles of pristine beach with white sand. Admission is $5.00 per car, $10.00 per camper, or $20.00 per bus, and all 150 parking spots often fill early. Walk-ins and bicycles are free. There are lifeguards, outdoor showers, and restrooms, and beach chair, boogie board, and umbrella rentals are available. (Also see the Kid-Friendly Beaches section of the Kidstuff chapter.)

## RECREATION

What follows is a good representation of the recreational opportunities scattered throughout the Lowcountry. Categories are in alphabetical order, and so are the businesses that are listed with each type of activity.

The following departments are also good clearinghouses for information on specific sports and recreational opportunities throughout the Lowcountry. In Charleston, call the City of Charleston Department of Recreation, (843) 724–7327, or the James Island Recreation Complex, (843) 720–3808. In Mt. Pleasant, call the Richard L. Jones Recreation Complex, (843) 884–2528. For Isle of Palms information, call the town's Recreation Department, (843) 886–8294. Sullivan's Island Town Hall, (843) 883–3198, can provide information on options on that island, and the North Charleston Recreation Department, (843) 745–1028, can answer recreation questions in that area.

## Aerobics

Individual recreation departments often offer aerobics classes. The parks and recreation departments and facilities listed in the Recreation introduction are good places to look for further information. Also, most full-service fitness centers offer a plethora of aerobics classes. (See the Fitness Centers section in this chapter.)

**Charleston County Community Education Program
Charleston County School District
75 Calhoun Street
(843) 937–6421
www.charlestoncoce.org**
This program offers moderately priced aerobic classes at locations all over the county. For a schedule and more information, write to the above address, or pick up a free brochure at one of the public libraries.

## Archery

**Carolina Rod & Gun Inc.
1319 Savannah Highway
(843) 571–7972**
Bow-and-arrow enthusiasts will find a fine source of archery equipment and information here. Carolina Rod & Gun employs full-time technicians and offers custom services such as bow-tuning and arrow-building. It is by far the most popular archery services vendor in the Lowcountry. (See the Hunting and Fishing chapter for more on Carolina Rod & Gun.)

## Aviation

Two companies in Charleston County offer flying lessons. One is based at the Charleston Executive Airport on Johns Island, and the other is located in East Cooper at the East Cooper Airport. Call either one to get advice on what's required by law.

**Palmetto Air Service
700 Airport Road, Mt. Pleasant
(843) 884–8914**
For primary flight instruction east of the Cooper River, talk to the instructors at Palmetto Air. Their lessons are $105 per hour for dual instruction and $70 per hour to learn solo in a Cessna 152. In a Grumman Tiger dual instruction is $140 per hour, and solo is $112 per hour. They also offer sightseeing flights over Charleston for those of us who are not yet ready to earn our wings.

**Pro Flight
2700 Ft. Trenholm Road, Johns Island
(843) 559–3331**
Open seven days a week, Pro Flight teaches all levels from primary flight training to instrument and commercial flight instruction. For instruction in a Cessna 150, the rental is $56.75 an hour plus $30.50 for the instruction. The cost is $80.75 an hour to rent a Cessna 172 and

$120.75 an hour for an Arrow, with the same $30.50 instructor's fee. Aircraft rental to licensed pilots is also available.

# Baseball

The area's recreation departments organize baseball leagues (T-ball for toddlers through baseball for teens), and there's a batting range for those who want to go it alone. Call the department in your area for information about spring registration, and plan to have on hand your child's birth certificate, social security card, and insurance as well as a registration fee of about $25 for city residents, $55 for nonresidents.

**Frankie's Fun Park**
**5000 Ashley Phosphate Road,**
**North Charleston**
**(843) 767-1376**
**www.frankiesfunpark.com**
You're never too old to swing it! Frankie's has a nine-position baseball batting cage with a variety of pitch-speed options. It costs $2.00 for 24 pitches or 144 swings for $10.00. (See the Kidstuff chapter for more about Frankie's.)

# Basketball

Public basketball courts are adjacent to most local playgrounds. Here are a few spots for shooting the rock convenient to various parts of the Greater Charleston area. More playgrounds are listed later in this chapter.

Both Moultrie Playground, across from Colonial Lake at 41 Ashley Avenue, and Hazel Parker Playground, next to the Carolina Yacht Club at 70 East Bay Street, have outdoor courts that are very convenient if you are downtown.

In Mt. Pleasant, the Richard L. Jones Recreation Complex on Egypt Road (see previous listing in Parks and Recreation Centers) has an indoor gymnasium and

active basketball programs for youth ages 5 to 17, adults, and seniors age 50 and older.

If you are on one of the East Cooper beaches, consider playing at the Isle of Palms Park, 24-28th Avenue, which has one outdoor lighted court and one indoor court. There are youth and adult basketball leagues organized by the recreation department there as well. Another island option is the lighted court at Sullivan's Island Park, conveniently located on Middle Street in the center of the business district and usually swarming with players eager to shoot some hoops.

If you are in West Ashley, try playing outdoors at St. Andrews Park on Playground Road or the St. Andrews Family Fitness Center on Sam Rittenberg Boulevard for indoor courts. The James Island Recreation Complex has an indoor court that is open for recreational play daily and organizes adult and youth leagues January through March. For more information, contact the area recreation departments.

St. John's Community School offers coed adult (18 and older) pickup basketball and a men's league for those age 20 and older. The school is at 1518 Main Road on Johns Island.

# Bicycling

**Coastal Cyclists**
**P.O. Box 32095, Charleston 29417**
**(843) 303-3334**
**www.coastalcyclists.org**
Coastal Cyclists is an organization of bike riders and racers that meets once a month (usually on the first Monday) at an area restaurant. Members enjoy supper together and have a meeting with a guest speaker. Coastal Cyclists organizes club rides for Class 1 to Class 4 riders covering 20 to 40 miles on average. The group has a racing team that travels to compete around the state. Annual family membership costs $25, single membership is $15 and includes a newsletter on upcoming

events. This group is open to riders of all levels.

# Bowling

Bowling is popular in the Lowcountry, with active leagues playing every night on area lanes right next to the occasional group or office outing. For information about leagues, talk to the management at the following lanes, and beware of those gutter balls!

### AMF Triangle Lanes
### 1963 Savannah Highway
### (843) 766-0241

Just off the Mark Clark Expressway, west of the Ashley, Triangle has automatic scoring, a pro shop, and a lounge. There are 24 lanes and leagues every evening. You can bowl here for $3.75 a game, with shoe rental for $4.00. This is a choice venue for birthday parties.

### Ashley Lanes
### 1568 Sam Rittenberg Boulevard
### (843) 766-9061

Ashley Lanes has numerous leagues and a total of 24 lanes. The per-game cost to bowl before 6:00 P.M. is $2.00 for adults and $1.30 for seniors, and the cost is

---

*Cyclists in South Carolina have the same rights on the road as a vehicle driver and are required to obey specific traffic laws: Ride on the right side of the road and in the same direction as traffic, obey all traffic signs and signals, do not ride on freeways (multi-lane divided highways), and form a single line in heavy traffic. Equipment must include a bell audible for 100 feet, and night use requires a front lamp with a white beam visible for 500 feet and a red rear reflector. Don't forget to wear a helmet!*

---

$3.00 after 6:00 P.M. It's $2.50 for shoe rental. In addition to bowling, you'll find an amusement center with a snack bar and several video games, plus a restaurant, lounge, and nursery.

### Twin River Lanes
### 613 Johnnie Dodds Boulevard,
### Mt. Pleasant
### (843) 884-7735

Twin River Lanes is the East Cooper venue for bowling and offers 16 lanes for play. Before 6:00 P.M., prices are $3.25 per game and $3.00 for shoe rentals. After 6:00, it goes up to $3.95 per game. You can rent lanes by the hour for $25. Other fun activities are the arcade with the laser tag room, the sports bar and grill, and the pizza counter.

# Camping

There are government-owned, public places for camping in the Charleston area as well as private options, and the best clearinghouse for information on them is the Charleston County Park and Recreation Commission, (843) 762-2172. We've included our favorites here.

If you've got a youngster who wants to get outdoors, the Boy Scouts are on top of things at their two campsites, Camp Ho Non Wah on Wadmalaw Island and Camp Moultrie on Lake Moultrie. For more information on joining the Boy Scouts of America or if you would like to volunteer to help out, call or write the Coastal Carolina Council of the BSA, 1025 Sam Rittenberg Boulevard, Charleston, (843) 763-0305.

The Girl Scout Outdoor Program Facility is a wonderful site in Cordesville (about 38 miles from Charleston) that's listed on the National Register of Historic Places. The summer resident camp is called Camp Low Country and runs June through August. The site includes a Junior Olympic-size pool, 20-stall stable, lighted riding ring, screened dining hall, three units of platform tents, and one cabin unit. For more information about the Outdoor Program Facility or other Girl Scout programs, call (800) 868–9911.

## Capers Island
### c/o SCDNR, P.O. Box 12559, Charleston 29412
### (843) 953-9300

This 2,000-acre barrier island can only be reached by boat but is well worth the effort of securing a ride. South Carolina's only primitive beachfront camping area, Capers has no facilities, and camping here is absolutely in the rough—exactly the way plenty of people want it. It is protected under the Heritage Trust Program and managed by the South Carolina Department of Natural Resources Marine Resources Division. Contact the Marine Resources Division at Fort Johnson on James Island at the number listed above for a permit.

## Francis Marion National Forest
### Pinckney Street, near intersection of US 17 and Highway 45, McClellanville
### (843) 887-3257, (843) 336-3248
### www.fs.fed.us/r8/fms

There are four sites in the Francis Marion National Forest, a little more than 2 miles past Awendaw. It's hard to beat this place for seclusion and an opportunity to get back to nature. The forest still bears scars from Hurricane Hugo, but it stands testimony to nature's resilience. To get there, take U.S. Highway 17 N. toward Georgetown. Just after the intersection of U.S. Highway 17 and Highway 45, about 33 miles from Charleston, turn right onto Pinckney Street and look for the ranger station. All the sites are free except at Buck Hall Campground, where they cost $15 per day for tents, $20 per day for full hookups, on a first-come, first-served basis. Call for information about availability, or write the Wambaw Ranger District, P.O. Box 788, McClellanville 29458.

## James Island County Park
### 871 Riverland Drive
### (843) 795-7275, (800) 743-7275
### www.ccprc.com

One lovely spot is the James Island County Park, with 125 camping sites. Campers can spend the night in tents or in recreational vehicles. Most sites are equipped with full water, sewer, and electricity hookups. Prices for tent sites range as follows: $20.80 for Charleston County residents; $23.40 for nonresident seniors; and $26.00 for nonresidents. For full hookups, these are the rates: $22.40 for Charleston County residents; $25.20 for nonresident seniors; and $28.00 for nonresidents. (Please note that these fees do not include the 12 percent accommodations tax levied here.) Round-trip shuttle service is available to downtown Charleston, Folly Beach County Park, and Folly Beach Fishing Pier for $5.00.

## KOA Kampground
### 3157 U.S. Highway 17 North, Mt. Pleasant
### (843) 849-5177, (800) KOA-5796
### www.koa.com

This Mt. Pleasant KOA campground offers large pull-through sites with 20-, 30-, and 50-amp hookups. Amenities include restrooms, showers, heated swimming pool, convenience store, laundry, firewood, and propane. There is a 30-acre lake fully stocked for fishing and water recreation. The 2.5-mile hiking trail and bike rentals offer other opportunities for enjoying the great outdoors. Deluxe and wilderness tent sites are available for those who really want to get away from it all. Located on US 17 N., this KOA has many nearby attractions including Boone Hall Plantation, Sewee Environmental Education Center, Patriots Point Maritime Museum, and historic Charleston. (See the Attractions, Kidstuff, and Lowcountry Day Trips chapters for more on these and other area points of interest.) Rates are $325 per month plus water and electricity. Nightly rates are around $35.

## Oak Plantation Campground
**3540 Savannah Highway**
**(843) 766–5936, (866) 658–2500**
**www.oakplantationcampground.com**
This is an RV campground with modern facilities. Campers park on concrete pads with 30- and 50-amp hookups available. The campground is landscaped with privacy in mind, and campers enjoy fishing for bream and bass in the freshwater lake. There is a playground with swings, a swimming pool, a small grocery with propane, and a shuttle bus for those who wish to leave the RV behind and catch a ride into the city. The office is generally open from 7:30 A.M. to 7:00 P.M., depending on the season, and nightly rates are in the $27.50 range.

# Fitness Centers

## Lifequest
**610 Coleman Boulevard, Mt. Pleasant**
**(843) 849–1414**

**35 Folly Road**
**(843) 571–2828**

**5101 Ashley Phosphate Road, Suite 149, North Charleston**
**(843) 767–1899**
**www.lqhw.com**
Lifequest centers are locally owned, state-of-the-art fitness centers. The three facilities are sparkling clean and attractive with

*For children (and adults) with physical, social, and behavioral disabilities, Anchors Away! is a special program for recreational opportunities designed by the Department of Neurology of the Medical University of South Carolina. Options include Jet Skiing, fishing, waterskiing, canoeing, harbor tours, sailing, swimming, kayaking, and more. For additional information call (843) 792-0721 or (800) 734-4785 or visit www.anchorsaway.info.*

an antibacterial aerobics floor, free weights, a dumbbell section, circuit-training machines (of Lifequest's own design), cardiovascular equipment (including steps, bikes, and treadmills), a ladies-only section, and a self-defense studio. Childcare for children 3 months and older is an option. Lifequest memberships for 12 months are about $56 a month for a single with each additional family member at $30 a month. Call for more information and special package rates.

## St. Andrew's Family Recreation Center
**1642 Sam Rittenberg Boulevard**
**(843) 763-3850**
**www.standrewsparks.com**
Affiliated with the St. Andrew's Park and Playground Department, this is a full-service health fitness facility. The whole family (even the little ones, who play in the nursery) can enjoy aerobics classes, six racquetball courts, a squash court, a basketball court, a Junior Olympic pool, Nautilus equipment, free weights, an indoor track, stair machines, treadmills, personal trainers, and more. Annual, three-month, student, and daily passes are available, and prices vary according to factors such as residence and age. St. Andrew's Public Service District residents pay about $37 a month for a single membership or $62 a month for a family membership with a $64 or $103 one-time enrollment fee. Full-time students pay on a month-to-month basis, usually about $43 a month. Daily passes are available for $10. Special discounts may apply, so call for more information. Hours are 5:00 A.M. to 10:00 P.M. Monday through Thursday, 5:00 A.M. to 9:00 P.M. Friday, 8:00 A.M. to 5:00 P.M. on Saturday, and 1:00 to 6:00 P.M. Sunday.

## Town and Country Inn Fitness Center
**2008 Savannah Highway**
**(843) 571-1000, (800) 334-6660**
**www.thetownandcountryinn.com**
Although it's in a motel complex, this $1-million 10,000-square-foot fitness center is open to the public for memberships. For an initiation fee and monthly payment,

members can use the Calgym exercise equipment, stair machines, stationary bikes, dumbbells, two racquetball courts, an indoor, heated lap pool, showers, and sauna. Memberships run $300 per quarter per person.

## Football

There are many leagues for youth football. For more information about children's teams, contact City of Charleston Youth Sports at (843) 724-7330. Registration is held throughout the month of August. Children must be ages 8 through 14 to play, and be sure to bring your child's birth certificate when you sign up. Play starts in mid-September and runs through the fall. Also, the Mt. Pleasant Recreation Department offers flag football for children ages 7 and 8 during the fall.

## Frisbee Golf

Charleston is on top of the Frisbee fun. On a pretty day, White Point Gardens (down by the Battery) is usually covered with young people throwing Frisbees. Call the City of Charleston Department of Recreation, (843) 724-7326, for more information.

## Gymnastics

It seems most extracurricular community programs and recreational department programs offer gymnastic courses. Another option we can recommend is Charleston Gymnastics Training Center.

**Charleston Gymnastics Training Center**
**1088 Quail Drive**
**(843) 720-3808**
This is a very serious, well-respected program that is safety-certified. Competitive

teams go to the state, regional, and national level. Preschool to advanced classes are offered throughout the school year. There is a $15 registration fee, and once-a-week one-hour classes cost $135 for an 18-week session.

## Horseback Riding

The equestrian set is quite active in the Greater Charleston area. We've included one stable each in Mt. Pleasant, West Ashley, Hollywood (south of Charleston on the way to Edisto Island), and Seabrook, and two on Johns Island.

**Brick Church Farm**
**1131 Wando Road, Mt. Pleasant**
**(843) 881-1310**
This is a popular riding school, away from city congestion, with caring, competent personnel. Call for directions and information. This is primarily a private show barn that prepares riders for hunter-jumper competitions on the local and southeastern levels. No horse rentals are available here, but boarding for hunters and jumpers is $750 a month. Lessons are offered on a limited basis (on your own horse), so call the number listed for more details.

**Middleton Riding and Hunt Stables**
**4280 Ashley River Road**
**(843) 556-8137**
**www.middletonplace.org**
A premier boarding and lesson facility, Middleton has a dressage arena, cross-country course, and lighted ring for evening riding. Stall boarding is $550 per month, and private lessons are offered for $35 per half-hour or $45 per hour. The nearby Middleton Inn (see the Bed-and-Breakfasts and Atmospheric Inns chapter) arranges trail rides for ages 10 and older for $40. Contact Middleton Inn, (843) 556-0500, for these walking trail rides through the Middleton woods and wetlands.

**Mullet Hall Equestrian Center**
**2662 Mullet Hall Road, Johns Island**
**(843) 795-4FUN (4386)**
**www.ccprc.com**
Opened in April 2001 by the Charleston
County Park and Recreation Commission,
this 60-acre equestrian center features
fenced warm-up and open-lunge areas,
four permanent show rings, and jump
sets. The center also has two barns with
140 stalls and areas for temporary stalls
and for exercising horses. For riders who
trailer their horses in, there are 20 miles of
riding trails through the 738-acre park
site. Passes are required for trail riding. A
one-year pass is $25 for individuals and
$50 for families. Ample parking is avail-
able for all kinds of vehicles. This facility
serves as the host site for a variety of
competitive horse shows. Call for more
information about upcoming events.

**Seabrook Island Equestrian Center**
**3772 Seabrook Island Road,**
**Seabrook Island**
**(843) 768-7541, (800) 341-4248**
**www.seabrookresort.com**
This center is at Seabrook but is open to
the public. Reservations should be made
for private lessons, trail rides into the
undeveloped portions of the island's
woods and marshes, rides on the beach in
the summer, and boarding. The walking
trail rides for ages 8 and older are $65 per
person. The advanced rider may go on a
trotting/cantering trail ride for $70 per
person; beach rides are $85 per person
for advanced riders. Parent-led pony rides
are $30 per half hour. Lessons cost $30
per hour for semi-private sessions, and
$40 per half-hour for private training.
Boarding fees here are $500 a month or
$25 per day. Advanced riders may also
call for more information on the monthly
adopt-a-horse program.

**Stono Ferry Stables**
**5304 Stono Ferry Course, Hollywood**
**(843) 763-0566**
**www.stonoferry.com**
Stono Stables offers lessons, dressage,

hunter-jumper training, boarding, and
sales. Staff members are involved in polo,
and this is a good source for information
about that sport as well. Stall boarding
runs $500 per month, and lessons for chil-
dren are $110 per month for one lesson
per week. These can either be one-hour
group lessons (with a maximum of five
riders) or half-hour private sessions.

**Stono River Stable**
**2962 Hut Road, Johns Island**
**(843) 559-0773, (877) 777-8951**
**www.stonoriverstable.com**
This established riding school offers
weekly and private lessons with a children's summer camp. The daily trail riding
lessons cover miles through the heart of a
sea island maritime forest area and cost
$35 per person. There is dressage, show
jumping, and a cross-country course at
this 200-acre facility. The owners welcome
visitors, and children regularly drop by to
feed a favorite pony a carrot. Lessons are
$45 per hour for a private lesson and $35
for a half-hour private lesson or a one-hour
group lesson. Stall boarding is available for
$450 per month. A new 10-stall barn is
offered for show and transit horses, so
bring your horse on vacation with you!

# Martial Arts

There are numerous martial arts studios in
the Charleston area. In addition, some
courses are also offered at many of the
recreation centers mentioned in the Parks
and Recreation Centers section in this
chapter.

**International Taekwon-Do Center**
**3545 Mary Ader Avenue**
**(843) 556-4391**
**www.allitc.com**
International offers classes for men,
women, and children ages five and older
who are interested in tae kwon do and
self-defense. Classes are taught at the
Savannah Highway studio and at Sunshine
House on Long Point Road in Mt. Pleasant.

There is a $65 registration fee, with a monthly lesson fee of $75, a four-month fee of $65 per month, and a yearly fee of $55 per month. Call for special packages, and check it out with a free trial class.

**Masters Studios of Self Defense**
**1021 Rifle Range Road, Mt. Pleasant**
**(843) 881–4866**

**1888 Wallenberg Boulevard**
**(843) 766–4376**

**7400-N Rivers Avenue, North Charleston**
**(843) 797–1031**

**1291-H Folly Road, James Island**
**(843) 762–1640**
**www.mastersstudios.com**
With four locations convenient to a good portion of the Greater Charleston area, Masters Studios offers classes for all ages in a variety of self-defense disciplines— shaolin kempo karate, jujitsu, kung fu, and t'ai chi. Group as well as private lessons are available. The twice-weekly, one-hour classes are about $80 per month for adults and $75 per month for kids ages 5 to 12.

# Minigolf

**Classic Golf**
**1528 Ben Sawyer Boulevard,**
**Mt. Pleasant**
**(843) 881–3131**
Classic Golf has two 18-hole courses and is a great place for a birthday party. Charges vary with age: Adults pay $7.00 per round; and children, $5.00. Special group and off-season rates are available. Hours are 11:00 A.M. to 10:00 P.M. or later in the summer. Chow down at the Island Clubhouse restaurant next door for Caribbean and island-style food after your round.

# Playgrounds

There are 16 playgrounds in the city, some of which are downtown and in West Ashley. The playground and special events coordinator for the Charleston Department of Recreation can be reached at (843) 724-7332. We've described some of our favorites.

**Hazel Parker Playground**
**70 East Bay Street**
**(843) 724-7332**
**www.charlestoncity.info**
Open sunup to sundown, this park has playground equipment as well as athletic fields, a tennis court, and basketball hoops. You can see Charleston Harbor from the grounds, and you are in skipping distance of the Battery.

**Mary Utsey Playground**
**1360 Orange Grove Road**
**(843) 724-7334**
**www.charlestoncity.info**
West of the Ashley, this playground's shady areas are much appreciated during the hot months in Charleston. It has swings and other standard playground equipment.

*If your faithful companion is your regular exercise pal, you may want to take note that the city of Charleston has provided some "dog" water fountains in two Peninsula playgrounds to quench "Fido's" thirst. One is located in Hazel Parker Playground on East Bay Street near Rainbow Row, and the other, in Moultrie Playground at the corner of Broad Street and Ashley Avenue at Colonial Lake. The fountains come with one lever but two basins, a high one for people and a low one for their four-legged friends. Most canines agree—this is a great way to beat the heat!*

**Moultrie Playground**
**41 Ashley Avenue**
**(843) 724-7398**
**www.charlestoncity.info**
Completion of an extensive renovation relocated four new tennis courts beside the existing two along Broad Street. The new baseball field moved to the old tennis court site and opened in spring 2001. New concrete walkways and bleachers were installed also. The playground has nice equipment for kids including climbing sets, swings, and a sand pit, plus basketball courts. Moultrie Playground is across from Colonial Lake and is a popular destination for families.

**St. Andrew's Park and Playground**
**1095 Playground Road**
**(843) 763-4360**
**www.standrewsparks.com**
This recently revamped playground features the basic fun stuff—monkey bars, slides, and swings. This is the headquarters for the St. Andrew's Park and Playground Commission, and up-to-date information on sporting events and activities is available here. There are lighted tennis courts, athletic fields for baseball, softball, football, and soccer, basketball

---

*High-flying fun for skateboarders can now be found in several Charleston area locations. Public skateboard parks are popping up to accommodate and provide safer sites for this growing sport. The City of Charleston committed $25,000 to build a ramp-and-rail rectangle at Ackerman Park behind Food Lion on St. Andrews Boulevard, and the Town of Mt. Pleasant recently opened a $17,000 skate park at the Richard L. Jones Recreation Center on Egypt Road near Belle Hall Elementary. For now the Ackerman Skate Park is free, and Mt. Pleasant Recreation charges a nominal daily fee or annual resident memberships of $25.*

---

courts, and a gymnasium. A picnic shelter is available.

# Racquetball

Racquetball enthusiasts can find camaraderie and court time at the fitness centers listed above and at some recreation centers and playground complexes. (See both categories in this chapter for phone numbers.)

# Running

Running is a very popular Lowcountry activity, and most every weekend offers a charity benefit run/walk for the serious and not-so-serious runners here. By far the largest race is the Cooper River Bridge Run, drawing an international field of competition of over 30,000 participants.

Along with the Cooper River Bridge Run, other annual races include a 5K and 10K that happen in conjunction with the Flowertown Festival in Summerville. Other 5K runs are the North Charleston Arts Festival run, the Holiday Festival of Lights run, and the South Carolina Race for the Cure. See our Annual Events chapter for more on these happenings. Also, Kiawah Island hosts a marathon, and the James Island County Park sponsors a triathlon series during June, July, and August. (See the Parks and Recreation Centers section of this chapter for more on this county park.)

**Charleston Running Club**
**P.O. Box 30224, Charleston 29417**
**(843) 856-4206**
**www.charlestonrunningclub.com**
The Charleston Running Club holds meetings the last Tuesday of every month at different locations around town such as Earth Fare grocery store and V Fitness Club and has about 600 members. The organization publishes a substantial newsletter monthly in booklet form (with results from races, stories, book reviews, and a calendar). The

club sponsors about a dozen races and a summer track series. They also organize a schedule of Charleston area group runs at Colonial Lake, MUSC Harper Student Center, and the James Island Post Office. Members enjoy a party after the Cooper River Bridge Run and discounts at local athletic stores. Membership costs $15 a year for an individual, $10 for a student, and $20 for a family. Write for more information and a membership application.

# Skating

People in this area skate indoors and outdoors and even have a club, the Charleston Roll Patrol, to promote their interests. Hampton Park and James Island County Park, where you can also rent in-line skates, are great outdoor skating sites (see the Parks and Recreation Centers section in this chapter).

With the advent of the professional ice hockey team, the South Carolina Stingrays, ice-skating has seen a surge of interest in the Lowcountry. For more about the Stingrays see our Spectator Sports chapter. The North Charleston Coliseum and the Carolina Ice Palace (see below) are the venues for this type of skating fun.

Here are some popular indoor rinks for roller-skating followed by one for ice-skating.

## Carolina Ice Palace
**7665 Northwoods Boulevard, North Charleston**
**(843) 572-2717**
**www.carolinaicepalace.com**
The Carolina Ice Palace has two NHL-sized ice rinks for public skating year-round. This is a fun atmosphere for family entertainment with youth and adult hockey and figure skating. The facility encompasses an arcade, virtual reality center, full service pro shop, party rooms, and a jumbo TV lounge. Hours are 11:00 A.M. to 3:00 P.M. Monday through Friday. After-school skating is scheduled from 3:00 to 5:30 P.M.

Monday and Friday. The palace is also open from 7:00 to 9:00 P.M. Wednesday and Thursday night. Friday and Saturday hours extend to 11:30 P.M., and Sunday hours are 1:30 to 6:00 P.M. Skating fees are in the $5.00 to $7.00 range with $3.00 for skate rental. (See the Kidstuff chapter for more on the Ice Palace.)

## Hot Wheels Skating Center, Inc.
**1523 Folly Road**
**(843) 795-7982**
**www.hotwheelsskating.net**
Even the little ones can skate here in clamp-on skates. The management at Hot Wheels is enthusiastic, and this is a very popular place for birthday parties, which are often booked weeks in advance. A snack bar stocks light refreshments. Skating prices range from $3.00 on Saturday from 11:00 A.M. to 1:00 P.M. up to $6.00 on Friday and Saturday nights from 7:00 to 11:00 P.M.

## Stardust Skate Center
**2035 Spaulding Drive, North Charleston**
**(843) 747-0111**
A popular skate center, Stardust is large and can accommodate several parties and many individual patrons at the same time. Supervision and safety are emphasized at this family-oriented center. The snack bar is extensive, and there are many video games to play. Skating prices vary, ranging from about $3.50 per person on school nights (and for children under 12 on Saturday mornings) up to $7.00 per person on Fridays and Saturdays between 7:30 and 11:30 P.M. Skating lessons for children 12 and younger are $2.50.

# Soccer

The popularity of soccer in this area has led to new venues for the sport. The recently dedicated Ansonborough Fields, downtown near the Charleston Maritime Center, are providing fields for soccer and football. In the fall of 2001, a new soccer

*Hiking enthusiasts may want to join in the healthy, relaxing, and fun activities of the Charleston Hiking Club, organized in 2002. Most of the hikes are in the scenic areas of the Lowcountry, but some are farther afield in other parts of South Carolina, North Carolina, and Georgia. Some of their trips have included the Swamp Fox passage of the Palmetto Trail, Santee Canal County Park, Raven Cliff Falls, Huntington Beach, Poinsette State Park, and Cumberland Island. They have also biked and canoed part of the Edisto River and Lake Moultrie. There is no membership fee, but participants must be reachable by e-mail. For more information on upcoming hikes, visit their Web site at www.angelfire.com/extreme3/chc.*

complex opened on James Island off Ft. Johnson Road.

Again, the area recreation departments are the clearinghouses for information on soccer. They can steer adults and children alike to a soccer team in their area. Sign-up includes a modest fee of $15 to around $25 and commitment to weekday practices and weekday and Saturday games or both. Birth certificates are required. Call the recreation departments previously listed for more information on youth and adult leagues.

## Softball

In the spring, it seems softball games pop up everywhere in the Lowcountry. To learn more about teams and competition for youth and adults, call the city and town recreation departments listed at the beginning of the Recreation section of this chapter. Also check with churches, as many sponsor their own teams.

## Tennis

An empty tennis court on a pretty day is hard to come by in this area. The City of Charleston maintains 61 hard courts, 47 of which are lighted and available on a first-come, first-served basis for free (except for a nominal fee at the Charleston and Maybank Tennis Centers). With headquarters at the Charleston Tennis Center, the city organizes leagues, round-robins, socials, and tournaments for tennis enthusiasts of all ages. Lessons can be arranged by calling (843) 724-7402. A new $9-million tennis complex was constructed on Daniel Island instigated by the announcement that the Family Circle Cup would move to Charleston from its long-standing run in Hilton Head. This is fostering the further growth of tennis here.

The very popular local United States Tennis Association league has 45 men's and ladies' teams competing at nearly every National Tennis Rating Program level of play on public and private club courts around the area. There are nine ladies' city league teams as well. Call the city tennis coordinator at (843) 724-7402, or one of the tennis centers listed below, for more information about specific locations, court reservations, and joining tennis leagues. The following list will give you some ideas about the options.

### Charleston Tennis Center
**19 Farmfield Avenue**
**(843) 724-7402**
**www.charlestoncity.info**
These city of Charleston courts are conveniently located in West Ashley and are popular with the tennis crowd. Hours are based on demand, but are generally Monday through Thursday 8:30 A.M. to 10:00 P.M.; Friday from 8:30 A.M. to 7:00 P.M.; Saturday from 9:00 A.M. to 6:00 P.M.; and Sunday, 10:00 A.M. to 6:00 P.M. Junior Tennis Summer Camps are held in July and August (see the Summer Camps section of the Kidstuff chapter). Court fees vary, so please call for information.

**Creekside Tennis and Swim**
**790 Creekside Drive, Mt. Pleasant**
**(843) 884-6111**
**www.creeksideclub.org**
Creekside Tennis and Swim has 12 lighted courts. Members enjoy use of lockers, a lounge, and a six-lane swimming pool. The club hosts active adult and junior programs. There are no court fees, but monthly dues and an initiation fee are charged. Nonmembers can take lessons. (See the Neighborhoods chapter for more on the Creekside community.)

**Kiawah Island Resort**
**12 Kiawah Beach Drive, Kiawah Island**
**(843) 768-2121, ext. 4012**
**www.kiawahresort.com**
In recent rankings, Kiawah was rated the No. 1 tennis resort in America by *Tennis* magazine, which bases its top-50 selections on quality of instruction, off-court amenities, and facilities. The resort has two separate tennis complexes open year-round. The West Beach Tennis Club has 14 Har-Tru clay courts, two lighted hard courts, and a backboard for practice. The East Beach Tennis Club boasts nine Har-Tru courts, three hard courts, two lighted courts, and a fully automated practice alley. Members and resort guests pay $22 per hour for court time. Nonmember play is available for a $32 per hour fee. (For more on Kiawah, see the Neighborhoods, Hotels and Motels, and Vacation and Beach Rentals chapters.)

**Maybank Tennis Center**
**1880 Houghton Drive**
**(843) 406-8814**
**www.charlestoncity.info**
Another city-owned tennis facility is the Maybank Tennis Center with a full-time staff on site. You'll find a total of 11 courts here, eight lighted hard courts and three Har-Tru. A fee of $3.50 per person per hour is charged for the hard courts, and $9.00 per hour for the clay courts. Annual city resident adult membership is $100 for hard courts and $240 for clay courts. The

hours are 8:30 A.M. to 10:00 P.M. Monday through Thursday, 8:30 A.M. to 7:00 P.M. on Friday, 9:00 A.M. to 6:00 P.M. on Saturday, and 10:00 A.M. to 6:00 P.M. on Sunday, or until you wind up that heated match.

**Wild Dunes Resort, Isle of Palms**
**5757 Palm Boulevard, Isle of Palms**
**(843) 886-2113**
**www.wilddunes.com**
Wild Dunes features 17 Har-Tru tennis courts, one hard court, a ball wall, and a stadium court for tournaments. Five of the courts are lighted. Resort guests and members have priority, but nonmembers can take part in clinics, lessons, and round-robins. (See the Neighborhoods, Hotels and Motels, and Vacation and Beach Rentals chapters.)

# Volleyball

Some bars on the beach provide a volleyball net and encourage random competition, which we hear can get pretty fierce among beer buddies. If you are interested in something more predictable and organized, there are teams put together by the Mt. Pleasant and Isle of Palms recreation departments. The Isle of Palms Recreation

*If you've "hit a wall" searching for a new outlet for your exercise regimen, give the climbing wall at the James Island County Park a try. The 50-foot-tall, 4,500-square-foot climbing surface or the 10-foot bouldering wall is perfect for working on your technique. The walls are open from noon to 5:00 P.M. on weekdays and 9:00 A.M. to 5:00 P.M. on weekends (or later in the warmer months). An all-day pass is $8.00 for county residents and $10.00 for non-county residents. Trained instructors are on hand for assistance and rental of harness and shoes. So, hit the wall, and scale new heights!*

Department, (843) 886–8294, organizes coed adult teams in January and February. The Mt. Pleasant folks can be reached at (843) 884–2528. There is a charge of about $35 for participation. Teams are also often sponsored by local restaurants and merchants. Inquire at one of the area recreation departments about signing up.

**Charleston Beach Volleyball
& Social Club
191 Line Street
(843) 343–7802
www.charlestonvolleyball.net**
The Charleston Beach Volleyball & Social Club organizes spring, summer, and fall leagues for coed teams at all levels. They welcome those new to the sport as well as highly competitive players with tournament experience. The action takes place on the sand courts on the beach in back of Charleston Harbor Resort & Marina at 20 Patriots Point Road on Sunday afternoons and weekday nights. Sunday afternoons are also pickup game days for anyone who cannot commit to play on a regular basis. After all that exercise, teamwork, and spiking, enjoy the social side too with food and beverages after the matches. The group even organizes other recreational events like dancing nights and hiking trips. Check out their Web site for a calendar of events, league schedules, and roster sign-ups.

# GOLF

Greater Charleston can take justifiable pride in the variety of golf challenges available to the area's visitors and residents.

If you're a serious tournament player with world-class experience, or if you're just one of those relatively harmless twice-a-year duffers, Charleston has you well covered when it comes to golf. After all, this is the site of America's very first golf course—among the city's many claims to fame. The actual site of the first course, laid out in 1786 and known as "Harleston Green," has long ago been overtaken by subsequent urbanization, but golf is always proudly mentioned when the list of Charleston's "famous firsts" comes up.

Today, Lowcountry golf is a wealth of opportunity. From the world-ranked resort courses to the ever-popular public tracks, from the private courses to the semi-private offerings, it's possible to golf every day for nearly a month and play a different 18-hole course each day.

Clearly, the great drawing card for Lowcountry golf is the weather. Here the winter chill hardly ever discourages the stouthearted player, and the summer's sweltering heat only adds another challenge to the dedicated would-be pro. Indeed, for the vast majority of the year, Charleston area golf courses sing the siren's call to golfers from (literally) all over the world.

We'll start with some of the famous designer names that are associated with Lowcountry golf courses. Then, we'll take you on a brief tour of some of our infamous signature holes, where even the best players are tested to make birdie.

We'll give you a tour of the area's public courses and then go out to the island resorts where an array of designer courses await the serious golfer determined to be tested by the very best.

## BETTER BY DESIGN

Every area course is different in some way. Each has its own charm and individual characteristics, not to mention frustrations. That, in part, may be because most of the world's best golf architects have designed courses here in the Lowcountry. You'll find the work of Pete Dye, Tom Fazio, Arthur Hills, Jack Nicklaus, Gary Player, Robert Trent Jones Sr., and Rees Jones, among them.

Pete Dye's name is one of the biggest in the industry. His most famous courses include Harbour Town on Hilton Head Island and the Stadium Course at PGA West in La Quinta, California. A more recent Dye offering is the Ocean Course at Kiawah Island, which hosted the 1991 Ryder Cup matches, the prestigious World Cup of Golf in 1997 and 2001, plus the 2003 World Cup. The 1997 World Cup was the world's most-watched golf competition when the event was transmitted via satellite to more than 80 countries. Won by the Irish for the first time since 1958, the team's four-day total of 31-under-par led the field by five strokes. Each team player pocketed $200,000 for his effort.

The Ocean Course rivals Tom Fazio's Lowcountry masterpiece, the Links Course at Wild Dunes Resort, which is ranked among the world's best by Golf magazine. Fazio's golf courses are possibly the best known here in the Lowcountry because he designed both courses on Wild Dunes (the Links and Harbor Course), and he also laid out Kiawah's popular Osprey Point.

Whereas Pete Dye frequently uses railroad ties (a signature of his work), Arthur Hills prefers to use more of a site's natural elements in his designs. Hills did the newest course at Dunes West, which opened in 1991 and showcased the 1992 Amoco Centel Championship. Hills' other famous golf course designs include Eagle

Trace, a TPC course in Coral Springs, Florida, cited in *Golf Digest's* "100 Best Courses in America."

Another name to note among the Charleston area's most popular golf designers is Willard Byrd, who gave us Patriots Point in Mt. Pleasant back in 1981. He's also responsible for the Ocean Winds course on Seabrook Island.

Newest of the "name" designers to provide Charleston-area golfers with a challenge to their skills is Dr. Michael Hurdzan. His contribution is the new 27-hole Golf Club at Wescott Plantation in North Charleston. Named "Architect of the Year" in 1997, Dr. Hurdzan's design allows players to enjoy the natural elements on the course and "play in various directions and lengths" around them.

## SIGNATURE HOLES

Here's a sampling of the flavor of Lowcountry golf—a few of the area signature holes you'll want to be prepared for.

Patriots Point has its famous No. 17, a par 3, 112-yard island green that catches the uninitiated off-guard. This hole requires the player to take into careful consideration the ever-changing winds off Charleston Harbor.

The No. 6 hole at Fairfield Ocean Ridge is another island hole that can be a spoiler. It's a tough 380-yard, par 4 challenge.

Crowfield Plantation offers its par 5, 500-yard No. 7 hole that features treacherous mounds that make players feel as if they've found a bit of old Scotland.

Rees Jones's Charleston National design, which opened in 1990, features the demanding No. 15 hole, a par 3, 183-yarder from the white tees. It plays 210 yards from the blue tees and has an innocent-looking pond on the right that attracts errant balls like a magnet.

On the Links Course at Wild Dunes, No. 9 is said to be the most difficult. It is a long, straight 451-yard par 4 that often plays even longer because it is usually played into the wind. The green is closely guarded on the left by a hidden pond. This green is also the most unforgiving on the course—it slopes severely from back to front. All things considered, a par on No. 9 is an excellent score.

The signature hole at Kiawah's Turtle Point is No. 11. There's water along the entire right side from the tee past the green. According to Jack Nicklaus, its designer, "You can drive the ball as far as you want, but the farther you drive it, the greater the chance of slicing it into the water. There is a secondary landing area, or an out where those who won't want to chance it can play the shot. Then putt it or chip it or, as the Scots say, 'play a bumble' back into the green."

## SCENERY

Pete Dye's Ocean Course on Kiawah and Tom Fazio's Links Course at Wild Dunes both make spectacular use of the Atlantic Ocean in their designs. Fazio's Harbor Course on Wild Dunes uses the Intracoastal Waterway as a backdrop. The Links at Stono Ferry, designed by Ron Garl in 1989, is another opportunity to play along the colorful and busy Intracoastal.

But most of the Lowcountry's golf courses take full advantage of the beautiful salt marshes, signature of the area itself, in their layout designs. Gary Player's recently redesigned Cougar Point on Kiawah is probably the best example. A curious alligator has even been known to occasionally wander onto the course.

In fact, the area's multiple charms make the Lowcountry a favorite destination for golf widows and widowers and the assorted family members who often get swept up in a spouse's or parent's pursuit of the sport. The rationalization usually goes something like this: While golfers are challenged to play the many private, semi-private, and public courses throughout the area, the unenlightened can always explore the beautiful Lowcountry plantations, the splendid museums, the beaches, and the interesting shops, thus staying contented and amused.

And that brings up another benefit of Charleston area golf: Because there are so many other things to do here, the area courses are relatively uncrowded. That means excellent starting times and an unhurried atmosphere.

Here we provide brief profiles of the area courses, so tee up when it suits you, and play at least 18 relaxing and scenic Lowcountry holes. You'll find descriptions of who designed the courses and when, plus who can play them, how much it costs (during high season), and where to call for more details. Greens fees quoted are in-season rates (unless otherwise noted) and exclude tax.

## CHARLESTON AREA GOLF COURSES

### Charleston National Country Club
1360 U.S. Highway 17 N.,
Mt. Pleasant
(843) 884-7799
www.charlestonnationalgolf.com

The idea for Charleston National Country Club was conceived more than 20 years ago, but the once-private golf community was just coming into focus when Hugo struck in 1989. Redesigned and refurbished with input from original designer Rees Jones, the par 72, 18-hole course (now semi-private) is 6,975 yards long. Charleston National has a beautiful 8,000-square-foot clubhouse with luxury amenities including a pool and tennis center. This is the home course for the College of Charleston and The Citadel golf teams. Charleston National's pro is Jeff Yost. Weekday greens fees are $65. Friday through Sunday fees are $85. Carts are included in the price.

### City of Charleston Golf Course
2110 Maybank Highway
(843) 795-6517

This public course, only five minutes from downtown Charleston, has been around

since 1927. Although it lost some 350 mature trees in Hugo's wrath, the course was beautifully replanted and is now in very good shape. The par 72 course is 6,411 yards long from the blue tees; it's 5,200 and par 72 from the forward tees. You'll find small greens, well-tended fairways, and an on-site pro shop with a snack bar. PGA- and LPGA-trained instructors are on hand for lessons, and this is the only public course in South Carolina with a Slazenger club-fitting system available for beginners and experts alike. Individual greens fees are $20 (for walkers). The rate goes up to $22 on weekends. Add $15 per person for a golf cart. Charleston residents get a $5.00 discount. Call about a week in advance for tee times.

### Coosaw Creek Country Club
4210 Club Course Drive,
North Charleston
(843) 767-9000
www.coosawcreek.com

Coosaw Creek, a 645-acre residential community in North Charleston, offers an Arthur Hills course designed in 1993. The par 71 semiprivate course is 6,593 yards long from the middle tees. The bonus here is on accuracy instead of length; good tee shots, as well as a deft short game, are the keys to low scoring. Hills had more natural topography to work with at Coosaw Creek than most Lowcountry layouts offer. You'll find rolling fairways, subtle mounding, and gradual elevation changes. The best opportunity to score low is on the front nine, as the back side brings more of the water and wetlands into play. Eric Landfried is the pro on hand. In-season, weekday greens fees are $64; Saturday and Sunday fees are $69, taxes and cart included. After September 15, the greens fees go down to $49 for weekdays and $55 on weekends.

### Crowfield Golf Plantation
300 Hamlet Circle, Goose Creek
(843) 764-4618

Crowfield Golf Plantation offers championship golfing on a semi-private course designed in 1990 by Tom Jackson and Bob Spence. Their par 72, 18-hole layout is 7,003 yards long. The course is slightly Scottish in that it has a rolling terrain accompanied by acres of fairway and green-side bunkers. Shooting ability is of prime importance here. Undulating greens and imaginative pin placements test the nerves of the most skilled players. Crowfield's pro shop is well stocked, and there's a restaurant and cocktail lounge on-site. Breakfast, lunch, or dinner may be ordered from the menu. Call pro Mark Hofstetter for lesson details. Tee times are accepted up to one week in advance. Monday through Thursday greens fees are $35; Friday through Sunday fees are $45, and that includes a cart.

## Dunes West
**3535 Wando Plantation Way,
Mt. Pleasant
(843) 856-9000, (888) 955-1234
www.golfduneswest.com**

Ten miles northeast of Charleston in the fast-growing East Cooper area, Dunes West is part of a 4,700-acre residential community that's been in development since the late 1980s. The highly rated course—set on a high, marshy peninsula bounded by three tidal creeks—was designed by Arthur Hills on the site of the historic Lexington Plantation house.

Like its sister course on Isle of Palms, Dunes West takes full advantage of its natural setting. The par 72 championship course is 6,859 yards long. The opening holes, cut from tall pines, have fairway corridors leading to elevated and bunkered greens. The back nine has a typical Lowcountry flavor with moss-draped oaks lining the fairways and expansive views of the marsh from several of the tees and greens. There's a handsome clubhouse with every modern luxury amenity. The pro is Kevin Zemnickas. The Hills course at Dunes West was the site of the 1992 Amoco Centel Championship, and it is now a semi-private course. High season greens fees Monday through Thursday are $70; Friday through Sunday, they are $85.

## Eagle Landing
**1500 Eagle Landing Boulevard, Hanahan
(843) 797-1667**

This semi-private golf course was constructed in 1987 and is slightly different in that it was built at "executive length." You play with a regulation ball, but the course itself is slightly shortened to use less land. The concept is very popular in Japan (where they know a thing or two about space limitations and miniaturization), but it's still fairly rare here. The par 65 course is 4,164 yards long from the middle (traditionally the men's) tees, but only par 62 and 2,910 yards from the forward (or ladies') tees. This foreshortened course takes some getting used to, but many of the residents of the associated Eagle Landing retirement community find the difference refreshing.

The Eagle Landing clubhouse features a fully stocked pro shop and snack bar. You'll also find a driving range and putting greens at this well-maintained facility. This unusual golf challenge is next to the Eagle Landing residential community. The course is public, but club memberships are available. Weekday fees are $15. Saturday and Sunday play will run you $19. Carts are included.

## Edisto Beach Golf Club
**1 King Cotton Road, Edisto Beach
(843) 869-1111**

The course closely associated with Fairfield Ocean Ridge resort on Edisto Island is a semi-private, 18-hole championship layout designed by Tom Jackson in 1976, and it has been considerably updated since then. The 6,400-yard course features water holes, dense subtropical vegetation, and (for early risers) frequent visits by native wildlife. Fairfield has its share of old bull gators, but local wisdom says they prefer sunning and running to fighting.

The course has dune ridges throughout. Where the Nos. 2 and 3 tees are now situated was once a Confederate stronghold. The overall feel of the course is natural, as it was primarily carved from tidal marsh and jungle-thick Lowcountry vegetation. The No. 1 green provides a spectacular view of the Atlantic.

Fairfield's other amenities add to the mix, and you'll find a fully stocked pro shop with club and cart rentals available. Clinics and private instruction are offered. Tee-time reservations are required. Daily rates are $50 for 18 holes before 2:00 P.M. and $43 after 2:00 P.M., but call direct for more information—rates change seasonally.

## The Golf Club at Wescott Plantation
## 5000 Wescott Club Drive,
## North Charleston
## (843) 871-2135, (866) 211-GOLF

Opened in the fall of 2000 with the full 27 holes up and ready for play early the following year, the Club at Wescott Plantation is North Charleston's worthy answer to the trendy designer courses on the resort islands closer to the coast. Designed by Dr. Michael Hurdzan, who took full advantage of the natural elements on the course, all 27 holes are tree-lined with plenty of definition to each hole. Each hole has five tees so golfers can choose tees from 5,120 yards up to 7,100 yards—depending on their ability. The course winds through streams, ponds, wetlands, and key sentinel trees, with holes playing in various directions and lengths from these features. The club also features a full driving range, a completely outfitted pro shop, a full-service restaurant, and meeting/conference spaces. Tony Sylvester is currently head pro. Weekdays (except holidays), fees are $37, weekend fees are $45. Prices are $27 during twilight hours.

## Legend Oaks Plantation
## 118 Legend Oaks Way, Summerville
## (843) 821-4077, (888) 821-4077

Located about 30 minutes from Charleston along scenic Highway 61 is Legend Oaks Plantation, a traditional-style golf layout on the site of an old rice plantation. A romantic avenue of 250-year-old live oaks leads to the Clubhouse, which is reminiscent of Augusta National. The par 72 course was designed by Scott W. Pool,

an associate of Pete Dye, and savvy players say it's akin to Pinehurst No. 2 with its presentation of challenges described as being "straightforward."

Spacious fairways, generous greens, and staggered tees give everyone a chance to enjoy the game, but water comes into play at half the holes, and huge live oaks stand between the golfer and the green. An ability to work the ball is required to score well here. From the blue tees, the course is 6,974 yards—a near-perfect test for the average bogey shooter. Joey Bradley is head pro, and greens fees are $38 on weekdays and $45 on weekends.

---

*The list of designers whose courses carve beautiful curves through the Lowcountry reads like a who's who in the industry. Pete Dye put his signature railroad ties to use at the Ocean Course on Kiawah Island, home of the 1991 Ryder Cup and 1997 World Cup of Golf. Arthur Hills designed the course at Dunes West, which showcased the 1992 Amoco Centel Championship. Tom Fazio crafted both the Links and Harbor Course at Wild Dunes. And Willard Byrd is responsible for Patriots Point and Seabrook's Ocean Winds, both of which are more than a decade old and maturing gracefully. Throw in Rees Jones (Charleston National), Gary Player (Cougar Point at Kiawah), and the Golden Bear himself, Jack Nicklaus (Turtle Point), and you see that Lowcountry courses have come off the drawing boards of the very best.*

---

## The Links at Stono Ferry
## 5365 Forest Oaks Drive, Hollywood
## (843) 763-1817
## www.americangolf.com

This 18-hole, par 72 course, owned and managed by Jim Colbert Golf, Inc., is on Highway 162, off U.S. Highway 17 S. near the little town of Hollywood, about 15 miles or a half-hour from Charleston. The Links opened in 1989 and was designed by Ron Garl to accompany the exclusive Stono Ferry Plantation development. In 2003 the course was upgraded with all-new greens of championship Bermuda grass—adding luster to the Stono challenge. The course is 6,606 yards long and open to the public seven days a week. It has three scenic holes on the Intracoastal Waterway, and it is a fair test from the back tees. You'll find a complete pro shop and a driving range, plus a full-service restaurant. PGA-trained teaching pro Dan Lorentz is on hand for tips and lessons. Rental clubs are available. Advance registration is required. Weekday greens fees are $59 before 2:00 P.M., $45 after. Saturday and Sunday, they are $69 before 2:00 P.M., $53 after. Locals get a discount before 1:00 P.M., and another price break after. There's a twilight fee after 4:00 P.M. Cart fees are included. Rates may vary in season.

**Patriots Point Golf Links**
**100 Clubhouse Road**
**(off U.S. Highway 17 Business),**
**Mt. Pleasant**
**(843) 881-0042**
**www.patriotspointlinks.com**
This 18-hole public course is across the Cooper River bridges in Mt. Pleasant, just off U.S. Highway 17 N., near the towering USS *Yorktown*, anchored in Charleston Harbor. (See our Attractions chapter.) The par 72 layout, open since 1980, has recently had a $2.1-million upgrade with a new state-of-the-art irrigation system installed. Patriots Point affords spectacular views of the harbor, with oceangoing cargo ships frequently passing by.

The course is 6,838 yards in length, with well-contoured fairways and well-bunkered greens. Pro Scott Holland is on hand for lessons and more information. Amenities include a complete pro shop, a driving range, rental clubs and carts. A grill and snack bar are available too. Call ahead for tee times. Greens fees vary by season but run about $68 Monday through Thursday, $82 Friday through Sunday.

**Pine Forest Country Club**
**1001 Congressional Boulevard,**
**Summerville**
**(843) 851-1193**
**www.pineforestcountryclub.com**
The 18 holes at Pine Forest Country Club in Dorchester County wind through the tall Summerville pines with some live oaks, dogwoods, and a lake system thrown in for good measure. Designed by architect Bob Spence in 1992, Pine Forest is noted for their well-kept golf challenges. It is one of the most talked about USGA courses in the Lowcountry. The course is 6,905 yards long from the middle tees, with an equal representation of straightaways, doglegs, and elevation changes. It is nicely balanced, with fun in store for golfers of all abilities. Rental clubs and carts are available. The head pro is Tom Sweeney. Call for reservations. Greens fees vary by season but weekdays are about $45. Saturday and Sunday fees are $55. Carts are included in the prices.

**Rivertowne Country Club**
**1700 Rivertowne Country Club Drive,**
**Mt. Pleasant**
**(843) 216-3777, (866) 216-3777**
**www.rivertownecountryclub.com**
Rivertowne Country Club, just off Highway 41 in Mt. Pleasant, is Arnold Palmer's first signature course in the greater Charleston area. Palmer is quoted as saying, "We wanted to create a golfing experience as distinctive and memorable as the city itself." His 7,188-yard championship layout features beautiful tree-lined fairways, spectacular views of the Lowcountry marsh, and 13 holes positioned along the Wando River and Horlbeck Creek. Club amenities include GPS-equipped golf carts with full-color graphics of each hole and tournament leader boards. There's also a driving range, chipping and putting greens, and a fully stocked golf shop with apparel, clubs, shoes, and accessories. Head pro is Marc Sunshine. Tee times for the public may be reserved by phone or on their Web site. Weekday greens fees are $110, weekends are $125.

**Shadowmoss Plantation
Golf and Country Club
20 Dunvagan Drive
(off Highway 61)
(843) 556-8251, (800) 338-4971
www.shadowmossgolf.com**
Public play is welcome at this scenic course, designed by Russell Breeden and opened in 1973 along Highway 61, the old Ashley River Road. In 1986, the 18-hole par 72 course was extensively renovated, and several water hazards were added to increase the challenge. Other modifications were made after Hurricane Hugo. The course is 6,701 yards long and cuts through pines, oaks, and hickories. A mosaic of ponds and streams comes into play in an area once dotted with early 18th- and 19th-century plantations.

You'll find a well-stocked pro shop, a snack bar, a grill with a lounge, and locker rooms. There's also a putting green as well as a chipping green and driving range. The golf pro at Shadowmoss is Bob Wolfe. Tee times can be arranged through a number of local hotels and inns or by calling Shadowmoss. Monday through Friday greens fees (with cart rental included) are $35, Saturday and Sunday fees are $45.

## COURSES AT LOWCOUNTRY RESORTS

# Wild Dunes

Only 15 miles from Charleston is Wild Dunes, which offers a total of 36 holes of Tom Fazio golf among its many upscale amenities.

**The Harbor Course
5881 Palmetto Drive, Isle of Palms
(843) 886-2164, (800) 845-8880, ext. 4
www.wilddunes.com**
The Harbor Course, which opened in 1985, has four holes set directly along the Intracoastal Waterway. The course is a par 70, with a 6,446-yard layout that really challenges players. Two holes play from one

island to another across the Yacht Harbor, where the wind can be a major factor. Frequent players say to beware the challenging 17th hole. The pro is Joe Stevens, and instruction is available through the fully stocked pro shop. From Monday through Sunday (March 25 through May 31), the greens fees are $120 ($99 after noon)—cart included.

**Wild Dunes Links
5757 Palm Boulevard, Isle of Palms
(843) 886-2164, (800) 845-8880, ext. 4
www.wilddunes.com**
The Links opened in 1980, with a 6,722-yard par 72 layout from the middle tees. Because two of the finishing holes (a par 4 and a par 5) are right on the Atlantic, you'll want to pray for a nonwindy day. Indeed, wind can make the course different every day, but the scenery compensates for its fickle nature. The course is in great condition from tee to green, with rolling fairways and oak and palm trees in abundance. The Links (and Wild Dunes' other offering, Harbor Course) have a new high-tech yardage system for golf guests. Using a golf-cart-mounted display screen linked to a Global Positioning Satellite System, players can determine the distance to a target with pinpoint accuracy. The pro shop is first rate, with Marty Mikesell riding herd on the whole golf program. *Golf Magazine* recently included Wild Dunes Links among its Top 100 courses in the country. From Monday through Sunday (March 25 through May 31), the daily greens fees are $185 ($119 after noon)—cart included.

---

*When you're playing on one of the Lowcountry's many marsh-front golf courses like Cougar Point on Kiawah or the Harbor Course at Wild Dunes, don't be surprised if you find yourself sharing the green with a curious alligator. The unofficial rule is: Let the gator keep the ball; no penalty stroke incurred.*

# Kiawah Island Resort

Internationally famous Kiawah Island offers no fewer than six separate, distinct golf layouts for the adventurous Lowcountry golfer. Popular PGA golf personality Roger Warren heads Kiawah's golf program. The River Course is exclusively reserved for property owners on the island, but Kiawah golf is so famous and popular there's still great opportunity for the tour elite, low handicappers, and the average player too. The Oaks, on Johns Island, is the newest acquisition. And four Kiawah courses—Cougar Point, Turtle Point, Osprey Point, and the Ocean Course, made famous by the internationally televised 1991 Ryder Cup Matches—are semi-private and open to homeowners, guests visiting the island, and Lowcountry vacationers who call specifically for reservations at least 24 hours in advance. Call Kiawah's main switchboard, and check with each course individually for tee times. Note that summer greens fees are slightly lower.

### Cougar Point
**West Beach Village**
**(843) 768-2121, (800) 654-2924**
**www.kiawahresort.com**
Cougar Point, formerly called Marsh Point, reopened in 1996 after a complete year-long makeover by original (1981) course designer Gary Player. Now, this par 72 course has a 6,925-yard layout from the championship tees. Ric Ferguson is the resident pro with a top-flight shop to boot. There's even a halfway house on the 10th hole. Sometimes, four-footed furry creatures, along with alligators, ospreys, hawks, and a few snakes, have been known to be in the gallery here. Daily greens fees in season are $155, cart included.

### Oak Point
**4255 Bohicket Road, Johns Island**
**(843) 768-7030**
**www.kiawahresort.com**
Recently acquired by Kiawah Island Golf, and now another part of its comprehensive golf package, is Oak Point. Tucked away within Hope Plantation adjacent to Kiawah and Seabrook islands, it was designed by Clyde Johnson and built in 1989. The par 72, 6,759-yard-long course is challenging to both the novice golfer and the experienced professional.

Wide areas of windswept fairways stretch along salt marshes and heavily foliaged woodlands. There are numerous vistas of freshwater ponds and winding creeks. Word is that some area golfers prefer this course to Kiawah's Turtle Point, and it's a great choice for 36-hole-a-day players seeking a variety of challenges in the Kiawah-Seabrook area. The pro shop was recently renovated, and PGA pro Stephen Youngner provides instruction for golfers at all levels of play. Hours can vary seasonally; call for tee times and more information. Daily greens fees in season are $88, cart included.

### The Ocean Course
**1000 Ocean Course Drive**
**(843) 768-2121, (800) 654-2924**
**www.kiawahisland.com**
The Ocean Course was designed by Pete Dye and completed just in time for the Ryder Cup matches in 1991. That year, *Golf Digest* named the Ocean Course "best new resort course of the year." Now the magazine calls it America's Toughest Resort Course, and a $2.5-million overhaul finished in the fall of 2002 means the challenge is even greater. The cliffhanger finish of the 1991 Ryder Cup put the course on the must-play list of pros and amateurs everywhere. Dye's beautiful design gives you a par 72, 6,824-yard challenge from the championship tees.

All 18 holes of the Ocean Course offer panoramic views of the Atlantic Ocean, and 10 holes play directly along the pristine, windswept beach. The clubhouse includes a restaurant, bar, pro shop, and locker rooms. The head pro at the Ocean Course is Brian Gerard. Daily greens fees are $245, cart included.

### Osprey Point
### Vanderhorst Plantation
**(843) 768-2121, (800) 654-2924**
**www.kiawahisland.com**

Tom Fazio designed Osprey Point in 1988. The par 72 course is 6,678 yards from the middle tees and has four large, natural lakes. At Osprey Point, Fazio used this superb natural canvas to create a golf challenge of amazing playability and variety. In addition to the natural lakes, there are fingers of saltwater marsh and dense forests of live oaks, pines, palmettos, and magnolias. Jim Kelechi is pro here, and the club has a restaurant, bar, lounge, and locker rooms. Daily greens fees in season are $155, cart included.

### Turtle Point
### East Beach Village
**(843) 768-2121, (800) 654-2924**
**www.kiawahresort.com**

Turtle Point, designed by Jack Nicklaus, is an 18-hole, par 72 course that's 6,914 yards long from the middle tees. It opened in 1981. Turtle Point is a low-profile design with fairway and green settings blended into the existing landscape. Nowhere is this more evident than along the spectacular three-hole stretch woven through rolling sand dunes directly along the Atlantic Ocean. Head pro at Turtle Point is Ronnie Miller. Turtle Point has been the site of the Carolina Amateur and the 1990 PGA Cup Matches. Daily greens fees in season are $155, cart included.

## Seabrook Island

Golf on Seabrook Island is limited to island residents, friends of club members, and visiting resort guests. There are two distinctly different golf challenges on the island: Crooked Oaks, designed by Robert Trent Jones Sr.; and Ocean Winds, designed by Willard Byrd. Both courses have been exe-cuted in beautiful, undisturbed surroundings for challenging championship play. Seabrook's golf courses are the only ones in all of South Carolina that have earned full certification in the Audubon Cooperative Sanctuary Program.

### Crooked Oaks
### 1002 Landfall Way
**(843) 768-1000, (800) 845-2475**
**www.discoverseabrook.com**

Crooked Oaks is an 18-hole, 6,832-yard, par 72 course that meanders through the lush maritime forest and around several black-water lagoons. When Jones designed it back in 1979, he described it as his "hard par-easy bogey" course. After its recent $2.3-million renovation, most of the greens are elevated or well-bunkered; there are no lucky shots to the bentgrass greens. It has rolling fairways weaving through stately live oaks, Spanish moss, sea marsh, and thick forest. Private and group instruction is offered by PGA pro Alan Walker. The fully stocked pro shop has sports fashions as well as equipment. Peak season greens fees are $140, cart included. The nine-hole rate is $90.

### Ocean Winds
### 1002 Landfall Way
**(843) 768-1000, (800) 845-2475**
**www.discoverseabrook.com**

Ocean Winds, designed by Willard Byrd, is slightly older (1973) and is a 6,765-yard, par 72 course from the middle tees. It plays a bit closer to the ocean. As a result, the Atlantic breezes can be a real test for even the best golfer. Ocean Winds golfers enjoy the benefits of a full-service clubhouse facility and a large pro shop, plus clinics and private instruction offered by an excellent teaching staff. Tournament coordination is available from PGA pro Alan Walker. Daily greens fees are $140 and include golf cart. The nine-hole rate is $90.

# BOATING AND WATERSPORTS

Boating is an integral part of the Lowcountry lifestyle. State figures reveal that Charleston County is home to the most boats in South Carolina—30,428 registered watercraft in 2004. That's an amazing statistic—about one boat for every four households on a per capita basis. The Trident area logged 55,120 registrations in 2004, which represents around 14 percent of the South Carolina total.

There seems to be no end in sight for the boating frenzy, as newcomers and old salts alike discover and rediscover the pleasures of spending time on the water. From moonlight sails and family picnics on barrier islands to morning hunts in the back creeks and deep-sea fishing adventures, many are the occasions when "by boat" is the only way to go.

You can bring your own, or you can buy, rent, or charter a boat while you are here. Whatever the case, make certain to acquire, in navigational terms, "local knowledge" before you leave shore. We recommend contacting the U.S. Coast Guard about its Auxiliary Public Education Courses. These cover information about navigational rules, aids to navigation, legal requirements, safety equipment, trailering, and coping with emergencies. State law requires that any person younger than 16 operating a boat or personal watercraft with an engine of 15 horsepower or greater without adult supervision must complete the boating safety training. The courses are held several times a year. For a schedule, call (843) 953-9382 or (800) 277-4301.

Note that laws governing boating under the influence are strictly enforced on South Carolina waters. Boat operators will be tested for blood-alcohol content in the event of accidents. For more information, call the Boating Safety Division of the South Carolina Department of Natural Resources at (843) 953-9382. The local Marine Resources Division is at 217 Fort Johnson Road and can be reached at (843) 953-9300. We suggest you request the department's pamphlet on equipment requirements, rules, and regulations. To find out specifically about licensing, boat titles, and registration, call (843) 953-9301.

Those who want to launch their boat in the Lowcountry will be happy to know that there are a number of landings for public use. On weekends they are generally crowded, and early risers will find it easier to park a car and trailer. The parks department is nearing completion of a major renovation project to improve the public access to 19 area boat ramps. For more information about the status of area landings, contact the Charleston County Park and Recreation Commission at (843) 795-2628.

## MARINAS

If you are interested in docking your boat at a Lowcountry marina, consider the following options. We offer several choices, scattered throughout the Trident area and listed alphabetically.

**Ashley Marina**
**33 Lockwood Drive**
**(843) 722-1996**
**www.ashleymarina.com**
This 180-slip marina, at intracoastal marker 470 on the Ashley River, is on the Peninsula and convenient to all areas of the city. Diesel and gasoline are available at the fuel dock, and there is room for 880 feet of boat docking. In addition to a captain's lounge, ship's store, showers, and a laundry, there is a fax machine, and a notary

public is on the premises. The marina also deals in new and brokered sailboats, trawlers, sportfish, and motor yachts. Marina managers can supply names and phone numbers of charter boats that leave from their marina. Some sample prices of charter opportunities are as follows: A captained fishing charter on either a 28- or 42-foot boat is around $900 for a full day offshore and $700 for a half-day. A three-hour rental for cruising inland waters is $300 plus $75 for each additional hour. (See the Hunting and Fishing chapter for more on charters.)

## Bohicket Marina & Yacht Club
## 1880 Andell Bluff Boulevard, Seabrook Island
## (843) 768-1280
## www.bohicket.com

Next to Kiawah and Seabrook resorts, Bohicket is 12 miles south of Charleston but just 6 miles from the Intracoastal Waterway. Within minutes, boaters are in the open sea. Bohicket's 200 wet slips and floating docks are on deep water, and dry storage is available. A recent renovation has expanded the dry stack storage and converted many of the wet slips to dockaminiums with 60 wet slips reserved for long- and short-term rentals. Shower and bathroom facilities, a laundry, shops, and restaurants make this marina a first-class destination. Boat charters, parasailing, and water tours are offered, and fuel is available at the ship's store. Bohicket Marina is a BoatU.S. facility with member discounts for transient dockage.

## Buzzard's Roost Marina
## 2408 Maybank Highway
## (843) 559-5516

Near Intracoastal marker 11, Buzzard's Roost is a deepwater marina that's just minutes from the city's municipal golf course. There are 190 wet slips along with dockage for transients. A laundry, shower, and gas and diesel fuel are available but no launch facilities. You will find a restaurant and small ship's store here.

## Charleston Harbor Resort & Marina at Patriots Point
## 24 Patriots Point Road, Mt. Pleasant
## (843) 856-9996, (888) 856-9996
## www.charlestonharbormarina.com

Opened in June 1998, the Charleston Harbor Marina created a lot of excitement among area boaters. This full-service marina offers convenient ocean access with its location at the southwestern tip of Patriots Point in Mt. Pleasant. (See more about Patriots Point Naval and Maritime Museum under the Museums and Other Sites section in the Attractions chapter.) This deepwater marina with 460 permanent and transient slips features state-of-the-art design with wide floating docks and protective breakwaters.

Amenities include gasoline and diesel fuel, a laundry, restrooms, and showers, electric and manual courtesy carts, a ship's store, and potable dockside water. Other special services are a shuttle service to downtown Charleston and the Charleston International Airport; rentals of power boats, sailboats, and windsurfers; and inshore and offshore fishing and sailing charters. Adjacent to the Hilton Charleston Harbor Resort (see the Hotels and Motels chapter) and the Patriots Point Links (see the Golf chapter), this resort complex provides endless opportunities for entertainment and recreation.

*Boaters, keep your eyes out for manatees in area waters during the summer months. The gentle, huge, seal-like mammals migrate northward from Florida by ocean, estuaries, and creeks, often swimming along the edges of waterways and in shallow water near marsh grass. Be sure to slow to no-wake speeds, and stay in deeper channels where manatees can dive to avoid collisions. If you see a manatee in South Carolina, call the state's Department of Natural Resources at (800) 922-5431. The department is tracking and recording sightings of this endangered species.*

## Charleston Maritime Center
**10 Wharfside Street**
**(843) 853-DOCK (3625)**
**www.ci.charleston.sc.us**

The Charleston Maritime Center has an all-season, deepwater marina with floating docks for 15 wet slips. Located on the Peninsula's Cooper River side, this facility is near the city market with loads of shops and restaurants for exploring and a major grocery store, Harris Teeter. The Maritime Center is part of Charleston's waterfront area development that includes the South Carolina Aquarium and IMAX Theatre complex nearby. (For more on these sites see the Attractions and Kidstuff chapters.) On-site there are showers, a dock shop, pump-out stations, gas and diesel fuel, ice, and 30- and 50-amp power. Transient boaters are a specialty here. BoatU.S. members receive a discount on fees.

---

 *Remember that Charleston Harbor is a busy "highway" for large ships coming in and out of the Port of Charleston daily. Recreational boaters (both power and sail) must stay clear by avoiding the ship channels, where possible, or crossing them quickly at right angles. Always be alert, and watch for ship or tug-boat traffic.*

---

## City Marina
**17 Lockwood Drive**
**(843) 723-5098**
**www.charlestoncitymarina.com**

This marina is close to all the action around the Peninsula. There are 300 slips and transient dockage, and there is a convenient downtown shuttle service. This marina can accommodate vessels as large as 300 feet at its new megadock. Electric 30-, 50-, and 100-amp power as well as gas and diesel fuel are available. The Marina Variety Store restaurant and Salty Mike's Deck Bar are adjacent for a little land-side dining and recreation. The

marina is nearing completion of a five-year expansion and improvement project adding more slips and facilities such as the ship's store, the reception center, and state-of-the-art control room.

## Cooper River Marina
**1010 Juneau Avenue, North Charleston**
**(843) 554-0790**
**www.ccprc.com**

Your fastest tack to Charleston Harbor may be the Cooper River Marina, located 2 miles north of the Cooper River bridges at the former Charleston Naval Base. This deepwater marina is operated by the Charleston County Park and Recreation Commission and has floating, concrete docks with electric hookups and plenty of free parking. Boat yard storage, security, laundry, fax and e-mail service, restroom facilities with a shower, a marina store, and ice are available. Charleston County residents receive a discount on slip fees.

## Daniel Island Marina
**669 Marina Drive**
**(843) 884-1000**
**www.danielislandmarina.com**

This 20-year-old marina has 44 wet storage slips and 300 in dry stack storage. With the development of Daniel Island (see the Neighborhoods chapter), the marina is seeing more traffic, and it now has a ship's store and deli, a shower, and restrooms. Fuel, ice, and live bait are available. No ramp is here, but work racks and a boat washing area are offered.

## Dolphin Cove Marina
**2079 Austin Avenue, North Charleston**
**(843) 744-2562**

Dolphin Cove is on very deep water on the Ashley between the Ashley River Bridge and the North Bridge. The marina offers 125 wet slips with an additional 250 in dry stack storage. Gas is available here, along with complete on-site engine, hull, and accessory service. Short-term dockage is available, and the facility is equipped with showers, a laundry, a lounge, and a restaurant.

**Duncan's Boat Harbour**
**4354 Bridge View Drive,**
**North Charleston**
**(843) 744-2628, (800) 287-2252**
**www.duncansboats.com**
Duncan's, on the Ashley River in North Charleston, is both a wet and dry storage marina. It has 60 wet slips, 30 outside dry slips, 225 inside dry stack spaces, and a ship's store plus restrooms and showers. Duncan's offers repair service for Mercruiser and Mercury and sells new boats, including the Bayliner, Trophy, Regal, and Cobalt Boats lines.

**Isle of Palms Marina**
**50 41st Avenue, Isle of Palms**
**(843) 886-0209**
**www.isleofpalmsmarina.com**
This marina, on the Intracoastal Waterway marker 116 at Wild Dunes Resort, is a full-service facility with 30 wet slips, floating docks, a restaurant, bathrooms, showers, a laundry, and a ship's store with supplies for boating. Isle of Palms Marina also offers inshore- and offshore-chartered trips, eco-tours, and Jet Ski and boat rentals. (See the Hunting and Fishing chapter.)

**Mariner's Cay Marina**
**3-A Mariner's Cay Drive, Folly Beach**
**(843) 588-2091, (800) 446-6194**
Mariner's Cay is part of Mariner's Cay Resort and is on the Folly River across from the Folly boat ramp. Just 2 miles from the ocean and 9 miles from the Intracoastal Waterway, this 77-slip marina is one of Charleston's closest facilities to the Atlantic and has gas and diesel fuel, ice, and 24-hour security. A laundromat, restrooms with showers, cable TV hookups, and a ship's store complete the amenities.

**Ripley Light Marina**
**56 Ashley Pointe Drive**
**(843) 766-2100**
Just west of the Ashley, in the shadow of California Dreaming (see the Restaurants chapter), you'll find Ripley Light. The 79-

wet-slip marina has showers, a laundry facility, a courtesy vehicle for transport to the Peninsula area, floating concrete docks, and boating supplies. Fuel, bait, and dry storage are available as well.

**Seabreeze Marina**
**50 Immigration Street**
**(843) 853-0932**
One of the newer marinas on Charleston's Peninsula is the dry stack storage facility called Seabreeze Marina. Conveniently located near the new Ravenel bridge on the Cooper River, this site is unobstructed with deepwater access to Charleston Harbor. The experienced marina staff is ready to make your day on the water hassle-free and fun. Call ahead to have your boat launched and fueled, and the cooler packed with your favorite refreshments and snacks from the ship's store. When you return they are ready to wash down the boat inside and out, flush the engine, drain the bilge, and return her to her storage berth. All this service practically guarantees an enjoyable boating experience. A fish cleaning station, maintenance work racks, air-conditioned restrooms and showers, and plenty of floating dock space and parking are other amenities featured here.

**Shem Creek Marina**
**526 Mill Street, Mt. Pleasant**
**(843) 884-3211**
Shem Creek offers 170 dry stacks for boat storage. Convenient for East Cooper residents, Shem Creek is often filled to capacity, but don't expect amenities other than fuel and ice. Adjacent to the Shem Creek boat ramp, this marina bills itself as "Mt. Pleasant's neighborhood marina."

**Stono Marina**
**2409 Maybank Highway, Johns Island**
**(843) 559-2307**
Just 4 miles from the Charleston Peninsula, Stono Marina is next to Buzzard's Roost Marina (see previous listing). Boat repair and service are available, and the ship's store carries boat supplies and ice.

There are restrooms and showers, but no fuel facilities.

**Toler's Cove Marina**
**1610 Ben Sawyer Boulevard,**
**Highway 703 at Intracoastal**
**Waterway, Mt. Pleasant**
**(843) 881-0325**
**www.tolerscovemarina.com**
East of the Cooper, Toler's Cove—surrounded by the Marsh Harbor development—is across the harbor from Charleston and across the Intracoastal Waterway from Sullivan's Island and the Isle of Palms. Toler's Cove can accommodate vessels up to 100 feet in length. The marina has showers and a laundry as well as gas, bait, ice, and other necessities. Discounts are offered to BoatU.S. members.

*Old salts (and new ones too) will want to pick up a copy of the* Boating News *for the latest scoop on all the area's waterfront info. The monthly tabloid, published in Charleston, is distributed along the coast from North Carolina to Florida. Along with news about legislation, boat shows, boatyards, marinas, and other maritime matters, commentary and letters make this a lively read. The free paper can be found at marinas, boating supply stores, and nautical shops, or call (800) 723-2703 or visit* www.theboatingnews.com *to subscribe.*

## BOAT SALES AND REPAIRS

If you are in the market for a new boat, shop the retail stores in the Trident area for reliable sales and service. Beware of fly-by-night operations selling boats out of cow pastures, however, as they are sometimes fronts for liquidation operations and may not be there to help mediate with the manufacturer when your new boat springs a leak.

From the city out to North Charleston, here's a sampling of some of the older establishments. These are also good places to start if you find yourself in need of a boat mechanic while visiting the Lowcountry. If you require a boatyard for more extensive repairs and maintenance contact one of the following: Charleston Boatworks at (843) 554-7775, Halsey Cannon Boatyard at (843) 884-3000, or Ross Marine at (843) 559-0379.

**Charleston Yacht Sales**
**3 Lockwood Drive, Suite 201**
**(843) 577-5050**
**www.charlestonyachtsales.com**
These knowledgeable yacht brokers handle both sail and powerboats with a large selection to choose from. They also offer service, repairs, appraisals, delivery, and surveys. They're next to the municipal marina and are a longtime fixture (since 1965) on the Peninsula.

**Longshore Marine**
**2650 Clements Ferry Road, Wando**
**(843) 216-4700**
**www.longshoremarine.com**
Located on Daniel Island at the entrance to Daniel Island Marina Village, Longshore Marine is a Mercury and Yamaha Outboards dealer. They continue to work on all models with parts, service, and accessories available. Some of their popular lines of new boats are Edgewater, Crownline, and Glacier Bay.

**Renken Boat Center, Inc.**
**2476 Savannah Highway**
**(843) 767-0515**
**www.renkenboatcenter.com**
Renken sells a variety of boats including Hurricane, Sea Fox, Mariah, and Mercury outboards. It also offers parts, service, and accessories. The Renkens have been doing business for many years in the Lowcountry, and theirs is a trusted name.

**Sea Ray of Charleston**
**4415 Sea Ray Drive (off Leeds Avenue),**
**North Charleston**
**(843) 747-1889**
**www.hallmarine.com**

This store is the area's exclusive Sea Ray dealer, selling sport boats, cruisers, and yachts as long as 68 feet. Boston Whaler, Mercruiser, and Mercury are other brand names here, and service and accessories are also offered.

**Seel's Outboard**
**1937 U.S. Highway 17 S.**
**(843) 556-2742**

**2910 U.S. Highway 17 N., Mt. Pleasant**
**(843) 849-8788**
**www.seelsoutboard.com**
Seel's carries Evinrude, Johnson, and Yamaha motors and Grady White boats as well as Chaparral, G3 Boats, Alumacraft, Stinger, Coral Bay, and Sea Hunt. With two locations, on Savannah Highway in West Ashley and the bypass in Mt. Pleasant, Seel's is an established boat dealership that has been in operation since the 1960s.

**St. Barts Yachts**
**3 Lockwood Drive, Suite 301**
**(843) 577-7377**
**www.st-barts.com**
In recent years, Beneteau USA moved its North American corporate headquarters to Charleston, and St. Barts is the local dealer for Beneteau Yachts. Beneteau's factory in Marion, South Carolina, builds sailboats from 31 to 46 feet long as well as custom lengths. St. Barts also represents the Wauquiez line and handles brokerage of all types of sailboats.

## SAILING INSTRUCTION

Sailors or aspiring sailors will find plenty of company in the Lowcountry. If you are interested in learning more about the sport or the local regatta schedule, talk to the enthusiasts at the College of Charleston Sailing Association. They are based at the Charleston Harbor Marina and can be reached at (843) 953-5549. (See listing.) Another good source for information as well as sails, rigging, and repairs is UKSailmakers at (843) 722-0823 or (800) 253-2002.

The following listings will steer your ship in the right direction when it comes to sailing instruction and service.

**College of Charleston**
**Sailing Association**
**Charleston Harbor Marina,**
**24 Patriots Point Road, Mt. Pleasant**
**(843) 216-8450, (843) 953-5549**
**www.cofc.edu/sailing**
The College of Charleston offers adult non-credit sailing classes that meet at the Charleston Harbor Marina. Equipment is furnished, and no advanced skills are required. Basic and intermediate classes are offered April through September. The cost is $295 for 15 hours of sailing instruction on J/22 boats and 4 hours of classroom instruction. Call the association for details.

**Ocean Sailing Academy**
**Charleston Harbor Marina,**
**24 Patriots Point Road, Mt. Pleasant**
**(843) 971-0700, (866) 971-0700**
**www.oceansailingacademy.com**
The Ocean Sailing Academy offers U.S. Sailing Certification courses from the Learn to Sail level on up through Open Ocean Passage Making. They even guarantee skippering ability at the conclusion of any of their courses. Completion of just one course will give you the freedom and certification to rent a boat and head out for a day of sailing. Instruction is given on a range of boats including J/24s, J/80s, Hunter 410s, and Beneteau 473s. Classes may be customized to fit your needs, or you may participate in one of their regularly scheduled courses. They operate Charleston's only public charter sailing club. For more information about classes, the sailing club, team-building programs, and prices, call the number above.

## CHARTERS

If you are dreaming of gliding across Charleston Harbor at sunset or entertaining your friends on a weekend outing, several area power and sailboat charter companies have all types and sizes of yachts to match your fantasy.

### AquaSafaris, Inc.
**P.O. Box 309, Isle of Palms 29451**
**(843) 886-8133, (800) 524-3444**
**www.aqua-safaris.com**

AquaSafaris is a watersport facility at Isle of Palms and Bohicket Marinas (see previous listings). Bareboat rentals of kayaks and 16- to 21-foot skiffs are available by the hour or half-day and full-day. Prices range from $30 per hour up to $455 for the full day. Other adventures here are private sailing charters, including day sails, harbor cruises, sunset sails, or island beach excursions. Their fleet of inshore and offshore fishing boats consists of all types—flats boats, sportfishing yachts, island hoppers, and head boats. Charters are arranged for 1 to 100 people by the hour, or half or full day. Group charters are offered for parties and special events, and catering with customized menus is available. AquaSafaris, Inc., also handles charters worldwide. Call the number listed for reservations and more details on pricing.

### Bohicket Boat Adventure and Tour Co.
**2789 Cherry Point Road,**
**Wadmalaw Island**
**(843) 559-3525**

**2408 Maybank Highway**
**www.bohicketboat.com**

With two locations at Bohicket and Buzzard's Roost Marinas, Bohicket Boat provides all kinds of boating fun for visitors and locals alike. They offer powerboat rentals, sailing charters, river and kayaking tours, and sunset cruises. Bohicket Boat even customizes tours geared to your special interest, be it dolphin-watching, crabbing, shrimping, shelling, or fishing around the barrier islands in the Lowcountry. Prices range from $30 per hour for a 16-foot skiff to $220 per day for a 22-foot Catalina sailboat. The custom tours cost $195 to $395 for two to four hours with up

to six passengers. Call for a monthly calendar of activities and reservations. (For more information on sportfishing trips, see the Hunting and Fishing chapter.)

### Schooner *Pride*
**360 Concord Street**
**(843) 559-9686**
**www.schoonerpride.com**

Sit back, relax, and take a two-hour harbor or sunset cruise on a three-masted, gaff topsail schooner (class C tall ship). What better way to enjoy the vistas of Charleston's historic waterfront? Reservations are recommended, and the fee is $20 for adults and children 12 and older and $15 for children ages 3 to 12. The Schooner *Pride* is also available for private parties of up to 49 people. The two-hour group rate is $800 Friday or Saturday after 6:00 P.M. and $700 all other times. The *Pride* departs from the Aquarium Wharf (near the South Carolina Aquarium). (See the Cruise and Boat Tours section of the Tours chapter for more on the *Pride*.)

## CANOEING

With the amazing system of waterways in the Lowcountry, there are many great opportunities for canoeing. The Charleston County Park and Recreation Commission, (843) 795-4386, can help with a list of community school courses in paddling. Also, each spring, it co-sponsors the East Coast Canoe & Kayak Symposium with the Trade Association of Paddlesports (TAPS). The event is held at James Island County Park. The symposium regularly attracts more than 1,000 paddling enthusiasts of all skill levels for a weekend of lectures, on-water demos, and classes. Reflecting the growing national interest in paddling, local support has made this one of the top events of its kind in the country. See the Annual Events chapter for more on this event.

Lowcountry Paddlers
P.O. Box 13242, Charleston 29422
(843) 556-5865
www.lowcountrypaddlers.net
Regular meetings are open to anyone
interested. Guest speakers talk about their
experiences as well as conservation issues
and upcoming trips. Meetings are held the
third Monday of each month at Provi-
dence Baptist Church on Daniel Island. An
all-day trip is planned for the third Saturday of the month. This family-oriented
group publishes a monthly newsletter and
has about 150 members. The annual membership (which includes membership in
the American Canoe Association) is $35
for an individual or $46 for a family with a
$10 per person surcharge for insurance.
Call the Charleston County Park and
Recreation Commission for contact information about this group.

Palmetto Islands County Park
444 Needlerush Parkway, Mt. Pleasant
(843) 884-0832
www.ccprc.com
This 943-acre nature facility is in a heavily
wooded area, with a two-acre pond and 1-
mile canoe trail. It is a perfect place to
canoe (rentals are no longer available, but
you can bring your own), and a nominal
admission fee of $1.00 a person is
charged. (See the Parks and Recreation
and Kidstuff chapters for more on this
exciting park.)

# KAYAKING

Not too many years back, Charlestonians
didn't know a whole lot about kayaks. But
this is the here-and-now, and kayaking has
definitely become a cool and popular sport.
The waterways around Charleston make an
ideal venue for both the beginning and
expert kayaker to take in the scenery and
tranquility. To find out more, check into the
following groups and venues.

Charleston Watersport Outfitters
1547 Johnnie Dodds Boulevard,
Mt. Pleasant
(843) 884-9098
www.charlestonwatersport.com
Charleston Watersport carries a complete
line of quality watersport equipment and
accessories. They handle sales and rentals
of the Ocean Kayak line of kayaks. The
store is conveniently located on the US 17
Bypass in the K-Mart shopping center to
serve vacationers on nearby Sullivan's
Island and the Isle of Palms. A full-day
kayak rental costs $40, plus $30 for each
additional day, and $60 for an entire
weekend. In addition to kayaks, Charleston
Watersport has a large selection of surfboards (Robert August, Maya, Stewart,
Hobie, and Orion), water skis (HO Sport
Extreme Ski Co.), and wakeboards (Hyper-
lite). The friendly staff can help you
choose your on-the-water fun.

Coastal Expeditions Tours
514-B Mill Street, Mt. Pleasant
(843) 884-7684
www.coastalexpeditions.com
Coastal Expeditions rents kayaks and
offers kayak tours all over the Lowcountry
from marsh creeks to secluded beaches.
Naturalists and instructors certified by the
American Canoe Association and British

*Witness a ship being built right before
your very eyes. The Spirit of South Carolina is taking shape on the Charleston
Peninsula at Ansonborough Field, just
south of the South Carolina Aquarium. A
small crew of boatwrights and volunteers are constructing a big timber pilot
schooner (138 feet in length) as part of a
two-year project initiated by the South
Carolina Maritime Heritage Foundation.
The tall ship project represents the
state's long shipbuilding history and
provides educational opportunities for
the youth of South Carolina. For more
information visit www.scmaritime.org.*

Canoe Union run this operation and take groups of 2 to 40 on nature tours. A quality operation, Coastal Expeditions welcomes beginners and experienced kayakers and also sells new and used equipment. It offers private and group lessons as well. The half-day tours are $58 per person and $88 per person for a full day. Single kayaks rent for $38 for a half-day and $48 for a full day; double kayaks are $48 for a half-day and $58 for a full day. Overnight expeditions for four or more people are a fun option too.

**James Island County Park**
**871 Riverland Drive**
**(843) 795–7275**
**www.ccprc.com**
James Island County Park offers lots of classes and clinics; and day, after-work, and overnight tours are offered in sea kayaking and canoeing. Canoe lessons range from $15 to $35 for Charleston County residents and $18 to $42 for non-residents.

Kayak classes and tours range from $20 for county residents and $24 for non-residents for a basic course, up to $70 for residents and $84 for nonresidents for more advanced offerings. Contact the park for their quarterly program guide to check out the variety of paddler offerings.

> *Practice Plus-One Boating, meaning what you take out on your boating trip be sure to bring back plus one—one piece of litter or debris, every time. If it floats, net it. If it blows out, go back and get it. Act ethically and responsibly to keep our waterways clean for the enjoyment of all.*

**Middleton Outdoor Program**
**4290 Ashley River Road**
**(843) 556–0500, (800) 782–3608**
**www.middletonplace.org**
Middleton offers nature-based kayaking

on the Ashley River year-round and in the black-water cypress swamp seasonally from December through April. Learn to roll and rescue while perfecting your paddle techniques, then follow your guide on a Lowcountry adventure. The basic kayak instruction with guided three-hour tour costs $35 per person ($25 per person for Middleton Inn guests). A two-hour private tour is available on a limited basis for $45 per person. Kayak rentals are also available for $20 per hour.

## WATERSPORTS

Other water recreation opportunities abound in our area and don't necessarily involve owning or chartering a boat. Local waters offer lots of spots that are waiting to be explored on personal watercraft or investigated by scuba diving. Surfing, windsurfing, and waterskiing provide ways to catch a wave or a breeze or jump a wake while demonstrating your finesse. Or maybe just plunging into a pool for a refreshing swim is your answer to the oft-daunting Lowcountry heat. A list of the folks who can help you get started follows.

## PERSONAL WATERCRAFT AND OTHER WET TOYS

To jump on your own Jet Ski and zip around the endless waterways, inlets, and creeks in the Lowcountry for the day, contact one of the following for rental or purchase of personal watercraft.

**Champion Honda Yamaha BMW**
**4155 Dorchester Road, North Charleston**
**(843) 554–4600, (888) 346–8026**
**www.championhondabmw.com**
Champion Yamaha sells the full line of Yamaha watercraft and accessories at competitive prices. It is a full-service center open Monday through Friday from 9:00 A.M. to 6:00 P.M. and Saturday from 10:00 A.M. to 3:00 P.M.

### H2Osmosis Sports at Trophy Lakes
**3050 Marlin Road, Johns Island**
**(843) 559-2520, (866) 213-7993**
**www.h2osmosis.com**
Trophy Lakes is the place for waterskiing, kneeboard, and wakeboard lessons taught by instructors who are nationally ranked on the pro tours. The lessons are taught on two private lakes on Johns Island and are scheduled by appointment. The rates are $50 for approximately 20 minutes. Water-ski and wakeboard pulls are $30 for 20 minutes. Weekly rates also are available. Waterskiing competitions are held here as well, so call H2Osmosis for a schedule of events.

### Tidal Wave Watersports
**69 41st Avenue, Isle of Palms**
**(843) 886-8456**

**1880 Andell Bluff Boulevard,**
**Johns Island**
**(843) 768-3482**
**www.tidalwavewatersports.com**
Tidal Wave Watersports' four locations have personal watercraft rentals, parasailing, and a water-ski school. The Jet Ski rental rates are $55 per half-hour for a single or $75 double and $75 an hour for a single or $95 double.

A special safari tour from Wild Dunes (that's the Isle of Palms address) is a very popular, 90-minute guided excursion by WaveRunner. You venture out into the ocean, up to Capers or Bulls Island (with a stop for beachcombing) and return on the Intracoastal Waterway. The 30-mile round trip starts at $95.

Parasailing choices are offered at all locations, with flights costing $55 (at Isle of Palms or Kiawah Island beach or at Charleston Harbor) for the 600-foot pull and $75 for the 800-foot thrill (it's a 1.5-hour trip). What a way to check out the beach from a bird's-eye view. Believe it or not, takeoff and landing are dry, and anyone age 2 and older may try it. (The minimum weight requirement is 80 pounds, or you fly with someone else.)

Tidal Wave Watersports also holds a waterskiing school at the Isle of Palms location, with U.S. Coast Guard–licensed and insured instructors. Ninety minutes of instruction is $195 for up to four people and includes a boat, captain, and equipment. Tidal Wave Watersports locations are open seasonally in the warmer months. Call ahead for more information.

### Yamaha Suzuki Sea-Doo of Charleston
**5870 Dorchester Road**
**(843) 552-7900**
**www.yssoc.com**
Representing the Sea-Doo line, Yamaha Suzuki Sea-Doo has the largest selection in the area of personal watercraft and jet-powered boats for sale. They run from 85 to 310 horsepower, with lengths up to 20 feet. These boats are good for touring, skiing, and all-around family fun.

## SCUBA DIVING

There are many scuba enthusiasts in this area. Diving the numerous wrecks under Charleston's waters is a real kick. For information about dive trips and activities, our listings give you some good places to start. The College of Charleston also offers a scuba class from time to time. Contact Coach Bruce Zimmerman at (843) 953-5960 to find out about the next scheduled class.

### Atlantic Coast Dive Center
**209 Scott Street, Mt. Pleasant**
**(843) 884-1500**
**www.atlanticcoastdivecenter.com**
Atlantic Coast Dive Center offers beginning dive classes and certification. The evening classes are held twice a week for three weeks and cost $225. Open-water certification is a $90 weekend fee (transportation not included) for training at Lake Jocassee in the upstate. Atlantic Coast Dive Center also organizes trips to many locations, including the Caribbean, the Bahamas, and Florida. To dive our local waters, call to schedule offshore dive charters.

**Charleston Scuba**
**335 Savannah Highway**
**(843) 763-DIVE**
**www.charlestonscuba.com**
This conveniently located store is a center for diving enthusiasts. It provides retail sales, gear rentals, on-site repairs, scuba charter trips, and classes—from open-water certification to dive master. Basic classroom and pool sessions are $295 for the twice weekly, three-week classes. An additional $155 covers four open-water dive sessions that are necessary for certification. Charleston Scuba is adjacent to the Holiday Inn Riverview west of the Ashley.

## SURFING

The surfing craze has been reborn among the young crowd, much to the delight of all those baby-boomer surfer dudes. The Lowcountry's most popular spots for wave action are on Folly Beach and the Isle of Palms. The Washout at East Ashley Avenue, a designated surfing area on Folly Beach, attracts all ages in search of the perfect wave. Other good surf can be found near the Folly Pier at East Atlantic Avenue, 10th Street on Folly Beach, and near the pier and the county park on the Isle of Palms. (Keep in mind that it is illegal to surf closer than 200 feet to a pier.) Bert's Break, at Station 22 on Sullivan's Island, is probably the best low tide break in the area. Local surf shops are equipped with surfing and beach-going needs. A couple of options follow.

**McKevlin's Surf Shop**
**8 Center Street, Folly Beach**
**(843) 588-2247,**
**(843) 588-2261 (Surf Line)**
**www.mckevlins.com**
Opened back in the '60s, McKevlin's carries a full line of surfboards, clothing, and accessories. Some of its better-known board brands are Gordon & Smith, Sharp Eye, Lost, T. Patterson, Harbour, and Seasoned. McKevlin's offers rental of surf and body boards and videos seven days a week. Call the Surf Line for the latest on wind and wave conditions, tides, and water temperatures.

**Ocean Surf Shop**
**31 Center Street, Folly Beach**
**(843) 588-9175**
**www.oceansurfshop.com**
Ocean Surf Shop sells surfboards and all the accessories you can think of to catch a wave. Just getting started? No problem—they give lessons and rent boards, too. Some of their major brands are Davo, Hobie, Surftech, Perfection, and Greg Loher. They carry fins, nose guards, leashes, car racks, decals, and sports watches to complete the gear. Wetsuits, tees, board shorts, sandals, and sunglasses from Billabong, Reef, Rainbow, Costa Del Mar, and Oakley outfit you wet or dry. This is the place to get "Edge of America" logo items to prove you've spent a day on the Edge. (See the Neighborhoods chapter for more on Folly Beach.)

*Are you ready to take the plunge? The annual Lowcountry Splash, a 2.4-mile open-water swim organized by Rehabilitation Centers of Charleston, is attracting more participants who are up to the challenge. The race through Charleston Harbor starts at Hobcaw Yacht Club on the Wando River in Mt. Pleasant and continues under the Cooper River bridge past the USS Yorktown, finishing at the Charleston Harbor Resort & Marina's floating docks. The Splash is held in late May or early June so that the water temperature has usually warmed up a bit, and, depending upon the tide and weather, swimmers may experience varying conditions—all part of the event. The cost to enter is $40 ($30 prior to May 1), and more information can be found at www.rcctherapy.com or by calling (843) 884-7880.*

# SWIMMING

### James Island Recreational Complex
### 1088 Quail Drive
### (843) 720-3806
### www.ci.charleston.sc.us

Operated by the city's Department of Recreation Aquatics Division, this 25-yard, outdoor pool with lifeguards is open June through August. Water fitness classes and swimming lessons are planned for the mornings, and open swimming is the norm in the afternoon. Adult city residents can swim for $2.00, nonresidents for $4.00; residents 17 and younger pay $1.50; nonresidents, $3.00. City residents pay $20 for youth swimming lessons and $25 for adult lessons; parent and tot swims are $15. Nonresidents pay $30 for youth lessons, $35 for adults, and $25 for parent and tot swimming.

### Palmetto Islands County Park
### 444 Needlerush Parkway, Mt. Pleasant
### (843) 884-0832
### www.ccprc.com

The outdoor water playground at Palmetto Islands County Park is open 10:00 A.M. to 6:00 P.M. on weekends in April and May and mid-August through Labor Day, and every day from Memorial Day until mid-August. Charges for county residents are $5.99 for an adult and $4.99 for a child under 42 inches tall; nonresidents pay $6.99 for an adult and $5.99 for a child. Children younger than 2 can swim for free. Swimming fees are in addition to a $1.00 per person park admission. (For more on this and other Charleston County parks, see the Kidstuff and Parks and Recreation chapters.)

### Richard L. Jones Recreation Center Pool
### 391 Egypt Road, Mt. Pleasant
### (843) 884-2528
### www.mtpleasantrec.com

There is a six-lane, indoor swimming pool at the Richard L. Jones complex. Swimming lessons, aquatic exercise classes, lap and recreational swimming are some of the many options. Membership is open to anyone. Mt. Pleasant residents pay only $2.00 for a one-year membership plus $2.00 each time they swim. Children 4 and younger swim free. Nonresidents pay $100 for yearly memberships plus the $2.00 swim fee. Swimming lessons range from $23 to $40 for residents and from $28 to $45 for nonresidents. A similar schedule of lessons is also offered at the Park West Complex Pool. Call (843) 856-2196 for more information.

### W. L. Stephens Aquatic Center
### 780 West Oak Forest Drive
### (843) 724-7343
### www.ci.charleston.sc.us

This is a good place to start your exploration of swimming pools in the Greater Charleston area, as the City of Charleston Aquatics Division has an office here. Open year-round, this indoor pool has six lanes and is 25 yards long. It is a popular winter birthday-party venue—nothing like a warm swim when there's frost on the windows—and draws its share of regular lap swimmers. There are full showers. The price to use the pool is $2.00 for adults and $1.50 for children younger than 17. Swimming lessons for residents are $15 for parent-tot, $20 for children, and $25 for adults; nonresidents, $25 for parent-tot, $30 for children, and $35 for adults.

# HUNTING
# AND FISHING

Hunting and fishing are major recreational traditions in the Trident area. When the Hon. William Elliott published *Carolina Sports by Land and Water* in 1846, it was called a "description and defense" of these sports in the Lowcountry. Today, the best defense of these outdoor activities is that many who participate in them are also conservation-minded people who help implement and adhere to laws protecting wildlife. Limits, seasons, and a licensing program are part of an overall system that fosters responsible sportsmanship and helps maintain diversity and numbers in fields and streams.

## HUNTING

Hunting is one of the most important industries in the state. Deer hunters alone contribute more than $180 million to South Carolina's economy. Overall, there are more than 200,000 licensed hunters here. To ensure the future of the industry, the South Carolina Department of Natural Resources sponsors a number of events to expose youth to hunting. Parent-child and adult-youth hunts for doves, ducks, and turkeys are among the outings they organize. The DNR also works closely with the many active conservation groups to promote youth and adult hunting. For more information on these and other programs, visit www.dnr.state.sc.us.

From raccoons to deer, turkeys to ducks, there is both variety and quantity in Lowcountry habitats. Deer hunting has overtaken dove hunting as the most popular type of hunting in South Carolina. The high deer population and the relative ease of accessibility, combined with the long

Lowcountry season (usually August 15 to January 1), are factors in its popularity. There are a lot of public and private lands set up specifically for deer hunting in this area.

The mourning dove continues to be popular quarry for hunters. It's ranked as the No. 1 game bird in South Carolina. Dove shoots are quite common in September, late November, and late December/early January and provide social events for many Lowcountry hunters. The sport is strong, but a slight decline in the dove population during the last few years has led to some restrictions, including the elimination of morning hunts during the first three days of the season and a bag limit of 12 doves per hunter per day. Turkey hunting has grown in popularity because of a very successful restoration project that moved turkeys from the Francis Marion National Forest in the 1950s and from the Piedmont and Savannah River Plant areas in the 1970s to other habitats across South Carolina. The season lasts four to six weeks in the spring and is an option in every county in the state.

Small game hunting for squirrel, rabbits, fox, raccoon, opossum, and quail provides more seasonal hunting opportunities. Most quail hunting takes place from late fall to early spring on public shooting reserves. On private lands in the Trident area, the season usually runs from late November to early March with a limit of 15 birds per hunter per day because of the limited numbers of coveys of quail.

Waterfowl hunting has experienced a big rebound after more than a decade of drought in the Canadian breeding grounds. More abundant moisture on the grounds and more acreage of nesting cover provided by the Conservation Reserve Program have increased the continent's water-fowl population. The past couple of years have seen the Lowcountry's numbers increasing as well. Blue-winged teals and northern shovelers are at all-time population highs, according to the Office of Migratory Bird Management for the U.S. Fish and Wildlife Service. Other species on the rise include greenwings, goldeneye, and buffleheads, in addition to the diving ducks such as canvasbacks and redheads.

## BEFORE TAKING TO THE FIELD

So how does the would-be hunter in the Lowcountry get set for those early-morning outings in a duck blind or late afternoons in a deer stand?

The South Carolina Department of Natural Resources publishes a booklet, *South Carolina Rules and Regulations for Hunting, Fishing, and Wildlife Management Areas,* that details hunting areas, regulations, education, limits, and check stations. For your free copy, write to the department at P.O. Box 167, Columbia 29202, or call locally at (843) 953–9307. The booklets can also be found at local sporting goods stores and the sporting goods departments at large retailers (such as Wal-Mart and Kmart), where you also can purchase hunting and fishing licenses. (Licenses are also available by phone 24 hours a day at (888) 434–7472 or on the Internet at www.dnr.state.sc.us with an additional $3.95 processing fee.) Turkey, migratory bird, and waterfowl hunting regulations and seasons are outlined in even more detail in separate brochures available just before the various seasons. Initiated in 1998, a migratory game bird permit is required in South Carolina. To get the free permit, hunters must obtain a migratory bird Harvest Information Program (HIP) permit by answering a few questions on forms available at all license vendors.

The South Carolina DNR Wildlife and Marine Resources Division designates private land in the Trident area as Game

*Hunters often ignore the danger of hearing loss, but prolonged exposure to the sounds of gunfire can lead to gradual, permanent deterioration. Non-electronic and electronic devices can alleviate the problem and are available at a wide range of prices. The over-the-counter models start as low as $8.00 or $9.00, a small price to pay to preserve good hearing.*

Zone 6. In addition to laws restricting hunting by personal invitation on private property, state game wardens also actively enforce regulations on other lands—marked as either Wildlife Management Areas (WMAs) or U.S. Forest Service property—where public hunting is allowed.

Obviously, residents or visitors must be licensed to hunt in the Trident area. Remember that seasons, prices, gender restrictions, and limits change virtually every year. Deer season generally lasts from mid-August to January 1. Migratory game bird season always comes in the fall. Other hunting season dates are available by calling (843) 953–9307. The annual price for a state resident to hunt in a management area is $30.50, with an additional $6.00 needed to hunt big game. For non-residents, it costs $125 for an annual license to hunt small game. A 10-consecutive-day, nonresident, small-game-only license costs $75, and a 3-consecutive-day one costs $40. Nonresident fees for hunting big game are $100 plus $76 for a management area permit.

For annual waterfowl season, hunters may buy a management area permit (in addition to their state hunting license and all necessary stamps) to hunt in designated areas (prices are the same as listed in the previous paragraph). Always make sure you know that you are within the scope of state and federal game laws before you head out to hunt.

For information about the South Carolina Department of Natural Resources' free 10-hour hunter education course, contact the department at the address given, and mark the letter: "Attention: Hunter Education." You can call the department at (803) 734–3885 or (800) 277–4301 or locally at (843) 953–9302. The course combines classroom instruction (covering hunting ethics, hunter-landowner relations, and basic conservation and wildlife management principles) and hands-on experience in hunter safety and hunting techniques. It is required that all residents and nonresidents born after June 30, 1979, successfully complete the course before a hunting license can be obtained. This course is accepted by other states that require safety certification for licenses, and South Carolina recognizes certification from other states.

## FISHING

The Trident area offers some of the best fishing on the East Coast. Charleston County, blessed with some 60 miles of protected coastline, is a fishing enthusiast's paradise. The fresh waters of the Ashley and Cooper Rivers, with their adjacent rice field breaks and salt creeks, bays, and (of course) the ocean are all open to the public. Fish for largemouth bass, bream, trout, flounder, or spottail bass in these rivers and bluefish in the harbor, or head out to the deep water to match wits with dolphin, wahoo, marlin, sailfish, or tuna.

Berkeley County's Marion and Moultrie Lakes cover 170,000 acres with striped bass, largemouth bass, sunfish, white bass, crappie, and catfish aplenty. Dorchester County includes part of the Edisto River, home to striped bass and American shad—

___

*Fishing for more information? Check out the area's source for weather, fishing reports, charters, tournaments, classifieds, recipes, and more. Visit www.charlestonfishing.com for the lowdown on local recreational fishing.*

the roe of which, often prepared and served with grits, is a Lowcountry delicacy. Largemouth bass, redbreast, and bluegill bream and catfish also swim the Edisto.

# Before You Drop a Line

Residents and out-of-state visitors pay fees to fish or shrimp, with rates varying according to the fishing venue and angler's age. (No license is necessary for dock or pier fishing.) For residents and nonresidents, saltwater fishing licenses (Marine Recreational Fisheries Stamps) are $10. Freshwater licenses are $10 on an annual basis for South Carolina residents. For out-of-state anglers, annual licenses to fish only fresh waters cost $35, and one-week freshwater licenses are $11. Ask the South Carolina Marine Resources Division about combination discounts if you plan to be both hunting and fishing.

In an effort to protect the fish population, South Carolina has also established regulations regarding limits on the sizes and number of fish that may be taken, the use of seines and gill nets, and guidelines concerning crabbing, shrimping, and other fishing activities. Saltwater fishing conservation and ethical angling practices are not only encouraged but enforced. Undersized fish and fish over the quantity limits should be released, helping to ensure future fish populations. Fortunately, the number of saltwater finfish tagged and released in South Carolina waters is increasing each year as more and more anglers take up this practice. Already, it is conserving resources and providing valuable information on the growth and movement of fish for further study and management. Again, for more specific information about seasons, rules, and licenses, refer to the South Carolina Department of Natural Resources' annually issued rules and regulations booklet (see Hunting for details on how to pick up a copy) or contact the Marine Resources Division at (843) 953–9300.

# Deep-Sea Fishing

Deep-sea fishing is a popular sport, and charter boats allow visitors and locals alike to enjoy the experience. Locals say that the best offshore fishing is during the months from May through September, when water temperatures are warmer, although, weather permitting, you can venture out at other times of the year. Charter trips are on luxury boats—air conditioned and large enough to ride out the ocean swells, yet small enough to put you on a first-name basis with the captain. The average cost for ocean reef charter trips—although prices can vary at the captain's discretion—is $700 for a half-day (that's for up to six passengers) and $1,100 for a full day (again, for six passengers).

Gulf-stream charters are only offered on a full-day basis and run about $1,000 for 10 hours, $1,150 for 12 hours, and $1,300 for 14 hours for six passengers. A gratuity is not included, and you'll want to tip the captain and mates whether the fish were biting or not. These guys earn their keep by charting the course, baiting the lines, and doing their best to find the fish. On both charter and "head" boats, which accommodate dozens more people on a "per head" basis at a fraction of a charter's cost, all rods, reels, bait, and tackle will be provided. Visiting anglers may be amazed to see that a little bit of everything is used to catch fish here—from ballyhoo with skirts to live bait to lures without bait. On charter boats, anglers usually bring along food and a drink cooler. On head boats, you can almost always count on a snack bar.

Call at least a month before you visit to book a charter. It is not normally necessary to contact a head boat more than a couple of days before you want to go out. Most captains are going to lead you to the reefs or the Gulf Stream and want you to plan on a long, physically challenging but exhilarating day. Be prepared: If you tend to get seasick, ask your doctor to recommend good over-the-counter preventive medicine. General common sense suggests you get a good night's sleep before your day on the boat, which will usually begin before dawn.

While on the sea, drink lots of nonalcoholic fluids, and don't forget your sunglasses and sunscreen, a long-sleeved shirt, a hat that shades your face, deck shoes with good traction, a couple of towels for drying off periodically, and a camera to prove the size of that mighty one that got away.

Expect to land fish such as king and Spanish mackerel, cobia, sea bass, and even barracuda if you are on the reefs. In the Gulf Stream, you'll likely pull blue or white marlin, wahoo, tuna, dolphin, or sailfish, so break out the recipes. Bottom fishing in the Gulf Stream could lead to good hauls of snapper, grouper, porgy, or amberjack—all good eating.

# Inshore Fishing

Perhaps inshore fishing is more to your liking. The ubiquitous winding rivers, creeks, and inlets in the Trident area offer lots of action without the lengthy trip out to the Gulf Stream. The quiet beauty of the setting and the salt marsh air can afford a memorable experience and, we hope, some good eating afterward. Go after flounder, king mackerel, trout, jack crevalle, spottail bass, or redfish.

The cooler months of the year, usually from September through April, are the best times to wet a line inshore. The clarity of the water is good then, and in shallow water, you may even see the fish and cast directly to them. (The summer months may be slightly less inviting for fishermen because of the heat and prevalence of gnats and mosquitoes.) Anglers use light-tackle rods and reels and saltwater fly rods for snagging most inshore catches.

# Charter Boats

The main charter operators in the area are based around five marinas: Charleston Harbor Marina, (843) 856-9996, Isle of Palms Marina, (843) 886-0209, and Toler's Cove, (843) 881-0325, in East Cooper; Ripley Light Marina, (843) 766-2100, west of the Ashley; and Bohicket Marina, (843) 768-1280, on Johns Island. Contacting them should provide the latest information on available charters for all kinds of fishing.

The following listings should give you a good head start on some of the head or charter boats available for offshore or inshore fishing. Take note that these salty seagoing veterans don't always like to be tied down to specific price ranges. Be ready to bargain. (For more information, see the Boating and Watersports chapter.)

**Bohicket Boat Charters**
**Bohicket Marina**
**1880 Andell Bluff Boulevard,**
**Johns Island**
**(843) 768-7294**
**www.bohicketboat.com**
Bohicket offers inshore, flats, offshore, and Gulf Stream fishing trips out of Bohicket Marina, near Kiawah and Seabrook Islands. Charters include full-, three-quarter-, and half-day trips on 24- to 43-foot passenger boats. Rates start at $300 for two people for four hours of flats fishing for redfish and trout. Inshore family fishing for four to six passengers begins at $295 for three hours. Offshore rates are $450 to $880 for half-days, $1,000 to $1,320 for three-quarter days, and $1,450 to $1,750 for full-day trips. Boat rentals from 15-foot skiffs to 23-foot deck boats are also available, along with tackle, trips to find shells, sunset cruises, and other customized journeys. Rates begin at $110 to $225 for half-days and $160 to $350 for a full day. (For more on Bohicket Marina, see the Boating and Watersports chapter.)

**Captain Ivan's Island Charters**
**805 Duck Hawk Retreat**
**(843) 762-2020**
**www.captainivan.com**
Specializing in live-bait and light-tackle fishing, Captain Ivan's 30-foot, wide-beam boat has custom rods, reels, and tackle and is Coast Guard certified. Half-day trips for up to four passengers are $550 with each additional passenger adding $100. Full-day trips for up to four are $900, adding $100 for each additional person. Gulf Stream trolling or bottom fishing runs $1,300 for up to four with additional passengers adding $100 each. Specialty trips for shark fishing and tournaments are available for booking, too.

**Capt. Peter H. Brown**
**522 Old Bridge Court, Mt. Pleasant**
**(843) 830-0448**
**www.saltcharters.com**
Full-time guide Capt. Peter Brown spends 280 days a year targeting gamefish along South Carolina's coast. And what does he do on his days off? Goes fishing, of course! His full-, three-quarter-, and half-day private charters are aboard an 18-foot flats skiff, ideal for stalking big fish in very shallow water. He also takes up to six people in his 23-foot center console for tarpon and near-shore fishing. Rods and tackle are provided for year-round inshore light-tackle and fly fishing. U.S.C.G. licensed and insured, Peter specializes in sight casting, and (depending on the season) he'll put you on the red drum, black drum, trout, flounder, Spanish mackerel, and jack crevalle. A four-hour trip is $300, a six-hour $400, and an eight-hour runs $500.

**Capt. Richard Stuhr**
**Inshore Light-Tackle and Fly Fishing**
**547 Sanders Farm Lane**
**(843) 881-3179**
**www.captstuhr.com**

Capt. Richard Stuhr, a native Charlestonian with lifelong experience on the water, offers custom trips into the inland waters of the Lowcountry on his 19-foot Action Craft. His specialties are inshore light-tackle and fly fishing. This Orvis-endorsed guide offers full- and half-day trips for one to three people (or two adults and two children) year-round. Prices range from $300 for half-days to $500 for full days.

### Carolina Clipper
**Shem Creek, 825 Creekside Drive, Mt. Pleasant**
**(843) 884-2992**
**www.carolinaclipper.net**
This large, comfortable boat, complete with snack bar and electric reels, is air conditioned and takes off each day, year-round at 7:00 A.M. Early-bird and overnight trips are available as well. Home base is on the north side of Shem Creek Bridge in Mt. Pleasant. Capt. Billy Knight is owner and operator.

### Fin Stalker Charters
**6 Hillcreek Boulevard**
**(843) 795-4707**
**www.backwaterfishing.com**
Lowcountry native Captain Chris Chavis really knows his way around the area's inshore estuaries, tidal creeks, and barrier island waters. He offers full- and half-day charters for light-tackle and fly fishing year round. The half-day rate is $350 and full-day is $550. All equipment is provided, and trophy photos are available. His Action Craft "flats boat" is ideal for stalking redfish, trout, jack crevalle, tarpon, Spanish mackerel, sharks, and cobia, among other sportfish challenges. No license is required. Call for more information and reservations.

### Harbor Fishing Charters
**1410 Downing Street**
**(843) 452-8844**
To fish the backwaters of the Lowcountry, including Charleston Harbor and the barrier islands, charter with Reid Simmons, an experienced inshore guide. Using light tackle and live bait, you will pursue spot-tail bass, trout, and flounder on his 19-foot flats boat. Half-day rates start about $350, and a full day is about $450.

### Isle of Palms Marina Charters
**41st Avenue at Intracoastal Waterway, Isle of Palms**
**(843) 886-0209**
**www.isleofpalmsmarina.com**
Isle of Palms Marina offers a variety of inshore and offshore fishing trips with three-quarter and full-day options. Inshore flats fishing for four hours is $325 for two people. For inshore fishing around the jetties, the cost starts at $550 for six hours. Offshore fishing on a nine-hour trip for four people is $1,175. Crabbing trips, shelling, beachcombing, motorboat rentals, as well as sunset and moonlight cruises are also available. (See the Boating and Watersports chapter for more on Isle of Palms Marina.)

### Palmetto Charters, LLC
**434 Brown Pelican Drive, Wando**
**(843) 849-6004**
**www.palmettocharters.com**
Palmetto Charters operates an offshore/inshore fishing charter fleet that departs from the Charleston Harbor Marina at Patriots Point as well as Ripley Light and Toler's Cove. The fleet encompasses a dozen boats ranging in size from 24 to 72 feet. Palmetto Charters offers some of the best guides and offshore fishers in the area with the better-known sportfishing yachts. The offshore trips for up to six passengers range from $675 for a half-day up to $1,550 for a full day depending on the size of the boat. Inshore rates for two people range from $400 to $600 depending on the length of time booked.

### Sea Fix Offshore Charters
**633 Royal Avenue, Mt. Pleasant**
**(843) 577-0800, (843) 881-0180, (800) 487-7565**
**www.seafix.com**
Sea Fix Charters offers a 54-foot Craig Blackwell sportfishing yacht designed for

*Anglers in privately owned boats need to remember that it is unlawful to fish within 150 feet of commercial fishing piers extending into the Atlantic Ocean.*

a comfortable ride with twin 800-horse-power diesel engines to get you to the Gulf Stream fast. An air-conditioned salon, top-of-the-line electronics, and tournament-grade tackle set you up for a great day of fishing. Book this boat for Gulf Stream, full-, three-quarter, half-day, and tournament charters. Up to six passengers may go, and the charters depart from Toler's Cove Marina in Mt. Pleasant. Rates range from $600 for a half day to $1,000 for a full day. This charter service also offers a 34-foot Atlantic.

# Fishing Piers and Bridges

Maybe you just want to escape for a couple of hours to see what you can find by dropping a line in the neighborhood waters. After all, scheduling a charter or putting the boat in the water often takes advance planning and a major commitment of time. Or perhaps you have the kids in tow—those attention spans may only be good for an hour or so. The Charleston area provides ample opportunity for this leisurely walk-up pastime. A number of piers and bridges for saltwater fishing are maintained and operated by the Charleston County Park and Recreation Commission and the City of Charleston.

### The Battery
### East Battery at Murray Boulevard
### (843) 724-7321
### www.charlestoncity.info
The seawall at White Point Gardens is a historic spot that has served as a promenade for Charlestonians for a couple of hundred years. This tip of the Peninsula is

where the Ashley and Cooper Rivers meet, as Charlestonians are fond of saying, to form the Atlantic Ocean. The confluence of the rivers here can make for some good fishing too, so drop a line anywhere along the 1.5-mile waterfront access. The Battery is open year-round and, with any luck, parking is found alongside.

### Breach Inlet Bridge
### Highway 703, Sullivan's Island,
### Isle of Palms
This bridge connecting Sullivan's Island and the Isle of Palms is almost never without some anglers. Because of the narrow inlet connecting the ocean with the creeks and waterway behind the islands, the currents are very strong, and swimming in the area is prohibited. But these currents can make for some lively fishing, as the fish are funneled through with the changing tides. Free parking is nearby on either side of the bridge, and the bridge's catwalks on both sides are open year-round.

### Brittlebank Park Pier
### Lockwood Drive
### (843) 724-7321
### www.charlestoncity.info
Operated by the city of Charleston, this pier with a floating dock extends 200 feet out onto the Ashley River on the west side of the Peninsula. At Lockwood Drive and Fishburne Street next to the Joseph P. Riley Ballpark, the 10-acre park is a venue for many large outdoor concerts and events. Parking is available, but there are no restrooms or other facilities. No fee is charged. It is open sunrise to 11:00 P.M. daily.

### Folly Beach Edwin S. Taylor Fishing Pier
### 101 East Arctic Avenue, Folly Beach
### (843) 588–FISH
### www.ccprc.com
Extending more than 1,045 feet into the Atlantic Ocean, this 25-foot-wide pier is noted for the distinctive design of a diamond-shaped platform at its end. The platform itself covers a 7,500-square-foot

area, with part of it under a covered shelter. The pier is 23 feet above sea level and affords great fishing, walking, birding, and viewing of Folly Beach and the ocean. Landward, a large facility provides restrooms (unisex restrooms are available, too, for people with disabilities and parents with small children), a tackle shop, and the Starfish Grille (see the Restaurants chapter). The pier is operated by the county park system and is open daily from 6:00 A.M. to 11:00 P.M. April through October, 7:00 A.M. to 7:00 P.M. March and November, and from 8:00 A.M. to 5:00 P.M. December through February. Parking is $5.00, and the fishing fees are $5.00 for an adult Charleston County resident ($8.00 for king mackerel fishing), $3.00 for children 12 and younger, and $8.00 for a nonresident adult ($10 for king mackerel fishing). You can also rent rods and get annual passes here.

### James Island County Park Dock
**871 Riverland Drive**
**(843) 795-7275**
**www.ccprc.com**
On a tidal creek on the Stono River, this floating dock offers tranquil fishing and crabbing with complete facilities and wheelchair access. Crabbing classes, which give pointers on catching and cooking crab, are offered here from time to time. Part of the dock is covered, and picnic tables are nearby. The park has plenty of parking and is open daily May through August, from 8:00 A.M. to 8:00 P.M.; October and March from 8:00 A.M. to 6:00 P.M.; September and April from 8:00 A.M. to 7:00 P.M.; and November through February 8:00 A.M. to 5:00 P.M. The individual admission price is $1.00, with no charge for children younger than three. (See the Kidstuff and Parks and Recreation chapters for more about the recreational opportunities at James Island County Park.)

### Palmetto Islands
**County Park Fishing Dock**
**444 Needlerush Parkway, Mt. Pleasant**
**(843) 884-0832**
**www.ccprc.com**

Wind down a paved walking trail to this large, floating dock at the Peninsula Center on Horlbeck Creek and Boone Hall Creek. There are also several smaller docks for peaceful fishing and crabbing within the Palmetto Islands County Park, which offers full facilities. Hours are 9:00 A.M. to 6:30 P.M. from April through September; 9:00 A.M. to 5:30 P.M. in March and October; and 9:00 A.M. to 4:30 P.M. from November through February. Park gate admission is $1.00 per person, with children younger than three free. (For more on the Palmetto Islands County Park, see the Kidstuff and Parks and Recreation chapters.)

### Pitt Street Bridge
**End of Pitt Street, Mt. Pleasant**
**(843) 849-2022**
At the end of Pitt Street, on the Intracoastal Waterway overlooking Charleston Harbor, is the old Pitt Street Bridge. The half-mile bridge is the former trolley car causeway, now closed to traffic, which used to connect Mt. Pleasant and Sullivan's Island. It's a good place to fish and a great spot for watching waterway boat traffic. The town of Mount Pleasant provides year-round access to the bridge at no fee.

### Waterfront Park Pier
**Cumberland Street to North Adgers**
**Wharf Charleston**
**(843) 724-7321**
**www.charlestoncity.info**
Waterfront Park is quite a popular spot for tourists and locals because of its setting overlooking Charleston Harbor toward Mt. Pleasant and Ft. Sumter. Fishing may be a good excuse to spend the day here, but there are many pleasant distractions like the passing boats and wildlife—don't forget to check your line every now and then. There is no entry fee, but you will have to search for a metered parking spot or enter one of the nearby garages for a charge. The park and pier are open daily year-round from 6:00 A.M. to midnight. No facilities are available, but an easy stroll

**CLOSE-UP**

# Lowcountry Lunkers

Several state-record-size gamefish have been landed in Lowcountry waters. Here's a listing of several, with the type of fish, weight (in pounds and ounces), port, year, angler, and angler's hometown noted.

**African Pompano**—35-8; Mt. Pleasant, 1997; by M.L. Wireman, Charleston.
**Albacore Tuna**—37-4; Charleston, 1976; by W. Crump, Johns Island.
**Bigeye Thresher Shark**—406-0; Edisto Island, 1978; by J.H. Mixson, Johns Island.
**Blackfin Tuna**—40-6; Charleston, 2005, by Mark Hartley, Mt. Pleasant.
**Bluefish**—21-0; Charleston, 1975; by J.A. Curtis, Charleston.
**Blue Marlin**—881-12; Charleston, 2005; by W.C. Taylor, Spartanburg.
**Bull Shark**—477-12; Stono Inlet, 1985; by C.R. Faust, Folly Beach.
**Croaker**—4-9; Charleston, 1979; by C.I. Frasier, Charleston.
**Dolphin**—74-6; Mt. Pleasant, 1994; by W.C. Etheredge, Columbia.
**Dusky Shark**—466-12; Charleston, 1981; by M. Almond, Charleston.
**Florida Pompano**—8-12; Charleston, 1975; by C. Mullinax Sr., Charleston.
**Gag Grouper**—48-8; Charleston, 1997; by R.L. Price, Summerville.
**Gray Snapper**—11-1; Charleston, 2002; by R.L. Price, Ladson.
**Hammerhead Shark**—588-3; Charleston, 1989; by B. Bass, Charleston.
**Jack Crevalle**—40-1; Charleston, 1993; by J. Benich, Mt. Pleasant.
**Jolthead Porgy**—18-4; Charleston, 1984; by J. Currie, North Charleston.
**King Mackerel**—62-0; Charleston, 1976; by J. Brownlee III, Charleston.
**Ladyfish**—5-14; Charleston, 1994; by B. Raver, Charleston.
**Lemon Shark**—370-0; Charleston, 2002; by R.L. Price, Ladson.
**Little Tunny**—29-7; Charleston, 1975; by C. Edwards Jr., Columbia.
**Longbill Spearfish**—53-0; Mt. Pleasant, 1986; by H.L. Johnson Jr., Mt. Pleasant.
**Red Grouper**—30-2; Charleston, 1976; by G. Frost, Belvedere.
**Sandbar Shark**—199-4; Charleston, 1984; by T. McGuiness, Charleston.
**Sand Tiger Shark**—350-2; Charleston, 1993; by M. Thawley, Summerville.
**Sheepshead**—15-12; Charleston, 2001; by D. Hoover, Charleston.
**Shortfin Mako Shark**—391-15; Charleston, 2002; by P. Ford, Charleston.
**Silky Shark**—248-0; Charleston, 1981; by R. Keenan, Charleston.
**Skipjack Tuna**—25-14; Charleston, 1986; by D.L. Stubbs, Charleston.
**Southern Flounder**—17-6; South Santee, 1974; by L.C. Floyd, Florence.
**Spinner Shark**—159-0; Mt. Pleasant, 1998; by J. Short, Ellenboro, N.C.
**Spot (tie)**—1-1; Charleston, 1967; by J. Stehmeyer, Charleston.
**Tautog**—5-4; Charleston, 2003; by T. Crull, Charleston.
**Vermillion Snapper**—6-10; Charleston, 1975; by D.H. Long, Charleston.
**White Marlin**—108-0; Charleston, 1981; by D.C. Critz Jr., Savannah, Ga.
**Yellowfin Tuna**—241-12; Charleston, 1979; by T.C. Lewis, Mt. Pleasant.
**Yellowtail Snapper**—10-8; Mt. Pleasant, 2003; by T. Snelgrove, Lexington.

This information is provided courtesy of the South Carolina Department of Natural Resources Marine Resources Division.

down Vendue Range leads to restaurants and shopping on East Bay Street. (See the Kidstuff and Parks and Recreation chapters for more on Waterfront Park.)

# Fishing Tournaments

Almost year-round (with the exception of the coldest winter months), a fishing tournament of some description can be found, usually benefiting conservation groups and charities in the Trident area. Some of the bigger ones offer large purses and prizes in the thousands of dollars. Competition can be pretty stiff, but the changing seas and good old-fashioned luck often come into play, and . . . anything can happen. If you are serious about getting into the competitive sportfishing tournament circuit, here are a few of the major ones to check out. For a more complete listing of the year's saltwater fishing tournaments held in South Carolina, pick up the brochure from the South Carolina Department of Natural Resources Marine Resources Division at area bait and tackle shops, or write to SCDNR, P.O. Box 12559, Charleston 29422.

**Bohicket Marina**
**Invitational Billfish Tournament**
**1880 Andell Bluff Boulevard,**
**Johns Island**
**(843) 768-1280, (843) 768-3461**
**www.dnr.state.sc.us**
One of the five tourneys in the Governor's Cup Series, the Bohicket Invitational is one of the major tournaments in the area. Held in early May, this one brings in the big boys competing for serious money; first prize for the largest marlin garners $7,500. Placing here can lead to even bigger prizes in the Governor's Cup competition. This tag-and-release tourney also awards $1,000 for the largest wahoo, dolphin, and tuna and the best female and youth angler. Get your crew, sportfishing yacht, and checkbook ready for an entry fee of $1,700 and a sportin' good time. It's called an invitational, but anyone can join in the fun.

**Carolina Lady Anglers "Fishing for the Cure" Open Tournament**
**P.O. Box 13141, Charleston 29422**
**(843) 345-6261**
**www.carolinaladyanglers.org**
The Carolina Lady Anglers is the only all-female saltwater fishing group in the area. They are dedicated to promoting sportfishing in the Lowcountry and raising funds for a cure for breast cancer. Proceeds from club events such as the "Fishing for the Cure" tournament are donated to breast cancer education and research. The inshore fishing tournament is held in late May/early June and takes place at the Charleston Maritime Center. The competition is open to all—female, male, and youth anglers—with an entry fee of $30. Eligible species include Spanish mackerel, king mackerel, trout, flounder, sheepshead, and black drum. First, second, and third place prizes are awarded as well as Outstanding Female, Outstanding Male, and Outstanding Youth (age 12 and under). A raffle, buffet supper, and live music add to the fun. (If you are interested in joining this group, attend a meeting on the first Wednesday of the month at 7:00 P.M. at Gilligan's Restaurant on Johns Island.)

**Charleston Trident Fishing Tournament**
**861 Riverland Drive**
**(843) 762-8023, (843) 795-4FUN**
**www.ccprc.com**
For over 35 years the Charleston County Park and Recreation Commission, area businesses, and individuals have cosponsored this free tournament, which covers the fishing season from March 1 through October 31. Competitors enter catches on entry blanks after weighing in at official weigh stations. Points are amassed for classes of eligible fish in both saltwater and freshwater divisions. Awards and certificates are given for outstanding saltwater and freshwater anglers, outstanding lady and youth (16 and younger) anglers, outstanding light-tackle and fly rod, ecology, and more. There are also awards for the largest fish caught in various cate-

*We really like the fact that Champ Smith, one of Toler's Cove Marina's captains, named his company Nervous Water Charters. For those of you new to fishing, note that nervous water is what you'll be looking for: It's a sign that lots of fish are moving around just waiting to take your bait.*

gories. The competition is restricted to the waters of Berkeley, Charleston, and Dorchester Counties, and boats leaving from and returning to the waters between the South Santee and South Edisto Rivers.

**Fishing for Miracles
King Mackerel Tournament
P.O. Box 13586,
Charleston 29422
(843) 766-0011
www.fishingformiracles.com**
Another of the South Carolina King Mackerel Governor's Cup Series tournaments in the area, the Annual Fishing for Miracles event is one of our favorite summertime competitions. Held in mid-August, this tournament is one of the largest fishing tournaments in South Carolina. Its proceeds benefit the Medical University of South Carolina Children's Hospital and the Coastal Conservation Association of South Carolina. There are some terrific prizes (first place could net you as much as $25,000), and it is all based out of the Charleston Harbor Resort & Marina just across the bridge in Mt. Pleasant. To get involved, contact the tournament committee by calling or writing. The boat entry fee in 2004 was $275 prior to August 1 and $325 after that date. See our Annual Events chapter for more on this tournament.

**James Island Yacht Club
King Mackerel Classic
P.O. Box 12840, Charleston 29422
(843) 795-6060
www.jiyc.org**

Held in late May, this tournament is one of the area's popular competitions (many of which offer less pressure than the billfish ones) with an emphasis on having a good time. Locals and visitors compete for cash and prizes, and the boat early entry fee is $125 or $150 late registration. First-, second-, and third-place prizes are awarded for the heaviest king mackerel, paying around $7,000. Other non-cash awards go for the outstanding catch by a James Island Yacht Club member, outstanding female angler, outstanding youth angler (14 and younger), and a tag-and-release award.

**South Carolina
Governor's Cup Billfishing Series
P.O. Box 12559, Charleston 29422
(843) 762-5025
www.dnr.state.sc.us**
The Governor's Cup is an annual, umbrella tournament that encompasses five billfish competitions along coastal South Carolina each spring and summer. Anglers and boats participate by entering two or more member events in the series and either landing or tagging and releasing billfish to accumulate points. More points are given for tagged and released fish, encouraging conservation of marine resources. A perpetual trophy is inscribed with the names of the winners in the categories of Outstanding Billfish, Outstanding Boat, and Outstanding Billfish Conservation. The tournament series runs from April through July and has included area events such as the Charleston Harbor Marina, the Charleston City Marina, and the Bohicket Marina Invitational billfish tournaments. The Governor's Cup is an official program of the South Carolina Department of Natural Resources in cooperation with the South Carolina Department of Parks, Recreation, and Tourism. North Carolina and Georgia have a Governor's Cup, too, and the three states compete in a shootout at the end of the year. For more information write to the address above.

# HUNTING AND FISHING OUTFITTERS

The Lowcountry is loaded when it comes to terrific stores that stock all the stuff you'll need to bag your limit or catch a mess of fish for cooking. Here are a handful of our favorite outdoor goods suppliers.

**Barton and Burwell**
**47 South Windermere Boulevard**
**(843) 766-3220, (877) 216-3474**

**675-B Johnnie Dodds Boulevard,**
**Mt. Pleasant**
**(843) 216-3711**
**www.bartonandburwell.com**
Serious anglers know the inventory at Barton and Burwell Fishing Supplies like they know the back creeks of the Lowcountry. Any and everything for the sport of fishing is here to be found. They carry tackle and supplies for inshore, nearshore, offshore, and blue-water fishing with brand names such as Star Rods, Penn reels, Shimano, Daiwa, Cape Fear, and C&H and Mold Craft lures. Clothing lines include Columbia, Aftco, and Tarponwear, and monogramming and embroidery of hats and shirts is available, too. Custom rod building is another plus at Barton and Burwell as well as the biggest rod and reel repair department in the area.

**Carolina Rod & Gun, Inc.**
**1319 Savannah Highway**
**(843) 571-7972**
In their big, newly expanded store, Carolina Rod & Gun has a large selection of sporting firearms, archery supplies, and outdoor clothing. A full-line Browning dealer, this shop also carries Benelli, Smith & Wesson, Glock, Kimbler, and Ruger. A full-time gunsmith is also on hand for all gunsmith service and repairs.

Their archery department is well known here in the Lowcountry for their inventory, including Browning, Darton, BowTech, and PSE bows. Sporting optics from Zeiss, Leica, and Schmidt & Bender provide a wide range of binoculars and scopes. Outdoor clothing by Browning, Mossy Oak, and Boyt/Bob Allen as well as shoes and boots from LaCrosse, Danner, and Chippewa complete your hunting gear.

**The Charleston Angler**
**654 St. Andrews Boulevard**
**(843) 571-3899**
**www.thecharlestonangler.com**
The Charleston Angler is out to improve your luck with everything you need for a day of inshore or flats fishing. They specialize in fly fishing and light tackle and carry fly and surf rods and reels from manufacturers such as G.Loomis, Sage, St. Croix, Shimano, and Ross Reels. They have live, frozen, and plastic bait and even offer fly-tying and casting lessons if you need a refresher. Men's, women's, and kids' clothing lines include Columbia, Patagonia, Woolrich, and Ex Officio. And if you want it personalized with the name of your new boat, they embroider on shirts, shorts, jackets, towels, or ballcaps. If you're just visiting, the helpful staff is happy to make suggestions for your selection of tackle or which guide to book. They are up on the recent conditions and what time of year which fish are running. Give 'em a call and try your luck.

**Haddrell's Point Tackle & Hunting Supply Center**
**885 Coleman Boulevard, Mt. Pleasant**
**(843) 881-3644, (800) 881-5201**
**www.haddrellspoint.com**
Haddrell's Point offers a complete line of inshore and offshore fishing equipment for the novice to the serious angler. It is one of a few local stores carrying a full line of saltwater and freshwater fly-fishing gear. Sage and G.Loomis rods, Star Rods, and Abel reels are a few of the brands the center carries, and it is the only Shimano warranty station in South Carolina. They handle warranty work for Penn reels too. Haddrell's also sells hunting accessories for turkey, duck, and deer hunters with clothing from Columbia, Woolrich, Aftco, and Kahala. Check this place out, and talk with the friendly, knowledgeable staff for

sales assistance, education, and instruction on hunting and fishing pursuits.

## Luden's
**78 Alexander Street**
**(843) 723-7829**
**www.ludensoutfitters.com**
Whether you are gearing up for hunting season, setting out on a harbor cruise, or just want to look the part at a Lowcountry regatta or oyster roast, Luden's is a good source for clothing, gear, and quality marine supplies. Some of the popular clothing lines include Henri Lloyd, Old Town, Filson, Woolrich, Barbour, Columbia, and Sperry Top-Sider. Marine supply brands include Camp, Zinc, Sampson Rope, Bristol Finish, Marinco, Harken, Seadog, Perko, and Racor.

It's also the place for safety equipment, compasses, gas tanks, sextants, and charts. It has more in-stock topo maps than any other South Carolina dealer. Luden's is the Lowcountry's authorized Orvis dealer, selling fly rods and flies, fly-tying materials, and Battenkill luggage. Special orders are welcome here. Enjoy the free parking (a rarity downtown) to spend lots of time browsing their location just off East Bay Street. (Also see Luden's in the Shopping chapter.)

# SPECTATOR SPORTS

When most people in the Lowcountry think of sports, they think of grabbing their equipment and getting involved directly in a game of tennis, a round of golf, a dip in the swimming pool, and other activities. However, neither visitors nor locals should overlook the excellent professional, amateur, and collegiate spectator sports available for our enjoyment.

There's nothing like taking off for a day at the stadium to watch the great American sport of baseball, and Charleston's own RiverDogs provide an action-packed brand of play. There's also the option of cheering for the big-name professionals who regularly show up at area golf and tennis matches. And who among us doesn't enjoy an autumn afternoon spent cheering on the college football team, even if our own college days are but a dim, gilded memory.

Tennis, sailing regattas, soccer, ice hockey . . . you name it—if it translates into action, it can probably be found somewhere in the Lowcountry. So take some time off from your own sports regimen to sit and watch the following folks in action. You'll probably find yourself screaming "Hey batter, batter, batter!" right along with the best of 'em!

## BASEBALL

**Charleston RiverDogs**
**360 Fishburne Street**
**(843) 723-7241,**
**(843) 577-DOGS (Ticket Office)**
**www.riverdogs.com**
Our minor league team, reborn the Charleston RiverDogs in 1994, is a Class A South Atlantic League farm team for the New York Yankees. The RiverDogs' season runs April through August. Locals turn out regularly and appreciate exciting baseball while enjoying the antics of Charlie the RiverDog, the giant costumed mascot who plays to the stands and brings out the kid in everyone. After 57 years at College Park, Charleston baseball moved to a new park. Home, as of 1997, is the 5,900-seat Joseph P. Riley Jr. Park on the banks of the Ashley River. This downtown location is next to Brittlebank Park, Stoney Field, and Lockwood Drive. General admission seats are $4.00 with a range of prices up to $8.00 for box seats. Watch for special, reduced-admission games and promotions such as fireworks displays after Friday night games and prize giveaways throughout spring and summer. Plenty of parking is available adjacent to the ballpark for $3.00.

## GOLF

**Rice Planters Amateur Golf**
**Championship**
**Snee Farm Country Club, U.S. Highway**
**17 N., Mt. Pleasant**
**(843) 884-8571, (843) 884-2600**
**www.riceplanters.org**
Since 1973, Snee Farm Country Club has hosted the Rice Planters Amateur Golf Championship, recently ranked by *Golf Week* magazine and Titleist as seventh in the top amateur golf events in the world. This tournament attracts top collegiate golfers, seasoned talent from across the United States, and terrific international amateur players. Past champions have included current pros Tom Lehman, Scott Hoch, Stewart Cink, Andy Bean, Hal Sutton, and Allen Doyle. Held Fourth of July week, this event is open to the public at no charge. Call Snee Farm for more information.

## ICE HOCKEY

**South Carolina Stingrays**
**3107 Firestone Road, North Charleston**
**(843) 744-2248, (843) 554-6060**
**(Ticketmaster)**
**www.stingrayshockey.com**
The North Charleston Coliseum reverberates with very vocal ice hockey fans who pack in to watch the Stingrays do their thing each season from October through March (even later if we make the playoffs). The team's loyal fans turn out in the red, white, and blue team colors and average more than 7,400 in attendance for each home game. The Stingrays, affiliated with the NHL's Buffalo Sabres, are in their ninth year in the Southeast Division of the East Coast Hockey League. In 1997, they ascended to the top of the heap by winning the ECHL Championship and the Kelly Cup. Again in 2001, they won this title. During intermissions, mascots Cool Ray and Li'l Puck keep the kids entertained. And when the frozen stuff has melted, the children come out to enroll for in-line hockey camps scheduled all summer long. The excitement never fades with the hockey crowd, so call for more schedule and ticket information. Tickets range from $12.25 to $17.00. Coliseum parking costs $4.00.

---

*Be in the know: Call the Joseph P. Riley Jr. Park "the Joe." Amid a flurry of modesty, Charleston Mayor Joseph P. Riley Jr. tried to dissuade officials from naming the new ballpark in his honor—to no avail. The official name has been unofficially shortened to "the Joe," and the nickname has stuck.*

---

## INTERCOLLEGIATE SPORTS

With several institutions of higher education in the area, opportunities for checking out college sporting events are abundant. The most popular are, of course, football, baseball, and basketball, but you can also find soccer, track and field, and other events if you are interested.

The College of Charleston's Cougars made it to the Trans-America Athletic Conference championships in previous seasons and in 1997 made some major noise by knocking off regional power Maryland in the NCAA tourney. Charleston Southern also cut the rug at the NCAA's Big Dance in '97. The College of Charleston and The Citadel are members of the Southern Conference. Former College of Charleston Coach John Kresse, with more than 500 Cougar wins to his credit, was inducted into both the NAIA and the South Carolina Athletic Hall of Fame.

The Southern Conference Basketball Championships are held at the North Charleston Coliseum in early March, and details can be found at www.socon tourney.com.

In 2001 and 2004, The Citadel Bulldogs won the Southern Conference Baseball Championship. (The College of Charleston captured the 2004 Southern Conference regular-season title.) This tournament is held in Charleston at Joseph P. Riley Jr. Park in late May and affords collegiate baseball fans an opportunity to see some of the best teams in action.

Citadel football fans gloated as one of their own, alumnus Travis Jervey, played for the 1998 NFC and the 1997 Super Bowl champions, the Green Bay Packers. So if you'd like to get up close to this college talent and competition while it's happening, get tickets by contacting The Citadel, (843) 953-5121, the College of Charleston, (843) 953-5479, and Charleston Southern University, (843) 863-7213.

## RUNNING

**Cooper River Bridge Run and Walk**
**45 Courtenay Drive**
**(843) 792-0345, (843) 937-4183**
**www.bridgerun.com**
Just because you don't feel up to walking

or running over the newly opened Arthur Ravenel Jr. bridge, don't give up on the 10-kilometer (6.2-mile) Cooper River Bridge Run. Each March or April (usually the weekend before Easter), you can be a spectator or a volunteer and get your own thrill from the collective energy of it all. Hit the streets and cheer the participants onward—hundreds of like-minded folks will be right out there with you. For more information, call the Medical University of South Carolina Wellness Center at the number above. (For more on the festivities, see the Annual Events chapter.)

## SAILBOAT RACING

With the popularity of the Around Alone (formerly the BOC Challenge), the solo sailor around-the-world yacht race, hosted by Charleston in 1994–95 and 1998–99, sailboat racing events have sprung up in this area. The Charleston Ocean Racing Association, established in 1967, holds 35 to 40 sailing events year-round in Charleston Harbor and offshore waters, promoting sailing and assisting members in obtaining competent crews and desirable berths. Also, a Charleston to Bermuda Race sailed its fifth competition from Charleston Harbor in May 2005.

Local regattas are popular events too, particularly in the warmer months. From the Carolina Yacht Club and Charleston Yacht Club regattas to those hosted by the Hobcaw, James Island, and Sea Island clubs, there are races throughout the summer. A schedule is set in January and posted in the area yacht clubs. Spectators enjoy watching these races, free of charge, from the Battery or from the grounds of the club hosting the event. Children are welcome and may even start asking about those Charleston Yacht Club Summer Junior Sail Program lessons (see Insiders' Tip in this chapter). Call the sailing department at the College of Charleston (which, by the way, traditionally has a fine sailing team) at (843) 953-5549 or visit www.cofc.edu/sailing for more information about

noncredit community sailing classes or sailing association memberships.

**Charleston Race Week '06**
**Charleston Ocean Racing Association**
**P.O. Box 123, Charleston 29402**
**(843) 722-0823**
**www.charlestonraceweek.com,**
**www.charlestonoceanracing.org**
The Charleston Ocean Racing Association (CORA) presents the eleventh annual Charleston Race Week during the month of April. Race Week comprises the Palmetto Cup regatta, an inshore competition for sailboats over 22 feet, selected one-design regattas, and a Wednesday evening harbor race. The Charleston Race Week Cup and overall Race Week winners are determined based on cumulative scoring results. More than 100 boats competed in 2005, and a good time was had by all.

**Charleston to Bermuda Race**
**(843) 722-1030**
**www.charlestontobermuda.org**
Alternating years with the Daytona to Bermuda Race, the Charleston to Bermuda Race leaves our city in May 2007. The 771-nautical-mile race is hosted on the receiving end by the Royal Bermuda Yacht Club (formed in 1844), and the finish line is off the St. David's Lighthouse in Bermuda. The 30-foot and larger sailboats are entered in either a double-handed class (two crew) or the fully crewed class with a minimum of four. Hundreds of spectators lined the Waterfront Park and the Battery and also watched from more than 100 spectator boats as the sailors set out on this challenge in May 2005.

## SOCCER

**Charleston Battery**
**Blackbaud Stadium,**
**1990 Daniel Island Drive**
**(843) 971-GOAL (4625)**
**www.charlestonbattery.com**

For more than 25 years, children have learned to sail in the Charleston Yacht Club Summer Junior Sail Program. If you have kids ages 7 to 15, this may be just what you're looking for to add a little excitement to their lives. Parents do not have to belong to the club, but nonmember participants pay slightly more than members—$350, compared with $300. Six three-week sessions are offered each summer. For more information, call (843) 722-4968, visit www.charlestonyachtclub.com, or write to the Summer Youth Sailing Program, Charleston Yacht Club, P.O. Box 20474, Charleston 29413.

In 1993, a professional men's soccer league team, the Charleston Battery, was formed, joining the United Systems of Independent Soccer Leagues. After placing at the top of the Atlantic Division in '94 and '95, the team advanced to the USISL finals in 1996, and won the league championship in a thriller: a 3-2 match decided in a shootout. In 1997, the Battery changed to the new Division II A-League (one notch below Major League Soccer), and in 2000, they won the Atlantic Division Championship. In 2003 the Battery claimed the A-League crown. You can catch all the action at the new $4.5 million soccer-specific Blackbaud Stadium on Daniel Island (just off Interstate 526 between the Cooper and Wando Rivers). The new facility provides fun for the whole family with an expansive kids' "Fun Zone" and the Three Lions Pub. The games run April through August.

Charleston Battery tickets range from $10.00 bleacher seats to $50.00 club seats. Kids younger than four are admitted free. Parking is $4.00 per car.

# TENNIS

**Family Circle Cup**
**Daniel Island Tennis Centre,**
**161 Seven Farms Drive, Daniel Island**
**(800) 677-2293**
**www.familycirclecup.com**
Spectator tennis took a major leap forward in the Charleston area with the announcement of a relocation of the Family Circle Cup to our city in 2001 after a long-time run in Hilton Head, South Carolina. As many as 100,000 tennis fans have attended the nine-day Women's Tennis Association Tier I event. A new $9-million tennis complex for the tournament was built within the new Town Centre Park in the planned community of Daniel Island. (See the Neighborhoods chapter for more on Daniel Island.) It served up an inaugural venue for this competition that attracts many of the top seeds in women's tennis. Some of the past competitors were Justine Henin-Hardenne, Conchita Martinez, Monica Seles, Arantxa Sanchez-Vicario, Mary Pierce, Serena Williams, Lindsay Davenport, and Jennifer Capriati. Held in mid-April, the Family Circle Cup is a hot ticket in Charleston's busy spring tourism events. Ticket prices range from $10 for qualifying matches up to $55 for the finals. Call the number above or write to Family Circle Cup for more information.

# RELOCATION

If you're among those thinking seriously about moving to the Lowcountry and making Charleston your permanent or part-time home, we have a news flash for you. This idea is not entirely original. It has occurred to others . . . with some frequency. Starting with the influx of military retirees who fell in love with the area during their World War II Navy days spent here, the concept of retiring to Charleston has only grown more popular with each passing year. And why not? The Lowcountry really has it all—sun, sea, golf, history, culture, plus educational and entertainment opportunities galore. Young people are similarly attracted to the area. Employment opportunities, especially for professionals, are getting more plentiful as the population surges upward. Therefore, a Relocation chapter is in order—as a helpful service to the next generation of insiders who will soon be calling Charleston and its environs "home."

Our Neighborhoods chapter will give you an overview of some areas where newcomers are currently finding homes. We've included a spectrum of price alternatives. And we've listed, below, a few of the major real estate companies ready and willing to help newcomers start their relocation process. Some newcomers choose to rent apartments, condos, or even homes while they acclimate to the area and select a neighborhood that's best for them. There's information for apartment dwellers, also. We've thrown in some practical information, too, such as where to get your new driver's license, how to register to vote, what are the utility hookup contacts, and even some recycling information for our new neighbors who, we hope, will be ecology-minded citizens here in the Lowcountry.

## REAL ESTATE COMPANIES

If you are new to the area and have turned to the Charleston Metro Chamber of Commerce (2750 Speisseger Drive, Suite. 100, North Charleston 29405; 843–577–2510; www.charlestonchamber .net), for any of its excellent visitor information, you might want to ask for its free list of area member real estate agencies too. This will give you a handy overview of the residential realtors as well as the commercial and industrial specialists who are currently chamber members and working here in the Lowcountry.

One of the best resources for specific real estate information in Greater Charleston is the Charleston Trident Association of Realtors (5300 International Boulevard, Suite C-105, North Charleston, 29418; 843–760–9400; www.charleston realtors.com). At last count, there were 3,000 member Realtors working throughout Charleston, Dorchester, and Berkeley Counties. And the association can easily recommend a professional to help you find the home that's right for you.

Naturally, choosing a real estate company is a very personal matter. Because it is such an important decision, be sure to find an agent who truly understands your priorities. Sometimes that's easier said than done.

An agent who specializes in investment properties may not understand why

*Look for the* Reader's Digest–*size catalog of listings called* The Real Estate Book, *which is a free pick-up in shops and restaurants throughout the Lowcountry.*

you want to see only pre-Revolutionary houses, or why an otherwise acceptable house won't do because your grandmother's furniture won't fit in the dining room. By the same token, an agent with a reputation for handling plantations and historic properties may not grasp the needs of a first-time buyer or the advantages of one school system over another. You can find agents who are such specialists if you ask the right questions. Be sure to be specific about your needs.

In general, the agents in the Greater Charleston area are well versed in the needs of a broad-spectrum market. And with computerized multiple-listing services, almost all agents can show you any house or property you might be interested in seeing. As with any business relationship, some frank discussions early on about your price range and what you're looking for can help avoid wasting your time and patience. Just remember that open communication with your real estate agent is the first key to finding the right home. And again, more information on the feel and price ranges in various Charleston-area neighborhoods can be found in the Neighborhoods chapter.

# Downtown Charleston Properties

Residential real estate in downtown Charleston is a very specialized market. You're looking at properties with historic and aesthetic values that often override the considerations of ordinary shelter. And then there's that awesome specter of restoration to consider—whether it's something already accomplished at someone's great expense, or it's something you feel you want to tackle yourself. These variables affect property values enormously. There are special tax strategies and things such as "facade easements" to learn about, which can actually make owning a home in the historic district a little more affordable. Pricing is also

affected by something called "comparables"—that's the price recently paid for a comparable house in the same neighborhood. That can change monthly or even (gasp!) weekly.

Sound complicated? It is, so it's best to get some help from people who deal with this on a daily basis. Here are some of the companies with plenty of experience selling residential real estate in downtown Charleston.

**Arthur Ravenel Jr. Co.**
**635 East Bay Street**
**(843) 723-7847**
**www.ravenelrealestate.com**
Ravenel is a small, family-owned company that has been in business since 1945. Its experienced agents can help you with purchases of historic downtown properties, waterfront properties, and commercial real estate. They also handle property management.

**Carriage Properties**
**19 Exchange Street**
**(843) 266-8000**
**www.carriageprop.com**
Early in 2002, six veteran sales associates from a top-producing downtown Charleston real estate company decided to form their own company. These agents—all major players in the fast-paced and highly competitive marketplace for historic homes in the Holy City—set up shop at a newly renovated downtown building and soon took on another agent to help handle their growing business. The company specializes in high-end luxury homes and condominiums in the Charleston area, particularly on the historic Peninsula.

**Daniel Ravenel Real Estate Co.**
**33 Broad Street**
**(843) 723-7150, (800) 382-2279**
**www.danielravenel.com**
This is a full-service independent agency with deep roots in the community. With offices in downtown Charleston, the agency provides customized residential, commercial, and waterfront real estate

services throughout the Lowcountry, from
the Battery to the beaches.

**Disher, Hamrick & Myers**
**196 King Street**

**480 East Bay Street**

**1 Beachwalker Drive, Suite B,**
**Johns Island**
**(843) 577-4115, (800) 577-4118**
**www.charlestonrealestate.net**
This company's agents primarily focus on
historic properties in downtown Charleston.
It is the leading brokerage firm in the historic district. The staff has more than 80
years of aggregate experience in the market. Many of these individuals are downtown residents who have been through
the restoration process themselves, giving
them a perspective that clients find
invaluable.

**Historic Charleston Properties**
**67 Broad Street**
**(843) 853-3000**
**www.historicrealestate.com**
Begun in 1997, this fledgling real estate
company came on fast and strong in the
Charleston market, earning $18 million in
sales their first year. The company now
focuses on upscale residential properties
and discreet, personalized service.

**Lane & Smythe Real Estate, LLC.**
**9 Broad Street**
**(843) 577-2900, (877) 451-4801**
**www.laneandsmythe.com**
This firm, founded in 1999, has agents with
35 years of combined service in the real
estate industry dealing in historic properties. It is proudly owned and operated by
women who are skilled at presenting a
total point of view, including the female
perspective, on relocating to the
Charleston area.

**Pate Properties, Inc.**
**960 Morrison Drive, Suite 200**
**(843) 577-3193**
This closely held company, with more than

25 years' experience in the market, has a
fantastic track record for handling downtown residential real estate, small investment properties, and property
management. The owner is one of the
city's few buyer representatives, sanc-
tioned by the National Association of
Realtors.

**Poston & Co. Real Estate, Inc.**
**304 Meeting Street**
**(843) 853-5300**
**www.postonco.com**
Marketing mostly residential real estate in
the upscale residential neighborhoods of
downtown Charleston, West Ashley,
James Island, Mt. Pleasant, and Daniel
Island, this firm has been in business for
over a decade. In 1997, their sales
exceeded $61 million. They focus on resi-
dential sales and relocation services,
including the marketing and sale of existing homes, new construction, and residential lots. They also offer property
management services.

# Tri-County Real Estate Companies

In addition to the independent real estate
companies that specialize in historic properties or beach homes, the giant franchise
networks are established here. These companies are eager to meet your real estate
needs and offer comprehensive, one-stop
real estate service—whether you're moving
across the country or across town. Look
for names such as Century 21, Prudential,
Coldwell Banker, RE/MAX, and the Agent
Owned Realty Co.

In fact, we're seeing an ongoing trend
among some of the older, larger, independent real estate companies toward joining
these nationwide franchise networks.
The idea here is that there's strength in
numbers—that teamwork and standardiza-
tion lead to better efficiency and greater
success.

**The Beach Company**
211 King Street, Suite 300
(843) 722-2615
www.thebeachcompany.com
Founded in 1945, this is the largest full-service real estate company in Charleston. In addition to residential sales and property management, they handle acquisition, development, construction services, and commercial brokerage.

**Prudential Carolina Real Estate**
49 Broad Street
(843) 577-0001

1315 Ashley River Road, West Ashley
(843) 571-7400

706 Orleans Road, West Ashley
(843) 556-5800

672 Marina Drive, Daniel Island
(843) 284-1900

3040 Highway 17 N., Mt. Pleasant
(843) 266-5000

195 West Coleman Boulevard, Mt. Pleasant
(843) 884-1800

628 Long Point Road, Mt. Pleasant
(843) 884-1622

1265 Folly Road
(843) 795-7810

125 Wappoo Creek Drive, James Island
(843) 795-5000

3714-K Betsy Kerrison Parkway,
Johns Island
(843) 768-4880

1400 Palm Boulevard, Isle of Palms
(843) 886-8110

---

*By far the major clearinghouse for Low-country real estate information is the* Saturday Real Estate *tabloid and the* Sunday Home and Garden *section of the* Post and Courier. *Here, the properties are listed by specific region, and all listings are comprehensive and coded for descriptive details.*

---

567 Crowfield Boulevard, Goose Creek
(843) 797-7799

900 North Main Street, Summerville
(843) 974-6200

1530 Old Trolley Road, Summerville
(843) 871-9000

**Relocation Services**
4024 Salt Pointe Parkway,
North Charleston
(843) 202-2030, (800) 476-1929
www.prudentialcarolina.com
Clearly, this company takes an aggressive stance in the local real estate market with a wide-reaching array of regional offices throughout the greater Charleston area. They also serve newcomers with a full-time staff in their Relocation Office. The relocation staff can help with school applications, tax forms, tuition fees, wheelchair-accessibility, and even career assistance. The relocation agent then refers you to a handpicked agent in one of the local offices.

**RE/MAX Professional Realty**
311 Johnnie Dodds Boulevard, Suite 131,
Mt. Pleasant
(843) 972-2400

102 Wappoo Creek Drive, Suite. A-3
(843) 406-9998

9209 University Boulevard,
North Charleston
(843) 767-7777, (800) 633-9275
www.remax-pros-charleston.com
This agency partnered with a well-known independent local realty company for several years when they were establishing their beachhead in the Lowcountry market. Today, they work out of three local offices and serve the entire tri-county area.

## APARTMENT RENTALS

There are many apartment and townhouse complexes in Greater Charleston, the majority of which are in West Ashley, Mt. Pleasant, North Charleston, and the

Ladson, Summerville, and Hanahan areas. Amenities vary wildly, with some including furnishings, balconies, fireplaces, ceiling fans, carpeting, or window treatments. Some apartment complexes have clubhouses, pools, and sports facilities; others have playgrounds or, especially downtown, reserved parking. Monthly rents range from $400 to $1,235 (more for luxury town houses and properties on the historic Peninsula), but the average hovers in the $750 to $800 range.

Lease agreements are usually for 6 or 12 months, although short-term leases, some with military-transfer clauses, are available. Security deposits also vary but are half to a full month's rent. Many places allow pets, but some complexes have size limits, and most require a deposit or a fee.

Apartment seekers will find these free real estate publications helpful: *Apartment Finder Blue Book* and *Charleston Apartment Guide.* Look for these pick-'em-up publications wherever newspapers are sold and at restaurants, sports facilities, and all information centers. Or you may want to write or call for a current issue and do some apartment shopping before you arrive.

## Apartment Directories

### Apartment Finder
**301 Broad Street, Suite 7**
**(843) 577-7882**
**www.apartmentfinder.com**
This magazine-format booklet of apartment options is published four times a year. It is colorful and includes Greater Charleston neighborhoods from downtown through North Charleston to Hanahan, Ladson, Goose Creek, and Summerville. West Ashley and East Cooper neighborhoods are included as well. Detailed maps help readers get acclimated to the various residential areas and transportation routes, and a handy comparison chart reduces the advertising hype to bare facts and figures for finding

the bottom line. Almost 160 pages in length, this is perhaps the most comprehensive apartment guide currently published in the Lowcountry. Distribution of this free publication is widespread. You can almost always find a kiosk or rack of them outside any area grocery store or post office. Some convenience stores have them next to where the newspapers are sold. Of course, the Charleston visitor center on Meeting Street always has an ample supply.

### Charleston Apartment Guide
**461 Jessen Lane, Suite G, Wando**
**(843) 388-0085**
**www.apartmentguide.com**
Formerly known as *An Apartment Guide to Charleston,* this revamped booklet is published four times a year. It is well organized with full-color photos, maps, and an easy-to-use color code for area neighborhoods from downtown to Moncks Corner. Sometimes hard to find, it is worth tracking down because of its comprehensiveness. One good bet is to look just outside area grocery stores and wherever newspapers are sold. Also, the Charleston Metro Chamber of Commerce always has copies on hand.

## MOTOR VEHICLE INFORMATION

New South Carolina residents may use a valid out-of-state driver's license for up to 90 days. Military personnel may use their home state license as long as it is valid.

*It's easy to suffer from serious sticker shock when you talk about real estate in downtown Charleston. If that seems to be your problem, simply look farther afield. Prices are far more reasonable once you're off that hallowed peninsular ground.*

Licensed newcomers must take a vision test and present their Social Security number to obtain a South Carolina driver's license. New drivers must bring their birth certificate and Social Security number and take the road, written, and vision tests. A quick review of the rules of the road booklet available in the South Carolina Department of Public Safety Division of Motor Vehicles offices may be beneficial prior to taking the written test. Drivers should apply at the SCDMV offices listed below.

New residents have 45 days to purchase South Carolina license tags for their vehicles. Before getting a tag, property taxes on the vehicle must be paid at your local county tax office. Then, new residents may apply by filling out Form 400 at any of the SCDMV locations below. General information on driver's licenses and tags/registration is available at (800) 442-1368 or www.scdps.org/dmv.

**3790 Leeds Avenue, North**

**180 Lockwood Boulevard**

**135 Wimberly Drive, Ladson**

**438 North Highway 52, Moncks Corner**

**1189 Iron Bridge Road, Suite 500, Mt. Pleasant**

**Express Office (No Road Tests or Tags/ Registration): 1119 Wappoo Road, Unit G**

## VOTER REGISTRATION

To register to vote, a new resident must be a U.S. citizen, 18 years old by the date of the election, mentally competent, and not under conviction of a felony. Proof of residency is required. Registration must take place at least 30 days prior to an election to vote in that election. Newcomers may register at the local county voter registration office, driver's license offices, or by mail. Call the following numbers for more information:

**Charleston County  (843) 744-8683**

**Berkeley County
(843) 719-4056 (Moncks Corner line)
(843) 723-3800, ext. 4056
(Charleston line)
(843) 567-3142, ext. 4056
(St. Stephen line)**

**Dorchester County (843) 832-0132**

## UTILITIES

For natural gas, electricity, water, and telephone services in Greater Charleston, call one of the following:

### NATURAL GAS:

**South Carolina Electric and Gas (SCE&G), (843) 554-7234, (800) 251-7234, www.scana.com/sce&g**

### ELECTRICITY:

**South Carolina Electric and Gas (SCE&G), (843) 554-7234, (800) 251-7234, www.scana.com/sce&g**

**Berkeley Electric Cooperative, (843) 572-5454, www.becsc.com**

**Santee Cooper (South Carolina Public Service Authority), (843) 761-4060, www.santeecooper.com**

### WATER:

**City of Charleston Commissioner of Public Works—Water & Sewer, (843) 727-6800, www.charlestoncpw.com
Berkeley County Water and Sanitation Authority, (843) 572-4400**

**Dorchester County Water & Sewer, (843) 767-2474**

**Mount Pleasant Waterworks & Sewer Commission, (843) 884-9626**

Many other municipalities have their own water and sewer commissions such as Isle of Palms, Kiawah Island, Folly Beach, Summerville, Goose Creek, Moncks Corner, and North Charleston. If you are relocating to one of these areas, consult the telephone directory for their individual numbers.

## TELEPHONE:

BellSouth provides telephone services for the majority of the area. For residential services call (888) 757–6500 and business services call (866) 620–6000. If calling outside of South Carolina or from a wireless phone, call (800) 336–0014 for residential and (800) 237–2802 for business. You may also visit their Web site at www.bellsouth.com.

## RECYCLING

Curbside recycling in blue bins is offered in most of the urban areas of Charleston County on an every other week basis. Some 40 drop-off containers are located throughout the county. Materials currently recycled include plastic containers (nos. 1 and 2), steel food cans, aluminum cans, and glass jars and bottles. Newspapers, magazines, office paper, and mail are recyclable as well, and corrugated cardboard can be brought to the drop sites. For more information about recycling in Charleston County call (843) 720–7111, in Berkeley County, (843) 572–4400, and in Dorchester County, (843) 832–0070.

# NEIGHBORHOODS

There was a time when living in Charleston meant hanging your hat somewhere on the Peninsula. Somewhere in the quarter-century between the world wars, all that started to change. Mind you, Charleston is and always will be largely defined by the geographic boundaries of the Peninsula and the charming old houses that exist in the prestigious neighborhood referred to as "below (meaning south of) Broad (Street)." Living in one of those grand old houses will always be part of the quintessential Charleston lifestyle. Earthquakes, storms, fires, and wars have worked their woes and done their best to alter that reality, but an address Below Broad will always be a prestigious one in Charleston.

Meanwhile, it's also true that thousands upon thousands of other certified Charlestonians are thriving in other neighborhoods—living full, complete, happy, and productive lives.

We'll start this description of Charleston's neighborhoods with some of the spectacular statistics surrounding real estate Below Broad. This includes the soaring values that have been asked and paid there since Charleston encountered tourism and the nation's growing fascination with historic preservation.

For better or worse, there's apparently a hot and heavy national market for Below-Broad property and the prestige of owning it. In 2004, no fewer than 62 Below-Broad properties sold for over $1 million. An out-of-town buyer paid $6,900,000 as the record price (so far) for residential property on the Charleston Peninsula.

Despite this kind of transaction, properties Below Broad are selling in the $600,000 to $2.5 million price range. And thanks to the efforts of our preservation-minded groups, institutions, and individuals, there are several other historic

neighborhoods on the Peninsula where residential properties are a little more affordable. According to the Charleston Trident Association of Realtors (Multiple Listing Service), the average selling price range of a single family residential house on the Peninsula during the first half of 2004 (including new and previously owned homes) averaged $796,937.

Naturally, real estate prices fluctuate greatly in different areas. And in a market as attractive as Greater Charleston, many homes and condominiums sell quickly and never make it to the Multiple Listing Service. But wherever real estate sales are a matter of public record, we've based our information on neighborhood home values on real numbers. Of course, this chapter is only a sampling of what is available, and the prices mentioned are indicators of the current values. Ask a real estate professional for more complete guidance.

Although the historic area south of Broad Street is considered the quintessential Charlestonian neighborhood, several other locales north of Broad (between Broad and Calhoun Streets) are now looked at very favorably too. The French Quarter—so-named for the French Huguenots who once lived and worked there—includes the area around Philadelphia Alley, State, Queen, and Chalmers Streets and is a mixture of commercial and residential buildings with inns, offices, restaurants, bars, and shops. Even the theatrical entity known as the Footlight Players (see the chapter on the Arts) coexists with busy families in this bustling cosmopolitan atmosphere.

Because the French Quarter is a small neighborhood of only a few square blocks, we're only talking about 40 town houses or so. Behind their relatively common facades, they vary in size, configuration, and building date. However, a late-18th-century to mid-19th-century, two-bedroom, two-bath home might average $750,000.

Ansonborough is one of Charleston's more famous examples of institutionally inspired restoration. In the early 1970s many architecturally significant homes in this neighborhood were in grievous disrepair. The Historic Charleston Foundation initiated a program that effectively and expediently changed the economic course of the entire area. A decade later, Ansonborough was one of the city's more sought-after neighborhoods, and it still is today. The advent of the South Carolina Aquarium, Liberty Square, the Ft. Sumter tour boat facility, and the other associated redevelopment along the western bank of the Cooper River just across East Bay Street from Ansonborough has added even more attractiveness to this downtown neighborhood. A typical 1830s house in Ansonborough with three bedrooms and two to three baths can sell in the $850,000 range.

Mazyck-Wraggborough includes the blocks between Calhoun Street and the Charleston Museum. Here you'll find an interesting mix of restored houses, beautiful churches, and light industry. Major historic anchors in this neighborhood include the Aiken-Rhett House, operated by the Historic Charleston Foundation, the Charleston Museum, and its neighboring house museum, the Joseph Manigault House. (See the House Museums section of the Attractions chapter.) In this neighborhood, a three-bedroom, three-and-a-half-bath house would sell for about $635,000.

The area around the Medical University of South Carolina, the College of Charleston, Colonial Lake, and all points in between is Harleston Village. Here you'll find an eclectic mix of bed-and-breakfast inns, condos, town houses, stately 18th- and 19th-century properties, and even a couple of high-rise apartment buildings. Two-bedroom rental houses are in the $1,500- to $1,800-per-month range. One-bedroom condos sell for about $275,000. But an average selling price for a three-

bedroom, two-and-a-half-bath home is in the $630,000 to $740,000 range.

Radcliffeborough is the area north of Calhoun Street, from the medical complexes east to Mazyck-Wraggborough. Ashley Hall, an independent school for girls, is situated here on a four-acre campus that includes the recently restored historic (ca. 1816) McBee House. There are several other fully restored mansions nearby plus rental properties, and many fixer-uppers can still be found in this area. Two-bedroom apartment rentals in Radcliffeborough average $1,200 per month. A three-bedroom, two-and-a-half-bath home recently sold for $432,000.

## EAST COOPER

Many neighborhoods east of the Cooper River—which include those in Mt. Pleasant, Sullivan's Island, and the Isle of Palms—are experiencing unprecedented growth. According to 2000 census figures, Mt. Pleasant was the second-fastest-growing city in the state with 58.1 percent growth in the last decade. In the fourth quarter of 2004 alone, more than 350 homes were sold here. The main corridor of growth seems to be along U.S. Highway 17 N. to Highway 41 and beyond.

All this projected growth will undoubtedly have a major impact on the real estate market east of the Cooper. However, recent figures from the Charleston Trident Association of Realtors (MLS) for the average East Cooper residence (south of Highway 41) was a very respectable $301,000.

Another major growth area is the southern end of the Isle of Palms. The IOP Connector, linking the island to the Mark Clark Expressway and Interstate 26, has fueled a flurry of new construction at both the southern tip of the Isle of Palms and at Wild Dunes Resort. In 2004 the average Wild Dunes residence was in the $800,000 range.

For newcomers who want a short list of lifestyle options, East Cooper offers a wide variety. There's the charm and quaintness of the Old Village in Mt. Pleasant. There are a number of older, established neighborhoods where families flourish—some of Mt. Pleasant's best are listed below. East Cooper's newer neighborhoods tend to offer several levels of home ownership to more easily accommodate first-time buyers as well as the upwardly mobile movers and shakers. And, of course, East Cooper's beach communities are always popular with laid-back folk and the second-home crowd.

# Established Neighborhoods

## CREEKSIDE

Just off US 17 N., Creekside is an established community and home to the Charleston Tennis Club. Residents have access to this facility with its courts and swimming pool. Winding streets and moderately upscale homes are handsomely individual. Many have a nice view of Shem Creek. An average four-bedroom, two-and-a-half-bathroom home in Creekside would be priced in the $595,000 bracket.

## THE GROVES

Between Coleman Boulevard and US 17 N. is the Groves. This neighborhood is one of few established Mt. Pleasant neighborhoods convenient to downtown Charleston. It consists of mostly one- or one-and-a-half-story brick homes built in the 1950s and 1960s. In this family neighborhood with a nice park for the children, you'll also enjoy the quiet streets for bike rides and leisurely strolls. A three-bedroom, two-and-a-half-bath ranch in the Groves might sell for about $359,000.

## HOBCAW

Off Mathis Ferry Road is Hobcaw, a large, established subdivision. Hobcaw has homes in many price ranges and is popular with longtime residents as well as young couples with children. Public

records show recent sales ranging from $325,000 to $860,000, with the average three-bedroom, two-and-a-half-bath home selling for $400,000. Proximity to the Hobcaw Yacht Club, with its outdoor swimming pool and other recreational facilities, is an appealing feature. Some houses are on the water, and these, of course, tend to be the priciest.

## OLD VILLAGE

This Mt. Pleasant neighborhood is one of the most appealing in the Trident area. Many of the restored antebellum homes are situated on large lots, while others are clustered along the tree-lined streets to form a village setting. One harborfront home here sold for $2,750,000 recently—the highest price paid in the Old Village in several years. Many houses were built in the last quarter-century, some even in this decade. Though certainly a real estate target for young affluent professionals, the Old Village has retained much of the unpretentious, casual charm it was known for a hundred years ago. An average home in the Old Village is in the $775,000 range.

## SNEE FARM

Just south of where Long Point Road intersects U.S. Highway 17 is Snee Farm, a large, established community with a country club. The golf course, tennis facilities, and the clubhouse are in great demand, and homes range in style from ranch to Georgian Colonial. Old oaks and gum trees soften the skyline and enhance a very attractive neighborhood. Here a three-bedroom, two-and-a-half-bath home sells for about $275,000.

# New Neighborhoods

A quick glance at the map will tell you the East Cooper area, especially Mt. Pleasant, is ripe for growth. Charleston's annexation of Daniel Island is a prime example; the corridor along Highway 41 is another. Look to these areas for some of the Lowcountry's best new communities.

## DANIEL ISLAND

If you've harbored a dream to sail into new territory, Daniel Island may give you that chance. Annexed as part of the city of Charleston but located east of the Cooper River, you're just minutes from downtown or North Charleston via Interstate 526. Daniel Island and its 20 miles of virgin waterfront on the Cooper and Wando Rivers are being developed into a town with public parks, residential neighborhoods, a town center with a waterfront park, and a corporate complex with two million square feet of office space. Ultimately, between 4,000 and 7,000 homesites are planned there. Residents are proud of the new Blackbaud Stadium, home of the Charleston Battery, a professional soccer team, and the tennis facility that is home to the Family Circle Cup (see the Spectator Sports chapter). One of Daniel Island's new assets is the recently opened private high school, Bishop England, which moved from downtown. It now sprawls on a 40-acre campus (see the Education chapter). Another new educational facility, this one a public school, is the 74,000-square-foot. elementary school, Hanahan Elementary, which houses over 900 students.

Many new families are living on Daniel Island now. Homes in one phase of a new condominium project are selling in the $265,000 range. More upscale, custom-built homes with four-bedroom, three-bath floor plans sell for $635,000 and more. It's reasonable to expect this rapid development to continue throughout the next decade and a half.

## DUNES WEST

A catalyst for the building boom off Highway 41 is Dunes West. This golf course community also offers swimming and tennis in a beautiful woodland and waterway setting. Many of these homeowners enjoy terrific views of the golf course and sur-

rounding waterways. The upscale, 2,011-acre private development was well under way by the mid-1980s, and complete build-out is scheduled for sometime after the year 2011. The variety of housing options in Dunes West is an unfinished story; major tracts of the vast acreage are still on the drawing board. For now the price of a four-bedroom, two-and-a-half-bath home near the golf course is in the vicinity of $400,000.

## I'ON

One of the newer planned communities on Mathis Ferry Road, I'On is known for its family-friendly feel with wide sidewalks, parks, lakes, and trees. The homes are designed with a nod to traditional Lowcountry architecture—reminiscent of downtown Charleston neighborhoods and Mt. Pleasant's Old Village. The new I'On Club houses upscale amenities for residents which include tennis and pool facilities, a community dock and a boat ramp on Hobcaw Creek. Homesites in I'On are priced from $90,000 up. Completed homes there start in the $475,000 range.

*Many of Charleston's downtown neighborhoods have very active membership associations that serve both social and economic (and sometimes even political) purposes. They have parties, sponsor tours, and work to govern future development. They also represent the neighborhood when resolving issues such as parking variances and utility construction.*

## LONG POINT

North of the Snee Farm Country Club community, just off US 17, is Long Point. Beautiful views of the marsh are among this neighborhood's best features. These upscale, newly constructed homes are nestled amidst mature gum and pine trees. Nearby are tennis and basketball courts, a soccer field, and Palmetto Islands County Park. (See the Parks and Recreation chapter.) Prices here range from $248,000 to $790,000, with an average four-bedroom, three-and-a-half-bath place going for $620,000.

## PARK WEST

This amalgam of 17 distinctive neighborhoods located along US 17, five minutes north of Mt. Pleasant's Towne Centre, has been created by some of the nation's leading builders. Park West has bike and jogging trails, forested habitats, sports complexes, retail shops, and professional offices. Charles Pinckney Elementary and Thomas C. Cario Middle School are within the community. Top-ranked Wando High School relocated here in 2004. A wide variety of pre-built and custom homes in Park West range from $200,000 to over $1 million.

## SEASIDE FARMS

Only minutes from Sullivan's Island and Isle of Palms, the community of Seaside Farms is a popular option in Mt. Pleasant with homes ranging in price from $310,000 to $700,000. Located near shopping, dining, and the convenience of I-526, residents of Seaside Farms can be near the beach and still commute to work almost anywhere in the Lowcountry. While family-sized homes of three bedrooms, two baths dominate this community, the latest trend in building is toward upscale condos—some with marsh and waterfront views.

# East Cooper Beaches

Sullivan's Island, Isle of Palms, Wild Dunes, and Dewees Island all have beautiful ocean or Intracoastal Waterway vistas. These upscale communities are among the Lowcountry's most popular. Land and real estate values are priced accordingly.

## DEWEES ISLAND

Billed as "Charleston's Only Private Island," Dewees is being developed carefully as an environmentally protected enclave. Modern homes are nestled discreetly among the island's vegetation, and a limited number of others are planned. Dewees's developers are hoping to preserve the natural integrity of this barrier island while they create a quiet, isolated upscale community. Bear in mind you must be willing to make your way to Dewees by boat—no bridge is available and none is planned. Most of the real estate activity on the island is new construction. Homesites in this unique community range from $375,000 to $1.1 million, and the few resale homes there have ranged in price from $480,000 to $1.4 million.

## ISLE OF PALMS

This beach community has an inviting, sandy beach and access to the creeks along the back of the island. In most cases, renovation after 1989's Hurricane Hugo has enhanced the real estate values here. Bigger and better houses, built high on stilts, will hopefully avoid future water damage. There are still many wonderful old beach houses, however, that have defied a century's worth of storms and tourism's relentless intervention.

The commute to peninsular Charleston from Isle of Palms is about a half-hour. Large beachfront homes (as in six bedrooms and four baths) can soar as high as $3 million. Condos sell for $340,000 and higher. The average three-bedroom, two-and-a-half-bath home fetches about $625,000.

## SULLIVAN'S ISLAND

There are no official subdivisions on Sullivan's Island, a laid-back beach community that's about a 20-minute commute from downtown Charleston. Rather, the location of property is described by its proximity to the water or local landmarks ("front beach" or "near Fort Moultrie," for example). This was the 19th-century summer community for many Below-Broad families of that time as well as today. The heightened real estate values of this historic island have encouraged more full-time residents. The current values range from $600,000 for a three-bedroom, two-bath house to $2.9 million for a four-bedroom, four-and-a-half-bath home on the beach front. The median price is in the $1 million range. The average price for a three-bedroom, two-and-a-half-bath home is $1.8 million.

## WILD DUNES

Just 15 miles from Charleston proper, Wild Dunes is a separate community at the north end of the Isle of Palms. This luxury resort has conference facilities, vacation rentals, villa accommodations, and homesites for sale. Homes here can go as high as $3.7 million for a four-bedroom, four-and-a-half-bath house, or as low as $300,000 for a more modest two-bedroom, two-bath place. (See the Boating and Watersports chapter for information on Wild Dunes Yacht Harbor facilities.)

## NORTH CHARLESTON

Although the city of North Charleston is largely outside the scope of this book, we'd be remiss if we didn't say there are many viable neighborhoods here that are both family oriented and affordable. According to the Charleston Trident Association of Realtors (Multiple Listing Service), the median selling price of a North Charleston home was $127,750 in 2004.

There's a notion (often an unfair one) among some Charlestonians that North Charleston is a good place to work but not a good place to live. It is mostly a city of main corridors where people clip through at the speed limit noticing all the business and industry but not the residential neighborhoods. The city is determined to remedy this perception with the encouragement of upscale neighborhoods such as Coosaw Creek, Whitehall, and Yeamans Hall. Newer options seem to appear on the

*The only way to get to Dewees Island is by private boat or a 20-minute ferry ride from the Isle of Palms. Once you're there, the only way to get around other than on foot is by electric vehicle. And get this: More than 65 percent of the island has been officially designated "development free" forever.*

city planner's drawing board with increasing regularity.

## WEST ASHLEY

Since 1960, the population in the West Ashley area has doubled. That fact alone speaks volumes about the neighborhoods in this part of the Lowcountry. The growth was accelerated by a major City of Charleston annexation in 1979. Many of these new residents have chosen apartments and subdivisions built since 1980.

West Ashley seems to thrive on the myriad small stores and businesses that line the major traffic arteries (Highways 171, 61, and 7, plus U.S. Highway 17 S.). Tucked behind these throughways are many neighborhoods that house families of every ilk and category. The Trident Association of Realtors (MLS) average price for a West Ashley home in 2004 was about $187,800. Some of the better-known neighborhoods in this section of Charleston follow.

# Established Neighborhoods

### BYRNES DOWN

Barely a mile from the Ashley River Bridge along US 17 is one of Charleston's first major subdivisions, Byrnes Down. It was built after World War II and named after James Byrnes, a South Carolina-born U.S. secretary of state. These small brick homes are popular with many first-home

CLOSE-UP

# Condo Living Appeals to Many Charleston Newcomers

Needless to say, the number of charming, old historic homes in Charleston is limited. Only so many were originally built, and fewer have survived the calamities of war, fire, storm, and earthquake—not to mention the ravages of neglect and time. This scarcity has driven real estate prices up and, some say, out of sight for most home buyers. Thus, the popularity of condominium living has seen a recent boom in Charleston's urban neighborhoods. From rehabilitated schools and updated commercial buildings to the new, upscale construction now seen along the downtown peninsula's waterfront, condo living is all the rage. The Greater Charleston area is a very popular choice for a second home—one that might someday serve the owners as a retirement nest for part or most of the year. Even older apartment complexes in many suburban areas are being converted into condos as more and more people move to the Lowcountry for its unique lifestyle. So, if buying a historic home is beyond your means, or you're thinking more along the lines of regular Charleston visits or just a carefree retirement, the condo option might be right for you. The choices are getting more plentiful, it seems, every year. Charleston's neighborhoods are nothing if not ever-changing and constantly evolving as fascinating places to live.

buyers who enjoy the advantage of being so close to the city. A recent average sales price for one of these trendy starter places was $230,000.

## THE CRESCENT

Folly Road and the Intracoastal Waterway border the Crescent. Described once as "the country, only 5 minutes from town," this highly desirable old neighborhood, built in the 1950s and 1960s, consists of established homes and yards with wonderful old trees. Generations of children have fed the resident ducks that inhabit the twin lakes, and all age groups take advantage of the quiet streets for walks and bike rides. A four-bedroom, three-and-a-half-bath home sells in the $700,000 range.

## PARKSHORE I, II, III, IV

The Parkshore family of subdivisions is bordered by Highway 7 and the Ashley River. These are newer executive homes with large lots and some availability remaining. Many have marsh views, and some have docks. Residents love the access to a community center within the Parkshore complex with its pool, park, and tennis courts. Most of these houses are three- and four-bedroom places with two-and-a-half to three-and-a-half baths. These homes recently ranged in price from $250,000 to $670,000, with an average home going for about $449,000.

## SHADOWMOSS

Shadowmoss is a mid-priced, country-club

community. It started in the 1970s and has been growing ever since. Many different builders have contributed to the development's housing mix, so there's something for every pocketbook here. Shadowmoss was designed around an 18-hole golf course and pool complex (see the Golf chapter). Residents enjoy community clubs and events and can make use of the on-site facilities. Real estate values range from $159,000 to $342,000, but an average three-bedroom, two-bath home might bring $185,000.

## JAMES, JOHNS, AND FOLLY ISLANDS, KIAWAH, AND SEABROOK

The islands west of the Ashley River, connected by a series of bridges, are a diverse and intriguing group. When the James Island Expressway (Highway 30) opened in 1993, it made these islands prime targets for developers.

Already densely populated, James Island has spectacular views of the Charleston Harbor and Peninsula and has many neighborhoods housing people who work throughout the Trident area. Much of Johns Island is still rural. Bohicket Road, the main highway through the island, has been widened in part near the resorts of Kiawah and Seabrook. New neighborhoods along this road are only a matter of time. Low-key Folly Beach is a casual, year-round island community with an eclectic mix of new construction and rustic old beach houses from Folly's days of yore. Real estate offerings include front beach, marsh and river, along with inland houses and lots. The median home price for a James Island home in 2004, according to the Charleston Trident Realtors, was $179,000. On outer James Island and on Folly Beach, the median was $438,000. Johns Island homes ranged from $247,250 all the way up to $7.5 million for a Kiawah resort home.

# James Island

## COUNTRY CLUB OF CHARLESTON

Across the Wappoo Bridge off Folly Road is Country Club of Charleston (sometimes called Country Club I). This older, established community with beautiful homes and well-kept lawns is one of the area's most desirable addresses. The private club, pool, and golf course are obvious assets, and the proximity to the Peninsula is another plus. Homes on the waterway are priced in the $1.5 million range for four bedrooms and three-and-a-half baths. Properties off the water sell in the $900,000 range for four bedrooms and two baths.

## PARROT CREEK

There is much to see in Parrot Creek. These newer houses and lots are large and beautifully landscaped—some fronting on deep water or marsh. Composed of mostly two-story homes on half-acre lots, Parrot Creek offers architectural variety and desirable extras such as wide porches to catch those prevailing breezes. A three-bedroom, three-and-a-half-bath home recently sold for $415,000. The average sale price is about $320,000.

## RIVERLAND TERRACE

Riverland Terrace, off Maybank Highway, is an established neighborhood with origins dating back to the 1920s. Today, you'll find a conglomeration of sizes, styles, and prices. There are interesting rehab possibilities as well as extraordinary turnkey dwellings throughout. Young people have been drawn to this area in recent years because of its tranquility and, in some instances, its affordability. The few houses on the waterway command the highest prices, while smaller houses in the middle of the neighborhood can be had for less. A three-bedroom, two-bath home might sell for as low as $225,000; a four-bedroom, two-bath house might be as high as

$470,000. The average price for a home that's not on the waterway would be about $378,000.

## HEADQUARTERS ISLAND PLANTATION

Across the Stono River from James Island are Johns Island and Headquarters Island Plantation. Incredibly, this spacious development on the vast open marsh is only 4.5 miles from downtown Charleston. This upscale, planned community is close to restaurants, shopping, and championship golf, but has the feel and openness of a far more distant setting. Property values for a four-bedroom, three-and-a-half-bath home reach $525,000. The low end of the price spectrum is about $220,000 for some three-bedroom, three-bath town homes.

# Folly Island

Real estate on this small resort island has exploded in price over the past several years. Articles describe the island as "the edge of America" with tongue only slightly in cheek. Like Key West in the 1970s, Folly is attracting a chic and mixed crowd who choose digs that range from dilapidated rental properties to impressive, dramatic, and upscale homes. Most properties fall somewhere in between. Many artists and dedicated surfers can still be found on Folly, but the buying

---

*New players on the real estate stage who fall in love with the proverbial historic fixer-upper can find solace in the Resource Center at the Preservation Society of Charleston. Therein lies a wealth of information on preservation and restoration techniques scripted by those who've performed that role in the recent past. This can be a major help in saving you time or money (or both).*

---

trend is moving toward the beach-loving executive types. In 2004, a beachfront home sold for $1.8 million. Most sales on Folly have been in the several new condominium developments that have recently been built. There, average prices can be around $332,000.

## SUNSET POINT

Near the west end of Folly, Sunset Point is an attractive newer subdivision. It is divided into six sections—some are a block from the beach; others front the marsh and deep water of Folly River. Prices here have been in the $595,000 range.

# Kiawah and Seabrook

These famous resort islands need no introduction here. (See the Area Overview, Golf, and History chapters.) The residents of these islands are among the wealthiest in Charleston County according to the latest figures from the Center for Business Research. Real estate on these barrier islands is blazing to new heights.

## KIAWAH

With 10 miles of beach and 10,000 acres of forest, marshes, creeks, and rivers, Kiawah is a world-class destination where you'll find some of the nation's most interesting resort architecture. Although the houses blend unobtrusively into the environment, they are by no means uniform. Palatial residences with creative use of glass and materials make the most of spectacular views from ocean to lagoon, and there is a consistency in landscaping throughout. In 2004, the average Kiawah home was $956,000, a dramatic increase over 1998's $116,644.

A variety of wildlife abounds, and the athletic facilities and social activities also lure homeowners. At your disposal are more than 18 miles of paved bike paths, a 20-station fitness trail, golf, tennis, swimming, and a 21-acre park and pool complex. Kiawah also has an active vacation rental program, which contributes to the real estate's value.

## SEABROOK

Bordered by the North Edisto, Bohicket, and Kiawah Rivers and the Atlantic Ocean, Seabrook Island is awash in spectacular water views. Kiawah's smaller next-door neighbor has more than 3 miles of beach and 2,200 private residential acres. The demographic makeup is similar to Kiawah, with Seabrook being another upscale island community with a wide assortment of real estate options and amenities. More residential than the other resort communities in the area, Seabrook incorporated as a town in 1987. There is a complete sports and recreation program, including a well-maintained equestrian center with aesthetically pleasing trail and beach rides. The average home price on Seabrook increased from $247,052 in 1998 to $832,000 in 2004. Seabrook, like Kiawah, also has a wide range of prices from $280,000 up to $3.2 million.

# RETIREMENT 🌴

With its mild climate and natural beauty, the Trident area is an attractive retirement destination. The mature market represents over 30 percent of the adult population here, and that number is growing every year. There are numerous residential communities, geared to different levels of independence, and a growing array of services in the business sector that are tailored to the needs of those enjoying their golden years. Many stores such as Revco, Eckerd, Kerr Drug, Harris Teeter, Lowe's, Belk, SteinMart and Waccamaw Home Superstore even run regular discounts for shoppers 60 or older. A 1 percent sales tax discount is given to seniors age 85 and over.

The Charleston County Public Library system maintains a community information database that provides detailed listings of organizations and resources, many geared toward senior citizens. It is updated on a continual basis and can be accessed by contacting any of the 15 county libraries. A listing of the county libraries can be found in the blue pages of the phone book or within the Education chapter. For more information about this useful resource, contact the Main Library at 68 Calhoun Street, (843) 805–6801.

## RESOURCES

**Advantage/Senior Services**
**Roper Hospital, 316 Calhoun Street**
**(843) 724–2489**
**www.ropersaintfrancis.com**
A senior services department at Roper St. Francis Healthcare is set up to deal with age-specific health issues. The Advantage program is a membership program for people 50 years and older that provides discounts on selected hospital services. Monthly meetings are held for an Alzheimers' support group, Mall Walkers,

and an AARP chapter with locations in Roper Downtown, Roper North, and Bon Secours-St. Francis hospitals. (For more on these hospitals, see the Health Care chapter.) Other community programs are offered throughout the year on topics such as Parkinson's disease. Additional benefits include a no-cost discount prescription card, eyewear discounts, and insurance assistance. Social activities include fitness classes and travel opportunities. Lifetime Advantage membership costs $15 per membership or $25 for spouses joining at the same time.

The Senior Resource Center is a clearinghouse of information about resources for seniors not only at Roper St. Francis Healthcare but also throughout the Greater Charleston area. Visitors will find a library full of senior-related topics. Internet access is available to provide more information. A dedicated phone line covers topics such as fitness programs, retirement planning, support groups, household safety, and continuing education. The Senior Resource Center is located in the Advantage Office on the first floor of Roper Hospital at 316 Calhoun Street.

**Center for Creative Retirement**
**Lightsey Center, College of Charleston,**
**160 Calhoun Street**
**(843) 953–5488**
**www.cofc.edu**
There is ample opportunity for seniors to join umbrella service organizations such as the Center for Creative Retirement at the College of Charleston, which is an affiliate of the Elderhostel Institute Network. Classes are held at the St. Joseph's Family Center, 1695 Wallenberg Boulevard in the West Ashley area, during fall, winter, and spring. Noncredit courses comprise educational seminars, tours, lectures, and discussion groups. Some past topics have included "History of Film," "Contemporary

Cuba," "Latest Trends in Medication," "History of Huguenots in Charleston," and "Legal Concerns of the Elder Population." The annual membership fee is $40.

## Charleston Area Senior Citizens Services Inc.
### 259 Meeting Street
### (843) 722-4127

This nonprofit agency serves older adults in the Tri-County area. Its information and assistance line operates from 8:00 a.m. to 4:00 p.m. Monday through Friday. The senior center offers a noon meal, programs, activities, and health education. For the homebound, home-delivered meals and transportation on the Peninsula are provided. The agency's major focuses, which are making a difference in our community, are sponsorship of the Foster Grandparent Program and a job-training program with subsidized employment for people 55 and older. The agency also operates a 77-unit housing complex for seniors.

## Charleston County Community Education
### Charleston County School District,
### 75 Calhoun Street
### (843) 937-6407
### www.charlestoncoce.org

For those who are ready to plunge into creative stimulation, an interesting option is the moderately priced Adult and Community Education Programs, sponsored jointly by the Charleston County School District and the Charleston County Park and Recreation Commission. Categories of classes encompass arts and crafts, business and vocational concerns, computers, culinary arts, fitness and health, language arts, sports, and special interests. Ten community schools across Charleston County are the sites of the classroom instruction. Offerings run the gamut from one-night, $5.00 sessions to six-week classes with fees of up to $150.00. Pick up information on the quarterly programs from the county school district offices on Calhoun Street or at Charleston County

*For active retired businesspeople who want to lend a helping hand to young entrepreneurs and their start-up businesses, there's the Service Corps of Retired Executives (SCORE). These counselors offer in-depth, one-on-one consulting to help their clients plan, market, manage, and package their ideas. They can be reached at (843) 727-4778, or visit www.score285.org.*

libraries. Please note that the district does not mail out class schedules.

## The Citadel
### 171 Moultrie Street
### (843) 953-5188
### www.citadel.edu/cgps

## College of Charleston
### 66 George Street
### (843) 953-5620
### www.cofc.edu

South Carolina resident seniors 60 or older who are eager for an intellectual challenge can take any of the wide array of courses offered (on a space-available basis) at these two outstanding Charleston colleges. The cost is just $25 a semester at the College of Charleston and only a $15 registration fee plus a one-time application fee of $25 at The Citadel. Another academic resource is the Senior Scholars Program for ages 55 plus, sponsored by The Citadel. For a $25-per-term fee, non-degree-seeking seniors become members and select lectures presented by Citadel faculty and staff and community leaders. Members are issued student ID cards allowing use of parking facilities, Daniel Library, computer labs, recreational facilities, and the college bookstore. Fall, spring, and summer term programs have covered such topics as "Lighthouses of South Carolina," "Charleston Gullah Connection," "Maritime Piloting in South Carolina," and "Everything Old is New Again: New Urban Legends." Social activities are offered as well. These include lectures, tours, picnics, and dancing classes. Anyone who is retired or semi-retired can enroll by calling (843) 953-5089.

**Lowcountry Senior Center**
**865 Riverland Drive**
**(843) 762-9555**

After more than five years of fundraising and planning, the new 10,500-square-foot Lowcountry Senior Center opened in the spring of 2002. The concept behind the center was to build a place for active seniors who want more out of life than "sitting in front of the tube all day." The center, managed by Roper St. Francis Healthcare, serves adults age 50 and older with a wide variety of programs and coordinated activities focused on wellness, education, fitness, recreation, and volunteer services. It also serves as a resource for senior-oriented information and houses a computer lab, fitness and arts and crafts rooms, and a main room for social activities like dancing, movies, and wine tastings. The Lowcountry Senior Center is located near the entrance to the James Island County Park on Riverland Drive and offers ample free parking. One-year memberships are $50 for Charleston County residents and $60 for nonresidents. Gold memberships including use of the fitness room are $85 for county residents and $95 for nonresidents.

**Shepherd's Center of Charleston**
**meets at First (Scots) Presbyterian Church**
**53 Meeting Street**
**(843) 766-2149**

**Shepherd's Center of West Ashley**
**meets at First Christian Church**
**1293 Orange Grove Road**
**(843) 556-1508**

**Shepherd's Center of East Cooper**
**meets at Mt. Pleasant Presbyterian Church**
**306 Church, Mt. Pleasant**
**(843) 216-6682**

All three facilities hold weekly meetings for a diverse program of lectures, workshops, and fellowship. Diverse topics covered have included "Noted S.C. Statesman,

Ben Tillman," "A Visit to China," "The Myth of Aging . . . Care for Life," and "Memoirs Done Write." Bridge, movies, and garden and plantation tours are offered as afternoon activities. The registration fee for the Charleston and West Ashley centers is $15, plus an annual $10 membership fee. East Cooper fees are $20, plus a $10 annual membership. Lunch is offered in between the morning and afternoon class periods for around $6.00. The Shepherd's Centers are interfaith senior centers with older adults organizing the programs for their peers.

## RETIREMENT HOUSING

Charleston offers retirement housing options ranging from resort living to private-patio or high-rise apartments to supervised care. The choice is yours, depending on the physical wants and needs of those involved, as well as budget. Note that we do not include the resort areas (Kiawah, Seabrook, and Wild Dunes) in this chapter. The resorts are upscale choices that are popular with many retirement-age residents, but they do not offer any provisions for assisted living. See the Hotels and Motels, Neighborhoods, and Relocation chapters for more specific information about resort properties and amenities. The following living arrangements for seniors in the Trident area are a sampling of what is available.

# Retirement Apartments

**Canterbury House**
**175 Market Street & 165 Market Street**
**(843) 723-5553**

Those interested in relocating into an apartment building for seniors will find the Canterbury House an appealing option. The Episcopal Church–sponsored complex added a new building in 2000 of 46 one-bedroom apartments to the original one of 204 apartments. The location on the Peninsula is within easy walking distance of shopping on King and Market Streets. The independent-living facility offers efficiencies, one-bedroom efficiencies, and one-bedroom apartments for seniors 62 years old and older whose income does not exceed certain specified levels for individuals or couples. Location and convenient parking make it handy for visitors and volunteers such as local musicians and children's choirs, who participate in special programs for residents. There is usually a lengthy waiting list for these apartments, so get your name on the list early if the Canterbury House is the place for you.

# Retirement and Life-Care Communities

**Bishop Gadsden Episcopal**
**Retirement Community**
**1 Bishop Gadsden Way**
**(843) 762-3300, (800) 373-2384**
**www.bishopgadsden.org**
Affiliated with the Episcopal Church, Bishop Gadsden is on a 54-acre site on James Island. Members enjoy the benefits of group living in a lovely setting and are often entertained and enlightened with lectures or presentations by volunteers from Episcopal churches in the community. An assisted-living option is also available. A 1999 expansion added 215 apartments and individual homes to the existing facility, and further expansion plans are in the works. A full range of amenities includes a wellness center, pool, casual and formal dining, beauty parlor, banks, and convenience stores on the premises. Services such as skilled nursing and dementia care make Bishop Gadsden the only nonprofit life-care community in the state.

**Cooper Hall Senior Living Community**
**937 Bowman Road, Mt. Pleasant**
**(843) 884-6949**
**www.cooperhall.com**

Several options are available at Cooper Hall, including apartments, lakefront villas, and assisted-living quarters. A 1999 $7.5-million expansion added to the full range of choices available here. Assisted-living options include studio and one- or two-bedroom apartments with kitchens and private bathrooms. Laundry service, medical observation, a continental breakfast and two meals a day, and a full slate of recreational activities are offered with transportation into town. Those in retirement living may choose from standard or deluxe one- or two-bedroom apartments with amenities such as an indoor swimming pool, pharmacy, beauty salon, laundry facility, and bridge rooms. Another popular feature is that pets are allowed in villa living areas. There is a licensed nurse on call at all hours, and residents can order from the dining room menu.

*One publication focusing on the interests and needs of Tri-County seniors is* Senior Sun. *The free pick-up is distributed all over town and covers senior events, health and wellness, gardening, finances, travel, entertainment, and timely information "for the young and active after 50!"*

**The Elms of Charleston**
**9102 Woodcreek Court,**
**North Charleston**
**(843) 572-5154, (800) 237-3460**
**www.elmsofcharleston.com**
The Elms is a beautifully landscaped, controlled-access community of custom-built patio homes, duplexes, town houses, and condominiums. Next to Charleston Southern University and Trident Regional Medical Center, the amenities at the Elms are extensive and include tennis and croquet courts and an 8,000-square-foot club with a fitness center, swimming pool, exercise area, spa, and library. The Wannamaker County Park with walking trails

borders the property. Shopping, dining, golf, and other cultural opportunities are minutes away. Management maintains the yard and home exteriors. Assisted living and long-term care are in nearby facilities.

### Franke at Seaside
**1885 Rifle Range Road, Mt. Pleasant**
**(843) 856-4700, (800) 940-7435**
**www.lutheranhomessc.com**
**www.frankeatseaside.org**
This residential-care facility, operated by Lutheran Homes of South Carolina, is located in Mt. Pleasant, just 1 mile from the beach at the Isle of Palms. It offers private and companion rooms with some assistance available. A full-time staff of licensed practical nurses and certified nursing assistants provides quality medical attention. One hundred fifty-eight one- and two-bedroom apartments in multiple buildings are options for independent living. Residents enjoy a wellness program, meals, housekeeping, and transportation. Emotional support is offered through family support groups, volunteer interaction, and a chapel program. A new 44-bed skilled nursing center was recently added to the community, and plans are under way for additional independent living cottages, patio homes, and apartments. A 24,000-square-foot resident's club and wellness center, the Burges Center, was just completed as part of an $18-million expansion.

### Oakdale Heights Senior Living
**601 Mathis Ferry Road, Mt. Pleasant**
**(843) 881-9809**
**www.oakdaleheights.com**
Opened in 2000, Oakdale Heights offers four floor plans in room or suite choices. Varying levels of care are available from short-term and traditional assisted living to a program for Alzheimer's patients. The 69-unit facility offers licensed nursing care on-site 24 hours a day. Independent living is available here as well. Amenities include activity/exercise rooms, lounges, a library, outdoor patios, a housekeeping/linen service, and a beauty and barbershop. A full-time social director is on staff.

### Presbyterian Home of South Carolina
**201 West Ninth North Street,**
**Summerville**
**(843) 873-2550**
**www.preshomesc.org**
The independent living options at Presbyterian Home in nearby Summerville include 59 outside cottages, 20 efficiency apartments, and 17 two-bedroom apartments. There are also 120 residential rooms with private baths, and residents are served three meals a day. Assisted living is an option here. On site are a beauty shop, barber services, and entertainment such as field trips to the Spoleto Festival, Monday night movies, ceramics, painting, and exercise classes. Bible classes and chapel are conducted, and transportation to the doctor or shopping facilities is furnished. Licensed nurses run a 90-bed infirmary. Opened in 1958, this community gives priority to South Carolina resident Presbyterians.

### Sandpiper Village
**1224 Village Creek Lane, Mt. Pleasant**
**(843) 884-5735, (888) 830-5105**
**www.sandpipervillage.com**
Locally owned and operated, Sandpiper is a campus-like community with independent living in one- and two-bedroom cottage-style homes. These attractive residences have front and rear entrances with convenient access to the Community Center. The Sandpiper Courtyard apartments offer assisted living. Meals, housekeeping, transportation to doctor appointments, and emergency call buttons are included. Rehab and skilled nursing facilities are available as well. Daily activities and social events, bingo, bridge, arts and crafts, church services, a beauty and barbershop, swimming pool, and a library are available. Small pets are allowed.

# HEALTH CARE (H)

Everyone is concerned about health care these days, and here in the Lowcountry we're very fortunate to have exceptional health care facilities offering high-quality professional services. Our hospitals provide comprehensive services ranging from state-of-the-art neonatal care to heart and liver transplants. Thanks to Roper St. Francis Healthcare's Lifelink ground and air mobile intensive-care units and the Medical University of South Carolina's Meducare Air, a helicopter transport service that extends across a 150-mile radius, patients can be placed in the hands of professionals by the fastest route possible.

## WALK-IN MEDICAL CENTERS

Visitors to Greater Charleston, and sometimes even locals, need a handy reference to the neighborhood medical clinics for those minor but often vacation-spoiling emergencies that can slow down the busy traveler. The following list contains some of the clinics that will see patients on short notice. Most clinics are open every day for extended hours, and no appointment is necessary.

## Charleston

Access Healthcare, LLC
235 Calhoun Street
(843) 853-8870

Peds Plus at Roper Hospital
316 Calhoun Street
(843) 724-2273

## Mt. Pleasant

Doctor's Care
631 Johnnie Dodds Boulevard
(843) 881-0815

Roper Mt. Pleasant ER and Diagnostic Services
570 Long Point Road
(843) 849-9339

## North Charleston

Doctor's Care
8091 Rivers Avenue
(843) 572-7000

## West Ashley

Doctor's Care
1851 Sam Rittenburg Boulevard
(843) 556-5585

Doctor's Care
3424 Shelby Ray Court
(843) 402-6834

## James and Johns Islands

James Island Medical Care
347 Folly Road, James Island
(843) 762-1440

Roper St. Francis Kiawah Seabrook Medical and Urgent Care
345 Freshfields Drive, Building J, Suite 101, Johns Island
(843) 768-4800

# Dorchester County

**Doctor's Care**
**10160 Dorchester Road, Summerville**
**(843) 871–7900**

## HOSPITALS AND HEALTH CARE FACILITIES

# Downtown Charleston

**Charleston Memorial Hospital**
**326 Calhoun Street**
**(843) 792–2300**
**www.musc.edu**
Charleston Memorial is dedicated to serving the needs of patients in Charleston County. This was the first area hospital to open a fully operational emergency room. Today, Charleston Memorial's emergency facility treats more than 20,000 patients annually. The hospital has a general medical unit, an intensive care unit, and a pediatric episodic unit. Charleston Memorial provides 24-hour emergency service and limited outpatient services. The McClennan Banks Clinic for outpatient ambulatory care next door contains 86 exam rooms and provides laboratory, radiology, and diagnostic services on site. It also houses prenatal clinics with ultrasound and amniocentesis. Charleston Memorial Hospital provides workshops and seminars on health-related topics free of charge. Visiting hours are from 9:00 A.M. to 9:00 P.M. daily.

**Kindred Hospital**
**326 Calhoun Street, 3rd Floor**
**(843) 876–8340**
**www.kindredhealthcare.com**
Kindred Hospital of Charleston is a private, long-term acute care hospital specializing in providing care for patients with complex medical needs. Patients are referred to Kindred Hospital for ongoing acute medical care because the severity of their medical condition precludes them from acceptance into a rehabilitation facility, sub-acute facility, or a skilled nursing unit.

They have 40 beds for these catastrophically ill, medically complex patients.

Kindred Hospital of Charleston is part of Kindred Healthcare, Inc., a national health care services company based in Louisville, Kentucky, that operates hospitals, nursing centers, institutional pharmacies, and contract rehabilitation services. The company's mission is "taking care of people who cannot take care of themselves." They are currently caring for more than 30,000 patients across the country.

**Medical University of South Carolina Medical Center**
**171 Ashley Avenue**
**(843) 792–2300**
**www.musc.edu/medcenter**
The MUSC Medical Center, a state-of-the-art teaching hospital, was named for the second year as one of the top 100 hospitals in the nation. This also is the heartbeat of the Medical University of South Carolina. (See the Education chapter.) This acute-care center, along with MUSC's outpatient clinic, serves not only patients from the Greater Charleston area, but also those attracted to it from all over the state and the nation. In addition to more than 50 certificate, baccalaureate, master's, and doctoral programs in virtually all areas of the health sciences, MUSC offers continuing education programs that help South Carolina's health professionals stay current with the latest medical treatments and procedures.

Under the umbrella of MUSC are several specialty facilities, including the Albert Florens Storm Eye Institute, MUSC Children's Hospital, MUSC Digestive Disease Center, MUSC Heart and Vascular Center, Hollings Cancer Center, MUSC Institute of Psychiatry, Women's Health Center, and MUSC Transplant Center. Work is under way on a new $292-million facility to house the Heart and Vascular Center. *Child Magazine* recently named the Children's Hospital the 10th-best children's hospital in the country. For more information on services, classes, physician appointments, or health information library topics, call the MUSC

# Physician Referral Services

**Bon Secours–St. Francis/
Roper Hospital**
(843) 402-2273, (800) 863-2273

**Charleston County Medical Society**
(843) 577-3613

**East Cooper Regional Medical Center**
(843) 884-7031, (800) 311-4803

**Medical University of South Carolina**
(843) 792-1414

**Trident HealthFinders**
(843) 797-3463, (866) 874-3368

---

Health Connection number at (843) 792-1414 or (800) 424-MUSC. General visiting hours are from 10:30 A.M. to 8:30 P.M. daily, and 9:00 A.M. to 9:00 P.M. for the pediatrics unit.

### Ralph H. Johnson VA Medical Center
**109 Bee Street**
**(843) 577-5011**
**www.va.gov**
This Department of Veterans Affairs medical center has 126 beds and 960 employees. The center provides acute medical, surgical, and psychiatric inpatient care plus primary and specialized outpatient care to veterans in a 13-county area of South Carolina. The VA Medical Center is affiliated with 50 different educational institutions but primarily works with MUSC, the main source of the center's paid resident staff. In fall 1996, the VA/MUSC Strom Thurmond Biomedical Research Center opened, providing a 42,000-square-foot location for the VA center's research staff. The hospital's 44 clinics work in a variety of health disciplines ranging from audiology to vascular surgery. Call the main switchboard at the number listed for additional information. Visiting hours are from 11:00 A.M. to 8:30 P.M. daily.

### Roper Hospital
**316 Calhoun Street**
**(843) 724-2000**
**www.ropersaintfrancis.com**
With 453 beds and more than 2,000 employees, Roper Hospital is one of the Lowcountry's oldest and largest health care facilities. In 1998, Roper merged with Bon-Secours–St. Francis Xavier Hospital to form CareAlliance Health Services, which has evolved into the new Roper St. Francis Healthcare. The hospital is in the midst of a two-year, $77.4-million construction project adding a seven-story, 245,000-square-foot tower that will replace its oldest hospital rooms. Included in its services are several special units: Roper Heart Center, a complete cardiac care facility that addresses education, prevention, diagnosis, and treatment, including surgery and rehabilitation; Roper Cancer Center, offering compassionate care, state-of-the-art diagnostic and treatment services, and special resources for cancer patients and their families; and Roper's NeuroScience Center, providing the area's only acute stroke unit and specializing in neurological treatment including epilepsy monitoring and surgery with advanced microscopy, ultrasound, and laser technology.

Women's, Infants', and Children's Services at Roper include a resource center, family-centered maternity care, lifestyle services, diagnostic breast and osteoporosis ser-vices, plastic and reconstructive surgery, the Bright Beginnings newsletter, and Peds Plus after-hours urgent care for infants, children, and adolescents.

The Roper St. Francis Rehabilitation Hospital is a 39-bed facility that focuses on rehabilitation and functional recovery. According to hospital statistics, patients who have been treated here consistently achieve higher levels of functional independence than the national norms. In addition to this inpatient facility, there are also outpatient rehabilitation services, such as physical therapy, occupational therapy, and speech therapy available in Summerville, Goose Creek, and Walterboro. The direct line for the Rehabilitation Hospital is (843) 724-2800.

Roper has diagnostic centers offering convenient access to lab, X-ray, and EKG services throughout the Trident area. To find the one nearest you, call (843) 402-2273 or (800) 868-4916. The centers are open from 8:00 A.M. until 5:00 P.M. Monday through Friday. Roper's downtown emergency room, (843) 724-2010, is open 24 hours a day with full-service emergency care. As a Heart and Stroke Emergency Network location, it also provides specialized heart care with its Chest Pain Observation Unit, which is next door to the E.R. The patient information desk can be reached at (843) 724-2111 and provides room numbers, or you may dial direct using 724, then 2, then the room number. General visiting hours are 9:00 A.M. to 9:00 P.M.

# East Cooper

### Daniel Island Medical Center
### 900 Island Park Drive, Charleston
### (843) 797-3463
### www.tridenthealthsystem.com
Recently opened in the East Cooper neighborhood of Daniel Island (see the Neighborhoods chapter), this medical facility is part of the Trident Health System. It offers

medical imaging (including mammography), lab collection, sports medicine, orthopedic rehabilitation, women's health, cardiac rehabilitation, and diagnostic services. Several primary and specialty care physicians maintain offices on-site.

### East Cooper Regional Medical Center
### 1200 Johnnie Dodds Boulevard,
### Mt. Pleasant
### (843) 881-0100
### www.eastcoopermedctr.com
This hospital serves the communities east of the Cooper River but also draws patients from throughout the Lowcountry. East Cooper Regional Medical Center has 106 beds and about 500 employees. Recent renovations focused on improved patient access. The hospital (formerly called East Cooper Community Hospital) has been in operation since 1986 and provides in-patient acute care and 24-hour emergency-room services. Additional special services include outpatient diagnostics, ICU/CCU, MRI, home health care, spinal care, ambulatory surgery, imaging, and OB/GYN. MUSC's Hollings Cancer Center (see earlier listing) opened a new outpatient treatment facility on the East Cooper Regional Medical Center campus in early 2005. Call the main switchboard for patient information and room assignments. Visiting hours are from 9:00 A.M. to 9:00 P.M. daily.

### Roper Mount Pleasant Medical Center
### 570 Long Point Road, Mt. Pleasant
### (843) 881-9678
### www.ropersaintfrancis.com
Located at Interstate 526 and Long Point Road, the Roper Mount Pleasant Medical Center opened in June 2001 as a part of CareAlliance Health Services. The two-story, 39,000-square-foot building contains doctors' offices and offers diagnostic services. A major part of the facility is the emergency room, which has five beds for full service, 24-hour emergency care. This is Mt. Pleasant's second emergency room, reflecting the population growth (up 58 percent in the 2000 census) of one of the

fastest growing cities in South Carolina. (See the Neighborhoods and Area Overview chapters for more on Mt. Pleasant.)

# North Charleston

**Archdale Medical Center**
**5300 Archdale Boulevard**
**(off Dorchester Road), Charleston Heights**
**(843) 552-8332**
**www.tridenthealthsystem.com**
Opened in the fall of 2000, this is one of the newest facilities of the Trident Health System. The center offers primary and specialty care physician practices as well as senior services. Diagnostic services include mammography and X-ray, a lab collection site, and occupational and physical therapy.

**Concentra Medical Center**
**8780 Rivers Avenue, North Charleston**
**(843) 572-0810**

**4115 Dorchester Road, Charleston**
**(843) 554-6737**
**www.tridenthealthsystem.com**
A part of the Trident Health System, these facilities offer a freestanding, comprehensive occupational medicine program serving more than 300 employers in Berkeley, Dorchester, and Charleston Counties since 1980. Services include post-offer physical examinations (when a prospective employee has been offered a job by a business pending the outcome of a physical exam), work injury treatment, drug and alcohol testing, and occupational injury and illness prevention programs. The physicians and staff are dedicated exclusively to the practice of occupational medicine.

**HealthSouth Rehabilitation**
**Hospital–Charleston**
**9181 Medcom Street, Charleston**
**(843) 820-7777**
**www.healthsouth.com**
Alabama-based HealthSouth opened HealthSouth Rehabilitation Hospital in Charleston in 1994, one of 2,000 facilities

in 50 states, Puerto Rico, Australia, and the United Kingdom. The full-service, 42-bed acute rehabilitation hospital spans patient care from injury or illness to maximum independence and function. Additional services include outpatient rehabilitation services, diagnostic imaging, outpatient surgery, and industrial rehabilitation. Their stated mission is "getting people back . . . to work . . . to play . . . to living." It is the only freestanding rehabilitation hospital in the Lowcountry and is accredited by the Joint Commission on the Accreditation of Healthcare Organizations (JCAHO).

**Roper Northwoods Emergency**
**and Diagnostic Services**
**2233 Northwoods Boulevard**
**(843) 824-8733**
**www.ropersaintfrancis.com**
Near Northwoods Mall, this facility offers full-service emergency care 24 hours a day. It also provides lab and X-ray and other diagnostic services.

**Trident Medical Center**
**9330 Medical Plaza Drive**
**(Interstate 26 and Highway 78)**
**(843) 797-7000**
**www.tridenthealthsystem.com**
The Trident Health System has 11 centers serving the health care needs of the Lowcountry by offering heart, cancer,

---

*Two local resource materials have more extensive listings of area health and social services. The* Tri-County Resource Directory, *published by Hotline, and the* Community Information Database, *compiled and continuously updated by the Reference Department of the Charleston County Library, are excellent sources. Both may be found in Charleston County libraries. You can get a copy of the former for $40 by contacting Hotline, (843) 747-3007 or visiting www.211help.org. The latter is accessible at no charge at Charleston County libraries.*

women's health, sports medicine, skilled nursing, industrial medicine, surgery, home health care, and senior services. The Trident Medical Center is the largest facility in the Trident Health System with a 296-bed, acute-care hospital employing more than 2,000 workers. The center provides diagnostic and outpatient and inpatient surgical services, and the hospital provides 24-hour emergency services. Other specialties include ICU/CCU heart care, cardiac rehabilitation, OB/GYN, pediatrics, sports/industrial medicine, physical rehabilitation, and a cancer center. Trident Medical Center is in the process of a $60-million expansion and renovation adding 64,000 square feet to its facility and a 400-space parking deck to improve patient access. For patient information, call (843) 797-5200, then dial 4 plus the room number.

**Trident Senior Health Center**
**2070 Northbrook Boulevard, Suite A-16, Charleston**
**(843) 797-0416**
**www.tridenthealthsystem.com**
Under the umbrella of the Trident Health System (see listing under Trident Medical Center), the Senior Health Center provides health care that meets the needs of residents age 65 and older. The center, which accepts Medicare assignments, is near Northwoods Mall. Staffed by two board-certified primary-care physicians with advanced training in geriatric medicine, the center also includes nurses, a geriatrician, and other health care professionals who are experienced in the special needs of the senior population. Primary medical care is provided for chronic illnesses such as heart disease, diabetes, and Alzheimer's. Trident Senior Health Center also takes a partnership role in wellness, with monthly health education programs, health screenings, and a senior health library. Additional assistance is offered with insurance or billing questions as well as other social service needs. The Archdale Medical Center (see previous listing) provides senior services also.

**Trident Surgery Center**
**9313 Medical Plaza Drive, Charleston**
**(843) 797-8992**

**Trident Eye Surgery Center**
**9297-B Medical Plaza Drive, Charleston**
**(843) 824-5024**
**www.tridenthealthsystem.com**
The Trident Surgery Center and Trident Eye Surgery Center specialize in same-day surgery, performing about 500 procedures a month. The centers feature state-of-the-art medical equipment, four operating rooms, and 10 private recovery rooms. Affiliated with the Trident Health System, the Trident Surgery Center is the only surgery center in the Lowcountry accredited by the Accreditation Association for Ambulatory Health Care.

# West Ashley

**Bon Secours–St. Francis Hospital**
**2095 Henry Tecklenburg Drive, Charleston**
**(843) 402-1000,**
**(843) 402-1010 (Healthline)**
**www.ropersaintfrancis.com**
Bon Secours–St. Francis Hospital is the oldest Catholic hospital in South Carolina and the only one in Charleston. Its long history in this community goes back to 1882, when five sisters of Charity of Our Lady of Mercy opened a small, wood-framed building called the St. Francis Xavier Infirmary. A 1998 merger with Roper CareAlliance made Bon Secours–St. Francis Xavier Hospital part of CareAlliance Health Services, now called Roper St. Francis Healthcare. Then and now, the emphasis has been on a devotion to caring for the whole person—physically, spiritually, and emotionally.

The hospital relocated in December 1996 from its previous downtown address to a new facility west of the Ashley River. The new hospital focuses on several signature services including spine and sports medicine, women's, infants', and children's health services, digestive disorders and urological care, heart and stroke emergency network, diabetes management, ambulatory surgery, and emergency services. The patient information and location number is (843) 402-1118, and Home Health Care services can be contacted at (843) 402-7000. (For information on Bon Secours' Senior Services, see the Retirement chapter.)

**Intrepid USA**
**2170 Ashley Phosphate Road,**
**Ste. 501, North Charleston**
**(843) 766-2929**
**www.intrepidusa.com**
Intrepid USA provides home care for both recovering, chronically ill, or disabled persons throughout Charleston, Berkeley, Dorchester, and Colleton Counties. Services include skilled nursing care, personal care, infusion therapy, medical social services, physical therapy, speech pathology, occupational therapy, respiratory therapy, home medical equipment, and hospice. Nationally, Intrepid USA has more than 100 offices in 24 states.

**Roper-St. Francis**
**Home Health Care, ProCare**
**1483 Tobias Gadson Boulevard,**
**Suite 208, Charleston**
**(843) 402-7000, (800) 353-7421**
**www.ropersaintfrancis.com**
Roper-St. Francis Home Health Care has two components: Home Health, and ProCare. Home Health provides home care by nurses, aides, medical social workers, and therapists. Services include skilled nursing, personal care, wound care, physical, speech, and occupational therapy, and a centralized intake department. ProCare provides in-home private duty nurses, homemaker and companion services, and temporary staffing for health care facilities. Home Infusion IV therapies are located at 7 Amy Elsey Drive and can be reached at (843) 763-2600.

**Roper West Ashley Surgery Center**
**18 Farmfield Avenue, Charleston**
**(843) 763-3763**
**www.ropersaintfrancis.com**

Opened in 1987, this West Ashley center performs more than 3,000 outpatient surgeries each year. Affiliated with the Roper Saint Francis Healthcare system, the Surgery Center provides general surgical services for adults and children.

## OTHER NEARBY HEALTH CARE FACILITIES

**Moncks Corner Medical Center**
**401 North Live Oak Drive,**
**Moncks Corner**
**(843) 761-8721,**
**(843) 577-9319 (Charleston phone no.)**
**www.tridenthealthsystem.com**
This Trident Health System outpatient diagnostic and rehabilitation facility serves the residents of Berkeley County. The center sponsors a number of community wellness programs in addition to providing laboratory testing, physical rehabilitation, radiology, and mammography services. Physician services are available by appointment at this location as well.

**Roper Saint Francis Medical Center**
**Berkeley**
**730 Stoney Landing Road,**
**Moncks Corner**
**(843) 899-7700, (800) 846-7707**
**www.ropersaintfrancis.com**
Roper Saint Francis Medical Center Berkeley has Berkeley County's only 24-hour emergency services department. The center also offers access to primary-care and specialty physicians as well as diagnostic services including laboratory testing, X-rays, mammography, CT scans, physical therapy, cardiopulmonary testing, endoscopy, and bronchoscopy.

**St. George Diagnostic Center**
**217 Parler Avenue, St. George**
**(843) 563-8452**
**www.tridenthealthsystem.com**
Serving Dorchester County residents, this Trident Health System center features general diagnostic procedures such as X-ray and mammography, a laboratory

drawing station, sports medicine, and rehabilitation services.

### Summerville Medical Center
**295 Midland Parkway, Summerville**
**(843) 832-5000**
**www.tridenthealthsystem.com**
The Summerville Center is a 94-bed, full-service facility with 24-hour emergency, general, medical, and surgical services, a heart center, intensive care and skilled nursing units, sports medicine and rehabilitation, and a sleep lab. It sponsors numerous wellness programs for the community in addition to providing medical imaging and X-rays, and diagnostic and physical rehabilitation services. The emergency room phone is (843) 832-5160.

Summerville Medical Center is a part of the Trident Health System.

---

**i**

*Here's a short list of health-oriented Web sites for your exploration:*
*www.aha.org*
*www.ama-assn.org*
*www.cdc.gov*
*www.healthweb.org*
*www.healthfinder.gov*
*www.ir-net.com (Information and Referral Resource Network)*
*www.211help.org*
*www.nlm.nih.gov (Medline)*
*www.webmd.com*

---

## MENTAL HEALTH CENTERS

### Berkeley Community Mental Health Center
**403 Stoney Landing Road,**
**Moncks Corner**
**(843) 761-8282, (888) 202-1381**
**(Charleston/Summerville)**
**www.state.sc.us/dmh**
This mental health center serves children, adolescents, and adults in Berkeley County with outpatient psychiatric services. The staff of 60-plus includes three full-time psychiatrists. Day treatment programs, short- and long-term therapy, and specialized clinics on such topics as attention deficit hyperactivity disorder and family preservation are offered. Private insurance coverage is accepted with prior approval, as well as Medicaid, Medicare, and the Civilian Health and Medical Program of the Uniformed Services. A sliding fee scale may be applied based on ability to pay. Transportation service is available for Berkeley County residents.

### Charleston/Dorchester Community Mental Health Centers
**2100 Charlie Hall Boulevard**
**(843) 852-4100, adults**

**3601-C Meeting Street Road**
**(843) 740-6136, children, adolescents, and families**

**106 Springview Lane, Summerville**
**(843) 873-5063, adults and children;**
**(843) 414-2350,**
**(800) 613-8379, after-hours emergency**
**www.state.sc.us/dmh**
With children and adolescent programs serving Charleston and Dorchester County residents, the Community Mental Health Center offers a comprehensive program of general mental health services for adults, adolescents, and children. The staff provides assessment and ongoing treatment, and the facility is affiliated with the South Carolina Department of Mental Health. A crisis stabilization center is operated to provide an alternative to hospital admission with early crisis intervention. The center accepts Medicare, Medicaid, and private insurance. A sliding fee scale is offered, based on ability to pay.

### MUSC Institute of Psychiatry
**171 Ashley Avenue**
**(843) 792-9888**
**www.musc.edu**
The Institute of Psychiatry at the Medical University of South Carolina serves not only as a center for professional education

and psychiatric research, but also as a provider of state-of-the-art care for a full range of psychiatric problems. Nationally recognized psychiatrists, psychiatric nurses, social workers, psychologists, and researchers work together to offer personalized treatment to individuals and families. The programs are designed to help people of all ages meet the impact of behavioral, emotional, and substance abuse problems. The Institute of Psychiatry's services include Adult Services, the Center for Drug and Alcohol Programs, Geriatric Services (including an Alzheimer's Care Program), Youth Services, and Specialty Services. Specialty Services include the Eating Disorders Program, Crime Victims Research and Treatment Center, Weight Management Center, Tic and Tourette Disorders Services, and Attention Deficit Disorders Services. To receive a brochure on any of the services or to make an appointment, call the number previously listed.

**Palmetto Lowcountry Behavioral Health**
**2777 Speissegger Drive**
**(843) 747-5830, (877) 947-3223**
**www.plbhs.com**
Palmetto Lowcountry Behavioral Health offers 24-hour help, assessment, and referral for treatment of depression, anxiety, drug and alcohol abuse, and other emotional problems. Formerly Charter Charleston Behavioral Health System, Palmetto Lowcountry provides inpatient, outpatient, and partial services for children, adolescents, and adults at the above location.

# ALTERNATIVE HEALTH CARE

Growing in popularity here in the Lowcountry and almost everywhere else are alternative health care practices such as chiropractic services, acupuncture, yoga, and holistic and homeopathic therapies. Here are some resources for those seeking new avenues toward well-being.

**Acupuncture Works**
**103 Rutledge Avenue**
**(843) 270-2228**
**www.acupuncturesmythe.com**
Trained in Asia, Gregg Smythe, DAc, is a national board-certified acupuncturist. Many receive effective relief from conditions such as back and neck pain, allergies, infertility, and incontinence. A native Charlestonian, Ms. Smythe returned to her hometown to practice this ancient Chinese treatment.

**Charleston Neck and Back Center**
**1835 Savage Road**
**(843) 763-2225**
**www.neckandbackcenter.com**
Charleston Neck and Back Center, open since 1988, has five licensed chiropractors and a total staff of 25 specializing in pain control, rehabilitation, family care, spinal injury care, plus full diagnostic and outpatient care.

**Charleston Therapeutic Massage**
**310 Broad Street, Suite 8, Charleston**
**(843) 723-7005**
**www.charleston-massage.com**
Five licensed and certified massage therapists work here specializing in relaxation, sports and deep tissue massage, as well as craniosacral therapy. Charleston Therapeutic Massage offers corporate on-site chair massage at your location, too.

**Cooper Spine Center**
**309 Coleman Boulevard, Mt. Pleasant**
**(843) 884-8444**
**www.chirolink.net/gscooperdc**
This center, with one licensed chiropractor, specializes in conservative chiropractic treatment of lower back pain, headaches, pinched nerves, scoliosis, and other difficult disorders of the back and neck. Sports and work injuries as well as auto accident injuries have been treated here since the center opened in 1983.

## CLOSE-UP

# Emergency and Health Care Numbers

Al-Anon/Al-Ateen
(843) 762-6999

Alcohol & Drug
Abuse Hotline
(800) 252-6465

Alcoholics Anonymous
(843) 723-9633

Alzheimer's Association,
Palmetto Chapter
(843) 571-2641, (800) 860-1444

American Cancer Society
(843) 744-1922

American Heart Association
Lowcountry Regional Office
(843) 853-1597

American Lung Association of
South Carolina, Coast Branch
(843) 556-8451

American Medical Association
(312) 464-5000

American Red Cross,
Carolina Lowcountry Chapter
(843) 744-8021

Berkeley County Health Department
(843) 723-3800,
(843) 723-0766 (Charleston line)

Berkeley County Rescue Squad
(843) 723-3800

Charleston County Health Department
(843) 579-4500

Charleston County Volunteer
Rescue Squad
(843) 745-6303

Child Abuse Hotline
(800) 422-4453

Coastal Crisis Chaplaincy
(843) 724-1212

Compassionate Friends
Charleston Chapter
(843) 884-2589

Dorchester County
Health Department
(843) 832-0041

Elderlink, Inc.
Trident Area Agency on Aging
(843) 745-1710

**Holy Cow Yoga & Holistic Center**
**10 S. Windermere Boulevard**
**(843) 769-2269**
**www.holycowyoga.com**
Located in South Windermere Center (see the Shopping chapter) across from Earth Fare health foods supermarket, Holy Cow offers a wide variety of yoga classes in a multi-disciplinary Hatha style with over 30 classes every week. They also offer workshops, seminars, and special guest speakers monthly to promote yoga knowledge, health and wellness, and spirituality. A staff of three massage therapists specializes in neuromuscular and Swedish deep tissue, full body, and deep relaxation massage, hot stone therapy, and Reiki.

Elder Support Line
City of Charleston Police Department
(843) 724-7180

Family Services
(843) 744-1348, (800) 232-6489

Grief and Loss Center of South Carolina
(843) 722-8371

HIV/AIDS/STD Hotline
(800) 342-2437

Hospice for the Carolinas
(800) 662-8859,
(803) 791-4220 (SC number)

Hotline
(843) 744-HELP, (800) 922-2283

Juvenile Diabetes Foundation
(843) 763-1973

Lowcountry Children's Center
(843) 723-3600

March of Dimes
Birth Defects Foundation
Lowcountry Division
(843) 571-1776

MUSC Health Connection
(843) 792-1414

Muscular Dystrophy Association
(843) 556-3654

Multiple Sclerosis Society
Mid-Atlantic Chapter
(800) 922-7591

Narcotics Anonymous
(843) 852-3001

National Foundation for Depressive Illness
(800) 248-4344

National Mental Health Association
(800) 969-6642

People Against Rape
(843) 745-0144,
(800) 241-7273 (hotline)

Poison Control Hotline
(800) 222-1222,
(800) 922-1117 (South Carolina number)

Roper Diabetes
Treatment Center
(843) 402-1099

Runaway Hotline
(800) 621-4000

STD Hotline
(800) 227-8922

Teenline
(843) 747-TEEN,
(800) 273-8255

**Island Chiropractic Centre**
**3546 Maybank Highway, Johns Island**
**(843) 559-9111**
www.charlestonchiropractic.com
Island Chiropractic is run by a certified sports physician with post-doctoral certification in X-ray interpretation, pain management, impairment ratings, CPR, and first aid. The staff of eight has been treating area patients at this location since 1987.

**Island Therapy Group**
**2201 Middle Street, Sullivan's Island**
**(843) 883-9497**
A staff of five licensed certified massage therapists provide services including Swedish deep tissue and sports massage,

craniosacral and neuromuscular therapy, and reflexology.

**Marti Chitwood, RD, CCN**
**1370 Ashley River Road**
**(843) 556-2123**
With a background in dietary therapy and healthful nutrition, Marti Chitwood is a good resource of holistic nutritional advice. Her approach considers the whole person, including lifestyle, emotions, attitudes, beliefs, and symptoms.

## OTHER SERVICES

**Center for Women**
**531 Savannah Highway**
**(843) 763-7333**
**www.c4women.org**
The Center for Women is a nonprofit organization dedicated to improving the lives of women in the Lowcountry through personal and professional success. Their services include information and referral resources and peer counseling for individual problem-solving strategies. The support groups include Depression and Anxiety, Separation and Divorce, Women in Transition, and Post Partum Depression. The Thursday Brown Bag Lunch Series is quite popular and has covered topics such as "Health After 40," "Financial Freedom," and "Motherhood." A recent seminar focused on "The Entrepreneurial Woman," with business professionals presenting financial, legal, marketing, and accounting information for women starting or running their own businesses. Most services and programs are held at the Center for Women and are free. Call the number above or visit their Web site for the latest on their innovative programs and events.

**Grief and Loss Center of South Carolina**
**150 Wentworth Street**
**(843) 722-8371**
The nonprofit Grief and Loss Center of South Carolina operates within the McAlister-Smith Funeral Home and serves as a clearinghouse of grief counseling and

support programs for men, women, children, and adolescents in the community. A current list of grief services is maintained here. The center sponsors community and professional workshops including an annual Grief Conference in the fall.

**Hospice of Charleston Inc.**
**3870 Leeds Avenue, Suite 101,**
**North Charleston**
**(843) 529-3100**
**www.hospiceofcharleston.org**
Licensed as both a hospice and home health agency, Hospice of Charleston has served the residents of Charleston, Dorchester, and Berkeley Counties since 1981. It provides medical, emotional, and spiritual care to terminally ill people and their families, with a staff of 57 full-time professionals and more than 170 trained volunteers. Grief recovery workshops are co-sponsored with area hospitals that meet once a week for six weeks. Stepping Stones is a one-day seminar for teens from 12 years up who have experienced a loss through death. Twice a year Shannon's Hope Camp (at Camp St. Christopher on Seabrook Island) is held for bereaved children. The camp involves the children in fun activities such as music, drawing, and arts and crafts designed to help them work out their grief. Each November, Hospice of Charleston sponsors the Candlelight Memorial Ceremony at Colonial Lake in downtown Charleston. For a $15 donation to Hospice, luminarias are lit surrounding the edge of the lake in memory of lost loved ones. A short program and music add to the remembrance ceremony. For more information on Hospice of Charleston programs, call the listed number.

**Lowcountry AIDS Services**
**3547 Meeting Street Road,**
**North Charleston**
**(843) 747-2273**
**www.aids-services.com**
Founded in 1985, Palmetto AIDS Life Support Services of South Carolina (PALSS) evolved into a statewide, community-based service agency now called Low-

country AIDS-Services (LAS). Lowcountry AIDS provides case management, counseling, and direct volunteer support to men, women, and children with HIV or AIDS in three counties—Charleston, Berkeley, and Dorchester. In addition to the practical and emotional support, this nonprofit social service agency works to educate and acts as an advocacy, resource, and referral agency for HIV/AIDS-infected people and their families. LAS is supported by the Community Foundation, Trident United Way, and private donations. (For information on LAS's Dining With Friends celebration, look under May in the Annual Events chapter.)

### Odyssey HealthCare of Charleston
**3870 Leeds Avenue, Suite 109,
North Charleston
(843) 554-4048, (800) 494-0418,
24 hours**
Serving Charleston, Berkeley, Dorchester, Colleton, and Beaufort counties (plus 11 other counties), Odyssey HealthCare provides interdisciplinary care for the terminally ill in their own homes. Providers are licensed to serve by the state and are Medicare-certified and accredited by the Joint Commission on Accreditation of Healthcare Organizations. Periodic educational and support programs are offered. Annual memorial services are held to provide rituals for grieving persons.

### Palmetto Chapter,
**The Alzheimer's Association
1941 Savage Road, Suite. 400-D
(843) 571-2641, (800) 860-1444**
Palmetto is a voluntary health, nonprofit organization dedicated to providing services and support to persons and families affected by Alzheimer's disease. An estimated 61,000 South Carolinians are afflicted with Alzheimer's. The Palmetto Chapter offers educational seminars, workshops, and literature. Other services include support groups, a help line, and referral information. They are also an advocacy group and publish a quarterly newsletter for their membership.

### Palmetto Health Hospice
**1815 Old Trolley Road, Suite 109
Summerville
(843) 821-4011, (800) 775-1392
www.palmettohealth.com**
Formerly Hospice Home Care Resources, Palmetto Health Hospice was the first Medicare-licensed hospice in South Carolina. Serving 21 counties in South Carolina, Palmetto Health Hospice specializes in providing comprehensive compassionate care to terminally ill patients and their families in their home of choice. Organized as a nonprofit charity, care is based on need, not the ability or inability to pay. Their Pathfinders Support Group helps adults who have experienced a loss through death. The group meets the third Tuesday of the month at 6:00 P.M. For more information on services, contact Palmetto Health Hospice at the numbers listed.

# EDUCATION ⬤

As in most communities its size, the academic options in Greater Charleston are greatly varied. Newcomers to the area with school-age children need to know specific details about the public and private schooling options and make their educational decisions accordingly. Sometimes this information is closely guarded (especially when the news isn't particularly good), but be diligent in your quest for detail. Finding good schools and good teachers is obviously extremely important.

If you're new to the city, one of your first sources of information about schools in your residential area should be your realtor. Ask about the area schools' comparative test scores, student-teacher ratios, college placement percentages, and athletic options. Don't hesitate to ask about any recorded incidents of violence. Another resource with reliable information is your county school district office. Addresses and phone numbers for offices in Charleston, Dorchester, and Berkeley Counties are listed in this chapter.

## PUBLIC SCHOOLS

Records from the first general public school system in the Lowcountry date back to 1856. Today, separate public school systems are in place in Charleston, Berkeley and Dorchester Counties. More than 88,000 students are enrolled in kindergarten through 12th grade at more than 134 schools in four school districts—Berkeley County, Charleston County, Dorchester II, and Dorchester IV.

The school year runs 180 days from mid-August until the end of May or early June. All children entering first grade must present a birth certificate and must be six years old by September 1. Those entering South Carolina schools for the first time must show a vaccination certificate. School bus service is available for students who live more than a half-mile from their assigned school.

Among the area's educational options are seven schools serving children with special needs, 12 magnet schools for academically gifted students, and a special South Carolina–mandated program in each district for children with high test scores and strong academic potential.

### Charleston County School District
**75 Calhoun Street**
**(843) 937-6300**
**www.charleston.k12.sc.us**
The Charleston County School District operates 86 schools in a 1,000-square-mile area along the South Carolina coast. About 48,500 students attend these schools. The county school system, governed by a nine-member board of trustees, is divided into eight constituent school districts, each one administered by an area superintendent. These eight districts, in turn, have elected school boards of various sizes that are responsible for establishing the attendance zones for local schools. The district employs 3,200 teachers and maintains an average pupil–teacher ratio of 19.9 to 1.

The district has been a trailblazer for the magnet school concept, with 12 locations—Buist Academy, Ashley River Creative Arts Elementary, Charleston Progressive Elementary, St. Andrews Elementary School of Math and Science, Charlestowne Academy, C. E. Williams, Jennie Moore Elementary, Military Magnet Middle School at Toole, Charleston County School of the Arts, Garrett Academy of Technology, Septima Clark, and the Academic Magnet High School. These special schools serve a student population that is academically or artistically gifted. Located on the Peninsula, in West Ashley, and in

North Charleston, they draw students from surrounding neighborhoods as well as areas spread throughout the district. Magnet school educational programs provide an alternative curriculum that integrates resources from the community, higher education, the arts, business, and technology. Call (843) 937-6413 for qualification information, as magnet schools can differ in entrance requirements.

SAIL—Students Actively Interested in Learning—is a state-mandated program in place in the Charleston County public school system. Offerings are innovative and challenging, designed to stimulate the academically talented students who are accepted into the program. Creative, critical problem-solving skills make up the focus of the curriculum content through programs such as the Academic Bowl and Odyssey of the Mind competitions, Advanced Placement courses, and a mentor program for grades 8 through 10. For more information on SAIL, call the supervisor at (843) 937-6566.

Special education programs for students with emotional, mental, or physical disabilities are available through the school district as well.

All told, Charleston County administers 42 elementary schools, 13 middle schools, 8 high schools, 12 magnet schools, 4 charter schools, and 8 programs. Relying on the phone book for numbers to reach specific offices for the different constituent school districts can be confusing, so we have compiled a list of important contacts in various Charleston County areas for easy reference.

**District 1 and 2, Mt. Pleasant**
**(843) 849-2878**

**District 3 and 9, James Island, Johns Island**
**(843) 762-2780**

**District 4, North Charleston**
**(843) 745-7150**

**District 10, West Ashley**
**(843) 763-1500**

**District 20, Charleston**
**(843) 937-6597**

**District 23, Hollywood, Edisto, Ravenel**
**(843) 889-2291**

**Berkeley County School District**
**229 E. Main Street, Moncks Corner**
**(843) 899-8600**
**(843) 723-4627 (in Charleston)**
**www.berkeley.k12.sc.us**
Berkeley County School District is the third largest in the state, with 36 schools serving over 26,000 students. The northern end of Berkeley County is rural and sparsely populated, while the area from Moncks Corner to Hanahan is suburban.

The curriculum is designed to meet the educational needs of all students, regardless of their academic achievement level. Accelerated students benefit from classes tailored to their advanced abilities. Call (843) 899-8640 or (843) 723-4627 extension 8640 for information on the ACE program (Academic and Creative Enrichment), Berkeley County's counterpart to Charleston County's SAIL program. Average students receive a steady diet of core courses designed to prepare them for the challenges posed by college and postgraduate jobs.

Remedial education is available for students requiring special attention. Special education programs are targeted to children with disabilities ranging from those who are visually impaired to the educable mentally retarded. All Berkeley County schools offer support personnel and services to students, including guidance counselors, psychologists, and speech therapists.

The breakdown shows Berkeley County administering 16 elementary, one elementary/middle, 12 intermediate and middle schools, 6 high schools, and 1 alternative.

## Dorchester County School District II
## 102 Green Wave Boulevard, Summerville
## (843) 873-2901
## www.dorchester2.k12.sc.us

District II in Dorchester County has been designated one of the fastest-growing public school districts in the state. A study conducted for the school district by The Citadel indicated that 95 percent of the residential growth projected for Dorch- ester County by the year 2000 would occur in District II, the Greater Summerville area. In addition, 98 percent of this growth was projected for the eastern or Oakbrook section of Summerville, where school enrollment bears this out by jumping from 10,106 in 1979–80 to 17,675 in 2003–2004.

District II operates 16 schools, specializ- ing in extracurricular activities for students in kindergarten through grade 12. Students graduating from Summerville High School have consistently scored above the state norms on the Scholastic Aptitude Test. The January 1996 issue of Money magazine listed Dorchester District II among the top 100 school districts in the nation, based on high student achievement in a location with a moderate cost of living and proxim- ity to a major metropolitan area.

GATE (Gifted and Talented Education) is Dorchester II's state-mandated program for those students who qualify for special enrichment and academic challenges. Call

(843) 873-2901 for more information on the qualifications needed to participate. Alternative programs for young people in District II high schools offer special coun- seling and basic skills aimed at lowering the dropout rate. These specialized pro- grams are conducted at an off-campus site—during the 2003–2004 school year at Givhans Community School—during regu- lar school hours.

Based on high achievement in stan- dardized testing, District II has several schools that earned "deregulation status" from the state for updating school curric- ula, allowing greater innovation in teaching methods, and meeting the increasingly complex needs of young people. There are nine elementary schools, five middle schools, and two high schools in Dorch- ester District II. The Givhans Community School and Rollings School of the Arts complete the list of schools in this district.

## Dorchester County School District IV
## 500 Ridge Street, St. George
## (843) 563-4535
## www.dorchester4.k12.sc.us

Dorchester District IV serves the outer region of Dorchester County and, with only about 2,600 students, is one of the smallest districts in the state. The district has a pupil-teacher ratio of one instructor for every 20.1 students. Setting high stan- dards for its faculty, the district provides incentives for the professional growth and advancement of its teachers and adminis- trators through in-service training pro- grams and membership in the Salkehatchie Consortium, which provides graduate courses at no cost to teachers.

The district's curriculum is designed for students looking to enter the work force after high school as well as students head- ing for college. District IV maintains two elementary schools, one middle school, and one high school.

# HOME SCHOOLING

Parents who wish to teach their children

at home can do so and should contact the school system in their county for specific guidelines and assistance. Standards are strict, so the number of home-schooled students fluctuates. Call (843) 937-6484 to find out more about home schooling in Charleston County. In Berkeley County, call (843) 723-4627, extension 8701; in Dorchester County, call (843) 873-2901.

## PRIVATE SCHOOLS

There is an excellent selection of over 100 independent schools in the area, ranging from parochial to all-girl. Some offer financial aid, and most sponsor open houses on campus for visitors. A good source for more information on private educational options in the Lowcountry is the Tri-County Admissions Council, which publishes an informational brochure complete with locator map, phone numbers, and important facts about member schools. A copy of this publication is available from local Realtors or the Charleston Metro Chamber of Commerce. Write for a copy to P.O. Box 39612, Charleston 29407 or visit their Web site, www.chastac.org. For contacts at nonmember schools, check the telephone directory. The following list of private schools is a sampling of what is available in the Greater Charleston area.

### Addlestone Hebrew Academy
**1639 Raoul Wallenberg Boulevard**
**(843) 571-1105**
**www.addlestone.org**
Addlestone accepts children from 18 months through grade 8 and provides secular as well as religious training. Conversational Hebrew classes are offered along with a full curriculum in the elementary grades.

### Archibald Rutledge Academy
**1011 Old Cemetery Road, McClellanville**
**(843) 887-3323**
**www.archibaldrutledgeacademy.com**
The Archibald Rutledge Academy, named for the South Carolina poet laureate, offers

full college preparatory and general curricula for students in kindergarten through grade 12. The school's small classes and updated facilities, as well as an emphasis on surrounding ecological and cultural resources, are important features.

### Ashley Hall
**172 Rutledge Avenue**
**(843) 722-4088**
**www.ashleyhall.org**
Founded in 1909, Ashley Hall is a college preparatory day school dedicated to educating girls from age 2 through grade 12. It remains the only all-girl independent school in the state. A full 100 percent of the school's graduates are accepted by colleges and universities across the nation. The school's early childhood program also admits boys ages two to four.

### Bishop England High School
**363 Seven Farms Drive**
**(843) 849-9599**
**www.behs.com**
Bishop England High School is a Roman Catholic coeducational secondary school operated under the auspices of the Diocese of Charleston. Grouping by academic ability is a unique feature of the school, whereby students of similar abilities are placed together for concentrated instruction. In summer 1998 the school relocated from its downtown campus to a state-of-the-art high school on a 40-acre site on Daniel Island. (See the Neighborhoods chapter for more on Daniel Island.)

### Catholic Schools
**1662 Ingram Road**
**(843) 402-9115**
**www.catholic-doc.org**
A full academic curriculum with all basic disciplines is offered at all six Lowcountry Catholic elementary, middle, and high schools, in addition to the study of religion and Christian values. The schools are Blessed Sacrament, Christ Our King-Stella Maris, Divine Redeemer, Nativity School, St. John's School and the Charleston Catholic School, Summerville Catholic School, and

Bishop England (see previous listing). For more information, contact the Catholic schools office at the address listed above.

## Charles Towne Montessori School
56 Leinbach Drive, Charleston
(843) 571-1140
www.ctmsedu.org

Situated on a 12-acre wooded campus in West Ashley, Charles Towne Montessori accepts children from 18 months to 12 years old. The school offers a learning environment in keeping with Montessori principles, encouraging creative expression in all aspects of a child's development. There is a studio program for the arts as well as an after-school sports program.

*For parents of Charleston County school students, a parent-teacher hotline number is available by calling the Community Bulletin Board at (843) 884-2278, then dialing in the four-digit extension, 2001. A directory follows for each of the schools, providing information on a variety of topics such as athletics, after-school programs, and PTAs.*

## Charleston Collegiate School
2024 Academy Drive, Johns Island
(843) 559-5506
www.charlestoncollegiate.org

Charleston Collegiate School, on a 30-acre site in the middle of Johns Island, offers a college preparatory curriculum stressing the fundamentals in all academic disciplines. The school accepts qualified students age 4 through grade 12.

## Charleston Day School
15 Archdale Street
(843) 722-7791
www.charlestondayschool.org

Charleston Day School is a coed day school enrolling about 185 students in grades 1 through 8. Graduates go on to local secondary schools and a variety of preparatory schools around the country.

## First Baptist Church School
48 Meeting Street
(843) 722-6646
www.fbschool.org

First Baptist Church School, established in 1949, offers a college preparatory education in a Christian setting for children age 4 through grade 12. The academic curriculum is enriched by Bible study and extracurricular activities.

## James Island Christian School
15 Crosscreek Drive
(843) 795-1762
www.jics.org

James Island Christian is a ministry of James Island Christian Church. It offers an interdenominational, comprehensive curriculum for students in kindergarten through grade 12. Their standards exceed the requirements for entrance into most colleges.

## Mason Preparatory School
56 Halsey Boulevard
(843) 805-6015
www.masonprep.org

The mission of Mason Preparatory School is to provide a solid academic foundation to students in grades one through eight. In addition to a well-rounded curriculum, a wide variety of after-school activities is offered.

## Northside Christian School
7800 Northside Drive, North Charleston
(843) 797-2690
www.northsideministries.net

Northside is a Christian school offering a complete educational program for students age 3 through grade 12. In addition to general, college preparatory, and advanced placement instruction, a fifth-quarter summer program is also available.

## Palmetto Academy
913 Wappoo Road
(843) 571-7740

Palmetto Academy has small classes emphasizing the basics in both general and college preparatory courses for students in grades 9 through 12. The school offers help for children with attention deficit disorder as well as for those who need more direct attention from teachers.

### Pinewood Preparatory School
**1114 Old Orangeburg Road, Summerville**
**(843) 873-1643**
**www.pinewoodprep.com**
This coeducational, college preparatory day school enrolls 700 students in preschool through grade 12. It offers a full developmental preschool starting at age four, a kindergarten program, and a challenging academic program for all students. A full athletic program as well as extracurricular activities such as art and music studies, student literary productions, and special interest clubs are available.

### Porter-Gaud School
**300 Albemarle Road**
**(843) 402-4771 (Lower School),**
**(843) 402-4775 (Middle/Upper**
**Schools)**
**www.portergaud.edu**
Episcopal-affiliated Porter-Gaud is a coeducational, college preparatory school with students in kindergarten through grade 12. All of its graduates go on to four-year colleges. In addition to its strong academic program, participation in a wide variety of sports and extracurricular activities is encouraged at all grade levels of this school on a West Ashley campus.

### St. John's Christian Academy
**204 W. Main Street, Moncks Corner**
**(843) 761-8539**
St. John's (formerly known as Lord Berkeley Academy) is a coeducational, college preparatory day school for students age 3 through grade 12. In addition to academics, St. John's offers extracurricular activities such as athletics and service clubs.

### St. Paul's Country Day School
**5139 Gibson Road, Hollywood**
**(843) 889-2702**
**www.stpaulscountryday.org**
St. Paul's Country Day School provides

academic instruction in a nondenominational Christian atmosphere. Students age 3 through grade 12 attend classes on a 10-acre consolidated campus.

*It's another one of those perfectly Southern traditions the Lowcountry is famous for: At graduation exercises each spring at Ashley Hall, college-bound girls descend the spiral staircase at McBee House (ca. 1816) in long white dresses with armloads of red roses.*

### Trident Academy
**1455 Wakendaw Road, Mt. Pleasant**
**(843) 884-3494**
**www.tridentacademy.com**
Trident Academy serves children age 5 through grade 12 who have been diagnosed with learning disabilities. The basic philosophy at Trident is to teach students to compensate for their differences in learning, allowing them to mainstream as quickly as possible.

## COLLEGES AND UNIVERSITIES

Higher education has been a priority in the Lowcountry since the founding of the College of Charleston in 1770. Today there are many academic institutions of advanced learning with expansive, formal campuses and wide-ranging course offerings. In addition, there are junior colleges, business colleges, and branches of out-of-state colleges and universities in the Trident area. Major institutions with strong ties to Greater Charleston are described below.

### Charleston Southern University
**9200 University Boulevard,**
**North Charleston**
**(843) 863-7000**
**www.csuniv.edu**
When it was founded in 1964, Charleston Southern was called Baptist College—the

only church-affiliated college in the area. Now elevated to university status and ranked as the second-largest church-affiliated university in the state, it offers 35 undergraduate degrees as well as masters degrees in business administration, education, and criminal justice. The student body has grown from an enrollment of 528 to more than 2,800. Sponsored by the South Carolina Baptist Convention, Charleston Southern University remains committed to its mission of "promoting academic excellence in a Christian environment."

**The Citadel**
**171 Moultrie Street**
**(843) 953-5000**
**www.citadel.edu**
Consistently ranked by *U.S. News and World Report* as one of the South's best colleges, The Citadel is a state-supported military college with an enrollment of more than 1,900 cadets. The 150-year, all-male tradition of the school was challenged in court, and the college accepted its first female cadets in fall 1996 with more entering every year.

With a formal campus and regimented activities, The Citadel combines academic requirements with military training in the areas of discipline, responsiveness, and leadership. Students select from 19 baccalaureate degree programs and must complete eight semesters of Air Force, Army, Navy, or Marine ROTC training, but they are not required to accept military commissions. Some undergraduate and a wide selection of graduate courses— including those leading to masters degrees in business administration, arts, science, and education—are offered through the College of Graduate and Professional Studies.

The Citadel Archives contain some very impressive collections: In 1966 Gen. Mark W. Clark, president emeritus of The Citadel, donated his personal, military, and official papers covering his career as commander of the Fifth Army in World War II, the Austrian Occupation, and the Korean War. Other notable collections include the Civil War letters of Gen. Ellison Capers

(Citadel class of 1857) and the papers of Pulitzer Prize–winning historian Bruce Catton.

**College of Charleston**
**University of Charleston**
**66 George Street**
**(843) 953-5507**
**www.cofc.edu**
Recognized as the first municipal college in the United States and the oldest institution of higher learning in South Carolina, the College of Charleston (founded in 1770) offers a broad range of undergraduate majors. This thriving academic institution provides a liberal arts education to 11,700 undergraduate and graduate students. The graduate studies program is called the Graduate School of the College of Charleston and offers degrees in such areas as education, marine biology, and public administration. The student-faculty ratio is 21-to-1, and 85 percent of the 467 faculty members hold doctorates or the highest degree in their field. For the second year in a row, the college was named "a top-rated college with the lowest costs" by *America's 100 Best College Buys 1999* survey book.

Three original buildings made up the College of Charleston for nearly 200 years. Now more than 100 buildings—from historic structures to high-tech classrooms—constitute the campus in the heart of historic downtown Charleston. Within this setting, the college showcases beautiful landscaping with botanical displays for every season.

**Medical University of South Carolina**
**171 Ashley Avenue**
**(843) 792-2300**
**www.musc.edu**
The oldest medical school in the South, MUSC was founded in 1824 and now is at the center of the largest medical complex in the state. The MUSC campus consists of 80 buildings covering 50 acres in downtown Charleston. The university includes six colleges—medicine, nursing, health-related professions, pharmacy, dental

medicine, and graduate studies. Student enrollment is 2,300, with a teaching staff of 1,200 full-time and 1,250 part-time faculty. The university coordinates statewide training of more than 800 interns and residents. Patient care is provided within the Medical University of South Carolina Medical Center (see the Health Care chapter), and faculty research is encouraged through facilities, funds, and administrative support provided by MUSC. MUSC is joining Johns Hopkins, Duke, the University of Kentucky, Case Western Reserve, Washington University, and University of Maryland to increase public awareness of its academic and clinical opportunities for medical students.

### Trident Technical College
### 7000 Rivers Avenue, North Charleston
### (843) 574-6111, (877) 349-7184
### www.tridenttech.edu

Trident Technical College is part of the state system and offers two-year programs for a variety of technical degrees. Trident Technical College also offers continuing education courses and customized training for business, industry, and government, helping to promote economic development in Charleston, Berkeley, and Dorchester Counties.

Merging with Palmer College (a private business college in downtown Charleston) in 1973, adding its Berkeley campus near Moncks Corner, and expanding its main campus in North Charleston gave Trident Tech a three-campus network. The newest additions are the Complex for Industrial and Economic Development adjacent to the main campus and the Veterinary Technology Building on the Berkeley campus.

The three campuses together serve around 12,000 undergraduate students, and 20,000 take continuing education classes each year. More than 150 associate degree, diploma, and certificate programs are offered. The curriculum includes programs in arts and sciences; business; health sciences; nursing; public service; hospitality, tourism, and culinary arts; community, family, and child services; and industrial and engineering technology. Classes are offered days, evenings, and weekends.

## CHARLESTON COUNTY LIBRARY SYSTEM

Twelve years in the making (from the public bond referendum for expansion of the library system to construction of the new main library), the new downtown branch of the Charleston County Public Library opened in the spring of 1998. The library building, relocated on Calhoun Street, is almost two and one-half times larger than its previous location on King Street. The old 200,000-volume library now has 300,000 books with the capacity for 570,000. The handsome edifice is a three-level structure with ground-level covered parking offering the first hour free with library validation. The first floor contains cataloging, circulation desks, fiction, large print, and young adult books and audiovisual materials. Expanded children's services include a youth services librarian and a children's story room. Conference rooms and a larger auditorium are available for public use.

The top floor houses the reference desk and materials, periodicals, nonfiction books, and the South Carolina Room. Banks of computers are available for research and general word processing by library patrons. Check it out, along with any of the other branch locations:

### Main Library
### 68 Calhoun Street
### (843) 805-6801
### www.ccpl.org

### Cooper River Memorial Library
### 3503 Rivers Avenue, North Charleston
### (843) 744-2489

### Dorchester Road Regional Branch Library
### 6325 Dorchester Road,
### North Charleston
### (843) 552-6466

Edgar Allan Poe Library
1921 I'On Avenue, Sullivan's Island
(843) 883-3914

Edisto Island Library
Thomas Hall, Highway 174,
Edisto Island
(843) 869-2355

Folly Beach Library
55 Center Street, Folly Beach
(843) 588-2001

Hollywood/St. Paul's Library
5151 Town Council Drive, Hollywood
(843) 889-3300

James Island Library
1248 Camp Road, James Island
(843) 795-6679

John L. Dart Library
1067 King Street
(843) 722-7550

John's Island Regional
3531 Manybank Highway
(843) 559-1945

McClellanville Library
222 Baker Street, McClellanville
(843) 887-3699

Mt. Pleasant Regional Branch Library
1133 Mathis Ferry Road, Mt. Pleasant
(843) 849-6161

Otranto Road Regional Branch Library
2261 Otranto Road
(843) 572-4094

St. Andrews Parish
Regional Branch Library
1735 North Woodmere Drive
(843) 766-2546

Village Library
430 Whilden Street, Mt. Pleasant
(843) 884-9741

West Ashley Library
45 Windermere Boulevard
(843) 766-6635

Bookmobile
(843) 805-6881

# CHILD CARE 🐻

Because many Charleston-area families are of the single- or two-career, working-parent varieties, there is a real need in the Lowcountry for full-time child-care facilities—reputable establishments that provide quality care for children from the early morning until after regular work hours.

The options that are out there for full-day, extended-hour centers are easy to obtain. The phone book and the local social services office are two good places to start. In this chapter, we provide some helpful hints to assist you in your search for this type of care provider, but we have concentrated on alternative care options and harder-to-find services and support groups.

## WHERE TO START

South Carolina licenses day-care centers only if they maintain standards in areas such as cleanliness, acceptable child-to-caregiver ratios, and adequate space-per-child allotments. There are three levels of regulation for child care facilities in the state. Level 1: Regulated. Meets basic requirements of the Department of Social Services, Division of Child Day Care Licensing and Regulatory Services, including fingerprinting and background check on all caregivers. Level 2: ABC Enhanced. Means that child care providers voluntarily meet higher educational requirements and are monitored (unannounced) yearly. Level 3: NAEYC Accreditation. Equates to even higher standards and accreditation through the National Association for the Education of Young Children. Call the local office of the South Carolina Department of Social Services at (843) 953-9780 or (800) 260-0211 to request more detailed information about this process. A visit to www.state.sc.us/dss/cdclrs/listings gives the licensed or registered child care providers by county. We encourage parents to investigate some of the options, listen for word-of-mouth tips, and read the classified section of the daily newspaper, *The Post and Courier,* for additional possibilities. Another helpful source of information is the Trident United Way's Child Care Resource & Referral program. Started in 2001, the free program provides education and guidance for finding quality child care, answers questions, and offers referrals based on a family's individual needs. Call (843) 747-9900 or (877) 227-3454, or visit www.tuw.org to access the information.

Before you make a decision about where to take your child, make sure the operation's license is up-to-date and the implemented programs fit your preference in terms of structure or freedom. Nose around the playground and check out the general atmosphere, but remember that this is real life, and kids will be kids. You could stumble upon a bad day for everyone at a good day-care or early childhood center. But overall, you should expect a day-care center to take care of your child in a way similar to a babysitter and expect an early childhood center to teach your child according to his age of development. Choose a center that allows drop-ins from parents; then do so regularly to ensure the center meets your standards.

---

*If you are a visitor to the Charleston area or a local parent, Lowcountry Kidsitters Inc. offers a babysitting referral service. Contact the Kidsitters at (843) 881-1862 for details on scheduling a responsible sitter to watch the kids in your hotel room or your home on your next evening out.*

---

There seem to be more centers in West Ashley and in other parts of Greater Charleston than on the Peninsula, and we hear parents complaining about that fact all the time. Mt. Pleasant residents have convenient access to several good child care facilities. Often there are waiting lists at these establishments, so it would be a good idea to think ahead and get your name on a few. We recommend you schedule visits during the center's working hours, so you will have a chance to observe the children, the care providers, and the facilities on a normal day.

The following listings will give you a rundown on some child care resources that can help guide you in your search for the most compatible solution for you and your child's needs. We have created a category with alternatives to traditional day-care centers, such as au pair care and Mother's Morning Out. While these are not total child care solutions, they are wonderful options. Samplings of some parent support groups and children's classes are included as well. Omitted are private, business-affiliated child care operations run strictly for the children of employees, as they are closed to the public.

## MOTHER'S MORNING OUT

# Local Area Churches

Depending upon the age of the children, Mother's Morning Out programs are offered throughout Lowcountry churches two or three mornings a week. They usually take newborns through preschool and kindergarten ages. You do not necessarily have to be a member of the church to enroll your child, but church members are given first priority.

## AN INTERNATIONAL OPTION

If you are able to provide lodging and would enjoy a cultural exchange experience to enhance your child's learning environment, you might consider contacting an au pair placement service. AuPair Care, at (800) 4AUPAIR or www.aupaircare.com, can help put you in touch with a live-in nanny. This service arranges for English-speaking European au pairs between ages 18 and 26 to come to the United States for a year. Host families supply lodging, meals, and a salary in return for 45 hours of child care a week.

Unlike employees, au pairs usually end up becoming much like family members, sharing meals and social occasions. A local community counselor is on hand to help the year go smoothly for both the au pair and the family. The folks we know who have used au pairs say it is a fun way to help solve the child care problem and broaden their children's vision of world boundaries.

## RESOURCES AND SUPPORT GROUPS

In 1994, the Peer Partnership for Civic Change selected Charleston as one of 14 communities around the country to receive a grant to participate in a community-building initiative.

The Charleston Civic Forum was formed as a result of this special funding. The forum was composed of a group of concerned citizens working to promote community discussions, to encourage collaboration among existing community organizations and to make Charleston a better place for its children, youth, and families.

In 1995, the Charleston Civic Forum held small discussion groups to identify priority issues affecting children, youth, and families. Based on this information, two issues were selected for further study in 1996 and 1997: improving race relations in the community and building civic capacity through community activism. Since then, several goals have been accomplished. A consensus of recommendations concerning race relations, improving public schools, and volunteerism in the nonprofit sector was developed. Seed support was established for creating the Mayor's Office on Children, Youth, and Families. (See subsequent listing.) A permanent, half-time researcher on Greater Charleston community issues was hired in partnership with the Graduate School of the College of Charleston. (See the Education chapter for more on the Graduate School of the College of Charleston.) Another partnership with Youth Service Charleston has funded dozens of community service groups and led to the development of a diverse new generation of young philanthropic leaders for the community.

The staff of the institute produced a resource directory, *Services and Resources for Families, Youth, and Children in the Charleston Area,* in the spring of 1995. The directory lists more than 800 different organizations under subject categories such as education, child care, counseling, community service and civic organizations, hospital and medical associations, parenting, recreation, and support groups. The directory is available for reference at the Charleston County Library and public school guidance counseling offices.

**Family Services Inc.**
**4925 Lacross Road, Suite 215,**
**North Charleston**
**(843) 744-1348, (800) 232-6489**
**www.familyserviceschassc.com**
Family Services, founded in 1888, is a private, nonprofit organization offering a full range of services designed to meet the needs of Trident-area families in the home, workplace, and community. The counseling staff is composed of social workers, marriage and family therapists, educational specialists, and budget and debt management counselors. Education and assistance are offered through seminars and workshops focusing on stress management, parenting, divorce adjustment, and self-esteem. Family Services groups have addressed anger management, helping children cope with divorce, and family violence intervention. For more information

on sessions, fees, and the complete range of services, call one of the listed numbers.

**Hotline, Inc.**
**P.O. Box 63305, North Charleston 29419**
**(843) 747-3007 (office),**
**(843) 744-HELP, (843) 747-TEEN,**
**(800) 922-2283, (800) 273-8255**
**www.211help.org**
Hotline provides a caring ear with information and referral services 24 hours a day to anyone in crisis or facing a problem. A Teenline is available for middle and high school students for discussing problems and concerns with others their own age. Educational programs and support groups are offered on a confidential and free basis. In addition to these services, Hotline compiles a frequently updated volume, the *Tri-County Resource Directory,* with cross-referenced listings of community organizations to assist families. The directory is available at the Charleston County Library Reference Department, or you may request a copy by calling the office number.

*The* Lowcountry Parent *is the Charleston area's parenting magazine full of good tips and information on education, family-oriented businesses, health and fitness, plus a calendar of family fun events. Pick up a free copy monthly and learn about preschools, camps, time management, birthday party planning, and other parent-helpful topics. You'll find the* Lowcountry Parent *at branch libraries, schools, health care offices, and local businesses, or call (843) 709-1906, or visit www.low countryparent.com.*

**Life Management Center**
**90 Alexander Street**
**(843) 577-2277**
**www.lifemanagement.org**
The Life Management Center helps people with learning differences and attention

deficit disorder (ADD/ADHD), as well as their families. Its services include individualized academic instruction, coaching, and time management and organizational strategies. Seminars, consultations, support groups, and referral services round out this valuable resource aimed at creating success for children and adults.

### Lowcountry Child Care Association
### 137 Keenan Avenue, Goose Creek
### (843) 572-2690

The Lowcountry Child Care Association's purpose is to promote, educate, and support family and group day-care providers. The association also provides parents with referral information about family and group day-care homes registered and licensed through the South Carolina Department of Social Services. Requests for information should be faxed to the number above.

### Mayor's Office for Children,
### Youth and Families
### 32 Ann Street, Charleston
### (843) 965-4190
### www.charlestoncity.com

This group serves as a clearinghouse for information about resources available to children, youth, and their families in the Trident area. The commission meets quarterly September through June. The office provides free listing information such as A Guide to Services for Families, published by the March of Dimes and the South Carolina Department of Health and Environmental Control. The guide contains phone numbers of area organizations involved in day-care, youth services, mentoring programs, infant and child health, parenting, and support groups. Contact the March of Dimes directly to obtain this publication at (843) 571-1776.

### MOMS Club
### Cooper Hall Senior Living Community,
### 937 Bowman Road, Mt. Pleasant
### (843) 971-2898

### James Island Recreation Complex
### 1088 Quail Drive, Charleston
### (843) 762-6059
### www.momsclub.org

The MOMS Clubs of Mt. Pleasant and Charleston were started as chapters of the national support group for mothers who stay at home with their children or work part-time. The group's broad range of activities includes special programs for mothers, play groups for children, and get-togethers for the whole family. Recent guest speakers presented talks on subjects such as college savings plans and children's dental care. The Mt. Pleasant MOMS Club meets every other Thursday at 7:30 P.M. at Cooper Hall Senior Living Community. The Charleston Club meets the first Friday of the month from 10:00 A.M. to noon at the James Island Recreation Complex. There is a one-time fee of $25. Children are always welcome at the meetings.

### Lowcountry Moms' Connection
### c/o Presbyterian Kindergarten
### 712 Wappoo Road
### (843) 556-6427
### www.charlestonmoms.com

The Lowcountry Moms' Connection is a spin-off of Mothers & More, an international, nonprofit organization that supports mothers who have altered their career paths to care for children at home. Membership includes stay-at-home moms as well as women who work part-time or run their own businesses. The West Ashley chapter meets the first Wednesday and third Tuesday of the month at 7:30 P.M. usually at the Presbyterian Kindergarten on Wappoo Road. The meetings include a broad range of parenting topics that support women's right to choose if and how they combine parenting and employment. In addition to the regular meetings, playgroups, parties, and activities are arranged for the children; a mothers' night out and couples get-togethers are organized to foster "parent sanity." Membership dues are $15 per year with prospective members welcome to attend a few events prior to joining.

## PARENTING CLASSES

Big Brother/Big Sister Class
Roper Hospital
316 Calhoun Street

Bon Secours–St. Francis Hospital
2095 Henry Tecklenburg Drive
(843) 402-2273
www.ropersaintfrancis.com
This sibling class is a fun way to help children prepare for their new role as big brother or sister. Games, a short film, refreshments, and a trip to see the babies in the nursery are all part of this class. It meets one Saturday morning at Roper Hospital or one Thursday evening at St. Francis each month, and parents should schedule attendance during the last month of pregnancy. The class is free and is designed for children ages 3 and older. Call the number above to register.

Exchange Club Parent/
Child Resource Center
1092 E. Montague Avenue,
North Charleston
(843) 747-1339
www.exchangeclubcenter.com
This parenting class focuses on families with children from early childhood through teens. The weekly classes use the S.T.E.P. model—Systematic Training for Effective Parenting. Some of the topics covered include understanding behavior, self-esteem, communication skills, developing responsibility, effective discipline, and nurturing social development. Classes

*Another helpful publication to keep handy (maybe in the car) is* Moms in the Know. *This guidebook for families in Charleston has sections such as "One's on the Way" (announcements, fitness, maternity clothes), "Doctor, Doctor" (family medicine, dentists), "Home Sweet Home" (contractors, realtors), "Not Just the Bear Necessities" (clothing, gifts, haircuts), "School Days" (child care, schools), "Out and About" (camps and community events), "We Got Through It" (parenting tips), and much more. It is a free pick-up at retail locations and public libraries, or visit* www.momsintheknow.com.

are held by child age groups Tuesdays, Wednesdays, and Thursdays in North Charleston. Additional classes are held on Wednesdays in Summerville and Thursday on Johns Island. Call for times and registration information. The fee is $90 for the six-week series.

### Parents and Children Together (PACT)
P.O. Box 675, Charleston 29402
(843) 769-5799
PACT is an educational and support program for parents of children ages six months to three years. The program is made up of three components: parent education, parent-child interaction, and early childhood education. The 10-week course meets once a week with fees ranging from $25 to $175. Sessions are held at area churches downtown, East Cooper, West Ashley, and North Charleston. Call the number above for a schedule and more information.

# WORSHIP

Charleston has been called the Holy City for at least a couple of hundred years. Newcomers may at first be taken aback by the reference, thinking it borrows too heavily against the true Jerusalem, but no such slight is intended. Instead, it's an old reference to Charleston's early tradition of religious freedom. Early on, that fact was demonstrated in the obvious proliferation of various church steeples in the city's skyline.

Apparently, early sailors enroute to Charleston first saw church spires on the horizon as they approached the Carolina coast. This may be where the term originated. Whatever its genesis, today that distinctive skyline is protected by Charleston law. One of the preservation ordinances passed by the city government many years ago was that no new building on the Peninsula could be taller than the steeple of St. Philip's Episcopal Church. Federal buildings are exempt from such laws, mind you, so the medical university and Veterans Administration hospitals loom like Goliaths on the upper Peninsula. One or two other tall buildings squeaked in before the height law was enacted. But generally speaking, Charleston's historic Peninsula will never be blighted by unsightly skyscrapers. It will remain the Holy City—by law.

Many of the church buildings in the Holy City are of particular architectural significance. Note that those are described in detail in our Attractions chapter under the subhead Historic Churches.

Charleston has every right to some kind of badge denoting its longstanding religious tradition. There's plenty of it, and religious diversification (some would say tolerance) has been a part of the city's heritage for a long, long time. A document called the Fundamental Constitutions of Carolina, penned in 1669, demonstrates this tradition:

"Therefore, any Seven or more Persons agreeing in any Religion, shall constitute a Church or Profession, to which they shall give Some name, to distinguish it from others. . . . No Man of any other Church or Profession shall disturb or molest any Religious Assembly. . . . It shall be lawful for Slaves as all others, to enter them selves, and be of what Church or Profession any of them shall think best, and therefore be as fully Members as any Freeman. . . . No Person whatsoever, shall disturb, molest or persecute another for his speculative Opinions in Religion, or his Way of Worship."

Into this somewhat idealistic ecclesiastical atmosphere streamed many divergent groups who would eventually call Charleston and its surrounding countryside home. The procession began as early as 1680, making this city one of the settings where the concept of separation of church and state evolved. This, of course, became one of the new nation's most treasured principles.

It may not be enough to point out that religious tolerance is a Charleston tradition. It's worth adding that religious diversification is, in fact, another of Charleston's remarkable survivors. Not only did many of the church edifices outlast the earthquakes, wars, hurricanes, and fires, their congregations did as well. So did liberal religious thought.

The first English settlers brought their Anglican tradition, and derivatives of that church still dominate the Lowcountry worship scene today. But early on, there were French Huguenots, Scottish Covenanters, Independents or Congregationalists, Jews, Baptists, and Quakers, whose congregations are still well represented in the Lowcountry today.

By most standards, today's religious climate in Greater Charleston would have to be called "traditional" . . . maybe even

# Lowcountry Chapels of Ease

The actual author of the term "chapel of ease" may be lost to the mists of time. However, when England's House of Commons created the Church Act of 1706, its purpose was very clear. England was adamant in its desire to establish its own official church as the dominant and official religion of the New World. Religion, after all, was power.

As distant and primitive as the colonies were at this early date, it was all too easy for upstart congregations and religious factions to take hold in the far-flung colonies. Thus, a tax was levied on skins and furs imported from the colonies in order to fund 10 Anglican parishes with churches (chapels of ease) and parsonages conveniently located at various points in the wilderness. This allowed England to get a jump on any other form of religion that might be evolving at the time.

The Church of England wanted to make it "easy" for settlers (and wealthy plantation owners) to have access to a "proper" house of worship. The chapels' convenient presence also made it more likely that wealthy planter families would patronize the establishment and generously tithe to the Mother Church.

Amazingly, some of these lovely little chapels survive in the Lowcountry. Unlike many early colonial dwelling houses that were made of wood, these religious "houses" were built to last—constructed of substantial materials (brick, slate, and sometimes tabby). Scattered as they are through the countryside, many of them escaped the destructive influence of urbanization. And as a result, they stand today as tangible evidence of the Lowcountry's important early religious tradition.

One of the easiest to find may be Christ Episcopal Church, first constructed in 1707, the year after the imposition of the Church Act tax. It's on U.S. Highway 17, about 8 miles north of the new Cooper River bridge (see the Lowcountry Day Trips chapter to learn more about this quaint little church). Unlike most of the old country chapels of ease, this one houses an active Christian congregation today.

But as for the name ascribed to these chapels, there remains an honest question: For whom was the "ease" really intended? Was it the isolated colonists or the Church of England?

*Pompion Hill was built ca. 1763 for planter families living along the east branch of the Cooper River. Locals call this little Georgian masterpiece "Pumpkin Hill."*
JOHN MEFFERT

*The small symmetrical building with its jerkin-head roof is Strawberry Chapel, ca. 1725, a chapel of ease built in St. John's Parish along the Cooper River.* JOHN MEFFERT "conservative." But the city's early acceptance of religious diversity is still alive and well. A wide range of choices is available here—whatever your spiritual path.

For instance, the Seventh-day Adventists have a church on upper King Street. And the Scientologists have a congregation in North Charleston. There's a Quaker Society of Friends, a Greek Orthodox congregation, as well as a group from the Church of Jesus Christ of Latter-day Saints, and a very strong Catholic archdiocese, too.

The Nation of Islam has a representation in the north area as well as the Buddhists. There are a Unity congregation and Unitarian Universalist church. There's a very strong presence of African Methodist Episcopal churches as well as a proliferation of Baptist congregations of many different designations scattered throughout the Lowcountry.

You'll find Christian Scientists, Charismatics, Evangelicals, and Full Gospel con-gregations in addition to the mainstream Methodist, Christian, Presbyterian, and Lutheran groups. Charleston's Jewish community is one of the country's earliest, and it has a strong presence in the community today. Plus, the interdenominational churches and nondenominational churches appeal to those without formal ties to any given group.

Not far from Charleston is the monastery called Mepkin Abbey, where about 30 Cistercian monks live the simple contemplative life of work, study, and prayer.

At this writing, the Yellow Pages contain more than 10 pages of church listings. Newcomers and visitors alike can easily find a number of worship options to explore. Also, the Saturday edition of *The Post and Courier* features a Religious Services page that lists the upcoming Sunday's church options, along with officiating clergy members and sermon topics.

# MEDIA 📺

As a result of relaxed federal ownership rules, the shift toward consolidation in media has swept across the nation's print and broadcast industries, and the Charleston market has been no exception. Local, privately-owned Evening Post Publishing Co., publisher of Charleston's daily newspaper, *The Post and Courier,* has expanded its holdings across the media spectrum. The company owns 11 television stations in Texas, Montana, Colorado, Arizona, Louisiana, California, and Kentucky, and eight newspapers in South Carolina, three in North Carolina, one in Texas, and one in Argentina.

This national trend is evident in the local radio and television businesses also. In recent years Covington, Kentucky–based Jacor Communications Inc., and New York–based Wicks Broadcast Group purchased radio stations in the Charleston market. More switches took place in 1999 as Clear Channel Communications of San Antonio, Texas, bought up Jacor's four stations while adding an AM talk radio format station. Four of these five stations consistently rank highly in the Arbitron ratings. Citadel Broadcasting Corp., based out of Las Vegas, gobbled up the Wicks Group's eight stations in a move to grow its eastern expansion. This purchase of combined listenership is said to reach about 40 percent of the Charleston market. A local sports-radio company, Kirkman Broadcasting, Inc., purchased one of Citadel's stations, adding to its group of three AM stations.

Overall, the radio market is young and trendy in its tastes, and the local stations respond accordingly. There are numerous choices on the dial in the Charleston area, and formats change frequently as a result of the fierce competition among the national broadcast groups and the independent stations. One constant, however,

is a large following for Christian, "family" radio in the Lowcountry.

Sinclair Broadcast Group of Baltimore, Maryland, has boosted its television holdings in mid-size markets with aggressive expansions. Locally, the group has purchased two stations, WTAT-TV (Fox Network) and WMMP-TV (UPN). Sinclair, one of the country's biggest broadcasting companies, owns or provides programming to 62 TV stations in 39 markets. Recent purchases have increased the company's reach to about 25 percent of U.S. television households.

The Greater Charleston area ranks 105th among the nation's television markets. There are affiliates for all three major television networks, plus Fox Broadcasting, the Public Broadcasting System, and an affiliate of the United Paramount Network (UPN). The larger cable television providers are Comcast Cablevision, serving the Greater Charleston area, Johns Island, Folly Beach, Kiawah/Seabrook, and Wild Dunes, (843) 554–4100; and Time Warner, (843) 871–7000, in the Summerville and Georgetown areas. Be sure to check in your specific area, since new cable, internet, and mobile communications providers are springing up across the Lowcountry.

## NEWSPAPERS
## Daily

*The Post and Courier*
**134 Columbus Street**
**(843) 577-7111**
**www.charleston.net**
As the oldest daily newspaper in the South, *The Post and Courier* is published by Evening Post Publishing. Today's newspaper is actually the combination of two of the town's longtime daily papers.

The *News and Courier,* founded in 1803, and the *Evening Post,* founded in 1894, merged as *The Post and Courier* on October 1, 1991.

Although for years the morning and evening papers maintained separate editorial staffs, they shared a common publishing plant still in use today. In 1990, the latest of several plant expansions took place, and another 10-unit press was installed, doubling press capacity. Additionally, computerization has advanced production to state-of-the-art, full-page pagination.

Weekly neighborhood sections are published every Thursday and provide local news to the communities making up the Trident area. Daily paid circulation is 95,588; the number for Sunday is 106,061.

Through the years, the staff has won numerous Associated Press awards and has been recognized for excellence by the Society for Professional Journalists. Editorially conservative, *The Post and Courier* gives the liberal point of view a nod on its op-ed page. However, the best airing of liberal opinion in the Lowcountry market will be found on the broadcast television stations.

# Weekly

### *Airlift Dispatch* (USAF)
**102 East Hill Boulevard, Suite 223, Charleston AFB**
**(843) 963-5536**
With 7,500 copies printed each week, this exclusive Charleston Air Force Base newspaper is published 50 weeks per year (excluding the two Fridays after Christmas). The paper covers base and military news. The *Dispatch* is distributed to on-base private residences and to 60 pick-up points throughout the base.

### *Berkeley Independent*
**320 East Main Street, Moncks Corner**
**(843) 761-6397**
The *Berkeley Independent* is a community-based weekly appearing on Wednesdays.

Circulation is 8,500, which is the largest paid distribution of any weekly in South Carolina. The *Independent* covers the economic, recreational, school, and entertainment news in Moncks Corner and surrounding, fast-growing Berkeley County.

### *The Catalyst* (MUSC newspaper)
**171 Ashley Avenue**
**(843) 792-3622**
**www.musc.edu/catalyst**
Published weekly, with 5,400 free copies distributed every Thursday evening, this tabloid is the Medical University of South Carolina's faculty and staff newspaper. Text and editorial content are produced by MUSC's public relations department. This publication reaches the highest concentration of degree-holding professionals in South Carolina. Dealing with issues of the medical community (including grants, awards, educational news, nursing, and medical breakthroughs), the *Catalyst* is highly respected among members of the medical profession.

### *Charleston Mercury*
**Island Publications,**
**1558-B Ben Sawyer Boulevard,**
**Mt. Pleasant**
**(843) 849-1778**
**www.charlestonmercury.net**
The *Charleston Mercury* was launched in March 2000 by way of the Internet and soon made its way into newsprint, mailing 12,600 copies every other week to households downtown, West Ashley, East Cooper, and Kiawah. This community newspaper with a "cosmopolitan attitude" presents a different perspective on news, analysis, and opinion. The *Mercury* covers a wide variety of information from correspondents' reports from Europe, South America, Africa, and beyond to the local hunting and fishing scene from a conservation viewpoint. Also included are the fine arts, family profiles (both historical and present-day), gardening, the buzz about town, travel, wine, and fine dining. The overall mission is to honor the

region's rich cultural heritage and the individuals and organizations that nurture it, making the *Mercury* an entertaining and stimulating read.

### The Chronicle
**1109 King Street**
**(843) 723-2785**
This African-American-oriented weekly is published on Wednesdays. Paid circulation is 6,000. Covering the Greater Charleston area, the *Chronicle* deals with issues related to African Americans, including news on schools, religion, business, and politics.

### Goose Creek Gazette
**205 Goose Creek Boulevard North,**
**Unit 11-A, Goose Creek**
**(843) 572-0511**
**www.goosecreekgazette.com**
The *Goose Creek Gazette* covers news of Goose Creek and Berkeley County and is published on Wednesdays. The free distribution is 11,200 copies. The *Gazette* focuses on business and industry news due to the explosive industrial growth in the county over the last several years. Local features also cover school and church news.

### Hanahan Goose Creek North Charleston News
**1928 East Montague Avenue,**
**North Charleston**
**(843) 747-5773**
This community-oriented weekly covers news of Hanahan, Goose Creek, North Charleston, and part of Berkeley County. It is published on Wednesdays. Circulation is 12,000. Church, school, and local news is covered.

### The Journal
**1558 Ben Sawyer Boulevard,**
**Mt. Pleasant**
**(843) 849-1778**
**www.islandpapers.com/journal**
The *Journal* carries community news for James Island and Folly Beach. It is published every Thursday. Paid circulation and rack sales are 8,670.

### Moultrie News
**1558 Ben Sawyer Boulevard,**
**Mt. Pleasant**
**(843) 849-1778**
**www.islandpapers.com/moultrie**
This is a free weekly carrying community news for Mt. Pleasant, Sullivan's Island, Daniel Island, and Isle of Palms. The focus is on the happenings in this fast-growing, East Cooper community. Published on Wednesdays, its total market coverage is 26,100.

### Summerville Journal Scene
**104 East Doty Avenue, Summerville**
**(843) 873-9424**
**www.summervillejournalscene.com**
This community paper is published on Wednesday and Friday with comprehensive coverage of the Summerville area and Dorchester County. National wire reports are interspersed with local news and features. The paid circulation is 10,700.

## Tabloids

The tabloid press in Greater Charleston is on the upswing, with several special-interest newspapers holding sway against the longtime survivors in this highly competitive advertising market.

### Carolina Arts
**P.O. Drawer 427, Bonneau 29431**
**(843) 825-3408**
**www.carolinaarts.com**
Published by Shoestring Publishing Co., this is a free monthly publication distributed throughout the Carolinas as a voice for the local arts scene. The writers take on difficult and controversial subjects (such as arts funding) and do extensive background research. Reviews of local arts offerings and gallery profiles are standard fare, and you'll find a comprehensive calendar of each state's arts exhibitions, shows, and special events. The publication was formerly known as *Charleston Arts*, which appeared in the Lowcountry from

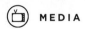 **MEDIA**

1987 to 1994, and as *South Carolina Arts,* from 1995 to 1996.

### Charleston City Paper
**1049 Morrison Drive**
**(843) 577-5304**
**www.charlestoncitypaper.com**
This alternative, weekly entertainment and review tabloid is a voice for Charleston's way-cool crowd. It is the successor to *Upwith,* which the Jones Street Publishers took over in 1997. The owners renamed the tab and have picked up the following of the college and young adult set. Look for reviews of the local club scene, movies, dining, and commentary on the area arts in general. *City Paper* circulation is 40,000, and copies are found in area restaurants and cafes, clothing stores, and college campus locations.

### Charleston Navy Shoreline
**Naval Weapons Station Charleston,**
**2316 Red Bank Road, Sutie 100,**
**Goose Creek**
**(843) 764-4094**
Published every other Friday, this tab is the official publication of the Charleston Naval Weapons Station. Started in June 2000, it covers the Navy news for the government and civilian employees in Charleston. Its 5,000 circulation is distributed free on base and to all base housing.

### Charleston Regional Business Journal
**389 Johnnie Dodds Boulevard,**
**Mt. Pleasant**
**(843) 849-3100**
**www.crbj.com**
Tapping into the success of business journal tabloids around the country, *Charleston Regional Business Journal,* published by Setcom Inc., was launched in 1995. After a year of providing in-depth business news coverage on a monthly basis, the publication doubled its frequency to twice a month in 1997. It is distributed free to area businesses with five or more employees, or it may be purchased by subscription. The circulation is 7,600.

### Island Life
**1413 Captain Sams' Road,**
**Seabrook Island**
**(843) 768-4404**
This monthly tabloid is delivered to seven sea islands in the Lowcountry: Edisto, Folly Beach, James Island, Johns Island, Kiawah, Seabrook, and Wadmalaw. It's also distributed in the downtown Charleston area and wherever books and newspapers are sold. Total circulation is 6,000 copies. Editorial content includes community news, entertainment, natural history, and political articles.

### Skirt!
**455 ½ King Street**
**(843) 958-0027**
**www.skirtmag.com**
This trendy monthly tabloid, launched in 1994, is dedicated to, but is not always exclusively about, women. It presents what's happening as viewed from the female perspective. Top-notch writers and smart, contemporary graphics make this idea really work. News, features, and regular columnists deal with local and national trends, political issues, creative arts, motherhood, and relationships—all delivered with a little cheek. In fact, *Skirt!* has dubbed itself "the monthly newspaper with an attitude." Total circulation is 30,000, and the tab is a free pick-up available throughout the Lowcountry.

### Vida Latina
**Vida Latina Publications, LLC,**
**976 Houston Northcutt Boulevard, Suite**
**3PMB140, Mt. Pleasant**
**(843) 388-8894**
**www.vidalatina.cc**
This all-Spanish language newspaper serves the rapidly growing population of Hispanics along the South Carolina, Georgia, and North Carolina coasts. It covers local as well as international news stories of special interest to its Spanish-speaking readership. The free publication distributes 9,500 papers every month to Charleston-area locations that cater to Hispanic patrons, primarily Mexican stores and restaurants.

# PERIODICALS

### Best Read Guide Charleston
**103 Broad Street, 2nd floor**
**(843) 722-8989**
**www.bestreadguide.com**
*Best Read Guide Charleston* is the local edition of the tour and travel, digest-size publication currently in 38 markets around the country. Morris Communications Corporation publishes 600,000 books quarterly in the Charleston market featuring the attractions and entertainment available here. Color-coded pages make it easy to find children's activities, golf course listings, a calendar of events, dining, tours, lodging, and maps. It is spiced up with short editorial features on local folklore, historical spots, nature trips, and other points of interest. The publication is a free pick-up in hotels, motels, restaurants, retail outlets, and visitor centers.

### Charleston Gateway
**255 King Street**
**(843) 723-8071**
**www.charlestongateway.com**
*Charleston Gateway,* founded in 1955, annually distributes 600,000 free copies to area hotels, motels, restaurants, galleries, and information centers. Issued every three months, this pocket-size publication is a handy guide to sightseeing, dining, shopping, and cooking. It contains a three-month calendar of events, a map of the Greater Charleston area, and a Peninsula street map.

### Charleston Magazine
**782 Johnnie Dodds Boulevard, Suite C,**
**Mt. Pleasant**
**(843) 971-9811**
**www.charlestonmag.com**
*Charleston Magazine* provides Charleston residents and visitors a lively, informative, entertaining, and sophisticated resource about our Peninsula and outlying districts on a monthly basis. Colorful features are offered on homes, gardens and architecture, dining, health and fitness, arts and entertainment, travel and style. Profiles of the region's most provocative and influential personalities, essays, and opinion columns tackle some of the tougher issues and concerns facing Lowcountry residents. Published by Gulfstream Communications, *Charleston Magazine* has a circulation of 28,000 and is available on newsstands or by subscription.

# TELEVISION

Three major cable providers serve the Greater Charleston area, so network channel numbers vary in different towns. Comcast Cable serves Charleston, Johns Island, Folly Beach, Kiawah, Seabrook, Wadmalaw, Wild Dunes, Awendaw, Edisto Beach, and the Hollywood–Ravenel area. Time Warner serves Summerville and Georgetown. The following is a list of local affiliates, with the channel numbers where each can be found in different area locales.

**WCBD, Channel 2 (NBC)—Comcast (Channel 3); Time Warner (2).**

**WCIV, Channel 4 (ABC)—Comcast (8); Time Warner (4).**

**WCSC, Channel 5 (CBS)—Comcast (9); Time Warner (5).**

**WITV, Channel 7 (PBS)—Comcast (11); Time Warner (7 in Summerville, 16 in Georgetown).**

**WTAT, Channel 24 (FOX)—Comcast (6); Time Warner (6).**

**WMMP, Channel 36 (UPN)—Comcast (13); Time Warner (13 in Summerville, 8 in Georgetown).**

# RADIO

Here is a fairly comprehensive list of the current radio station options arranged by format. Remember, radio stations are after the listener's attention, which is a moving target. Formats practically change with the weather. Your best bet is to use your radio dial and go exploring.

## COUNTRY

WEZL 103.5 FM
WNKT 107.5 FM

## NEWS/TALK

WSCC 730 AM/94.3 FM
WTMA 1250 AM
WQNT 1450 AM
WQSC 1340 AM

## OLDIES

WXLY 102.5 FM
WCOO 105.5 FM

## PUBLIC RADIO

WSCI 89.3 FM

## RHYTHM AND BLUES

WXST 99.7 FM

## URBAN

WWWZ 93.3 FM
WPAL 100.9 FM (Adult contemporary)
WMGL 101.7 FM

## ROCK

WSSX 95.1 FM (Contemporary Hits)
WAVF 96.1 FM (Alternative)
WYBB 98.1 FM
WRFQ 104.5 FM (Rock Classics)

## SPORTS

WQTK 950 AM
WTMZ 910 AM

## ADULT CONTEMPORARY

WALC-FM 100.5
WCSQ-FM 92.5 FM
WSUY 96.9 FM

## CHRISTIAN, GOSPEL, FAMILY

WFCH 88.5 FM
WYFH 90.7 FM
WKCL 91.5 FM
WJNI 106.3 FM
WXTC 1390 AM
WZJY 1480 AM
WTUA 106.1 FM

## MEXICAN REGIONAL

WAZS 98.9 FM

# MILITARY

Throughout our country's wars, both domestic and foreign, the strategic location of Charleston's port and the energy of the city's defenders have both played important roles. Volumes have been written on the subject, movies have been made, and there's no small amount of high drama, colorful characters, genuine courage, and even a bit of Nazi intrigue involved.

For most of the Cold War years, the Greater Charleston area served as the U.S. Navy's third-largest home port and the country's largest submarine base. North Charleston is currently home to the U.S. Air Force's 437th Airlift Wing. And the Marines, the Army, and Coast Guard still work to underscore the military's presence in this area.

But how do Charlestonians feel about the military?

Many of Greater Charleston's proudest citizens are former military people who have chosen to retire here. More former personnel from Charleston's military past return to the Lowcountry every year. Their loyalty to the military is unquestioned. But the real answer as to how they feel may be best illustrated by Charleston's fierce patriotism during the anxious days in 1991 pre- on Desert Storm in the Gulf s mounted in the Persian ians watched quietly as from the Navy Base slid port facilities, under the ridges, out into Charleston o the pages of history. ships from some faraway ere men and women from —Charleston's own fathers sons, and daughters.

Commuters on their way to work, tourists en route to the beaches, lovers strolling in Waterfront Park—almost everyone who saw the ships heading out—felt a pull on the heart.

But such a scene is hardly new in this old port city. Generations of Charleston-based military families have watched the same heart-rending parade head out into the Atlantic. The same is true of the more recent conflict in Iraq. This time, it was the Air Force and the 437th Airlift Wing's fleet of massive C-17s lifting tons of soldiers and war materiel into the air for their rendezvous with destiny. And while the individual soldiers, airmen, sailors, and their vessels may have changed, the deep feeling of pride in many patriotic Charlestonians, native or adopted, has not.

Historically, the importance of Charleston to the military defense of our country is almost impossible to calculate. On the other hand, the importance of the military to Charleston is a matter of clear and impressive economic record.

Even though the Charleston Navy Base and shipyard were officially closed in 1996, the Lowcountry's military presence still packs plenty of economic heat. According to figures released by the Charleston Metro Chamber of Commerce, the 40-plus military units still active in greater Charleston account for more than 18,000 jobs (both civilian and active duty) with a total payroll of $672 million in 2002.

The vast area that comprised the former Charleston Navy Base has tremendous economic potential—as do the remaining facilities in place at the site and the deep water access along the Cooper River. In the years since 1996, a number of proposals have been suggested that would "adaptively reuse" this asset to benefit the greater Charleston community. The plan that seems to have gained the greatest support to date is one that grants the northern part of the base to the city of North Charleston. The southern end of the base would become a new container terminal for the State Ports Authority—said to have the potential for unleashing a giant economic boom for North Charleston and the Lowcountry in general.

## GONE, BUT NOT FORGOTTEN: UNITED STATES NAVAL BASE, CHARLESTON

As many of the Lowcountry's proud military retirees are quick to point out, Charleston used to be "a Navy town." And what seems like only a few years ago, the economic security blanket the U.S. Navy provided Charleston for generations started to unravel almost overnight.

In the spring of 1993, the March 13 headline in the *Post and Courier* shouted, "A Direct Hit!" In Washington, the Defense Base Closure and Realignment Commission had announced the names of the U.S. military installations under consideration for closure or "realignment" in response to the end of the Cold War. It was part of the government's all-out effort to curb the nation's suffocating deficit. With that announcement, the 200-year-long journey of Charleston and the United States Navy veered onto a new course. In May 1993 the final hearings were held, and Charleston's arguments to sweep back the tide were unsuccessful. The official announcement came in June: Both the Charleston Navy base and the Charleston shipyard were casualties.

The history of the Navy's official presence in Charleston dates back to only 1900—although there were Naval battles in and off Charleston's waters since the American Revolution. In 1900 the 56th Congress authorized the establishment of a new Navy yard on the west bank of the Cooper River. A site comprised of three antebellum plantations about 6 miles north of the Custom House was selected, and surveying began in early 1902.

In 1909, the dry dock was the first project to be completed, followed by the red brick buildings and the main power plant. With a workforce of some 300 civilians, the first ship was placed in dry dock, and

work began on vessels of the American fleet in 1910. By 1915, 800 were employed at the yard.

During World War I, a naval training center was established at the yard, and there was a considerable expansion of facilities, land area, and work force. Employment soared to 6,500 personnel by November 1918. But after the war, the work force was gradually reduced, and only minor vessels were sent to Charleston for repairs. By 1922, the future of the Navy yard had become uncertain.

The beginning of a second surge of activity for the yard came in 1933. A large government-ordered workload created the need for more facilities and a much larger workforce. These men and women formed the nucleus of the group that would soon meet the demands of shipbuilding and repair work during World War II. More expansion included what is now known as the south yard, the Naval Air Station, and the Noisette Creek Area.

During the war, Navy yard employees built some 200 vessels of various classes including destroyers, destroyer escorts, tank-landing ships, amphibious landing ships, and destroyer tenders. There was also much battle damage repair work to be done. Civilian employment at the yard peaked in 1943 with almost 26,000 employees sharing the workload in three shifts daily.

Meanwhile, the Sixth Naval District (which included South Carolina, most of North Carolina and Florida, plus Alabama, Tennessee, Mississippi, Louisiana, and Texas) was responsible for the protection of the sea lanes and convoy routes along 540 miles of coastline on the eastern seaboard.

The record for reported submarine contacts in coastal waters off the United States was set in April 1943, with 35 hostile contacts investigated. Unbeknownst to most people living in the Lowcountry at the time, the busiest area for antisubmarine patrols was right off the coast of Charleston. As a result of an intensive defense strategy, only three American ships were torpedoed off the Carolinas and Georgia coasts after May 1942.

Just before the outbreak of World War II, the naval complex had again been enlarged with the establishment of the Charleston Naval Ammunition Depot. It was 20 miles from downtown on the west bank of the Cooper River, set on land that had once made up five plantations in the Goose Creek area of St. James Parish. Throughout the war, the depot was receiving, storing, reworking, and issuing vast amounts of ammunition.

On November 30, 1945, the U.S. Naval Base, Charleston, was officially established, and the old Navy yard became the Charleston Naval Shipyard, a component of the base.

The ammunition depot was placed in "partial maintenance" status in 1950 during the Korean War, and that status was upgraded to active in 1952. In 1954, an additional tract known as the Liberty Hall Annex was acquired for further expansion. In another area on the Navy yard property, the Marine Barracks, Charleston, was established in March 1959.

During the 1950s, the Naval Shipyard became the major overhaul facility on the East Coast for submarines as well as the outfitter for new ships constructed for the Navy in private shipyards in the district. New piers, barracks, and buildings for mine warfare ships and personnel were started in 1956. Later, Charleston became home port for combatant ships and submarines of the Atlantic fleet. The Naval Ammunition Depot was renamed the Naval Weapons Station in 1965, and by 1990, the station covered 16,344 acres.

The Gulf War provided a major test of Charleston's continuing naval presence and strategic importance, and by all accounts, the Lowcountry representatives in the conflict passed with flying colors.

As dark a cloud as the 1993 news of the closures was to the entire Trident area, the story turned out to have a silver lining. First, Congress passed an economic growth package that one local member of the House said would eventually foster up

*Many so-called experts predicted that Charleston would experience a dire economic disaster of hurricane proportion when the U.S. Navy Base finally closed. Indeed, commuters over the Cooper River bridge rarely see a U.S. Navy vessel of any kind these days in Charleston Harbor. Instead, they're more likely to see huge container ships laden with goods from all over the world coming and going from this busy port. Faced with the impending Navy pull-out, our tri-county leaders unified, cooperated, and succeeded not only in keeping the economy afloat, but they also helped propel it toward a whole new era of prosperity.*

to 132,000 jobs in South Carolina. It was said that a large percentage of those opportunities might eventually come here to the Lowcountry.

Also, the base closure commission chose not to close Charleston's NAVELEX facility, its Naval Electronics Engineering Command, but to expand it. That brought hundreds of high-tech jobs into the area. Later, NAVELEX was reorganized and became the Space and Naval Warfare Systems Center, or SPAWAR. Their mission is to provide command, control, compu communications, intelligence, surveill and reconnaissance (C4ISR) enginee and integrated solutions to the war fi in support of the Department of Defe in their global war on terrorism. SPAW Systems Center, Charleston, is focusec providing a comprehensive assessmen future needs, as well. They are applyin revolutionary advances in information a communication technologies to transfo the Navy into a knowledgeable, networked force.

Today, the Naval Weapons Station in Charleston has expanded its mission and Department of Defense support role. Now it is a training center with the Naval

Nuclear Power Training Command, the Nuclear Power Training Unit, and the Border Patrol Satellite Academy; and an engineering center with SPAWAR and its nearby Southern Division. It includes the Naval Facilities Engineering Command, which, as the Army logistics hub, is the busiest CONUS surface port in the defense transportation system.

The ironic conclusion to the story of Charleston's 1993 naval yard closure (if any conclusion can be drawn) is that our national defense is dynamic. In other words, another round of base closures is always as near as the next session of Congress.

Another agency that bloomed in the vacancy of Charleston's former Navy base is the NOAA Coastal Services Center (National Oceanic and Atmospheric Administration) at 2234 South Hobson Avenue. This division of the U.S. Department of Commerce fosters and sustains the environmental and economic well-being of the coast by linking people, technology, and information.

The Coastal Services Center employs about 100 people with experience in many disciplines and organizations related to the conservation and management of coastal resources. Planners, geographic information specialists, marine scientists, oceanographers, natural resource scientists, physicists, and ecologists are represented. They work with private industry, state coastal programs, local, county, and state planning offices, NASA, the Central Intelligence Agency, and various divisions of NOAA, the parent organization.

## CHARLESTON AIR FORCE BASE

The 3,500 acres of North Charleston that serve as home for the Charleston Air Force Base are about 16 miles from downtown, nestled between Interstate 26 and Dorchester Road (Highway 642). The main gate is off Dorchester, but there is easy access from I-26 via Aviation Avenue and the Rivers Avenue base gate.

The base is not open to the public, but visitors may be cleared for admittance onto the base by base residents or employees. Both gates are manned around the clock by security police, and government or military identification is required to gain access. If you need more information about gaining access to the base, call the Security Police Law Enforcement desk at (843) 566-3600.

# Base History

As the popularity of flying grew, air operations in Charleston began in 1928 on a small field north of the city at what later became Charleston Municipal Airport. During those first years, the airfield was used primarily by commercial and private aircraft. In 1931, the city floated bonds and sold stock for the purchase of 432 acres at a cost of $25,000 and established the area's first municipally sanctioned airport. In 1935, a Work Projects Administration group was given the job of modernizing the airfield, and, with a $313,000 grant, a new 3,500-foot paved runway with modern lighting was completed and another runway started.

The day after the Japanese attacked Pearl Harbor, the Eastern Defense Command met in New York City and made immediate plans for the defense of the East Coast. Those plans included the establishment of military operations at existing municipal airports up and down the coast. Thus, in December 1941, the Army Air Corps took full control of the field in Charleston for coastal operations.

In early 1942, the first flights from the newly designated Charleston Army Air Field consisted mostly of antisubmarine missions. As the year wore on, operations expanded to include the training of B-17 Flying Fortress and B-24 Liberator combat crews and their support crews bound for the European theater of war. At the same time, the airfield was being used by commercial aircraft. This was a successful early example of the "joint-use" concept that is still in place here today.

Joint-use operations continued until 1946, when the military portion of the airfield was closed and officially returned to the city. By war's end, the airfield consisted of 2,050 acres and had received $12 million in improvements. Military operations were re-established in 1952, when the city of Charleston and the Air Force agreed to establish a troop carrier base and, once again, allow joint use of the runways.

The Troop Carrier Wing became the host unit under the Tactical Air Command. The base was transferred to the Military Air Transportation Service (MATS) on March 1, 1956. The Air Transport Wing (ATW) was activated in 1954 and became the host unit until 1966.

On January 8 of that year, the Air Force revamped all MATS units and their missions. MATS became the Military Airlift Command and the ATW was discontinued.

It was Air Force policy at the time to renumber active duty units using the same numerical designations as those units showing distinguished service during World War II. When the 437th Military Airlift Wing was activated, it was assigned to Charleston Air Force Base. Personnel and equipment formerly assigned to the 1608th ATW were reassigned to the 437th MAW.

In October 1991, the 437th MAW was redesignated to the present-day 437th Airlift Wing as part of an Air Force-wide reorganization effort.

In June of 1993, the 17th Airlift Squadron became the first fully operational C-17 base in the Air Force. By 1993, they had converted to the C-17A Globemaster III. It was inactivated in 2000—marking the end of 35 years of C-141s flying out of Charleston. At one time there had been 58 C-141s assigned here.

History called again in 2001. From Charleston C-17A crews flew the first night-combat and humanitarian-coalition missions into Afghanistan. And in 2001, the 16th Airlift Squadron was reactivated. Today, Charleston is home to 54 C-17A Globemaster III aircraft (each one costing approximately $207 million). The 437th Airlift Wing and 315th Airlift Wing (Reserves) are also responsible for a radar site in Jedburg, South Carolina, an airstrip at North Auxiliary Airfield near Orangeburg, South Carolina, and various off-base housing in the North Charleston area.

## Air Park Tours

Currently on static (that's the military term for "permanent") display at the Charleston AFB are four aircraft that (with prior arrangement) can be toured by groups of 20 to 40 accompanied by an Air Force–qualified guide. Included are a Douglas C-47 (DC-3) Skytrain, a Lockheed C-121 Constellation, a Douglas C-124 Globemaster, and a Lockheed C-141 Starlifter. Although tours of the air park have been somewhat curtailed following the events of 9/11, you can call for information about tour schedules. Contact the 437th Airlift Wing public affairs office at (843) 963-5608.

## Lodging

There are about 167 temporary quarters (lodging) on base available to active duty and retired military personnel and their dependents. While priority is given to those on official government orders, military personnel traveling for leisure may make reservations 24 hours prior to their arrival date. There are 69 single rooms with private baths, 40 rooms with shared baths, 36 family units (with two to four bedrooms), and 12 "distinguished visitor" suites that may be reserved. For more information, call (843) 963-3806 or (843) 963-8000.

## CHARLESTON'S LITTLE-KNOWN ARMY PRESENCE

The fact that a considerable number of U.S. Army personnel are stationed in Charleston may come as something of a surprise. But indeed, the U.S. Army has several commands housed as tenants at the Naval Weapons Station. Their Combat Equipment Group—Afloat, the 841st Transportation Battalion, and the Army Corps of Engineers are headquartered at various locations around Charleston. These commands have played an integral role in homeland security and the war on terror.

CEG-A, a component of the U.S. Army Materiel Command, projects logistics power in contingencies through 12 pre-positioning ships of equipment and fuel. CEG-A occupies 51 buildings on 320 acres of the Naval Weapons Station property, formerly occupied by the Polaris Missile Maintenance Atlantic Facility. The Army has since invested $36 million in modifications on the 25-acre Wharf Alpha site. Wharf Alpha is the Naval Weapons Station's strategic pier location for the upload and download of the Army's $1.8-billion pre-positioning equipment inventory.

Charleston can also be very proud of the 841st Transportation Battalion, the Military Surface Deployment and Distribution Command's South Atlantic Port Manager, whose mission is to synchronize defense transportation and cargo movements. This tenant of the Naval Weapons Station is responsible for coordinating with various commands including Military Sealift Command, local labor, port authorities, and transportation firms to expedite the movement of major military equipment to troops. The battalion was proud to facilitate the largest cargo load in history onto a U.S. Navy large, medium-speed, roll-on/roll-off vessel.

During Operations Enduring Freedom and Iraqi Freedom, the 841st Transportation Battalion has moved six Army pre-positioned vessels carrying over 1.5 million square feet of equipment. The unit also has several reserve components attached

to it that have been responsible for numerous equipment deployments from Charleston. The 841st is the busiest terminal in the Army, shipping more than 30 percent of the Army cargo deployed by sea through Charleston during the global war on terrorism.

The Army Corps of Engineers' mission is to meet the needs of the citizens of South Carolina and the nation by providing quality projects and services for water resource, environmental, and military customers. They manage a variety of technical activities, including a multi-disciplined engineering design program. The Corps of Engineers is responsible for local projects including the execution of the $135-million Charleston Harbor deepening and widening project, operation of the St. Stephen's Powerhouse, and support to the Federal Emergency Management Agency's Public Works and Engineering mission responding to natural and man-made disasters. The Corps' workforce comprises a diverse range of disciplines including engineers, economists, and biologists contributing over $9 million annually to the local economy.

Charleston's U. S. Army presence is relatively modest but extremely important to the Department of Defense and the war fighters defending freedom in our country and around the world.

## U.S. COAST GUARD, WATCHING OUR SHORES

The U.S. Coast Guard presence in Charleston, known as "Base Charleston," is headquartered on a little more than eight acres. The base is located within the historical district of the City of Charleston at 196 Tradd Street on the east side of the Ashley River. It was first commissioned at its present site in 1914. The government purchased the land from West Point Mill Company, Andrew B. Murray, and the City of Charleston. The land was dedicated to the U.S. Lighthouse Service and originally was used as a buoy depot. The U.S. Coast

Guard absorbed the U.S. Lighthouse Service in 1939, including Base Charleston.

The main Administration Building, commonly known as the Rice Mill building, is a three-story, 30,000-plus-square-feet, heavy timber structure with exterior brick walls built in 1859. It was once known as Chisolm's Mill. At the zenith of its heyday as a rice mill, it processed $1 million in rice annually and was capable of containing 150,000 bushels of rice in the rough.

Judging from historical news accounts describing the mill's construction in 1859, what is now the Coast Guard's Administration Building was once a storehouse attached to the original mill. The building was rebuilt upon the foundations of an earlier (1826) mill that had burned to the ground. The brick foundation walls are up to 30 inches thick, decreasing to 14 inches thick at the roof gables.

The Coast Guard's Rice Mill building has an interesting structural feature that came as a result of the earthquake of 1886. Earthquake rods and turnbuckles were run through the floors and into the walls.

These rods were installed on many buildings in Charleston in an (unsuccessful) attempt to provide tensile reinforcing and help close large cracks opened by that earthquake.

The building is still being used and recently underwent a $750,000 facelift. The Rice Mill is eligible for inclusion on the National Register of Historic Places. The base recently received the local coveted Carolopolis Award from the Preservation Society of Charleston.

In December of 2004, the U.S. Coast Guard raised its flag on a new law enforcement training academy in Base Charleston. Their mission is to teach nearly 2,000 servicemembers a year how to stop and board vessels that could be potentially carrying drug smugglers or terrorists to the nation's shores.

The Coast Guard and all of Charleston's military facilities have strong partnerships and joint missions with one another and other federal facilities throughout the United States.

# INDEX

# ABOUT THE AUTHORS

## J. MICHAEL MCLAUGHLIN

J. Michael McLaughlin has been living in and writing about the Lowcountry since 1979. During that time, his interests in history, architecture, and the legendary Charleston lifestyle have led him into countless adventures.

His writing has found its way into numerous regional and national magazines, and his freelance work as an advertising and public relations consultant has captured national marketing awards.

Michael was raised on a farm in Indiana, but he's quick to point out it was in southern Indiana, and "in Charleston, that makes a big difference." He graduated from Indiana University in 1967 with a B.S. degree in business-journalism, aiming for a Madison Avenue career in advertising. Instead, his first writing job turned out to be in Vietnam, where, as a war correspondent, he won a Bronze Star for his coverage of the 101st Airborne Division during the ill-fated 1968 Tet Offensive.

After a decade back home in Indiana as an award-winning writer-producer for several Midwestern ad agencies, he joined the writers' colony in Key West, Florida. And that's where he was living when 1979's Hurricane David forced him to evacuate the island and he discovered Charleston. Since then, he's considered himself "a born-again Southerner," writing about Charleston and the Lowcountry's charming, if idiosyncratic, ways.

## LEE DAVIS TODMAN

Lee Davis Todman was raised in Charleston and returned to her beloved city in 1987 after pursuing her education and a nine-year stint away in "the urban fast lane." Lee received a journalism degree from the University of Georgia in 1976 and did graduate work there in public relations. In 1979 she began her career in Atlanta, working for several ad agencies, among them J. Walter Thompson USA, where she was a senior media planner.

The pull of the ocean and the traditions of her childhood proved too strong to abandon for long, though: "Who says you can't go home again? Being away from Charleston only sharpened my focus on the city's enduring appeal." Since returning, Lee has worked as a freelance advertising and marketing consultant on local and regional accounts, creating and implementing many award-winning campaigns.

Lee and Michael have also collaborated on a short volume of stories relating South Carolina history, Globe Pequot's *It Happened in South Carolina*.

Succumbing to the allure of the historic district, Lee has undertaken the renovation of an old house (ca. 1803) in the downtown Peninsula area, and it has proved to be both a test of her endurance and a labor of love. But it provides the perfect setting from which to ponder the timeless beauty and vitality of old Charleston.